Blackstone's Guide to the

# FINANCIAL SERVICES & MARKETS ACT 2000

**Key Text**

## REFERENCE

Blackstone's Guide to the

# FINANCIAL SERVICES & MARKETS ACT 2000

*General Editor*
Michael Blair, QC

Loretta Minghella
Michael Taylor
Mark Threipland
George Walker

BLACKSTONE
PRESS LIMITED

Published by
Blackstone Press Limited
Aldine Place
London
W12 8AA
United Kingdom

Sales enquiries and orders
Telephone + 44-(0)-20-8740-2277
Facsimile + 44-(0)-20-8743-2292
E-mail: sales@blackstone.demon.co.uk
Website: www.blackstonepress.com

ISBN 1 84174 116 7
© Michael Blair 2001
The contributors hold the copyright for their respective chapters.
First published 2001

**British Library Cataloguing in Publication Data**
A catalogue record for this book is available from the British Library

Typeset in 10/12pt Times by Style Photosetting Ltd, Mayfield, East Sussex
Printed and bound in Great Britain by Antony Rowe Limited,
Chippenham and Reading

# Contents

# Preface

The Financial Services and Markets Act 2000 has finally been produced after a prolonged and innovative parliamentary process. Its central tenet, that there should be integrated financial regulation based on clear objectives, proportionality and fairness, has attracted general support, though there has been much contention round the edges. The Act creates a fresh start for the oversight of this crucially important sector of the United Kingdom economy, and is being widely studied elsewhere in the world. A centrepiece of this new government's legislation agenda over the last two years, it provides the framework for a more detailed working out of its principles and requirements that is yet to be finalised.

The focus now shifts from Parliament itself to the Treasury and to ministers, who have to put in place a layer of secondary legislation, and to the Financial Services Authority, which is planning and consulting on its *Handbook* to contain the rules and guidance needed to make the Act into a fully workable system.

This book is largely focused on the new Act, and has gone to press without waiting for certainty or completeness in either of these supporting layers. In particular, it does not analyse in any depth the crucially important Regulatory Activities Order and Financial Promotion Order, on which the Treasury propose further consultation in the autumn of 2000. Nor is it able to grapple with issues about transition or commencement, which also depend on policy development in the Treasury.

Nonetheless the authors hope that an early account and analysis of the Act itself may be useful to the very many people who will be affected by the legislation when it commences, and to those who are preparing to advise them.

The financial services industry is innovative and fast-moving. The systems for regulation of it have to be effective and fast-moving too. No sooner had the ink dried on the Act but it was already in need of amendment. The Credit Institutions Directive (2000/12/EC) of 20 March 2000 entered into force on 15 June, the day after royal assent to the Bill, and rendered out of date some parts of sch. 3 on EEA passport rights. In this work we have sought to be as up to date as we can in a rapidly evolving world.

Two of the authors are employees of the Financial Services Authority, and I have recently retired as general counsel to its board. None of us should be taken as writing on behalf of, or as expressing any view of, the Authority in this work.

The publishers envisage a possible further and expanded edition of this book when more of the underlying detail has been settled. Meanwhile the law is stated as at 6 July 2000.

*Michael Blair QC* (h.c.)
*3 Verulam Buildings*
*Gray's Inn*
*London WC1R 5NT*

# Contributors

**Michael Blair** QC is in independent practice at 3 Verulam Buildings, Gray's Inn, London, specialising in financial services law. From 1998 to April 2000 he was General Counsel to the Board of the Financial Services Authority (FSA). Prior to that he was General Counsel to, and latterly also Deputy Chief Executive of, the Securities and Investments Board. He is a Member of the Competition Commission (Appeals Panel), and is the Chairman of the Personal Investment Authority (PIA), of the Personal Investment Authority Ombudsman Bureau (PIAOB) and of the Investment Management Regulatory Organisation (IMRO). He is also a Director of the Financial Services Compensation Scheme.

Before coming to the City in 1987, he was an Under Secretary in the Lord Chancellor's Department (LCD), with responsibility first for the Midland and Oxford Circuit (as Circuit Administrator) and then for the Courts and Legal Services Group at LCD Headquarters. Called to the Bar in 1965, Michael was elected a Bencher of the Middle Temple in 1995 and was granted the rank of Queen's Counsel (*honoris causa*) in 1996. He served on the General Council of the Bar for nine years, latterly as Chairman of the Professional Standards Committee (1994) and as Treasurer (1995–98).

A Visiting Professor at the University of Reading, Michael is the author or editor of a number of legal textbooks, including *Financial Services: The New Core Rules* (1991) and *Blackstone's Guide to the Bank of England Act 1998* (1998) (both Blackstone Press).

**Loretta Minghella** is the FSA's Head of Enforcement Law and Policy. She trained with Kingsley Napley, and practised as a white-collar defence lawyer there after qualifying as a solicitor in 1987. She later joined the Investigations Division of the Department of Trade and Industry, advising on companies and insider dealing investigations. In 1990, Loretta moved to the Legal Division of the Securities and Investments Board and became its Head of Enforcement Law and Policy Support in 1993. She took up her current role for the wider FSA in 1997. In that role, she has led the team responsible for FSA Enforcement Division's contribution to legislative change, and for the development of the FSA's enforcement policies and practices.

**Michael Taylor** is currently a Senior Economist at the International Monetary Fund (IMF) where he works on systemic banking and bank restructuring issues. He was formerly a noted commentator on the British regulatory scene, contributing regularly to publications such as the *Financial Times Financial Regulation Report* and to the *Financial Regulator*, which he also edited. His paper for the Centre for the Study of Financial Innovation, '"Twin Peaks": A regulatory structure for the new century' (1995) sparked a wide-ranging debate in both the UK and elsewhere on reform of the organisational structure of financial regulation. He has also worked on banking supervisory policy at the Bank of England, and has held a number of academic appointments at leading British universities. A Visiting Professorial Fellow at the Centre for Commercial Law Studies, Michael has published widely in both academic and professional journals. His most recent books include *Blackstone's Guide to the Bank of England Act 1998* (Blackstone Press, 1998) (with Michael Blair, Ross Cranston and Chris Ryan) and *Bond Markets: Law and Regulation* (Sweet & Maxwell, 1999) (editor with Tamasin Little and Helen Parry).

**Mark Threipland** manages the Handbook Unit in the FSA General Counsel's Division, advising on the preparation of the FSA's *Handbook of Rules and Guidance*, having previously been part of the FSA's team which liaised with the Treasury during the passage of the Financial Services and Markets Bill. He trained as a solicitor with Linklaters & Alliance and then spent six years in their Financial Markets Group. He is a member of the Financial Services sub-committee of the Law Society's Company Law Committee.

**George Walker** is a Fellow and Lecturer in Banking and Finance Law at the Centre for Commercial Law Studies, University of London. He is an Affiliate Lecturer in Law at Cambridge University and a Visiting Professor at SMU School of Law, Dallas, Texas. He is a Legal Consultant with Farrier & Co, Solicitors, London and to the IMF in Washington, DC. He is Executive Editor of the *Financial Regulation Report* and an Assistant Editor of the *Encyclopaedia of Banking Law*. He is co-author of *Banking and Financial Services Regulation* and author of the forthcoming *International Banking Regulation — Law, Policy and Practice*. He is a solicitor in Scotland, England and Wales and a member of the New York Bar.

# Table of Cases

# Table of Statutes

# Table of Statutory Instruments

# Abbreviations

| | |
|---|---|
| ATS | alternative trading system |
| DGFT | Director General of Fair Trading |
| DTI | Department of Trade and Industry |
| FOS | Financial Ombudsman Service |
| FSA | Financial Services Authority |
| FSA 1986 | Financial Services Act 1986 |
| FSAMA 2000 | Financial Services and Markets Act 2000 |
| ICS | Investors Compensation Scheme |
| ICVC | investment company with variable capital |
| IMRO | Investment Management Regulatory Organisation |
| IOSCO | International Organisation of Securities Commissions |
| LDT | licensed deposit-taker |
| NAO | National Audit Office |
| NCC | National Consumers Council |
| OEIC | open-ended investment company |
| OTC | over the counter |
| PIA | Personal Investment Authority |
| RCH | recognised clearing house |
| RIE | recognised investment exchange |
| RPB | recognised professional body |
| SEC | Securities and Exchange Commission |
| SFA | Securities and Futures Authority |
| SIB | Securities and Investments Board |
| SRO | self-regulating organisation |
| UCITS | undertaking for collective investments in transferable securities |

# Chapter One
# The Policy Background

*Michael Taylor*

The Financial Services and Markets Act 2000 (FSAMA 2000) gives legal basis to the radical reform of the UK's system of financial regulation announced by the government soon after the May 1997 general election. The extent of the government's radicalism in reforming financial regulation took many practitioners and commentators by surprise. The Labour policy handbook, *New Labour, New Life for Britain* had, perhaps deliberately, been vague about the new government's plans for financial regulation. It promised only to 'reform and strengthen the regulatory system' and 'to simplify both the structure and the nature of the system so that it commands the confidence of both the public and the industry'. While FSAMA 2000 is consistent with both these statements, it goes much further than many observers had expected.

The obvious respect in which the Act is a radical measure is in providing statutory underpinning for the Financial Services Authority (FSA), which combines the regulation of banking, securities and insurance business, and replaces no fewer than nine pre-existing regulatory bodies. Indeed, the FSA is practically unique among regulatory agencies in the industrialised world in terms of the diversity of businesses regulated, and its very broad scope, encompassing both prudential and business conduct regulation. (Prudential regulation is concerned with the financial soundness of regulated institutions, whereas business conduct regulation is concerned with the way in which their products are marketed and sold.) While other integrated financial regulators have been in existence for some years, most notably in the Scandinavian countries, none has been established in a country with a financial sector as large as the UK's, and all have a largely prudential focus. It should not be surprising, therefore, that such a radical reform of regulation, especially as it affects one of the world's leading international financial centres, should have attracted such widespread attention far outside Britain.

A second respect in which the new Act is radical is in the range of enforcement powers it grants to the FSA. These go a significant way beyond the combined powers of the bodies which the FSA replaces. Especially significant are the FSA's enforcement powers in respect of its Code of Market Conduct. The FSA will be able to levy penalties against individuals or firms who breach the Code through insider dealing or attempted market manipulation. It will also be able to apply to the High Court for disgorgement or restitution orders. This aspect of the Act's radicalism had received greater public discussion than the unification of supervision, as speeches by Sir Andrew Large, the former chairman of the Securities and Investments Board, had strongly argued the case for a civil route for the disposal of such cases in parallel to the existing criminal law. Nonetheless, this change represents a substantial departure from past City regulation, while also conferring on the FSA a range of powers that are practically unique among regulatory bodies in the world.

While the Act's radicalism is apparent on the surface, in another sense it is also the product of a long process of evolution. Although the Government's May 1997 announcement was as sudden as it was unexpected, it reflected the UK's experience of financial regulation over a period of many years. Thus, as well as representing a radical departure from past practice, the Act can also be regarded as the outcome of a long process of gradual change in the regulation of Britain's financial sector. The process of regulatory change was itself motivated by, and was at times a catalyst for, more fundamental changes in the structure of the regulated industry. Thus to understand the policy background to the Act it is necessary to understand the processes of both industry and regulatory change extending back over several decades.

The evolution of the UK's financial sector since the early 1980s can be thought of as the gradual confluence of three previously quite separate streams. These are the 'primary' banking sector, monitored and supervised by the Bank of England; the organised markets in the City, such as the Stock Exchange and Lloyd's; and the rest of the financial sector, including building societies and insurance companies and licensed securities dealers. Each of these streams exhibited significant differences in the style and nature of regulation, especially in the balance between statutory and self-regulation.

The story since the early 1980s has been one of the gradual erosion and disappearance of the distinctions and boundaries between these different streams. Once distinct financial activities have become more closely integrated, and many financial institutions have become active in at least two of the activities of banking, insurance and securities. Moreover, in parallel to this process, another has been in evidence in which the balance between statutory and self-regulation shifted decisively in favour of the former in each of the three component parts of the financial sector. This has resulted in a primarily informal and extra-legal system of financial regulation giving way to one largely based on statute. The two processes of regulatory and industry change are closely linked and have exercised a fundamental influence on the need for the type of regulatory consolidation represented by the formation of the FSA.

## FINANCIAL REGULATION AT THE TIME OF THE
## WILSON COMMITTEE

To understand the process described above it is necessary first to give an account of the regulation of Britain's financial sector circa 1978, at the time of an inquiry into Britain's financial system chaired by Sir Harold Wilson. The report of this inquiry described a set of arrangements that even then were on the verge of passing away, but for this reason it is a valuable snapshot of a now vanished world. This description can then serve as the prelude to tracing the subsequent developments that have given rise to the formation of the Financial Services Authority. A notable feature of the pre-1980 period was the relative absence of statute law from two of the three streams, in contrast to the third stream where statutory regulation played a very significant role from an early stage.

Prior to the enactment of the Banking Act 1979, Britain had lacked any system of formal authorisation or supervision of its banking sector, at least since the repeal in 1856 of Peel's 1844 Banking Act (7 & 8 Vict c. 113). (For a history of banking regulation in Britain see Heidi M. Schooner and Michael Taylor, 'Convergence and competition: the case of bank regulation in Britain and the United States' (1999) 20 Mich J Int'l L 595). Although the Bank of England was empowered, by s. 4(3) of the Bank of England Act 1946, to issue directives to the banking sector, this power was never formally invoked. Instead, the Bank exercised informal powers of moral suasion over the banks, relying largely on its ability to dispense favours (especially access to its lender of last resort facilities) in return for cooperation on the part of the institutions with which it dealt. These were principally the clearing banks, discount houses and accepting houses, which together constituted the 'core' or 'primary' banking sector. In addition to its powers of moral suasion the Bank also relied to a substantial extent on the forces of self-regulation, especially that exercised by organised committees of institutions like the Accepting Houses Committee or the London Discount Market Association. The efficacy of this approach to regulation was based to a substantial degree on the relatively small and concentrated nature of the constituency with which the Bank dealt. The widespread acceptance of informal norms of behaviour, including the acceptance of the Bank's unique responsibilities in relation to the rest of the banking sector, also served to ensure that the Bank's writ ran large.

The Bank of England's relationship with the primary banking sector extended far back into the nineteenth century when the Bank evolved from the dominant commercial bank into one discharging many of the functions of a recognisable modern central bank.

Informal monitoring of the banking sector was conducted by the Bank's Discount Office which developed a number of characteristics that were later to inform the Bank's approach to statute-based banking supervision: the approach was informal, flexible, and — unlike the United States — based neither on law nor on formal on-site examinations. The cornerstone of the Discount Office's approach to supervision was the interview — as it was to remain for much of the period following the advent of statutory regulation. The Bank regarded this type of regulation as 'non-statutory' rather than 'self-regulatory', since it followed from the 'customary' and 'traditional' role of a central bank in ensuring orderly markets and prudently run banks (see the Bank's submission published in Committee to Review the Functioning of Financial Institutions, *Second Stage Evidence* (London: HMSO, 1979), vol. 4, p. 96).

The second component of the pre-1980 financial sector comprised the organised markets, including the Stock Exchange, Lloyd's of London and the various commodities exchanges. Like the supervision of the banking sector, the regulation of these markets relied to a substantial degree on informal norms of behaviour rather than on statute law. The Bank of England took a keen interest in the functioning of these markets, albeit relying for its authority on City tradition rather than on any statutory function. It would not have been too wide of the mark to describe the Bank's self-appointed role in this period as the City's 'chief prefect', imposing informal disciplinary norms on the primary banks and organised markets alike, and representing the City's interests to government. It was in this capacity, for example, that the Bank played the leading role in organising the Council for the Securities Industry (CSI) a short-lived attempt to bring a greater measure of coordination to City self-regulation.

Notwithstanding the Bank's 'prefectorial' interest in them, the organised markets were genuinely self-regulatory bodies, displaying many of the characteristics of club-type arrangements, albeit subject to varying degrees of oversight by government departments. As the Stock Exchange explained in its evidence to the Wilson Committee, 'the principal feature of the regulatory system in the UK is that, within the general framework of the law, the authority of the supervising bodies is drawn not from statute but from the consent of the users of the market. It is a system in which the Stock Exchange has throughout played and still fulfils the central role.' (Committee to Review the Functioning of Financial Institutions, *Second Stage Evidence*, vol. 4, p. 16.) Stock Exchange rules were intended to provide protection to users of the market, of which the cornerstones were the companies listing requirements (administered alongside the Companies Act 1948) and the system of single capacity, which prohibited members from acting as both broker and dealer (or 'jobber' in the old Stock Exchange terminology). Fixed commissions were also in theory supposed to provide the investor with a degree of protection.

Similarly, in its evidence to the Wilson Committee, Lloyd's insurance market also outlined a self-regulatory system in which 'the Committee of Lloyd's plays a very considerable part in supervising the operations of Lloyd's underwriters, subject to the overall control of the Department of Trade. Before admitting a new Underwriting Member, the Committee satisfies itself as to the candidate's integrity and financial standing. Thereafter, the Committee supervises the conduct of the annual audit of accounts of every Underwriting Member. . . . This form of self-regulation, which operated at Lloyd's for many years prior to the introduction of statutory requirements, works extremely well.' (Committee to Review the Functioning of Financial Institutions, *Second Stage Evidence*, vol. 2, pp. 76–7.) What was true of the Stock Exchange and Lloyd's was also true of other City organised markets, such as those for commodities or the fledgling market for financial futures. These organised markets represented City 'self-regulation' in the truest sense of the word, in that the setting of rules for conduct in these markets was left to the determination of self-governing committees of practitioners subject to only the most limited statutory oversight.

The role of statute law was completely different in relation to the third component of the financial system. This comprised a diverse group of institutions that had in common only that they were not subject to the City's self-regulatory traditions, and that their regulation was to a substantial degree based on statute law. It embraced securities dealers who were not members of the Stock Exchange, the building societies, savings banks, insurance companies, and friendly societies.

The origins of the legislation governing this sector can be traced back into the middle of the nineteenth century, when Victorian social reformers attempted to encourage the habits of thrift among the great majority of the working population by facilitating new forms of saving institution. For example, the first Building Societies Act was enacted in 1836, followed by another in 1874. To ensure the security of the modest savings of working people, the legislation provided a high degree of regulation. It limited the types of activities in which these institutions could engage, and subjected them to governmental supervision either through dedicated regulatory bodies (most recently, the Building Societies Commission and the Friendly Societies Commission) or by the Board of Trade.

In some instances legislation was introduced specifically in response to certain types of financial scandal: this was true of the introduction of legislation on insurance companies, which was influenced by a series of Victorian scandals, in particular the failure of the Albert Life Assurance Co. in 1869 which gave rise to the Life Assurance Companies Act 1870. A series of scandals also contributed to the regulation of non-Stock Exchange securities dealers following a number of 'share-pushing' incidents in the 1930s. The report of the commission of enquiry established to examine the matter, the Bodkin Committee, made recommendations that resulted in the Prevention of Fraud (Investments) Act 1939, which was effectively re-enacted in 1958. This required securities dealers who were not members of the Stock Exchange to be licensed by the Board of Trade.

An important feature of the pre-1980 system was that although the UK had never enacted statutory measures analogous to the US Glass–Steagall Act (the Banking Act 1933), which separated commercial and investment banking, its financial markets were nonetheless highly fragmented and compartmentalised. Stock Exchange rules effectively prohibited membership by banks, which were therefore prevented from evolving into Continental-style universal banks. The activities limitations on building societies prevented them from becoming serious competitors to banks in the provision of consumer and commercial credit or the provision of payments services. Cross-ownership of banks and insurance companies was discouraged by the Bank of England and the Board of Trade. Furthermore, various customs and practices served to limit competition, ranging from officially sanctioned cartels (such as that among dealers in the government bond market) to the convention that banks did not compete with building societies for the latter's core business, mortgages. As a result the three streams of the financial sector remained largely separate and the degree of convergence between them was negligible. Until the end of the 1970s it was still largely possible to regard these three main elements of the financial system as belonging to distinct spheres, with their own traditions and styles of regulation.

## THE 1980S AND THE ADVENT OF STATUTORY REGULATION

The pre-1980 system came under pressure from a number of distinct sources which served to undermine it from both within and without. The first factor, at least in terms of time, was the secondary banking crisis of 1973–5. The so-called 'secondary' banks were, by definition, outside the 'primary' sector, which formed the focus of the Bank of England's non-statute-based supervision. Secondary banks were recognised as banks by the Board of Trade under the Companies Act 1967, s. 123, the sole purpose of which was to exempt them from the need to obtain a licence under the Moneylenders Acts 1900 to 1927. Section 123 recognition gave legitimacy to the formation of a large number of 'secondary' banks, which were not subject to authorisation and supervision by either the Board of Trade or the Bank of England. The existence of this secondary banking sector, combined with loose monetary and fiscal policies in the early 1970s, combined to produce a speculative property bubble. When this burst the secondary banks were left heavily exposed to a property sector that was unable to meet its repayment obligations. A number of institutions faced serious liquidity problems, and as the crisis wore on a growing number of them became insolvent. In response the Bank of England launched the 'lifeboat', which was a rescue package for troubled secondary banks to which it and the clearing banks committed £1,200 million. (For a detailed account see Margaret Reid, *The Secondary Banking Crisis* (London: Macmillan, 1982).)

The Banking Act 1979 was a direct consequence of the secondary banking crisis. Central to that Act was an attempt to preserve the Bank of England's traditional relationship with the core banking sector while requiring authorisation and supervision of the secondary sector. It thus drew a distinction between 'recognised banks' — the former primary sector — and 'licensed deposit takers' (LDTs). The surviving secondary banks were licensed as deposit takers and were subject to more intensive supervisory monitoring than were the recognised banks. The distinction was a way of preserving the Bank of England's long-cherished principle of applying a flexible supervisory regime to institutions with which it historically had enjoyed a close relationship. Although the Bank of England gained responsibility for banking supervision under the new Act, significantly from the point of view of more recent developments, both the then Prime Minister (James Callaghan) and Chancellor (Denis Healey) apparently had their reservations about its suitability for the role (see Michael Moran, *The Politics of Banking: The Strange Case of Competition and Credit Control*, 2nd edn. (London: Macmillan, 1986), p. 120).

Even some within the Bank argued against it taking on this responsibility, and consideration was briefly given to establishing a separate banking commission. Ultimately, however, the traditionalist position that regarded banking supervision as an essential central banking function prevailed.

The Banking Act 1979 was replaced in short order by another, the Banking Act 1987. The collapse of Johnson Matthey Bankers, a recognised bank under the 1979 Act, revealed the deficiencies of the two-tier system, especially the Bank of England's limited powers to require information of the recognised banks. Thus, the 1987 Act abolished the two-tier banking system and introduced a single banking authorisation based on the concept of an 'authorised institution'. It also granted the Bank significantly more extensive information-gathering powers, including the ability to require banks to commission reports from audit firms to verify the information they sent it. Yet despite the extensive powers it was granted under the new Act, the Bank was perceived in some quarters to be struggling with its statutory responsibilities and, as Sir Thomas Bingham noted in his report on the closure of the Bank of Credit and Commerce International (BCCI), on occasion seemed reluctant to use its powers to the full. The Bank's role in both the BCCI episode in 1991 and the collapse of Barings in 1995, attracted widespread public criticism and again raised doubts about whether it was the right body to conduct banking supervision.

The switch from a non-statutory to a statutory system of banking supervision was accompanied by equally fundamental change in the City of London's organised markets, and especially the Stock Exchange itself. A number of factors combined to undermine the City's old-established self-regulatory traditions and to pave the way for a statute-based system. Among them was the growing internationalisation of the City, as increasing numbers of foreign institutions began to play an active part in its markets, especially after the end of exchange controls in 1979. The telecommunications revolution, which laid the foundation for today's integrated, global financial markets, also facilitated this process. The government's privatisation programme, which aimed to create a new class of shareholders who had never before owned shares (the 'Sids' of the famous British Gas advertisement), also meant that changes to the system of investor protection were necessary. As a result, the old systems of City self-regulation, which had relied to a substantial extent on the existence of a network of relationships underpinned by shared norms of behaviour, came under increasing strain.

Although each of these factors was a major driver of legislative and structural change in City regulation, there were several other more specific factors that gave rise to the 1980s revolution. The first was the Stock Exchange's Big Bang. This was the result of Roy Hattersley's referral of the Stock Exchange's rulebook to the Office of Fair Trading under the Restrictive Trade Practices legislation. Following the change of government in 1979 the referral was eventually dropped, but subject to an agreement (the 'Parkinson–Goodison agreement') between the then Secretary of State for Trade and Industry and the then Chairman of the Stock Exchange. Under the terms of this agreement, the Exchange agreed to abolish minimum commissions, to put an end to single capacity (thus allowing the development of broker-dealers) and to permit outside firms to take over member firms (previously outside firms had been limited to a 30 per cent shareholding.) The result of these changes was further to dilute the sense of the Stock Exchange as a club with the ability to enforce its own membership rules. The abolition of single capacity removed what had been seen as one of the bulwarks of investor protection under the old regime.

In parallel to these changes was the review of investor protection conducted by Professor L. C. B. ('Jim') Gower. This was established following a series of financial scandals in the late 1970s and early 1980s, culminating in the collapse of the investment manager Norton Warburg which was regulated by the Board of Trade. Gower's remit was almost that of a one-man royal commission, with terms of reference that required him '(a) to consider the statutory protection now required by (i) private and (ii) business investors in securities . . .; (b) to consider the need for statutory control of dealers in securities, investment consultants and investment managers; and (c) to advise on the need for new legislation'. Gower had long supported the concept of a Securities and Exchange Commission for the UK (at least since his work on an earlier Company Law Committee in 1960), and in his initial discussion document expressed support for it as the ideal. However, he also recognised that it was not practical politics, not least because of the City's 'rooted opposition to a commission'. He accordingly went on to propose a system of self-regulating organisations which he believed would fill some of the gaps in the coverage of the old system. Importantly, it involved repeal of the Prevention of Fraud (Investments) Act 1958 and subjecting all securities dealers, whether or not they were members of the Stock Exchange, to the same Securities Act. Under the proposed arrangements the Stock Exchange would become a self-regulating organisation (SRO), while there would be another SRO dealing with public issues and takeovers. Gower's proposed structure of SROs was to be completed by one for the over-the-counter market and another for the unit trust industry. The government's role in this system was to be relatively hands-off, limited only to the authorisation and on-going monitoring of the activities of the SROs.

The completion of Gower's report was pre-empted by the government introducing a Bill which subsequently became the Financial Services Act 1986 (FSA 1986). The FSA 1986 contained a number of significant departures from Gower's original proposals. Although it stopped short of establishing a statutory securities commission, as advocated by the opposition Labour party, it nonetheless envisaged that the powers vested in the Secretary of State could be delegated to a body that had been established specifically to oversee the work of the SROs. This body, the Securities and Investments Board (SIB), although a private company limited by guarantee, exercised powers transferred to it from the Department of Trade and Industry, and had the general responsibility to ensure that the SROs regulated in the public interest. Its first chairman, Sir Kenneth Berrill, argued strongly that, although the new body would not be responsible for the regulation of securities offerings, it would 'to all intents and purposes be exercising the powers of an SEC in this country'. Nonetheless, many commentators continued to compare the powers of the new agency unfavourably with those of the US Securities and Exchange Commission.

Also significant was the structure of the system of SROs: instead of following the US system, as proposed by Gower, in which the Stock Exchange would have become an SRO, the regulation of brokers and dealers was separated from market regulation, and a new SRO was established to regulate brokers and dealers. There were also SROs for futures brokers and dealers, for investment managers, and for investment advisers. In addition, whereas Gower's original terms of reference had referred only to securities, the authorisation regime introduced by the new Act also encompassed complex products like life assurance and personal pensions. Hence the marketing and sales practices governing these products became subject to regulation for the first time, and an SRO was established to regulate the providers of these products. However, despite its otherwise broad coverage, FSA 1986 did not extend to Lloyd's of London, an omission which drew criticism from the Labour opposition.

The need to reassure a sceptical, and sometimes hostile, City community meant that the government stressed the self-regulatory element in the new system (in the words of David Lomax in his early study, *London Markets after the Financial Services Act* (London: Butterworths, 1987), there was 'obeisance to the principle of self-regulation'). In fact, however, FSA 1986 introduced a substantial degree of statutory regulation into the affairs of the City's organised markets for the first time. It also went a substantial distance towards eroding the distinction between the second and third streams of financial sector regulation. In particular, the non-Stock Exchange securities dealers, previously subject to the Prevention of Fraud (Investments) Act 1958, were brought within the same regulatory apparatus as the Stock Exchange's membership. While it is possible to criticise FSA 1986 and its regulatory bodies both for matters of conception and execution (some of these criticisms will be examined later) this should not detract from the fact that the new regime resulted in a substantial change in City attitudes towards regulation. The Financial Services and Markets Act 2000 would simply have not have been feasible without the groundwork of its predecessor. In this context it is significant that although the Labour Party opposed several aspects of the FSA 1986, they did nothing to prevent it reaching the statute book.

The third stream of the UK's financial sector also experienced significant legislative change in the 1980s. The most obvious development, as just mentioned, was the replacement of the Prevention of Fraud (Investments) Act 1958 with the Financial Services Act 1986. However, other legislation also powerfully affected this stream. Most notably, the Building Societies Act 1986 introduced a significant measure of deregulation into this previously highly regulated sector, permitting the societies to compete with banks in retail financial products, including current accounts. Given that the banks had a few years earlier moved into the market for mortgages, once the exclusive preserve of the societies, competition between joint stock and mutual institutions was now intense. The privatisation of the Trustee

Savings Bank in 1988 also added an extra dimension to competition in high street banking.

An overarching development in each of these separate sectors was the growing influence of EC law on the pattern of UK financial regulation. The Banking Act 1979 had, significantly, been in part necessary to comply with the First Banking Coordination Directive (77/780/EEC). However, as part of the regulatory harmonisation required to complete the European Internal Market in financial services, the late 1980s and early 1990s also saw a series of Directives on specific aspects of regulatory policy. A number of these were based on the concept of a 'credit institution', which embraced both banks and building societies, thus laying a common platform for their prudential regulation. Moreover, the banking Directives were premised on the Continental European model of a universal bank. Thus the Capital Adequacy Directive, which set capital requirements for market risk for both banks and investment firms, raised the issue of how competitive equality between banks and securities firms could be preserved if the same Directive was implemented by different sets of regulators. (Many of these, though not the Capital Adequacy Directive (93/6/EEC), have now been gathered together into the consolidating Credit Institutions Directive (2000/12/EC).)

EC law also resulted in the rules relating to banking regulation becoming more prescriptive than the Bank of England had traditionally favoured, given its preference for a flexible style of regulation. This preference had meant that the Bank had attempted to keep the number of detailed rules with which banks had to comply to the bare minimum, relying instead on the judgment of its individual supervisors. By contrast, the regulators established under FSA 1986 had formulated extensive rule books governing the behaviour of securities firms. The arrival of EC Directives that applied to both classes of institution resulted in a growing convergence between the Bank's techniques of regulation and those traditionally practised by the securities regulators.

## THE CONFLUENCE OF THE THREE STREAMS

The three streams of finance, which had been kept separate by custom, practice and cartels operated by the leading institutions, had begun to converge. By the end of the 1980s the regulatory system of the City of London had been radically transformed compared with that of a decade earlier. Nonetheless, the pace of regulatory change was itself soon outrun by developments in the industry itself that within a few years had put the new regualtory system under increasing strain. From being largely distinct sectors, the banks, building societies, unit and investment trusts, and insurance companies had become competitors, both as repositories of the savings of individuals and as providers of finance. The largest UK commercial banks acquired investment banking arms, while linkages between banks and insurance companies began to form. Financial conglomerates, straddling the banking, securities and insurance sectors, thus began to emerge. Parallel to these developments were the emergence of new types of financial product which did not fit readily into traditional regulatory distinctions; for example, futures contracts on the stock indices made it possible for insiders to deal or manipulate markets without acquiring any of the underlying securities.

These developments presented regulators with a number of profound challenges. For example, financial conglomerate groups found themselves subject to a plethora of different regulatory bodies, which both increased their regulatory burden and impeded the ability of any one regulator to obtain an overview of their risk profile. One illustration of this problem was the collapse of Barings in 1995, in which an old-established merchant bank was brought down by problems in its securities arm. But other, less spectacular, instances of the strains on the regulatory system were beginning to show. As a result, a regulatory system built on assumptions about clear dividing lines between different types of financial institution and product was increasingly poorly adapted to the realities of the financial market-place as it had evolved by the end of the twentieth century. Hence a reconfiguration of regulatory structure, the better to reflect these new economic realities, was becoming a matter of necessity.

The debate in the UK that followed the publication of Michael Taylor's report for the Centre for the Study of Financial Innovation, *Twin Peaks: A Regulatory Structure for the New Century*, considered some of these issues, although it did not do so in the depth of the Commission of Inquiry appointed by the Australian government which reported in March 1997 and which drew broadly similar conclusions (*Financial System Inquiry Final Report* (Canberra: Australian Government Publishing Service, 1997)). Both reports argued that industry convergence required regulatory convergence if regulation was to remain effective. However, there was little sign that this analysis had much influenced official thinking until the Chancellor's statement to the House of Commons on 20th May 1997. In consequence the latter was as unexpected as it was radical.

Announcing the decision to create what has subsequently become the Financial Services Authority, the Chancellor, Mr Gordon Brown MP, said:

[I]t is clear that the distinctions between different types of financial institution — banks, securities firms and insurance companies — are becoming increasingly blurred. Many of today's financial institutions are regulated by a plethora of different supervisors. This increases the cost and reduces the effectiveness of supervision.

In making the 'blurring the boundaries' argument the centrepiece of his justification for the government's new initiative, the Chancellor appeared to accept the arguments of those who had claimed that there was a need for a radical overhaul of the financial regulatory system as to reflect the new economic realities of the industry. The formation of the FSA, and the associated statutory changes in the Financial Services and Markets Act 2000, represented the government's response to these developments. The formation of a single regulatory authority, with oversight of the entire financial services sector, eliminated problems of regulatory jurisdiction in an environment in which the old, institutionally based regulatory structure had become increasingly outmoded. The enactment of a single statute, the Financial Services and Markets Act 2000, reflected the reality of the fact that having separate banking, securities and insurance legislation to regulate rapidly integrating financial services sectors was becoming increasingly redundant and possibly an obstacle to further beneficial change.

## OTHER INFLUENCES ON THE LEGISLATION

Although this blurring of boundaries argument was undoubtedly influential, other factors were equally, if not more, important in giving the Financial Services and Markets Act 2000 its final shape. At least as important as the desire to bring the regulatory structure up to date were three other considerations: the decision to award the Bank of England greater independence in the formulation of monetary policy; the government's desire to end what it described as 'City self-regulation' and especially to respond to what it regarded as the scandal of the mis-selling of personal pensions; and the long-standing desire on the part of the regulators, strongly supported by the new government, to obtain greater powers to combat financial crime. These different factors combined to give the Financial Services and Markets Act 2000 a very different character to the one it would have had, had it merely been an attempt to introduce a modernised regulatory system.

### Central bank independence

Like the decision to create a single 'super-regulator', the decision to grant the Bank of England autonomy in monetary policy did not feature in the Labour Party's election manifesto. The intellectual ground for this surprise move had been laid well in advance by a number of influential supporters of the case for central bank independence, including several former Conservative Chancellors of the Exchequer. Nevertheless, one issue that had received comparatively little prior attention was whether the Bank of England, as an independent central bank, should also conduct banking supervision. The evidence of other countries provides two different possible models.

   The first, Federal Reserve, model stresses the synergies between the conduct of monetary policy and banking supervision. In particular, since banks are the conduit through which changes in short-term interest rates are transmitted to the wider economy, the central bank needs to be concerned about their financial soundness as a precondition for an effective monetary policy. A subsidiary argument stresses the synergies which exist between the information needed for monetary policy purposes and that needed to assess the soundness of the banking system. The alternative, Bundesbank, model stresses instead the risks to the central bank of it directly conducting banking supervision. First, a central bank which is also responsible for supervision may err on the side of laxity if it fears that tight monetary conditions may lead to bank failures. Secondly, bank failures inevitably will occur and when they do they will be blamed on the supervisor. If the supervisor is the central bank, its credibility will be undermined, and with it its credibility in the conduct of monetary policy. Thus the Bundesbank model stresses that the relationship between the central bank and the banking supervisor should be sufficiently distant to limit the scope for such 'reputational contagion'.

The arguments for combination or separation of function were therefore finely balanced, and in practice the different arrangements are found in approximately equal measure in countries with independent central banks. However, in the British case two factors seem to have been decisive. First, as we have seen, the Labour Party had a long history of being unimpressed by the Bank of England's capability as a bank regulator. This dated back to the debates on the first UK Banking Act, in 1979, but was subsequently reinforced by episodes like BCCI and Barings, although neither episode resulted in a firm policy commitment to remove banking supervision from the Bank. Secondly, the Bank of England Act 1998 presented an opportunity to effect a transfer of powers under the Banking Act from the Bank to the Securities and Investments Board (see Michael Blair et al., *Blackstone's Guide to the Bank of England Act 1998* (London: Blackstone Press, 1998).) The 1998 Act permitted the government to change the regulatory arrangements in a way which supported its general objective of modernising the system, but without the immediate need to establish a new regulatory agency. Given the circumstances of a crowded legislative timetable, such an opportunity must have seemed very attractive to the Treasury ministers. Thus, shortly after the Bank of England was granted monetary policy independence, the government announced that it would also lose responsibility for banking supervision to what subsequently became the Financial Services Authority.

## An end to 'self-regulation'

As we have seen, 'self-regulation' in its truest sense had ceased to exist in the City a decade and a half before the Act. Nonetheless, Labour Party spokesmen criticised the decision in 1986 not to create a statutory securities commission in the UK, and continued to insist that in the absence of such a body the resulting system remained largely 'self-regulatory'. Bryan Gould, the party's then spokesman on City affairs, said in a parliamentary debate on the Bill for FSA 1986 that 'failure to put in place a proper independent statutory commission will be regretted by the government and is already being regretted by the City', and he also criticised the Conservative government for its failure to bring Lloyd's within the framework provided for by the Bill. The characterisation of the arrangements brought in by FSA 1986 as 'self-regulatory' provided ammunition for opposition spokesmen as evidence emerged of various regulatory failings by the new agencies it had established, and the emerging scandals at Lloyd's cast doubt on the wisdom of exempting the insurance market from the Act's scope.

Of the various scandals that afflicted FSA 1986 regulators, none had a greater impact than that of pensions mis-selling. The 'mis-selling' issue concerned the way in which personal, portable pensions, introduced by the Conservative government in the mid 1980s, were marketed and sold. These pensions were provided through the life insurance companies, and were intended to be an alternative to occupational pensions which, it was argued, led to rigidities in the labour market by encouraging workers to remain with the same employer for long periods of time. The protection of individuals against the sale of unsuitable pension plan products was to have been provided by the regulatory framework established by the Financial Services Act 1986, which was completing its parliamentary passage at the same time as the legislation for the new portable pensions. In the words of John Major, then a junior minister concerned with the introduction of the new system, FSA 1986 would 'safeguard people against the unscrupulous overselling of personal pensions'.

Approximately eight million personal pensions were sold in the UK between 1988 and 1995. Some were sold to people who were in occupational schemes and who were advised to transfer out of these schemes and to take out personal pensions in their place. For those prospective pensioners who were in well-funded schemes and where the prospective pension was protected against inflation, as was the case with many public-sector employees, it would be very difficult to argue that it was good advice to leave those schemes in favour of personal pensions with no employer contribution and an uncertain return. In at least some cases this mis-selling seems to have been due to the fact that insurance company salesforces were poorly controlled and were remunerated on a commission-only basis, thus leading to high-pressure sales tactics. These sales practices continued notwithstanding a regulatory regime that included as its key concepts 'best advice' and 'suitability', both of which had been introduced into the regulatory framework as a way of regulating the sale of complex, packaged financial products such as pensions.

Nonetheless, the extent of pensions mis-selling still remains a matter of dispute and depends on a number of assumptions, for example, about the investment return and the buyer's perceived financial needs at the time. Estimates of mis-selling have varied widely. When the issue first came to public prominence in 1993, a report commissioned by the SIB suggested that as many as 1.5 million pensions had been mis-sold with compensation costs amounting to some £4 billion. Subsequently, these figures have been disputed by both the industry and some independent commentators, but the results of the subsequent regulatory review of the mis-selling cases suggests total compensation costs may be at least double the original estimate. There can be little doubt that, whatever the true scale of the problem, it did cause a significant loss of public confidence in personal pensions and in the system set up to regulate them.

The essence of the government's response to the mis-selling episode was to attribute it to the failings of self-regulation. The reason that mis-selling had not been detected and dealt with by regulators at a sufficiently early stage, it was argued, was because the SROs failed to take adequate enforcement action. This was due to the fact that they were hamstrung by their industry-dominated boards.

Meanwhile, the SIB lacked sufficient enforcement powers to ensure that appropriate regulatory actions were taken. The SIB possessed only the power to 'derecognise' an SRO, an option that was too draconian to be an effective basis for intervention. In the absence of the kinds of intervention powers available to the United States SEC in its dealings with its SROs, the SIB was thus constrained from ensuring that the SROs regulated in the public interest.

While this analysis can be disputed in a variety of ways, it formed the basis for the Labour Party's conclusion, while in opposition, that the complex two-tier system of the SIB and SROs needed to be replaced by a single, statutory body responsible for the regulation of all securities and investments business. Although the model most often cited was that of the US SEC, this overlooked the fact that the latter body itself made substantial use of SROs. Instead, a completely unitary system was proposed in which the functions of the existing SROs would be absorbed into a reformed and enhanced SIB, reconstituted as a proper statutory body. This proposal formed the nucleus for what has subsequently become the FSA, although the latter has gained the important additions of banking, building society and insurance regulation, as well as the function of acting as the competent authority for listing which was transferred to the FSA from the London Stock Exchange in May 2000. Moreover, the FSA, like the SIB, remains a private company discharging a public function, and hence the proposal for a 'statutory commission' has never in fact been enacted.

## Dealing with financial crime

The third influential factor behind the new regime introduced by the Act derives from a long-standing sense on the part of the financial services regulators that they lacked adequate powers to combat financial crime, especially market manipulation and insider dealing. For several years prior to the Act in speeches made by its then chairman, Sir Andrew Large, the SIB argued that there were serious shortcomings in the investigation and disposal of cases of insider dealing and market abuse. In part these shortcomings were due to fragmented jurisdictions, with the SIB having no powers over market abuse resulting from the conduct of individuals who were not authorised persons under the Financial Services Act 1986. In part they were also due to the fact that such cases could only be prosecuted under the criminal law, with a criminal rather than a civil burden of proof. As Sir Andrew remarked in a speech delivered on 29 October 1996:

> . . . under the criminal system the evidential and public interest hurdles to be cleared before commencing a successful prosecution in the criminal courts are, quite correctly, high. But, as a result, activities which take place outside the scope of the regulators, whether the actions of company directors or end users of markets, may finish up not being taken to court. And since there is no sufficient civil alternative, what we would deem unacceptable actions from a regulatory viewpoint, and which we could often deal with if entered into by someone who was subject to regulation, can currently go unchallenged.

In often complex cases, with evidence that could only be interpreted on the basis of specialist knowledge, this meant that the number of prosecutions brought for market abuse was very small and the number of convictions even less. The regulators spent several years pressing for a revision to the law that would permit them to dispose of cases of market abuse through civil rather than criminal channels. Significantly, this was one aspect of UK regulatory reform where its proponents seem to have drawn direct inspiration from US law and practice. This is the basis for the new Code of Market Conduct and the provisions of the Act relating to the FSA's powers in relation to individuals who breach that code.

This aspect of the Act has also proved to be the most controversial. It resulted in the draft Bill being criticised in an opinion of Lord Lester of Herne Hill QC, commissioned by a Joint Committee of the Lords and Commons that had been established to scrutinise it, on the grounds that the proposed new regime was incompatible with the European Convention on Human Rights. In consequence the government introduced a number of important amendments, most notably to the proceedings of the proposed new Financial Services and Markets Tribunal which will now hear cases involving a breach of the Code of Market Conduct at first instance. Moreover, the regime has now lost its 'civil' tag, which counsel's opinion had strongly argued was something of a misnomer.

## CONCLUSION

As we have seen, the Act is an attempt to modernise the UK's regulatory system by reflecting the realities of the new financial landscape that has emerged over the last decade and a half. But it is also much more than this. In abolishing the SROs its aim is to remove some of the last vestiges of the old self-regulatory practices of the City. In introducing a new regime for market abuse it aims also to ensure that the incidence of financial crime and sharp market practice is reduced. It also reflects a changing role for the Bank of England, which has to a large extent lost its role as the City's 'head prefect'. The transfer of banking supervision to the FSA was simply the most striking example of how the old informal norms that once ruled the City, with the Bank as their accepted enforcer, have given way over the years to a regime based more explicitly on statute law and on detailed rules and regulations. The Act has been possible because the balance between statutory and self-regulation had long ago shifted decisively in favour of the former.

# Chapter Two
# Accountability and Objectives of the FSA

## Michael Taylor

This chapter is concerned with the mechanisms for ensuring the Financial Services Authority's (FSA's) accountability in the broadest sense. Two distinct strands of Part I of the Financial Services and Markets Act 2000 (FSAMA 2000) put in place a framework for the FSA's accountability: the first creates *institutional* mechanisms for accountability by specifying a series of provisions relating to the FSA's constitution and governance arrangements. The second specifies a number of *objectives and principles* that the FSA must observe in the exercise of its functions. These represent the criteria according to which the FSA's performance of the functions conferred on it may be judged. This chapter considers both these aspects of the arrangements for the FSA's accountability. However, it begins with a brief section considering the reasons for the FSA having been established with a rather unusual constitutional status, as a private company discharging a public function.

## A PRIVATE COMPANY DISCHARGING A PUBLIC FUNCTION

The arrangements for the regulation of the financial sector envisaged in FSAMA 2000 are somewhat unusual, although not unprecedented. In conferring regulatory powers on a body corporate (s. 1), the Act departs from the practice adopted in the UK for the regulation of most other industrial sectors. (It is worth noting, however, that the government has since proposed to transform the Office of Fair Trading into a corporation governed by a board on the model of the FSA.) Vesting these powers in a private company has a number of important consequences. In the first place the FSA is not to be regarded as acting on behalf of the Crown, and its members, officers and staff are not Crown servants (sch. 1, para. 13) This is a status that they share in common with the staff of the Bank of England, who are similarly not Crown servants, although the Bank is a public, rather than a private, corporation.

Secondly, it avoids the personalised approach to regulation that has been a feature of the approach adopted for utilities like water, electricity, gas and telecommunications. The regulation of each of these sectors has been entrusted to a 'Director General' in whom powers are vested personally by statute. In this arrangement 'one sees a reflection of the highly personal style of UK government through ministers, and it has been a key influence on the way in which regulation operates' (T. Prosser, 'Regulation, markets and legitimacy' in J. Jowell and D. Oliver (eds), *The Changing Constitution*, 3rd edn. (Oxford: Clarendon Press, 1994). However, the conditions in the financial services sector are substantially different from those in the utilities. Not only is the financial sector much larger and more diverse (accounting on one measure for 14 per cent of national output) than any of the industries regulated by a Director General, but the range of regulatory tasks is much broader. Moreover, as discussed elsewhere in this book, the range of powers conferred on the FSA by the Act is very extensive; arguably the Act creates the most powerful regulatory body for financial services anywhere in the world. It would be obviously inappropriate for such a broad range of powers to be vested personally in a single individual, especially as the way that the more limited powers of the utilities regulators have been exercised has itself been the subject of much criticism. These factors argue for a much less personalised approach to the regulatory arrangements for financial services than would have been inevitable had the Director General model been adopted.

The most commonly discussed alternative to the creation of the office of Director General is to establish the regulatory body as a multi-member commission. In the UK this administrative arrangement has been adopted for a variety of regulatory and quasi-judicial functions including those of the Equal Opportunities Commission, the Independent Television Commission, the Building Societies Commission, the Health and Safety Commission and the Civil Aviation Authority. Despite a passing interest in the concept while in opposition, the Labour Party in government has not been disposed significantly to extend the use of regulatory commissions, although in many other countries they are widely used for the regulation of financial services as well (for example, it is the organisational form of the United States Securities and Exchange Commission and Federal Deposit Insurance Corporation). In theory, a multi-member commission has a number of advantages compared with vesting powers in a single individual. It arguably leads to greater consistency of decision-making over time and may also result in greater regulatory independence from either government or the industry. On the other hand, it is sometimes urged against the multi-member commission that it is not well-adapted to speedy decision-making, which can be of the essence in the regulation of financial services, especially when responding to a possible systemic crisis.

Vesting powers in a body corporate represents a departure from either of the main administrative forms used for the regulation of other industries and in other countries of the world. Nonetheless, it has been argued that this arrangement is able to combine the best elements of the Director General and multi-member commission models discussed above. The FSA's governance arrangements display aspects of both approaches and the Act requires that its constitution provides both for a board of directors and a chairman, who is also a member of the governing body (sch. 1, para. 2(2)). This arrangement, it has been argued, provides a balance between the need for rapid decision-making informed by special expertise (provided by the chairman and executive members of the board) while maintaining an element of collegiality in the decision process as well as a degree of independent oversight (provided by the non-executive members). A further advantage claimed for the board arrangement is that it enhances the transparency and accountability of regulatory bodies, and this was one of the primary reasons cited for adopting the same governance arrangements for the Office of Fair Trading and, prospectively, for the Gas and Electricity Markets Authority as well.

Nonetheless, the issue of whether or not the roles of chairman and chief executive should be combined, as at present, has been a controversial one. Many concerns have been expressed about the power that a combined role confers on a single individual. For example, the authors of a pamphlet for the Centre for Policy Studies argued that the combination of chairman and chief executive roles was a 'move almost unprecedented in the public sector' which might reduce rather than improve public accountability (Andrew Tyrie and Martin McElwee, *Leviathan at Large: The New Regulator for the Financial Markets* (London: Centre for Policy Studies, 2000)). Although the Act does not explicitly require the roles to be split, there was a good deal of support for the proposal during debates on the Bill and in the report of the Joint Committee of the Lords and Commons established to scrutinise the draft Bill (Joint Committee report, para. 113). Although the government strenuously opposed this proposal, it was ultimately obliged to accept a late compromise amendment tabled in the Lords that 'In managing its affairs, the [FSA] must have regard to such generally accepted principles of good corporate governance as it is reasonable to regard as applicable to it' (s. 7). In the Combined Codes on corporate governance the separation of roles is recommended, although not mandated.

Although unusual, the decision to vest regulatory powers in a body corporate was not entirely unprecedented in the UK. As noted in the previous chapter, many of the 'governmental' functions under the Financial Services Act 1986 (FSA 1986) were delegated to the Securities and Investments Board (SIB), which was established as a company limited by guarantee. The exercise of statutory powers by a private-sector body was there adopted in an effort to ensure that regulation remained rooted in the financial markets; in theory a private-sector body would be more alert to the concerns of the industry, especially regarding the regulatory burden, than a government department or agency would be. The decision to vest powers in a body corporate in the successor to FSA 1986 may also have been influenced by similar considerations, although administrative expediency may have played at least as great a part in the decision to adopt this form. A new governmental agency could not have become operational until it had been legislated into existence; this would have necessitated a long delay in setting up the new regulatory arrangements for the financial sector. By vesting powers in a body corporate rather than a new governmental agency the considerable logistical and administrative problem of merging nine separate regulatory agencies into one was significantly eased since an existing regulatory body, the SIB, could be made the core of the new arrangements.

As part of the transition arrangements the SIB changed its name by special resolution to the Financial Services Authority in October 1997 and continued to exercise both its existing powers under FSA 1986 and those powers under the Banking Act 1987 which were transferred to it by the Bank of England Act 1998. The discharge of other regulatory functions was then governed by a series of contracts between the FSA and other regulatory bodies, including the self-regulating organisations established under the FSA 1986, and the statutory regulatory bodies like the Building Societies Commission, the Friendly Societies Commission, and the Insurance Division of the Treasury. Under the terms of these contracts, the FSA provided these regulatory bodies with services (including but not limited to those of its professional staff) to enable them to discharge their regulatory functions. Thus formal rule-making and enforcement decisions remained with the existing regulatory bodies, e.g., the boards of the self-regulating organisations or the statutory commissions, but the operational aspects of regulation were discharged by the staff of the FSA. This arrangement was adopted to permit the single regulatory agency to be created *de facto* in advance of the legislation coming into force. It permitted the staff of the existing regulatory bodies to be integrated into a single management structure and to be placed on the same terms and conditions of service. It also permitted a large amount of detailed planning and preparation to be completed before the Act came into force. The Act's effect is to replace this ad hoc arrangement with a broad range of powers for the FSA, covering the authorisation and supervision of banking, securities, investment, and insurance business.

## INSTITUTIONAL MECHANISMS FOR ACCOUNTABILITY

Vesting such a broad range of powers in any body, whether a governmental agency or a private company, places a special premium on ensuring that they are used in a responsible and accountable manner. The need for accountability has to be balanced by the need to ensure that the regulatory body is independent of improper influence, whether exercised on it by politicians or by the industry it regulates; the necessity of such independence as a prerequisite for effective regulation is a common theme throughout the various recent international statements of regulatory best practice (for example, Basel Committee on Banking Supervision, *Core Principles for Effective Banking Supervision* (1997) and International Organisation of Securities Commissions (IOSCO), *Objectives and Principles of Securities Regulation* (Montreal: IOSCO, 1998)). The task of ensuring a proper balance between regulatory independence on the one hand and accountability on the other is a complicated one, and has proved to be one of the most controversial aspects of the Act.

The model of accountability adopted is closely aligned with that applied to public corporations, like the Bank of England, notwithstanding the fact that the

FSA's legal form is that of a private company. Indeed, there are some important parallels between the accountability arrangements established by the Act and those put in place by the Bank of England Act 1998. At the same time there are also significant differences.

In both cases, the accountability arrangements reflect the traditional constitutional doctrine that incorporated bodies should not be directly answerable to Parliament, and that it is for ministers to answer for the exercise or non-exercise of whatever powers they may possess. Thus for both the Bank and the FSA the primary line of accountability is to HM Treasury. The Treasury have four main mechanisms for holding the FSA to account. The first is the power of appointment or dismissal of the FSA's board and chairman, powers reserved to the Treasury by para. 2(3) of sch. 1 to the Act. However, there are two main differences from the appointment of the Bank of England's governor and court. The first is that the latter are formally Crown appointments, whereas the FSA board appointments are not. Secondly, the Act does not specify any formal criteria for the appointment or dismissal of members of the governing body, other than they cannot be currently serving members of Parliament or of the Northern Ireland Assembly. Unlike the governor of the Bank of England, for example, the chairman of the FSA does not have a statutory fixed term in office. In this respect the Act is less prescriptive than the Bank of England Act 1998, which contains a number of provisions relating to the terms of office, the qualifications for appointment, and conditions for the dismissal of the Bank's governor and court of directors (Bank of England Act 1998, sch. 1, paras 1 to 8). Accordingly, there are fewer statutory requirements for ensuring the security of tenure, independence and appropriate qualifications of appointees to the FSA's governing board than for the Bank of England's court. On the other hand, appointments to the FSA board will in practice be governed by the principles set out by the Nolan Committee on Standards in Public Life which provides a degree of non-statute-based transparency to the appointments process.

In addition to the power of appointment and dismissal of the members of the FSA's governing body, the Act confers on the Treasury three other mechanisms for holding the FSA to account. In the first place, the FSA must submit to the Treasury, at least once each year, a report covering such matters as the FSA's discharge of its functions; the extent to which its objectives have been met; the extent to which it has complied with the principles that should govern the discharge of its functions set out in s. 2(3) of the Act; and any other matters the Treasury may direct (sch. 1, para. 10(1)). This report is to be accompanied by a report from the non-executive directors of the governing body (sch. 1, para. 10(2)) and will be laid before Parliament (sch. 1, para. 10(3)).

In addition, the Treasury are empowered, by ss. 12 to 18 of the Act, to commission reviews and inquiries into aspects of the FSA's operations. A review is to be conducted by a person who appears to the Treasury to be independent of the FSA (s. 12(7)) and is confined to considering the economy, efficiency and effectiveness with which the FSA has used its resources in discharging its functions (s. 12(1)). The merits of the FSA's general policies and principles are explicitly excluded from such reviews (s. 12(3)). They are thus, in broad terms, equivalent to a 'value for money' review conducted by the National Audit Office (NAO), for which they are intended to be substitutes (see below). These reports must also be laid before Parliament (s. 12(5)(a)) and the Treasury may decide on the extent of further publication (s. 12(5)(b)).

By contrast, inquiries under s. 14 relate to specific, exceptional events occurring within the FSA's range of regulatory responsibilities. If events concerning a collective investment scheme or the activities of a person carrying out an authorisable activity (whether or not authorised to do so) either could have posed a grave risk to the financial system or caused or risked causing significant damage to the interests of consumers, and these events might not have occurred but for a serious failure either in the regulatory system or its operation, then the Treasury are empowered to commission an independent inquiry into those events (s. 14(2)). Similar powers may also be exercised where the event concerns listed securities or the issuer of listed securities which caused or could have caused significant damage to holders of listed securities and when those events might not have occurred but for a serious failure in the regulatory system for listing (or in the operation of that system) (s. 14(3)). Section 14 thus creates a formal basis for a practice that had developed during the previous decade and a half of commissioning reports on various aspects of the regulators' discharge of their responsibilities (e.g., the report by Sir Thomas Bingham on the supervision of the Bank of Credit and Commerce International). The Treasury may also decide on whether the report of such an inquiry is published, in whole or in part (s. 17(2)). If any report or part of a report is published then it must be laid before Parliament (s. 17(5)). Hence, unlike reviews, it is not automatic that the report of an inquiry will be laid before Parliament.

The Act's intention is clearly, therefore, to place the Treasury at the centre of the FSA's accountability arrangements. Several other accountability mechanisms are envisaged by the Act. An important element in the FSA's accountability is provided by the requirement that a majority of the members of the governing body should be non-executive (sch. 1, para. 3(1)(a)). The Act gives a statutory role to the non-executive members of the Board, similar to the arrangements introduced for the Bank of England under the Bank of England Act 1998. There is to be a committee of the governing body, consisting solely of non-executive members, with a chairman is appointed by the Treasury. This committee is charged with a special role in respect of the FSA's efficiency, internal controls and determining the remuneration of the chairman and the executive members of the board.

A second, company-like aspect of the FSA's accountability is that it will be obliged to hold an annual meeting, analogous to a shareholders' meeting for a public limited company, but in the present case open to any interested parties. The annual public meeting must be held within three months of the report under sch. 1, para. 10, being made to the Treasury, and the purpose of the meeting is to permit the report to be considered by facilitating a general discussion of its contents and by providing an opportunity for questions to be put to the FSA about any of its acts or omissions in the discharge of its functions (sch. 1, para. 11(2)). The FSA must prepare and publish a report of the meeting no later than one month after the meeting's conclusion (sch. 1, para. 12).

The FSA's accountability to two further important stakeholder groups — consumers and practitioners — is to be advanced by two statutory bodies, a Consumer Panel and a Practitioner Panel (originally Forum), both of which were initially established on a non-statutory basis in November 1998. The Consumer Panel exists to advise the FSA on the interests and concerns of consumers and to report on the FSA's effectiveness in meeting its consumer protection and public awareness statutory objectives (see below.) This Panel can raise its own concerns, initiate research and publish its own reports. The Practitioner Panel was also established in November 1998, and is now placed on a statutory basis by the Act. Its membership comprises senior representatives of the businesses that are regulated by the FSA. Both Panels may make representations to the FSA, and the Act requires that the FSA 'have regard' to such representations. By s. 11, if the FSA disagrees with the view expressed or proposal made in the representation it must give the panel a statement in writing of its reasons for disagreeing, and this statement may be made public. The membership of both Panels is determined by the FSA itself, although the Treasury's approval is required for the appointment and dismissal of the chairmen of these Panels (s. 9(3) and s. 10(3)).

The only explicit mention of accountability to Parliament in the Act is the requirement that the FSA's report to the Treasury, and the reports commissioned under s. 12, should be laid before Parliament, and inquiries commissioned under s. 14 may be so laid. Although reflecting a traditional constitutional doctrine, the absence of a more formal mechanism of parliamentary accountability formed the subject of much debate during debates on the Bill. The House of Lords Delegated Powers and Deregulation Committee argued that if ministers were to exercise the same kind of rule-making power that the Act vests in the FSA, there would undoubtedly be a case for parliamentary control. The Joint Committee on Financial Services and Markets also recommended that a parliamentary committee should scrutinise the FSA's annual report and take regular evidence from a broad section of consumers and practitioners. In addition, a number of expert commentators argued for a 'dual-key' approach to appointments of the FSA's chairman and board, with nominations by ministers being subject to confirmation hearings by Parliament (as proposed, among others, by Robert Laslett and Michael Taylor in *Independence and Accountability: Tweaking the Financial Services Authority* (London: Centre for the Study of Financial Innovation, 1998) and by Tyrie and McElwee in *Leviathan at Large*). However, as already discussed, the Act does not envisage a substantial role for parliamentary accountability and cleaves to the traditional constitutional doctrine of accountability through ministers. Furthermore, because the FSA is funded by a levy on the financial services industry rather than by public funds, the government held that there was no case for making it subject to oversight by the National Audit Office, including NAO 'value for money' reviews, on the grounds that no public money was involved. Hence involvement of the NAO, which traces the use of public money and reports to the Public Accounts Committee of the House of Commons, would be inappropriate. The commissioning of reviews by the Treasury, discussed above, has been adopted as an alternative to NAO oversight.

Judicial review and scrutiny of the FSA's actions will be a further important component of the network of accountability mechanisms. Although established as a private company, the FSA will be subject to judicial review and to the panoply of administrative law since it clearly performs a public function and is empowered to do so by statute. On the other hand, the Act applies a number of largely subjective criteria to the way in which the FSA is required to discharge its tasks: for example, the FSA is required to act in a way which is compatible with the regulatory objectives and in a way which is most appropriate for meeting them. But, while the former of these (compatibility) is not subjective, the latter refers to the way which the FSA considers most appropriate for meeting the objectives (s. 2(1)(b)). It could be argued that the introduction of such a personalised criterion constrains, to some degree, the scope for judicial review.

Moreover, the Act confers on the FSA a broadly drafted immunity from suit. Although the importance of ensuring that individual officers of the FSA are immune from suit for actions taken in furtherance of their official duties is widely recognised, the extent to which the FSA is immune from suit as a body corporate has been much more controversial. The FSA has immunity from suit for all its acts except those taken in bad faith or in breach of the Human Rights Act 1998 (sch. 1, para. 19). This broad immunity from suit was also enjoyed by a number of the regulatory agencies that the FSA replaced, but has become more controversial given the concentration of powers in the FSA's hands, making it a much more powerful body than those it replaced. In these circumstances, it has been argued, such a broadly drafted immunity from suit needs to be accompanied by a strong and independent complaints procedure. By sch. 1, para. 7, the FSA is required to establish a complaints scheme for dealing with any complaints arising from the discharge of its functions, or the failure to discharge its functions (other than its legislative functions). The Act also provides for an investigator who can act independently of the FSA (sch. 1, para. 7(1)(b)). The complaints procedure is necessary to give some redress to regulated businesses and individuals who are damaged by the FSA's maladministration. However, serious doubts were expressed in debates on the Bill about the adequacy of the arrangements provided for under the Act, and this remains a controversial feature of it. In agreeing not to disturb the substance of a late amendment the government accepted that the scheme must confer power on the independent investigator to recommend compensatory payments, payable by the FSA, to a justified complainant (sch. 1 para. 8(5)).

## OBJECTIVES AND PRINCIPLES

In addition to the institutional arrangements for holding the FSA to account, the Act also contains a number of regulatory objectives and principles that are intended to provide criteria by which the FSA's performance of its functions may be judged. The emphasis that is given in the Act to regulatory objectives makes it unusual compared to the Acts that it supersedes, including the Banking Act 1987 and the Financial Services Act 1986. Rather than appearing prominently in the first part of these Acts, the objectives of regulation were neither clearly articulated nor prominently displayed. Giving such prominence to the FSA's objectives is intended to help to ensure that regulation is effective and appropriate and that the FSA can be held accountable for the way in which its functions are exercised. In this respect the Act crystallises the experience gained by a number of regulatory agencies since the 1980s in defining more clearly their role and functions.

While the approach in the Act greatly contributes to the clarity of regulation and establishes an entity which should enjoy a firm understanding of its aims and purposes, the very broad range of financial activities regulated by the FSA has required careful balancing in the formulation of these objectives. A balance has had to be struck across two different dimensions: the first involves developing a single set of objectives that can embrace the different aims and purposes of banking, securities and insurance regulation. The second has involved finding a regulatory middle way between, on the one hand, the demands of consumers for security and protection, and the need to maintain and promote suitably high industry standards, and, on the other, the recognition that unnecessarily burdensome regulation can stifle innovation and competition in financial markets, and that regulation should not aim to absolve individuals from the responsibility for making their own financial decisions.

The statutory objectives that define the FSA's overall purpose are four in number: maintaining market confidence; promoting public awareness; protecting consumers; and reducing financial crime. The Act applies these objectives, together with the associated principles of regulation, directly to the FSA's general functions, including rule-making, the preparation and issuing of codes, and the regulator's general policies. As the competent authority under Part VI (the 'UK Listing Authority') the FSA also has a specific general duty, under s. 73, which is similar to but not quite the same as the principles of regulation laid down in s. 2(3). However, in its capacity as the listing authority the FSA does not appear to have objectives that are equivalent to those in s. 2(2) that apply to its regulatory functions. This issue is considered further in chapter 8.

## Market confidence

The FSA's market confidence objective is defined as 'maintaining confidence in the financial system' (s. 3(1)), including financial markets and exchanges, regulated activities and connected activities. The term 'confidence' is generally used in the context of the regulation of securities markets, where the purpose of regulation is often said to be to provide investors and potential investors with confidence in the integrity and orderly conduct of the market. In the words of the IOSCO *Objectives and Principles*, the aim is to ensure that markets are 'fair, efficient and transparent'.

Markets with these characteristics are ones in which the process of price discovery will operate on the basis of the information available to all investors. To guard against the risk that market prices may be distorted by insiders exploiting their superior information, market integrity regulation embraces such matters as the authorisation of exchanges, ensuring a reliable price formation process, and the prevention of improper trading practices including market manipulation and insider dealing. Thus market integrity regulation at one extreme shades off into dealing with conduct that falls within the purview of the criminal law, while at the other extreme it is concerned with ensuring that markets operate efficiently. Market integrity regulation, combined with regulation of the disclosure of information in securities offerings (discussed below), has formed the core of the traditional functions of securities regulators throughout the world.

However, the objective as formulated in the Act goes beyond this relatively limited conventional sense in which regulation is concerned with market confidence. The objective refers to confidence 'in the financial system', which indicates a comparatively extended meaning. An important element in this extended meaning relates to the *stability* of the financial system, which the Treasury and the FSA itself have made clear that they regard as being integral to the market confidence objective. As the FSA explains in its document *A New Regulator for the New Millennium* (hereinafter referred to as *'New Millennium'*), maintaining confidence 'involves . . . preserving both actual stability in the financial system and the reasonable expectation that it will remain stable' (ch. 1, para. 2).

It is consistent with the existence of financial stability that individual firms should fail; this is the natural consequence of a competitive market economy in which investors incur risks in response to the prospective returns of their risk-taking. When a financial firm miscalculates the trade-off between risk and return, investors and its creditors (including depositors) may lose money. Thus the users of financial services need also to understand that different types of investment carry different levels of risk, and it is not the purpose of financial regulation to remove risk from the financial system altogether. As the FSA remarks in the *New Millennium* document, a regime that attempted to eliminate all risks for users of financial services would be excessively burdensome and uneconomic, and would encourage excessive levels of risk taking. Hence the 'market confidence' objective contemplates the possibility of the failure of individual firms (*New Millennium*, Ch. 1, para. 6).

By contrast, *financial instability* can be thought of as arising where financial distress in one financial institution is communicated to others. Contagion may occur as a result of problems in one institution triggering a crisis of customer confidence in other institutions; alternatively it may occur because the failure of one institution to settle its obligations causes the failure of other, fundamentally sound, institutions. Traditionally, the risk of this type of contagion was thought to be highest among banks, i.e., deposit-taking institutions. This is because of the inherent difficulty of the financial service they provide, which is to transform illiquid assets (loans) from and into liquid liabilities (deposits). A commitment to pay a depositor can be met in normal times, because customers' demand for access to their funds is reasonably predictable and liquid assets can be held to meet this demand. However, when a sufficiently large number of customers demand convertibility at the same time, the bank's commitment to provide them with liquid funds cannot be met without some form of outside assistance. Since all deposit-takers suffer from the same potential weakness, and it can be difficult for depositors to distinguish between a sound bank and an unsound one, a crisis of confidence in one entity can quickly spread to others that are perceived to share the same characteristics. Further, the nature of the weakness is such that concern about insolvency, whether or not well-founded, may be sufficient actually to cause insolvency if assets have to be liquidated at reduced prices ('fire sale prices') to meet the demands of withdrawing depositors.

A further source of potential contagion among banks is that they participate in the payments system, where obligations are settled between financial intermediaries. The failure of one participant in that system to meet its obligations can have serious implications for the ability of other participants to meet their own obligations. Disruption to the payments system can in turn precipitate a wider economic crisis. Arguably, it is in the core of the payments system that the greatest systemic risk arises. However, other elements of the financial system infrastructure, including settlements and clearing systems, also contain the potential to act as a transmission mechanism for contagion between financial institutions. Hence the FSA also stresses that its concern with financial sector stability is not limited to ensuring the financial soundness of the banking system, but is also concerned with other elements of the financial system — including clearing houses and settlement systems — that are a vital part of the system's infrastructure.

In view of the overarching importance attached to the systemic stability objective of regulation it is, perhaps, surprising that it is only implicit in the market confidence objective. This was the view of the Joint Committee on Financial Services and Markets which proposed that the 'market confidence' objective be amended to refer explicitly to systemic risk, so that the FSA's objectives would include 'maintaining confidence *in the soundness* of the financial system' (emphasis added.) The committee was also of the view that some reference to the FSA's role as a crisis manager, in collaboration with the Treasury and the Bank of England, should be incorporated in this objective. However, ministers were not persuaded by this argument. The government's position on the systemic protection objective was that public and market confidence in the financial system clearly requires confidence in the soundness of the system as a whole. However, other aspects are also relevant, notably maintaining confidence in the effective prudential supervision of individual institutions. Singling out one aspect could throw doubt on the FSA's role in this area and narrow its remit. The government agreed with the committee that cooperation with the Bank of England and the Treasury is very important, but claimed that this had been adequately covered in a published memorandum of understanding (MoU). (The text of the MoU is published in Michael Blair et al., *Blackstone's Guide to The Bank of England Act 1998* (London: Blackstone Press, 1998), app. 5.)

The MoU divides responsibility for systemic stability between the Bank and the FSA on the following lines: the Bank is responsible for 'the overall stability of the financial system as a whole' (para. 2) which involves, *inter alia*, the financial system infrastructure (in particular the payments system) and the 'broad overview' of the system (para. 2 (iii)). By contrast, the FSA's responsibilities are primarily institution-specific, relating to individual firms, markets, and clearing and settlement systems (para. 3). However, within this broad distinction, the Bank is also permitted to undertake official financing operations in 'exceptional circumstances' in order to 'limit the risk of problems in or affecting particular institutions spreading to other parts of the financial system' (para. 2(iv)).

Quite how the distinction between system-wide and institution-specific responsibilities will be resolved in practice remains to be seen. The test of such an arrangement is how it will handle the failure of an individual firm which is sufficiently large potentially to pose a threat to the stability of the wider financial system. Paragraph 11 of the MoU states that the Bank and the FSA 'would immediately inform and consult each other' if either should become aware of a potentially systemic problem, while para. 12 envisages the appointment of a 'lead institution' to manage the situation and to co-ordinate the authorities' response in the event that a problem develops. There is no presumption that the 'lead institution' should be the Bank and para. 3(iii)(b) of the MoU would appear to envisage that in at least some cases the FSA will take on a crisis resolution role, at least as it relates to an individual institution, and may assume the role of attempting to broker a private-sector solution that has previously been the exclusive preserve of the central bank.

A difficulty will, however, arise because it is unlikely that a problem in a single financial institution would obviously be confined only to that institution. Since the spread of contagion is inherently unpredictable, any problem could on this definition become potentially systemic, and hence fall within the Bank's area of responsibility. This means that the relationship between the Bank and the FSA with regard to crisis management remains ambiguous, at least in the abstract. On a case-by-case basis it may be relatively easy to determine whether the problems in an individual institution are sufficiently serious to give rise to systemic problems and hence to decide on the allocation of crisis management roles. Nonetheless, one consequence is that the respective roles of the Bank and the FSA will not become entirely clear until the crisis management arrangements are tested in practice.

**Public awareness and consumer protection**

These two objectives need to be considered in parallel since they are in practice closely related. The public awareness objective is defined as 'promoting public understanding of the financial system' (s. 4(1)), which includes both awareness of the benefits and risks associated with different kinds of investment and financial dealing and the provision of appropriate information and advice (s. 4(2)). By contrast, the consumer protection objective refers in quite general terms to 'securing the appropriate degree of protection for consumers' (s. 5(1)). Both these objectives are concerned with the problem of correcting the imbalances of information between producers and consumers of financial services.

Economists refer to such information imbalances as 'information asymmetries'. If a market is to function well, buyers must have adequate information to be able to evaluate competing products. They must be able to identify the range of buying alternatives and understand the characteristics of the buying choices they confront. However, these conditions are often absent from the market for retail financial products. The essence of a financial contract is that it involves a promise: money is exchanged today for an (often vague) promise of money in the future. Most ordinary consumers have only a limited ability to assess the extent to which the promisor (i.e., the supplier of the financial contract) is in a position to make good the promise made to them. Moreover, the fact that the nature of a financial contract involves a promise, means that transactions of this type are especially vulnerable to fraud and the exploitation of the unwary. It was in the context of these types of information imbalance that the father of the Financial Services Act 1986, Professor Jim Gower, used his now famous phrase about the purpose of regulation being 'to prevent reasonable people from being made fools of'.

The traditional method for correcting these information imbalances has been to institute regulatory requirements for firms to disclose information to their clients. This type of disclosure is intended both to alert users and potential users of financial services to the risks of the transactions into which they may enter and also to inform them of such matters as costs and terms and conditions. This type of regulation is explained in the IOSCO *Objectives and Principles of Securities Regulation* as follows: 'The most important means for ensuring investor protection is the requirement of full disclosure of information material to investors' decisions. Investors are, thereby, better able to protect their own interests.' In other words, the essence of this type of regulation is to ensure that investors are placed in a position to make a fully informed judgement of the costs and potential risk and return characteristics of a financial contract. Beyond this, regulation does not seek to absolve them of responsibility for the decisions taken on the basis of the information so disclosed, and in this sense it might be described as a form of *caveat emptor* — let the buyer beware. However, a more accurate description of this principle is 'freedom with disclosure', and it has long been a central pillar in Britain of the regulation of many forms of financial contract, dating back at least to the Joint Stock Companies Act 1844. It leaves the producer and the consumer free to enter into transactions subject to the important proviso that the consumer does so on the basis of full and accurate disclosure. The principle of freedom with disclosure is also closely related to other forms of regulation, for example, the labelling of foods so that potential consumers can judge for themselves whether they wish to consume the contents. Indeed, the connection between disclosure regulation of securities and food labelling was explicitly made by the American Justice Louis D. Brandeis. In his 1914 book *Other People's Money* he remarked:

it is now recognised in the simplest merchandising, that there should be full disclosures . . . The law has begun to require publicity in aid of fair dealing. The

Federal Pure Food Law does not guarantee quality or prices; but it helps the buyer to judge of quality by requiring disclosure of ingredients. Among the most important facts to be learned for determining the real value of a security is the amount of water it contains.

Nonetheless, in recent years there have been many who have argued that the complexity of financial products like pensions and life assurance means the doctrine of freedom with disclosure cannot reasonably be applied to them, and that some higher degree of consumer protection is required than mere disclosure. Disclosure might provide the consumer with a good deal of information, but the consumer might then be unable to interpret it properly or to understand the significance of what he or she was being told. This thinking informed the concepts of 'best advice' and 'suitability' as they appeared in the rulebooks of the SROs that operated under the Financial Services Act 1986. Thus rule 5.1 of the SIB's Conduct of Business Rules required that the firm should not effect for a customer any transactions which the firm believed to be unsuitable for the customer, and the 'know your customer' requirements of the SRO rule books placed heavy emphasis on the firm's need to obtain sufficient detailed information regarding a customer and his current investment and financial position to ensure that the proposed investment was appropriate and affordable and that the customer fully understood the nature and risks of the product. These concepts represented a partial shift away from the freedom-with-disclosure regime, since they placed an obligation on the provider of financial services to offer the consumer products that were appropriate to the consumer's financial needs. To continue the food analogy, it is equivalent to requiring a shopkeeper or a waiter to recommend a certain food to a customer — other than one who positively insists on making his own choice — based on a detailed assessment of his needs, tastes and financial resources. Failure to observe these requirements was a breach of regulatory rules and also provided the consumer with a cause of action.

The suitability and best advice regime was clearly ineffective in preventing the mis-selling of personal pensions (see chapter 1). This has led some observers to argue for a more restrictive approach, usually referred to as product regulation. This type of regulation seeks to guarantee that a financial product meets certain government-prescribed minimum quality standards; and it would also ban certain types of product from sale altogether. Although product regulation has a long history on the Continent of Europe, where it is now being gradually phased out as the result of deregulation, this type of regulation has been relatively rare in Britain. While the recent introduction of a voluntary CAT (conditions, access, terms) mark and the concept of a 'stakeholder pension' have moved Britain more in the direction of product regulation, the consensus of opinion is against a significant extension of this type of regulation. It is argued that it would excessively lower customers' standards of care and would reduce competition and innovation to the ultimate detriment of consumers.

The Act attempts to strike a careful balance between the range of possible responses to information imbalances between firms and their customers. The first draft of what is now s. 5(2) was very close to the principle of freedom with disclosure in that it emphasised the 'general principle that consumers should take responsibility for their decisions'. As the Joint Committee noted in its report on the draft Bill, 'This is a version of the time-honoured principle, *caveat emptor*, "Let the buyer beware"'. This initial formulation of the statutory objective was very controversial. On the whole it was welcomed by representatives of the industry, particularly on the grounds that it avoided raising public expectations about what the regulatory system could reasonably be expected to deliver. On the other hand, it met with a good deal of criticism from representatives of organised consumer interests. The National Consumers Council (NCC) argued for the principle of *caveat emptor* to be disapplied from non-business customers or at least strongly qualified; the FSA's own consumer panel proposed deleting the *caveat emptor* principle altogether. In evidence to the Joint Committee, Mr Davies (the FSA's chairman) acknowledged fears that the provision as drafted might be taken not merely to qualify the consumer protection objective, but to negate it entirely. The government responded to concerns about the possible negation of consumer protection by the principle of *caveat emptor* by inserting a new para. (c) in clause 5(2) of the Bill. This provision now requires the FSA, in considering what is the appropriate degree of protection, to take into account the need that consumers may have for advice and accurate information. The government's intention is that s. 5 taken as a whole strikes a balance between what it is reasonable for consumers to expect, and their responsibility for decisions in the context of this expectation.

This balance is further developed in the FSA's *New Millennium* document, which distinguishes between a number of different risks, including what it terms 'prudential risk', 'bad faith risk', 'complexity/unsuitability risk' and 'performance risk'. The FSA argues that it has a role to play in reducing the first three of these risks, but that regulation is not intended to guard against 'performance risk', i.e., the risk 'that investments do not deliver the hoped-for returns'. Hence regulation can reasonably be expected to protect the consumer against the risks of firm collapse, fraud, misrepresentation or deliberate mis-selling and the risk that consumers are sold a product that is unsuitable for their needs, but not the inherent risks of investing.

Despite the careful balance that has been struck in the formulation of the consumer protection objective, one factor that might have received more attention is the role of competition in ensuring that consumers are provided with high-quality, good-value products. Although, as we have seen, the proper functioning of a market depends on consumers' ability to assess the products they are being offered, to the extent that this condition can be met, a greater degree of competition is to be preferred to a lesser one. The role of competition as a *partial* substitute for regulation has most recently been recognised by the Cruickshank report on the British banking industry. Nonetheless, this important observation does not form part of the FSA's objectives as formulated. Indeed, as will be discussed below, the extent to which the promotion of competition should feature among the FSA's objectives was one of the most controversial issues in their formulation.

A final issue that arose in the context of this objective is the precise nature of the 'consumers' who require protection. Information imbalances between a firm and unsophisticated retail investors are obviously acute. At the other extreme, financial intermediaries which deal with each other frequently and which employ teams of specialist traders, lawyers and other experts might be reasonably expected to be able to protect their own interests. Hence there is a strong case for disapplying the kinds of conduct of business rules applied to retail transactions to those that only involve financial intermediaries (i.e., 'wholesale' transactions) and for formally incorporating this distinction in the Act.

The degree to which the distinction between the professional and retail investor should be enshrined in statute became a controversial matter during the drafting of the Bill. The experience of the Financial Services Act 1986 regime, in which unnecessary and burdensome conduct of business rules had been initially applied to interprofessional markets, had made the industry wary of a repeat performance under the new Act. Even representatives of organised consumer interests were inclined to support such a distinction. For example, the NCC proposed that language akin to that of a 'business customer' from the Unfair Contract Terms Act 1977 could be adopted in the Act, to exempt this category of user of financial services from the Act's protections. However, against this proposal it was urged that there were certain categories of business customer (e.g., small businesses) which might also need a high degree of protection from improper sales practices by financial intermediaries. This point illustrates the difficulty of defining the wholesale/retail distinction in a way that can accommodate the varying degrees of sophistication of a wide range of users of financial services. Ultimately, therefore, the argument that this distinction was best captured in the rules and codes promulgated by the FSA prevailed over the argument that it was sufficiently important to ensure that there was a clear statutory basis for applying a different, less onerous conduct-of-business regime to markets in which professional investors deal only with other professionals.

As a result the Act does not formally incorporate the wholesale/retail distinction, although the requirement in s. 5(2)(b) that in determining what is an appropriate level of consumer protection the FSA should have regard to 'the differing degrees of experience and expertise that different consumers may have in relation to different kinds of regulated activity' clearly reflects this thinking. Section 5(2)(a) also requires the FSA to have regard to the different degrees of risk in different kinds of investment or other transaction. The FSA's gloss on its statutory objectives reflects the important issue that the necessary degree of regulatory protection for consumers will depend in part on their degree of sophistication. The *New Millennium* document states that the level of protection provided will depend on the sophistication of the consumer, and that professional counterparties need (and want) much less protection than the retail consumer.

While the FSA will pursue the objective of an 'appropriate' level of consumer protection, the public awareness objective provides it with an alternative basis on which to address the information imbalances that are characteristic of financial markets. Well-informed, knowledgeable consumers will obviously be in a better position to understand and evaluate the characteristics of different types of financial products as well as their own financial needs. Thus the FSA's second statutory objective (s. 4) requires it to promote 'public understanding of the financial system'. This is a wholly new objective, in the sense that none of the regulatory agencies that the FSA replaces was explicitly charged with a consumer education role. The prominence of this objective in the FSA's statutory responsibilities suggests that the government assigns it a very high priority. It is argued that if markets are to function efficiently consumers also need to become more financially literate, especially if they are to be able to make proper provision for their old age and periods of unemployment in a time of a diminishing role for the State.

The FSA has stated in its *New Millennium* document that it will pursue two main aims under this objective. It will endeavour to promote a higher level of general financial literacy and it will aim to improve the information and advice available to consumers. The second aim clearly involves significant overlap with the consumer protection objective from which it is arguably indistinguishable. Thus the FSA proposes to make greater use of league tables and relative performance indicators, which a number of the previous regulatory bodies had also sought to develop under their consumer protection remit; it would appear that the FSA's intention is to extend this work. However, the promotion of financial literacy does involve a significant new departure and the FSA has stated that it interprets this aim as involving the provision of programmes to enable consumers to acquire the knowledge and skills they require to become better informed consumers. This will also involve it in fostering public understanding of retail financial products, in particular on the part of vulnerable or inexperienced consumers.

Assigning a role to the FSA in promoting consumer understanding of the financial system also represents an innovation in the sense that this type of regulation serves a social purpose as well as contributing to the efficient working of financial markets. Regulation in Britain has been overwhelmingly concerned with ensuring market efficiency and other social objectives have generally been promoted by the use of government spending programmes rather than regulatory action. (From an economic perspective even the prevention of fraud and other types of financial crime promotes market efficiency.) This contrasts with the situation in some other countries where regulation has been used to serve social ends. An example is the community service obligation embodied in the Community Reinvestment Act of 1977 (12 USC § 2901–2906) in the United States; the purpose of this Act is to ensure that the supply of credit is not cut off to particular communities, especially in low-income areas.

Although this type of social regulation has been rare in Britain, the issue of whether it should be extended by incorporation in the FSA's statutory objectives was considered during the public consultation exercise on the draft Bill. The NCC requested the Treasury to add to the list of objectives 'the need for reasonable access to financial services for those who have difficulty in getting access to products appropriate to their needs'. The House of Commons Treasury Select

Committee also suggested that the FSA could become involved in matters of financial and social exclusion. However, the government, supported by the report of the Joint Committee of the Houses of Lords and Commons, resisted calls for the FSA's objectives to be amended to include these explicitly 'social' objectives. As the Joint Committee commented, the addition of such an objective 'would make life excessively difficult for a regulator responsible for prudential supervision, and would damage lines of accountability'. It recommended instead that if the government wished to impose social obligations on financial firms it should do so directly. With the exception of the public understanding role of the FSA, therefore, an extension of regulation as a means to promote certain 'social' objectives has not been significantly extended.

**The reduction of financial crime**

The fourth of the statutory objectives is the 'reduction of financial crime', which means 'reducing the extent to which it is possible for a business carried on by a regulated person to be used for a purpose connected with financial crime' (s. 6(1)). In this context financial crime includes 'misconduct in, or misuse of information relating to, a financial market'. Hence one intention of this objective is to provide statutory underpinning to market integrity regulation, especially that aspect of it that shades off into combating certain forms of criminal conduct (e.g., insider dealing.) As discussed elsewhere in this book, the Act gives the FSA new powers in this area.

In addition, the financial crime objective covers a number of other functions previously discharged by the FSA's predecessor agencies. These include the important function of protecting consumers of financial services from fraud or dishonesty; as noted earlier, financial transactions are especially prone to this type of abuse since their essence is a promise to pay a sum of money at some future date. Thus financial crime is defined (by s. 6(3)(a)) as including any criminal offence involving 'fraud or dishonesty'. The prevention of money laundering has also become an issue on which regulators have been expected to play an enhanced role in recent years. This has important linkages with certain prudential issues, most notably the adequacy of a firm's systems and controls, of which controls on money laundering are an element. Moreover, as the FSA notes in the *New Millennium* paper, the exposure of a financial firm to being used for criminal purposes may also damage public confidence in that institution and possibly in the wider financial system. Hence there is a clear sense in which the financial crime objective also links with the first statutory objective of fostering public confidence in the financial system.

## PRINCIPLES OF REGULATION

In discharging its objectives under the Act, the FSA will be required to have regard to obligations set out in s. 2(3) of the Act. These represent 'principles of good regulation' and are intended to provide the FSA with guidance on the way in which Parliament expects it to discharge its duties.

The first principle (s. 2(3)(a)) refers to the way in which the FSA will allocate and deploy its resources. The Act requires it to do so in 'the most efficient and economic way'. In the *New Millennium* paper the FSA gives an undertaking that in deference to this principle it will go beyond the statutory requirement to consult on fees and will also consult on its budget. Moreover, the FSA will also seek to develop a 'thematic' and risk-based approach to regulation, in which resources are allocated according to what are perceived as being the institutions and sectors that pose the greatest risk to consumers and users of financial services and the wider financial system.

The second principle concerns the corporate governance of financial firms, and especially the role of management (s. 2(3)(b)). A long-standing matter of concern in Britain and in many other countries has been that a regulatory regime might result in a shifting of responsibility from the firms' management to the supervisory authorities. No supervision, however effective, could — or should — ever replace sound management in the firm. It is important that supervisors and regulators do not become a kind of superior management board, and that sound corporate governance remains the depositors' and consumers' first and most important protection. In recognition of this important point, the Act's second principle of good regulation requires the FSA to have regard to 'the responsibilities of those who manage the affairs of authorised persons'. The FSA interprets this to mean that the senior management are to be held responsible for risk management and controls within firms and that as a regulator it should not be too intrusive into firms' commercial decisions (*New Millennium*, p. 10).

The third principle requires the FSA's regulation to be 'proportionate to the benefits, considered in general terms, which are expected to result' from it (s. 2(3)(c)). In having regard to this principle the FSA will take into account the costs incurred by firms and consumers, including extensive use of cost/benefit analysis of proposed regulatory requirements. The proportionality of regulation is also relevant to distinction between wholesale and retail consumers referred to earlier in this chapter. However, while a laudable principle, the experience to date of introducing cost-benefit analysis into regulation has been disappointing, both in the UK and elsewhere. Cost-benefit analysis is well adapted to relatively static situations, whereas regulators inevitably have an impact on the future behaviour of regulated persons in a way that is hard to predict in advance. Serious conceptual difficulties will, therefore, need to be resolved before cost-benefit analysis could ever meaningfully play the pivotal role in regulation that this principle would seem to envisage.

The remaining principles can be considered together since they are closely related. The fourth principle requires the FSA to have regard to the desirability 'of facilitating innovation in connection with regulated activities'; the fifth principle requires the FSA to have regard to the 'international character of financial services and markets' and the desirability of 'maintaining the competitive position of the

United Kingdom'; while the sixth and seventh principles concern minimising the possible adverse impact on competition of the FSA's regulation. Thus each of these principles is a different formulation of the concern that regulation should not unnecessarily impede or distort competition and innovation.

The prominence given to competitiveness issues in the principles of regulation reflects its prominence in the debate on the formulation of the regulator's objectives. Many in the industry (and some commentators) were concerned that creating such a powerful regulatory agency, with a clear focus on consumer protection, would in time prove to be a recipe for over-regulation. These concerns were heightened by the widespread belief that historically the City of London had flourished as a financial centre in part because it has enjoyed a relatively light regulatory burden (an argument advanced, for example, in the City Research Project's *Final Report* published in March 1995). This sense of unease found expression in the argument that the promotion of competition should explicitly feature as one of its statutory objectives, a position that found many influential supporters in the City. The primary justification for making the competitiveness of the UK financial sector an explicit statutory objective was the belief that it would provide a needed counterbalance to the pressures the FSA would inevitably face to expand its consumer protection remit. Despite suggestions at certain stages of the legislative process that the government was minded to accept their arguments, ultimately the case put by several senior officials of the FSA, that an additional competitiveness objective would make their task impossibly complex, appears to have prevailed. Nonetheless, the government went some way towards meeting the concerns of the FSA's critics by incorporating competitiveness as a principle to which the FSA must have regard, albeit not one of its statutory objectives.

# Chapter Three
# Regulated and Prohibited Activities

## *Mark Threipland*

Part II of the Financial Services and Markets Act 2000 (FSAMA 2000) sets the basic scope of the Act by prohibiting persons who are not authorised (or exempt) from:

(a)  carrying on regulated activities in the United Kingdom (the 'general prohibition': s. 19); and
(b)  falsely claiming to be authorised or exempt (s. 24).

Part II also contains two further prohibitions which are not described in this chapter. First, it prohibits an authorised person from carrying on regulated activities without permission (s. 20), as described in chapter 6. Secondly, it restricts the communication of financial promotions by an unauthorised person (s. 21), as described in chapter 4.

The general prohibition in s. 19 will replace the authorisation requirements of three existing statutes, FSA 1986, the Banking Act 1987 and the Insurance Companies Act 1982. Consistent with the Act being framework legislation, the detail of the regulated activities is left to secondary legislation.

## THE GENERAL PROHIBITION

### Elements of the general prohibition

The general prohibition is as follows (s. 19(1)):

No person may carry on a regulated activity in the United Kingdom, or purport to do so, unless he is—
(a)  an authorised person; or

(b)   an exempt person.

To decide if a person's activities breach the general prohibition, the following principal elements need to be considered, each of which is described in more detail later in this chapter:

(a)   Is the person carrying on regulated activities, that is, activities specified as regulated activities in the Regulated Activities Order?
(b)   If so, are those activities carried on by way of business?
(c)   If so, is the person carrying them on in the United Kingdom?
(d)   If so, is the person an exempt person or can the person benefit from another exemption?
(e)   If not, the person contravenes the general prohibition unless he is an authorised person.

As the general prohibition covers purporting to carry on a regulated activity as well as actually carrying one on, it is clear that an unsuccessful attempt to carry on a regulated activity is within the scope of the prohibition.

## Authorised persons

The routes to authorisation are described in chapter 5. An authorised person cannot breach the general prohibition, even if the authorised person's permission (see chapter 6) does not include the regulated activity in question. This 'single perimeter' will be of assistance in avoiding problems of defining the boundaries between different regulated activities. An authorised person carrying on a regulated activity without permission will contravene s. 20 and may be subject to FSA enforcement action as well as an action for damages if the Treasury so prescribe (s. 20(3)). But an authorised person need not be concerned about the criminal offence and potential unenforceability of agreements that result from contravention of the general prohibition (s. 20(2)).

## Exempt persons and other exemptions

'Exempt persons' are appointed representatives (s. 39(1)), recognised investment exchanges (s. 285(2)), recognised clearing houses (s. 285(3)) and persons exempt as a result of a s. 38(1) exemption order (s. 417(1)). But a person is only an 'exempt person' in relation to a regulated activity to which the exemption relates (s. 417(1)). So an exempt person carrying on a regulated activity outside the scope of the relevant exemption will contravene the general prohibition. There are also specific exemptions from the general prohibition in Part XIX (Lloyd's names and former Lloyd's names) and Part XX (members of certain professions carrying on limited regulated activities incidental to professional services). A person benefiting from one of these specific exemptions is not an 'exempt person'. This is important in view of the many particular dispensations for exempt persons, such as a proposed exemption from the restriction on financial promotion (see chapter 4).

## REGULATED ACTIVITIES

### Treasury's power to specify the regulated activities

The Treasury are entitled to specify what is a 'regulated activity' by order (s. 22) and this power will be used to make the Regulated Activities Order. Generally, a regulated activity must be described in terms of a specified activity relating to a specified investment (s. 22(1)(a)), which can be any asset, right or interest (s. 22(4)), for example, the specified activity of dealing as agent relating to the specified investment of shares. However, the Treasury may also specify an activity which does not relate to any investment, but rather is carried on in relation to property of any kind (s. 22(1)(b)). Section 22(1)(b) will be used, for example, to specify that the activity of operating a collective investment scheme is a regulated activity irrespective of the type of property to which the collective investment scheme relates. There are no express limitations on this power although, under rules of statutory interpretation, the long title of the Act may set an outer limit. Both the first order specifying the regulated activities and further orders which, in the opinion of the Treasury, extend the meaning of regulated activity are subject to the affirmative resolution procedure and therefore require approval by resolutions of both Houses of Parliament (sch. 2, para. 26).

Schedule 2 to the Act describes the Treasury's power in more detail, but without limiting it (s. 22(2) and (3)). In particular:

(a)   it lists in general terms particular activities (sch. 2, part I) and investments (sch. 2, part II) which may be specified for the purposes of s. 22(1);

(b)   it permits the Regulated Activities Order to include exemptions (sch. 2, para. 25(1)(a));

(c)   it empowers the Treasury to give themselves or the FSA discretionary decision-making powers in the Regulated Activities Order (para. 25(1)(b)) and powers to make rules or regulations or to provide information or documents relating to the definition of regulated activity (para. 25(1)(c) to (e)). An example of how the first type of power may be used is to replicate the FSA's existing power to certify a newspaper as within an exclusion for investment advice (FSA 1986, sch. 1, para. 25(2)).

The mechanism for amending the scope of the Act is similar to that under the FSA 1986; extensions of the scope of FSA 1986 are permitted by statutory instrument subject to the affirmative resolution procedure (FSA 1986, s. 2(3)). But, significantly, the initial scope of FSA 1986 was set out in that Act (FSA 1986, sch. 1), with the result that it was subject to the full parliamentary legislative process which the Regulated Activities Order will be spared. The Treasury's power to amend the scope of the Banking Act 1987 is more restricted: the initial definition of the prohibition on accepting deposits is set out in that Act, but changes to the definitions of deposit and deposit-taking business are possible by statutory instrument subject to only the negative resolution procedure (Banking Act 1987, s. 7). There are no specific powers to amend the scope of the Insurance Companies Act 1982 by secondary legislation.

### Regulated activities and European Directives

Various European Directives in the financial services area and forming part of the Single Market Programme set a minimum level for the scope of the general prohibition. These are the Investment Services Directive (93/22/EEC), the banking Directives now consolidated as the Credit Institutions Directive (2000/12/EC) and various directives in the life and non-life insurance areas. These Single Market Directives require each EEA State, including the United Kingdom, to introduce in its national law an authorisation requirement for persons established in that State who carry on specified financial services. But EEA States are permitted to extend the authorisation requirement to activities beyond the minimum in the Directives and the scope of the authorisation requirement of the Act, as set out in the February 1999 draft of the Regulated Activities Order, goes well beyond the Directives in many respects where the government has perceived a need to protect consumers or regulate markets in other areas.

### Draft Regulated Activities Order and changes in scope

The regulated activities in the Regulated Activities Order will replace the authorisation requirements under FSA 1986, the Banking Act 1987 and the Insurance Companies Act 1982. A draft of the Regulated Activities Order was published for consultation in February 1999 (in the Treasury's *Regulated Activities — A Consultation Document*), and the Treasury have published a further draft for consultation during autumn 2000. Tables 3.1 and 3.2 at the end of this chapter contain a tabular summary of the regulated activities and the principal exclusions based on the February 1999 draft of the Order.

The February 1999 draft of the Regulated Activities Order contained a large number of proposed changes from the existing legislation described as clarificatory. In addition, a number of major changes in scope have been announced by the Government as follows:

(a) *Mortgages.* Following extensive consultation, the government announced that it intends to bring mortgage lending within the scope of the Act in 2001 (HM Treasury news release, 26 January 2000). This will probably be achieved by making lending on mortgage a regulated activity under the Regulated Activities Order. It is included in para. 23 of sch. 2 to the Act but not in the February 1999 draft of the Regulated Activities Order. The government does not intend, for the present, to bring mortgage advice and arranging within the scope of the Act, although many mortgage intermediaries already require authorisation or exemption because advising on and arranging endowment policies is investment business under FSA 1986 and will be a regulated activity. Mortgage advertising will also be regulated by the FSA, probably through the financial promotion regime. Regulation by the FSA will complement rather than replace the voluntary code operated by the Council of Mortgage Lenders. Consumer credit will continue to be regulated under the Consumer Credit Act 1974, which is not being replaced by the Act.

(b) *Professional firms.* Firms which are regulated by professional bodies to be designated by the Treasury (likely to be solicitors, accountants and actuaries) will be exempted from the need for authorisation if their regulated activities are merely 'incidental' to their professional services. This will be through Part XX and regulations made under that Part rather than through the Regulated Activities Order. This is expected to relieve around 13,000 professional firms, currently authorised under FSA 1986 by the recognised professional bodies, from the need for authorisation.

(c) *Lloyd's insurance market.* The Lloyd's insurance market is currently regulated for solvency purposes by the FSA under delegation from the Treasury while other aspects of Lloyd's business are regulated by the Council, which is the governing body of Lloyd's. Part XIX of the Act gives the FSA extensive authorisation and intervention powers over Lloyd's. The February 1999 draft of the Regulated Activities Order proposed that making arrangements relating to Lloyd's syndicate membership and capacity, advising on syndicate membership and managing syndicate capacity will all be regulated activities from the time when the general prohibition comes into force. In addition, the exemption in the FSA 1986, s. 42, for the Society of Lloyd's and underwriting agents will be dropped. Accordingly, the Society of Lloyd's (which runs facilities supporting the market) as well as underwriting agents and members' advisers will need to be authorised for all regulated activities which they carry on (paras. 3.8 to 3.15 of part 1 of the Treasury's *Regulated Activities — A Consultation Document*, February 1999).

(d) *Offering.* In a change from the FSA 1986, the government has proposed that 'offering' to carry on a regulated activity will not be a regulated activity. The government did not 'consider it appropriate additionally to regulate firms which carry on the business of offering in the UK, but which do not then subsequently deal, arrange deals or give advice in the UK. Where the offering is targeted at the UK, it is thought that the offering will be appropriately dealt with under the financial promotion regime' (para. 3.18 of part 1 of the Treasury's *Regulated Activities — A Consultation Document*, February 1999). However, there are some differences between the general prohibition and financial promotion regimes, in particular, their scopes. Of course, purporting to carry on a regulated activity and falsely claiming to be an authorised or exempt person will be offences (ss. 19(1) and 24).

(e) *Credit unions.* The government has announced that credit unions, which currently are exempt from the banking authorisation (Banking Act 1987, sch. 2, para. 10) will come within the scope of FSAMA 2000 following further consultation between the FSA and the sector (Treasury press release of 16 November 1999). The timing remains uncertain.

The Treasury have consulted on a number of possible future changes in scope, including:

(a)  *Long-term care.* At the time of writing, a Treasury committee is considering the need for regulation of long-term care contracts. Should that committee confirm that that regulation will be proportionate and effective, the government aims to include long-term care products in the Regulated Activities Order (*Hansard*, HL, 18 April 2000, col. 582). The timing remains, of course, uncertain.

(b)  *Pre-paid funerals.* The Treasury have consulted on various options for the regulation of pre-paid funeral plans (*Regulation of the Pre-paid Funeral Industry — a Consultation Document*, January 1999). At the time of writing, no announcement has been made, but this is another potential new matter for inclusion within the scope of the Act.

## ACTIVITIES CARRIED ON 'BY WAY OF BUSINESS'

For an activity to be a regulated activity, it must be carried on 'by way of business' (Financial Services and Markets Act 2000, s. 22(1)). 'By way of business' is not defined in the Act, but the Treasury have the power by order to specify circumstances in which a regulated activity is or is not to be regarded as carried on by way of business (s. 419). The explanatory notes to the Act explain that this power may be used for the purposes of s. 22(1).

At the time of writing it is premature to predict what provision the Treasury may make under s. 419, but it is nonetheless possible to consider the meaning of 'by way of business' at general law. There is much case law in other contexts on the word 'business', but in general it seems that its interpretation depends on the context in which it is used. Two factors that are likely to be particularly relevant to a determination of whether an activity is carried on by way of business are frequency and commercial purpose. However it seems that, for an activity to be carried on 'by way of business' is a lower hurdle than for the carrying on of it to be a business. In interpreting the meaning of 'by way of business' in the context of FSA 1986, s. 63 (whether a gaming contract was entered into by way of business), it was held in *Morgan Grenfell and Co. Ltd* v *Welwyn Hatfield District Council* [1995] 1 All ER 1 at p. 13 that there was:

no reason . . . to place a narrow meaning on the word 'business'. It clearly should not be given a technical construction but rather one which conforms to what in ordinary parlance would be described as a business transaction as opposed to something personal or casual.

Further:

Regularly entering into a certain type of transaction for the purpose of profit is a good indication that the party . . . is doing so by way of business. But it is equally possible that the very first time it enters into such a contract it is doing so by way of business because it is doing so as part of its own overall business activities.

It is important to distinguish the 'by way of business' test in s. 22(1) from that relating to financial promotion (s. 21(1)), which restricts communicating financial promotions 'in the course of business'. This seems to be an even lower hurdle, and s. 21(1) seems merely to require that the person be engaged in a business (of any sort) in the course of which the financial promotion is communicated; there is no need to consider whether the communication itself is made 'by way of business'. So advice about a pension scheme given by an employer to its employees might arguably not be given 'by way of business' but a financial promotion relating to it would be communicated 'in the course of business'.

## TERRITORIAL SCOPE OF THE GENERAL PROHIBITION

The territorial scope of the general prohibition has three elements. First, the requirement in s. 19(1) that a regulated activity must be carried on in the United Kingdom, for which no further definition is given so that interpretation will depend on the general law. Secondly, s. 418 extends the application of the general prohibition in cases where it might otherwise not apply under the general law: this extends the *outward* application. Thirdly, it seems that the Regulated Activities Order will cut back the *inward* application of the general prohibition for overseas persons. It is convenient to look separately at activities *within*, *outward* from and *inward* into the United Kingdom, although this approach may not be appropriate in complex cases involving, say, multiple parties or multiple jurisdictions.

### Regulated activities within the United Kingdom

Where both the person carrying on the regulated activity and the client or counterparty are located in the United Kingdom, and all aspects of the activity are carried on here, it is clear that the regulated activity is carried on in the United Kingdom. That is the case even if the person has no establishment in the United Kingdom but acts through an agent here, whether a permanently established UK agent or an employee on a temporary visit here. But an overseas person acting through an agent in the United Kingdom may be able to take advantage of exemptions or exclusions for overseas persons in the Regulated Activities Order (see further 'Regulated activities inward into the United Kingdom' below).

### Regulated activities outward from the United Kingdom

Where a person performs an activity from a UK location, but the client or counterparty is outside the United Kingdom, the territorial application of the general prohibition is less clear. It is necessary to analyse this situation by reference to the general law. The approach taken under English law is as follows:

(a)   For the proposed regulated activities of establishing etc. a collective investment scheme, arranging deals for another, making arrangements enabling or facilitating deals, safeguarding and administering investments and managing investments, the traditional approach for the equivalent FSA 1986 investment activities has been to regard these as, by their nature, carried on where the firm is, rather than the client. There is no reason to regard the treatment under the Act as different, and this appears to be the appropriate treatment for managing the underwriting capacity of a Lloyd's syndicate as well.

(b)   Advice is generally regarded as given where it is received by the client, and this appears to be the appropriate treatment for the proposed regulated activities of investment advice and advice on syndicate participation at Lloyd's.

(c)   For accepting deposits, it seems that 'accepting' will be defined as assuming the liability to repay the deposit (February 1999 draft of the Regulated Activities Order, art. 2(1)). Such liability has generally been regarded as assumed when (and where) the deposit is first received by the acceptor or its agent. In practice, for non-cash transactions, the currency of the deposit has been regarded as significant because the first receipt by the acceptor (or its agent) is often only in the United Kingdom where UK sterling payment facilities are used.

(d)   For the other regulated activities, the law of contract may be of assistance. Where communication is instantaneous, transactions are normally treated as entered into where and when the acceptance of the offer to enter into the transaction is received by the offeror. Where communication is not instantaneous, for example, by post, the transaction is treated as entered into when the acceptance is posted, and so probably where the offeree is located. The position can become even more complicated where agents receive and pass on orders, as is commonly the case in relation to the effecting of insurance contracts.

Where a person might not otherwise be regarded as carrying on a regulated activity in the United Kingdom, FSAMA 2000, s. 418, provides that the person is to be so regarded in four cases, which are particularly relevant to activities outward from the United Kingdom. In each of these cases, the person will require authorisation or exemption under the general prohibition (s. 19(1)) and, if an authorised person, permission under s. 20. The first two cases seem to be intended to implement the requirement for 'home State' authorisation under the Single Market Directives (see chapter 5). The first three cases apply to a person who has a registered office (or head office, where it does not have a registered office) in the United Kingdom, and provide that the person is to be regarded as carrying on a regulated activity in the United Kingdom if:

(a)   Under the *first case*, the person is entitled to exercise passport rights under a Single Market Directive and is carrying on a regulated activity to which that Directive applies in another EEA State.

(b)   Under the *second case*, the person is the manager of a fund which is entitled to passport rights and persons in another EEA State are invited to become participants in the fund (currently, this would cover funds within the scope of the UCITS Directive (85/611/EEC)).

(c)    Under the *third case*, the day-to-day management of a regulated activity is the responsibility of the person's registered or head office or another establishment maintained by the person in the United Kingdom. The meaning of 'day-to-day management' is unclear and this case seems to represent a potential widening of the authorisation requirement under all of the existing regimes, where activities of a non-UK office are under the day-to-day management of a UK office. On the other hand, it seems that activities of a UK person carried on from a UK office but under the day-to-day management of an overseas office would not fall under any of these three cases, and whether they are carried on 'in the United Kingdom' will depend on the general law.

The *fourth case* applies to a firm which does not have its head office in the United Kingdom; the firm will be regarded as carrying on a regulated activity in the United Kingdom if it is carried on from an establishment maintained by it in the United Kingdom. The use of the word 'establishment' is a change from the phrase 'permanent place of business' in FSA 86, s. 1(3), but looking at the judicial interpretation of *establishment* there seems to be little change in practice. For example, the tests or indications include 'exclusive occupation of premises', 'some degree of permanence' and 'some organisation on the premises' (*Lord Advocate* v *Babcock and Wilcox (Operations) Ltd* [1972] 1 WLR 488 at p. 492 per Lord Morris of Borth-y-Gest) and an 'established place of business' is 'some more or less permanent location not necessarily owned or even leased by the company, but at least associated with the company and from which habitually or with some degree of regularity business is conducted' (*Re Oriel Ltd* [1985] 3 All ER 216 at p. 219 per Oliver LJ). There is considerable European case law on the meaning of establishment, but as this provision does not seem to be intended to implement a requirement of a Single Market Directive this is unlikely to be relevant. The establishment must also be *maintained* by the firm. Clearly, the payment of rent or other overheads would be regarded as maintaining the establishment. But it seems that 'maintained' should be interpreted more broadly than this to include other forms of use, provided there is some sort of responsibility for or control over the establishment. On the other hand, it seems that a place of business of an agent or subsidiary of a firm would not be 'maintained' by the firm without something more.

## Regulated activities inward into the United Kingdom

The analysis of the general law position for activities outward from the United Kingdom is applicable also in relation to activities carried on from overseas with a client or counterparty in the United Kingdom. But where an activity would be regarded as carried on in the United Kingdom under the general law, it may still be outside the scope of the general prohibition because of a 'by way of business' exemption for an overseas person (that is, broadly, a person who does not carry on a regulated activity from an establishment maintained by the person in the United Kingdom) and also exclusions for an overseas person applicable to particular regulated activities in the Regulated Activities Order.

## FALSE CLAIMS TO BE AUTHORISED OR EXEMPT

Section 24 of the Act creates an offence of falsely describing oneself, or holding oneself out, as an authorised or exempt person in relation to a particular regulated activity. It is a defence for the accused to prove that all reasonable precautions were taken and all due diligence exercised to avoid committing the offence. The Act does not recreate the regimes under Parts III and IV of the Banking Act 1987 which restricted the use of banking names and required notification of representative offices of overseas banks, not authorised to accept deposits in the United Kingdom. It is not entirely clear whether such a representative office might be regarded as contravening s. 24 merely by describing itself as a bank. Provided it is made clear that no authorisation to accept deposits under the Act has been obtained, it seems that no offence will be committed.

## SANCTIONS FOR BREACH OF THE GENERAL PROHIBITION

The sanctions for breach of the general prohibition are potentially severe, namely criminal liability, unenforceability of agreements, compensation and action by the FSA or the DTI to obtain an injunction and restitution.

### Criminal sanctions

Breach of the general prohibition is an offence punishable by up to two years' imprisonment and an unlimited fine (s. 23). It is a defence for the accused to prove that all reasonable precautions were taken and all due diligence exercised to avoid committing the offence (s. 23(3)). For example, in determining whether a defendant took 'all reasonable precautions and exercised all due diligence' a court might take into account whether the defendant acted reasonably in accordance with legal advice or FSA guidance that activities did not amount to carrying on regulated activities in the United Kingdom. This defence is identical to those available for the authorisation offences under FSA 1986 (s. 4(2)) and Banking Act 1987 (s. 96(4)) but there was no equivalent defence to the authorisation offence in the Insurance Companies Act 1982.

### Unenforceability of agreements and compensation

There are two ways in which contravention of the general prohibition may lead to an agreement being unenforceable (neither is applicable if the regulated activity is 'accepting deposits', see below):

(a)    An agreement made by an *unauthorised person* in the course of carrying on any regulated activity in contravention of the general prohibition, the making or performance of which constitutes or is part of the regulated activity, is unenforceable against the other party (s. 26). Section 26 does not apply if the unauthorised person is an EEA firm with a right to passport under any of the Single Market Directives (sch. 3, para. 16(2); see chapter 5 for further details relating to passporting).

(b)    An agreement made by an *authorised person* is unenforceable against the other party if it is made in the course of carrying on a regulated activity but in consequence of action by an *unauthorised person* which contravened the general prohibition (s. 27). It is irrelevant whether the authorised person was acting within or outside the scope of his permission. In contrast to the equivalent provision in FSA 1986 (s. 5), s. 27 of FSAMA 2000 does not apply to an agreement made by an exempt person acting as principal within the scope of the exemption. Section 27 also does not apply if the unauthorised person is an EEA firm with a right to passport under a Single Market Directive (sch. 3, para. 16(3)).

Subject to the above, the Act makes it clear that agreements are not illegal or invalid as a result of a contravention of the general prohibition (s. 28(9)). This ensures that the innocent party to the agreement may continue to enforce it against the other party, notwithstanding that performance of the agreement may be a criminal offence. In addition, since ss. 26 to 29 provide civil remedies for a contravention of the general prohibition, even if the general prohibition were to be regarded as a 'duty', it seems that no action may be brought under the tort of breach of statutory duty in accordance with the general principles of that tort (*Lonrho Ltd* v *Shell Petroleum Co. Ltd (No. 2)* [1982] AC 173, per Lord Diplock).

Under both ss. 26 and 27, the innocent party to the agreement may recover money or property transferred under the agreement as well as compensation for any loss sustained as a result of having parted with it, but not profits made by the other party (ss. 26(2) and 27(2)). The compensation is in the amount agreed between the parties or determined by the court (s. 28(2)); how remote the recoverable losses can be is not expressly provided for. If property transferred under the agreement has passed to a third party (seemingly even one aware of the circumstances), the third party is not affected by the rescission of the agreement (s. 28(8)) although equitable remedies may still be available. The innocent party is entitled instead to recover the value of the property at the time of its transfer, even if that value has since increased. If the innocent party elects not to be bound by the agreement or recovers money under these provisions, money or property already received by the innocent party under the agreement must be returned (s. 28(7)).

The court has a discretion to allow an agreement to be enforced or assets transferred under the agreement to be retained if it is satisfied that this is 'just and equitable' (s. 28(3)). The Act sets out issues that the court must have regard to in exercising this discretion. In a change from the existing position for investment agreements and insurance contracts these are not preconditions to a court allowing enforcement. The matters to which the court must have regard are:

(a)    In the case of an agreement within s. 26, the court must have regard to whether the *unauthorised person* reasonably believed that he was not contravening the general prohibition (s. 28(5)). 'Reasonable belief' seems to be a lower hurdle for the unauthorised person than the defence against the criminal offence described above (s. 23(3)).

(b)    In the case of an agreement within s. 27, the court must have regard to whether the *authorised person* knew that the *unauthorised person* was contravening the general prohibition (s. 28(6)). Actual knowledge appears to be required so that an authorised person is not under an obligation to exercise reasonable diligence in checking, for example, the authorised status of an adviser who introduces clients.

These effects on private rights as between two parties to an agreement are similar to those that exist in relation to contravention of the authorisation offence for investment business (FSA 1986, ss. 3 and 5) and for insurance business (Insurance Companies Acts 1982, s. 2; FSA 1986, s. 132). One important difference is that FSAMA 2000 does not continue the express provision that contravention of the authorisation offence for insurance business does not affect the validity of a reinsurance contract entered into in respect of an unenforceable insurance contract (FSA 1986, s. 132(6)). Section 28(9) of the 2000 Act expressly provides that the unenforceable contract, in this case an insurance contract, is not otherwise illegal or invalid. So it seems unlikely that the courts would revert to the line of reasoning in cases prior to the FSA 1986, s. 132, which precluded reliance on an illegal insurance contract to establish a cause of action under a related reinsurance contract (see, for example, *Phoenix General Insurance Co. of Greece SA* v *Halvanon Insurance Co. Ltd* [1988] QB 216).

## Accepting deposits in breach of the general prohibition

The sanction of unenforceability of agreements and compensation does not apply in relation to the regulated activity of 'accepting deposits' in contravention of the general prohibition (ss. 26(4) and 27(4)). This continues the position under the Banking Act 1987 (s. 3(3)). 'Accepting deposits' is not defined but presumably, by virtue of s. 22(1), means the regulated activity of that description in the Regulated Activities Order. The logic appears to be that the depositor should be able to recover the deposit pursuant to the terms under which it was accepted. Section 29 provides a new remedy against an *unauthorised person* accepting deposits in contravention of the general prohibition: where the depositor is not entitled under the agreement to recover the deposit without delay, he may apply to the court for an order directing its return. As under s. 28, the court need not make such an order if this is 'just and equitable' and the court must have regard to whether the deposit-taker reasonably believed that he was not contravening the general prohibition. Section 29 does not apply if the unauthorised person is an EEA firm with a right to passport under any of the Single Market Directives (sch. 3, para. 16(4)).

## Right of the FSA and the DTI to seek injunctions and restitution

The FSA and the DTI are entitled to seek injunctions to restrain anticipated contravention of the general prohibition and orders to disgorge profits and require restitution of losses arising from such contravention (ss. 380 and 382).

| Regulated activities | Deposits (art. 23) | General insurance contracts (art. 24) | Long-term insurance contracts (not contractually based) (art. 25) | Long-term insurance contracts (contractually based) (art. 25) | Shares etc. (art. 26) | Debt instruments (art. 27) | Government securities (art. 28) | Instruments giving entitlement to securities (art. 30) | Certificates representing securities (art. 30) | Units in a collective investment scheme (art. 31) | Options (art. 32) | Futures (art. 33) | Contracts for differences (art. 34) | Lloyd's syndicate capacity and syndicate membership (art. 35) | Rights to or interests in investments (art. 36) | Any assets |
|---|---|---|---|---|---|---|---|---|---|---|---|---|---|---|---|---|
| | | | | | | | | *Investments* | | | | | | | | |
| Accepting deposits (art. 4) | X | | | | | | | | | | | | | | | |
| Effecting contracts of insurance (art. 5) | | X | X | X | | | | | | | | | | | | |
| Carrying out contracts of insurance (art. 6) | | X | X | X | | | | | | | | | | | | |
| Establishing etc. a collective investment scheme (art. 7) | | | | | | | | | | | | | | | | X |
| Making a market (art. 8) | | | | | X | X | X | X | X | X | | | | | X | |
| Buying with a view to selling (art. 9) | | | | | X | X | X | X | X | X | | | | | X | |
| Regularly soliciting the public to deal (art. 10) | | | | X | X | X | X | X | X | X | | | | | X | |
| Dealing as principal in contractually based investments (art. 11) | | | | X | | | | | | | X | X | X | | X | |
| Dealing as agent (art. 12) | | | | | X | X | X | X | X | X | X | X | X | | X | |
| Arranging deals for another (art. 13) | | | | | X | X | X | X | X | X | X | X | X | | X | |
| Making arrangements, enabling or facilitating deals (art. 14) | | | | X | X | X | X | X | X | X | X | X | X | X | X | |
| Safeguarding and administering investments (art. 15) | | | | X | X | X | X | X | X | X | X | X | X | | X | X¹ |
| Sending dematerialised instructions (art. 16) | | | | | X | | X | X | X | X | | | | | | |
| Causing dematerialised instructions to be sent (art. 17) | | | | | | | | | | | | | | | | X¹ |
| Managing investments (art. 18) | | | | | X | X | X | X | X | X | X | X | X | | X | X¹ |
| Certain investment advice (art. 19) | | | | | X | X | X | X | X | X | X | X | X | | X | |
| Advice on syndicate participation at Lloyd's (art. 20) | | | | | | | | | | | | | | X | | |
| Lloyd's managing agents (art. 21) | | | | | | | | | | | | | | X | | |
| Agreeing to carry on regulated activities within arts. 7 to 21 (art. 22) | | | | Depends on the regulated activity to which the agreement relates | | | | | | | | | | | | |

¹ In particular circumstances.

**Table 3.1**  Regulated activities and the investments to which they relate. The Table is based on the draft Regulated Activities Order published in February 1999 and is therefore subject to change. (References to articles are to articles of the February 1999 draft Regulated Activities Order.)

| Regulated activities | Exclusions | | | | | | | | |
|---|---|---|---|---|---|---|---|---|---|
| | Deals with or through authorised persons | Groups and joint enterprises | Supply of goods and services | Employees' share schemes | Sale of body corporate | Trustees and personal representatives | Necessary activities in course of profession | Overseas persons | Other specific exclusions |
| Accepting deposits (art. 4) | | | | | | | | | paras 2, 3 |
| Effecting contracts of insurance (art. 5) | | | | | | | | para. 5 (reinsurance) | para. 4 |
| Carrying out contracts of insurance (art. 6) | | | | | | | | para. 5 (reinsurance) | para. 4 |
| Establishing etc. a collective investment scheme (art. 7) | | | | | | | | | |
| Making a market (art. 8) | | para. 10 | para. 11 | para. 12 | para. 13 | para. 15² | | para. 14 | paras 6, 16 |
| Buying with a view to selling (art. 9) | | para. 10 | para. 11 | para. 12 | para. 13 | para. 15² | | para. 14 | para. 7 |
| Regularly soliciting the public to deal (art. 10) | | para. 10 | para. 11 | para. 12 | para. 13 | para. 15² | | para. 14 | paras 8, 16 |
| Dealing as principal in contractually based investments (art. 11) | para. 9 | para. 10 | para. 11 | para. 12 | para. 13 | para. 15² | | para. 14 | |
| Dealing as agent (art. 12) | para. 18 | para. 19 | para. 20 | para. 21 | para. 22 | para. 23² | | para. 24 | |
| Arranging deals for another (art. 13) | para. 28 | para. 31 | para. 32 | para. 33 | para. 34 | para. 35 | para. 36 | para. 37 | paras 26, 27, 29, 30 |
| Making arrangements, enabling or facilitating deals (art. 14) | | para. 42 | para. 43 | para. 44 | para. 45 | para. 46 | para. 47 | para. 48 | paras 39, 40, 41 |
| Safeguarding and administering | | para. 53 | para. 54 | para. 55 | | para. 56 | para. 57 | para. 59 | paras 50, 51, 52, 58 |
| Sending dematerialised instructions (art. 16) | | para. 64 | | | | para. 65 | | para. 66 | paras 61, 62, 63 |
| Causing dematerialised instructions to be sent (art. 17) | | para. 64 | | | | para. 65 | | para. 66 | paras 61, 62, 63 |
| Managing investments (art. 18) | | para. 68 | para. 69 | | | para. 70 | | para. 72 | para. 71 |
| Certain investment advice (art. 19) | | para. 74 | para. 75 | | | para. 76 | para. 77 | para. 80 | paras 78, 79 |
| Advice on syndicate participation at Lloyd's (art. 20) | | | | | | | | | |
| Lloyd's managing agents (art. 21) | | | | | | | | | |
| Agreeing to carry on regulated activities within art. 7 to 21 (art. 22) | Depends on the regulated activity to which the agreement relates | | | | | | | | |

² Exclusion only applicable to a bare trustee and (in Scotland) a nominee.

**Table 3.2** Exclusions and their application to the regulated activities. The table is based on the February 1999 draft of the Regulated Activities Order and is therefore subject to change. Many of the exclusions are subject to conditions and limitations or apply in different ways to different regulated activities or investments. Reference should therefore be made to the full text of the exclusion in each case. (References to articles and to paragraphs are to articles of, and to paragraphs of sch. 3 to, the February 1999 draft Regulated Activities Order.)

# Chapter Four
# Financial Promotion

## *Mark Threipland*

This chapter describes the restriction on financial promotion by unauthorised persons in s. 21 of the Financial Services and Markets Act 2000 (FSAMA 2000) and the consequences of contravening this restriction. It also briefly describes how financial promotion by authorised persons will be regulated. The Act represents a change in approach to the regulation of marketing financial services. To put the new regime in context, this chapter contains brief descriptions of the existing regimes and other relevant legislation and also contains a discussion of why the restriction is needed at all and how it fits in with other provisions of the Act.

The principal elements of the new financial promotion regime are as follows:

(a)   The restriction on financial promotion in s. 21 applies to unauthorised persons only. Financial promotion by authorised persons will be regulated by the FSA's rules, although there are particular restrictions on financial promotion of unregulated collective investment schemes by authorised persons in FSAMA 2000, Part XVII.

(b)   An unauthorised person may communicate a financial promotion only if an exemption applies or if the content of the financial promotion has been approved by an authorised person. This approval will be regulated by the FSA's rules, so that the authorised person will have to ensure that relevant disclosures are included and take responsibility for the accuracy of the promotion, thereby giving the recipient a right of redress and the FSA a right to bring enforcement action.

(c)   The financial promotion regime is built around a wide restriction in s. 21 subject to exemptions which the Treasury may make in secondary legislation to cut back the scope of the restriction to workable proportions. At the time of writing, the final version of these exemptions is not available. In October 1999 the Treasury published a draft of the Financial Services and Markets Act (Financial Promotion) (Exemptions) Order (referred to in this chapter as the 'draft Financial Promotion

Exemptions Order') and a further draft was issued for consultation during autumn 2000.

(d)   The financial promotion regime has abandoned the traditional concepts of 'advertisement' and 'unsolicited call'. It covers communications in any form or medium, including written advertisements, telephone calls, visits, letters, faxes, e-mails, broadcasts and Internet websites. The draft Financial Promotion Exemptions Order distinguishes between *real-time communications* and other forms of financial promotion.

(e)   The distinction between 'solicited' and 'unsolicited' calls has been discarded at the level of the Act, although the draft Financial Promotion Exemptions Order exempts most *solicited* real-time communications.

(f)   The existing three legislative regimes concerning the marketing of deposits, insurance and other investments have been consolidated at the level of the Act. However, the draft Financial Promotion Exemptions Order contains broad exemptions for financial promotions relating to deposits and general insurance, which is consistent with there being less regulation of the conduct of deposit-taking and general insurance business.

The government's stated intention in developing the financial promotion regime was to modernise and streamline the legislative framework applying to financial promotion in the UK, 'to ensure that the UK is best placed to reflect . . . the opportunities of new and rapidly evolving communications technology' and 'to create a regime that is capable of standing up to the developments of modern technology while remaining effective against the more traditional methods of promoting financial services' (HM Treasury, *Financial Promotion — Second Consultation Document*, October 1999; *Hansard* HC Standing Committee A, 22 July 1999). The legislation does not use the phrase 'financial promotion' other than in the title of s. 21 (and in empowering the FSA to make 'financial promotion rules' in s. 145). In this chapter, 'financial promotion' has been used as a shorthand to refer to an invitation or inducement of the type restricted by s. 21.

## EXISTING UK LEGISLATION

This section briefly describes the existing UK legislation on financial promotion that is likely to be repealed when FSAMA 2000, s. 21, comes into force.

### Financial Services Act 1986

The new approach to the regulation of financial promotions is radical in many ways. But those familiar with the investment advertisement and unsolicited call regimes in FSA 1986 will find much that is familiar to them in the financial promotion regime, although presented with new terminology and in a more unified way. FSA 1986 and the rules and regulations made under it make detailed provision for the control of investment advertisements (s. 57), unsolicited calls

(s. 56), promotion of unregulated collective investment schemes (s. 76) and promotion of certain long-term insurance contracts (s. 130). There is a comparison of the two regimes in Table 4.1 at the end of this chapter.

## Banking Act 1987

There are currently few statutory controls specific to the marketing of deposits, reflecting the prudential focus of the supervision of banks and other deposit-taking institutions. The Banking Act 1987 (Advertisements) Regulations 1988 (SI 1988/645) (contravention of which is a criminal offence) require the inclusion of specified information in UK deposit advertisements and apply primarily to persons who are not carrying on deposit-taking business in the United Kingdom or another EEA State. The Credit Institutions (Protection of Depositors) Regulations 1995 (SI 1995/1442) apply to UK-authorised and passporting EEA banks operating in the UK and require certain disclosures about compensation schemes. The FSA also has a power under the Banking Act 1987, s. 33, to order a bank to change the contents of a misleading deposit advertisement.

## Insurance Companies Act 1982

There are also few statutory controls specific to the marketing of insurance contracts (other than long-term insurance contracts that constitute 'investments' under FSA 1986). The Insurance Companies Regulations 1994 (SI 1994/1516) require certain disclosures to be made in insurance advertisements issued by UK and overseas insurance companies and in invitations (both written and oral) made by insurance intermediaries. Contravention of the regulations is a criminal offence.

## OTHER UK LEGISLATION RELEVANT TO FINANCIAL PROMOTION

This section describes the other principal UK legislation that will continue to be relevant to financial promotions when FSAMA 2000, s. 21, comes into force.

## General advertising regulation

Most advertising targeted at UK consumers is subject to self-regulatory mechanisms through the Advertising Standards Authority and codes of practice (such as the Banking Code for deposits). There are also statutory controls on advertising. The Trade Descriptions Act 1968 makes it an offence to offer goods using a false trade description and gives enforcement powers to local weights and measures inspectors. There are specialist regimes, such as the statutory regulation of consumer credit and consumer hire advertisements, and the media-specific controls for commercial television, cable and radio. The Control of Misleading Advertisements Regulations 1988 (SI 1988/915) (which implement the EC Misleading Advertisements Directive, 84/450/EEC) give the Director General of Fair Trading powers to obtain injunctions against regular issuers of misleading advertisements and put the burden of proof on the advertiser to show that the advertisement is not misleading. These Regulations currently do not apply in relation to FSA 1986 investment advertisements issued by authorised persons or appointed representatives (the Directive being implemented in this context through regulatory rules), and it remains to be seen whether implementation of the Directive in the context of financial promotions by authorised persons will be left to FSA rules.

## Restrictions on offers of securities

Under the Public Offers of Securities Regulations 1995 (SI 1995/1537), if unlisted securities are offered to the public for the first time in the UK, the offeror must publish a prospectus, unless an exemption in the Regulations applies. Where a prospectus is prepared in accordance with the Regulations, it will benefit from an exemption from the restriction on financial promotion (draft Financial Promotion Exemptions Order, art. 63), but other financial promotions connected with the offer must still comply with the restriction. Where the offer falls under the exemptions in the Regulations, the restriction on financial promotion will still apply, and any offering document must be communicated or approved by an authorised person or fall under an exemption from the restriction. The government has stated that, where similar exemptions exist in the Regulations and under the restriction on financial promotion, it is intended, in general, that the exemptions should be compatible (HM Treasury, *Financial Promotion — A Consultation Document*, February 1999, part 4, para. 5.2). In the case of an offering to the public of shares to be officially listed, listing particulars or a prospectus under FSAMA 2000, Part VI, will be required, and there will be an exemption for such documents (draft Financial Promotion Exemptions Order, art. 62).

## Telecommunications (Data Protection and Privacy) Regulations 1999

Restrictions on the use of telecommunications equipment for cold calling are imposed by the Telecommunications (Data Protection and Privacy) Regulations 1999 (SI 1999/2093) which implement the European Telecoms Data Protection Directive (97/66/EC) (commonly known as the 'ISDN Directive'). In summary, unsolicited communications to individuals transmitted by automated calling mechanisms or by fax are prohibited without prior consent. Other forms of unsolicited telecommunications to individuals (e.g., telephone calls and e-mails) are permitted without consent, unless the individual has notified the caller that he or she does not wish to receive such calls or if the individual's name is recorded on a public register maintained by the Director General of Telecommunications.

## OTHER PARTS OF FSAMA 2000 RELEVANT TO FINANCIAL PROMOTION

### Unregulated collective investment schemes

FSAMA 2000, Part XVII, contains restrictions on authorised persons who communicate or approve financial promotions relating to unregulated collective investment schemes.

**Financial promotion and regulated activities**

Persons engaged in financial promotion will need to consider whether they are carrying on a regulated activity, potentially in contravention of the general prohibition (s. 19). The most relevant regulated activities are investment advice and arranging.

**Offences and market abuse**

The communication of financial promotions could potentially amount to market abuse (Part VIII) or an offence under s. 397 (misleading statements and practices).

## WHY IS A FINANCIAL PROMOTION REGIME NEEDED AT ALL?

Why are the general advertising controls not sufficient for financial services? General advertising controls focus on accuracy, and there is a strong consumer protection case for a separate and additional regulatory regime on the grounds that promoting financial services can lead consumers into making significant, long-term and sometimes high-risk commitments. Statutory controls can go beyond ensuring the accuracy of advertising to requiring the disclosure of risks associated with an investment and also full disclosure of terms and charges. Controls have arguably become more important with the increase in direct sales of financial services through off-the-page, telephone and Internet marketing, without the consumer receiving advice from an intermediary.

In addition, reliance on the general prohibition on carrying on regulated activities is arguably not sufficient. This is, first, because of the probable link between the financial promotion regime and the territorial scope of the general prohibition through the overseas persons exclusions and, secondly, because the promotion of regulated activities is often concerned with the stage before any regulated activities are actually carried on, enabling the FSA to take preventative action. This is particularly true now that it is proposed that 'offering' should not be a regulated activity (in contrast to FSA 1986), so that an unauthorised person contravenes the general prohibition only at the stage of 'agreeing' to carry on a regulated activity and not before.

## RESTRICTION ON FINANCIAL PROMOTION

**Elements of the restriction on financial promotion**

Subsections (1) and (2) of s. 21 are the keystones of the regime. They provide that:

(1)  A person ('A') must not, in the course of business, communicate an invitation or inducement to engage in investment activity.

(2)  But subsection (1) does not apply if—

(a)  A is an authorised person; or

(b)   the content of the communication is approved for the purposes of this section by an authorised person.

To decide if a person 'A' is contravening the restriction on financial promotion, the following elements need to be considered, each of which is described in more detail later in this chapter:

(a)   Is A acting 'in the course of business'?
(b)   If so, is A 'communicating' anything, which includes 'causing a communication to be made' (s. 21(13))?
(c)   If so, is the communication an 'invitation or inducement'?
(d)   If so, is it an invitation or inducement to 'engage in investment activity'?
(e)   If so, is the content of the communication 'approved' by an authorised person?
(f)   If not, is the communication within the territorial scope of the restriction?
(g)   If so, does an exemption apply?
(h)   If not, A is contravening the restriction unless A is an authorised person.

## In the course of business

The restriction on financial promotion is contravened only when a person communicates 'in the course of business'. Communications between private individuals in a personal capacity are therefore not restricted. Under s. 21(4), the Treasury have the power, by regulations, to define the circumstances in which a person acts in the course of business. At the time of writing, it seems that they do not intend to exercise this power (HM Treasury, *Financial Promotion — Second Consultation Document*, October 1999, part 1, para. 4.6).

Chapter 3 contains a discussion of the interpretation of the requirement that an activity be 'carried on by way of business' to be a regulated activity under s. 22(1), and what constitutes a 'business'. Section 21(1) seems merely to require that the person be engaged in a business (of any sort) in the course of which the financial promotion is communicated; there is no need to consider whether the communication itself is made 'by way of business' or whether making such communications constitutes a business of the person. During debate on s. 21 (*Hansard* HC Standing Committee A, 20 July 1999), the minister said:

It seems reasonable to regulate people promoting investments or investment services in the course of their business, whether or not such services are carried on as a business. A company might, for instance, promote its own shares in the course of business, but it would not necessarily be carrying on the business of selling those shares.

For a communication to be 'in the course of' a business, it seems that there must be some connection between the business and the communication such that the person potentially derives a direct or indirect financial benefit from the communication. An example of a financial promotion that is likely to be regarded as communicated in the course of business, but which might not immediately be obvious as such, is an employer's leaflet promoting a group personal pension scheme to its employees.

## Communicate

'Communicate' seems to encompass both the activity of physically transmitting or giving information to another person and the activity of imparting information. Under s. 21(13), 'communicate' includes causing a communication to be made, which confirms that pre-transmission activities are potentially caught by the restriction on financial promotion. It appears that all of the following are potentially within the restriction:

(a)   A person transmitting his or her own financial promotions. Examples of this are making a telephone call, holding a face-to-face conversation and handing over a leaflet.

(b)   A person transmitting a financial promotion without being aware of its contents or being involved in the preparation of its intellectual content. Examples of this are a person distributing leaflets prepared by another person, a broadcaster transmitting a television or radio advertisement, a telephone company transmitting a telephone call, an Internet service provider transmitting an e-mail, a direct mail firm distributing advertisements and a newspaper publishing an advertisement. The Treasury have proposed an exemption for 'mere conduits' (draft Financial Promotion Exemptions Order, art. 23).

(c)   A person involved at a stage prior to the transmission of the communication who instigates its communication. Examples are a person who submits an advertisement to a newspaper for publication or to a broadcaster for broadcasting. But it appears that a person who does not personally transmit a financial promotion must directly cause it to be communicated to be caught by the restriction. Taking the example of a television advertisement, the advertising agency which creates the intellectual content of a television advertisement, the production company which records the advertisement and the company which maintains the transmitter which transmits it are unlikely to contravene the restriction when the financial promotion is communicated, unless otherwise involved with the financial promotion.

It is clear that more than one person can potentially contravene the restriction in relation to a single communication. Continuing the example of a television advertisement, it would appear that the advertiser communicates it (i.e., causes it to be communicated), the television station which determines whether and when the advertisement will be transmitted communicates it (either by transmitting or causing transmission by others) and the cable company down whose cables it is transmitted also communicates it.

It is arguable that all persons who communicate (including causing the communication) of a financial promotion need to be authorised persons, unless an authorised person approves the content of the financial promotion or an exemption applies. The involvement of an authorised person in communicating the financial promotion or causing it to be communicated would not appear to prevent unauthorised persons from contravening the restriction in relation to the same financial promotion. Although s. 25(2)(a) provides a defence to the criminal offence if the person concerned believed on reasonable grounds that the content of the communication was '*prepared*, or approved' by an authorised person (emphasis added), there is no equivalent defence against an agreement being treated as unenforceable as a result of an unlawful communication. Of course, if the authorised person who communicates the financial promotion also approves its content, this relieves other persons involved in the communication from potentially contravening s. 21(1).

## Invitation or inducement

The phrase 'invitation or inducement' is a departure from the existing legislation which use alternative formulations based on whether an advertisement contains an invitation or information intended or calculated to lead to the relevant activity. The dictionary definitions of 'invitation' suggest that it includes a request or solicitation. An 'inducement' would seem to be a wider concept, and some dictionary definitions suggest that no promotional intent is necessary — something can be an inducement if it merely brings something about or causes it to happen. In the Race Relations Act 1976, 'to induce' was held to mean 'to persuade or to prevail upon or to bring about' (*Commission for Racial Equality* v *Imperial Society of Teachers of Dancing* [1983] ICR 473 at p. 476). The fact that purposive wording has been used in conjunction with the word 'inducing' in FSAMA 2000, s. 397(2) might support this interpretation. But to apply this wide interpretation of 'invitation or inducement' in this context would extend the restriction to many types of communication which the existing legislation does not restrict. To require an unauthorised person to obtain approval from an authorised person for non-promotional correspondence and conversations seems potentially unworkable.

Pressed on this matter during the passage of the Bill, the minister confirmed the government's stated policy was 'to capture promotional communications only', that ' "inducement", in its Bill usage, already incorporates an element of design or purpose on the part of the person making the communication' and that 'design or purpose is implicit in this context' (*Hansard* HL, 18 May 2000, cols 387 and 388). It seems likely that a court would have regard to these clear statements under the rule in *Pepper* v *Hart* [1993] AC 593. Under that rule, a court may have regard to certain classes of material contained in *Hansard* where an enactment is obscure or ambiguous, or where its literal meaning would lead to an absurdity (meaning, in this context, a result which is unworkable, impracticable or productive of a disproportionate counter-mischief).

If that is right, it seems that non-promotional materials are not caught. In the same debate, the minister said that the restriction 'will not catch . . . public announcements, exchange of draft share purchase agreements in corporate finance transactions or cases in which the recipient of a communication simply misunderstands its contents and engages in investment activity as a result'. But that is not to say that it is necessary for a communication to contain a recommendation for it to be an 'invitation or inducement'. A selection of factual information that would tend to influence a recipient's decision may be an inducement, although factual information that is provided in a fair and balanced way may not. In the context of actionable misrepresentation at common law it has been held that, although mere incompleteness might not make a communication into an inducement, an omission that makes the communication one-sided so as to amount to a travesty and not an accurate summary may do so (*Oakes* v *Turquand and Harding* (1867) LR 2 HL 325 at p. 342 per Lord Chelmsford). Some communications that fall within the definition of the regulated activity of investment advice are likely to be inducements.

Must actual promotional intent on the part of the communicator be proved, or may an objective test be applied? An objective test appears appropriate for whether a communication is an 'invitation' and it seems reasonable to assume that an objective test may be applied to 'inducement' as well. To quote the minister again, whether something is an inducement 'will depend on the actual or perceived intent behind the communication'. So all the circumstances of the communication are likely to be relevant to a determination of whether it is an invitation or inducement, including its content, its character, its context and the experience, both general and particular, of the recipients. The restriction on financial promotion looks to the act of communication rather than any result flowing from it, so there is no need for any investment activity to be engaged in as a result of the communication, nor for the communication to be actually received by anyone. On the other hand, it is clear that the restriction cannot be contravened without a communication being made, even if there is some duty to make a disclosure.

**Engage in investment activity**

'Engaging in investment activity' is defined in s. 21(8) as:

> (a)  entering or offering to enter into an agreement the making or performance of which by either party constitutes a controlled activity; or
>
> (b)  exercising any rights conferred by a controlled investment to acquire, dispose of, underwrite or convert a controlled investment.

An important question is whether non-specific or 'image' financial promotions are caught. It seems that they are, and that the references in s. 21(8) to 'an agreement' and 'a controlled investment' should not be regarded as relating to a *particular* agreement or investment. The wording is similar to FSA 1986, ss. 44(9) and 57, which were always regarded as catching generic advertisements. This interpretation may be supported by the references to 'particular investment' in the proposed exemption for generic promotions (draft Financial Promotion Exemptions Order, art. 17) and in the definition of 'certain investment advice' (draft Regulated Activities Order, art 19), if the references are retained in the Orders as made.

For an agreement to fall within limb (a) of the definition in FSAMA 2000, s. 21(8), it does not matter whether the recipient of the communication is to enter the agreement by acceptance of an offer or by making an offer which is accepted by the other party (who need not be the communicator). Making or performing the agreement must constitute a 'controlled activity', but it does not matter whether the controlled activity is conducted by the recipient (e.g., by purchasing a share) or the other party (e.g., by managing the recipient's assets). But a communication that induces the recipient not to take action (e.g., a defence document in a takeover bid) will not be a financial promotion. A communication will fall within limb (b) if it promotes the exercise of certain rights conferred by an investment. Examples include a notice inducing the recipient to exercise a warrant or option. But inducing the exercise of voting rights is not restricted.

The Treasury have the power to specify what is a controlled activity and a controlled investment in secondary legislation just as they can specify what is a regulated activity for the purposes of the general prohibition (see chapter 3). A draft specification of controlled activities was published for consultation in October 1999 (draft Financial Promotion Exemptions Order, sch. 1) and a further draft has been published for consultation during autumn 2000. From the published draft it seems, logically, that the controlled activities will track the regulated activities almost exactly. The likely principal difference is that the exclusions applicable to regulated activities will not apply to the controlled activities. In general this would follow the approach that was taken under FSA 1986 investment advertisement regime (FSA 1986, s. 44(9)). For example, an overseas broker whose dealing services would not contravene the general prohibition because it can benefit from the overseas persons exclusions could still contravene the restriction on financial promotion if it promotes those services to UK persons.

### Approval of financial promotions by authorised persons

The restriction on financial promotion does not apply to a communication if 'the content of the communication is approved for the purposes of this section by an authorised person' (FSAMA 2000, s. 21(2)(b)). The mechanism of 'approving' investment advertisements applies under FSA 1986, s. 57, but the words 'for the purposes of this section' in FSAMA 2000, s. 21(2)(b), are new. These make it clear that the approval must be specifically for the purposes of enabling the financial promotion to be communicated by unauthorised persons free of the restriction on financial promotion. For example, if a solicitor who is an authorised person approves an advertisement for legality generally, that would not suffice unless the solicitor does so specifically for the purposes of s. 21 as well. Further, approval for the purposes of communication by the authorised person itself, rather than by unauthorised persons, would not suffice. An unauthorised person would therefore be well advised to obtain specific confirmation of the purposes of an approval before relying on it. The requirement is for the 'content of the communication' to be approved. Where an invitation or inducement forms part of a larger communication, does this mean that the entire communication needs to be approved or just the part constituting an invitation or inducement (for example, an advertisement in a newspaper or parts of an Internet website)? Although it is not completely clear, it seems that 'communication' in s. 21(2)(b) means the invitation or inducement communicated (compare s. 21(13)).

The FSA will make rules that an authorised person must comply with when approving financial promotions for communication by others and a draft of those rules has been published (FSA, *The Conduct of Business Sourcebook* (Consultation Paper 45), annex a, ch. 3). It is proposed that the steps to be taken by an authorised person in approving a financial promotion (in particular, as to the disclosures to be included in an approved communication and ensuring that it is not misleading) will be broadly similar to those required if the communication was made by the authorised person, and require the authorised person to take responsibility for the accuracy of the financial promotion. An unauthorised person who communicates a financial promotion will not contravene the restriction on financial promotion merely because the authorised approver contravenes the rules (there is an exception regarding unregulated collective investment schemes in s. 240(2)). But the authorised person may face an action for damages (s. 150) and FSA enforcement action.

The application of the approval process to all forms of financial promotion could lead to some areas of major difference when compared to existing regimes, as follows.

*Oral financial promotions*    Oral financial promotions by unauthorised persons that are approved will not contravene the restriction on financial promotion, in contrast to the position under FSA 1986, s. 56. The requirement is for the content of the communication to be approved, and given the difficulty in controlling the content of real-time oral communications, this may not always be practicable. In recognition of this, the FSA has proposed to prohibit such approvals (*The Conduct of Business Sourcebook* (Consultation Paper 45, annex a, COB 3.12.1(2)).

*Deposits and insurance*    Financial promotions relating to deposits, general insurance contracts and long-term insurance contracts which are not FSA 1986 investments may be approved, in contrast to the position under the Banking Act 1987 and the Insurance Companies Act 1982. Although it seems likely that such financial promotions will benefit from wide exemptions in the Financial Promotions Exemptions Order, the approval process will represent an alternative method of avoiding a contravention of the restriction on financial promotion.

*Unregulated collective investment schemes*   Under FSA 1986, approval of investment advertisements relating to unregulated collective investment schemes is
permitted by FSA 1986, s. 57(1), but prohibited by SRO and FSA rules (e.g., the
FSA's Core Conduct of Business Rules, r. 5(3)). This means that advertisements
relating to such schemes can be issued by authorised persons only (subject to the
restrictions in FSA 1986, s. 76). FSAMA 2000, s. 240, now includes a mechanism
whereby an authorised person may approve such financial promotions if it would
be permitted to communicate the financial promotion itself under s. 238. Importantly, contravention of this condition leads to the approval being invalid and to the
unauthorised person contravening the restriction in s. 21.

## TERRITORIAL SCOPE

Under FSAMA 2000, the restriction on financial promotion has an unlimited
territorial scope, subject to a restriction in s. 21(3) for promotions originating
outside the United Kingdom. The Treasury has proposed cutting back the territorial
scope in the Financial Promotion Exemptions Order.

Financial promotions *within the United Kingdom*, i.e., that originate within the
United Kingdom and are communicated to persons in the United Kingdom, are
within the territorial scope of the restriction. The draft Financial Promotions
Exemption Order proposed no exemptions for *outward financial promotions*. This
was despite concerns about dual regulation of financial promotions by UK persons
into other jurisdictions which impose their own requirements on incoming promotional material. The Treasury's view was that these concerns were outweighed by
the need for the FSA to be able to take action against a UK promoter in support
of an overseas regulator which was facing inappropriate promotions. The restriction on *inward financial promotions* applies only if a communication which
originates outside the UK is 'capable of having an effect in the United Kingdom'
(FSAMA 2000, s. 21(3)). This phrase seems to be open to a wide interpretation
and to include any invitation or inducement which is capable of resulting in a UK
person engaging in investment activity. The intention of the communicator to
promote to UK persons seems to be irrelevant. However, the draft Financial
Promotions Exemption Order proposes an exemption for a financial promotion
communicated from a place outside the UK and not *directed at* persons in the UK.
It includes a number of (non-exhaustive) tests for interpreting what is 'directed at'
and a safe harbour if all tests are satisfied. The draft exemption does not apply to
financial promotions relating to deposits or general insurance contracts.

Further consideration of the territorial scope of the restriction on financial
promotion would be premature until the Financial Promotion Exemptions Order
has been finalised. An important factor may be the need to implement the
Electronic Commerce Directive (2000/31/EC) by January 2002. The Directive
adopts, as a starting point, home State control of electronic commerce, so that an
EEA State from whose jurisdiction an electronic communication is sent would
regulate the communication's content and use and would oblige disclosure of the

country of origin. This recognises the difficulty of regulating electronic services being offered from overseas and broadly follows the recommendation of the IOSCO report (*Securities Activity on the Internet — a Report by the Technical Committee*, International Organisation of Securities Commissions, September 1998). FSAMA 2000, s. 21, is flexible enough to enable the Treasury, through exemptions, to amend the restriction on financial promotion to a home State approach. The government has agreed that 'the UK must be prepared to relinquish regulation of inward promotions in favour of a move to home-state regulation when the latter is provided for in the future by EC legislation or other multilateral agreements' (HM Treasury, *Financial Promotion — Second Consultation Document*, October 1999, part 2, para. 2.14). This is a move away from the Single Market Directives which permit host States to impose their own marketing rules on services offered cross-border where these are in the interest of the 'general good'.

## INTRODUCTION TO THE FINANCIAL PROMOTION EXEMPTIONS ORDER

The Treasury have a wide power, under FSAMA 2000, s. 21(5), to make exemptions from the restriction on financial promotion in secondary legislation (subject to an affirmative resolution procedure). In October 1999, the Treasury published the Financial Services and Markets Act (Financial Promotion) (Exemptions) Order in draft for consultation along with a consultation document (HM Treasury, *Financial Promotion — Second Consultation Document*, October 1999). A further draft for consultation appeared during autumn 2000. The following paragraphs discuss the main features of the draft Order, other than in relation to territorial scope, which is discussed above.

### Types of communications

The draft Financial Promotion Exemptions Order draws a distinction between *real-time communications* and *non-real-time communications* and between *solicited* and *unsolicited real-time communications*. These distinctions are important and many of the draft exemptions apply differently to different types of communication. But no distinction is drawn between solicited and unsolicited non-real-time communications. The terminology does not lend itself to instant understanding — as a rule of thumb, the distinction between real-time and non-real-time communications broadly replicates that between advertisements and calls under the previous regimes, but in a technology-neutral way, and the distinction between solicited and unsolicited real-time communications broadly replicates that between solicited and unsolicited calls.

### Application of the exemptions to real-time communications

The exemptions in the draft Financial Promotion Exemptions Order apply in different ways to real-time communications. The principal features are as follows.

*Deposits and general insurance* The restriction on financial promotion does not apply to real-time communications which relate to deposits or general insurance contracts, carrying forward the position under the existing legislation.

*Solicited real-time communications* Most solicited real-time communications are exempt. The overall effect is therefore similar to FSA 1986, s. 56, which did not regulate solicited calls.

*Unsolicited real-time communications* Some exemptions apply to unsolicited real-time communications only, some do not distinguish between real-time and non-real-time communications and some do not apply to unsolicited real-time communications. The effect of this is that unsolicited real-time communications are exempt from the restriction on financial promotion in broadly the same circumstances in which unsolicited calls were exempt from FSA 1986, s. 56, under the Common Unsolicited Calls Regulations made by the FSA. Where the exemptions for investment advertisements and unsolicited calls were similar, they have been consolidated.

### Exemptions for deposits and general insurance contracts

In addition to exempting all real-time communications relating to deposits or general insurance contracts, non-real-time communications relating to those investments are exempt provided that they contain certain disclosures relating to the deposit-taker or insurance company concerned.

### Exemptions for other investments

There are extensive exemptions in the draft Order for financial promotions that relate to investments other than deposits and general insurance contracts which, in many cases, carry forward those previously contained in FSA 1986, s. 58(1), the Treasury's two investment advertisement exemption orders (Financial Services (Investment Advertisements) (Exemptions) Order 1996 and 1997, SI 1996/1586 and 1997/963 respectively) and the FSA's Common Unsolicited Calls Regulations. There are, however, some new exemptions which will be of interest if they are included in the Order when it is made.

## SANCTIONS

The sanctions for breach of the restriction on financial promotion are potentially severe, namely, criminal liability, unenforceability of agreements, compensation and action by the FSA or the DTI to obtain an injunction and restitution.

### Criminal sanctions

Contravention of the restriction on financial promotion is an offence punishable by up to two years' imprisonment and an unlimited fine (FSAMA 2000, s. 25). There are two defences, for the accused to prove. The first is that the accused believed on reasonable grounds that the content of the communication was prepared or approved by an authorised person. For example, a newspaper publisher or website operator who undertakes reasonable enquiries to ascertain that an advertiser is an authorised person should be able to rely on this defence. But it should be noted that there is no equivalent of the 'prepared' limb of this defence in relation to the other sanctions. The second defence is that the accused took all reasonable precautions and exercised all due diligence to avoid committing the offence, which is identical to the defence under the general prohibition (see chapter 3 for further details).

## Unenforceability of agreements and compensation

Civil sanctions apply for contravention of the restriction on financial promotion. They are available to a person entering a 'controlled agreement', or exercising rights conferred by a controlled investment, 'as a customer', 'in consequence of an unlawful communication' (s. 30(2) and (3)). The controlled agreement, or obligation to which the customer is subject, is unenforceable against the customer and the customer can recover amounts transferred under the agreement or obligation as well as compensation for losses that resulted from having parted with those amounts. A 'controlled agreement' is an agreement, the making or performance of which by either party constitutes a controlled activity (s. 30(1)). 'As a customer' is not defined and seems to depend on all the circumstances such as the nature of the relationship and whether one party is using the services of the other rather than merely being a counterparty.

The words 'in consequence' suggest that the unlawful communication must be a direct cause of the agreement being entered into. But the agreement need not be with the person who communicated the unlawful financial promotion. So it would be possible, subject to the court's discretion discussed below, for there to be no connection between the communicator and the person who is unable to enforce the agreement. It seems that, in such circumstances, both the communicator and the person entering into the agreement with the customer could be required to pay compensation for the customer's losses. This corresponds to the position under FSA 1986 for unsolicited calls (FSA 1986, s. 56(1)). But it differs from that for investment advertisements; only agreements with the person issuing or causing an unlawful investment advertisement were unenforceable but there was no requirement for a causal link between the unlawful investment advertisement and the agreement (FSA 1986, s. 57(6)).

The court has a discretion under FSAMA 2000 to allow an agreement to be enforced or assets transferred under the agreement to be retained if it is satisfied that this is 'just and equitable' (s. 30(4)). Issues that the court must have regard to in exercising this discretion are set out in s. 30(5), (6) and (7). They are:

(a)   if the other party to the agreement made the unlawful communication, whether he reasonably believed that he was not making such a communication;

(b)   if some other person made the unlawful communication, whether the other party to the agreement knew that the agreement was entered into in consequence of an unlawful communication.

These conditions are very similar to those applicable in relation to the general prohibition (see Chapter 3 for further details).

## Right of the FSA and the DTI to seek injunctions and restitution

The FSA and the DTI are entitled to seek injunctions to restrain anticipated contravention of the restriction on financial promotion and orders to disgorge profits and require restitution of losses arising from such contravention (ss. 380 and 382).

## FINANCIAL PROMOTION BY AUTHORISED PERSONS

The restriction on financial promotion in FSAMA 2000, s. 21, does not apply to authorised persons. In communicating a financial promotion, an authorised person will have to comply with the following:

(a)   Rules on financial promotions made by the FSA. The FSA has published a draft of such rules in ch. 3 of *The Conduct of Business Sourcebook* (Consultation Paper 45, annex a). Broadly, authorised persons will be able to communicate financial promotions subject to certain due diligence and disclosure requirements. The draft rules adopt many of the concepts used in the Act, so that the analysis of those concepts in this chapter will be relevant.

(b)   Restrictions on communicating and approving financial promotions relating to unregulated collective investment schemes in Part XVII of the Act, and exemptions from those restrictions in any Treasury regulations made under s. 238(6) and in the FSA's rules (*The Conduct of Business Sourcebook*, 3.11).

(c)   The other UK legislation relevant to financial promotions referred to earlier in this chapter.

**Table 4.1** Comparison of the financial promotion regimes in the Financial Services and Markets Act 2000 and the Financial Services Act 1986. (This is based on the October 1999 draft Financial Promotion Exemptions Order which is subject to change.)

| Topic | Financial Services Act 1986 | Financial Services and Markets Act 2000 | Principal differences |
|---|---|---|---|
| Advertisements | Issue of 'investment advertisements' by unauthorised persons is restricted by s. 57. The concept of 'advertisement' is potentially very wide, but incorporates a promotional element and possibly a requirement to be more than 'one-off'. | The communication of relevant 'invitations or inducements' by unauthorised persons is restricted by s. 21. | The financial promotion regime is technology-neutral. 'Communicate' seems to catch a wider range of activities than 'issue'. 'One-off' invitations and inducements are caught. It is not clear that a financial promotion must be promotional in nature, although ministerial statements support this interpretation (under the rule in *Pepper v Hart*). |
| Calls or real-time communications | Unsolicited calls are not themselves regulated under s. 56, but rather the entering into of relevant agreements in the course of or in consequence of such calls by authorised or unauthorised persons. There is potentially some overlap between what is a call caught by s. 56 and what is an investment advertisement caught by s. 57. | The communication of relevant 'invitations or inducements' by unauthorised persons is restricted by s. 21. The draft Financial Promotion Exemptions Order introduces the concept of 'real-time communication', which is broadly equivalent to an FS Act 'call'. | The financial promotion regime is technology-neutral. Real-time communications must now be 'invitations or inducements' to be caught, but it is the communication that is regulated not the entering into of agreements. |
| Whose communications are regulated? | Only investment advertisements issued or caused to be issued by unauthorised persons are restricted by s. 57. Investment advertisements of authorised persons are regulated by SRO, RPB or FSA rules. Unsolicited calls of both authorised and unauthorised persons are regulated by s. 56. Authorised persons must also comply with relevant SRO, RPB or FSA rules. | Only financial promotions communicated by unauthorised persons are restricted by s. 21. Financial promotions communicated by authorised persons are regulated by FSA's rules (for unregulated collective investment schemes, see the last row of this table). | The financial promotion restriction in s. 21(1) applies only to unauthorised persons (for unregulated collective investment schemes, see the last row of this table). |

| Topic | Financial Services Act 1986 | Financial Services and Markets Act 2000 | Principal differences |
|---|---|---|---|
| Solicited and unsolicited communications | There is no distinction between solicited and unsolicited investment advertisements. Solicited calls are not regulated. Section 56 applies to unsolicited calls only. | There is no distinction at the level of the Act. The draft Financial Promotion Exemptions Order exempts 'solicited real-time communications', except those by UK persons which are part of a coordinated promotional strategy (arts 16 and 22). There is no exemption for solicited non-real-time communications. | Although the approach has changed, in many cases the result will be the same. The draft Financial Promotion Exemptions Order applies a stricter test of when a communication is 'solicited'. |
| By way of business | The investment advertisement regime applies to all advertisements, whether or not issued in the course of business. Unsolicited calls are regulated only if the call results in an investment agreement being entered into in the course of business. But the caller need not be engaged in a business. | Financial promotions are regulated only if communicated in the course of business. | All personal financial promotions (i.e., those not made in the course of a business) are outside the financial promotion regime. |
| Sanctions for contravention | The investment advertisement regime carries criminal and civil sanctions (including potential unenforceability of contracts). The unsolicited call regime has civil sanctions only (including potential unenforceability of contracts), not criminal sanctions. | The financial promotion regime carries both criminal and civil sanctions (including unenforceability of contracts). | Sanctions for contravention are uniform. |

| Topic | Financial Services Act 1986 | Financial Services and Markets Act 2000 | Principal differences |
|---|---|---|---|
| Territorial scope | Investment advertisements issued 'in the United Kingdom' are caught. The generally accepted view is that this covers advertisements issued within and into the UK, but not from the UK. There remains doubt regarding whether s. 57 catches investment advertisements on the Internet not directed at UK persons, although the FSA has given some comfort regarding use of its enforcement powers (Guidance Release 2/98).<br><br>Unsolicited calls within, into and from the UK are caught. | Financial promotions within, into and from the UK are caught, except that:<br>(a) financial promotions originating outside the UK which are not capable of having an effect in the UK are not caught (s. 21(3)); and<br>(b) the draft Financial Promotion Exemptions Order contains exemptions for most promotions originating outside the UK which are not 'directed at' the UK. | Territorial scope of the regime for unauthorised persons will be uniform irrespective of the medium of promotion.<br><br>The application of the regime to Internet promotions that originate outside the United Kingdom but are not directed at the United Kingdom will be clarified.<br><br>The application of controls to outward promotions has been extended. |
| Exemptions | Exemptions for investment advertisements are in s. 58 or Treasury regulations.<br><br>Exemptions for unsolicited calls are in the FSA's Common Unsolicited Calls Regulations. | All exemptions for unauthorised persons will be made by the Treasury, and contained in the Financial Promotion Exemptions Order.<br><br>Financial promotions by authorised persons will be regulated by FSA rules, but Treasury exemptions will be relevant (s. 145(3)). | Many of the exemptions will be aligned. Exemptions will be technology-neutral.<br><br>The Treasury have proposed a number of significant new exemptions. |
| Approval by authorised person | An unauthorised person may issue an investment advertisement if an authorised person has approved its contents.<br><br>There is no concept of 'approval' of unsolicited calls. | An unauthorised person may communicate any form of financial promotion if an authorised person has approved its content. | In theory, an unauthorised person may communicate a real-time communication whose content is approved by an authorised person. But the FSA has proposed to prevent authorised persons from approving real-time communications (FSA, *The Conduct of Business Sourcebook* (Consultation Paper 45, annex a), 3.12.1(2)). |

| Topic | Financial Services Act 1986 | Financial Services and Markets Act 2000 | Principal differences |
|---|---|---|---|
| Promotion of long-term insurance contracts | Section 130 restricts advertising of long-term insurance contracts constituting investments by both authorised and unauthorised persons, except those issued by authorised insurers or those from EEA or designated States. | No equivalent restriction. | Promotion of long-term insurance contracts by unauthorised persons is not subject to any special restrictions. |
| Promotion of unregulated collective investment schemes | Promotion of unregulated collective investment schemes by authorised persons is restricted by s. 76, subject to exemptions made by the FSA in the Financial Services (Promotion of Unregulated Schemes) Regulations 1991.<br><br>Promotion of such schemes by unauthorised persons is restricted by ss. 56 and 57 and the authorisation requirement for investment advice. SRO rules prohibit approval of investment advertisements relating to unregulated collective investment schemes for issue by unauthorised persons. | Communication of financial promotions relating to unregulated collective investment schemes by authorised persons, and approval by authorised persons of financial promotions of unauthorised persons, is restricted in Part XVII, subject to exemptions to be made in Treasury regulations and in FSA rules.<br><br>Communication of financial promotions relating to such schemes by unauthorised persons is restricted by s. 21(1). | The restriction on authorised persons only applies to financial promotions, not the giving of advice which is not a financial promotion.<br><br>Authorised persons will be able to approve financial promotions of unregulated schemes for communication by unauthorised persons, in the same circumstances in which they can communicate them. |

# Chapter Five
# Authorisation and Exemption

## *Mark Threipland*

Part III of the Financial Services and Markets Act 2000 (FSAMA 2000) sets out who has authorisation and how authorisation ends, how firms from other EEA States can obtain authorisation by exercising rights under European law and how UK firms can exercise similar rights in other EEA States. It gives the Treasury power to exempt persons, by order, from the general prohibition. It also provides an exemption for appointed representatives of authorised persons.

## AUTHORISATION

### What is authorisation?

FSAMA 2000 creates a single authorisation regime for the regulated activities within its scope. This contrasts with the existing legislation, under which persons wishing to carry on different kinds of financial services activities may need to be authorised under more than one statute, for example, the Banking Act 1987 for deposit-taking and FSA 1986 for investment business. Authorisation under FSAMA 2000 will bring a person inside the criminal perimeter in the sense that an authorised person cannot commit the criminal offences in Part II, which are contravention of the general prohibition (ss. 19 and 23), contravention of the restrictions on financial promotion (ss. 21 and 25) and falsely claiming to be authorised or exempt (s. 24). Instead, the ability of an authorised person to carry on regulated activities is controlled through the permission regime (see chapter 6) and by the FSA's rules.

Being authorised confers a number of rights, in addition to the ability to carry on regulated activities in the United Kingdom lawfully, including the ability to approve financial promotions under s. 21 and the ability to appoint appointed representatives under s. 39. But authorisation brings with it a host of obligations. In particular, authorised persons have to comply with the FSA's rules, pay fees to the FSA and, in most cases, contribute to the compensation scheme.

**Who is authorised?**

Section 31 sets out the following four routes to authorisation.

*(1) Part IV permission* A person with a 'Part IV permission' is an authorised person. This covers:

(a) A person who *applies for and is given permission by the FSA* under Part IV to carry on one or more regulated activities (s. 31(1)(a)).

(b) A person who receives a Part IV permission because his authorisation under existing legislation is *grandfathered* under transitional provisions to be made by the Treasury (ss. 426 and 427). At the time of writing, the transitional provisions have not been published, but the Treasury have confirmed that persons currently authorised under the Banking, Financial Services, Insurance Companies, Building Societies, Friendly Societies, Credit Union and Lloyd's Acts (including members of the self-regulating organisations and certain members of the recognised professional bodies) will be grandfathered into authorisation under the Act (Explanatory Notes to FSAMA 2000, para. 79). The FSA is expected to be able, for a limited period of two years after the Act comes into force, to require particular persons or groups of persons to re-apply for authorisation, if it has reason to believe that they do not meet the common standard for authorisation (HM Treasury, *Financial Services and Markets Bill: A Consultation Document*, July 1998, part 1, para. 21).

(c) *The Society of Lloyd's*, which is an authorised person with a Part IV permission by virtue of s. 315(3).

*(2) EEA firms* A person established in another EEA State who exercises passport rights to carry on activities in the United Kingdom under a Single Market Directive is an authorised person (s. 31(1)(b) and sch. 3). Such a person is referred to in the Act as an 'EEA firm' (the definition is in sch. 3, para. 5) and the rights exercised are commonly called a 'passport'. The Directives mentioned in FSAMA 2000 are the Second Banking Coordination Directive (89/646/EEC) for banks and other credit institutions (now replaced by the Credit Institutions Directive, 2000/12/EC), the Investment Services Directive (93/22/EEC) for investment firms and the various life and non-life Directives for insurance undertakings. See further under 'Passport Rights under the Single Market Directives' later in this chapter.

*(3) Treaty firms* A person established in another EEA State who exercises rights under the Treaty Establishing the European Community is authorised (FSAMA 2000, s. 31(1)(c) and sch. 4). These are rights anterior and in addition to those governed by the Single Market Directives. A person who seeks to exercise such rights is referred to in the Act as a 'Treaty firm' (the definition is in sch. 4, para. 1). See further under 'Exercise of Treaty rights by Treaty firms' later in this chapter.

(4) *Others* Persons may be otherwise authorised under FSAMA 2000 (s. 31(1)(d)). This covers:

(a)　*UCITS qualifiers*. The operator, trustee or depositary of a fund established in another EEA State is an authorised person, if that fund has exercised passport rights under the UCITS Directive (85/611/EEC) and become a recognised collective investment scheme under s. 264 of the Act (sch. 5, para. 1(1)). This implements a requirement of the UCITS Directive and carries forward the position under FSA 1986, s. 24. Such persons are called 'UCITS qualifiers' in the FSA's draft *Handbook*. FSAMA 2000, s. 264 and sch. 5, are flexible enough to permit the Treasury to extend their provisions should the mutual recognition of funds be extended beyond the UCITS Directive. Currently, the Directive applies only to funds, known as 'UCITS', constituted as unit trusts or open-ended investment companies, which meet detailed criteria covering matters including investment scope. The operator of a unit trust UCITS will normally be its manager and the operator of an open-ended investment company UCITS will be the company itself (FSAMA 2000, s. 237(2)). In either case, if the fund has a separate investment manager, that firm will need to seek authorisation by another route if it wishes to carry on regulated activities in the United Kingdom. A UCITS qualifier has permission under sch. 5, para. 2(1), to carry on any activity, appropriate to the person's capacity, amounting to establishing, operating and winding up collective investment schemes as described in sch. 2, para. 8.

(b)　*Investment companies with variable capital (ICVCs)*. An open-ended investment company, authorised under regulations made under s. 262, is an authorised person with permission to operate the scheme and carry on other connected activities, which would include marketing (sch. 5, paras. 1(3) and 2(2)). Such firms are called 'ICVCs' or 'investment companies with variable capital' in the FSA's draft *Handbook*. Authorisation of an ICVC as an authorised person, in addition to its 'product' authorisation under Part XVII, is necessary as it is a separate legal entity carrying on regulated activities in its own right, unlike a unit trust, and this carries forward the position under FSA 1986, s. 24A. The automatic authorisation of an ICVC does not extend to its authorised corporate director, which must seek authorisation by an alternative route.

### Can a person be authorised by more than one route?

It is possible for a person authorised through one of these routes to be authorised to carry on regulated activities by other routes. A person is either an authorised person or not, so it would not be correct to regard a person as having more than one authorisation. But authorisation through more than one route may result in a person having more than one permission to carry on regulated activities in the United Kingdom (see chapter 6).

### Authorisation of partnerships and unincorporated associations

FSAMA 2000, s. 32, makes particular provision for partnerships and unincorporated associations. Such a firm may be authorised under the Act, in which case it is authorised to carry on regulated activities in the name of the firm (s. 32(1)(a)). This clarifies the position of a firm without separate legal personality, for example, an English partnership. Section 32(1)(b) provides that the authorisation of the firm is not interrupted by changes in its membership. A change of partners in a partnership, or a change of the membership of an unincorporated association, may amount to a dissolution of the existing firm and the formation of a new partnership or association. But s. 32(2) allows the authorisation to pass to a successor partnership or association in the event of dissolution, provided that the members and the business of the successor are substantially the same as the original. Section 32 does not apply to a partnership constituted under the law of any place outside the United Kingdom which is a body corporate. What is a 'body corporate' will be determined under the general law, as the inclusive definition in s. 417(1) is of little assistance in interpretation.

## PASSPORT RIGHTS UNDER THE SINGLE MARKET DIRECTIVES

FSAMA 2000 sch. 3, gives effect in UK law to European single markets in banking, investment services and insurance. The Directives concerned (referred to in the Act as the 'Single Market Directives') are the Second Banking Coordination Directive (89/646/EEC, now replaced by the Credit Institutions Directive 2000/12/EC), the Investment Services Directive (93/22/EEC) and the various life and non-life Directives. Schedule 3 will replace the equivalent provisions contained in the Banking Coordination (Second Council Directive) Regulations 1992 (SI 1992/3218), the Investment Services Regulations 1995 (SI 1995/3275) and sch. 2F to the Insurance Companies Act 1982.

### What is a passport?

Under the Single Market Directives, credit institutions, investment firms and insurance undertakings established and authorised under the law of one EEA State have the right to carry on certain activities in other EEA States without the need to obtain a further authorisation in those other EEA States. These Directive rights are referred to in the Act as 'EEA rights' (sch. 3, para. 7) and commonly known as a 'passport'. The State where a passporting firm is established is commonly known as its 'home State'.

### Which firms are entitled to a passport?

To have a passport, a firm must be authorised in an EEA State to carry on:

(a) deposit-taking, in which case it may be a credit institution with a passport under the Credit Institutions Directive;
(b) a core investment service (listed in sch. A to the annex to the Investment Services Directive), in which case it may have a passport under that Directive unless it is also a credit institution; or

(c)   specified life or non-life insurance business, in which case it may have a passport under the insurance Directives.

Not every firm authorised in an EEA State to carry on the activities in (a) to (c) above has a passport. Most importantly, this may be because it is not incorporated in the EEA (or, if an unincorporated entity, does not have its head office in the EEA). For example, a branch of a US corporation authorised in the United Kingdom does not have a passport. In addition, a firm may not have a passport because it does not carry on activities in a way specified in the Directives, or because it falls within an exemption under the Directives. Under the Credit Institutions Directive, subsidiaries of credit institutions that meet certain criteria are also entitled to a passport. Such firms appear to be entitled to exercise passport rights under both the Credit Institutions Directive and the Investment Services Directive.

**Responsibilities of the home and host State regulators**

The competent authority in the home State (referred to in the Act as the 'home State regulator') retains full responsibility for authorising a passporting firm, and for prudential supervision of the firm (that is, supervision of its financial soundness and ensuring that it and its controllers are fit and proper). The competent authorities in the EEA States where a passporting firm carries on business under its passport (referred to as 'host State regulators') may impose only limited rules. These must relate to the conduct of business under the passport in their States and must be adopted in the interest of the 'general good'. This requires those rules to be proportionate, non-discriminatory and non-duplicative of home State rules with equivalent effect. Express provision is made in certain areas such as compensation, custody and liquidity of branches of credit institutions (the latter is the joint responsibility of the home and host State regulators).

**What activities are covered by a passport?**

A passport entitles a passporting firm to carry on activities within a host State either by establishing a branch in the host State or by providing services cross-border into the host State. A passporting firm may also exercise passport rights to carry on activities by these two means in parallel. A passporting firm is only entitled to passport activities which it may lawfully carry on under its home State authorisation.

The passports under the Single Market Directives cover a range of financial services, which include deposit-taking, certain investment services and life and non-life (or general) insurance business. The Credit Institutions Directive passport covers the listed activities in annex 1 to the Directive. The Investment Services Directive passport covers the core investment services and non-core investment services (listed in schs. A and C to the annex to the Directive). The insurance Directives passports cover the specified insurance business activities.

The passported activities do not necessarily correspond with the activities which are regulated under the law of any EEA State. The passported activities may go wider because the Directives specify minimum activities that must be regulated in each EEA State, being deposit-taking, the core investment services and specified insurance business activities, but provide for activities which are wider than that minimum to be passportable (in the case of the Credit Institutions Directive and the Investment Services Directive). In addition, the passports may not cover all the activities that are regulated in any EEA State, because EEA States are entitled to impose an authorisation requirement on non-passportable activities. To carry on such activities in the host State, a passporting firm may require authorisation from the host State regulator (commonly referred to as a 'top-up authorisation'). The most important examples of non-passportable regulated activities in the United Kingdom under existing legislation are investment services relating to commodity derivatives and advice on life policies.

### Exercise of passport rights by an incoming EEA firm

A firm which is established in an EEA State other than the United Kingdom and has a passport is referred to in the Act as an 'EEA firm'. Schedule 3 adopts a uniform approach to the exercise of passport rights by an incoming EEA firm, except where the Directives diverge in their operation. In particular, the Act treats an EEA firm which exercises its passport rights in the United Kingdom as an authorised person under the Act, just as EEA insurance companies were treated as authorised under the Insurance Companies Act 1982. This is a new approach for EEA credit institutions and investment firms, which were not treated as authorised persons under the Banking Act 1987 and FSA 1986, but instead did not need authorisation.

To become authorised under sch. 3, an EEA firm needs to make a notification through its home State regulator. The detailed procedures depend on whether a branch is being established or services provided cross-border and are set out in part II of sch. 3. There is no need for the FSA to be satisfied as to the fitness and propriety of the EEA firm, or as to the other threshold conditions in sch. 6.

### When should an incoming EEA firm make a notification?

FSAMA 2000 does not expressly require an EEA firm to notify its home State regulator that it will be carrying on business in the UK, unlike the previous legislation implementing the Investment Services Directive and what is now the Credit Institutions Directive (Investment Services Regulations 1995 (SI 1995/3275), reg. 6; Banking Coordination (Second Council Directive) Regulations 1992 (SI 1992/3218), reg. 6). Under FSAMA 2000, an EEA firm will only need to notify where, in the absence of notification, the firm would contravene the general prohibition in s. 19 and hence commit a criminal offence (s. 23). An EEA firm will therefore not need to notify for activities carried on outside the territorial scope of the general prohibition (described in chapter 3), for example where it can take

advantage of the overseas person exclusions. But the law of the EEA firm's home
State should impose a notification requirement for services provided in other EEA
States. Contravention of the general prohibition by an EEA firm which has not
exercised its passport rights does not carry with it the sanctions of unenforceability
of contracts or requirement to return deposits (sch. 3, para. 16; ss. 26 to 29). An
EEA firm which has not exercised its passport rights in the United Kingdom will
be able to benefit from an exemption from the restrictions on financial promotion,
provided it complies with the FSA's financial promotion rules (October 1999 draft
of the Financial Services and Markets (Financial Promotion) (Exemptions) Order,
art. 27).

### Effect of authorisation of an incoming EEA firm under sch. 3

On qualifying for authorisation under FSAMA 2000, sch. 3, an EEA firm will have
permission to carry on the passported regulated activities covered by its notification
to its home State regulator and, where the notification covers consumer credit, will
be exempt from the need for a licence under the Consumer Credit Act 1974. The
FSA must inform the EEA firm of the UK rules that it must comply with.
Regulations to be made by the Treasury under FSAMA 2000, sch. 3, will set out the
procedures to be followed should an EEA firm wish to change certain matters
covered by its passport notification, such as the types of activities carried on in the
United Kingdom. But if an EEA firm with a passport to provide services
cross-border into the United Kingdom wishes to establish a branch here (or vice
versa), it will need to go through the notification procedure in part II of sch. 3 again.

### Exercise of passport rights by an outgoing UK firm

A firm that is established in the United Kingdom and has a passport is referred to
in the Act as a 'UK firm' (sch. 3, para. 10). Part III of sch. 3 sets out the
notification procedures by which UK credit institutions (banks and building
societies), investment firms and insurance undertakings (insurance companies and
some friendly societies) may exercise passport rights to establish branches in, or
provide services cross-border into, other EEA States. Only a firm with a Part IV
permission which has its registered or head office in the United Kingdom has
passport rights under part III of sch. 3. In addition, its permission must cover
activities within the scope of the Directives and it must not be exempt from the
application of the Directives. Schedule 3 also gives the Treasury the power to make
regulations governing the continuing regulation of passporting UK firms, including
procedures for modifying the activities carried on under a passport.

### When should an outgoing UK firm make a notification?

If an authorised UK firm with a passport provides services in another EEA State
through a branch, or by the provision of services cross-border, without going

through the notification procedure, it will contravene a requirement imposed by the Act (sch. 3, paras 19(1) and 20(1)) with all the usual consequences (including discipline under Part XIV). It is an offence for an unauthorised UK firm with a passport, such as a credit institution subsidiary, to do so (sch. 3, para. 21). A UK firm should also take into account the law of the relevant EEA host State.

Determining when a branch is established or services are provided cross-border may be difficult, particularly in the case of cross-border services. EEA regulators have taken different views on this question. Some have adopted a 'solicitation test', under which a firm is regarded as providing services to a resident of that State if a particular transaction, or the relationship under which the transaction is conducted, was solicited by the firm. The United Kingdom has generally adopted a less expansive view of when services should be regarded as provided cross-border. The European Commission has favoured a 'characteristic performance' test in the banking sector, which broadly treats a service as provided in the place with which the service is most closely connected (European Commission Interpretative Communication, SEC (97) 1193). On the other hand, the European Commission has taken the view that the provision of insurance services via the Internet does amount to the provision of insurance services into the EEA State where the risk is situated (European Commission Interpretative Communication, C (1999) 5056). There has been no equivalent Commission communication regarding investment services.

## EXERCISE OF TREATY RIGHTS BY TREATY FIRMS

Schedule 4 to FSAMA 2000 gives effect in UK law to the rights of establishment and to provide services cross-border under arts 43 to 55 of the Treaty Establishing the European Community which go beyond the passport rights covered by FSAMA 2000, sch. 3. These 'Treaty rights' permit a person, established and authorised under the law of one EEA State (its 'home State'), to carry on an activity in other EEA States ('host States') so long as the law of its home State provides equivalent protection to that of the host State or meets EU harmonised minimum requirements applicable in that area of law. These rights are given specific effect for many financial services firms through the Single Market Directives. However, as explained above, the Directives do not cover the full range of financial services or financial service providers. Schedule 4 provides a mechanism for EEA persons to exercise Treaty rights in the UK in the absence of passport rights, potentially enabling, for example, a passporting EEA insurance company to carry on reinsurance business in the UK without applying for Part IV permission. The Act contains no equivalent mechanism for a UK firm to exercise Treaty rights in another EEA State; this is a matter for the local law in that State.

Schedule 4 does not define the extent of Treaty rights, which are the subject of developing case law in the EU, but sets the conditions that must be met for authorisation by this route. The FSA must receive confirmation from the Treaty firm's home State regulator that it has authorisation in the home State for the regulated activities that it seeks to carry on in the United Kingdom. The laws of the home State must provide equivalent protection — a certificate from the Treasury to this effect is conclusive evidence of that fact. Alternatively, those laws must satisfy EU harmonised minimum requirements applicable in that area of law. If the regulated activities that the firm is seeking to carry on are covered by the firm's passport rights under sch. 3, then those rights must be exercised instead of Treaty rights. A Treaty firm is also required to give notice of its intention to exercise its Treaty rights and to provide such information as the FSA may require. Failure to give proper notice may be a criminal offence. On qualifying for authorisation, a Treaty firm has permission to carry on each regulated activity which it sought to carry on under sch. 4.

Similar rights were recognised under FSA 1986, s. 31, but were rarely exercised. Schedule 4 goes somewhat beyond FSA 1986, s. 31; in particular it permits Treaty rights to be used to establish branches as well as for cross-border services.

## ENDING OF AUTHORISATION

The ending of a person's authorisation results in the provisions of the FSAMA 2000, and the FSA's rules, applicable to authorised persons ceasing to apply to that person, with certain exceptions. For example, some of the FSA's information-gathering and investigation powers under Part XI continue to apply even after a person's authorisation has ended and the compensation scheme (Part XV) and the ombudsman scheme (Part XVI) will continue to apply with respect to activities carried on while authorised. The method of ending authorisation depends on the route through which authorisation was obtained. If a person is authorised under more than one of the routes under s. 31 (for example, if it is an EEA firm authorised under sch. 3 and has a top-up permission under Part IV), then the person will cease to be an authorised person only when authorisation under each of those routes ends (ss. 34(3), 35(3) and 36(2)).

### Persons ceasing to have a Part IV permission

For a person authorised by having a permission under Part IV, authorisation ends when that person's Part IV permission is cancelled, whether at the initiative of the person (s. 44(2)) or of the FSA (s. 45(2)). If, on cancellation of the Part IV permission, the person no longer has permission to carry on any regulated activity, the FSA must give a direction withdrawing authorisation (s. 33(2)).

### EEA firms

The FSA may cancel an authorisation under sch. 3 on request from an EEA firm (s. 34(2)). But the FSA may not, on its own initiative, cancel an EEA firm's authorisation under sch. 3, so long as it retains its home State authorisation. An EEA firm will only cease to qualify for authorisation under sch. 3 if its home State authorisation under the relevant Directive is withdrawn (s. 34(1)(a)). This is because the Single Market Directives reserve withdrawal of authorisation to the home State regulator, which has a duty to notify the FSA of such a withdrawal. The authorisation of a passporting unauthorised subsidiary of an EEA credit institution ends when its right to passport under the Credit Institutions Directive ceases (s. 34(1)(b)).

## Treaty firms, UCITS qualifiers, ICVCs

As for an EEA firm, the FSA may cancel an authorisation on request from a Treaty firm or UCITS qualifier (ss. 35(2) and 36(1)). A Treaty firm will also cease to qualify for authorisation under sch. 4 if the relevant home State authorisation is withdrawn (s. 35(1)). Although the Act does not make specific provision, a UCITS qualifier will cease to be authorised if it ceases to be the operator, trustee or depositary of a recognised UCITS. Similarly, an ICVC will cease to be authorised when it ceases to be an ICVC (i.e., when its product authorisation is withdrawn).

## EXEMPTION ORDERS

FSAMA 2000, s. 38, gives the Treasury the power to make orders exempting specific persons or classes of person from the general prohibition in s. 19, and therefore from the need to be authorised. Section 38(2) provides that a person with a Part IV permission may not benefit from such an exemption, so cannot have the status of both an authorised person and an exempt person. The Treasury have published a draft order (HM Treasury, *Financial Services and Markets Bill: Regulated Activities — A Consultation Document*, February 1999). The Treasury propose to carry forward a number of exemptions under existing legislation, but not including those where a person is to be subject to regulation under the Act. So the Treasury have not carried forward exemptions currently enjoyed by the Society of Lloyd's and underwriting agents at Lloyd's, and exemptions under the Banking Act 1987 for deposit-taking currently enjoyed by persons authorised under FSA 1986. It appears that activities previously covered by those exemptions will instead have to be covered by the authorised person's permission.

## EXEMPTION OF APPOINTED REPRESENTATIVES

FSAMA 2000, s. 39, creates a particularly significant exemption from the general prohibition. This is for appointed representatives of authorised persons and is similar to FSA 1986, s. 44. The exemption applies only if:

(a)   the appointed representative is a party to a contract with an authorised person, referred to as the principal, which permits the appointed representative to carry on regulated activities; and

(b)   the principal has accepted responsibility in writing for the conduct of those regulated activities.

An appointed representative can be any person, including an individual or company. An appointed representative does not need authorisation, but may need to be approved by the FSA under Part V. The Treasury have the power to prescribe further conditions that the contract between principal and representative has to meet. The Treasury's stated intention is that this power will be used to reproduce the detailed requirements in FSA 1986, s. 44(4) and (5), which require the principal, by contract, to be able to exercise certain controls over activities of the appointed representative.

The Treasury have the power to limit, by regulation, the types of regulated activities that may be carried on under this exemption, and have stated that their intention is that this will broadly reproduce the scope of FSA 1986, s. 44. This means that the relevant permitted regulated activities are likely to be arranging deals and giving investment advice. One important difference is that, under s. 39(1) of the 2000 Act, it will not be possible for an authorised person to be an appointed representative. Under FSA 1986, s. 44, a person could be authorised under the Banking Act 1987 or the Building Societies Act 1986 and exempt as an appointed representative under FSA 1986. Arrangements of this type are fairly common. The appointed representatives under such arrangements will need to have permission under FSAMA 2000 for all the regulated activities previously carried on as appointed representatives and will be directly regulated by the FSA for such activities, rather than indirectly through their principals. It seems likely that arrangements for grandfathering existing authorisations into the new regime will mean that appropriate permission will automatically be granted.

In general, the FSA's rules will apply to the principal only, not to the appointed representative. But any business conducted by an appointed representative for which the principal has accepted responsibility will be treated as having been done by the principal (s. 39(3) and (4)). So the principal must have permission for any such business that is a regulated activity. Further, the authorised principal may be liable to FSA enforcement action or a claim for damages in respect of any action or omission of the appointed representative in carrying on the regulated activities which would amount to a contravention of FSA's rules if carried on by the principal. So the principal will have an interest in ensuring compliance by the appointed representative with those rules. In addition, certain of the FSA's powers, including information-gathering and investigation powers under Part XI, apply directly in relation to an appointed representative. There is, however, a limitation of the responsibility of the principal in respect of criminal offences, when the knowledge and intentions of the appointed representatives are not attributed to the principal in most circumstances (s. 39(6)).

An appointed representative, as an exempt person, is expected to be exempt from the financial promotion restriction when communicating financial promotions relating to the exempted activities (October 1999 draft of the Financial Services and Markets (Financial Promotion) (Exemptions) Order, art. 28). But the principal will be concerned to ensure that such communications comply with the FSA's financial promotion rules as described above.

# Chapter Six
## Permission to Carry on Regulated Activities

### Michael Blair

Having dealt with the requirement for *authorisation* (chapter 5), the Financial Services and Markets Act 2000 (FSAMA 2000) moves on, in Part IV, to deal with the closely related concept of permission.

### WHAT IS PERMISSION?

Under the FSA 1986, the concepts of authorisation and permission were separate and not overlapping: under that Act, there were authorised persons, and there was also a separate class of permitted persons, who were permitted to remain outside the scope of the requirement for authorisation, but were not in any sense regulated as such. That concept of permission is not carried forward in the new legislation. Instead, it is more helpful to think of the new permission regime as carrying forward the relevant approved business scopes of authorised persons, whether in the rules of any of the SROs, or in the specific relevant statute, such as the Banking Act 1987.

Under FSAMA 2000, therefore, the two concepts of authorisation and permission are designed to work together to achieve the single integrated regime. The key to understanding the two is in ss. 19 and 20. It is a breach of the general prohibition, and thus a criminal offence, for a person to carry on a regulated activity in the United Kingdom without being an authorised person. (The separate category of exempt person is not relevant to permission.) That results from s. 19, which is dealt with in chapter 3 above. Under s. 20, an authorised person who carries on a regulated activity in the United Kingdom without permission is taken to have contravened a requirement imposed by the FSA under the Act. This means that the permission is not in itself relevant for criminal prosecution purposes. And the only people who have permission are authorised persons. So it follows that the permission regime is, as it were, internal to the authorised regime: permissions can be thought of as internal subdivisions within the class of authorised persons, or internal membranes within the concept of authorisation. While acting outside a permission is deemed to be a contravention of a requirement imposed on the person by the FSA, that deemed contravention does not adversely affect related transactions, or give rise to an action for breach of statutory duty, though the Treasury have the power, under s. 20(3), to make a contravention of s. 20 actionable by persons who suffer loss as a result, rather like breach of the FSA's rules (s. 150).

An authorised person will in the ordinary way *have only one permission* under Part IV to carry on regulated activities under the Act. Colloquially, it may be convenient for a firm to be described as having a permission to carry on deposit taking, and another to carry on fund management business etc. But, technically, each firm will have its own permission, and will have one only. The only exception to this is what might be described as 'top-up' permission. If an incoming firm, which is entitled to carry on certain regulated activities pursuant to its 'passport', or under the Treaty or the UCITS Directive, wishes to be able to carry on other non-passportable regulated activities in the United Kingdom, it will need to apply to the FSA for that purpose: and it will then have its authorisation and permission under Part III, and its permission under Part IV to carry on the additional activities. That permission under Part IV will in turn lead to a separate basis for the person's authorisation under s. 31(1)(a), though the Act does not contemplate multiple authorisations as such.

To underline this conceptual approach, s. 40(2) prevents an authorised person from applying for permission if he already has extant permission under Part IV. Instead, an application to vary the permission is the way ahead. Further, an EEA firm, as defined in para. 5 of sch. 3 to the Act, may not apply for permission under Part IV to carry on any regulated activity which it is or would be entitled to carry on in exercise of an EEA right (as defined in para. 7 of sch. 3). This applies whether the EEA firm is seeking to operate through a branch in, or by providing cross-border services into, the United Kingdom. Interestingly, there is no equivalent prohibition for so-called Treaty firms, that is, those relying on the Treaty alone and not on any of the relevant single market directives.

For most firms, the means of becoming authorised for the purposes of the Act is, ignoring European and transitional aspects, the obtaining of a Part IV permission to carry on one or more regulated activities: see s. 31(1). The application to the FSA will therefore technically be an application for permission, and the granting of permission will lead to the status of authorised person. An application for permission, under s. 40, may be made by an individual, a body corporate, a partnership or an unincorporated association. The FSA may, under s. 42(2), give permission for the applicant to carry on the regulated activity or activities concerned. If the FSA gives permission, it must, under s. 42(5), specify the permitted regulated activity or activities, described in such manner as the FSA considers appropriate. Under s. 347, the FSA must maintain a publicly accessible record of every authorised person, and the record must include information about the services which each authorised person holds himself out as able to provide: so, though the language of permission is not used in Part XXIII, it can be expected that the record will track the permission granted to UK authorised persons.

The procedure on an application for permission is set out in ss. 51 to 53. An application must be determined before the end of six months from receipt of the completed application. If an application is incomplete, the deadline is 12 months, though incomplete applications can nevertheless be determined without requiring them to be perfected. If an application is to be refused, a warning notice (as to which see chapter 28) has to be served. This gives an unsuccessful applicant the FSA's reasons and an opportunity to make representations to the FSA though not, in this case, access to evidence relied on by the FSA in reaching its decision. The disappointed applicant will also have the opportunity to have the matter referred to the Financial Services and Markets Tribunal if a subsequent decision notice is served, refusing the application.

## CONDITIONS, LIMITATIONS AND REQUIREMENTS

It is convenient now to deal with three other concepts relevant to the permission regime. The first is the so-called 'threshold conditions' dealt with in s. 41 and sch. 6. The second is the limitations which may be included in a permission under s. 42(5). And the third is the selection of requirements that may be included in a permission under s. 43.

*The threshold conditions* are dealt with in s. 41. When giving or varying permission, or any requirement under s. 43, the FSA is obliged by s. 41(2) to ensure that the person concerned will satisfy and continue to satisfy the threshold conditions in sch. 6. The test is to be applied in relation to all the regulated activities for which that person has or will have permission. The particular conditions will be described later in this chapter.

The inclusion of *limitations* is specifically enabled by s. 42(7)(a), which enables the FSA to incorporate in the description of regulated activity for which permission is given such limitations as it considers appropriate. An example given in the paragraph itself is a limitation as to the circumstances in which the activity may, or may not, be carried on. Parliament may here be contemplating that a permission may be given on terms that the business may not be done with private customers, or that a broker may deal within the EEA only on recognised exchanges, or must not undertake transactions in contingent liability investments. The limitation may be incorporated at the outset or when a variation is applied for (s. 44(5)). The limitations envisaged will be of permanent effect unless the permission is varied (see below). Under s. 52(6) a proposal to incorporate a limitation attracts the warning and decision notice procedure, but, as with an application for permission, on the basis that the FSA does not have to offer access to used and unused material (this is because s. 52(6) does not appear in the lists in s. 394(a) or (b)).

The FSA is also enabled, by s. 43, to include in a Part IV permission such *requirements* as the FSA considers appropriate. These requirements may be positive or negative, that is, requiring the person concerned to take specified action, or not to take action, and the requirement may extend to activities which are not regulated activities. They can also cope with the issues confronting the firm as a member of a group, where appropriate. Examples might be to obtain additional capital within a particular time following the granting of the permission, (or to secure an undertaking from a parent company to supply capital when required) or to refrain from taking on a particular director or significant member of staff. Another example of a negative requirement might be that client money should not be held. It appears from s. 43(5) that the requirements may be permanent or of limited duration, though, by s. 43(6), the FSA may vary the permission under s. 44 or s. 45 after the expiry of the period. Accordingly, a prime purpose of the requirements is to act as a temporary expedient to assist an applicant in the early months or years following authorisation, though, as with a limitation, a requirement may be varied, indeed imposed afresh, where a variation of permission is applied for (s. 44(1)(e) and (5)). For a particular form of requirement, 'an assets requirement', see s. 48 and the discussion on it below. Section 52(6) provides for the warning notice and decision notice procedure described above to be used in the case of a proposed requirement.

## THRESHOLD CONDITIONS

The FSA is obliged to ensure that applicants for permission satisfy the threshold conditions on a continuing basis. The test is to be applied in relation to all the regulated activities concerned. Loosely described as the 'fit and proper' requirements, both in the period before the reform was commenced, and during the time FSAMA 2000 was in preparation, sch. 6 in fact contains rather more substance, though the fit and proper concept, known as 'suitability', is the most significant of the conditions.

In sch. 6, there are five conditions, concerning permission under Part IV (s. 40), and there are three more relating to incoming passport holders and foreign insurers which are not dealt with further in this work. The five general threshold conditions are as follows:

(a)   legal status;
(b)   location of offices;
(c)   close links;
(d)   adequate resources; and
(e)   suitability.

### Legal status

The first threshold condition (sch. 6, para. 1) deals with required legal status for insurance business and for deposit taking. To carry on insurance business an authorised person must be a body corporate, registered friendly society or member of Lloyd's. Deposit takers must be bodies corporate or partnerships.

## Location of offices

Paragraph 2 of sch. 6 deals with a problem which has caused difficulty in the context of the Single Market Directives in that, until now, there were no domestic statutory provisions requiring a body incorporated in the EEA to have its head office and registered office in the same country. Bodies corporate constituted under the law of any part of the United Kingdom now must have their head offices and registered offices in the same country. A body incorporated in one part of the United Kingdom can, however, have its head office in any other part.

## Close links

Paragraph 3 of sch. 6 makes a threshold condition for the grant of permission which deals with problems, most recently prominent in the BCCI case, which arise when persons seeking authorisation here have close links with another person of such a kind as to prevent the FSA from supervising the applicant effectively. The lead test in the paragraph is that, if there are close links (see below) with another person, then two tests must be satisfied:

(a)   those links are not likely to prevent effective supervision by the FSA; and
(b)   if the person to whom the applicant is linked is himself regulated outside the EEA, then that foreign regulation does not prevent effective supervision of the applicant.

Close links are defined at para. 3(2) in classic company law terms, involving the concept of parent undertakings, subsidiary undertakings and 20 per cent control.

## Adequate resources

The fourth threshold condition concerns the adequacy of the resources of the applicant in relation to the regulated activity to be carried on. The resources may be taken to include:

(a)   the provision which the applicant makes in respect of liabilities (including contingent and future liabilities); and
(b)   the means by which the applicant manages the incidence of risk in connection with his business.

Resources thus is to be construed in a broad way as substantially more than capital and guarantees etc. The reference to risk management in particular indicates that the real test is not the simplistic one of amount of capital, but rather a subjective assessment of the probability of the firm concerned surviving any particular level of disturbance or shock.

**Suitability**

The fifth general threshold condition is the so-called 'fit and proper' test. The applicant has the burden of satisfying the FSA that he is a fit and proper person having regard to all the circumstances. The paragraph specifically includes as relevant to the circumstances the connection which the applicant has with any person, the nature of the regulated activity concerned and the need to ensure that affairs are conducted soundly and prudently.

The reference in para. 5 to connection overlaps to some extent with the close links issue discussed above, though here the existence of individuals is much more prominent than in the case of para. 3 (close links). A 'connection' is undefined, though s. 49(1) makes it plain that the FSA may regard as connected for this purpose any person in or likely to be in a 'relationship' with the applicant. So this will include connected persons in the company law sense as well as others who might be thought to be bad apples capable of infecting a barrel. The reference in para. 5 of sch. 6 to sound and prudent conduct of affairs is an echo of the provisions in the Banking Act 1987 and the Building Societies Act 1986 concerning sound and prudent management, and it can be expected that a large part of the practice under those sections will be carried forward by the FSA in its policy development and casework under this threshold condition.

**Protection of consumers**

The topic of threshold conditions would not be complete without referring to FSAMA 2000, s. 41(3). The FSA's obligation to ensure that the threshold conditions will be satisfied does not prevent it from taking such steps as it considers are necessary, in relation to a particular authorised person, in order to secure its regulatory objective of the protection of consumers. Parliament here seems to be saying that, as long as the FSA pays due regard to the threshold conditions, it does not need to be enslaved by them if it needs to take action, for instance, by an own-initiative variation of permission, in order to protect consumers. The most obvious way in which this might be relevant could be where the FSA concluded that the firm's resources were not adequate, under para. 4 of sch. 6, but then decided not to cancel the permission straight away, because of the need to allow some time for positions to be unwound or transactions to be completed.

## VARIATION AND CANCELLATION OF PERMISSION

Sections 44 to 46 of FSAMA 2000 deal with two quite separate cases of variation or cancellation of permission. Section 44 deals with the natural tendency of firms to expand their range of activities, or to contract them. The initiative, under s. 44, rests with the authorised person concerned. It proposes, and the FSA disposes. If the FSA proposed to refuse an application to reshape the permission, it would have to apply the tests of adverse effect on the interests of consumers, or desirability in the interests of consumers.

The second class of variation is quite different, and in substance is the equivalent of the powers of intervention in some if not all of the statutes which the Act replaces. Here the initiative is with the FSA and its power to take regulatory action can be triggered by one or more of three preconditions set out in s. 45(1). These are, broadly speaking, breach or anticipated breach of the threshold conditions; not carrying on a regulated activity for a year or more; and protection of the interests of consumers or potential consumers. The FSA's powers on an own-initiative basis are to vary the permission or cancel it. There is in s. 46 an additional, free-standing, power to 'intervene' where the trigger event is more restricted, but where the test for 'intervention' is much lower. If the FSA considers that a person has acquired control over a UK authorised person with a Part IV permission and it appears to the FSA that the likely effect of the acquisition of control on the authorised person or on any of its activities is *uncertain*, then the FSA has a new and immediate power to impose or vary a requirement under s. 43 as if the authorised person were applying afresh for permission.

Because an own-initiative variation (other than that under s. 46) is akin to disciplinary or enforcement action, there is procedure for review of the FSA's decision. If the FSA proposes to cancel the permission, the full warning notice and decision notice procedure is available (s. 54). In this case, the FSA must also, under s. 394, allow the firm to have access to FSA material relevant to the decision. If, however, the proposal is to vary the permission, but not cancel it altogether, there is one procedure for urgent cases (where the variation can take effect immediately or on a stated date) and another for less urgent cases.

Either way s. 53 requires written notice (known as a 'supervisory notice' — see s. 395(2)) with details of the variation, reasons and an offer to consider representations made about the proposal. If, having considered those representations, the FSA decides to go ahead (or not to rescind an immediate variation), then there must be written notice of the decision which informs the person of his right to refer the matter to the Tribunal. The procedure in s. 53 is similar to but not the same as the more usual warning notice and decision notice procedure.

The exercise of own initiative power with immediate (or on a stated date) effect and without allowing the time for prior representations and tribunal proceedings is available only if the FSA reasonably considers that it is necessary to do so having regard to the ground on which it is acting (s. 53(3)). However, the FSA has to give written notice, including the reasons for its decision on timing, and the authorised person has a chance to make representations to the FSA either after the variation takes effect or, if the timing permits, beforehand. Either way the authorised person has the right to refer the matter to the Tribunal, which will be able to test the reasonableness of the FSA decision to proceed with immediate or near-immediate effect.

The scheme of the Act also contemplates that the person concerned can refer the matter to the Tribunal straightaway, on receipt of the first supervisory notice, whenever there is actual, as opposed to proposed, exercise of the own-initiative power (s. 55(2) and s. 53(5)(c) and (e); see also s. 133(1)(a)).

## ASSETS REQUIREMENTS

Under s. 48 of FSAMA 2000, the FSA has a special power, either at the outset, when giving a permission to an authorised person, or thereafter, when varying it, to impose an 'assets requirement' on the person. Assets requirements are defined in s. 48(3) as a special sort of requirement which either prohibits the person from dealing or places restrictions on his dealing with his assets, or which requires some or all of those assets, or customer assets held by that person, to be transferred to and held by a trustee approved by the FSA. These powers reproduce the substance of the statutory powers of intervention which were available to the FSA under the FSA 1986, ss. 65, 66 and 67. But the restatement has procured some improvements which no doubt reflect the experience of using the 1986 powers and their equivalents in the rule books of the SROs. The improvements are as follows:

(a)   Under FSAMA 2000, s. 48(5), the consequence of a requirement addressed to the person concerned has legal effect in relation to that person's bank and other places where the person keeps an account. The bank or other institution is relieved of any relevant contractual obligations to that person, and is made liable to the FSA if it acts in breach of the requirements after it has had notice of them.

(b)   While the requirement to transfer assets to a trustee does not have immediate legal effect, but depends upon compliance with the requirement by the authorised person, nonetheless s. 48(7) renders void any charge created by that person over any assets of his which are held in accordance with the requirement. Accordingly, while the trusteeship direction depends upon the person concerned executing the transfer, the Act prevents subversion of the transfer by charges over any beneficial interest.

Compliance with the regime for assets requirements is enforceable under Part XIV (disciplinary measures), etc., though s. 48(9) creates a special criminal offence to support the provision securing that assets held by the trustee may be released or dealt with only with the FSA's consent. The trustee may well not be an authorised person, and thus not open to the disciplinary measures in Part XIV.

## OVERSEAS REGULATORS

There remains one section in Part IV of FSAMA 2000 to deal with. This is s. 47, which specifies the power of the FSA to vary or cancel permission on its own initiative, but at the request of an overseas regulator of a kind prescribed by the Treasury. The background to this section, plainly enough, is the obligation in the Single Market Directives on home State regulators to take measures relating to the home State authorisation if properly requested to do so by the host State regulator. Accordingly, if a United Kingdom firm has a branch in Portugal, and the Portuguese regulator (assuming that it is prescribed by the Treasury under s. 47) requests the taking of measures in relation to the UK firm because of improprieties of a prudential character in the Portuguese branch, then s. 47 provides the machinery, powers and conditions upon which that intra-European cooperation is to take place. The own-initiative power becomes exercisable at the request, or in order to assist, the Portuguese regulator even if Part XIII (incoming firms: intervention by FSA) is not available. So the s. 47 powers are available for Portuguese purposes even in respect of a United Kingdom firm. The section divides into two parts, depending on whether there is a need to comply with a Community obligation.

If there is such a need, that criterion for action appears to be sufficient on its own, and to replace the other tests in s. 45(1) (breach of threshold conditions etc.). The FSA has to act at its own expense in that case (s. 47(6)).

If not, s. 47(4) empowers the FSA to take into account factors such as reciprocity, the nature of the foreign law or requirement that may have been broken, extraterritorial jurisdiction, seriousness of the case and the public interest. The list is virtually the same as that in s. 195(6). Here, too, the criteria for action in s. 45(1) appear to be displaced: this emerges not from s. 47 itself or from s. 45(5) but from the fact that the s. 195 criteria appear to justify intervention even if the criteria in s. 194(1) are not available (see s. 195(2)).

In this case, where there is no Community obligation, the FSA may expect the requesting regulator (if a request has been made) to contribute to the costs involved.

# Chapter Seven
## Performance of Regulated Activities

*Michael Blair*

Part V of the Financial Services and Markets Act 2000 (FSAMA 2000), in contrast with almost all of the rest of the Act, focuses its attention on individuals, whether within the financial services industry or in its fringes. It contains two quite separate forms of control in relation to individuals, one 'negative' and the other 'positive'. The negative one, effectively prohibiting a person from staying in or entering the financial services industry, is in ss. 56 to 58. The positive one, under which certain people carrying on specific activities in financial services firms have to be positively vetted and approved, is in ss. 59 to 71. The negative power bears directly upon the individual, though there are consequential obligations on firms (see s. 56(6)): the positive one, however, is fashioned so as to impinge on individuals through firms and relates to the individual when acting for the firm in a particular specified capacity. Technically, the positive power can impinge on corporate persons (and on externally employed contractors) as well, but the main focus is on individuals in or working for firms.

### PROHIBITION ORDERS

Sections 56 to 58 of FSAMA 2000 deal with the negative form of control. If it appears to the FSA that an individual is not fit and proper, it can prohibit him or her from the industry, either totally or in part. This power is derived from that contained in FSA 1986, s. 59, which was used on a number of occasions in the period 1988–2000. As with that power, a prohibition order under FSAMA 2000, s. 56, leads to criminal sanctions for breach (s. 56(4)) and authorised persons must take reasonable care to avoid any function of theirs being performed by someone who is prohibited in relation to the function in question (s. 56(6)). If an authorised person is in breach of s. 56(6), a private person who suffers loss as a result of that contravention has a right of action against the authorised person under s. 71. That section is built on similar lines to its equivalent in relation to contravention of an FSA rule in s. 150(1) and the Treasury have powers to define who are private persons (and to make the right of action available to other persons) for both purposes. Sections 57 and 58 provide the necessary machinery for adjudication and subsequent variation in this context.

## POSITIVE POWER OF APPROVAL

Section 59 of FSAMA 2000 establishes a new fundamental principle that when an authorised person enters into an arrangement in relation to carrying on a regulated activity, any person performing a 'controlled function' under the arrangement needs to be approved by the FSA to perform that function. This requirement depends, crucially, on the definition of controlled function, and s. 59 goes on to set the framework for establishing which functions in firms are to be controlled functions. Section 59(2) deals with the problems that can arise in the commercial world when a person working for a firm is not necessarily doing so under an arrangement entered into between him or her and the firm, but under an arrangement entered into by a person who has contracted with the firm to provide services. Consultants, matrix management and, indeed, appointed representatives (as to which see s. 39) are all within the scope of this extended form of control over individuals.

A controlled function is a function of a description specified by the FSA in rules (s. 59(3)). And, in order for the rules to be validly made, the FSA has to fit the descriptions of functions into one or more of three conditions. These are broadly as follows:

(a)  the 'management' condition (s. 59(5)), which is that the function is likely to enable the person responsible to exercise a *significant influence* on the *conduct* of the firm's *affairs*;

(b)  the 'customer-relations' condition (s. 59(6)), which is that the function will involve the person *dealing with customers* of the authorised person and

(c)  the 'customers' property' condition (s. 59(7)), which is that the function will involve the person *dealing with property* of customers.

All three conditions have to relate to the regulated activity, and in the second and third conditions there has to be a substantial connection with that activity. Until the relevant rules are made, it is not possible to be more precise about the reach of s. 59, but the FSA is currently consulting on a set of controlled functions which follow the managerial, customer relations and customer property structure laid down by s. 59. As an example board members of the company, the money laundering reporting officer, the internal auditor and advisers and salespersons are likely to be included.

Sections 60 to 62 deal with the machinery whereby approval can be obtained for the performance by an individual of a particular controlled function in a firm. The application is made by the firm (and s. 60(6) deals with the case where the applicant firm is not yet authorised at the time when it needs to make its application). The test for granting the application, in s. 61(1), is that the FSA is satisfied that the so-called 'candidate' is a fit and proper person to perform the function to which the application relates. Ancillary tests such as qualification, training and competence are mentioned in s. 61(2). The FSA has, by s. 61(3), three months in which to determine whether to grant the application or to start the statutory machinery enabling review of a proposed refusal. The three-month period is interrupted during any time when the firm is responding to a request by the FSA to provide further information. It is expected that in practice applications under Part V will be dealt with in substantially less time than the three months permitted.

Section 62 provides the machinery for a warning notice on a proposal to refuse, and a decision notice on a refusal of an application: rights to have the matter referred to the Financial Services and Markets Tribunal then ensue for firm and individual alike. Equally, if the FSA is minded to withdraw an individual approval given under Part V, on the grounds that the person is not fit and proper, then there has to be the warning notice and decision notice procedure followed by a right to refer the matter to the Tribunal (s. 63).

## STATEMENTS OF PRINCIPLE ON THE CONDUCT OF APPROVED PERSONS

Sections 64 and 65 provide for statements of principle to be issued by the FSA, coupled with a code of practice, relating to the conduct expected of approved persons. Parliament has concluded that the machinery for approval and withdrawal of approval on fit and proper grounds for individuals is unlikely to be sufficient on its own to provide a satisfactory regime for the standards of conduct expected of approved persons. Accordingly, the FSA is empowered (though not required) to issue statements of principle for that purpose. If any statement of principle is issued, the FSA is obliged to follow it up with a code of practice. The purpose of the code is to help to determine whether or not a person's conduct complies with the statement of principle.

These statements of principle are different in character from the so-called FSA principles for businesses. The latter are rules, made under Part X; they are addressed to firms and breach of them leads to all the consequences set out in the Act for breach of a rule. Statements of principle made under s. 64, however, are addressed to approved persons and a special code of discipline is set up at ss. 66 to 69 (see further below) to enforce them against the individual personally.

As just mentioned, statements of principle do not stand on their own, but have to be coupled with a code of practice which has evidential value in helping to determine whether or not the person is in breach of the principle. The machinery relating to this code of practice is markedly similar to that provided in s. 122 for the code of market conduct, though there are some differences. Essentially, in the context of individual approval, the code may be relied on in so far as it tends to establish:

(a)   that the conduct complies with a statement of principle, or

(b)   that the conduct is in contravention of a statement of principle.

In the market abuse context, however, the effect of s. 122(1) and (2) is that (a) and (b) above apply, but subject to the proviso that behaviour described in the market abuse code as not amounting to market abuse is *conclusively* taken not to be market abuse.

The procedural requirements in s. 65 for making statements and codes are not unlike those relating to rules, as to which see chapter 12.

## DISCIPLINARY POWERS

Sections 66 to 69 provide a special disciplinary system in relation to the enforcement of the statements of principle and the code. The central concept, in s. 66(1) and (2), is 'guilty of misconduct'. That misconduct is either:

(a)   failure to comply with a statement of principle, or

(b)   being knowingly concerned in a contravention by the firm of a requirement imposed on the firm.

This definition of misconduct therefore requires approved persons to comply with the statements of principle, and also to avoid any knowing participation in a breach by the firm of any requirement imposed upon it. Individuals who do not require approval cannot be disciplined for 'knowing concern' in a firm's contravention of a rule etc., except in a case where the FSA takes proceedings for injunctions or restitution under Part XXV (see chapter 27). This underlines the importance of the borderline to be drawn between those functions which require Part V approval and those which do not.

The sanctions available against approved persons are, by s. 66(3), an unlimited penalty of a financial character, or a statement of misconduct. These are similar to, though dealt with in a different order from, the financial penalties and public censure sanctions available against firms under Part XIV. Section 66 contains, however, a provision not to be found in Part XIV, namely that, once the FSA has become aware of misconduct, it has two years in which to begin proceedings against the individual, after which the disciplinary powers cease to be exercisable, though, presumably, the court-based powers in Part XXV remain at least technically available. Section 67 deals with the rights to a warning notice, decision notice and reference to the Financial Services and Markets Tribunal.

Part V (like s. 123 for market abuse penalties) does not actually specify that the penalties are payable to the FSA, though ss. 91(5) and 206(3) so provide for other penalties payable by issuers of securities and by firms: but the implication of part III of sch. 1 to the Act is that penalties under s. 66 (and s. 126) are indeed payable to the FSA.

## STATEMENT OF POLICY

Part V of FSAMA 2000 deals with one other adjectival matter concerning approved persons and discipline of them. Under s. 69(1) the FSA is obliged to prepare and issue a statement of its policy about penalties payable by approved persons, dealing with the imposition and with their amount. This section is one of a number in the Act which require the FSA to produce statements of policy relating to disciplinary matters: others are at s. 93 (listing), s. 124 (market abuse) and s. 210 (general discipline). Certain elements of that required policy are laid down by s. 69(2), including the seriousness of the misconduct, the question of deliberate or reckless misconduct and (thus emphasising that approved persons do not have to be individuals) whether the approved person is an individual. The meat of the section is in subsection (8), which requires the FSA to have regard to the statement of policy in force at the time of the misconduct (not of the decision-making) in taking decisions about penalties.

# Chapter Eight
# Official Listing

## *George Walker*

The maintenance of an effective capital market is essential to the efficient and orderly operation of any developed economy. The capital markets provide a mechanism through which a range of equity and debt instruments or securities can be made available to the public.

The capital markets allow investors to receive an income in the form of a dividend or interest payment and to make a gain in the event that the value or price of the security rises. This, in turn, allows companies to raise funds through first or primary issues of securities to the public. The existence of a formal or informal market also allows securities to be bought and sold in secondary trading. The existence of liquid markets then facilitates further investment and dealing in relevant corporate stock.

Before securities of any form can be issued to the general public they generally have to comply with certain requirements in terms of content and presentation. In the United Kingdom, the principal method of achieving this is by the admission of the securities to an official list which is maintained by the competent authority for listing.

The relevant requirements concerning the operation of the official list and the powers and functions of the competent authority in the United Kingdom are now set out in Part VI of Financial Services and Markets Act 2000 (FSAMA 2000). This replicates the earlier provisions contained in the Financial Services Act 1986 (FSA 1986), together with new powers to impose penalties for breaches of the listing rules.

It was originally intended that the London Stock Exchange would continue as the competent authority for listing within the United Kingdom. The Chancellor then announced on 4 October 1999 that responsibility for listing would be transferred to the FSA. This followed the Stock Exchange's decision to de-mutualise and convert itself into a public company. It was thought that it would no longer be appropriate for the Exchange to continue as the listing authority and the Treasury were asked to transfer authority and competence in this regard to the FSA. This was effected in May 2000 by the Official Listing of Securities (Change of Competent Authority) Regulations 2000 (SI 2000/968). When carrying out its duties as competent authority, the FSA is referred to as the United Kingdom Listing Authority (UKLA).

As the competent authority for listing, the FSA has become responsible for the maintenance of the official list and the admission of qualifying securities to listing. The listing authority also approves documentation issued by listed companies, provides guidance on the application of listing rules and investigates breaches of the rules.

Although the FSA is now responsible for the admission of securities to listing, the Stock Exchange and the other exchanges in the United Kingdom continue to determine admission to trading. Listing is then concerned with the admission of securities to the approved list, which means that they have satisfied the requirements set with regard to structure, content and presentation. Admission to trading is only concerned with allowing securities to be admitted to dealing on a particular exchange. This may or may not involve approved or listed securities. Both of these functions were formerly undertaken by the Stock Exchange before demutualisation. Following their separation, certain consequential amendments have had to be made to the terms of the Act and Listing Rules.

The conditions with regard to listing (the Listing Rules) were formerly published by the London Stock Exchange but are now published by the FSA. The Listing Rules give effect to the requirements set out in the European 1979 Admission to Listing Directive (79/279/EEC), 1980 Listings Particulars Directive (80/390/EEC) and 1982 Interim Reports Directive (82/121/EEC) as well as the later 1989 Prospectus (Public Offers) Directive (89/298/EEC). The statutory provisions governing admission to listing were formerly set out in the Companies Act 1985 and the FSA 1986. The European Directives were given effect, in particular, through the Public Offers of Securities Regulations 1995 (SI 1995/1537) and the Traded Securities (Disclosure) Regulations 1994 (SI 1994/188).

The purpose of this chapter is to explain the background to the listing regime in the United Kingdom and the main types of pubic offering. The provisions with regard to listing set out in Part VI of FSAMA 2000 are considered in further detail. The general content of the current listing rules is then discussed.

## LISTING

The provisions contained in Part VI of FSAMA 2000 replace the earlier rules set out in FSA 1986. The 1986 Act had been enacted to create a formal statutory framework for the regulation of all investment business within the United Kingdom based on an underlying system of self-regulation through a number of sector-specific agencies and separate professional bodies (see chapter 1).

Part IV of FSA 1986 introduced basic provisions concerning the admission to listing of defined securities. This included a prohibition on the admission of any security to the Official List of the Stock Exchange unless it complied with the listing rules of the competent authority (defined in s. 142). The Council of the Stock Exchange (as it was then known) was designated as the competent authority. Persons responsible for the preparation of prospectuses had to ensure that they contained all such information as investors and their professional advisers would reasonably require irrespective of whether the information was expressly required by the Listing Rules (s. 146).

FSA 1986 also contained provisions in Part V relating to offers of securities that were not to be listed. It was intended that Parts IV and V would replace the earlier prospectus provisions contained in Part III of the Companies Act 1985. While Part IV was implemented in 1987, replacing the 1985 Act provisions relating to listed securities, Part V was never brought into force. New provision had to be made following the adoption of Directive 89/298/EEC by the European Community in 1989. This sets out the requirements for prospectuses for the initial public offerings of securities not already listed on a stock exchange of any member State and gives member States the option to ensure that any offer of transferable securities to the public within their territories is subject to the publication by the issuer of pre-vetted or approved prospectuses. The Directive was implemented on 19 June 1995 by the Public Offers of Securities Regulations 1995 (SI 1995/1537) and sch. 3 to the Companies Act 1985 and Part V of FSA 1986 were repealed.

Official listing of securities is subject to three European Directives. The Admission to Listing Directive (79/279/EEC) was adopted in 1979 and established minimum conditions for all securities to satisfy before admission to official listing on any stock exchange within member States. This included the legal status of the company and its shares, minimum size of the company and negotiability of shares. Each member State had to designate a national authority or authorities to determine decisions relating to the admission of securities to official listing.

The Listings Particulars Directive (80/390/EEC) was adopted in 1980. This coordinated the requirements for the compilation, scrutiny and distribution of listing particulars. The admission of securities to official listing was also made conditional on publication of an information sheet (referred to as the listing particulars), the contents of which had to enable investors and their investment advisers to make an informed assessment of the assets and liabilities, financial position, profits and losses and prospects of the issuer and of the rights attaching to such securities.

The Interim Reports Directive (82/121/EEC) was adopted in 1982 requiring companies admitted to listing to publish specified information on a regular basis including half-yearly profit and loss statements.

## PUBLIC OFFERINGS

A public offering may be made in one of a number of ways. In the United Kingdom, the main methods of marketing shares comprise offers for sale or subscription, placements and rights issues. These are, however, only the main categories of initial offering with a number of other types being available (see, for example, ch. 4 of the FSA's Listing Rules).

## Offerings

An offer for subscription takes place when a company invites people to purchase its shares, the persons offering to buy being known as subscribers. An offer for sale is where the offer is made by an existing shareholder and not by the company itself with the acquirers being known as purchasers rather than subscribers.

Both offers for subscription and sale are generally conducted through issuing houses. The sale price may either be fixed by the seller (a fixed-price offer) or through tender (a tender offer). An underwriter may also be used to take up any shares not purchased by the public. This is important as a company cannot allot any shares if all those being offered have not been taken up unless this is specifically provided for in the terms of the offer or certain specified conditions have been satisfied (Companies Act 1985, s. 84).

Advertising an offer of shares will only constitute an invitation to treat under English law. The offer to purchase is made by the investor completing the application form. Successful applicants will receive a letter of acceptance although they will not become shareholders until formal registration on the company's register. Acceptance letters are normally renounceable, which allows the applicant to sell the right to acquire the share in the same way as the share itself.

## Placings

While public offerings generally involve considerable delay and cost, shares may alternatively be placed by a sponsoring broker selling the shares directly to a much smaller group of persons who will often be professional investors.

## Rights issues

A rights issue takes place where a company offers shares to existing shareholders in proportion to their shareholding. Shareholders in listed companies are allotted shares and informed through a renounceable letter of allotment. A company is generally obliged to make a rights issue where it wishes to issue new equity shares for cash unless the shareholders have agreed otherwise. To the extent that a rights issue is also relatively expensive, many companies may still prefer to raise finance through a placement. Shares may be issued to existing shareholders through a capitalisation or bonus issue, for which the company will not receive any new money.

Shares which are already listed may also be marketed through either an intermediaries offer, an introduction or such other method as may be approved in addition to the offer for sale, subscription or placing referred to above.

## OFFICIAL LIST

The provisions with regard to official listing are now set out in Part VI of FSAMA 2000. These set out the powers and functions of the competent authority and requirements with regard to the maintenance of the official list, applications for listing and the discontinuance and suspension of listings. The Act also contains separate provisions concerning the content and registration of listing particulars and prospectuses. The Listing Rules may require that listing particulars must be issued before securities can be admitted to the official list (s. 79(1)). A general duty of disclosure is imposed on those preparing the listing particulars (s. 80(1)). The Act also contains provision with regard to the issuance of supplementary listing particulars where there has been a significant change since preparation of the particulars but before dealings have started (s. 81(1)). Particulars must be registered with the registrar of companies on or before the date on which they are published (s. 83(1)).

The Act requires Listing Rules to secure that a prospectus must be published before any securities which are to be listed are offered to the public in the United Kingdom for the first time (s. 84(1)). No person may offer new securities for which an application for listing has been made without publishing a prospectus (s. 85(1)). The requirements as to listing are to apply equally to prospectuses (s. 86(1)). Non-listing prospectuses may also be approved by the competent authority where securities are to be offered to the public although no application is to be made for listing (s. 87(1)). This allows the prospectus to be used in other EU States where the relevant authorities are obliged to give it full effect on a mutual recognition basis.

Persons responsible for the preparation of listing particulars, prospectuses and non-listing prospectuses are liable to pay compensation to those who suffer loss as a result of any untrue or misleading statement or the omission of any information which is required to be contained in these documents (s. 90(1)). The competent authority is also given a new power to impose financial penalties on issuers who have breached their listing rules (s. 91(1)).

### Competent Authority

Section 72(1) of the Act provides that the functions conferred on the competent authority under Part VI are to be exercised by the FSA.

A set of general functions with regard to listing is specified in s. 73(2) in similar terms to those in s. 2(4) for the FSA's other functions. However, only six of the seven prudential principles in s. 2(3) are applied by s. 73(1), the missing requirement being s. 2(3)(b) (responsibility of managers). Certain amendments to other provisions of FSAMA 2000 are set out in sch. 7 to apply where the FSA acts as competent authority.

The Treasury are given power by s. 72(3) to transfer these functions by order to another person in accordance with the provisions set out in sch. 8. Such a transfer of functions may be effected if the FSA agrees in writing that the order should be made, or the performance of the transferred functions would be significantly improved by the transfer, or it would otherwise be considered to be in the public interest that a transfer should be effected (sch. 8, para. 1(2)). Two other specific possible public interest grounds were set out in the Bill, although they were deleted before the Bill was enacted. They related to improving competition having regard to the control of the official list and the rules and practices of the competent authority being liable to restrict, distort or prevent competition to a significant extent.

A transfer order does not affect anything previously done by any person acting as competent authority for listing. The order may also include various ancillary matters set out in sch. 8, para. 2(2).

## Official list

The FSA, as competent authority, is obliged to maintain the official list (s. 74(1)). The competent authority may admit to the official list only such securities or other instruments ('things') as it considers appropriate (s. 74(2)). For the purposes of Part VI of the Act, a security means anything which has been, or may be, admitted to the official list and listing means being included in the official list in accordance with Part VI (s. 74(5)). A security must comply with all relevant conditions set out in Part VI of the Act or rules issued under it and not otherwise fall within a description or category set out in a disqualification order issued by the Treasury (s. 74(3)).

## Listing

Admission to the official list may be granted only on an application made in such manner as may be specified in the Listing Rules and the FSA must be satisfied that the requirements of the listing rules and any other requirements imposed have been satisfied (s. 75(1) and (4)). An application may be refused if the FSA considers that granting it would be detrimental to the interests of investors, but only having regard to factors relating to the issuer (s. 75(5)). Applications can be made only by or with the consent of the issuer of the securities (s. 75(2)). If the securities are already officially listed in another EEA State, an application may be refused if the issuer fails to comply with any relevant obligations relating to that listing (s. 75(6)).

The FSA's decision must be notified to the applicant within six months of the original date of receipt of the application or the date on which any further information requested has been provided (s. 76(1)). If due notice is not given, the application will be deemed to have been refused (s. 76(2)). Once admitted, however, the admission may not be challenged on the ground that any relevant requirement or condition had not been satisfied (s. 76(7)).

The listing of any securities may be discontinued where there are special circumstances which preclude normal regular dealings as provided for in the

Listing Rules (s. 77(1)). Listing may also be suspended in accordance with the Listing Rules (s. 77(2)). This power applies irrespective of when the securities were admitted to the official list (s. 77(4)).

Where securities are delisted, s. 77(5) now allows the issuer to refer the matter to the Financial Services and Markets Tribunal. A detailed procedure concerning the suspension or discontinuance of listing is set out in s. 78. This generally provides for notice which must contain specified material including details and date of effectiveness, reasons for suspension or discontinuance, the right to make representations and relevant period as well as the right to refer the matter to the Tribunal. This is, however, without prejudice to the right of the FSA to delist with immediate effect. The notices under s. 78 are supervisory notices within the definition in s. 395(13).

## LISTING PARTICULARS

The Listing Rules may provide that securities (other than new securities) may not be admitted to the official list unless appropriate listing particulars have been submitted to and approved by the FSA and published or such other document as may be required has been published (s. 79(1)). Listing particulars means a document in such form and containing such information as may be specified in the Listing Rules (s. 79(2)). The persons responsible for listing particulars are to be determined in accordance with regulations issued by the Treasury (s. 79(3)).

Section 80(1) imposes a general duty of disclosure in relation to listing particulars. Listing particulars are to contain all such information as investors and their professional advisers would reasonably require or expect to find there for the purpose of making informed assessments of the assets and liabilities, financial position, profits and losses and prospects of the issuer and of the rights attaching to the securities. This is without prejudice to any specific information required by the Listing Rules or by the FSA (s. 80(2)). This only relates, however, to information within the knowledge of the person responsible for the listing particulars or which it would be reasonable for him to obtain by making enquiries (s. 80(3)).

Supplementary listing particulars must be issued where there has been any significant change to the matters set out in the original particulars (s. 81(1)). This applies to any matters required to be set out in the listing particulars or to any significant new matters which subsequently arise which would otherwise have had to be included (s. 81(1)(a) and (b)). The supplementary listing particulars are to be issued in accordance with the provisions set out in the listing rules. Significant means, by s. 81(2), significant for the purpose of making any informed assessment of the kind set out in s. 80(1). There is no duty to issue supplementary particulars unless the issuer is aware of the change or new matter or is notified of it by a person responsible for the listing particulars (s. 81(3)). That person is, however, required to give appropriate notice (s. 81(4)).

The competent authority may, under s. 82(1), permit certain information to be omitted from the listing particulars where its disclosure would be contrary to the public interest, seriously detrimental to the issuer or otherwise considered unnecessary for the type of persons expected normally to buy or deal in the particular types of securities concerned. This may not, however, apply to essential information (s. 82(2)(a)). Essential information means information which a person considering acquiring securities of the kind in question would be likely to need in order not to be misled about any facts which it is essential for him to know in order to make an informed assessment (s. 82(6)). The Secretary of State or the Treasury may issue a certificate confirming that the disclosure of certain information would be contrary to the public interest (s. 82(3)).

A copy of the listing particulars must be delivered to the registrar of companies on or before the date on which they are published under the Listing Rules (s. 83(1)). A statement that a copy has been delivered to the registrar must be included within the listing particulars (s. 83(2)). Failure to provide the registrar with a copy of the listing particulars is an offence (s. 83(3) and (4)). These requirements apply equally to supplementary listing particulars (s. 83(5)).

## Compensation

Any person responsible for listing particulars is liable under s. 90(1) to pay compensation to any person who has acquired securities to which the particulars apply and has suffered loss as a result of any untrue or misleading statement in the particulars or the omission of any matter which should otherwise have been set out in the particulars. This is subject to certain exceptions set out in sch. 10. Any person who fails to comply with the requirements with regard to the issuance of supplementary particulars is also liable to pay compensation to purchasers who have suffered loss as a result (s. 90(4)), though, again, there are relevant exceptions in sch. 10. These statutory liabilities are without prejudice to any other liability which may arise (s. 90(6)).

## PROSPECTUSES

Listing Rules must provide that no new securities for which an application for listing has been made may be admitted to the official list unless a prospectus has been submitted to and approved by the FSA and published (s. 84(1)). The prospectus must accordingly be published before the securities are offered to the public in the United Kingdom. It is an offence for any person to offer new securities for which an application for listing has been made without publishing a prospectus as required by the Listing Rules (s. 85(2)). This may also lead, for example, to discipline under Part XIV if the offer is made by an authorised person. Any person who suffers loss may sue the person who made the offer of securities subject to the defences which are generally applied to breaches of statutory duty (s. 85(5)).

The provisions applicable to listing particulars, including the obligations of issuers and other parties under Part VI of the Act, are to apply equally to prospectuses required by Listing Rules and supplementary prospectuses of that kind (s. 86(1) and (2)).

The Listing Rules may (under s. 87(1)) provide for prospectuses to be submitted and approved by the FSA where securities are to be issued to the public in the United Kingdom for the first time although no application for listing is to be made. Once approved by the FSA, such a 'non-listing prospectus' must be recognised by all competent authorities in other EEA States. Certain amendments are made under sch. 9 to apply the listing provisions contained in the Act to non-listed prospectuses.

## SPONSORS

Under the previous regime in the FSA 1986, sponsors acted as intermediaries between the issuer and the London Stock Exchange (later the FSA), but their legal status and the enforceability of their responsibilities were unclear. FSAMA 2000 therefore clarifies their position and rights and duties. Sponsor means any person approved by the FSA for the purpose of the listing rules (s. 88(2)). The Listing Rules may require any person to make arrangements with a sponsor for the carrying out of certain specified services and for the maintenance of a list of relevant sponsors and conditions for listing (s. 88(3)). The Act also now includes provisions by way of warning notices and decision notices and the right to apply to the Tribunal where an application for approval as a sponsor is to be refused or an existing approval cancelled (s. 88(4) to (7)). The FSA may also, under special provisions in the listing rules, proceed against the sponsor for breach of a requirement imposed on him or her under the rules (s. 89(1)). This would result in a public censure of the sponsor, again subject to notice and the right to apply to the Tribunal (s. 89(2), (3) and (4)). Third parties who could be prejudiced by the proposed discipline are given appropriate due process rights (ss. 392–3).

## PENALTIES

Under s. 91(1), by way of major change, penalties may now be imposed by the FSA on any person (issuer or applicant for listing) who has breached the Listing Rules. This will extend to include present and former directors who have been knowingly involved in a breach of the Listing Rules (s. 91(2)). Penalties are to be paid directly to the FSA. As with approved persons under Part IV (s. 66(4)), no proceedings for a penalty may be started after two years from the date on which the authority knew of the contravention or of the circumstances from which the contravention could reasonably be inferred (s. 91(6)). Alternatively, as with sponsors, a public censure may be issued. These are important new powers. Formerly, the competent authority could only issue private or public censures or suspend or cancel listing. This will accordingly allow the competent authority additional flexibility in dealing with listing breaches.

Where a penalty is to be imposed, the authority must give the person concerned a warning notice stating the reasons for the proposed action and the amount of fine or content of the censure statement (s. 92(1), (2) and (3)). This must then be followed by a decision notice (s. 92(4), (5) and (6)). Any other persons who may be prejudiced must also be notified (ss. 392 and 393). If action is to be taken against a person, the matter may be referred to the Financial Services and Markets Tribunal (s. 92(7)).

The FSA's policy with regard to the imposition of penalties and amount is to be set out in a published policy statement (s. 93(1)). Criteria on amount are to include the seriousness of the contravention, the mental element (deliberate or reckless) and whether the person was an individual. The penalty is otherwise unlimited, and, once paid to the FSA, has, under s. 100(2), to be applied for the benefit of issuers of listed securities.

## COMPETITION

FSAMA 2000 contains new provisions allowing the Treasury to order the regulating provisions and practices of the competent authority to be kept under review having regard to possible significant adverse effects on competition (s. 95(1) and (2)).

## OBLIGATIONS OF ISSUERS

The Listing Rules may specify requirements to be complied with by issuers of listed securities and the action to be taken by the FSA in the event of non-compliance (s. 96(1)). This may include authorising the authority to publish the fact that an issuer has breached the rules or publish relevant information in the event that the issuer has failed to do so (s. 96(2)).

## INVESTIGATIONS

Under s. 97(1) and (2), the FSA may appoint one or more persons to conduct an investigation where it considers that there has been a breach of the Listing Rules or requirements of the Act with regard to registration or publication of prospectuses or the advertising rules. This may include situations where a director of an issuer or applicant company has been involved with a breach of the rules (s. 92(1)(b) and (c)).

## ADVERTISEMENTS, PENALTIES, FEES AND IMMUNITY

Under s. 98(1) and (2), advertisements in connection with applications for listing must either be approved or be authorised by the FSA in advance. It is an offence to fail to do so (s. 98(2)). Reasonable belief that the advertisement or information had been approved or authorised is a defence (s. 98(3)). Once the information has been approved or authorised, no civil liability can arise with regard to any statement or omission in the information if, taking the information and listing particulars together, a person would not be likely to have been misled (s. 98(4)).

Listing Rules may require the payment of fees to the competent authority in respect of applications for listing and the continued inclusion of securities in the official lists (s. 99(1)).

Additional provisions were added to the Act in connection with penalties. In determining its policy with regard to amount, the competent authority cannot have regard to anticipated costs in carrying out its functions under Part VI (s. 100(1)). The penalty structure must be applied to benefit the issuers of securities admitted to the official list (s. 100(2)). Up-to-date information must also be set out in the scheme details issued by the authority (s. 100(4)).

Section 101 contains general provisions in connection with the content of the Listing Rules. The Listing Rules may make different provisions for different types of cases (s. 101(1)). Listing rules may authorise the competent authority to dispense with or modify the application of the rules in particular cases and by reference to any particular circumstances (s. 101(2)). Listing Rules must be made by an instrument in writing (s. 101(3)). This must be printed and made available to the public with or without payment (s. 101(4)).

Section 102(1) contains a general exemption from liability and damages for the FSA and its staff in connection with anything done or omitted in the discharge, or purported discharge, of its functions as competent authority under the Act (s. 102(1)). This will not apply to acts or omissions shown to have been in bad faith or awards in connection with unlawful acts or omissions under s. 6(1) of the Human Rights Act 1998 (s. 102(2)).

## LISTING RULES

The FSA became the competent authority in succession to the London Stock Exchange on 1 May 2000. It is now responsible for making and publishing the Listing Rules, which used to be published by the London Stock Exchange in a loose-leaf yellow binder known as the Yellow Book. The FSA has continued the tradition of publishing earlier Stock Exchange conditions for admission of securities to listing.

Following the announcement that the FSA would assume responsibility for admission to listing, it was agreed that the Stock Exchange's Yellow Book would effectively be transferred to the FSA. This would include provisions not required under the European Directives or other United Kingdom legislative enactments. The objective was to continue the operation of the existing standards, minimise duplication and ensure continuity in so far as possible, at least, in the short term. Some minor consequential amendments were considered necessary. These stand-alone FSA Listing Rules were to take effect from the date of transfer. Over time, it was intended that the Listing Rules would be integrated as a discrete source book within the FSA Handbook.

Before the announcement of transfer of responsibility for admission to listing was made, the London Stock Exchange had published a consultative document entitled 'Listing Rules 2000' setting out proposed amendments to its listing rules on 16 September 1999. These changes were subsequently finalised and, although the initial draft of the FSA Listing Rules did not contain these amendments, they were subsequently included.

As with earlier versions, the FSA Listing Rules apply to additional securities not set out in the European Directives or under the FSA 1986. Before the Stock Exchange (Listing) Regulations 1984 (SI 1984/716) came into effect, the requirements of the Yellow Book applied to all listed securities. The listing also had no legislative basis although the rules still had some statutory effect with, for example, the then Stock Exchange being able to exempt certain companies from having to comply with the prospectus requirements set out in the Companies Act 1948, ss. 39 and 418. The November 1984 Yellow Book contained separate provisions which gave effect to the requirements of the 1984 Listing Regulations and those which were simply imposed by the Council of the Stock Exchange without any statutory basis. The 1984 Listing Regulations were replaced by Part IV of the FSA 1986, which applied only to a sub-set of the investments set out in sch. 1 to that Act (s. 142(2)). This did not include such securities as those issued by overseas governments or local authorities outside the EEA which were admitted to listing in London. This was significant in that the Treasury could issue directions to the London Stock Exchange only to the extent that it acted as competent authority under relevant Community provisions (FSA 1986, s. 192).

While some confusion may also have arisen with regard to the extent of judicial review available in relation to securities which fell outside the scope of the Admissions Directive, it is now clear that judicial review applies generally in connection with any decisions taken by the competent authority for listing.

The Listing Rules will consequently give effect to:

(a)   requirements that are mandatory under the European Community Directives;

(b)   additional requirements of the UK Listing Authority under its powers as competent authority in relation to securities covered by Part VI of FSAMA 2000 (formerly Part IV of FSA 1986); and

(c)   corresponding requirements in relation to other securities admitted to listing.

Applications for listing were until 1 May 2000 processed through the London Stock Exchange's Listing Department. This was transferred to the FSA with responsibility for admission to listing. The transfer included the Listing Department's groups dealing with monitoring and enquiries, equity markets, capital markets and policy. On transfer, the other advisory bodies to the UK Listing Authority, the Listing Authority Advisory Committee (LAAC) and the Listing Rules Committee (LRC) continued in operation although they were then answerable to the Board of the FSA.

The listing process now generally operates by the FSA considering applications for admission to listing with a view to determining whether all of the relevant conditions for listing (including any special conditions) have been complied with. Relevant listing particulars and other documents prescribed are examined and approved provided they satisfy all relevant requirements. While further information may be requested in connection with matters set out in the particulars or supporting documents, the FSA is not responsible for the investigation or verification or the accuracy or completeness of the information provided. Primary responsibility for the accuracy of documents remains with the directors of an issuer.

The current FSA Listing Rules include separate rules for approval of prospectuses where there is no application for admission to listing (non-listing prospectuses). The listing rules also now contain provisions designed to encourage observance by listed companies of the Combined Code which sets out the principles of good governance and code of best practice derived from the Hampel, Cadbury and Greenbury Reports.

## Contents of listing particulars

Chapter 6 of the Listing Rules sets out the information required to be provided in listing particulars and prospectuses. This varies according to the nature and circumstances of the issuer and type of security to be listed. Separate requirements are imposed with regard to information required for admission of shares or convertible debt securities to listing, admission of debt securities to listing and certificates representing shares.

## Listing application procedures

The Listing Rules must set out the procedures for the receipt and processing of applications. Admission will become effective only once the decision to admit has been announced electronically or on a designated notice board (when electronic systems are inoperable).

Certain papers ('the 48 hour documents') must be lodged in final form with the FSA no later than mid-day, at least, two business days prior to consideration of the application for listing (Listing Rules, para. 7.5). Further items must be lodged no later than 9 a.m. on the day of consideration of the application including payment of fees, an undertaking not to offer the securities to the public prior to admission and the duly completed shareholder or pricing statement. Other documents are to be lodged as soon as practicable after consideration of the application but no later than five business days after they have become available (Listing Rules, para. 7.7). The FSA may also require other documents to be provided at any time before or after admission to listing.

Where an issuer issues securities on a regular basis, a simplified application procedure (a formal application) or an application only to list a specified number of securities (a block listing) may be used.

## Publication and circulation of listing particulars

The Listing Rules contain provisions with regard to the prior approval, publication and circulation of listing particulars and supplementary particulars.

## Continuing obligations

As well as obtaining the original admission to listing, a number of further continuing obligations must be complied with by the issuer and certain other parties. The Listing Rules accordingly include a number of general continuing obligations and additional obligations in connection with specific matters.

The main obligations are listed in ch. 9 of the Listing Rules under the headings: general obligation of disclosure for companies, notifications relating to capital, notification of major interests and shares, notification when the Company Announcements Office is not open for business, rights as between holders of securities, communication with shareholders and certain other miscellaneous obligations. Further obligations are imposed in connection with companies without listed equity securities and certificates representing shares.

# Chapter Nine
# Control of Business Transfers

## *Michael Blair*

Part VII of the Financial Services and Markets Act 2000 (FSAMA 2000) deals with a new scheme for effecting, with the approval of the court, transfers of insurance business or of banking business. Until the commencement of this part, the position has been as follows:

(a)   There was statutory machinery for the transfer of insurance business, which could be achieved with an order of the court for transfers involving long-term business, and with the approval of the Treasury (or more recently the FSA) for transfers involving general insurance.

(b)   There was no such procedure for transferring banking business, and mergers between banks and takeovers within the banking community often necessitated a private Act of Parliament where the process of securing a contractual variation was unduly difficult. English law does not have the doctrine of 'universal succession' which enables transfers of banking business in many other jurisdictions without the need for individual novation.

The new scheme is essentially an amalgam of three elements:

(a)   the replacement (with some changes) of the machinery for long-term insurance business, currently in part I of sch. 2C to the Insurance Companies Act 1982, and required by the EC insurance Directives;

(b)   the conversion of the general insurance transfer machinery (in part II of that schedule) into a court-based system, and

(c)   the invention of a wholly new scheme for banks.

The geographical reach of the three elements is complex and each is different. Broadly, element (a) above respects the home/host State divide in the Directives and is thus limited to insurance undertakings which are based in the UK or outside the EU. Element (b) above is similar, but with a 'host State' capacity for reinsurance business as well (branches of EEA firms in the UK). Element (c), being free of Directive requirements, is available whether the connection with the UK is UK incorporation (or the equivalent) or the carrying on in the UK of deposit-taking business.

This Part of the Act did not appear in any of the earlier drafts of the Bill, but was introduced at the report stage in the House of Commons, with little if any advance notice. During the standing committee proceedings, an opposition spokesman had asked whether the government had any intention to solve the problem relating to mergers of banks, which were much in the news at the time, and the government responded with the new clauses to constitute Part VII at the next parliamentary stage.

The fact that the scheme was introduced at a late stage is apparent from the Act, since Part VII contains two powers for the Treasury to make regulations, either to impose requirements on persons applying for court approval for a transfer (s. 108), or to modify the Part itself for certain categories of transfer or even just to provide for its 'more effective operation' (s. 117). This latter power was inserted on the third reading in the House of Lords of the Bill for the Act, that is, at the very last stage for amendment.

Part VII, with sch. 12, deals with the interrelationship between court approval and regulatory oversight. The FSA is entitled to be heard in the proceedings (s. 110(a)), and the schedule lists the various regulatory certificates that have to be produced to the court. The most significant ones are certificates confirming the necessary margin of solvency, for insurance, and adequate resources, for banks.

The effect of an order of the court transferring the business is to achieve a seamless conveyance of the rights and obligations under the previous contract. The powers of the court are set out in some detail in s. 107, the underlying purpose being to secure that the scheme of transfer is fully and effectively carried out.

Part VII, with sch. 12, also deals with the regulatory certificates that may be required under the EC Directives for use in other countries in the EEA or, for insurance, in Switzerland. As with so much in the European context, machinery has to be devised to work in both directions, into and out from the UK.

# Chapter Ten
# Penalties for Market Abuse

*George Walker*

One of the most innovative and controversial aspects of the new Financial Services and Markets Act 2000 (FSAMA 2000) is the inclusion of provisions concerning market abuse.

Financial markets must be protected from abuse or malpractice. Otherwise, their effective operation would be significantly damaged. Liquidity and efficiency would be undermined and the stability and continued development and prosperity of the economy as a whole threatened.

In attempting to control abusive practice, the interests of legitimate market participants in the conduct of normal trading operations must also be fully protected. Without the maintenance of a free and open market place, competition and innovation would necessarily be constrained. A correct balance must accordingly be secured between the prohibition of illegitimate market activity and the promotion or protection of normal trading practices. It is in achieving this balance that most of the difficulties surrounding the introduction of the new regime have arisen.

The market abuse provisions are set out in Part VIII of the Act. Their objective is to make the operation of the markets more open, transparent and fair through the penalisation of various forms of behaviour considered to constitute market abuse or malpractice.

Market abuse is defined in general terms in the Act with the Treasury being required to prescribe the markets and investments to which the regime is to apply. The FSA is directed to prepare and issue a code of practice to assist in determining which types of behaviour may be considered to constitute market abuse and is given the power to impose penalties or censure where market abuse takes place. The Act also contains a number of procedural provisions in connection with the imposition of fines with a statement of policy being required in this regard.

## MARKET OFFENCES

The introduction of penalties for market abuse was considered necessary to correct the perceived omissions in the earlier legislative framework which existed in the United Kingdom. The original objective was to create a new civil regime to parallel the various criminal controls which were already in place. Insider dealing is currently a criminal offence under the Criminal Justice Act 1993, and misleading statements and practices were prohibited under FSA 1986, s. 47 until this was replaced by FSAMA 2000, s. 397. Fraud and similar offences are also prohibited at common law although their specific meaning and relevance are not altogether clear in many cases.

While these measures have created important and necessary deterrents against market manipulation and insider trading, their success has been limited. The existing criminal offences apply generally and not just to market operators but only include a narrow range of defined abuses. The more general disciplinary regime set up under FSAMA 2000 will cover a wider range of possible abuses, but it will apply only to authorised or approved persons. The existing offences are also interpreted strictly and a high standard of proof beyond reasonable doubt has to be established to secure a successful prosecution. When fines are imposed, they will rarely be proportionate to the gain or loss involved in economic or financial terms and will consequently have little, if any, compensatory or other redistributive effect in practice. The new market abuse regime is accordingly intended to include a greater number of abuses while at the same time allowing a wider range of more relevant penalties to be imposed.

It was not intended that FSAMA 2000 would repeal all of the existing criminal provisions which apply to market conduct and market offences. Indeed, the practical effect of many of these has been extended by allowing the FSA to undertake criminal prosecutions itself. The objective of the market abuse measures is then to create a new parallel quasi-civil regime to act as a complement or supplement to the existing criminal provisions already in operation.

While the existing prosecuting authorities including the DTI, the Serious Fraud Office and the Crown Prosecution Service, will continue to be able to proceed against such offences, it is hoped that the knowledge and expertise of the FSA will allow it to make an increasingly important contribution in this area. It is also intended that the FSA should be able to prosecute breaches of the Money Laundering Regulations, at least, in so far as these affect firms' systems and controls.

## DRAFTING AND REVISION

The history of the drafting of what is now Part VIII of FSAMA 2000 clearly demonstrates the difficulties which arise in attempting to establish an appropriate level of control over abusive practices in the financial services area.

Under the original provisions contained in the July 1998 Bill, the FSA was to be given power to impose unlimited financial penalties for market abuse. Market abuse was defined in the Bill and the Treasury were given an order-making power to specify which markets and which investments would be covered. The Bill stated that market abuse occurred wherever behaviour was likely to damage the confidence of informed participants in the market or produce the result that the market was otherwise unfair. In order to constitute market abuse, behaviour had to be based on restricted information, it had to create a mistaken impression as to the supply, demand or price or value of an investment and had to be of such a nature as to be likely to distort the market. The FSA was empowered to impose a financial penalty on any person, whether an authorised person or not, who had engaged in market abuse or induced another to engage in abuse.

Although the conditions applicable to the basic sanction have been retained, the provisions in the original Bill have been materially amended, in particular, in response to concerns with regard to legal certainty and to compliance with the European Convention on Human Rights. Other critics questioned the basic idea of creating a new civil regime and suggested that the only change needed was to revise and extend the existing criminal provisions, but this was rejected by the government.

A Joint Committee on Financial Services and Markets was then set up to consider a number of the provisions in the Bill, which it did in its First and Second Reports. These were followed by the government response document of June 1999. In its First Report of 27 April 1999 (House of Commons Papers, Session 1998–99, 328), the Joint Committee questioned the perceived lack of certainty of the proposed regime, in particular, with regard to the general drafting of the original clause 56, the absence of any intent requirement and the lack of any statutory safe harbour for conduct in compliance with the FSA's proposed Code of Market Conduct which was to be issued under the Act. The report also doubted the fairness of the new regime and its compatibility with the European Convention on Human Rights.

The possibility of infringement of the European Convention on Human Rights was considered separately in a joint opinion by Lord Lester of Herne Hill QC and Javan Herberg to the Joint Committee. Incorporation of the Convention into United Kingdom law by the Human Rights Act 1998 means that from October 2000 the courts must construe legislation in a manner compatible with the Convention in so far as possible and that the FSA will be potentially liable in damages for any breach of Convention rights (FSAMA 2000, sch. 1, para. 19).

Although the draft Bill had attempted to classify the disciplinary and market abuse offences as civil, the report of the Joint Committee considered that most, if not all, would, in fact, be criminal in nature for the purposes of the Convention. Article 6 would then require that there had to be an independent and impartial court and a fair trial, involving equality of arms, the right to proper legal assistance and full protection of the presumption of innocence and privilege against self-incrimination. Article 7 also requires that the offence charged must be clearly defined in law while art. 4 of Protocol 7 (which is not incorporated into UK law by the Human Rights Act 1998) may prevent dual prosecution under the criminal law and the market abuse provisions of the Act.

The government subsequently took advice from Sir Sidney Kentridge QC and James Eadie and announced a series of changes to the Bill to increase certainty and reduce the possibility of a successful challenge under the Convention. These included applying the revised rules only to 'market participants', imposing restrictions on the FSA's use of compelled evidence, ensuring the provision of subsidised legal assistance 'in appropriate cases', protection for those who took 'reasonable steps' to avoid breach of the primary rules and creation of an absolute safe harbour in respect of compliance with the Code of Market Conduct. Although these revisions were generally approved by the Joint Committee in its Second Report of 27 May 1999 (House of Commons Papers, Session 1998–99, 465), opinion was reserved with regard to the clarity of the conceptual basis of the regime following the government's decision not to revise the original definition of market abuse.

While further concerns were expressed with regard to the degree of intent required in relation to the constitution of the wrongful conduct, the government insisted that the purpose of the legislation was to focus on the effect of the course of action adopted and not the intention of the individual involved. Even unintentional effects of behaviour could undermine the proper operation of a market, and for this reason an express intent requirement would not be introduced.

Further comments had also been received following the FSA's publication of its Consultation Paper 10, *Market Abuse: a Draft Code of Market Conduct*, in June 1998. The FSA responded to a number of the issues raised in its feedback statement on 10 March 1999. This considered, in particular, the problem of intent within the Code, the evidential status of and issuance of further guidance on the Code, interaction with the rules of recognised investment exchange, the Panel on Takeovers and Mergers and other FSA provisions as well as certain other more specific points.

The definition of market abuse was subsequently amended during the examination of the Bill by Standing Committee A of the House of Commons in November 1999. Rather than continue to apply the original 'informed participant' standard, a revised test was introduced based on a 'regular user' with further safeguards being inserted with regard to reasonable care and belief, in an attempt to ensure that the sanction was not unnecessarily wide in scope nor unfairly penal in effect.

The latest amendments considered to the Bill (which almost delayed its royal assent) concerned the creation of statutory safe harbours to separate the market abuse regime from the work of the Panel on Takeovers and Mergers. It had been argued that the FSA could be drawn into takeover battles with either predatory or target companies attempting to challenge rulings of the Panel on the basis of possible market abuse infractions. This could then have the effect of undermining the authority of the Panel and the continued speedy, efficient and effective nature of its highly respected work.

Against this, the government argued that the FSA, as the statutory regulator, should remain responsible for determining the meaning of market abuse and the scope of any permitted exceptions. The FSA should be empowered to grant safe harbour status where it was satisfied that conduct sanctioned by particular provisions of the City Code on Takeovers and Mergers did not constitute market abuse, but only with the agreement of the Treasury and on the basis of the actual text or words used and not the rulings of the Panel as such.

The prolonged disagreements which arose in connection with the impact of the market abuse provisions on the continued authority and viability of the takeover system within the United Kingdom led to amendment No. 180 being put forward again by the opposition in the Lords on 12 June 2000 following its earlier rejection in the Commons. Lord McIntosh of Haringey for the government had proposed that the Commons amendment 180A be accepted in place of 180. While 180A revised the market abuse provisions to allow the FSA to insert 'City Code' safe harbours within its Code of Market Conduct (with the consent of the Treasury) and to impose an obligation on the FSA to keep itself informed of developments in the area, 180 would have amended the takeover clauses appearing later in the Bill to include a statutory exemption from liability in the event of compliance with the City Code as interpreted by the Panel on Takeovers and Mergers. Lord Alexander of Weedon had also proposed a further amendment 180B, which would have allowed the Panel to determine for the purposes of market abuse which behaviour was to be considered to be in conformity with the City Code.

After a further hour of debate, amendment 180B was rejected on a 188 to 183 vote in favour of the government. It was accordingly accepted that City Code exemptions would be included within the FSA's Code and not the statute and that the FSA, and not the Panel, would determine which conduct was to be considered to be in compliance with the terms of the City Code. The Bill then received royal assent two days later on 14 June.

Following the government's rejection of any statutory takeover exemption, Sir Howard Davies, Chairman of the FSA, confirmed that the FSA would include various safe harbour clauses within a revised Code of Market Conduct that would apply expressly to various types of conduct permitted by the City Code. The scope of exemption would then be determined by the FSA in consultation with the Treasury and not through the rulings of the Takeover Panel. The FSA would, however, cooperate closely with the Takeover Panel to ensure that these safe harbours were kept up to date and to avoid duplication of action in practice. This would include agreeing a clear policy of non-intervention in takeover situations where the Panel had all necessary power to act. Only in exceptional circumstances would the FSA consider exercising its market abuse powers and then only following consultation with the Panel.

How all of this will operate in practice remains to be seen. There is general agreement on the need for more inclusive and relevant sanctions against market abuse and malpractice. A number of important concerns were, however, raised during the consultation period especially with regard to legal certainty, human rights compliance and possible jurisdictional overlap, although the Treasury and FSA have shown themselves to be receptive to comment and, at least, partial adjustment. A considerable degree of care will still have to be taken in giving effect to the new provisions and, in particular, in ensuring that all of the safeguards agreed are properly implemented and operate in an effective but fair manner in practice.

## MARKET ABUSE

The statutory definition of market abuse is set out in FSAMA 2000, s. 118(1), which applies to such markets as the Treasury may prescribe by order under s. 118(3). The FSA is empowered to impose penalties under s. 123(1) on persons who are or have engaged in market abuse.

The new regime operates by creating three general statutory conditions (s. 118(1)(a), (b) and (c)) supported by three more specific behaviour tests (s. 118(2)(a), (b) and (c)). The third of the general statutory conditions is the main element: market abuse is behaviour by one or more persons which is likely to be regarded by a regular user of a market who is aware of the behaviour as being a failure on the part of the person or persons concerned to observe the standard of behaviour reasonably expected of a person in his or their position in relation to the market (s. 118(1)(c)).

In order to constitute market abuse, behaviour must also apply in relation to qualifying investments traded on a market to which the section applies (s. 118(1)(a)) and fall within one of the three statutory tests set out in s. 118(2) (s. 118(1)(b)).

The three statutory behaviour tests in s. 118(2) are:

(a)  the behaviour is based on information which is not generally available to those using the market but which, if available to a regular user of the market, would or would be likely to be regarded by him as being relevant in deciding the terms on which transactions in investments of the kind in question should be effected (s. 118(2)(a));

(b)  the behaviour is likely to give a regular user of the market a false or misleading impression as to the supply of, or demand for, or as to the price or value of, the investments in question (s. 118(2)(b)); or

(c)  a regular user of the market would, or would be likely to, regard the behaviour as behaviour which would, or would be likely to, distort the market in the particular investments (s. 118(2)(c)).

These are summarised as misuse of information, false or misleading impressions and distortion in the FSA's draft Code of Market Conduct (see below).

A regular user of a particular market is defined as a reasonable person who regularly uses the market in investments of the kind in question (s. 118(10)). Behaviour includes any action or inaction (s. 118(10)) although it will be taken into account only if it occurred in the United Kingdom or in relation to qualifying investments on a market which is situated in the United Kingdom or accessible electronically in the United Kingdom (s. 118(5)). Information is to be treated as being generally available if it can be obtained by research or analysis (s. 118(7)). Market abuse may be behaviour by one person alone or with one or more other persons (s. 118(9)) either acting jointly or in concert (s. 118(1)).

The FSA may impose a penalty on any person who either is or has engaged in market abuse (s. 123(1)(a)) or has required or encouraged another to do so by taking or refraining from taking any particular action (s. 123(1)(b)). In determining whether a penalty is to be imposed, account must be taken of the extent to which the person (or persons) believed, on reasonable grounds, that his or her (or their) behaviour did not amount to market abuse or to requiring or encouraging another to behave in that way (s. 123(2)(a)) or took all reasonable precautions and exercised all due diligence to avoid engaging in market abuse or requiring or encouraging another to do so (s. 123(2)(b)). The FSA may issue a public censure rather than impose a financial penalty (s. 123(3)). The imposition of a penalty under Part VIII will not render any transaction void or unenforceable (s. 131).

While drafted as three general conditions (s. 118(1)) with three further statutory behaviour tests (s. 118(2)), the concept of market abuse is essentially based on the failure to uphold relevant standards in the three particular areas of activity referred to in s. 118(2). The first of these (s. 118(2)(a)) will generally apply to information misuse (such as insider trading) and the latter two (s. 118(2)(b) and (c)) to most instances of market manipulation. These are developed further in the FSA's Code of Market Conduct which is considered further below.

Even if behaviour is considered to be below the recognised standards for the particular market, it will not constitute market abuse unless it falls within one of the statutory activities listed in s. 118(2). While the purpose or objective of the conduct may be taken into account to determine whether a defence may be available under s. 123(2), the conditions imposed under s. 118 are generally to be applied on an objective rather than subjective basis looking only to effect rather than intent.

The effect of the revisions made to the market abuse provisions especially at the Commons committee stage should be to make the operation of the new regime more transparent and workable in practice. A considerably more sensitive set of relevant standards and supporting definitions has been adopted which should allow the authorities more effectively to balance the interests of legitimate market operators as against the need to penalise market abuse and malpractice. Much will, however, depend upon how the core statutory provisions are developed and applied by the FSA over time especially through its Code of Market Conduct.

## CODE OF MARKET CONDUCT

Section 119(1) of FSAMA 2000 requires the FSA to prepare and issue a code for the purpose of determining whether or not particular behaviour amounts to market abuse. Consultation Paper 10, *Market Abuse: a Draft Code of Market Conduct*, was issued by the FSA in June 1998.

Following the publication of Consultation Paper 10, the FSA established a series of working groups made up of market practitioners, the RIEs and the DTI to discuss the draft Code. The practitioner group comprised representatives from the securities, derivatives and commodities markets nominated by the RIEs and trade associations as well as from the Law Society. Consultation with the exchanges and other regulators took place through a market abuse sub-group of MERLIN (the Markets and Exchange Regulatory Liaison Information Network) comprising representatives of each of the RIEs and the DTI.

Following the amendments made to the Bill, a revised draft Code was issued in July 2000 (Consultation Paper 59). It was expected that a supplement would be issued to incorporate the additional provisions required with regard to the Panel on Takeovers and Mergers, authorised activity under the City Code on Takeovers and Mergers and revisions to the Listing Rules following transfer of responsibility for listing from the London Stock Exchange to the FSA (see chapter 8).

The revised draft Code sets out the standards of conduct expected of those using prescribed markets. The purpose is to assist market participants to identify relevant standards of conduct which, if complied with, will avoid market abuse.

Although it was originally intended that the Code would only have evidentiary weight, the government subsequently decided, in response to parliamentary pressure, that compliance would constitute a full defence against any allegation of market abuse. This is now provided for in s. 122(1).

The draft Code sets out a number of activities which the FSA considers will constitute market abuse. The Code is, however, neither conclusive nor exhaustive. Whether a particular activity constitutes market abuse is for the FSA to determine on a case-by-case basis, subject to recourse to the Financial Services and Markets Tribunal and possibly to the courts. Conduct not set out in the Code may still amount to market abuse for the purposes of the Act. Section 122(2) accordingly provides that the Code may be relied on in so far as it indicates whether or not behaviour should be taken to amount to market abuse. The Code is thus only evidential with regard to breaches (s. 122(2)) but conclusive with regard to exemptions (s. 122(1)).

The draft Code begins by defining its scope of application (MAR1.1), provides guidance on the new regular user test (MAR1.3) and lists a number of prescribed activities and supporting safe harbours under the headings of misuse of information (MAR1.5), false or misleading impressions (MAR1.6) and distortion (MAR1.7). The draft Code explains the two statutory exceptions available (MAR1.8), expands the meaning of requiring or encouraging (MAR1.9), considers the relationship between the new regime and the criminal law and other regulatory requirements (MAR1.10). It also refers to the FSA's separate statement of policy on penalties (MAR1.11 which was set out in app. B to Consultation Paper 59).

**Regular user standard**

The concept of the regular user is essential to the market abuse regime. This is, in particular, used to define the standard by which market behaviour is to be judged. Its meaning and use are developed further in the draft Code. The FSA describes the concept in Consultation Paper 59 as being the equivalent of the court's reasonable man or the man on the Clapham omnibus (para. 6.6).

The regular user is a hypothetical user of the market rather than any particular or actual user, although the test will be applied to the circumstances of the specific case including the nature of the market and investment in relation to which the behaviour occurrs (MAR1.3.1). The draft Code recognises that although the actual standards of conduct which generally apply in a market at any particular time are relevant, they do not define the standards of the regular user as such. There may be occasions when the standards which are in fact accepted by actual users may not be deemed to be objectively acceptable to the regular user, such as where the misuse of information is knowingly tolerated on a regular basis (MAR1.3.2).

The standard against which behaviour is to be assessed will depend partly on the characteristics of the market and partly on the investments concerned. The FSA also recognises that practices will vary across markets especially having regard to the positions held and the experience, skill and knowledge of the persons concerned (MAR1.3.3).

The FSA states that the standard of behaviour to be reasonably expected of a person using a market will take into account the need for the market to operate fairly and efficiently as a whole. The regular user will then expect those using and benefiting from a market to have regard to the wider interests and longer-term continued operation of the market (MAR1.3.5).

Although the regular user is a hypothetical user, the test will not operate in a vacuum. The regular user will take into account compliance with the rules of an RIE or other rules or codes of conduct and good practice when deciding whether behaviour falls short of reasonably expected standards so as to amount to market abuse (MAR1.3.6). This will include the rules and standards of overseas markets when conduct on those markets is relevant to determining whether or not there has been an abuse of a prescribed market (MAR1.3.4).

As breach of relevant standards is possibly the core element of market abuse and as this is defined in terms of the regular user, how this is interpreted and applied in practice will be of crucial importance to the effective operation of the new regime. Although an objective standard is generally to be adopted this can only be assessed having regard to all of the circumstances of the particular case.

The application of the objective test is supported by the use of an effect rather than intent trigger. It is not essential that there is any actual intent or purpose to engage in market abuse (MAR1.3.7). Intention may be considered in some cases to determine whether particular conduct falls within any of the statutory behaviour tests but this is not to be applied as a condition in its own right. Where intention may be relevant and there is more than one purpose, the FSA will have regard to the 'actuating purpose', which is defined to mean 'a purpose which motivates or incites a person to act'.

While the FSA will principally look to effect rather than intent, a mistake or omission will not generally amount to market abuse provided that reasonable care has been taken to prevent and detect its occurrence (MAR1.3.8).

Although the guidance provided by the FSA in the draft Code with regard to the regular user standard is of value, how the test will be understood and applied in practice remains to be seen.

## Market abuse

To constitute market abuse, conduct must fall within one of three categories of behaviour set out in FSAMA 2000, s. 118(2), as well as breach the regular user standard already discussed (s. 118(1)(c)). The three categories are essentially abuse, appearance and distortion based. While each involves information in some manner, the first is essentially concerned with information abuse. The other two are more conduct based with the second principally being concerned with false pricing and the third with the creation of some other form of false market.

The first can also be considered to be more use based or passive in operation while the other two involve some more immediate or direct form of active market manipulation. The third would also appear to be more general than the second and potentially include the second, at least, in certain price-related circumstances. The three categories are clearly alternative rather than cumulative for the purposes of the Act and a particular course of conduct may fall within more than one category.

The three behaviour categories are expanded in the draft code.

*Misuse of information*    The draft Code (MAR1.5) refers to the first type of possible abuse (FSAMA 2000, s. 118(2)(a)) as misuse of information.

The FSA will apply four initial tests to determine whether this category of possible market abuse may be relevant (MAR1.5.5). Behaviour will be a misuse of information where it is based on material information, the information is not generally available, the information is investment relevant and relates to matters which a regular user would reasonably expect to be disclosed to other users in the market.

Information is to be treated as being generally available if it can be obtained by research or analysis (FSAMA 2000, s. 118(7); draft Code, MAR1.5.6). Information will be generally available where it has been disclosed through an accepted channel for dissemination or otherwise under the rules of a prescribed market, it is contained in records which are open to pubic inspection, it has otherwise been made public or derived from public information or it can otherwise be obtained through observation (MAR1.5.7). This will apply even if the information is only available overseas and has not been directly published in the United Kingdom, it has only been communicated to a section of the public and not generally or it is only available on payment of a fee (MAR1.5.8).

Relevance will be determined having regard to the circumstances of each case. Factors to be taken into account will include how specific and precise, material, current and reliable the information is as well as the nature and content of other information already available and the extent to which the information differs from information which is generally available (MAR1.5.10). Examples of relevant information would include business affairs or prospects, commodity delivery factors or official statistics or fiscal and monetary policy announcements (MAR1.5.12).

Information will fall within the fourth condition (reasonable expectation of disclosure) where it has to be disclosed to the market in accordance with any legal or regulatory requirement (referred to as disclosable information) or is usually the subject of a public announcement although not subject to any formal disclosure requirement (referred to as announceable information).

The draft Code creates four information misuse safe harbours based on required dealings, behaviour not based on information, trading information and takeover-related activity. Dealing will not amount to market abuse if the person was required to comply with a legal (including contractual) or regulatory obligation (MAR1.5.21). Dealing will not be caught if the decision to deal was taken before the relevant information was available and the terms were not subsequently changed (MAR1.5.22). Normal dealing on trading information will not constitute market abuse although it may, for example, amount to front running which is prohibited under the FSA's Conduct of Business Rules (MAR1.5.16). A person who is (or is acting for) an actual or potential takeover bidder may develop an equity position in a target company without being liable for market abuse, provided it is for the benefit of the offeror or potential offeror and was carried out solely for the purposes of pursuing the bid (MAR1.5.28).

*False or misleading impression*    Behaviour will be considered to amount to market abuse where it is likely to give a regular user of the market a false or misleading impression as to the supply of, or demand for, or the price or value of any particular investment (FSAMA 2000, s. 118(2)(b); draft Code, MAR1.6.2). The purpose is not to prohibit behaviour which may raise or lower the price of or value of investments as such but to maintain an open and free market and one in which users can be confident about the operation of the underlying price mechanism in place.

To constitute market abuse, the draft Code requires that the behaviour must be likely to give a regular user a materially false or misleading impression (MAR1.6.4(1)). There must also be a real likelihood that the behaviour will have that effect (MAR1.6.4(2)). A number of factors are to be taken into account to determine whether or not behaviour is likely to create a false or misleading impression (MAR1.6.5). These include the experience and knowledge of the regular user, the structure of the market including reporting, notification and transparency requirements and relevant legal and regulatory rules.

Examples of the conduct covered by the prohibition will include artificial transactions, dissemination of incorrect information, dissemination through an accepted channel without care and a course of conduct involving false or misleading impressions.

The test for artificial transactions in the draft Code is that a person must not enter into a transaction where he knows (or could reasonably be expected to know) that the principal effect of the transaction (or series of transactions) will be, or is likely to be, artificially to inflate or depress the apparent supply of, or demand for, or the price or value of, a qualifying investment or relevant product. The principal rationale for the transaction in question may, however, be objectively considered a legitimate commercial purpose, in which case the draft Code will not have been breached (MAR1.6.7).

Artificial transactions may include wash trades (without any change in or transfer of beneficial interest in the underlying security), simultaneous purchase and sales (to offset market risk), sales (other than repos) without transfer of market risk and fictitious transactions (MAR1.6.9).

There may be market abuse where a person knows, or could reasonably be expected to know, that the information is false or misleading and disseminates the information to create a false or misleading impression (MAR1.6.12). The factors to be taken into account in determining whether information is relevant are listed in MAR1.5.10.

Market abuse may also occur where information is placed in an accepted channel for dissemination, such as a regulatory news service, without reasonable care having been taken to ensure that it was not false and misleading (MAR1.6.16).

A person may otherwise engage in a course of conduct which he knows or could reasonably be expected to know would have a principal effect of conveying a false and misleading impression to a regular user in the market (MAR1.6.19). This may, for example, be particularly relevant to commodity derivatives markets.

Behaviour will not be considered to constitute market abuse where its principal rationale is, objectively, a legitimate commercial purpose or where it involves required transaction reporting or a required or permitted cross-trade or price-maintenance operation. Legitimate trading may include the unwinding of positions to benefit from differences in taxation or capital returns or price differentials across locations. The rules of a particular market may also permit or require members to engage in behaviour that may otherwise be regarded as creating a false or misleading impression. This may include regular or exceptional transaction reporting, cross-trades and price maintenance and such behaviour will not be market abuse provided that the relevant rules are fully complied with in each case.

*Distortion*    Behaviour may be market abuse when a regular user of the market would consider that it would, or would be likely to, distort the market in investments of the kind in question (FSAMA 2000, s. 118(2)(c); draft Code, MAR1.7).

A person may not engage in behaviour that will impede the general operation of the market and, in particular, interfere with the normal forces of supply and demand. The purpose of the prohibition is to prevent behaviour which would distort the market to the detriment of market users including investors (MAR1.7.3).

The draft Code repeats the statutory requirement that the behaviour must be such that a regular user would, or would be likely to, regard it as behaviour which would, or would be likely to, distort the market (MAR1.7.4(1)). As with false and misleading impressions, there must also be a real likelihood that the behaviour would have such an effect (MAR1.7.4(2)).

A number of general factors are taken into account in determining whether or not the behaviour may fall within this category and amount to market abuse

(MAR1.7.5). These include the extent and nature of the visibility or disclosure of the person's activity in taking or retaining control over the supply or demand in question, the extent to which other market users have failed to protect their interests or fulfilled their obligations, the person's willingness to relax control or other influence to help maintain an orderly market, the risk of settlement default and differences in delivery prices under the market's delivery mechanisms.

Distortions may, in particular, arise as a result of either abusive squeezes or price positioning. An abusive squeeze occurs where a person acts to distort prices for the settlement or release of obligations to him or those acting in concert or colluding with him (MAR1.7.8). The person must have a significant influence over the supply of the relevant product or delivery mechanism and hold positions on a prescribed market either directly or indirectly in respect of which the person expects others to deliver to him or take delivery from him (or those acting in concert or colluding with him) of quantities of the qualifying investments or relevant products concerned.

Behaviour will also constitute market abuse where a person enters into a transaction or series of transactions with the purpose of positioning the price of a qualifying investment or relevant product at a distorted level dictated by the person concerned (MAR1.7.11). Factors to be taken into account will include the size of the position held, transaction size and transaction volume, market liquidity and market or credit-risk hedging (MAR1.7.12). Examples of the behaviour covered include entering into a series of transactions to ramp or drive up or down the price of a qualifying investment or value of an index.

Safe harbours in this case include acting in accordance with the London Metal Exchange 1998 rules on market aberrations (MAR1.7.15).

**Statutory exceptions**

The draft Code considers the two exceptions contained in the Act in relation to market abuse (MAR1.8.1). These comprise behaviour which in the opinion of the FSA does not amount to market abuse (s. 122(1)) and behaviour that conforms with a rule which includes a provision to the effect that that behaviour does not amount to market abuse (s. 118(8)). Both of these direct and indirect exceptions are referred to as safe harbours for the purposes of the draft Code. The rules-based exception will include permitted price stabilisation provisions as well as Chinese walls and Listing Rules concessions.

The statutory exceptions are distinct from the immunity from a penalty created where a person has either reasonably believed that behaviour did not constitute market abuse or took all reasonable precautions and due diligence to avoid engaging in market abuse (s. 123(2)(a) and (b)).

**Requiring or encouraging**

Under FSAMA 2000, s. 123(1), market abuse may be committed directly or by requiring or encouraging others to do so.

The draft Code provides some guidance with regard to determining whether a person's conduct or inaction amounts to requiring or encouraging (MAR1.9). Behaviour may, for example, amount to market abuse where a director of a company instructs an employee to deal in qualifying investments or relevant products (MAR1.9.3(1)). A person may recommend or advise others to engage in any activity which would constitute market abuse or try to persuade or otherwise incite them to engage in such behaviour (MAR1.9.3(2)). An employer who is aware of and permits an employee to engage in market abuse is encouraging market abuse (MAR1.9.3(3)).

There will be no market abuse where a person has passed information on to employees in connection with the proper performance of their functions, professional advisers, commercial counterparties, employee representatives or trade unions, or some other official body such as a government department, the Bank of England, the Competition Commission or any other statutory or regulatory body or authority (MAR1.9.6).

## DESIGNATED MARKETS AND INVESTMENTS

The Treasury is to prescribe by order which markets and investments are to be covered (s. 118(3)). The Treasury issued a consultation document on *Market Abuse: Prescribed Markets* in June 1999, which included a draft statutory instrument (draft Financial Services and Markets Act [2000] (Market Abuse) (Prescribed Markets and Qualifying Investments) Order). In preparing the draft Order, the Treasury stated that they took into account the expectations of market participants as to the integrity of the market, the reliance participants placed on the market for the dissemination of information relevant to the value of the investments traded and on the market facilities that enabled people to enter into transactions as well as the wider economic importance of the market.

While the specific listing to be adopted was not coterminous with market recognition under the Act, they would generally correspond. The draft Order accordingly applies to the six currently recognised investment exchanges (the London Stock Exchange (LSE), the London International Financial Futures and Options Exchange (LIFFE), the London Metal Exchange, the International Petroleum Exchange, OM London Exchange Ltd and Tradepoint Financial Networks). The Order also applies to each of the separate markets operated on each exchange, including for example, SEAQ-I and the main market on the LSE. It is expected that the final Order will also include Coredeal, which came into operation during the course of 2000. Qualifying investments were defined in the draft Order as all investments admitted to trading under the rules of any of the markets prescribed.

## PROCEDURE

Where the FSA proposes to impose a penalty, it must first provide a warning notice, which must, in particular, state the amount of the penalty or proposed censure statement (FSAMA 2000, s. 126(1), (2) and (3)). This initiates the procedure set out in Part XXVI of the Act (see chapter 28). If the FSA decides to take action, it must issue a decision notice which must again state the amount of the penalty or content of the statement (s. 127(1), (2) and (3)). This is subject to reference of the matter to the Financial Services and Markets Tribunal (under s. 127(4)), which is considered further in chapter 11.

The FSA may direct any RIE or recognised clearing house to terminate, suspend or limit the scope of any existing inquiry where it considers it desirable or expedient to do so (s. 128(1)).

The FSA may also apply to the court under ss. 381 or 383 to consider whether the circumstances are such that an injunction should be issued to restrain the market abuse or a restitution order should be made.

The Treasury (in Scotland, the Lord Advocate) may from time to time issue written guidance for the purpose of assisting relevant authorities to determine the action to be taken in relation to instances of market abuse where there is also the possibility of a criminal prosecution (s. 130).

## PENALTIES

On finding that market abuse has occurred, the FSA may impose a financial penalty (FSAMA 2000, s. 123(1)), publish a public censure (s. 123(3)), apply to the court for an injunction (s. 381) or restitution order (s. 383) or itself order restitution (s. 384).

The FSA may apply for an injunction where there is a reasonable likelihood that a person may engage in market abuse or where a person has already engaged in market abuse and there is a reasonable likelihood of him continuing to do so (s. 381(1)) or where steps could be taken to remedy or mitigate the market abuse (s. 381(2) and (6)). A court may also restrain a person from disposing of or otherwise dealing in any assets (s. 381(3) and (4)).

A court may order a person to pay to the FSA such sum as may be considered just having regard to the profits accrued or loss or other adverse effect suffered as a result of market abuse (s. 383(4)). The FSA is to pay the amounts received to such qualifying persons as the court may direct (s. 383(5)). A qualifying person is a person to whom the profits would otherwise have been attributable or who has suffered the loss or other adverse effect (s. 383(10)). The court may also require such accounts or other information to be supplied as it may require (s. 383(6)). The accounts and information may also have to be verified in such manner as the court may direct (s. 383(7)).

While the FSA is not obliged to impose any particular penalty in respect of market abuse under s. 123 of the Act, it is required to issue a statement of policy with regard to the imposition and amount of penalties and the operation of at least the main basis of the exception regime provided in respect of reasonable belief or reasonable precaution (s. 124(1)). The general approach of the FSA to enforcement is considered in chapters 16, 27 and 29.

The FSA's proposed approach to sanctions for market abuse is now set out in section 15 of its forthcoming Enforcement Manual (ENF15). The specific nature and amount of any compensation required or other penalty imposed will depend upon the particular circumstances. A number of factors are to be taken into account depending upon the nature of the penalty being considered. These may include matters relating to the seriousness of the contravention (such as nature and seriousness of breach, the extent to which it was deliberate or reckless, duration and frequency, adverse impact, profit or loss avoided, loss or costs imposed on other market users and possible repetition) or the behaviour of the person concerned (such as degree of cooperation with the FSA, corrective action or other compliance). The FSA may also consider the degree of sophistication of relevant market users, the extent to which the infraction may be dealt with by other authorities, its previous response, the impact of the penalty on the market or consumers and the disciplinary record and history of the firm in question (see, for example, ENF15.6.2).

The particular factors to be taken into account in determining the amount of a financial penalty include adverse effect on the market, deliberate or reckless conduct, whether the person to be penalised is an individual or a firm, the profit or loss avoided, conduct following contravention, disciplinary record and compliance history, previous action taken by the FSA and action taken by any other regulatory authorities (ENF15.9.4).

Where the same course of conduct may give rise to both a criminal offence and a breach of the market abuse provisions, the FSA will initially consider whether a criminal prosecution should be commenced either by itself or some other authority. Where it is considered not appropriate to commence criminal proceedings, the FSA will determine whether it would be appropriate to exercise any of its civil or regulatory enforcement powers under FSAMA 2000 having regard to all of the factors referred to above. The FSA's concern in all cases will be to determine whether the action is desirable for the protection of investors or for the purpose of maintaining public confidence in the integrity of financial markets. This is subject to any guidance given by the Treasury or Lord Advocate under s. 130.

The Enforcement Manual also includes special provisions dealing with the FSA's possible future endorsement under s. 143 of the City Code on Takeovers and Mergers (ENF15.12) and with action involving overseas authorities (ENF15.13). The provisions relating to the Takeover code contained in s. 143 are distinct from s. 120 and not yet addressed by the FSA. Section 143 is concerned with discipline for breach of the Takeover Code at the request of the Panel and s. 120 with the use of the Code as a defence to allegations of market abuse.

# Chapter Eleven
# Hearings and Appeals

*Loretta Minghella*

Part IX of the Financial Services and Markets Act 2000 (FSAMA 2000) establishes the Financial Services and Markets Tribunal, which is to be fully independent of the FSA and will be run by the Lord Chancellor's Department. This is different from the current Financial Services Tribunal under the Financial Services Act 1986 (FSA 1986), which sits very infrequently and is run by the Treasury. The new Tribunal will hear cases referred to it by those who wish to contest the FSA's decisions to issue them with decision notices and supervisory notices, e.g., to impose penalties or withdraw approval or authorisation. Given that it will hear referrals in relation to a much larger number of firms across such a wide range of business, it is to be expected that it will be more active than the old Tribunal. Its design therefore assumes a rather greater significance.

The Act deals with the conduct of Tribunal proceedings in a number of different places. First, the Lord Chancellor is given power (under s. 132(3)) to make rules about the conduct of proceedings before the Tribunal. Schedule 13 and s. 133 also make provision about Tribunal proceedings, to varying extents subject to rules made under s. 132(3).

Being an independent and impartial tribunal established by law, with full first instance jurisdiction, the Tribunal is the Act's principal mechanism for ensuring that the administrative-based enforcement process satisfies the requirements of art. 6 of the European Convention on Human Rights. The Tribunal will, of course, itself be subject to the provisions of the Human Rights Act 1998.

## COMPOSITION OF THE TRIBUNAL

The composition of the Tribunal is a subject which has excited significant industry and parliamentary interest. Schedule 13 to FSAMA 2000 provides that the Lord Chancellor must appoint a panel of persons to serve as chairmen of the Tribunal, who must be lawyers with a seven-year general qualification in England and Wales or equivalent professional qualifications in Scotland or Northern Ireland (sch. 13, para. 3). From that panel the Lord Chancellor must appoint one person to be President and one to be Deputy President (sch. 13, para. 2). The President and Deputy President must have 10-year general qualifications or their equivalent.

The Lord Chancellor must also appoint members of a lay panel, who must be people who appear to him to be qualified by experience or otherwise to deal with matters of the kind that may be referred to the Tribunal (sch. 13, para. 3(4)). The FSA has indicated that the Committee which will take disciplinary decisions will include practitioner appointees. Some have voiced concerns that the broadly drawn criteria in sch. 13 would allow the Tribunal to be staffed without any industry practitioners at all: the wording is certainly broad enough to allow the Lord Chancellor to look for experience outside the industry as well as within it.

The terms on which Tribunal members are appointed (including remuneration and expenses) are matters for the Lord Chancellor, who may remove them on the ground of incapacity or misbehaviour (sch. 13, paras 4 and 5).

The Lord Chancellor may appoint staff for the Tribunal to be paid from his own budget (sch. 13, para. 6).

## REFERENCES TO THE TRIBUNAL

### Time limits for references

Section 133 provides that a reference to the Tribunal must be made within 28 days of the decision notice or supervisory notice, or such other period as may be specified in rules of procedure made under s. 132(3). The period may be extended by the Tribunal, if there is nothing in the rules to the contrary (s. 133(2)).

### The FSA's role after the issue of a decision notice

The FSA must not take the action specified in a decision notice, for example, to impose a penalty, during the period within which the matter could be referred to the Tribunal (s. 133(9)(a)). If the matter is so referred, the FSA must wait until the matter has been determined by the Tribunal and, if appropriate, any appeal from the Tribunal's decision has been finally determined (s. 133(9)(b)). This provision does not apply to supervisory notices, some of which can have effect in advance of the decision of the Tribunal.

## PROCEEDINGS BEFORE THE TRIBUNAL

### Constitution of the Tribunal

The President of the Tribunal is to make standing arrangements for the selection of persons to act as members of the Tribunal for the purposes of a reference

(FSAMA 2000, sch. 13, para. 7(1)). On any reference at least one member must be from the panel of chairmen (sch. 13, para. 7(2)). Where it appears to the Tribunal that a matter involves a question of fact of special difficulty, it may appoint one or more experts to assist it (sch. 13, para. 7(4)).

## Tribunal procedure

Paragraph 9 of sch. 13 sets out the matters for which rules made under s. 132(3) may make provision. It is interesting to note that the rules may specify the circumstances in which hearings may be held in private. The Tribunal will generally be required by art. 6 of the European Convention on Human Rights to hold a public hearing unless the right to a public hearing is waived by the person whose rights or obligations are being determined, though art. 6 does contemplate some exceptions to this.

Practice directions about the Tribunal's procedure may be given by the Tribunal President (sch. 13, para. 10).

## What evidence may the Tribunal consider?

When the Bill was only in draft, the Tribunal was to be called an Appeal Tribunal and it looked possible that its jurisdiction in relation to factual matters could be limited. This provoked an enormous amount of controversy and resulted in clarification from the government that the Tribunal would have full jurisdiction to entertain all matters of fact. This is provided for by s. 133(3), which states that the Tribunal may consider any evidence relating to the subject-matter of the reference, whether or not it was available to the FSA at the material time.

The Tribunal may summon any person to give evidence or produce documents to it (sch. 13, para. 11(1)). Evidence may be taken on oath (sch. 13, para. 11(2)). A person who fails to comply with a Tribunal summons or who interferes with or suppresses documentary evidence is guilty of an offence (sch. 13, para. 11(3)). Less serious cases may be dealt with by magistrates imposing the maximum fine available to them (which is £5,000) (sch. 13, para. 11(4)). A conviction in the Crown Court may result in a term of up to two years' imprisonment and/or an unlimited fine (sch. 13, para. 11(5)).

## Legal assistance before the Tribunal: coverage of the scheme

The government decided to make provision in FSAMA 2000 for the protections of art. 6(2) and (3) of the European Convention on Human Rights to be afforded in market abuse proceedings. One of these protections, the provision of free legal assistance in appropriate cases to those who cannot afford their own, is included in Part IX of the Act. Sections 134 and 135 authorise the Lord Chancellor to establish and administer an assistance scheme. Section 136 makes provision for the funding of the scheme.

It is largely for the Lord Chancellor to decide the scope of any scheme by regulations. It is worth noting that any scheme would cover legal assistance 'in connection with proceedings before the Tribunal' (s. 134(1)). It would not appear capable of covering the administrative stages before a Tribunal reference is made.

There is only one category of person for whom the scheme, if one is made, can make provision, namely, an individual who has, pursuant to s. 127(4), referred to the Tribunal an FSA decision to impose a penalty or publish a statement in respect of that individual's market abuse under s. 123. There may be other criteria in the regulations for such a person to satisfy (s. 135(1)(d)).

The Act makes detailed provision about the scope of the scheme. For example, the scheme may make provision for the kind of assistance and who may provide it and the process for making and determining applications. It will be possible for assistance to be provided subject to conditions, such as a requirement on the applicant to make a contribution to the cost of the assistance.

## Legal assistance before the Tribunal: funding the scheme

Legal aid is normally funded by the ordinary taxpayer. The funding arrangements for legal assistance before the Financial Services and Markets Tribunal are contained in s. 136 of FSAMA 2000.

Unusually, the government decided that this scheme, which had been introduced into the Bill following industry pressure to provide additional protections in the market abuse context, would be paid for by the industry. Whilst the Lord Chancellor will use money provided by Parliament, he will be able to issue demands to the FSA from time to time to cover the actual or anticipated cost of the scheme. The FSA will pay that money to him and he will pay it into the Consolidated Fund. In this way, the scheme should effectively be self-financing.

The FSA will have power to make rules requiring authorised firms (or a subset of them) to pay for the scheme. The government's decision here is an interesting one. Whilst the market abuse regime applies to authorised and unauthorised market abusers, and is designed to reinforce market confidence as a whole, the costs of the legal assistance scheme are to be borne only by the authorised community. Indeed, the FSA has discretion to limit the funding to a class of authorised firms.

## DECISIONS OF THE TRIBUNAL

### What is the Tribunal's role?

FSAMA 2000, s. 133(4), provides that it is for the Tribunal to determine what, if any, is the appropriate action for the FSA to take in relation to the referred matter. It is not for the Tribunal to take the action itself. On determining a reference, the Tribunal must remit the matter to the FSA with such directions as the Tribunal considers appropriate for giving effect to its determination. Under s. 133(8), the Tribunal may, on determining a reference, also make recommendations as to the

FSA's regulating provisions or its procedures. Whilst the FSA is not bound to follow any such recommendations, they would be bound to carry significant weight.

## Extent of the Tribunal's determinations

Given that the Tribunal has full jurisdiction to hear all matters of fact, it might have been expected that it could order the FSA, following a reference, to take *any* action which it is open to the FSA to take under the Act. However, the Tribunal's powers of determination are somewhat narrowed by s. 133(6) and (7).

To understand these provisions it is necessary first to recall that decision notices may be issued under various provisions of the Act. They may relate to penalties for market abuse, for example. In those cases, the government has decided, as a matter of policy, to apply the protections of the ECHR relating to criminal proceedings, limiting what use can be made of compelled statements and providing free or subsidised legal assitance in cases of hardship. However, decision notices may relate to disciplinary penalties which do not attract these protections. The FSA may issue a decision notice under one Part of the Act only if the warning notice which preceded it was issued under the same Part. In turn, s. 133(6) prevents the Tribunal from going further than the FSA could. For example, in hearing a case about a disciplinary penalty, the Tribunal is prevented from concluding that a market abuse penalty should be imposed. This is designed to reduce further the possibility that any relevant Convention rights have not been afforded during the process.

Furthermore, different procedures apply prior to the issue of decision notices and supervisory notices, notably in relation to the disclosure of evidence and in relation to third-party rights. Section 133(7) ensures that these procedures cannot be circumvented. It does this by precluding the Tribunal, when the reference follows a supervisory notice, from directing the FSA to do something which would have otherwise required the giving of a decision notice.

## Form of decision

A decision of the Tribunal must be committed to writing, signed by the chairman, and must state the reasons for the decision and whether it was unanimous or by majority (FSAMA 2000, sch. 13, para. 12(2)). The decision must be communicated to each party, and the written reasons sent as soon as reasonably practicable to each party and any authorised person concerned (if not a party) (sch. 13, para. 12(3)). The Treasury must also be sent a copy (sch. 13, para. 12(4)).

## Costs

The question of who should bear the costs of Tribunal proceedings was hotly debated in Parliament. FSAMA 2000, sch. 13, para. 13(1), provides that the

Tribunal may order costs against any party if it considers that the party has behaved vexatiously, unreasonably or frivolously. Such order may extend to all or part of the costs or expenses of other parties in connection with the proceedings. It is submitted that this would not extend to any costs incurred prior to the giving by the FSA of the notice which resulted in referral.

There is also provision in sch. 13, para. 13(2), for the FSA to be ordered to pay costs or other expenses of other parties if the FSA's decision which is the subject of the reference was unreasonable.

### The FSA's role in response to a determination

The FSA must act in accordance with the Tribunal's determination and any directions it gives (s. 133(10)). It may revise its regulating provisions or its procedures following any recommendation which accompanies the determination, but would have to follow the ordinary statutory procedures, including consultation, before doing so.

### How may the Tribunal's order be enforced?

The Act provides that the Tribunal's order may be enforced as if it were an order of a county court or an order of the Court of Session in Scotland (s. 133(11)).

## APPEALS

Appeals from decisions of the Tribunal are to the Court of Appeal (or the Court of Session in Scotland) on a point of law only (FSAMA 2000, s. 137(1)). Such appeals may only be brought with the permission of the Tribunal or the relevant appellate court (s. 137(1) and (2)). Moreover, the point must arise from a decision of the Tribunal disposing of the reference (s. 137(1)).

Where the appellate court decides that the Tribunal's decision was wrong in law, it may remit the matter to the Tribunal or itself make a determination (s. 137(3)). There are no provisions corresponding to s. 133(5) to (11) which describe how the FSA is to respond to any determination of the appellate court and how any order of that court is to be enforced. It may perhaps be assumed that the intention was to enable the appellate court to do anything the Tribunal could have done and to require the FSA to act accordingly. Rules made under s. 132 can deal with matters related to these appeals (s. 137(6)).

Appeals from the Court of Session and the Court of Appeal lie, with leave, to the House of Lords (s. 137(4) and (5)).

# Chapter Twelve
# Rules and Guidance

## Mark Threipland

Part X of the Financial Services and Markets Act 2000 (FSAMA 2000) confers upon the FSA its principal rule-making powers for authorised persons. In addition, it gives the FSA power to issue guidance on regulatory matters. It also sets out the procedures that the FSA must follow in exercising its rule-making powers, including those conferred in other Parts of the Act, and the procedures for competition scrutiny of the exercise of those powers. The FSA is engaged in a comprehensive consultation exercise on its proposed *Handbook of Rules and Guidance*. Table 12.1 shows the proposed contents of the *Handbook* and the progress of consultation.

**Table 12.1** Proposed structure of the FSA's *Handbook of Rules and Guidance*
CP = Consultation Paper

| Block | Topic | Latest proposals as at October 2000 (all available on the FSA's website: www.fsa.gov.uk) |
| --- | --- | --- |
| 1 High-level standards | Principles for Businesses | Policy Statement, October 1999 CP 57, annex E |
| | Threshold Conditions | CP 63 |
| | Statements of Principle and Code of Practice for Approved Persons | Policy Statement, June 2000 'High level standards' |
| | Criteria for Assessing Fitness and Propriety of Approved Persons | Policy Statement, June 2000 'High level standards' |

| Block | Topic | Latest proposals as at October 2000 (all available on the FSA's website: www.fsa.gov.uk) |
|---|---|---|
| 1 High-level standards | Senior Management Arrangements, Systems and Controls | Policy Statement, 2000 'High level standards' |
| | General provisions | CP 71 |
| 2 Business standards | Prudential Sourcebook | |
| | Interim (banks) | CP 52 |
| | Interim (building societies) | CP 51 |
| | Interim (insurers) | CP 41 |
| | Interim (friendly societies) | CP 41 |
| | Interim (investment business) | CP 54, CP 68 |
| | Integrated Prudential Sourcebook | CP 31 and Response Statement outline the approach |
| | Conduct of Business Sourcebook | CP 45, CP 57 |
| | Market Conduct Sourcebook | |
| | Inter-professional Code | CP 47 |
| | Code of Market Conduct | CP 59 |
| | Price Stabilising Rules | CP 40 |
| | Training and Competence Sourcebook | CP 34, CP 60 |
| | Money Laundering Sourcebook | CP 47 |
| 3 Regulatory processes | Authorisation Manual | CP 63 |
| | Supervision Manual | CP 53 (Controlled functions rules), CP 64 |
| | Enforcement Manual | CP 65 |

| Block | Topic | Latest proposals as at October 2000 (all available on the FSA's website: www.fsa.gov.uk) |
|---|---|---|
| 4   Redress | Complaints Sourcebook | CP 49 |
|  | Compensation Sourcebook | CP 58 |
|  | Pensions Review Materials |  |
| 5   Specialist sourcebooks | Collective Investment Schemes | CP 62 |
|  | RIE/RCH | CP 39 |
|  | Exempt Professional Firms | CP 69 |
|  | UK Listing Authority |  |
|  | Lloyd's | CP 48, CP 66 |
|  | Credit Unions |  |
| 6 | Glossary |  |
|  | Index |  |

## EXISTING LEGISLATION

The existing regulators impose obligations in significantly different ways. The FSA 1986 gives the FSA (as the 'designated agency') explicit powers to impose obligations on authorised persons through its rules, which have the status of secondary legislation. These are unusual in that the provisions made under them carry the force of law but do not require the approval of Parliament. The self-regulating organisations (IMRO, PIA and SFA) also impose obligations directly on their members, based largely on contract law, and the recognised professional bodies (such as the Law Society) impose direct obligations under the terms of their constitutions. In contrast, under the Banking Act 1987, Building Societies Act 1986, Friendly Societies Act 1992 and Insurance Companies Act 1982, obligations are set out in primary and secondary legislation, which the prudential regulators have supplemented by means of prudential guidance. The harmonised approach of FSAMA 2000 means that the FSA is potentially able to take a significantly different approach to regulation in some areas of financial services.

## FSA'S POWERS TO IMPOSE REQUIREMENTS

FSAMA 2000 broadly follows the model of FSA 1986. The FSA is entitled to impose binding requirements on authorised (and in some circumstances unauthorised) persons which have the force of law without parliamentary approval. It is constitutionally unusual for a private company like the FSA to be given powers to make secondary legislation, and secondary legislation made by government departments normally requires parliamentary approval, whether by the affirmative or negative resolution procedures. The Act therefore represents a significant shift of power (and responsibility) from Parliament and the government to the FSA when compared with the prudential regulators, and these powers have been conferred within a defined framework of responsibilities and accountability arrangements. These include the constitutional accountability framework in Part I, and the constraints attached to the individual powers, including consultation requirements.

As well as the express constraints set out in the Act, the FSA's rule-making powers, as powers to make secondary legislation, are subject to constraints under public law. Judicial review of the FSA's rules would be possible on the usual grounds, including acting unreasonably, use of the powers for an improper purpose and so on. In addition, and in contrast to the prudential guidance of the prudential regulators and contractually based rules of the self-regulating organisations, the rules of the FSA are subject to the public law prohibition on unauthorised sub-delegation of a legislative power conferred by Parliament. The normal principle is that a delegate may not sub-delegate unless expressly or impliedly authorised to do so. Both by reason of this doctrine, and the express constraints in the Act, the FSA's ability to modify the application of its rules on an individual basis is limited, except where permitted by the Act .

There are therefore essentially two ways in which the FSA may impose and vary requirements on authorised persons (and others): by using powers to make general provisions applying to classes of persons or by using powers in the Act to vary and interpret requirements on a case-by-case basis. Both types of powers are described below.

## GENERAL PROVISIONS APPLYING TO CLASSES OF PERSONS

The FSA's powers to make provisions applicable to classes of persons may be conveniently categorised using the terminology used by the FSA in its *Handbook* (which is not always that of the Act) as described below.

### Principles

The FSA has proposed 11 broad 'principles for businesses', laying down standards that the FSA expects authorised persons to meet and expressed at a fairly high level of generality (*The FSA's Principles for Businesses: Response on Consultation Paper 13* (October 1999)). Breach may lead to enforcement action by the FSA, but the FSA has determined that contravention should not trigger private rights of action for damages under FSAMA 2000, s. 150. The terminology is potentially confusing, as these principles will be made under the rule-making powers and will have the status of rules under the Act. They should be distinguished from the statements of principle for approved persons to be issued under Part V, which will not be rules but have a distinct status under the Act (FSA, *High Level Standards for Firms and Individuals* (Policy Statement), June 2000). Detailed consultation procedures apply to both types of principle.

## Rules

Rules are provisions binding on authorised (and in certain cases unauthorised) persons, contravention of which will generally trigger the full range of sanctions, that is, enforcement action by the FSA and private rights of action for damages. Although most rules will be made under the general rule-making power in s. 138, there are many other rule-making powers for specific purposes in Part X and in other parts of the Act. Rules may apply in different ways to different persons or activities (s. 156(1)), so cannot be struck down as unreasonable merely because they are unequal in their operation as between different classes (see *Kruse* v *Johnson* [1898] 2 QB 91). Rules may also contain incidental and supplemental provisions and, importantly, transitional provisions (s. 156(2)). The FSA proposes clearly to mark binding rules in the *Handbook* with an 'R' in the margin. Detailed consultation procedures apply to a proposal to make rules.

### Evidential provisions and codes

FSAMA 2000 gives the FSA three powers to make evidential provisions, or codes with similar effect. Section 149 enables the FSA to make rules (called 'evidential provisions') which, if contravened, will not lead to enforcement action or other sanctions. An evidential provision must be linked to another rule and must indicate that its contravention can be relied on as tending to establish contravention of the linked rule, or that compliance with the evidential provision can be relied on as tending to establish compliance with the linked rule (or both). This power enables the FSA to elaborate on rules that are framed at a higher level of generality, including the principles for businesses. The FSA proposes clearly to mark evidential provisions in the *Handbook* with an 'E' in the margin. Because they are rules, the detailed procedures for making rules also apply to making evidential provisions. Evidential provisions are new to financial services regulation. The classic example of material with this type of evidential status is the Highway Code, which is non-mandatory but which is given similar legal significance by s. 38(7) of the Road Traffic Act 1988 in determining whether road traffic offences have been committed. Breach of the Highway Code does not necessarily establish negligence, nor is the observance of the code of itself an answer to an allegation of negligence (*Croston* v *Vaughan* [1938] 1 KB 540 at p. 552) but a contravention may as a matter of fact amount to strong evidence to prove lack of proper driving (*Trentham* v *Rowlands* [1974] RTR 164). It seems that compliance or contravention of an evidential provision with the relevant evidential effect will place an evidential burden on the FSA or the firm, respectively, to prove contravention of or compliance with the linked rule.

There are separate powers to issue a code relevant to the statements of principle for approved persons (s. 64) and a code relevant to the commission of market abuse (s. 119). These codes are also given express evidential status and there are specific consultation procedures for making them.

## Published guidance

FSAMA 2000, s. 157(1), gives the FSA power to issue and publish guidance on a wide variety of matters, including its own rules and the criminal perimeter created under the Act. This guidance may consist only of 'information and advice' and cannot therefore impose binding requirements, vary binding requirements or change the burden of proof. But even if it does not formally impose or vary requirements, firms and other persons may in practice heed guidance as an expression of the FSA's views on the application of its requirements and the Act, to avoid possible enforcement action by the FSA.

The FSA proposes clearly to mark guidance in the *Handbook* with a 'G' in the margin. Where guidance is given to persons subject to the FSA's rules and is intended to have continuing effect, it will generally fall within the definition of 'general guidance' in s. 158(5). This means that it must be issued by the FSA's Board (sch. 1, paras. 1(2) and 5(2)) and is subject to competition scrutiny (s. 159(1)) as well as being subject to the FSA's general duties (s. 2(4)(c)) and judicial review. Further, the issue of guidance under s. 157 in relation to rules to a class of regulated persons requires prior consultation in the same way as rules, recognising its regulatory effect (s. 157(3)). The FSA can use its resources to support the giving of information and advice by third parties (s. 157(2)), which may assist the FSA in pursuing its public awareness objective (s. 4).

What reliance can persons place on the FSA's guidance? The Act is silent on this issue, but it seems that some reliance can nonetheless be placed on it in appropriate circumstances for the reasons described below.

*FSA enforcement action*    The FSA has stated that 'if a firm acts in accordance with general guidance in the circumstances contemplated by that guidance, then the FSA will proceed on the footing that it has complied with the aspect of the rule to which the guidance refers' (*The FSA's Approach to Giving Guidance and Waivers to Firms* (Policy Statement), September 1999). Where the FSA is taking enforcement action against a person who has properly relied on guidance from the FSA, it seems that person may be able to prevent the action under the public law doctrine of 'legitimate expectation'.

*Contravention of the criminal perimeter*    Contravention of the general prohibition (s. 19) or the restriction on financial promotion (s. 21) is an offence. But there is a defence if the defendant can prove that he took all reasonable precautions and exercised all due diligence to avoid committing the offence (ss. 23(3) and 25(2)(b)). It seems that acting in reliance on guidance from the FSA may assist in proving this defence, even if the prosecuting authority is not the FSA itself, as was recognised by the minister (*Hansard* HL, 27 March 2000, col. 562). If the FSA is the prosecuting authority, the doctrine of 'legitimate expectation' may also be relevant as discussed above. A further sanction for contravention of the general prohibition or the restriction on financial promotion is unenforceability of contracts. But a court may allow agreements to be enforced if this is 'just and equitable', having regard to whether there was a reasonable belief that the offence was not being committed (ss. 28(3) to (5) and 30(4) and (6)). It seems that reliance on guidance from the FSA may assist in proving such belief.

*Actions for damages*   If an action for damages is brought against an authorised person for contravention of a rule (s. 150), it seems that the FSA's general guidance is likely to have some influence on the courts, although it clearly cannot bind the courts. Where there is a question of construction of the contents of existing rules made under FSA 1986, the FSA has a right to make representations to the court (Civil Procedure Rules 1998, sch. 1; RSC Order 93, rule 22). Although rarely if ever used, it seems likely that this will be continued under the new Act. This will also be relevant in relation to a claim for damages under s. 71 alleging failure of an authorised person to obtain approval for a person performing a controlled function, as the scope of those functions is set by rules (s. 58(3)).

### Directions and other requirements imposed on classes of persons

The FSA has many administrative powers under the Act to issue directions and other requirements applicable to classes of both authorised and unauthorised persons. Examples are a direction that the exemption from the general prohibition for members of designated professional bodies is not to apply to classes of professionals (s. 328(1)) and a direction stating how to apply for a Part IV permission (s. 51(3)). The constraints on the FSA's use of these powers are the FSA's general duties (as regards the FSA's general policy and principles: s. 2(4)(d)) and judicial review, and certain additional constraints attached to particular powers. The consequences of contravention of an administrative direction or requirement depends on its nature. For authorised persons, it seems that all the consequences of contravention of 'requirements' imposed under the Act will apply (including discipline under Part XIV and injunctions and restitution under Part XXV), in addition to any specific consequence attached to a particular direction. The FSA proposes clearly to mark administrative directions or requirements appearing in the *Handbook* with a 'D' in the margin.

### VARYING AND INTERPRETING REQUIREMENTS CASE-BY-CASE

The FSA has various powers to set regulatory requirements on a case-by-case basis, as described below. Each has its own accountability arrangements.

**Variation of permission and intervention**

The FSA is able to vary an authorised person's Part IV permission on its own initiative, including by imposing limitations or requirements (FSAMA 2000, s. 45). For firms from EEA States exercising passport rights or Treaty rights in the UK, there are similar but more limited powers under Part XIII (there described as intervention powers). In each case, the grounds on which the FSA may act are specified, the FSA is required to follow a published procedure and its decisions may be referred to the Financial Services and Markets Tribunal.

**Waiving or modifying the application of rules for individual firms**

Section 148 confers a power on the FSA to waive or modify its rules. Before granting a waiver, the FSA is required to satisfy itself of a number of matters, essentially that compliance with the rule concerned is unduly burdensome or does not achieve its purpose, and that the waiver will not result in undue risk to persons protected by the rule. A major transitional issue for authorised persons will be whether, and if so how, waivers from existing requirements will be 'grandfathered' into the new regulatory regime. The SROs are currently able to waive their rules, but there are some significant differences in the ability of the FSA to waive its rules under the Act, as follows:

(a)   The waiver power applies to rules applicable to authorised persons made under most, but not all, of the FSA's rule-making powers. An applicant for a waiver will have to consider whether the rule concerned can be waived (there are similar waiver powers for collective investment scheme rules and recognised body rules in ss. 250 and 294).

(b)   The FSA is entitled to waive a rule only on request or with consent. So it will not be possible to continue, in the same way, the current practice of SROs of granting interim waivers to large groups of firms on their own initiative.

(c)   The FSA is required to publish waivers, unless it is 'inappropriate or unnecessary' (s. 148(6) to (8)). The FSA is, amongst other things, required to consider commercial interests in deciding whether to publish. Publication should aid transparency.

**Individual guidance**

The FSA's power in s. 157(1) to issue guidance includes power to give guidance on an individual basis both to authorised and unauthorised persons. Just like published guidance, individual guidance cannot impose binding requirements, but may provide information and advice, such as the FSA's interpretation of how a rule applies in a firm's particular circumstances. The constraints on the FSA's use of this power are the FSA's general duties (as regards the general policy and principles underlying its use: s. 2(4)(d)) and judicial review. Although the FSA has the power to charge for individual guidance, it is not the current practice to do so. The ability to rely on individual guidance from the FSA was the subject of much controversy during the passage of the Bill through Parliament, particularly in the context of the market abuse regime. The government resisted pressure to give the FSA specific powers to operate a 'no action letter' procedure with formal status, or to put the FSA under a formal obligation to give guidance on request. But even in the absence of any formal status for the FSA's guidance, it seems that some reliance can nonetheless be placed on it in appropriate circumstances as described above for published guidance. The FSA has stated that 'the FSA would not take regulatory action against a firm for behaviour in line with current written guidance to it in the circumstances contemplated by the guidance' (*The FSA's Approach to Giving Guidance and Waivers to Firms* (Policy Statement), September 1999).

## Exercising administrative powers of direction or powers to impose requirements

There are many administrative powers to make directions or impose requirements on an individual basis, applicable to both authorised and unauthorised persons. For example, a requirement to provide additional information imposed on an authorised person seeking to vary permission (s. 49(4)). The constraints on the FSA's use of these powers are the FSA's general duties (as regards the general policy and principles underlying their use: s. 2(4)(d)) and judicial review, and in certain cases constraints attached to a particular power. The consequences of contravention of administrative directions were described above. When introduced into Parliament, the Bill included an administrative power that would have enabled the FSA to set the financial resources requirements of authorised persons on an individual basis, but this was removed by government amendment. So the FSA will have to use the other tools described above to continue its current policy of setting capital and other ratios for banks and building societies on an individual basis.

### GENERAL RULE-MAKING POWER

### Persons to whom general rules apply

FSAMA 2000, s. 138, confers power on the FSA to make 'general rules' applying to authorised persons, and the bulk of the rules in the *Handbook* will be made under this power. The application of general rules to EEA firms exercising passport rights in the UK is limited, because general rules may not restrict the activities that they may carry on or regulate matters (such as financial resources) which are reserved to home State regulators under the Single Market Directives.

### Activities to which general rules apply

General rules apply with respect to the carrying on of regulated activities and other activities which are not regulated activities. For example, the general rule-making power will enable the FSA to make financial resources rules imposing capital adequacy and liquidity requirements, rules relating to a firm's systems and controls and rules regulating the conduct of a firm's business with customers. The power to make rules with respect to non-regulated activities was subject to some controversy during passage of the Bill through Parliament. An important constraint on the FSA's ability to impose rules on a non-regulated business of an authorised person is that the purpose of general rules must be the protection of consumers of regulated activity services (see below). For example, the FSA will be able to impose financial resources requirements relating to non-regulated aspects of an authorised person's business, to prevent risk to the solvency of the authorised person.

There is no specific restriction on the ability of the FSA to extend conduct of business regulation to areas where this is currently limited, such as general insurance business and deposit-taking. However, the FSA has indicated that it does not intend to do so (*The Conduct of Business Sourcebook* (Consultation Paper 45a), part I, para. 2.8). FSAMA 2000, s. 138(3), clarifies that the power to make general rules is not limited by the FSA's other powers. For example, the fact that Part V gives the FSA specific power to issue broad statements of principle for approved persons does not imply that the high-level principles for businesses cannot be made under s. 138.

## Purpose for which general rules can be made

The purpose for which general rules may be made is the protection of consumers of regulated activity services. It is important to distinguish between this purpose and the FSA's regulatory objectives. Furtherance of the regulatory objectives alone is not a valid purpose, but rather in making rules for the purpose of protecting consumers, the FSA must ensure they are compatible with the objectives (s. 2). Under s. 138(4), there need not be a direct relationship between the authorised persons to whom the rules apply and the consumers who are protected by the rules, so rules to prevent systemic risk are possible. The definition of 'consumer' in s. 138(7) is sufficiently wide to include those with interests derived from the use of services by others (e.g., beneficiaries of a life policy), the interests of beneficiaries of trusts (whether the user of services or the authorised person is the trustee) and counterparties to principal-to-principal transactions.

## Territorial scope of general rules

There is no territorial limit on the FSA's general rule-making power. Subject to the constraints discussed in 'Procedures for making rules' below, the FSA could, in theory, apply general rules to the worldwide activities of an authorised person (other than a passporting EEA firm), including activities carried on from an overseas place of business with overseas persons. In practice some requirements, such as financial resources rules, apply in relation to a firm as a legal entity and territorial limitations would make no sense. In other instances, the FSA is required by the Single Market Directives to apply some rules with extraterritorial effect. For example, rules protecting client money and assets are the responsibility of the home State under the Investment Services Directive (93/22/EEC) and must be applied to UK investment firms carrying on business from branches in other EEA

States under the passport. In many other cases, the FSA has proposed limitations on the territorial scope of its rules (for example, *The Conduct of Business Sourcebook* (Consultation Paper 45a, annex A, COB 1.4), limits the territorial scope of the draft conduct of business rules). During progress of the Bill through Parliament, there was considerable opposition pressure to include express territorial limitations on the scope of the FSA's rule-making powers, but these were resisted by the government.

**Miscellaneous ancillary matters**

FSAMA 2000, s. 139, supplements the FSA's general rule-making power. Section 139(1) enables the FSA's rules on the handling of clients' money to override certain principles of the general law, and is similar to s. 55 of FSA 1986. In particular, rules may create a statutory trust designed to protect clients' money from an authorised person's general creditors in the event of its insolvency, which is an important principle of investor protection. Rules may also permit authorised persons to retain interest earned on clients' money held under such a trust, for which the firm might otherwise be accountable. The FSA is proposing to make extensive client money rules, carrying forward similar rules of the FSA and SROs under FSA 1986 (*The Conduct of Business Sourcebook* (Consultation Paper 45a), annex A, COB 9.3). There is a large body of case law on the liability of a bank as constructive trustee for money wrongfully withdrawn from a client account. Section 139(2) clarifies that a bank is liable for wrongful withdrawal of money from an authorised person's client account only where the bank had knowledge that the withdrawal was wrongful and 'deliberately' failed to make enquiries.

Section 139(4) enables the FSA's cancellation rules to override a contract between an authorised person and its customer by granting the customer unilateral 'cooling-off' rights to cancel or withdraw from a contract after it has been entered into and recover any premium paid. Again, this carries forward a similar FSA 1986 provision (s. 51) and the FSA has proposed to make cancellation rules similar to existing rules which apply mainly to sales of packaged products such as unit trusts, life policies, PEPs and ISAs (*The Conduct of Business Sourcebook* (Consultation Paper 45a), annex A, COB 6.7). Cooling-off rights are an important mechanism for investor protection as a means of mitigating the effects of high-pressure selling, particularly where this is associated with cold-calling. Various EC Directives do or will require cooling-off rights to be given, for example, the Third Life Directive (92/96/EEC, art. 15) and the proposed Distance Marketing Directive.

## OTHER SPECIFIC RULE-MAKING POWERS IN PART X

Part X of FSAMA 2000 contains a number of specific rule-making powers (and a power for the Treasury to supplement certain rules by order) in addition to the general rule-making power. Those of particular interest are described below.

## Rules restricting the activities of managers of unit trusts and insurance companies

FSAMA 2000, s. 140, enables the FSA to make rules to implement art. 6 of the UCITS Directive (85/611/EEC) prohibiting a manager of an authorised unit trust scheme from carrying on activities other than management of schemes, in a similar way to FSA 1986, s. 83. Section 141(1) enables the FSA to make rules implementing requirements of insurance Directives to prohibit insurance companies from carrying on business other than insurance business in a similar way to the Insurance Companies Act 1982, s. 16 (FSA, *Prudential Sourcebook Insurers*, vol. 1, Rules (Consultation Paper 41b), r. 1.3).

## Rules endorsing the Takeover Code

FSAMA 2000, s. 143, enables the FSA to make rules endorsing the City Code on Takeovers and Mergers and the Rules Governing Substantial Acquisitions of Shares, just as the FSA was able to endorse them under FSA 1986 following its amendment in 1989. Endorsement would provide a mechanism enabling the FSA to exercise its disciplinary powers over an authorised person or approved person for a contravention of the endorsed provisions, but only at the request of the Takeover Panel. Endorsement would also give some statutory backing to the regulation of takeovers in the United Kingdom which are otherwise regulated under voluntary arrangements. This may become particularly important should statutory backing be required under an EC Directive relating to takeover regulation. The procedural requirements in s. 143, which the FSA must follow in order to make endorsing rules, are similar to those for other rules.

## Price stabilising rules

FSAMA 2000, s. 144 enables the FSA to continue arrangements under FSA 1986, s. 48(2)(i), for making rules relating to stabilising the price of new issues of securities. The FSA has issued draft rules (*The Price Stabilising Rules* (Consultation Paper 40)). Stabilisation is regarded as a legitimate method of enabling the market to absorb new issues, but could in some circumstances constitute the misleading statements and practices offences (s. 397(2), (3)) and insider dealing (Criminal Justice Act 1993, Part V) and constitute market abuse (FSAMA 2000, s. 118). Compliance with price stabilising rules provides a defence, or 'safe harbour', for both authorised and unauthorised persons against these criminal offences (s. 397(4), (5)(b); Criminal Justice Act 1993, sch. 1, para. 5) and under the market abuse regime (FSAMA 2000, s. 118(8); FSA, *The Price Stabilising Rules* (Consultation Paper 40), annex A, S1.1(2)(c)). One particular innovation from FSA 1986 is that FSAMA 2000, s. 144(3), enables the FSA to endorse overseas price stabilising rules for the purposes of s. 397(5)(b) only, so that persons may comply with those rather than the FSA's own price stabilising rules — endorsement of US and Japanese rules has been proposed.

## Financial promotion rules

FSAMA 2000, s. 145 enables the FSA to make rules regulating the communication of financial promotions by authorised persons and their approval of financial promotions of others. These rules may not apply to a financial promotion that falls under an exemption from the restriction on financial promotion. The FSA has proposed rules that will largely carry forward existing advertising and cold calling rules in a more unified way (*The Conduct of Business Sourcebook* (Consultation Paper 45a), ch. 3).

## Money laundering rules

FSAMA 2000, s. 146, enables the FSA to make rules applying to authorised persons concerning the prevention and detection of money laundering. This is a new power and the FSA has proposed a regulatory regime 'parallel, but separate' to the existing Money Laundering Regulations 1993 (SI 1993/1933), which will continue in force (FSA, *Money Laundering: the FSA's New Role* (Consultation Paper 46)).

## Control of information rules

FSAMA 2000, s. 147, enables the FSA to make rules requiring or permitting an authorised person not to disclose information or use information for the benefit of another person with whom it does business, which the authorised person would otherwise have to disclose or use. Section 147 is similar, although expressed somewhat differently, to FSA 1986, s. 48(2)(h). The FSA can therefore make rules relating to the operation of 'Chinese walls' within multidisciplinary authorised persons and groups. Chinese walls are procedures which are designed to prevent the flow of information between different entities in a group and between different departments within a single firm, and are an important tool in dealing with conflicts of interest and the flow of inside information. The problem is that, under the general law, knowledge held by an individual in one part of a firm may be imputed to individuals in another part of the firm, even if they are the other side of a Chinese wall. For example, knowledge about an impending bid in the corporate finance department may be imputed to the broking department of the same firm. Recent cases, although not directly applicable, have provided some support for the efficacy of Chinese walls in overriding this general law principle (*Prince Jefri Bolkiah* v *KPMG* [1999] 2 AC 222; *Young* v *Robson Rhodes* [1999] 3 All ER 524).

The FSA has proposed draft rules similar to existing Chinese wall rules (*The Conduct of Business Sourcebook Supplement* (Consultation Paper 57)). Acting in conformity with these rules will provide a person (authorised or unauthorised) with a defence (or 'safe harbour') against:

(a) contravention of another FSA rule, compliance with which relates to disclosure or use of information for customers, where the individual dealing with the matter is the other side of a Chinese wall from the information;

(b)   the misleading statements and practices offences (s. 397(4) and (5)(c)); and

(c)   engaging in market abuse (s. 118(8)), as the FSA proposes to specify that compliance with its control of information rules will have this effect.

The establishment of effective Chinese walls may also protect an individual within an authorised person from committing an insider dealing offence under Criminal Justice Act 1993, Part V, as commission of these offences is predicated on actual knowledge by the individual.

There remains the question of the extent to which compliance with control of information rules will protect a person from a civil action based on breach of fiduciary duties or the duty of confidentiality. This is a complex topic, for which readers are referred to the detailed, although somewhat out-of-date, consideration of the issues in the Law Commission's 1992 consultation paper *Fiduciary Duties and Regulatory Rules* (No. 124) and its follow-up 1995 report (Law Com. No. 236, Cm 3049), which recommended express legislative provision in this respect. The Treasury originally intended to include such express provision in the Act (*Financial Services and Markets Bill: A Consultation Document* (July 1998), para. 5.11). But the government believed that developments in case law since 1998, in particular, *Prince Jefri Bolkiah* v *KPMG* referred to above, meant that express provision for a defence to a civil claim was not necessary (*Hansard* HL, 9 May 2000, cols 1405–9). The minister stated that 'These provisions are aimed specifically at displacing the fiduciary duties that would otherwise arise. If the Bill states that information can be withheld or not used in certain circumstances, then in those circumstances it can be withheld or not used. Nothing else is needed to achieve that result.' (*Hansard* HL, 18 May 2000, col. 421.) It is possible that a court may find s. 147 sufficiently ambiguous to have regard to this statement under the rule in *Pepper* v *Hart* [1993] AC 593.

## SANCTIONS FOR CONTRAVENTION OF RULES

This section describes the potential sanctions for contravention of rules by authorised persons, which are FSA enforcement action and actions for damages. These consequences apply equally to contravention of any requirement in or under the Act by an authorised person. Of course, some rules confer rights or privileges (for example, the safe harbours for persons who comply with price stabilising rules) in addition to, or rather than, imposing requirements. Also, some rules apply to persons other than authorised persons (for example, listing rules under Part VI and compensation rules under Part XV); the consequences of contravention of rules by unauthorised persons will depend on the nature of the rule concerned and are beyond the scope of this book.

### FSA enforcement action

Breach of a rule by an authorised person enables the FSA to take a number of different types of enforcement action, as follows:

(a) Discipline, that is, public censure and fines (Part XIV).

(b) Injunctions and restitution (Part XXV).

Breach of a rule by an authorised person may also be relevant to other types of enforcement action by the FSA against that person, as follows:

(a) Variation of the firm's Part IV permission potentially including cancellation of permission and hence ending of authorisation. For firms from EEA States exercising passport rights or Treaty rights in the UK, there are similar but more limited intervention powers (Part XIII) and the FSA may request the firm's home State regulator to take action.

(b) Information-gathering and investigation powers (Part XI).

**Claims for damages**

FSAMA 2000, s. 150, creates a right of action in damages for 'private persons' (to be defined by the Treasury) who suffer loss as a result of a rule contravention by an authorised person. This section does not remove any common law cause of action that a person might otherwise have. It allows a person to recover losses just by showing that there has been a contravention of a rule as a result of which the person has suffered loss rather than having to rely on that contravention as evidence of negligence. It is similar in effect to FSA 1986, ss. 62 and 62A, which created similar rights of action for contravention of FSA, SRO and RPB rules.

FSAMA 2000, s. 150(1), creates a presumption that a private person will have such a right of action for damages. But the FSA may remove that right from particular rules, and has proposed to do so for certain high-level rules, such as the principles for businesses (*The FSA's Principles for Businesses: Response on Consultation Paper 13* (October 1999)). The Treasury are also able to prescribe that contravention of a particular FSA rule is actionable by non-private persons. But there can be no right of action under s. 150 for contravention of financial resources rules or listing rules. See Part XVI (chapter 18 below) regarding the ability of a consumer to seek a compensatory award under the Ombudsman scheme.

## PROCEDURE FOR MAKING RULES

The detailed procedure for making rules is an important part of the accountability framework for the FSA, and goes well beyond what was required of any of the existing regulators. The same procedure applies to all provisions with the status of 'rules' made under FSAMA 2000, other than listing rules, which have their own procedures (sch. 7, para. 4, and Part VI). These procedures also apply to guidance in relation to rules given to a class of regulated persons, recognising its regulatory significance (s. 157(3)). The procedural requirements are set out below.

(a) The general duties apply to the function of making rules (s. 2(4)(a)).

(b)   The FSA must consult on draft rules, unless the delay would be prejudicial to consumers. It must also specify a time during which representations may be made, must have regard to such representations and must publish a response to them (s. 155).

(c)   The FSA must perform and publish cost-benefit analysis of proposed rules (s. 155(2)(a)). There is a clear link between the results of such cost-benefit analysis and the duty that the FSA must have regard to the proportionality of any burden (s. 2(3)(c)). The requirement for cost-benefit analysis does not apply if the FSA considers that the proposed rules will not result in a significant increase in the overall cost position (s. 155(8)). Nor does it apply to proposed rules for funding the compensation scheme, the ombudsman scheme, the legal assistance scheme or the FSA itself, although consultation on the FSA's fees must be accompanied by a budget (s. 155(3) and (9)).

(d)   Consultation drafts of rules must be accompanied by explanations of the purpose of the proposed rules and of how they are compatible with the FSA's general duties (s. 155(2)(b) and (c)).

(e)   The FSA is required to specify in every rule-making instrument the powers under which the rules have been made (s. 153(2)).

(f)   Rules must be made by the FSA's board as the board cannot delegate its legislative functions (sch. 1, paras 1(2) and 5(2)).

(g)   If the rules as made differ significantly from the consultation draft, the FSA is required to publish details of the difference and perform a further cost-benefit analysis (s. 155(6)).

(h)   The FSA must consult with a Practitioner Panel and a Consumer Panel 'on the extent to which its general policies and practices are consistent with its general duties' (ss. 8 to 11).

(i)   The FSA is subject to judicial review in making rules, like any other public authority. Further, an FSA rule, as secondary legislation, is liable to be struck down (or simply disapplied) where it is impossible to interpret it so as to be compatible with rights under the European Convention on Human Rights (Human Rights Act 1998, s. 3(2)(c)).

## COMPETITION SCRUTINY OF THE FSA

Chapter III of Part X of FSAMA 2000 provides for competition scrutiny of the FSA's rules, general guidance, policy statements, codes and practices (although there is a separate regime for competition scrutiny relating to recognised bodies in Part XVIII). Special provisions are necessary because s. 164 creates a safe harbour from the Competition Act 1998: conduct encouraged by the FSA's regulating provisions does not contravene the prohibition imposed by the Competition Act 1998, s. 2(1) (of agreements preventing, restricting or distorting competition within the United Kingdom) or s. 18(1) (of abuse of a dominant position in a market which may effect trade in the United Kingdom).

## The role of the Director General of Fair Trading

The Director General of Fair Trading (DGFT) is under a duty to keep the FSA's regulating provisions and practices under review, and to report on any which have a significantly adverse effect on competition (ss. 160 and 161). This continues a similar regime under FSA 1986. The DGFT has used FSA 1986 powers on a number of occasions, most recently in a report on the polarisation rules (*The Rules on the Polarisation of Investment Advice* (OFT 264) (August 1999), on which Treasury action has been deferred pending the outcome of a research study by the FSA).

## The role of the Competition Commission

Following an interim report by Don Cruickshank, head of the Review of Banking Services in the UK, in July 1999, in the context of banking services, the government somewhat strengthened the regime in the Bill for competition scrutiny of the FSA's regulating provisions to include a role for the Competition Commission established under the Competition Act 1998 (Review of Banking Services in the UK, *Competition and Regulation in Financial Services: Striking the Right Balance* (July 1999)). The Commission must consider and report on two types of report from the DGFT (FSAMA 2000, s. 162 and sch. 14). The first is a report by the DGFT which concludes that particular regulating provisions or practices of the Authority have a significantly adverse effect on competition. The second is a report by the DGFT which concludes that particular regulating provisions or practices do not have such an effect, but where the DGFT has referred the matter to the Commission for further consideration. The Commission's report must state whether, in its opinion, the provisions or practices have a significantly adverse effect on competition. If it concludes that there is no such effect, then that is the end of the matter. If the Commission concludes that there is such an effect, then it must go on to state in its report whether it considers that the effect is justified, taking into account the FSA's functions under the Act. It must also state what action, if any, ought to be taken by the FSA.

## The role of the Treasury

The final arbiter on the matter of competition will be the Treasury, but its ability to overturn the conclusions of the Commission is limited (s. 163). If the Commission's opinion is that an adverse effect on competition is not justified, the Treasury must direct the FSA to take appropriate action, unless there are exceptional circumstances or action is unnecessary because the FSA has already taken action. The Act does not specify what might constitute exceptional circumstances, but the Treasury have stated that this might include, for example, a grave risk to the financial system if the regulating provisions were changed. In addition, the

Treasury cannot direct the FSA to take any action which the FSA has no power to take or which would be incompatible with the FSA's functions or obligations under the Act. If the Commission's opinion is that the adverse effect on competition is justified, then the Treasury may override that decision and direct the FSA to make changes only in exceptional circumstances.

# Chapter Thirteen
## Information Gathering and Investigations

*Loretta Minghella*

Part XI of the Financial Services and Markets Act 2000 (FSAMA 2000) contains the FSA's specific, formal powers to obtain the information it requires to pursue its statutory objectives. There are five discrete sets of powers in Part XI, which may be summarised as follows:

(a)   powers to gather information directly from authorised and other regulated persons;

(b)   powers to require reports from skilled persons about authorised persons;

(c)   powers to carry out general investigations relating to authorised persons and their appointed representatives;

(d)   powers to investigate where circumstances suggest particular breaches; and

(e)   powers to investigate to assist overseas regulators.

Some of the powers are also conferred concurrently on the Secretary of State (i.e., the DTI) recognising the potential relevance of the powers to the Department's role in relation to compliance with company law.

Part XI, which attracted a great deal of parliamentary attention at the legislative stage, goes into considerable detail about the scope and extent of each power, and the rights of those under investigation at key stages. It also deals with the admissibility of compelled answers, powers to enter premises and the consequences of failing to cooperate with the FSA in the exercise of the powers.

### POWERS TO GATHER INFORMATION

The first power in Part XI is one to require information and documents from authorised persons (s. 165(1)), past and present (s. 165(8)), where the information and documents are reasonably required in connection with the FSA's statutory functions (s. 165(4)). This kind of power was a common feature of predecessor legislation such as FSA 1986, s. 104. It may be used in a wide variety of circumstances, not just to look into what may be a firm-specific problem, e.g., in support of a consumer education initiative.

The FSA may require a past or present authorised person, by written notice, to provide information or documents (FSAMA 2000, s. 165(1) and (8)). The notice must be specific as to the information or documents required, or must describe them in specific terms (s. 165(10)). The notice must be complied with by the date and at a place reasonably specified by FSA (s. 165(2)).

The FSA may also give written authorisation to an FSA officer, including a member of staff or agent, to exercise similar powers (s. 165(3)). The officer may require the information or documents without delay (s. 165(3)).

The FSA may ask for the information provided to be provided in some particular form, and to be verified or authenticated in any particular manner, provided that such requests are reasonable (s. 165(5) and (6)).

The powers may be used to require information from operators, trustees or depositaries of certain overseas collective investment schemes, as well as from recognised investment exchanges and clearing houses (s. 165(7)).

Information may also be required to be provided by persons 'connected' with authorised firms (s. 165(7)(a)). 'Connected' is defined for the purpose in s. 165(11) as a person who is or has been a member of the authorised person's group, its controller, a member of the same partnership, or a person mentioned in part I of sch. 15. Broadly speaking, 'connected' is further expanded in sch. 15 to include officers, managers, employees and agents of the authorised person.

## REPORTS BY SKILLED PERSONS

The second formal set of powers in Part XI allows the FSA to require an authorised person to produce a report on any matter which could have been the subject of the information gathering powers in s. 165 mentioned above (s. 166(1) and (2)). The report must therefore reasonably be required in connection with the discharge of FSA's functions (s. 165(4)).

By s. 166(2) the requirement can be imposed on an authorised person, any other member of that person's group, or a partnership of which the authorised person is a member (a more limited class of persons than 'connected persons' under s. 165). In each case, it does not matter if the person concerned no longer has that status if the person had it at the relevant time, provided that the person is, or was at the relevant time, carrying on a business.

The person making the report has to be nominated or approved by the FSA and must be someone whom the FSA believes to have the necessary skills (s. 166(4)). This power has its origins in s. 39 of the Banking Act 1987 and in similar provisions of SRO rule books, where the report has commonly been commissioned to be produced by accountants. A skilled person might also be a lawyer, an actuary or a person with particular commercial experience such as a banker. The FSA has indicated that it will seek to avoid conflicts of interests arising in cases where serious compliance failures are suspected by appointing someone other than the firm's auditors or regular advisers to produce the report.

The cost of producing such a report falls on the firm. A factor influencing FSA in the use of this power is likely to be the extent to which any such report would assist the firm itself to remedy breaches, compensate consumers or improve systems and controls within the firm.

It is the duty of those providing services to the authorised person to cooperate with whoever is appointed to make the report by giving such assistance as may reasonably be required (s. 166(5)). For example, the company's in-house accountants would be under a duty to co-operate with accountants appointed to write a report. The FSA may apply to the Court for a mandatory injunction (in Scotland, an order for specific performance) in the event of non-compliance (s. 166(6)).

## GENERAL INVESTIGATIONS

The FSA or the Secretary of State may initiate a general investigation, if it appears to either of them that there is good reason to do so, into the business of an authorised person or appointed representative, any particular aspect of that business, or the ownership or control of an authorised person (s. 167(1)). The power is to appoint one or more competent persons to carry out the investigation on behalf of the FSA (or Secretary of State, as the case may be) (s. 167(1)).

It does not matter whether the person under investigation is authorised at the time of the investigation. The power extends to former authorised persons and appointed representatives in relation to business carried on when they had that status and can cover the ownership and control of a former authorised person at any time when he was an authorised person (s. 167(4)). Nor is the investigation limited to regulated business: the power to investigate the business or any aspect of it is expressly defined to include unregulated activity (s. 167(5)).

If he thinks it necessary for the purposes of the investigation to do so, the person appointed to investigate may extend the investigation by virtue of s. 167(2). This allows the investigator to investigate the business of a person who is or was a member of the group of which the person under investigation is part; or a member of the same partnership. An investigator who decides to extend the investigation in this way must given written notice to the person whose business will be investigated as a result of the decision.

## PARTICULAR INVESTIGATIONS

The FSA may, under s. 168, appoint investigators in a number of circumstances suggesting particular contraventions of various kinds, both criminal and non-criminal. Some of these powers are shared with the Secretary of State. Those appointed to investigate in these specific circumstances have wider powers of investigation than those appointed under s. 167.

The triggers for investigations by either FSA or DTI are contained in s. 168(1) and (2). The main triggers for these concurrent powers include circumstances suggesting that certain criminal offences may have been committed, such as insider dealing, market manipulation, misleading statements, and unauthorised business. Other key triggers include circumstances suggesting that market abuse may have taken place.

In addition, the FSA (but not the DTI) may appoint investigators under ss. 168(4) and (5) in other circumstances, e.g. where a person is suspected of having committed an offence under prescribed money laundering regulations, where circumstances suggest that an authorised person may have broken FSA rules or that a person approved under s. 59 may be guilty of misconduct or may not be fit and proper to perform the controlled function for which approval has been given.

These powers are much wider than the statutory powers available to FSA under the predecessor statutes and Parliament debated whether the threshold for their exercise should be higher. The words 'reasonable grounds to suspect' were considered as an alternative to 'circumstances suggesting' a possible breach. Before Standing Committee A the Economic Secretary to the Treasury explained that 'reasonable grounds to suspect' would require the FSA to have a degree of certainty that an offence had been committed before an investigation could be launched. 'The test is too stringent . . . to deal effectively with the issues which the FSA will have to tackle.' The words 'circumstances suggesting' were adopted so as to enable the FSA (and DTI) to exercise its powers in a broader range of circumstances than the other wording would allow.

## INVESTIGATIONS IN SUPPORT OF OVERSEAS REGULATORS

The express power to gather information and investigate to assist an overseas regulator conferred by FSAMA 2000, s. 169, is a new power for the FSA (whereas the DTI have such powers already under, s. 82 of the Companies Act 1989). Section 169 has the effect that the FSA may use its s. 165 information-gathering powers and by extension its powers to require a report from skilled persons. It may also appoint investigators 'to investigate any matter'.

An 'overseas regulator' means an authority, whether in the EU or elsewhere, which exercises functions corresponding to any function of the FSA under the Act, any function of the competent authority for listing, the companies regulatory responsibilities corresponding to those of the DTI under the Companies Act 1985, and any function of investigating insider dealing whether criminally or otherwise. There is a residual power for the Treasury to make regulations specifying additional companies or financial services functions for this purpose (s. 195(3) and (4) applied by s. 169(13)).

Where there is a discretion to assist, the FSA may take a number of factors into account (s. 169(4)). These include whether such assistance would be reciprocated, whether the matter to be investigated involves a breach of a law with no close parallel in the UK or assertion of a jurisdiction not recognised here, the seriousness of the case and importance to people in the UK, and whether it would otherwise be in the public interest to assist. The FSA may make it a condition of assistance that the overseas regulator contributes to the costs of the investigation (s. 169(5)).

In some circumstances, the FSA will be required as a matter of its Community obligations under Single Market Directives to investigate, and s. 169(3) obliges it to consider whether it must do so. If the FSA considers that Community obligations oblige it to investigate, the factors listed above which are relevant to discretionary assistance fall away and no contribution to costs may be sought (s. 169(6)).

The FSA may allow a representative of the overseas regulator to attend and take part in any interview conducted for the purposes of the investigation (s. 169(7)). This will be signalled by FSA direction to the person appointed to investigate. Such a direction cannot be given unless the FSA is satisfied that any information obtained by the overseas regulator as a result of the interview will be subject to obligations to keep the information confidential (s. 169(8)). These obligations must be equivalent to those imposed on the FSA, which are contained in Part XXIII of the Act.

No 'sitting-in' direction can be given unless the FSA has published a statement, approved by the Treasury, setting out its policy on the conduct of interviews carried out with overseas regulators sitting in (s. 169(9) to (12)).

## INVESTIGATION POWERS: GENERAL PROVISIONS

The investigating authority, whether it is the FSA or Secretary of State, must notify a person whom they have decided should be investigated under s. 167 or 168 that investigators have been appointed (s. 170(2)). The notice must be in writing and must specify the provisions under which the investigator has been appointed and the reason for the appointment (s. 170(4)).

The investigating authority (i.e., the FSA or the Secretary of State) may appoint any competent person to investigate on its behalf. Section 170(5) provides that the investigator may be a member of staff. The investigator must make a report of the investigation to the investigating authority (s. 170(6)).

Under predecessor and related legislation allowing the appointment of investigators, it has not always been entirely clear to what extent investigators should be regarded as independent of those appointing them. FSAMA 2000, s. 170(7) makes clear that it is for the investigating authority to control the scope, conduct, duration and reporting of the investigation by the giving of directions. These directions are generally a private matter between the investigating authority and the investigator, but where there is a change in scope or conduct of the investigation, the position may be different. Where the investigating authority believes that there is a real risk of significant prejudice to the person under investigation if he remains ignorant of the change, he must be given written notice of it (s. 170(9)).

By virtue of s. 170(3), notices do not need to be given under section 170 if the investigating authority believes that this would be likely to result in an investigation under s. 168(1) or (4) being frustrated. Nor do notices need to be given in certain types of case such as insider dealing, market abuse and other investigations under s. 168(2), where the investigation at the outset may be into a set of facts rather than persons and, indeed, it may be unclear who, if anyone, is to be suspected of any wrongdoing (s. 170(3)(G)).

## POWERS OF INVESTIGATORS

### Powers of investigators appointed under section 167

The general power to investigate under FSAMA 2000, s. 167, is available in a wide range of circumstances. The detailed powers conferred on such investigators are accordingly limited, since they may be exercised in circumstances of varying seriousness (s. 171).

By virtue of s. 171(1), the investigator may require people to attend for interview at a specified place and time or to provide such information as the investigator may require. These requirements may be imposed only on those under investigation and those 'connected' with them within the meaning of s. 171(4). There is an additional power in s. 171(2) which enables the investigator to require *any* person to produce documents. In every instance, the investigator must reasonably consider the question, information or document to be relevant to the purposes of the investigation (s. 171(3)).

### Additional powers of investigators appointed under section 168

The powers of investigators appointed under s. 168 are wider than those available to s. 167 investigators, reflecting the more specific and inevitably serious circumstances in which they are appointed (ss. 172 and 173).

In addition to the powers available to s. 167 investigators (s. 172(1)), those investigating under s. 168(1) or (4) may require any person to attend for interview and otherwise to provide such information as the investigator may require for the purposes of the investigation (s. 172(2)). The investigator must be satisfied that the requirement is necessary or expedient for those purposes (s. 172(3)). Those investigating on behalf of overseas regulators under s. 169 have the same powers as investigators appointed by virtue of s. 168(1) (see s. 169(2)).

Those investigating the specific misconduct mentioned in s. 168(2), which includes insider dealing, market abuse, unregulated business and unlawful promotion, have yet broader powers of investigation conferred by s. 173. Reflecting the fact that such investigations may need to be mounted without any idea who may be responsible, there is no need to identify and notify a person under investigation and no notion of connected person. The powers available to the investigator include the ability to require any person who may be able to give relevant information to attend for interview, and to give such information or particular documents which may be required for the investigation. They may also be required to give all and any other assistance which they are reasonably able to give.

## Supplemental powers of investigators

Where a person could be compelled under Part XI to produce a document, but that document is in the hands of a third party, the requirement may imposed on the third party (s. 175(1)).

Where a document is produced in response to a Part XI requirement, copies and extracts may be taken, and the person producing it and any 'relevant person' may be required to provide an explanation of it (s. 175(2)). 'Relevant person' is defined in s. 175(7) and includes directors, controllers, certain professional advisers and employees of a person. The decision in *Attorney-General's Reference (No. 2 of 1998)* [1999] 3 WLR 961 suggests that this provision should not be narrowly construed.

A person who is required to produce a document but fails to do so may be required to state where, to the best of his or her knowledge and belief, the document might be found (s. 175(3)).

These provisions do not affect any rights a third party might have over any documents, e.g., a solicitor's lien (s. 175(6)). A lawyer may be required to furnish the name and address of his or her client (s. 175(4)) but, by virtue of s. 413, none of the powers in Part XI may be used to require the disclosure of privileged information defined in that section under the heading of 'protected items'.

## Banking confidentiality

Special provisions apply to information or documents in respect of which a person owes a duty of banking confidence (s. 175(5)). Such material may not be required of a person unless one of four conditions is present. First, the person required to disclose or produce is the person under investigation or is a member of the same group as the person under investigation. Second, the person to whom the confidence is owed is the person under investigation or a member of that person's group. Third, the person to whom the confidence is owed consents. Fourth, there has been specific authorisation by the investigating authority.

## ADMISSIBILITY OF STATEMENTS MADE TO INVESTIGATORS

Until recently, a common feature of financial services legislation was the power of the authorities to compel answers to questions on the basis that those answers could be used against the provider of them in criminal proceedings. The European Court of Human Rights in the case of *Saunders* v *United Kingdom* (1996) 23 EHRR 313 found the use of answers compelled under the Companies Act 1985 in criminal proceedings against Ernest Saunders to be an infringement of his right to a fair trial contained in art. 6 of the Convention. The UK responded by amending a large number of statutes (the amendments were enacted by s. 59 of the Youth Justice and Criminal Evidence Act 1999) including the predecessor statutes to FSAMA 2000. It was always to be expected, therefore, that this Act would generally disable the authorities from adducing in evidence in criminal proceedings against the maker of them answers compelled in the course of statutory investigations.

Accordingly, where a statement has been compelled as a part of a general or specific investigation under s. 167 or s. 168 — what will be called here a *Saunders* statement — the statement will only be able to be adduced in criminal proceedings against the maker of the statement in limited circumstances (s. 174). These arise where the *Saunders* statement is, in effect, put in issue in the proceedings by or on behalf of the maker of it. This does not prevent the prosecutor from adducing in evidence *documents* produced by the person making the statement or from adducing *Saunders* statements in evidence against others.

There are some types of criminal cases where, exceptionally, it may be possible to adduce *Saunders* statements whether or not the maker of the statements puts them in issue. These are proceedings under s. 177(4) relating to the provision of false or misleading information in purported compliance with a person exercising Part XI powers; proceedings under s. 398 for misleading the Authority; and certain offences under perjury legislation.

Subject to one exception, the Act expressly allows for *Saunders* statements to be used in non-criminal cases, provided that they meet the ordinary tests for admissibility which apply to such cases. The exception relates to the market abuse regime. Where the proceedings relate to action to be taken under s. 123 — which enables the FSA to impose a financial penalty or to censure a person for market abuse — any *Saunders* material obtained from that person will not be admissible against him or her. The government inserted this provision to ensure that, if the market abuse regime was found by a court to be criminal in nature, the legislation would already provide all the safeguards required in criminal proceedings by art. 6 and would not, therefore, need altering on ECHR grounds.

## ENTRY OF PREMISES UNDER WARRANT

One of the most controversial proposals in the draft Bill was a power of entry *without* warrant. That did not survive in the Bill as eventually introduced. As enacted, FSAMA 2000, s. 176, provides for warrants to be issued to the police to enable them to search premises for documents and information required for an investigation which a person has refused, or is likely to refuse, to hand over voluntarily.

A warrant is to be issued by a justice of the peace, or, in Scotland, a sheriff on an application which must be supported by information given on oath by or on behalf of the FSA, the Secretary of State or an investigator.

There are three bases on which a warrant may be issued. The first is that there are reasonable grounds for believing that a person who has been required to produce documents or information under Part XI has not complied in full and that there are documents or information on the premises concerned which have already been required to be produced.

The second basis is that there are reasonable grounds for believing that the premises specified in the warrant are premises of an authorised person or an appointed representative, that there are documents or information on the premises which could be required to be produced under Part XI, and that if they were required to be produced, they would not be produced, or they would be removed, tampered with or destroyed.

The third basis is that there are reasonable grounds for believing that one of the offences which may give rise to an investigation under s. 168 (power to appoint investigators in particular cases) has been or is being committed, provided that it is one of the offences for which a prison sentence of at least two years could be imposed. (Such offences include 'perimeter offences', such as carrying on unauthorised business; insider dealing and market manipulation; and 'misleading statements', whether by authorised or unauthorised persons.) There must also be reasonable grounds for believing that there are documents or information on the premises specified in the warrant which could be required to be produced, under Part XI, and that if they were required to be produced they would not be produced, or they would be removed, tampered with or destroyed.

Warrants issued under s. 176 authorise a constable to enter the premises concerned, to search and take possession of documents or information of the relevant kind or to take any other steps which may appear to be necessary for preserving them or preventing interference with them. Section 16(2) of the Police and Criminal Evidence Act 1984 enables persons named on the warrant to accompany the constable in the execution of the warrant and will enable FSA investigators to attend during the execution of the warrant.

Copies of documents or information may be taken and anyone at the premises may be required to say where the relevant kind of documents or information may be found and to provide an explanation of any such document or information. The constable may use such force as may be reasonably necessary to gain entry to the premises.

In England and Wales, provisions of the Police and Criminal Evidence Act 1984 apply to warrants issued under this section. These provide safeguards for the execution of warrants and their wording. Similar provisions apply in Northern Ireland.

Where a document is seized under a warrant, it may be retained for three months or until the end of any relevant criminal proceedings commenced within the three-month period (s. 176(8)).

## CONSEQUENCES OF FAILURE TO COOPERATE

If any person (other than an investigator) fails to comply with a requirement imposed on him by FSAMA 2000, Part XI, the fact may be certified in writing to the court (s. 177(1)). If the court is satisfied that the defaulter had no reasonable excuse, it may deal with the defaulter as though there were a contempt of court. Where the defaulter is a company, the court may deal with any director or officer as though they were in contempt. This contrasts with the position under FSA 1986, which makes failure to comply with requirements imposed by investigators appointed under, for example, s. 106, a criminal offence.

FSAMA 2000, Part XI, does, however, contain three different offences relating to failure to cooperate.

First, it will be a criminal offence to interfere with documents which are known or suspected to be relevant to an existing investigation or one which is likely to be conducted, whether by falsifying, concealing, destroying or otherwise disposing of them. It will be a defence to show that there was no intention to conceal relevant facts from the investigator (s. 177(3)).

Secondly, a person who knowingly or recklessly provides information which is materially false or misleading in purported compliance with a Part XI requirement commits an offence (s. 177(4)).

These first two offences may be tried in the magistrates' court or Crown Court and the maximum sentence is two years' imprisonment and an unlimited fine.

Thirdly, intentional obstruction of a warrant is a criminal offence (s. 177(6)), triable only in the magistrates' court and carrying a maximum sentence of three months' imprisonment and a level 5 fine (currently £5,000).

# Chapter Fourteen
## Control over Authorised Persons

*Michael Taylor & Michael Blair*

Part XII of the Financial Services and Markets Act 2000 (FSAMA 2000) concerns the control of authorised persons. It creates an obligation to notify the FSA of an intended acquisition of a controlling interest in an authorised person, of an intended increase in that interest or of an intention to reduce such an interest. This Part creates an obligation on the FSA either to approve (with or without conditions) such acquisitions or changes in control, or to issue an objection to an acquisition or change in a controlling interest, and includes criteria according to which the FSA's approval is to be granted or withheld. It also contains provisions relating to controlling interests that have been acquired in breach of these notification or approval requirements, and creates a number of offences relating to such breaches.

## EC LEGISLATION

Controls over the owners and controllers of authorised persons have become increasingly governed by European legislation, which creates a number of requirements that apply to the competent authorities of the member States. First, before authorising an entity to conduct financial services business the competent authorities must have been informed of the identity of the shareholders and members who have a qualifying interest in a credit institution, as well as the amount of such holdings (e.g. Credit Institutions Directive (2000/12/EC), art. 7 (formerly in the Second Banking Coordination Directive (89/646/EEC), art. 5); Investment Services Directive (93/22/EEC), art. 4; Third Non-life Insurance Directive (92/49/EC), art. 8). The legislation defines a 'qualifying holding' as 'a direct or indirect holding in an undertaking which represents 10 per cent or more of the capital or the voting rights or which makes it possible to exercise a significant influence over the management of the undertaking in which a holding subsists' (e.g. Credit Institutions Directive, art. 1(10); Investment Services Directive, art. 1(10); Third Non-life Insurance Directive, art. 1(g)).

The competent authorities must also require each prospective purchaser to give prior notification of a proposed direct or indirect acquisition of a qualifying holding that would result in a person's holding reaching or passing the threshold of 20, 33 or 50 per cent of the voting rights or capital, or would result in the credit institution becoming such a person's subsidiary. Thus the Investment Services Directive, art. 9(1), states that:

> Member States shall require any person who proposes to acquire, directly or indirectly, a qualifying holding in an investment firm first to inform the competent authorities, telling them of the size of his intended holding. Such a person shall likewise inform the competent authorities if he proposes to increase his qualifying holding so that the proportion of the voting rights or of the capital that he holds would reach or exceed 20, 33, or 50 per cent or so that the investment firm would become his subsidiary.

See also, for example, the Credit Institutions Directive, art. 16(1) and the Third Non-life Directive, art. 15(1).

Likewise, any shareholder or member owning a qualifying holding in a financial institution who proposes to dispose of that holding, to reduce it below 20, 33 or 50 per cent measured by voting rights or capital, or to reduce the holding below the subsidiary level must inform the competent authorities (see, for example, the Credit Institutions Directive, art. 16(3)). In addition, the financial institution itself must, on becoming aware of it, inform the competent authorities of any acquisition or disposal of holdings in its capital that causes the holdings to exceed or fall below the 20, 33 and 50 per cent thresholds and must at least once each year furnish to the competent authorities the names of its shareholders and members owning qualifying holdings and the size of their holdings (see, for example, the Credit Institutions Directive, art. 16(4)).

## IMPLEMENTATION IN UK LAW

The statutes or regulations that FSAMA 2000 replaces implemented the relevant European legislation in the domestic legal order, and hence they already made the required provisions. Indeed, a number of the provisions in European Directives were modelled on pre-existing British practice. For example, the Banking Act 1987, s. 21, required any person whose intention was to become a shareholder controller of an authorised institution to issue a notice in writing to that effect to the Bank of England (subsequently the FSA). Section 105(4) of the Banking Act 1987 defined a shareholder controller in terms of the same 20, 33 and 50 per cent thresholds as those set out in the European Directives.

Since FSAMA 2000 also implements the European legislation it also adopts these thresholds and notification requirements. Interestingly, however, it goes beyond the EU requirements in applying the control provisions to all UK authorised persons as defined at s. 178(4): this goes beyond the previous UK legislation which covered only those benefitting from EU 'passports'. The Act requires a potential acquirer to notify the FSA of a proposal to acquire a controlling interest in an authorised person or of any proposal to acquire additional control over an authorised person (s. 178(1) and (3)); it also creates an obligation for a person who inadvertently acquires a controlling interest in an authorised person to notify the FSA within 14 days of becoming aware that he has acquired control (s. 178(2)). The latter provision is intended to provide some degree of protection to a market maker in bank shares, for example, who may inadvertently acquire a controlling interest as part of his inventory of securities held for trading purposes.

The first threshold at which the notification of proposed acquisition of control over an authorised person becomes obligatory is 10 per cent of the shares or voting rights in the authorised person itself or of shares or voting rights in the parent of an authorised person (s. 179). The Act then follows the European legislation in requiring the notification of acquisitions that increase the relevant shareholdings or voting rights beyond the 20 per cent, 33 per cent and 50 per cent thresholds (s. 180). The obligation to notify is symmetrical, to the extent that a controller who wishes to reduce his shareholding or voting power must also notify the FSA if his intention would result in the shareholding or voting power falling below any of the above thresholds (s. 190). Ability to exercise significant influence over the management of the authorised person or its parent, by virtue of shares or voting rights, is also regarded as control (ss. 179(1) and (2)).

## APPROVAL BY THE FSA

The purpose of requiring notification of the controllers of an authorised person is to permit the FSA to vet them. FSAMA 2000 would appear to require positive vetting by the FSA, rather than the negative vetting that was the surface characteristic of at least one of its predecessor statutes. The Act's language is cast in terms of the FSA issuing its 'approval' of shareholder controllers, whereas the Banking Act 1987, s. 21 to 24, referred instead to the FSA (formerly the Bank of England) issuing only a 'non-objection' to a proposed shareholder controller. Since, however, there was a free-standing test of fitness and propriety of controllers (see below) this difference is more apparent than real. The FSA may require a person proposing to become a controller of an authorised person to provide it with such information or documents as it reasonably considers necessary in order to reach this assessment (s. 182(2)).

The Act requires the FSA to be satisfied on two 'approval requirements' (s. 186) before approving a proposed controller: it must be satisfied that the proposed controller is a fit and proper person to have the relevant degree of control over an authorised person, and it must be satisfied that the interests of consumers would not be threatened by the control (s. 186(2)). In deciding whether these approval requirements are met, the FSA must have regard to its duty (under s. 41) to ensure that the authorised person will satisfy, and be able to continue to satisfy, the 'threshold conditions' for authorisation set out in sch. 6 to the Act. This requirement mirrors the requirement previously in the Banking Act 1987, s. 22(1)(c), which also required the FSA (formerly the Bank of England) to have regard to the implications that a potential controller might have on an institution's ability to fulfil the authorisation criteria contained in sch. 3 to that Act.

The requirement that a controller of an authorised person should be 'fit and proper' was an established feature of the statutes that FSAMA 2000 replaces. For example, the Banking Act 1987 stated that one of the criteria for regulatory approval as a shareholder controller of an authorised institution was that the person (either natural or a body corporate) should be a 'fit and proper' person to become a controller of an authorised institution (s. 22(1)(a)). The concept of fitness and propriety will continue to play a key role in the assessment of shareholders and potential shareholders, since FSAMA 2000 states that the FSA may object to a controller unless it is satisfied, *inter alia*, that 'the acquirer is a fit and proper person to have the control over the authorised person that he has or would have if he acquired the control in question' (s. 186(2)(a)).

The concept of fitness and propriety is not defined in FSAMA 2000, nor was it in the statutes that the Act replaces. However, fitness and propriety have been elaborated to encompass such matters as ability, probity, judgment, compliance with relevant laws and codes, reputation and record. Clearly, there is a need to ensure that the shareholder controllers of all regulated financial intermediaries are persons of probity. This follows from the fiduciary responsibilities that exist between a financial intermediary and its customers, and the scope that exists for financial entities to be used as a vehicle for fraud by unscrupulous persons. Furthermore, evidence of illegal or unethical behaviour by an owner or controller of an authorised person might undermine the public confidence on which all financial entities ultimately depend. In addition, the prevention of conflicts of interest or the use of the authorised person to obtain cross-financing for the owner on favourable terms are all matters that justify the need for controls over the owners and controllers of authorised persons. The ability and judgment of the owners of a financial intermediary — and even more of its managers — are clearly matters of overriding concern in deciding whether or not it should be licensed to undertake regulated activities.

However, the concept of fitness and propriety extends beyond personal probity, experience or judgment. It is also essential to ensure that a shareholder controller is a potential source of strength to the authorised person, especially with regard to banks, where the nature of the financial contract they offer makes the confidence of depositors a matter of overriding concern. Commenting on the fitness and propriety criterion in 1987, the then Governor of the Bank of England, Robin Leigh-Pemberton, stated that 'confidence remains the central and indispensable requirement of a bank, and anything in the character of the business of a prospective controller that may threaten confidence must concern us' ('Ownership and control of UK banks', *Bank of England Quarterly Bulletin*, November 1987).

Of particular concern in assessing the fitness and propriety of a bank's shareholder controller is whether it could provide strength to the authorised entity.

Thus if the owner or controller is a body corporate, its ability to provide support to the authorised person in times of stress — either directly through financial assistance or indirectly by providing depositors with confidence that such support will always be available — is a significant factor in determining whether or not it is fit and proper as an owner or controller. Among matters that the FSA has indicated that it takes into account, under the pre-2001 regime, in assessing the fitness and propriety of shareholder controllers is:

> any possible contagion which might undermine confidence in the bank. If, for example, a holding company or another company which is a major shareholder in the bank were to suffer financial problems, this could lead to the bank's experiencing difficulties obtaining deposits or other funds, or in raising new equity from other shareholders or potential shareholders, and could lead to a run on the bank. (FSA, *Guide to Banking Supervisory Policy*, FP, s. 2, para. 9.)

Considerations of this kind will continue to form part of the FSA's judgment of fitness and propriety under the new Act, but it will need to tailor the standards it applies to the very diverse range of institutions it will regulate. While the FSA will be required to make judgments about the fitness and propriety of all owners and controllers of authorised persons, different standards and thresholds will be appropriate depending on the nature of the institution. The standards of fitness and propriety applied to the owners or potential owners of a bank will obviously differ from those applied to the owners or potential owners of an insurance company or investment manager given the differences in the nature of the fiduciary relationship between these types of institution and their customers. These differences can more adequately be captured by detailed regulations and guidance than in statute. The fact that the concept continues not to be defined in statute gives the FSA potentially very broad discretion in its application, and this is essential if the FSA is to be able to apply the standards of fitness and propriety with an appropriate degree of flexibility.

A second issue on which the FSA must be satisfied in approving controllers of authorised persons is that 'the interests of consumers would not be threatened by the acquirer's control or by his acquiring that control' (s. 186(2)(b)). At first sight this seems to lay down a similar test to the one which existed in the Banking Act 1987, s. 22(1)(b), by which the FSA had to be satisfied that the interests of depositors and potential depositors would not be threatened by a person becoming a shareholder controller. Since the Act applies to all types of financial intermediary, not just banks, a specific reference to 'depositors' would have defined its locus too narrowly. Hence the reference to 'consumers' is intended to broaden the range of interests which the FSA must take into account to reflect the broad scope of its regulatory responsibilities. 'Consumers' are defined in s. 186(6) by reference to s. 138(7). They include persons who use, have used, or are or may be contemplating using any of the services provided by authorised persons in carrying on regulated activities, or who have rights or interests that may be derived from or are otherwise attributable to the use of such services by other persons. The definition was amended in the House of Lords to expand it further, especially in the fiduciary or trust context. What matters for this purpose is that the range of parties whose interests the FSA will need to consider is much more extensive than in the predecessor statutes like the Banking Act 1987.

FSAMA 2000 permits the FSA three months ('the period for consideration') in which to determine whether it will issue its approval or objection to the acquisition of control over an authorised person. It must issue its determination in the form of a notice served on the potential controller. It may either approve the acquisition of control unconditionally (s. 184) or (by the warning notice and decision notice procedure) attach conditions to its approval of control (s. 185). Conditions may be cancelled by the FSA either on application from the person to whom the decision notice is addressed or by the FSA acting on its own initiative (s. 185(5) and (6)); the person to whom the decision notice is addressed may also request a variation in its terms. In the event that the FSA objects to the acquisition of control, it must issue its objection (again through the warning notice and decision notice procedure). If issued, the decision notice may also specify steps that the acquirer could take to be approved as a controller of an authorised person (s. 186(4)). The acquirer can object to the FSA's decision by referring the matter to the Financial Services and Markets Tribunal (ss. 185(7) and 186(5)).

The FSA may also, by s. 187, serve a notice of objection on a person who is an existing controller of an authorised person, although before doing so it must provide that person with a warning notice (s. 188(1)) and consult with other relevant competent authorities outside the United Kingdom (s. 188(2)). The objection may relate to either the failure to notify the FSA prior to the acquisition of control (s. 187(1)) or arise from the FSA becoming aware of matters that satisfy it that the approval requirements in s. 186 are not met or that a condition has been breached (s. 187(3)).

The Act also makes provision for the disposal of improperly acquired shares, meaning shares that have been acquired despite the FSA's issue of a notice of objection or in breach of a condition imposed by the FSA (s. 189). The FSA may serve a 'restriction notice' on the acquirer (with a copy being served on the authorised person or its associates if appropriate) which can direct, *inter alia*, that the transfer of the shares is void; that no voting rights are to be exercisable in respect of them; that no further shares are to be issued to their holder; and that no payments (e.g., of dividends) are to be made on the shares (s. 189(2)). The FSA may also apply to the High Court (or Court of Session) for an order requiring that the shares be sold, the proceeds of the sale being paid into court for the benefit of the beneficial owners of the shares (s. 189(3) and (6)).

## OFFENCES

Part XII of FSAMA 2000 creates a number of offences relating to the failure to notify the FSA of an intention to acquire control over an authorised person and the acquisition of control notwithstanding the FSA's objection or in breach of a condition required by the FSA. Failure to notify the FSA either of a proposed acquisition of control or of a proposed disposal or reduction of a controlling interest is an offence by s. 191(1). A criminal offence, as opposed to disciplinary sanction, is appropriate here, as the person concerned may well not be regulated by the FSA. Section 191(9) makes available a defence for a person charged with such an offence that he had, at the time of the alleged offence, no knowledge of the act or circumstances by virtue of which the duty to notify the FSA arose.

Acquiring or disposing of control before having received the FSA's approval or warning notice, while still within the three-month consideration period granted by the Act, is an offence (s. 191(3)). Similarly, if a person carries out his intention of acquiring control over an authorised person while a warning notice issued by the FSA remains in force, he is guilty of an offence (s. 191(4)). Failure by an 'inadvertent' controller to notify the FSA within the 14 day period allowed for by s. 178(2) is also made an offence by s. 191(2). The offences created by s. 191(1) to (4) are punishable by a fine not exceeding level 5 on the standard scale.

Going ahead with the acquisition of control in spite of the FSA's having issued a notice of objection is the most serious offence created by this Part of the Act (s. 191(5)). A person guilty of this offence may be convicted either summarily or on indictment. On summary conviction the person is liable to a fine not exceeding the statutory maximum, while on indictment the person is liable to imprisonment for a term not exceeding two years or a fine, or both (s. 191(7)).

# Chapter Fifteen
## Incoming Firms: Intervention by the FSA

*Michael Blair*

Part XIII of the Financial Services and Markets Act 2000 provides a self-contained code for the oversight, within the United Kingdom, of firms coming into the UK in reliance on a Community right to do so. Those rights themselves are described in Part III of and sch. 3 and sch. 4 to the Act (chapter 5 above). The central concept in Part XIII is a power of intervention in the hands of the FSA. 'Intervention' was a creature of the Insurance Companies Act 1982 (see ss. 37 to 41 in particular) and of the Financial Services Act 1986 (see, for instance, Chapter VI of that Act, 'powers of intervention'), but the concept of intervention has now no meaning in relation to domestic cases, and the phrase is reserved for Part XIII of FSAMA 2000 with its inward passporting flavour. The equivalent, for domestic cases, is in Part IV and, in particular, the power of the FSA to impose requirements upon a Part IV permission and to vary a Part IV permission on the FSA's own initiative (see, in particular, ss. 43 and 45).

Part XIII follows the standard pattern established in the Single Market Directives, which divides regulatory jurisdiction into home State matters, which are prudential in character, and host State ones, where the interest of consumers etc. are involved. The clearest explanation of this is in arts 10 and 11 of the Investment Services Directive (93/22/EEC), but the principle applies in the other sectors as well.

Following this pattern, Part XIII contains s. 194, which relates to the power to intervene on a host State basis, and s. 195, which enables the FSA to exercise a power of intervention at the request of or for the purpose of assisting the home State regulator.

Because of the detail in the relevant Directives, particularly where there is an 'irregular situation', the Act deals with domestic requirements providing for fairness to the firm and with the need to proceed immediately: and it has to make all that fit with the Directive requirement for cooperation with other regulators. The result is quite complex.

## DOMESTIC GROUND FOR INTERVENTION

FSAMA 2000, s. 194, provides the criteria of which the FSA must be satisfied before it exercises a power of intervention in respect of an incoming firm. These are that:

(a)   there is an actual or likely contravention of a host State requirement under the Act;

(b)   the firm has knowingly or recklessly given false or misleading information to the FSA; or

(c)   intervention is desirable to protect the interests of actual or potential customers.

The decision-making under this section will be complex and intricate, since the tests require not only a clear understanding of the borderline between the home State and host State responsibilities, but may also involve two other aspects of Community law. These are, first, the arrangements in the several Single Market Directives relating to cooperation between competent authorities and, secondly, the impact on this aspect of the law of the European doctrine of 'the general good'. This is not the place for a full description of these issues, but it may be worth stressing the requirements in the relevant Directives for cooperation between competent authorities. Article 19 of the Investment Services Directive (93/22/EEC) and arts 22 and 28 of the Credit Institutions Directive (2000/12/EC) are different aspects of this point. (Insurance has some special features; see further below.) In particular, in the Investment Services Directive, the host member State which is faced with an 'irregular situation' in an incoming institution can require the institution to put an end to that situation, and, if that requirement is not complied with, the home State authorities have to be informed and are obliged to take all appropriate measures to ensure that the irregular situation is resolved. On persistence in violating the host State requirements, the host State authorities may, after informing the home authorities, take appropriate measures to prevent or penalise further irregularities. Intervention under Part XIII of FSAMA 2000 relates to the second stage, following the communication to and from the home member State. The 'requirement' mentioned above and envisaged in, for instance, art. 19(3) of the Investment Services Directive, is not itself intervention: this emerges from FSAMA 2000, s. 199(3), which contemplates in that case a simple requirement in writing.

The domestic side of the procedure is set out in s. 197, in terms that are very similar to the equivalent section, s. 53, in Part IV.

The additional procedure for certain EEA cases is set out in s. 199 and tracks very closely the structure envisaged by art. 19 of the Investment Services Directive, and that under the Credit Institutions Directive, though the host State responsibilities in that Directive are of course much less than in the investment services context. Interestingly, s. 199(2)(b) expressly refers to the provision in the Single Market Directives as a gateway to the use of the statutory procedure. The procedure applies, says this paragraph, if any of the Directives requires it.

In the insurance area, there is a slightly different structure, stemming from art. 20.5 of the First Non-life Insurance Directive (73/239/EEC) and art. 24 of the First Life Insurance Directive (79/267/EEC). Here, the authority for dealing with prohibitions on disposals of assets rests with the home member State, though there may be other member States concerned, that is, member States of the 'commitment'. Communication is therefore required. No specific powers are conferred on the host State authorities, however, except that each member State must be able to take measures to prohibit free disposal of assets in its own territory at the request of the home State. Since this may involve orders relating to persons not authorised in the host State concerned, the solution, in s. 198 of the Act, is to enable the court on the application of the FSA to grant injunctions, or interdicts, to restrain the firm from disposing or otherwise dealing with any of its assets, and otherwise to enable the FSA to perform its functions under the Act.

## SCOPE OF THE POWER OF INTERVENTION

Under FSAMA 2000, s. 196, the kind of requirement that can be imposed under Part XIII is the same as under Part IV. Effectively, the FSA has to contemplate, notionally, that the incoming passport is a Part IV permission, and that satisfying the criteria for exercise of the power of intervention has actually triggered the power under Part IV to vary a Part IV permission. This is dealt with in chapter 6 above, centring on ss. 44(1) and 45(2). Removing a regulated activity, or narrowing its description, or varying a requirement imposed under s. 43, are the options most likely to be used in the Part XIII context. However, this construction depends on giving a non-technical meaning to the word 'requirement' in s. 196. A narrower construction would confine the FSA in this context to the structure in s. 43.

## EXERCISE OF POWERS IN SUPPORT OF OVERSEAS REGULATORS

FSAMA 2000, s. 195, offers the second avenue for use of powers of intervention. This contemplates exercise at the request of or for the purpose of assisting an overseas regulator. On analysis, this section breaks down into two separate parts. First, if the request or the purpose of assisting relates to a so-called Community obligation, then the existence of the Community obligation, assuming that the FSA concludes that it exists, is a sufficient ground in itself for the exercise of the power. This follows from s. 195(5), which requires the FSA, in deciding whether or not to intervene, to consider whether intervention is necessary in order to comply with a Community obligation. Community obligation is undefined in the Act, but the analysis will presumably be the same as in the other places in the Act, especially Part IV, where if the FSA diagnoses a Community obligation, it is then required to act accordingly. The most likely circumstance where an obligation would be found to exist would be in a flagrant case where the home State had itself taken intervention action, or even withdrawn authorisation. Here, the general duty to cooperate with other competent authorities (see, in particular, s. 354) might well mean that something similar or parallel had to be put in place in the UK. Since these cases are also referable to the Financial Services and Markets Tribunal (see s. 195), the existence of the Community obligation, and the basis on which the home regulator had acted if relevant, will be capable of judicial reconsideration.

Where there is no Community obligation, the criteria for exercise of power of intervention at the request of or to assist an overseas regulator are set out in s. 195(6). These correspond, virtually word for word, to the equivalent criteria for exercise of the FSA's own-initiative power at the request of or to assist specific overseas regulators in s. 47(4).

## CONSUMER CREDIT

The power of intervention is also available to the FSA in relation to consumer credit, if the Director General of Fair Trading informs the FSA that one of the conditions precedent to the exercise of power of intervention has arisen (FSAMA 2000, s. 194(3)). The effect of the subsection is to bring to bear on an incoming EEA firm the FSA's powers of intervention in relation to the firm's passport as a whole. This may seem an odd provision, but it derives from the fact that the Single Market Directives allow incoming financial firms to exercise their passport in relation to consumer credit (see for instance the Credit Institutions Directive, annex A, para. 2 and footnote; Investment Services Directive, annex, sch. C, para. 3).

There is a second set of sanctions, in ss. 203 and 204, which are in the hands of the Director General of Fair Trading himself, and which are modelled on the procedure available to him under the Consumer Credit Act 1974. It may be expected, therefore, that the Director General would seek to use his own powers, to prohibit the carrying on of Consumer Credit Act 1974 business, in any case where, in his view, that was a sufficient response to the problems in the firm concerned. The requirements in the Directives are to take measures to put an end to the irregular situation: so if that irregular situation were limited to consumer credit aspects, ss. 203 and 204 might be the appropriate response. If, however, the matter complained of went beyond that ambit, then the FSA's powers would be available at the request of the Director General. The criterion in both cases is virtually the same, that is, the Director General's conclusion that the firm has done anything of the kind specified in s. 25(2)(a) to (d) of the Consumer Credit Act 1974. This list is as follows:

(a)    commission of any offence involving fraud, dishonesty or violence;

(b)    contravention of any provision made under the Consumer Credit Act 1974 or other legislation on individual credit or individual transactions;

(c)    discrimination in a business context on the grounds of sex, colour, race, or ethnic or national origin;

(d)    engaging in business practices appearing to the Director General to be deceitful, oppressive, or, whether unlawful or not, unfair or improper.

Where, however, the Director does not make a finding about past conduct and is concerned about likely future contraventions, he is limited to his own powers in ss. 203 and 204.

# Chapter Sixteen
# Disciplinary Measures

*Loretta Minghella*

Part XIV of the Financial Services and Markets Act 2000 (FSAMA 2000) sets out the two disciplinary tools available to the FSA to deal with the misconduct of authorised persons: the power of public censure in s. 205 and the power to impose a financial penalty in s. 206. There is no statutory limit to the amount of a penalty which the FSA can impose.

Whilst these powers have been a familiar component of UK financial services regulatory tool kits since 1988, and widely used by other financial services regulators internationally for decades, the decision to include them in this Act attracted significant debate. None of the relevant statutory financial services regulators had previously had the power to impose a financial penalty, and not all had shared the Securities and Investments Board's power to issue a public statement of misconduct. The approach to managing the behaviour of regulated firms had developed in what was therefore largely a non-public environment. Against this background, the temperature of the debate was perhaps unsurprising.

In response to concerns raised during the Bill's passage through Parliament, additional safeguards were introduced in relation to the FSA's policies and procedures for the exercise of these powers which are more fully described below.

## WHAT CONTRAVENTIONS MAY BE DISCIPLINED?

The FSAMA 2000 powers of public censure (s. 205) and imposition of a financial penalty (s. 206) may be invoked in relation to a contravention of a requirement imposed by or under the Act. The most obvious requirements are those contained in the FSA's rules, made under Part X of the Act (see chapter 12). Many other requirements are imposed by or under the Act itself, or deemed to be so imposed. In particular, s. 20 has the effect that where an authorised person carries on a regulated activity in the UK otherwise than in accordance with his permission to do so, he is to be taken to have contravened a requirement imposed on him by the FSA under the Act. Specific requirements may include those imposed under s. 43 in relation to the way the firm carries on its particular activities (see chapter 6) and those imposed in the context of investigations under Part XI (see chapter 13). It appears that where a firm commits an offence under the Act, it will breach a requirement imposed by or under the Act, and will therefore be capable, in theory at least, of being disciplined under Part XIV for the breach.

## FSA APPROACH TO DISCIPLINE

The FSA is required by FSAMA 2000, s. 210, to publish a statement setting out its approach to financial penalties under Part XIV. This must cover its policy in relation to the use of the power in the first place, and, where it decides in favour of a financial penalty, the factors it will consider when deciding on the amount. This policy statement must be published first in draft, and the FSA must take appropriate steps to bring it to the public's attention. Regard must be had to representations made in consultation before the statement is finalised. The FSA is then obliged to publish an account of representations received and its response. Where the final statement differs significantly from the consultative draft, the FSA must point out the differences. The finalised statement must be appropriately published, and a copy sent to the Treasury without delay. Changes to the statement will have to go through the same consultation and publication procedure. Section 210(7) requires the FSA to have regard to the statement in force at the time of a contravention when exercising its powers to impose a penalty.

Although not obliged to do so, the FSA has indicated that it will publish a statement of its approach to both disciplinary powers, not just its power to impose a penalty. It is evident that the censure power is destined generally to be used in the less serious disciplinary cases, or in cases which would have resulted in a penalty if the firm's resources were sufficient to pay it.

The factors which the FSA has indicated that it proposes to take into account in deciding whether to take disciplinary action include: the nature and seriousness of the breach, the conduct of the firm after the breach, the previous disciplinary record of the firm, relevant guidance given by the FSA, action taken by it in previous similar cases, and action taken by other regulatory authorities. The FSA has indicated in its Consultation Paper 65a that not every breach will warrant disciplinary action. Indeed, the FSA has repeatedly said that it will be a minority of breaches which are likely to fall into this category. It is clear that many breaches will be resolved by discussion between a firm and its supervisors, perhaps leading to agreement to improve the firm's systems and controls. In other cases, an informal warning may be given.

## FSA APPROACH TO FINANCIAL PENALTIES

The FSA does not have an entirely free hand when framing its policy in relation to financial penalties. Quite apart from its ordinary public law duty to behave reasonably, the FSA has a general duty under FSAMA 2000, s. 2(3)(c), to have regard to the principle that a burden imposed on a person should be proportionate to the benefits. More particularly, s. 210(2) requires that the FSA's policy on determining what the size of any penalty should be must include having regard to the seriousness of the breach, the extent to which it was deliberate or reckless and whether or not the person on whom the penalty is to be imposed is an individual.

In relation to the first factor, the seriousness of the breach, the FSA has indicated that the following may be relevant: the duration and frequency of the contravention, whether it revealed serious or systemic weakness of management systems or internal controls; the impact on orderliness of financial markets; the loss or risk of loss caused to consumers or other market users.

The requirement in s. 210 to have regard to whether the person concerned is an individual was inserted during the Bill's passage through Parliament and reflects recommendations by the Joint Committee on Financial Services and Markets. How this is supposed to work in practice is not entirely clear. There was a perception that one of the problems with predecessor regimes was the potential for unfairness where individuals were concerned. This appears largely to do with the perceived difficulties individuals may have in defending themselves, as compared with large corporate organisations, which in turn appears to be based on the relative financial positions of individuals and large corporates. However, the authorised community includes many small companies giving financial advice on the high street. These may be much less well-off than many individuals who may be the subject of a financial penalty.

Nevertheless, size and resources of a firm may be relevant to financial penalties in a number of ways. Systemic failure in a large firm could damage or threaten to damage more consumers than a similar failure in a small firm. The size and resources of a firm may be relevant to mitigation: in particular what it might be reasonable for the firm to do in response to a breach may vary according to the resources of the firm concerned. Moreover, the purpose of a penalty is not to threaten solvency, and it will be necessary to have regard to financial resources where a financial penalty of the usual amount in such cases might have the effect of putting the firm out of business. It is clear that any other approach would risk compromising the FSA in respect of s. 206(2), which states that it may not both impose a penalty and withdraw authorisation in respect of the same contravention. With this in mind, the FSA has indicated that its proposed approach is to have regard to the size, financial resources and other circumstances of the person concerned, including whether or not the person is an individual.

As a general rule, the FSA has said that it does not generally propose to impose penalties on any kind of tariff basis. As an exception to its general policy, however, the FSA has indicated that it proposes to use an indicative scale of penalties for the late submission of reports and other documents which firms are required to submit to it. This indicative scale would provide a framework for taking into account the lateness of the return and the annual fees paid by the firm to the FSA, these being barometers of seriousness and resources.

## DISCIPLINARY PROCEDURE

Although FSAMA 2000, Part XIV, purports to deal with disciplinary measures, most of the substantive provisions on process are to be found in Part XXVI of the Act (see chapter 28), following significant amendment to Parts XIV and XXVI in the House of Lords.

The procedure for the exercise of the powers of public censure (s. 205) and imposition of a financial penalty (s. 206) involves the issue by the FSA of a warning notice setting out the proposed statement of censure, or the amount of the penalty as the case may be (s. 207; see also s. 387 in chapter 28). Certain material must then be disclosed by FSA (see s. 394 in chapter 28). The firm may make representations at this point and so may certain third parties. Section 393 deals with third-party rights in this context. If the FSA decides to proceed further, it is then obliged to give a decision notice, setting out the statement or penalty (s. 207) in accordance with s. 388. Chapter 28 sets this out in more detail. The firm may accept the outcome at that stage. Alternatively, the matter may be referred to the Financial Services and Markets Tribunal in accordance with the provisions of Part IX of the Act (see chapter 11). For present purposes, it is worth noting that the Tribunal is to be a first-instance tribunal with full jurisdiction over all matters of fact and law.

While the firm is considering whether or not to exercise its right to refer the matter to the Tribunal, the FSA may not publish the statement or seek to recover the penalty (s. 133(9)). Once the period in which referral can be made has expired, or any decision so referred has been confirmed by the Tribunal (or on appeal), the FSA may publish the statement or seek to recover the penalty as the case may be. There is a requirement to give the person concerned a final notice at that point (s. 390). After a statement has been published, a copy must be sent to the firm concerned (s. 209). A copy must also be sent to potentially prejudiced third parties, being persons to whom a copy of the decision notice was given under s. 393(4).

## FINANCIAL PENALTIES: WHAT HAPPENS TO THE MONEY?

FSAMA 2000, sch. 1, para. 16, requires the FSA to operate a scheme to apply for the benefit of the authorised community the money it receives by way of penalties. The FSA's penalty policy must take no account of the expenses incurred in discharging its functions (sch. 1, para. 16(1)). The scheme must be prepared in draft, consulted upon, refined in the light of consultation and published in the same way as the FSA's penalty policy.

## ARTICLE 6 OF THE EUROPEAN CONVENTION ON HUMAN RIGHTS

Some have suggested that the safeguards outlined here and in related chapters do not go far enough in relation to discipline, on the basis that disciplinary action is criminal for the purposes of art. 6 of the European Convention on Human Rights.

Such action is certainly not criminal for domestic purposes, but that is not determinative for art. 6 purposes. Were discipline to be criminal for art. 6 purposes, certain additional safeguards would automatically flow: for example, in the context of a presumption of innocence, there would be a privilege against self-incrimination in the disciplinary proceedings. There would also be an express right to legal assistance for those of insufficient means when the interests of justice so require. The question whether art. 6 applies in its civil or criminal guise to disciplinary proceedings was debated at length in the Joint Committee on Financial Services and Markets and mentioned at various points in the Parliamentary process. The government, advised by Sir Sidney Kentridge QC and James Eadie, took the view that the disciplinary regime was not criminal for art. 6 purposes and that, unlike the market abuse regime, there was not sufficient doubt about it to warrant introducing criminal safeguards in case the courts took a different view. It is generally accepted that art. 6 applies in full to the disciplinary process as a whole in its civil form. As further explained in chapters 10 and 28, compliance with art. 6 is ultimately secured by the availability of referral to an independent tribunal of full jurisdiction, the Financial Services and Markets Tribunal.

# Chapter Seventeen
# Compensation

## *Michael Blair*

Part XV of the Financial Services and Markets Act 2000 (FSAMA 2000) requires the FSA to establish a new body to run a system for compensation. The essential nature of the scheme is to provide a safety net for the benefit of users of regulated services. If they have justified claims against a firm which was authorised at the time when the claims arose, and the firm is unable or likely to be unable to satisfy those claims, the scheme steps in to satisfy the claims, and raises money from within the authorised community in order to pay them.

As with much else in the Act, the provisions made at the level of the statute itself are fairly general. Part XV itself has, for instance, no more than 13 sections, and there is no relevant schedule to the Act. As with the previous schemes which are replaced by the Act (see below), much of the detail will, therefore, be in rules made by the FSA, which has the task of establishing the machinery for the scheme.

## PREVIOUS BODIES

Before the commencement of FSAMA 2000, compensation in the financial services field was dealt with by five central schemes (one of which was voluntary), and a number of others that were specific to particular legal, accountancy and actuarial professions. Deposit-taking business, for instance, was covered by the Deposit Protection Scheme, for banks, and the Building Societies Investor Protection Scheme, for building societies. There was also a Policyholders Protection Scheme, for most though not all insurance business, and a very similar but voluntary Friendly Societies Protection Scheme for insurance business carried on by friendly societies. For investment business as in the Financial Services Act 1986, there was an Investors Compensation Scheme (ICS). Furthermore, under the same Act of 1986, each of the eight professional bodies recognised under that Act, in relation to 'investment business', was required to have compensation arrangements. So far as members of those professional bodies will become authorised by the FSA under the Act, they will be brought into the new central compensation arrangements.

The various previous schemes each had separate structures, financial limits, definitions of eligible claims and claimants and procedural requirements, often set down in the main statute. Each of them also had their own claims history and characteristics. For instance, the scheme for building societies has never been called upon, whereas the ICS has had a regular stream of defaults, mainly among independent financial advisers, and has accordingly built up a staff of over 100. In the years 1988 to 1999 it has paid out compensation totalling £142 million, in 726 separate cases. In between is the scheme for banks, which has paid out over £150 million during its life, and the scheme for insurance companies which has paid out around £220 million. These, however, have occurred in a much smaller number of much larger defaults compared with the regular annual task of the ICS in handling numerous smaller cases.

Under the provisions of FSAMA 2000, the extent to which the different arrangements are unified hereafter is left very largely in the hands of the FSA. Section 214, for instance, enables, but does not require, 'the establishment of different funds for meeting different kinds of claim' (s. 214(1)(b)). There is, however, in the Act itself some special machinery, discussed below, to deal with the specific issues that arise about continuity in the insurance sector, whether in the life or the non-life context.

## EUROPEAN REQUIREMENTS

Part XV of FSAMA 2000 is designed to enable the United Kingdom to continue to comply with the relevant Directives in the field of consumer compensation for financial services. These are the Deposit Guarantee Directive (94/19/EC) and the Investor Compensation Directive (97/9/EC). There is presently no European requirement for compensation in relation to general or life insurance.

## THE CONSUMER'S VIEW OF COMPENSATION

If a bank has a person's money on deposit, or a policy has been taken out with an insurance company, or an investment firm has a consumer's assets or client money, it may be a source of great anxiety to discover that the firm has ceased trading and may be or has been declared insolvent. The scheme is designed to maintain consumer confidence and offer a certain level of protection by assuring consumers that in such cases the debts due to them and proper claims of theirs will be met (or largely met) by the industry as a whole.

The scheme is designed to relate to 'claims made in connection with regulated activities carried on . . . by relevant persons' (s. 213(3)(a)). It does not matter that the relevant business was carried on in breach of an FSA permission, so long as the person carrying it on was authorised at the time of the act or omission giving rise to the claim.

'Claim' is undefined but may be taken to include, assuming that rules are made on the lines currently proposed, any claim that has been or could be enforced in a court of law. This will include claims for return of deposits from banks and building societies, and claims for breach of actionable rules made by the FSA (as to which see s. 150). This class of case will be highly significant, at least for the securities and investment advice sectors, in view of the large number of cases disposed of by the relevant predecessor scheme (ICS) which related to breach of rules made by the relevant SRO, such as suitability of the investment for the customer. Claims will also include awards made by the ombudsman but remaining unpaid at the time of default (see chapter 18). This is because, in the compulsory jurisdiction, once the complainant has accepted the determination, it becomes binding on the authorised person and becomes enforceable as a money award. The awards made in the voluntary jurisdiction are also enforceable as a matter of contract.

The next question of relevance to the consumer is whether he or she is an eligible claimant. Section 214(1)(f) envisages rules that specify particular kinds of claimant. It is expected that compensation cover should primarily be available to private individuals and very small businesses: if so, that would be a change, in some areas, from the pre 2001 position, with large companies no longer being able to claim deposit protection, but small companies being able to claim policyholder protection when they could not before.

A third question of interest to the consumer is how much he or she is likely to recover through the scheme, and whether there are any financial limits relating to large claims. The Act contemplates that the amount payable on a claim may be limited to a specified maximum amount (s. 214(1)(j)). These limits can, it appears, be of two kinds. There may be an overall maximum and, instead or in addition, there may be a percentage of the claim that is not met, because of the so-called principle of 'co-insurance'.

In the previous schemes, speaking generally, there was a mixture of different approaches. The schemes relevant for deposit taking had an overall limit of £20,000, with a co-insurance element of 10 per cent, thus yielding a maximum payable of £18,000. In the investment field, there was an overall maximum of £50,000, with no co-insurance up to £30,000 and 10 per cent for the remaining £20,000, yielding, accordingly, a net maximum of £48,000. In the insurance area there was no overall limit, no co-insurance where insurance was compulsory, and up to 10 per cent co-insurance for the remaining areas. Since the new scheme is likely to be segmented along broadly similar lines, it appears that part of the difference in approach just described will be carried forward. It is likely that there will be different limits for the deposit and investment schemes, and that there should be no overall limit on the amount payable in the insurance field. It is also possible that there will be a co-insurance-free tranche in future in the deposit protection and insurance areas.

A final question which a claimant may ask relates to geography. Section 214(4) enables the scheme to be made so as to apply differently in relation to different territories, areas or localities. The purpose is to secure a clear statement of the extent to which the scheme will benefit those doing business abroad, and foreign claimants, bearing in mind that, under the Single Market Directives compensation is regarded as a home State matter, and therefore has to have a geographical coverage across the European Union as a whole for firms based in the United Kingdom and authorised here.

Equally, the UK-based consumer may wish to know what kind of compensation he or she might expect if a French, Danish or other EEA firm were to default on its obligations. The basic rule is that the consumer would look to the home State for compensation, but there are two exceptions to this. First, policyholders protection is still on a host State basis (see, for instance, s. 3(2) of the Policyholders Protection Act 1975 as prospectively amended in 1997). Secondly in the credit institutions and investment services areas, the Directives envisage that incoming passport holders can 'top up' into the host State regime where it is more generous than their own home State one. This recognises that unevenness in compensation regimes could be a competitive disadvantage when consumers are choosing a company or other firm to supply their needs.

## THE INDUSTRY'S VIEW OF COMPENSATION

From the point of view of the firms in the financial services community, the main topic of interest is the overall amount of compensation payable, and the arrangements made for distribution of the amount payable within the industry. When there were different schemes, part of this was regulated automatically by the structure and the relevant legislation for the sectors concerned. Even then, there was still a good deal of debate and difficulty about the distribution, within the ICS, as between the constituencies represented by the three main SROs. Indeed, until the arrival of the Personal Investment Authority (PIA), which was brought about by a merger between a relatively well funded and a relatively poorly funded regulated sector, there were annual difficulties about meeting the liability arising in the latter, which also happened to be the sector in which most of the defaults took place. With a single scheme, these issues become internal to the scheme; and the Act recognises that, by enabling the establishment of different funds for meeting different kinds of claim (s. 214(1)(b)). The present intention is to divide the scheme into three funds, broadly to cover deposit protection, investment services and insurance. There may have to be some 'contribution groups' within two of the three sub-schemes (probably not in deposit protection) in order to provide an appropriate relationship between the defaulting firm and its own peer group.

In the end, there may be as many as eight contribution groups, ranging from banks and building societies to independent advisers.

This structure then raises the question whether there should be cross-contribution between the different funds (or sub-schemes) and, within them, between the different contribution groups. The current proposal is that each of the three funds or sub-schemes should stand on its own feet, and that, while cross-contribution between contribution groups within a particular fund or sub-scheme should be possible, this should be made as infrequent an occurrence as possible.

## OBTAINING INFORMATION

Part XV of FSAMA 2000 contains new unified provision enabling the compensation scheme to obtain the information necessary for it to do its job. Under s. 219, the scheme has a power to require the person in respect of whom a claim is made under the scheme to provide information and documents. The previous scheme for investment business (ICS) lacked such a power, and, it is understood, not infrequently found that a source of difficulty. The Act, therefore, remedies that deficiency, though, it should be noted, the information-gathering powers are less extensive than those available to the FSA itself under s. 167, since the FSA may impose requirements on persons connected with the authorised person, such as directors, employees, agents and other group companies, whereas the powers in s. 219 are limited to the person who is the subject of the claim or to persons knowingly involved in the act or omission giving rise to the claim (s. 219(1) and (10)).

The machinery enabling the scheme to obtain information extends (with modifications) through into the period after a default has occurred. As soon as an insolvency is declared, the scheme's power to obtain information under s. 219 becomes inoperable, at least in domestic cases. Instead, there is provision enabling the scheme to inspect documents in the hands of the liquidator (s. 221) or the official receiver (s. 224).

The new machinery is available to the compensation scheme itself. In this, the Act follows s. 65 of the Banking Act 1987, which dealt, in subsections (3) and (4), with the power of the Deposit Protection Board to obtain information from insolvent institutions and from those concerned in their winding up. The provision in s. 65(1) of the 1987 Act enabling the FSA at the request of the Deposit Protection Board to obtain information about surviving institutions, so as to determine the contributions, has not appeared afresh in FSAMA 2000, Part XV.

## INSURANCE ISSUES

Insurance, and in particular long-term insurance, can pose special problems in relation to compensation. If, for instance, a life policy is payable only upon death or, say, age 65, and the policyholder is still alive and under any such age, there is no immediate ability to claim at law, and, indeed, it would be strange if the mere fact that the insurance company went into default prompted an acceleration of the obligation to pay out on the policy, whether in the sum assured or some actuarially abated sum. Accordingly, ss. 216 and 217 of FSAMA 2000 make provision to enable the scheme to secure continuity of insurance, typically by transferring the benefit and burden of the contract to another authorised person, and making relevant safeguards for the benefit of policyholders. If it is not reasonably practicable for the scheme manager to secure these transfers, the scheme is empowered, if rules are made, to make payment in cash, but, under the structure of the Act, this is seen as very much a second best. It is noticeable that the Act does not envisage applications for compensation in these cases, and the scheme manager may need to act independently and on its own initiative to deal with these special cases. Indeed in some cases policyholders may not be aware that their insurer is in financial difficulties.

Equally, when a general insurer goes into default, it is necessary to provide in one way or another for continuity of cover. Compulsory motor cover is a good example of this.

Some of these special arrangements for insurance liabilities were derived from the Policyholders Protection Act 1975, which in turn was prospectively amended by the Policyholders Protection Act 1997. Limited parts of the 1997 Act have only recently been commenced by the Policyholders Protection Act 1997 (Commencement No. 1) Order 2000 (SI 2000/971), and it can be expected that the rules under the Act will deal with its content as far as appropriate.

## STRUCTURE OF THE SCHEME

Under FSAMA 2000, s. 212, the FSA is obliged to establish a body corporate to operate the scheme, and the Financial Services Compensation Scheme Ltd has been formed to meet that need. Its chairman is Mr Nigel Hamilton, a noted insolvency practitioner. The chairman and other members of the board have to be appointed on terms to secure their independence from the FSA in the operation of the scheme. The Act makes a number of specific provisions about how the scheme is to be run. In particular there must be an annual report to the FSA (s. 218), and management expenses for the administrative purposes of the scheme are not recoverable as part of the levy to be imposed by the compensation company unless a budgetary limit has been fixed in relation to the period in question, and the amount to be raised does not exceed that budget (s. 223). These two elements of external accountability reflect some of the equivalent requirements for the FSA itself (annual report, and obligation to consult on fees). The compensation company and its staff are immune on the same basis as for the FSA itself (s. 222). In consequence, the only method of recourse for those dissatisfied with a decision on the payment of a claim is by way of judicial review, or, under s. 222(2), by establishing bad faith or a breach of the Human Rights Act 1998.

# Chapter Eighteen
# The Ombudsman Scheme

## *Michael Blair*

Part XVI of the Financial Services and Markets Act 2000 (FSAMA 2000) has as its purpose the establishment on a statutory basis of a broadly based scheme of alternative dispute resolution for the customers of the financial services industry. The aim is to provide for relevant disputes to be resolved quickly and with minimum formality by an independent person.

Although referred to in the Act as the ombudsman scheme, the legislation leaves the operating name to be chosen by the scheme operator, and the name so chosen is the Financial Ombudsman Service (FOS).

## STRUCTURE OF THE SCHEME

The FOS replaces eight previous dispute resolution services operating across the financial services sector. Some of these were organised on a voluntary basis (as with the Insurance and Banking Ombudsmen and the Personal Insurance Arbitration Scheme). Others were set up on the basis of a statutory requirement (the Building Societies Ombudsman) or of a regulatory one (PIA Ombudsman, Investment Ombudsman (IMRO firms), SFA Complaints Bureau and Arbitration Service, and the FSA Independent Investigator). In providing a single, one-stop shop, service it is a cardinal point of the architecture of the FOS that anything previously capable of being dealt with by any of those bodies (even if the body worked on a voluntary basis and even if the firm in question did not participate) should find a home in the new service. This unification is expected to handle about 30,000 complaints a year, making the FOS (with 350 staff, and a budget of £20m or so) in all probability the largest scheme of its kind in the world.

A second cardinal point of the scheme's architecture is that the FOS will follow the model of its predecessor ombudsman schemes, in accepting cases only where there has been prior attention to the complaint by the firm concerned. If the relevant rules are made as proposed, consumers will have had to have ventilated their complaints with the firm in question before invoking the jurisdiction of the scheme. Further, the FSA has new powers to require regulated firms to set up and maintain, across the whole relevant field, complaints-handling and resolution procedures of their own. These two measures, taken together, should filter out of the FOS arrangements a very substantial number of disputes which might otherwise have overwhelmed it.

A third cardinal point is the creation of two separate and non-overlapping jurisdictions. One is the compulsory jurisdiction and the second is the voluntary one. Essentially, the compulsory jurisdiction is imposed on authorised firms, and in relation to the general subject matter covered by the schemes in the previous era. Most of the subject matter will be within the anticipated Treasury Regulated Activities Order, but there will be some exceptions in both directions.

REGULATED ACTIVITIES ORDER          COMPULSORY JURISDICTION

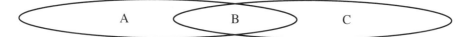

All the business in the Regulated Activities Order will be divided, for ombudsman purposes, into classes A and B. The compulsory jurisdiction will consist of all the business in classes B and C. While all the business in class B will be regulated activities subject to FOS compulsory jurisdiction, there will be some regulated activities not so subject (class A). Corporate finance is a possible example, since there will be no possibility of relevant complainants (see below) coming into contact with such business. Similarly reinsurance will fall into class A, because the counterparty will not be an eligible complainant for ombudsman purposes. Equally, but at the other end of the spectrum, there may well be some unregulated activities which will be made to fall within the compulsory jurisdiction (class C); examples could include the marketing of general insurance by authorised firms, which was covered by the previous Insurance Ombudsman arrangements. The decision by the government in January 2000 to include mortgage lending (though not mortgage advice or broking) within the scope of the authorisation requirements means, however, that the content of class C is likely to be less than if mortgage lending had been left out of the regulatory scope.

Essentially, therefore, the compulsory jurisdiction will cover the carrying on of regulated activities by authorised firms, but in some areas other activities are included and in other areas not all regulated activities are included. Stockbroking, advice on packaged products and handling of the affairs of depositors with, or mortgage borrowers from, credit institutions are therefore included, along with much else.

The voluntary jurisdiction, on the other hand, is intended to relate principally to unauthorised persons, though the Act does not limit it in that way. The outer limit for business to be covered by the voluntary jurisdiction is, loosely speaking, whatever would be capable of being regulated if the Treasury were to decide to bring it within the regulatory scope. This concept of 'potentially regulated activities' is specified in s. 227(4) of the Act, which throws the reader back to s. 226(4) and thus to the test in s. 22. All activities in relation to investments (in the new, broad, sense of that word as an asset, right or interest), and all activities carried on in relation to property of any kind, are thus potentially covered. It is hard to think of an activity that could be described in any sense as 'financial' that would not fall within the power. And the wording is apt to include much that is not financial (car sales or lawnmower repairs would be examples); so it is not surprising that the FOS and the FSA have indicated that the voluntary jurisdiction will be proceeded with on a cautious and incremental basis.

The voluntary jurisdiction may also cover authorised firms, where a complaint relates to something covered by the voluntary jurisdiction, but not covered by the compulsory jurisdiction rules. If therefore the voluntary jurisdiction were to cover, say, mortgage broking, or aspects of consumer credit, the rules would be able to extend that scope to authorised and unauthorised firms alike. But if, say, mortgage broking by authorised firms were to be made a regulated activity and were also to be brought into the compulsory jurisdiction, then the voluntary jurisdiction could no longer deal with complaints of that sort (s. 227(2)(e)).

The voluntary jurisdiction can operate only if the respondent firm has agreed to join the scheme and is thus participating in it, though it is to be expected that market competitiveness and transparency (and indeed the influence of relevant trade associations and professional bodies) will create some commercial pressure to join up.

## OPERATION OF THE COMPULSORY JURISDICTION

It is not possible to describe in full detail the operation of the compulsory jurisdiction rules until the relevant rules are made by the FSA, and so far as relevant by FOS. Nonetheless the broad approach which will be adopted by the FOS in applying the provisions of Part XVI of the Act is already clear. It can be summarised under the following headings.

### Consent by an eligible complainant

The Act indicates clearly (in ss. 228 and 229) that the compulsory nature of the jurisdiction extends only to compelling the firm complained of ('the respondent'); the customer or other complainant is not compelled to submit to the jurisdiction, nor indeed, to accept the outcome (as to which see further below). To be able to use the Service, however, the complainant has to be eligible (s. 227(2)(a)): 'eligible' is to be defined by the FSA, and the expectation is that the access to the scheme will be limited to private individuals and to small businesses, whether incorporated or not, within specific turnover and size limits.

## Investigative procedure

Under the scheme provided for by the Act, both the FSA and the FOS have power to deal with different aspects of the procedure for dealing with complaints. Under para. 13 of sch. 17, the FSA deals with two of the conditions for making a complaint (the time limit, and the requirement, referred to above, to seek prior informal resolution of the complaint through the firm's own complaints procedure). The FOS is to deal, by 'scheme rules', with the procedure for reference of complaints, and investigation, consideration and determination of them by the Ombudsman.

So the Act calls for an investigative process, rather than the adversarial one familiar to those who practise in the courts. Further, by s. 231, the ombudsman has a statutory power to require either party to provide such information or to produce such documents as he considers necessary for the determination of the complaint. In effect, therefore, the ombudsman is in charge of the process, and he can require answers to questions and the delivery to him of files, correspondence and other records to help him deal with the issues before him. And his power to obtain answers and papers is enforceable by contempt proceedings in the High Court (or Court of Session) unless the defaulter has a reasonable excuse for failing to comply (s. 232).

## 'Fair and reasonable'

Each ombudsman operating the compulsory jurisdiction is required, by s. 228(2), to determine complaints by reference to what, in his opinion, is fair and reasonable in all the circumstances of the case. This is likely to include many of the considerations which would be relevant in a court of law in determining legal liability, but is not limited to that strictly legal approach. The concept is designed to achieve fairness on a case-by-case basis in accordance with the merits. While, therefore, the ombudsmen will have to respect the nature of the contractual bargain, if there is one, and will need to be wary of setting aside or modifying contracts where a court itself could not do so, they will be able to reach conclusions favourable to complainants in cases where the courts would not be able to find a relevant legal relationship. Unfairness in administration, delays in dealing with correspondence, and unreasonable behaviour in relation to quality of service are all potentially within the scope of 'fair and reasonable' determinations.

Consistency is, however, answered by the need for a written and signed statement of the determination, given to both sides, and containing the reasons for the determination. There is no appeal from any determination once it becomes final and binding (as to which see below), and, indeed, the purpose of the scheme is to produce swift, consistent and summary justice. Technically, therefore, any challenge by the respondent (and under the scheme he alone could be bound by a finding with which he disagreed) would have to be brought by way of judicial review. With the test being 'what is, in the opinion of the ombudsman, fair and reasonable' (s. 228(2)), the only realistic basis for challenge appears to be that of irrationality in the '*Wednesbury* unreasonable' sense, or some element of procedural unfairness in breach of the FOS rules, or an error of law relating to the ombudsman system itself.

## The award

Part of the ombudsman's determination is the amount and type of redress to be awarded. There may be a money award of fair compensation for loss or damage, and there may also be, with or without a money award, a direction to take just and appropriate steps in relation to the complainant (s. 229(2)). So where the ombudsman decides that money is the correct form of recompense he may make a money award (subject to some special limits discussed below); but if he thinks it just and appropriate to require something more specific, that is also within his power. Reinstatement of an inappropriately surrendered life policy or the back-dated reissue of specific units in a unit trust scheme are examples of the taking of steps. It does not matter that the court could not make such a direction (s. 229(2)(b)). The Act specifies, however, that the direction operates only as between the parties (s. 229(2)). If, therefore, the inappropriate surrender of the life policy were caused by poor quality advice, not by the insurance company but by the complainant's own adviser, the direction could not be aimed at the insurance company, and the best the ombudsman could do would be to direct the adviser to seek, at his own expense, the reinstatement of the consumer, and with a money award becoming payable instead if he was unable to achieve the primary result.

There are specific provisions in s. 229 about the amount of money awards. The basic rule is that 'financial loss' lies within the ombudsman's power. The actual 'quantum' is not limited to that which a judge would award in a court (the ombudsman has to assess the amount which would be 'fair compensation for loss or damage'); but the kinds of financial loss (direct loss, consequential loss etc.) are those in the textbooks on damages for financial loss. In addition, the FSA has power to specify (with or without a special upper financial limit) other kinds of loss or damage where the 'fair compensation' rule can then operate. Examples would be distress or inconvenience, pain and suffering, or even damage to reputation. Costs incurred in the making of the complaint are not to be included in the award as there is special provision about costs. It is understood that the FSA proposes to include some additional heads of loss or damage, but not to specify any financial limit for any of them (other than the overall limit, as to which see the next paragraph).

There has to be an overall monetary limit, and it is expected that the FSA will specify, under the power in s. 229(6), an overall maximum of £100,000. Actual awards will therefore be at or under this, but the complainant may find that he or she is able to receive, under the compulsory jurisdiction, more than this in money or money's worth. This is because the monetary limit does not apply to:

(a)    'directions' to take steps, which could have a monetary value;
(b)    interest, which is payable on the award and therefore is in addition; and

(c)   costs, for which a special regime is erected under s. 230.

Further, even where the £100,000 limit does apply, and cuts down what would otherwise be fair compensation, the ombudsman can make an (unenforceable) recommendation to the respondent that he should pay the difference on a voluntary basis.

**Legal effect of the determination**

This subject was touched on earlier in the context of the fairness and reasonableness of the determination. The scheme is essentially one-sided, in the sense that the respondent can be bound by the award if the complainant accepts it (s. 228(5)); but the respondent has no option of that kind. If the complainant does not like any element of the determination, or indeed if there is no award in the determination because the ombudsman finds for the respondent, the complainant is entirely free to pursue his hopes of a remedy elsewhere. In this respect the structure is similar to the predecessor ombudsman schemes, but quite unlike arbitral proceedings, where the submission of the dispute to arbitration means that the rights of the parties are (barring most unusual circumstances) to be determined in the arbitration in a conclusive way.

At one stage it was thought by some that the fact that the complainant was not bound unless he signalled his acceptance would be of some assistance to the scheme in relation to art. 6 of the European Convention of Human Rights. The ombudsmen in some of the previous schemes have operated very informal arrangements, with the majority of the work done on the papers and without any right to an oral hearing. There was concern that this informality might have to be tightened up to comply with art. 6, if 'civil rights' were to be 'determined'. The one-sided nature of the jurisdiction appeared to offer some comfort, until it was realised that, in any event, the procedures could have the effect of compulsorily determining the civil rights of the respondent firm. The Bill for the Act has been certified by Ministers as 'human rights compliant', and so it is to be expected that the relevant civil guarantees under art. 6 will be accorded in the procedure.

Once the determination is accepted it is binding on both sides and final. There is no appeal as such; and enforcement is available in the county courts (or sheriff court in Scotland, or the equivalent in Northern Ireland) for money awards (sch. 17, para. 16) and by injunction (or the equivalent) for directions to take steps (s. 229(9)).

The question of the relevance of the determination, if not accepted, in subsequent proceedings is not determined by the Act. There plainly can be no '*res judicata*' effect since s. 228(6) is clear about that; and there probably can be no 'issue estoppel' since there has been no determination of any kind to generate any authoritative finding on any issue. The only determination in question has been 'rejected'. The courts and tribunals are likely, therefore, if the issue presents itself, to regard the written determination of the ombudsman as no more than an expression of opinion, the admissibility of which, without any question of cross-examination, is likely to depend on the specific rules of evidence applicable to the legal proceedings. Moreover, since the merits test for the ombudsman is 'fair and reasonable', the court or tribunal will almost always find that the issues it has to determine are different. That said, the determination may on occasion be found useful for its analysis of the case, for the 'fact finding' resulting from the investigation, and for the light it sheds on the conduct of the parties before and during the proceedings before the ombudsman.

## THE VOLUNTARY JURISDICTION

The voluntary jurisdiction is in essence a second scheme, operated by the same ombudsmen within the same organisational structure, but according to legally separate rules and separate financial arrangements. Much of the detail about the scheme remains to be filled in by voluntary jurisdiction rules (made by the scheme operator with FSA consent under FSAMA 2000, s. 227(3) and (6)) and by the standard terms of reference (fixed by the scheme with FSA approval). It is understood that the powers will be exercised so as to produce as much similarity between the compulsory and voluntary jurisdictions as is legally possible. The main elements are as follows:

(a)   the firm in question has to be a willing member of ('participant in') the scheme;

(b)   the complainant has to fall into the class of eligible complainants, (a class that *can* be different from the class of those who can use the compulsory jurisdiction, but is likely to be the same) and has to be willing to use the scheme for his complaint;

(c)   the complaint has to relate, as mentioned above, to business that is not at the time within the compulsory jurisdiction and is business specified in rules;

(d)   though voluntary up to this point, once the machinery starts it can proceed with an element of compulsion; the investigative powers of the ombudsman are the same in the two jurisdictions, as are the arrangements for securing obedience to them; and it can be expected that the terms of reference will by the contract of submission to the jurisdiction import a certain element of compulsion to secure compliance with eventual awards;

(e)   the procedure and the terms of reference deal with all the remaining detail, including the question of fees for the service involved, and, presumably, costs between parties (though the power to write costs rules is limited to the compulsory jurisdiction).

## THE OMBUDSMEN AND THE SCHEME OPERATOR

FSAMA 2000, s. 225 and sch. 17 provide for the FOS to be administered by a corporate body known in the Act as the 'scheme operator'. The company has been established, under the chairmanship of Mr Andreas Whittam-Smith. The chairman and the other directors are appointed by the FSA, but the terms of their appointment must be such as to secure their independence from the FSA in the operation of the scheme (sch. 17, para. 3). The company has operational and financial responsibilities, and legislative powers, both for the compulsory and the voluntary jurisdiction, but subject to the approval of the FSA.

The Act envisages the appointment and maintenance, by the scheme operator, of a panel of persons with appropriate qualifications and experience to act as ombudsmen. The panel consists of the chief ombudsman, and other members to act as ombudsmen. The chief ombudsman is Mr Walter Merricks. The functions of the chief ombudsman are not specified in detail in the Act, beyond his obligation to report to the FSA annually on the discharge of his functions (in parallel with a report required from the scheme operator on the discharge of its functions). As things have developed, however, the chief ombudsman has become the spokesman for and champion of the scheme, and is effectively the chief executive as well as the principal 'quasi-judicial' officer in the scheme itself.

The relationship between the FSA and the scheme is specified with some clarity. Any legislative function of the scheme requires the FSA's consent or approval, as do the annual budget and the standard terms of reference for the voluntary jurisdiction. It seems plain from the Act that Parliament does not envisage any direct relationship between the FOS and the Treasury or Treasury ministers: accountability is exclusively to the FSA, as in the case of the compensation scheme (see chapter 19).

In establishing the arrangements for the voluntary jurisdiction, part IV of sch. 17 to the Act contemplates that there may be arrangements whereby part of the voluntary jurisdiction is exercised, on behalf of the scheme, by outside bodies which are concerned, whether by statute or otherwise, with operating broadly comparable schemes for the resolution of disputes. The Mortgage Code Compliance Board and the General Insurance Standards Council are possible bodies which might fit the description of those to whom part of the voluntary jurisdiction can be delegated.

# Chapter Nineteen
# Collective Investment Schemes

*George Walker*

Statutory provisions concerning collective investment schemes are now set out in Part XVII of the Financial Services and Markets Act 2000 (FSAMA 2000). These generally replicate the earlier requirements set out in the Financial Services Act 1986 (FSA 1986) although a number of new provisions are included, such as with regard to approving changes to authorised unit trusts' investment and borrowing powers by the FSA. Part XVII also restates with amendment the powers previously dealt with under the European Communities Act 1972 for regulations to be issued by the Treasury in connection with the creation and operation of open-ended investment companies (OEICs). Many of the earlier regulations governing the operation of collective investment schemes will now be reissued (as rules) by the FSA.

Unit trust and similar schemes remain important investment vehicles in the UK and abroad. The essence of such schemes is that they provide for the collective holding, management and investment of a pool of assets from which the earnings or gains on disposition are shared. These attributes are reflected in the definition of a collective investment scheme set out in FSAMA 2000, s. 235(1). While such schemes may be constituted either in an unincorporated or incorporated form, the distinct characteristic of UK schemes has been that they have traditionally been based on the concept of a trust. This provides for the collective holding of the property concerned as well as determining the general rights and liabilities of the parties concerned.

The principal advantages of unit trusts and similar schemes is that they allow the unit holder to share in the gains derived from the holding of a portfolio of shares, commodities or other assets but without the need to have any investment management experience or to be involved in the management of the fund as such. The use of professional managers allows the portfolio to be better managed while a separate trustee acts as a custodian and generally protects the interests of the unit holders. The authorisation of schemes will also ensure that they are subject to proper regulation with restrictions being imposed on the promotion of unregulated schemes to the general public. Managers are subject to various requirements concerning the assets in which trust funds may be placed depending upon the nature of the particular scheme. Borrowing or gearing is generally prohibited or, at least, subject to strict control. Tax advantages are also available such as with regard to the capital gains treatment of authorised unit trust schemes. Over 1,250 unit trust schemes are currently authorised in the UK with assets under management of over £400 billion.

The provisions set out in FSAMA 2000 apply to collective investment schemes as defined in s. 235(1), subject to exemptions made by Treasury regulations. The Act will then cover such schemes as authorised unit trusts, OEICs and recognised schemes as well as certain unregulated schemes. Unregulated schemes may, for example, include unauthorised unit trusts or unauthorised OEICs or such other collective holding arrangements as bloodstock syndicates, many limited partnerships or certain other pooling arrangements. The provisions will not apply to investment trust companies which are incorporated under the Companies Act and governed by that Act and the separate provisions in FSAMA 2000 concerning the issuance of listed and unlisted securities. An OEIC falls within the definition of a collective investment scheme and is to be governed by Treasury regulations made under Chapter IV of Part XVII of FSAMA 2000 and FSA rules made under those regulations. Schemes not covered will include life assurance schemes, partnerships and other forms of business association and other forms of parallel management which do not provide for the pooling of assets or gains.

Part XVII of the Act is in six Chapters. Chapter I contains relevant definitions and gives the Treasury power to exclude by order certain arrangements from being collective investment schemes. Chapter II prohibits authorised persons from promoting participation in a collective investment scheme unless an exemption applies. Authorised unit trust schemes, authorised OEICs and recognised schemes are exempt. Chapter III sets out the procedures and general rules to apply to the authorisation of unit trust schemes. Chapter IV gives the Treasury power to issue regulations in connection with OEICs. While this generally continues the earlier provisions, it also allows regulations to be issued concerning the establishment and regulation of new forms of OEICs in the UK which go beyond the UCITS Directive of 1985 (see below). Chapter V provides for the recognition of overseas schemes. This generally includes schemes authorised in other EEA States, designated territories or other individually recognised countries. Powers of investigation are set out in Chapter VI in connection with authorised unit trusts and overseas schemes. Equivalent provision in connection with OEICs are to be set out in Treasury regulations.

## ORIGINS AND DEVELOPMENT

The earliest forms of unit trusts set up in the UK were fixed schemes which provided for the purchase of a predetermined number of investment or portfolio units by a manager and held by a trustee. Sub-units were then sold to investors.

The amount of sub-units could be increased only if the trust deed provided for the creation of further investment units. The first scheme was the Foreign and Colonial Government Trust which was advertised for subscription on 20 March 1868. This was followed by various other schemes including the Submarine Cables Trust. Although this was held to be illegal in *Sykes* v *Beadon* (1879) 11 ChD 170 to the extent that it constituted an unincorporated association of more than 20 persons carrying on business contrary to s. 4 of the Companies Act 1862, this was overturned on appeal in *Smith* v *Anderson* (1880) 15 Ch D 247. The Court of Appeal considered that the certificate holders were not in association, the management of the trust did not amount to carrying on business and, at any rate, the business was not carried on by the certificate holders but by the trustees. Flexible trust schemes, which allowed for the investment portfolio to be managed on a discretionary basis, began with the Foreign Government Bond Trust in 1934. Although flexible as opposed to fixed structures became almost standard practice over time, fixed schemes have since become more important again with the recent emergence of single property schemes.

**Early controls**

Unit trusts became subject to statutory regulation under the Prevention of Fraud (Investments) Act 1944. This was subsequently replaced by the Prevention of Fraud (Investments) Act 1958. This provided for the authorisation of unit trust schemes by the Board of Trade (subsequently the Department of Trade and Industry) subject to certain conditions, in particular, concerning the duties of the manager and trustee and certain other matters as set out in the schedule to the 1958 Act. Only authorised schemes could be promoted to the general public. The 1958 Act was subsequently repealed by FSA 1986, which created a new statutory framework for the regulation for collective investment schemes. The detailed requirements were developed in the SIB's rule book although day-to-day supervision was generally delegated to IMRO and LAUTRO. While a considerable degree of self-regulation had already been developed within the unit trust industry, in particular, under the Association of Unit Trust Managers (subsequently the Unit Trust Association), this was replaced by the new provisions given effect to under FSA 1986.

**UCITS**

The provisions of FSA 1986 and relevant rules were drafted to give effect to the provisions set out in Directive 85/611/EEC of 20 December 1985 on the coordination of laws, regulations and administrative provisions related to undertakings for collective investments in transferable securities (UCITS). The Directive was adopted to harmonise laws relating to collective investment schemes throughout Europe and to facilitate the cross-border marketing of qualifying schemes. To qualify as a UCITS, a scheme had to comply with a number of requirements in connection with its establishment, operation and management.

The Directive applies to undertakings the sole object of which is the collective investment in transferable securities or capital raised from the public and which operate on the principle of risk spreading and the units of which may be repurchased or redeemed out of the undertakings' assets at the request of holders. Action taken by a UCITS to ensure that the stock exchange value of its units does not significantly vary from their net asset value is to be regarded as equivalent to such repurchase or redemption. Excluded from the definition are close-ended schemes, schemes which raise capital without promotion of units to the general public or only to the public in non-member States and certain other schemes in which the investment and borrowing powers are considered inappropriate.

All UCITS must be authorised by competent authorities in a member State. This requires approval of the manager, depository or trustee and the fund's rules. The trustee is responsible for ensuring that the sale, issue, repurchase, redemption and cancellation of units by the management company takes place within the law and the fund rules. The trustee must also ensure that valuations are carried out in accordance with the law and fund rules, observe the instructions of the manager (provided that these do not conflict with the law or fund rules), ensure that transaction consideration is remitted within the usual time and that the scheme's income is properly allocated. The manager and trustee must, in particular, act independently of each other and comply with the other conditions contained in the Directive.

The Directive sets out certain general principles in connection with the investment policies to be pursued by UCITS. The types of property into which funds may be placed are specified and restrictions placed on the amounts of any individual investment to spread risk. Investments must generally be made in transferable securities although a certain portion of the assets may be made up of debt instruments or units in other UCITS. A scheme may be permitted to borrow up to 10 per cent of the value of the fund.

The Directive provides for the regular publication of information to unit holders including a prospectus and an annual and half-yearly report by the managers. These must comply with requirements set out in sch. A and B to the Directive.

While the pricing of units is left to be determined within each member State, it must reflect the underlying value of the assets held within the scheme less relevant charges or costs. The dealing prices of units must be regularly published.

Schemes which are authorised in accordance with the terms of the Directive may be marketed in other member States. This is subject to a two-month notification requirement only, accompanied by certain specified information. The host member State may otherwise apply rules only if justified by the general good. This may include more detailed advertising requirements. General provisions in connection with the revocation of authorisation are also set out in the Directive with procedures for authorities to act in cooperation in connection with breaches of relevant provisions.

The provisions set out in the Directive were reflected in the earlier regulations issued by the FSA (or the SIB as it earlier was). These will now be reissued under

FSAMA 2000. They include the Financial Services (Regulated Schemes) Regulations 1991 (originally made under FSA 1986) and the Financial Services (Open-Ended Investment Companies) Regulations 1997 (under the Open-ended Investment Companies (Investment Companies with Variable Capital) Regulations 1996 (SI 1996/2827)).

## COLLECTIVE INVESTMENT SCHEMES

Collective investments schemes are defined in FSAMA 2000, s. 235(1). This replicates the definition set out in FSA 1986, s. 75. A collective investment scheme means any arrangements with respect to property of any description, including money, the purpose or effect of which is to enable persons taking part in the arrangements (whether by becoming owners of the property or any part of it or otherwise) to participate in or receive profits or income arising from the acquisition, holding, management or disposal of the property or sums paid out of such profits or income.

The essence is accordingly shared profit or income through collective investment. By s. 235(2), persons who participate must not have any day-to-day control over the management of the property (although this does not exclude the right to be consulted or provide directions). The arrangements must involve the pooling of contributions (and profits or income) and the central management of property by or on behalf of the operator of the scheme (s. 235(3)). Where pooling may take place in connection with separate parts of the property, the arrangements will only constitute a single collective investment scheme if the participants are entitled to exchange or switch between the parts (s. 235(4)).

The Treasury may by order provide that certain arrangements do not constitute a collective investment scheme either in specified circumstances or within particular categories of arrangement (s. 235(5)). These exceptions were formerly contained in FSA 1986, s. 75(5) to (7). They include parallel management arrangements, schemes not operated by way of business or not as an investment business as well as corporate group arrangements, employee share schemes, deposit-taking business, franchise agreements, timeshare-type agreements, contracts of insurance and occupational pension schemes.

A unit trust is a collective investment scheme under which the property is held in trust for the participants (s. 237(1)). An authorised unit trust scheme is a unit trust scheme which is authorised for the purposes of the Act by virtue of an authorisation order issued under s. 243 (s. 237(3)).

An open-ended investment company (OEIC) is a collective investment scheme which satisfies both a property and investment condition (s. 236(1)). The property must belong beneficially to and be managed by or on behalf of a body corporate for the purpose of spreading investment risk and distributing the results of the management of the funds. Under the investment condition, a reasonable investor must expect to be able to realise within a reasonable period his investment (represented by the value of the shares or securities held in the scheme) on a basis calculated wholly or mainly by reference to the value of property in respect of which the scheme makes arrangements. This is without regard to any actual or potential redemption or repurchase of shares under company law in the UK or elsewhere within the EEA. This amends the earlier definition which referred only to the rights of participants being represented by shares in or securities in the company which may either be redeemed or repurchased or sold on an investment exchange at a price related to the value of the underlying property held. An authorised open-ended investment company means a body set up and authorised in accordance with regulations issued under s. 262 (s. 237(3)).

A recognised scheme is a scheme recognised under the provisions governing the recognition of other EEA schemes, schemes authorised in designated countries or territories or other individually recognised schemes (s. 237(3)). Units means the rights or interests (however described) of the participants in the scheme (s. 237(2)).

The trustee is the person holding the property in question on trust for the participants and the operator is either the manager of a unit trust scheme with a separate trustee or the company if the scheme is an OEIC (s. 237(2)). Depository means any person to whom the property subject to the scheme is entrusted for safekeeping.

## RESTRICTIONS ON PROMOTION

The core restriction on promotion is set out in FSAMA 2000, s. 238(1). An authorised person must not communicate or cause to be communicated an invitation or inducement to participate in a collective investment scheme, unless it is an authorised unit trust scheme, on authorised OEIC or a recognised scheme. There may also be promotion of other schemes in ways subject to rules made by the FSA, which do not involve promotion to the general public (s. 238(5)). Promotion otherwise than to the general public includes promotion in a way designed to reduce, so far as possible, the risk of participation by persons for whom participation would be unsuitable (s. 238(10)). This would apply where, for example, a promotion aimed at a specific class of potential investors (such as employees of a particular firm) was received by a member of the general public. The restriction does not apply to a communication originating outside the UK unless it is 'capable of having an effect' in the UK (s. 238(3)).

The Treasury may specify circumstances in which the general prohibition is not to apply (s. 238(6)) and have further power in s. 239(1) to exempt single property schemes by regulation. Single property schemes are defined in s. 239(3)(a) as schemes involving the management of specific buildings or a group of adjacent or contiguous buildings managed as a single enterprise with or without ancillary land or furniture, fittings and contents. In order to be exempted, the scheme units must be dealt in on a recognised investment exchange (s. 239(3)(b)). If exemption regulations are issued in connection with single property schemes, the FSA may issue rules imposing duties on the operator and trustee or depositary (s. 239(4)).

An authorised person may not approve a financial promotion if he would not be entitled to issue it directly under the general prohibition on the promotion of collective investment schemes (s. 240(1)). An authorised person may be liable to private persons in damages following breach of the general restriction on promotion or restriction on approval of promotion (s. 241).

## AUTHORISED UNIT TRUST SCHEMES

Chapter III of Part XVII of FSAMA 2000 provides for the authorisation by the FSA of unit trust schemes. This includes detailed provisions in connection with applications for authorisation, authorisation orders, certificates, rules, scheme particulars, alteration, withdrawal and intervention.

### Authorisation

An application to the FSA for an order declaring a unit trust scheme to be authorised must be made by the manager and trustee (s. 242(1)). The manager and trustee (or proposed manager and trustee) must be different persons (s. 242(2)). The application must be made in such manner as may be directed and contain all such information as may be required at the time of the application or subsequently (s. 242(3)).

An authorisation order may be issued by the FSA if the scheme complies with the requirements set out in the Act (s. 243(1)(a)). The scheme must comply with the trust scheme rules which are to be made by the FSA (ss. 243(1)(b) and 247) and a copy of the trust deed and solicitor's certificate confirming compliance with the relevant requirements must also be provided (s. 243(1)(c)). The manager and trustee must be independent of each other (s. 243(4)) and be bodies incorporated in the UK or another EEA State with a place of business in the UK (s. 243(5)). They must be authorised persons with permission to manage or to act as a trustee as appropriate (s. 243(7)). The name of the scheme must not be undesirable or misleading (s. 243(8)). The scheme's purposes must be reasonably capable of being successfully carried into effect (s. 243(9)) and participants entitled to have the units redeemed at a price related to the net value of the property determined in accordance with the scheme rules (s. 243(10)).

Applications must be considered within six months of receipt of the completed application (s. 244(1)). If an application is to be refused, warning notice must be given to the applicants (s. 245(1)). If the application is refused, a decision notice must be issued with either applicant being able to refer the matter to the Financial Services and Markets Tribunal (s. 245(2)). Under the previous legislation, there was no right of appeal to a tribunal and the only recourse was by way of judicial review.

A separate certificate of EEA compliance may also be issued by the FSA on request (s. 246(1)). The request may either be made at the time of the original application or subsequently (s. 246(2)). This will entitle UCITS compliant schemes to be marketed in all other European jurisdictions.

## Trust scheme rules

The FSA may issue trust scheme rules containing requirements with regard to the constitution, management and operation of authorised unit trust schemes (s. 247(1)(a)). These rules will generally also set out the powers, duties, rights and liabilities of managers and trustees, the rights and duties of the participants and provisions concerning the winding up of schemes (s. 247(1)(b), (c) and (d)). The trust scheme rules may make provision for various other matters (s. 247(2)). The FSA is now entitled to approve changes to investment and borrowing powers (s. 247(2)(d)). This replaces the earlier provisions which reserved this right to the Treasury. Trust scheme rules may make provision as to the contents of trust deeds (s. 247(3). Trust scheme rules bind managers, trustee and participants irrespective of the terms of the trust deed (s. 247(4)). The FSA has proposed to reissue the earlier Regulations subject only to minor amendment.

Auditors may be disqualified by the FSA from auditing authorised unit trust schemes or authorised OEICs if the auditor has breached the terms of the trust scheme rules (s. 249(1)). The FSA must follow the warning and decision notice procedure provided for in the Act (s. 249(2)).

## Scheme particulars rules

The FSA may also issue scheme particulars rules (s. 248(1)). These may require the manager to submit scheme particulars to the FSA and publish the particulars or otherwise make them available to the public on request. They may provide for the notification of any significant changes as well as for compensation to be paid to qualifying persons in the event that loss is suffered as a result of an untrue or misleading statement in or omission from the particulars (s. 248(3), (4) and (5)). Qualifying persons will include all persons having any legal or beneficial interest in the scheme (s. 248(6)).

The FSA may modify or waive the application of any of the trust scheme rules or scheme particulars rules in connection with a particular scheme (s. 250(1), (2) and (3)). The general rules with regard to modification or waiver of rules contained in s. 148 will apply subject to certain amendments set out in s. 250(4) and (5).

## Alterations

Any proposed alteration to a scheme or proposal to replace the trustee or manager must be approved by the FSA. The manager must notify the FSA of any proposal to alter the scheme or to replace the trustee and the trustee must notify the FSA of any proposal to replace the manager (s. 251(1) and (3)). Replacement trustees and managers must satisfy the relevant conditions concerning independence, incorporation, authorisation and permission referred to above (s. 251(5)). The changes can take effect only if the FSA approves the proposals or does not serve a warning notice within one month (s. 251(4)). A warning notice is required within one month if the FSA proposes to refuse approval of a replacement trustee or manager (s. 252(1) and (3)) and both trustee and manager must receive the warning notice if the proposal is to refuse other alterations to a scheme (s. 252(2) and (3)). This must then be followed by a decision notice, which may be referred to the Financial Services and Markets Tribunal (s. 252(4)).

## Exclusion clauses

Section 253 restrains the inclusion of certain exclusion clauses in trust deeds. Any provision of a trust deed is void in so far as it would have the effect of exempting the manager or trustee from liability for any failure to exercise due care and diligence in the discharge of their functions.

## Revocation

The authorisation of a unit trust may be revoked by the FSA under s. 254(1) (otherwise than by consent) in one of five cases:

(a)  if one or more of the requirements for the making of the authorisation order are no longer satisfied;

(b)  if the manager or trustee of the scheme has breached a requirement set out in the Act;

(c)  if the manager or trustee has knowingly or recklessly given the FSA false or misleading information in any material particular;

(d)  if no regulated activity has been carried on for more than 12 months; or

(e)  it is otherwise desirable to protect the interests of participants or potential participants.

If the FSA proposes to issue a revoking order, separate notice must be given to the manager and trustee which may be referred to the Financial Services and Markets Tribunal by either the manager or the trustee (s. 255(1)). A decision notice must be issued where the FSA decides to make a revoking order having issued a warning notice (s. 255(2)).

Requests for revocation may also be made by the manager or trustee although this will be granted only where no matters have arisen which may require investigation or where revocation would not be in the interests of participants or would breach Community obligations (s. 256(1) and (3)).

## Intervention

The FSA may issue directions under s. 257(2) to require a manager to cease issuing or redeeming units or require the manager and trustee of a scheme to wind it up. Directions may be issued in any case in which a revoking order might be made under s. 254 (except in the case of inactivity) (s. 257(1)). Further directions may be issued once a revoking order has been made provided earlier directions are already in place (s. 257(4)). A person breaching a direction may be liable to any person who suffers loss (s. 257(5)). Directions may be revoked or varied by the FSA independently or on the application of the manager or trustee (s. 257(6)). The FSA may also apply to the court for an order removing, or removing and replacing, the manager or trustee in any case where it is empowered to issue a direction under the Act (s. 258(1)).

Separate procedures apply to the giving and varying of directions on the FSA's own initiative (s. 259), refusals to revoke or vary (s. 260) and notification of revocations and requested variations (s. 261). Supervisory notices must be given to the manager and trustee setting out the terms of a proposed direction or, if the FSA considers it necessary for the direction to take effect immediately, the actual direction (s. 259(1), (2) and (3)). The notice must contain specified matters (s. 259(4)) including the right to make representations (s. 259(4)(d)) which must be considered by the FSA (s. 259(8) and (9)). If a direction is to be issued, an existing direction not revoked or directions varied on the FSA's initiative (s. 259(13)), the manager or trustee may refer the matter to the Financial Services and Markets Tribunal (s. 259(10)). A warning notice must be given where the FSA proposes to refuse a request to revoke or vary a direction (s. 260(1)(a) and (b)) and such a decision may be referred to the Tribunal (s. 260(2)). Notice is also to be given where the FSA decides to revoke on its own initiative (s. 261(1)) or to revoke or vary on request (s. 261(2)).

## OPEN-ENDED INVESTMENT COMPANIES

The same level of statutory detail is not provided with regard to open-ended investment companies (OEICs) as for authorised unit trust schemes. Section 262(1) empowers the Treasury to make regulations concerning OEICs which generally cover the same matters as, and replace, the Open-ended Investment Companies (Investment Companies with Variable Capital) Regulations 1996 (SI 1986/2827). In the 1986 Regulations, OEICs are referred to as investment companies with variable capital (ICVCs). FSAMA 2000, s. 263, amends s. 716 of the Companies Act 1985, which prohibits the formation of unincorporated companies with more than 20 members.

The regulations made under FSAMA 2000, s. 262 by the Treasury may make provision for OEICs corresponding to those made for unit trust schemes in Part XVII, Chapter III, including provision for authorisation by the FSA (s. 262(2)(l)). They may also confer functions on the FSA, which will presumably include making rules (s. 262(3)(b)).

The current FSA regulations made under the Treasury Regulations of 1996 and governing OEICs are the Financial Services (Open-ended Investment Companies) Regulations 1997. These provide for the constitution of OEICs and the drawing up and publication of prospectuses. They also contain detailed provisions concerning pricing and dealing, including initial offers, issuing, cancellation, sale and redemption, dilution levy, forward and historic pricing requirements and valuation. The investment and borrowing powers of OEICs are set out in detail. These regulations give effect to but also develop the requirements set out in the UCITS Directive. Specific provisions are included with regard to securities companies, warrant companies, umbrella companies, efficient portfolio management, stock lending, cash borrowing and lending. The powers and duties of the directors and depository are set out in some detail as well as other provisions on income, reports and accounts, shareholders' meetings, umbrella companies and suspension and termination. The Regulations will now be reissued, as rules, with amendments once the Treasury have made their regulations under s. 262.

The FSA has subsequently proposed certain amendments to the Regulations in connection with the tax implications of certain transactions, conversion of authorised unit trusts to OEICs and charging to capital (see Consultation Paper No. 36, November 1999).

## RECOGNISED OVERSEAS SCHEMES

FSAMA 2000 continues the earlier provisions concerning the recognition of overseas schemes which may be marketed in the UK. These provisions apply to schemes constituted in other EEA States, designated territory schemes and other overseas schemes on separate application. Recognition under these provisions makes a scheme a recognised scheme for the purposes of Part XVII (s. 237(3)) which entitles an authorised person to communicate an invitation or inducement to participate in it (s. 238(1) and (4)(c)).

### Schemes constituted in other EEA States

A collective investment scheme constituted in another EEA State is recognised if it satisfies the requirements set out in Treasury regulations, the operator of the scheme gives two months' notice to the FSA of its intention to invite persons in the UK to participate in the scheme (as required under Directive 85/611/EEC) and the FSA does not give notice that the invitation may not comply with relevant UK law (s. 264(1)). This gives effect to the requirement contained in the Directive that the UK must recognise other compliant schemes subject to any general good or public interest reasons. The notice of intention to invite must be accompanied by a certificate confirming Directive compliance, an address for service in the UK and such other information or documents as may be required (s. 264(3)). If the FSA intends to object, notice must be given to the operator and the home State authorities (s. 264(2)). This notice must set out the reasons and specify a reasonable time (not less than 28 days) within which representations may be made (s. 264(4)). Representations must be considered by the FSA within a reasonable time (s. 265(2)). If the notice is withdrawn, the scheme becomes recognised from the date of withdrawal (s. 265(3)). If the notice is not to be withdrawn, the operator and home State authorities must be given a decision notice (s. 265(4)) and the operator may refer the matter to the Tribunal (s. 265(5)). This is a rare example of a decision notice that follows an earlier notice which was not itself a warning notice (see ss. 264(2) and 265(4)). Unusually, these formalities attract no third-party rights (see s. 392).

By FSAMA 2000, s. 266(1), rules made by the FSA under the Act, apart from financial promotion rules made under s. 145 (see chapter 12) and facilities rules made under s. 283(1) (see below), do not apply to EEA schemes recognised under s. 264.

The FSA may suspend the exemption given by s. 238(4)(c) from the restriction on promotion set out in s. 238(1) where the operator of an EEA recognised scheme has contravened the financial promotion rules (s. 267(1), (2) and (8)). This enables the FSA to stop promotion of a scheme even though it cannot suspend the scheme's recognition. Here the supervisory notice procedure will apply (ss. 267 and 395(13)(e)). The home State authorities and operator must also be informed if the FSA proposes to direct suspension (s. 268(3)). The operator must be informed that he or she may refer the matter to the Financial Services and Markets Tribunal (s. 268(4)(e), (10) and (11)).

## Schemes authorised in designated countries or territories

Schemes managed in and authorised under the law of a country or territory outside the UK and the EEA may also be promoted in the UK if they emanate from a jurisdiction which is designated by order by the Treasury (s. 270). A scheme from a designated country or territory will be recognised if it is of a class specified in the order, the operator has given written notice to the FSA that he wishes to be recognised and the FSA has approved the recognition or has not issued a warning notice within two months of the date of application (s. 270(1)(a), (b), (c) and (d)). The Treasury may not make an order designating any country or territory unless satisfied that the law under which relevant collective schemes are authorised and supervised affords investors in the UK protection, at least, equivalent to that provided under FSAMA 2000 in connection with comparable authorised schemes (s. 270(2)). The Treasury must ask the FSA for a report on the law in the country or territory including its opinion as to whether adequate protection is provided (s. 270(5)(a)). The FSA must provide the report and it must be taken into account by the Treasury (s. 270(5)(b) and (c)). The Treasury will, however, have the final decision.

A warning notice must be issued by the FSA if it intends to refuse approval of a particular scheme (s. 271(1)). The warning notice must be received by the operator before the end of two months of the date of the application or it will have no effect (s. 271(2)). A decision notice must subsequently be issued if the FSA is to refuse approval (s. 271(3)(a)). The matter may be referred by the operator to the Financial Services and Markets Tribunal (s. 271(3)(b)).

## Individually recognised overseas schemes

FSAMA 2000, s. 272(1), provides for the recognition of overseas schemes on an individual basis. An order declaring a scheme to be recognised may be issued by the FSA if it is satisfied with regard to certain requirements set out in s. 272. These include affording adequate protection to participants, the adequacy of the scheme's constitution and management and the adequacy of the powers and duties of operator and trustee or depositary in so far as relevant having regard, in each case, to the trust scheme rules and corresponding rules relating to authorised OEICs (s. 272(2), (3), (4), (5) and (6)). The operator and trustee or depositary must be authorised persons or otherwise fit and proper (s. 272(8) and (9)). The name of the scheme must not be undesirable or misleading and its purposes reasonably capable of being successfully carried into effect (s. 272(11) and (12)). There must be entitlement to redemption at a price related to net value or at a reasonably similar market price (s. 272(13)). These generally reflect the requirements set out in the Act for authorisation of unit trusts. Certain matters must also be taken into account in considering whether these requirements are satisfied (s. 273). These include any matter relating to any person who will be employed by, or associated with, any director of or any other person exercising influence over the operator, trustee or depositary.

The Act includes further provisions concerning the procedures for making applications for recognition and their refusal. Applications must, in particular, be considered within six months (s. 275(1)), with warning and decision notice procedures applying in connection with proposed refusals (s. 276(1) and (2)).

Section 277(1) requires notice to be given to the FSA of any proposed alteration of an individually recognised scheme. The proposal must not be implemented unless it is approved by the FSA (s. 277(2)). At least one month's notice of any replacement of the operator, trustee or depositary must be separately provided to the FSA (s. 277(3)).

The FSA may make rules imposing liabilities on the operation of a recognised scheme equivalent to those set out in the scheme protection rules of an authorised unit trust (s. 278). Recognition may also be revoked on similar grounds to those applied to authorised unit trusts and OEICs (s. 279). Less drastically, the same grounds can also lead under s. 281 to directions to suspend the recognition until problems have been rectified. In both cases, there are similar procedures including the issuance of supervisory notices with powers to act immediately in cases of urgency (ss. 280 and 282).

## Facilities and information in the UK

The FSA may make rules requiring operators of recognised schemes to maintain in the UK such facilities as are considered desirable in the interests of participants (s. 283(1)).

The FSA may give a written notice to the operator of any recognised scheme requiring invitations or inducements to participate in the scheme which are communicated by the operator to include explanatory information specified in the notice (s. 283(2)). Such a requirement may apply to communications originating outside the UK only if they are 'capable of having an effect' in the UK (s. 283(3)).

## INVESTIGATIONS

The FSA or the Secretary of State may appoint a person to conduct an investigation into most types of collective investment schemes (s. 284(1)). An investigation under s. 284 may be into the affairs of any authorised unit trust scheme or its manager or trustee, the affairs of any recognised scheme or its operator, trustee or depositary in so far as they relate to activities carried on in the UK, or the affairs of any other collective investment scheme or its operator, trustee or depositary (s. 284(11)). However, s. 284 does not apply to OEICs, for which separate provision will be made in Treasury regulations made under s. 262 (see s. 262(2)(k)). The distinction reflects the fact that investigation of companies is generally regarded as a matter for the Secretary of State, not the FSA. An investigation may be ordered under s. 284 in any case in which it is considered in the interests of the participants or potential participants to do so or that the matter is otherwise of public concern (s. 284(1)).

The person appointed to conduct the investigation may also investigate any other scheme with the same manager, trustee, operator or depositary as the scheme which he or she is appointed to investigate (s. 284(2)), and, here, OEICs are included in light of the need of an investigator to form a complete picture. The investigator may require any person to produce documents in his possession or under his control which are considered to be relevant, attend before the investigator or otherwise provide any assistance as may reasonably be required (s. 284(3)). Various of the provisions of Part XI concerning investigations are applied to s. 284 investigations by s. 284(4) to (7). Section 284(8), (9) and (10) contains provisions on banking confidentiality similar to those in s. 175(5).

# Chapter Twenty

# Recognised Investment Exchanges and Clearing Houses

## George Walker

A substantial part of all securities issuance and trading is conducted through formal exchanges and their connected clearing systems. Many transactions may be entered into directly between market counterparties including, for example, on the increasingly large over-the-counter (OTC) derivatives markets although trades in most company shares and corporate and government debt instruments are dealt with through formal exchanges. The main reason for this is the transparency, certainty and security provided by the formal market and supporting clearing arrangements.

Dealing in shares and debt instruments in the United Kingdom has traditionally been conducted on the London Stock Exchange (LSE), which is the single largest market, although electronic orders can now be processed through Tradepoint or any of the new more specialist alternative trading systems or platforms (ATSs) which have recently been set up. All types of financial derivatives contracts may also be bought or sold on the London International Financial Futures and Options Exchange (LIFFE) or on the OM Exchange, which is linked to the Stockholm Exchange. Coredeal is one of the most recently recognised new investment vehicles, pioneered by the International Securities Markets Association with its focus on the bond markets, including Eurobonds.

Financial contracts in many commodities may be traded on either the London Metal Exchange (LME) or the International Petroleum Exchange (IPE). There are a number of other commodities exchanges, salesrooms and auction houses in London and elsewhere, although to the extent that they do not create a market in securities-related instruments as defined in the Financial Services and Markets Act 2000 (FSAMA 2000), they do not have to be recognised.

There are two major clearing houses in London which provide clearing and settlement facilities for the main markets. The London Clearing House (LCH) has acquired responsibility for a number of distinct clearing functions over a long period of time and now provides services for LIFFE, the LME and the IPE among others. The electronic (dematerialised) settlement of registered securities may be effected through CREST. The settlement of transactions conducted through the Central Gilts Office (CGO) and the Central Moneymarkets Office (CMO) are also now to be carried out through CREST following agreement between the Bank of England and CRESTCo Ltd.

The recognition of these exchanges and clearing houses for supervisory and regulatory purposes was dealt with in the Financial Services Act 1986 (FSA 1986), sch. 4. Those provisions have been substantially re-enacted in Part XVIII of FSAMA 2000. The government considered that these recognition arrangements had proved an appropriate way of maintaining high standards within the markets and therefore decided to continue the recognition regime under FSAMA 2000. The only major changes have been to confer on the FSA a power to issue directions and to confer on the recognised investment exchanges (RIEs) and recognised clearing houses (RCHs) the same immunity as the FSA has from civil action by members, and others, in respect of anything done in the performance of their regulatory functions. The Treasury's power to bring exchange disciplinary proceedings into the statutory review procedure (s. 300) may also prove to be a major change.

Separate competition law rules are included in Chapters II and III of Part XVIII. These replicate the competition provisions contained in other Parts of the Act and create a parallel regime for recognised bodies. The Act also provides for the recognition of overseas exchanges and clearing houses.

Draft recognition requirements for investment exchanges and clearing houses were issued by the Treasury in February 1999. The draft regulations contain various conditions which must be satisfied by applicant exchanges and clearing houses. These will include being fit and proper, having sufficient financial resources and being able and willing to promote and maintain high standards of integrity and fair dealing in the carrying on of regulated activities. They must also cooperate in the sharing of information with other agencies. Special rules will apply in relation to exchanges which offer or propose to offer clearing services in respect of the market contracts that are protected in the insolvency of any party by Part VII of the Companies Act 1986.

The FSA subsequently issued a consultation paper with its draft RIE and RCH Sourcebook for comment in January 2000. The FSA also issued a separate paper on market infrastructure providers in January 2000 (*The FSA's Approach to Regulation of the Market Infrastructure* (Discussion Paper D02)). This is concerned with other exchange providers, ATSs and non-exchange trading systems, clearing houses and other market service providers. One of the most significant recent developments which has occurred in this area has been the general move from dealing on traditional exchange-based markets to the new electronically driven systems or platforms which can match, buy and sell orders as well as provide for contractual completion. A number of such ATSs have been set up since 1999, which has placed increasing competitive pressures on the established markets and created a number of new regulatory challenges for the authorities.

The origins and nature of operation of each of the major exchanges and clearing houses in the United Kingdom are outlined in turn. The specific content of the revised recognition regime set up under the Act and the content of the new recognition rules are then examined in further detail.

## EXISTING RECOGNISED INVESTMENT EXCHANGES AND CLEARING HOUSES

There are currently six main RIEs and two RCHs in the United Kingdom. A number of new exchanges have also recently been recognised, or applied for recognition, with further growth expected in ATS facilities. The main existing RIEs and RCHs are considered further below.

### London Stock Exchange

The largest formal securities market in the United Kingdom remains the London Stock Exchange (LSE). As with many of the other London markets, the exchange originated in the dealings which were entered into between merchants and early capital providers in the old coffee houses in the City of London and nearby. During the eighteenth century, as entrepreneurs required increasingly large sums for investment in overseas trading expeditions and long shipping voyages, the practice developed of buying and selling shares in these ventures in the coffee houses. The Muscovy Company was, for example, the world's first joint stock-company and was set up in London in 1553 (see the LSE's website at www.londonstockexchange.com).

A number of specialist brokers then began to act as intermediaries between the merchants and investors. In 1760, a group of 150 of these brokers formed a club at Jonathan's Coffee House to buy and sell shares, after apparently being removed from the Royal Exchange for bad behaviour. The name of the club was then changed to the Stock Exchange in 1773. The original deed of settlement of the Stock Exchange was entered into in 1802 and revised in 1875. It was replaced with a new memorandum and articles of association in 1986 when the Exchange became a private limited company after the Big Bang on 27 October 1986.

With Big Bang, ownership in member firms was for the first time opened to non-Exchange members, minimum commissions were abolished and the earlier distinction between brokers and jobbers was abandoned with all firms becoming dual capacity broker-dealers. The former open outcry market was replaced by screen trading with the introduction of SEAQ (the Stock Exchange Automated Quotations system) and SEAQ International for international equities. While SEAQ provides a quote-driven dealing system which is generally conducted by telephone, SETS (the Stock Exchange Trading Service) was launched on 20 October 1997 to create an automated matching service for orders which were placed electronically by prospective buyers and sellers. This is considered to provide more choice, increased transparency, lower costs, larger volumes and improved competition.

The LSE now comprises a number of separate markets including the main market on which listed securities are traded, the Alternative Investment Market (AIM) for new and growing companies and techMARK for high-technology stock. AIM was set up in June 1995 to create a separate market for smaller or younger companies which sought access to the capital markets but without all of the requirements imposed on main market companies. AIM companies do not have to comply with the UK Listing Rules (see Chapter 8) and are subject to a less stringent and more flexible regulatory regime. While over 2000 listed companies are traded on the LSE, about 400 companies are currently traded on AIM.

TechMARK is described as being a market within a market which began operation on 4 November 1999 with over 190 companies from the main market. The stocks are grouped together with a common identity and given their own FTSE indices. The LSE also has a specialised part of the listed market, called extra-MARK, devoted to exchange traded funds (ETFs). ETFs are OEICs which track market indices. OEICs are considered with collective investment schemes in Chapter 19.

In anticipation of possible future expansion and technical developments, the LSE entered into a strategic alliance with the Frankfurt Deutsche Börse in July 1998. This was to have allowed them to harmonise markets in leading stocks and develop a joint trading platform. Following the creation of a common access facility in January 1999 for both exchanges, it was subsequently announced on 3 May 2000 that the two exchanges would merge to create iX-international exchanges, but this plan was subsequently abandoned in September 2000.

As part of its longer-term reform programme, the LSE has introduced a new ownership structure including the creation of transferable shares and the re-registration of the exchange as a public company. Work continues in this area.

### Tradepoint Stock Exchange

Tradepoint is an electronic order-driven stock exchange. Tradepoint was established in January 1992 and began trading in UK equities with over 45 member firms in September 1995. By January 2000, Tradepoint had 150 member firms worldwide. Tradepoint is now owned by a consortium of investment banks and other investors (see www.tradepoint.co.uk).

Tradepoint provides for the direct trading in securities by fund managers, market makers and brokers. Orders are posted anonymously in the Tradepoint order book and are automatically matched in price and time priority. Total pre- and post-trade transparency is secured through the instant publishing of all trades. The LCH acts as a central counterparty which removes counterparty risk on all order book transactions carried out on the exchange. This allows trades to be settled on a net position basis. Almost all UK listed companies can be dealt with on Tradepoint.

Tradepoint was approved by the Securities and Exchange Commission in March 1999 which allowed US firms to have direct membership of a non-US stock exchange for the first time.

## LIFFE

LIFFE, the London International Financial Futures and Options Exchange, is the largest derivatives exchange in Europe. LIFFE was originally set up in September 1982 to provide financial market participants with a better means of managing risks in relation to foreign exchange and interest rates following the removal of UK foreign exchange controls in 1979. LIFFE initially operated at the Royal Exchange, but new trading facilities were opened at Cannon Bridge House in December 1991.

LIFFE began by only trading financial futures and options on interest rates in the world's major currencies. Since 1992 it has also offered options on UK equities, and the FTSE 100 and FTSE 250 Indeces following its merger with the London Traded Options Market (LTOM). Contracts in soft commodities and agricultural products, including cocoa, robusta, coffee, white sugar, grain, potatoes and the Baltic Freight Index were added following the merger with the London Commodity Exchange (LCE) in 1996. LIFFE is claimed to be the only exchange in the world which can offer a full range of contracts including financial, equity-related (original and indices) and commodities-based products (see www.liffe.com).

## London Securities and Derivatives Exchange

The London Securities and Derivatives Exchange (OM London Exchange or OMLX) is a specialist derivatives market which is run in parallel to the Stockholm Stock Exchange and is managed by the Swedish OM Group. OM had begun to offer Swedish options trading in June 1985 and was listed on the Stockholm Stock Exchange in 1987. The OM London Exchange was established in 1989 with the first electronic link between exchanges being set up between OM London and Stockholm. The Stockholm Stock Exchange was privatised in 1992 and then merged with OM in 1998. An electronic link was set up between the Copenhagen and Stockholm Stock Exchanges in 1999 and the Oslo Stock Exchange is now in discussion with the Swedish-Danish alliance Norex. OM also provides a range of exchange technology support services through its subsidiary operations.

OM and Morgan Stanley set up a new joint venture exchange for European share dealing in February 2000. The exchange is known as Jiway and is a screen-based order and quote-driven electronic market. Brokers can connect to Jiway electronically with orders being executed within the Jiway order book. Access is initially to be limited to the UK, Sweden and Germany, and it is proposed to extend it to France, Italy, the Netherlands and Switzerland in 2001. Jiway became operational in autumn 2000 and is designed for the growing on line cross-border retail market (see www.jiway.com).

The OM London Exchange also set up the UK Power Exchange (UKPX) in June 1999 for trading in electricity contracts. It is also intended to set up an integrated exchange and clearing house dealing in electricity spot and futures under the New Electricity Trading Arrangements (NETA). The five largest electricity providers in the UK are members of UKPX. The intention is to take advantage of the opportunities created by the deregulation of electricity trading within the UK. OM subsequently became involved in discussions concerning the possible takeover of the LSE, however these have since terminated.

## International Petroleum Exchange

The International Petroleum Exchange (IPE) provides a futures exchange for crude oil and gas contracts. It is the second largest energy futures exchange in the world and supports benchmark prices in two thirds of the world's crude oil and the majority of middle distillate traded in Europe. IPE futures and options contracts can either be entered into by locals on the floor or through brokers following completion of an execution and clearing agreement with a floor member. Trading is by open outcry on standardised terms (see www.ipe.uk.com).

## London Metal Exchange

The London Metal Exchange (LME) was established in 1877 as the London Metal Exchange Company, which initially traded from Lombard Court (see www.lme.co.uk). It opened its current headquarters in Leadenhall Street in 1994. The LME is the largest base metals market in the world. It provides a range of futures and options contracts in the main industrially used non-ferrous metals (copper, primary aluminium, aluminium alloy, lead, nickel, tin, zinc and silver). Trading is either by open outcry between ring dealing brokers or on a 24-hour inter-office basis. Of the Exchange's 100 member firms, 14 participate in the ring dealing. The open outcry trading sessions take place twice a day. Other broker members join the ring dealing firms in inter-office trading. Both floor and inter-office trading contracts are cleared through LCH.

Historically, most hedging was conducted through forward contracts entered into on the Exchange. Traded options were introduced in 1987. While most trade hedging contracts are cancelled out by equal and opposite buy/sell back contracts, LME provides for physical delivery through an international network of approved warehouses. LME traded options contracts are also settled through LCH.

## LCH

The London Clearing House (LCH) was originally established as the London Produce Clearing House Ltd in 1888 and was renamed the International Commodities Clearing House Ltd in 1973 and the London Clearing House Ltd in 1991. LCH was acquired in October 1996 by LIFFE, the IPE and LME from a syndicate of UK banks. It provides clearing services to its members and the exchanges (see www.lch.co.uk).

LCH clears trades for LIFFE, IPE, LME and Tradepoint. Minimum financial resources and reporting requirements are imposed on members with further initial and additional margin requirements being required in respect of trading volumes. All open positions must be covered on a daily basis either by liquid funds or other collateral. Payments are made through a protected payments system. By acting as a central counterparty, LCH removes credit or counterparty risk. CRESTCo and LCH have also announced that they will set up a central counterparty service for trades executed through the LSE's SETS order book and settled through CREST.

## CREST

CREST was set up following the establishment of a Task Force on Securities Settlement by the Bank of England in June 1993. The objective of the Task Force was to develop a new system for the electronic settlement of registered securities in London. It had originally been intended that the TAURUS system would be introduced for the holding and settling of equities and fixed-interest debts to replace the LSE's earlier TALISMAN system of 1979. Despite early progress, increased costs and delays led to the TAURUS project being abandoned in March 1993.

CREST is operated by CRESTCo. Ltd which is a recognised clearing house for the purposes of FSA 1986. Members are generally authorised by the FSA in respect of their dealings as well as custody business (see www.crestco.co.uk).

CREST operates on an optional basis. Issuers may make their securities CREST eligible and investors can elect whether to hold securities in a certificated form or an uncertificated form within CREST. All corporate registered securities in London may be brought within CREST. CREST does not accept bearer securities unless a separate register is created to allow them to be de-materialised. CREST is governed by the Uncertificated Securities Regulations 1995 (SI 1995/3272), which were made under the Companies Act 1989, s. 207. The Regulations allow title to securities to be evidenced otherwise than by way of a certificate and transferred otherwise than by means of written instrument. Under the Companies Act 1985, share certificates otherwise have to be issued by all companies with transfers only being effected on receipt of executed instruments of transfer.

Securities transfers are made electronically through the CREST system. This operates by notifying the registrars of the issuing companies that are required to register executed transfers. While title is still determined by registration, the system operates by integrating the individual registrars' departments into an electronic processing framework. Transfers are normally given effect within two hours of notification, although credit risk is removed by creating an equitable right in the securities in favour of the transferee. An assured payment system is operated through the use of settlement banks which are irrevocably obliged to effect necessary payments following book entry settlements. Partial delivery against payment can be effected as payments are synchronised although settlement may still be interrupted. CREST provides for the simultaneous exchange of payment and securities, which allows transactions to be settled on a real-time basis.

CRESTCo Ltd has been responsible for the settlement of government gilts and money market instruments since May 1999 when responsibility for the Central Gilts Office (CGO) and the Central Moneymarkets Office (CMO) was transferred to CRESTCo from the Bank of England. The CGO had been set up in 1986 by the Bank and the LSE to provide an electronic transfer system for gilt-edged securities. The CMO was set up by the Bank in 1990 to act as a depositary and electronic settlement system for a range of securities including sterling-denominated bearer securities, Treasury bills, local authority bills, trade bills, bank and building society certificates of deposit and building society commercial paper. Rather than de-materialise securities, CMO operates by immobilising them in a vault and effecting transfer through book entries. Although the instruments are negotiable, book-entry settlement allows them to be securely held at all times while title may be easily transferred through electronic transfer.

## RECOGNITION REGIME

The main features of the FSA 1986 recognition and exemption regime for investment exchanges and clearing houses have been re-enacted in Part XVIII of FSAMA, which will be supplemented by orders issued by the Treasury under the Act. Draft regulations were issued in February 1999. The Act also gives the FSA a new power to issue directions to RIEs and RCHs to take steps to comply with the recognition requirements.

Some concerns had arisen during the consultation period as to whether an RIE or RCH should have a right of appeal against the use of the power to issue directions. The government considered that this was unnecessary in light of the high degree of discretion conferred on the RIEs and RCHs under the Act although the FSA would be required to give notice of intention to issue a direction and provide for representations to be made. The government also initially rejected the need to extend the right of statutory immunity to cover action taken by anyone and not just action by members, though s. 291 eventually provided the wider immunity. The FSA will, however, be required to consult on any rules it makes applying to RIEs and RCHs and conduct a cost-benefit analysis in the same way as it would when making other rules. The government also agreed that domestic and overseas exchanges and clearing houses should be treated on an equal basis although some differences in reporting rule changes would be permitted as overseas bodies were already subject to regulation in their home country.

The recognition requirements formerly in FSA 1986, sch. 4, in relation to exchanges (and s. 39 in relation to clearing houses) are made more flexible by allowing the Treasury to set out and amend the relevant criteria by regulations. It is likely that these will include amendments, for example, to the Traded Securities (Disclosure) Regulations 1994 (SI 1994/188). The exemption achieved by recog-nition will also be extended to include OTC trades which do not occur on an RIE, but are part of the exchange's business.

The additional requirements for recognition made in the Companies Act 1989, sch. 21, in relation to market contracts (as defined in s. 155) are to continue in effect. These prevent liquidators from attempting to unwind contracts made through exchanges or clearing houses.

Responsibility for determining whether overseas exchanges and clearing houses should be recognised is transferred from the Treasury to the FSA (s. 292). As these bodies are already subject to extensive controls in their home territories, they will not be subject to the full set of requirements imposed on domestic applicants. The test applied will continue to be whether the home State supervision together with the rules and practices of the particular body are such that the protection secured is, at least, equivalent to that provided in relation to domestic recognised bodies.

Grandfathering provisions are to be included in the recognition regulations to allow existing recognised bodies three months to comply with the new requirements. The new regulations are intended only to bring all of the requirements together in a single measure, improve certainty in some respects, provide for the recognition of stand-alone clearing houses which do not provide services for an RIE and allow for greater delegation of functions to other fit and proper bodies.

## RECOGNITION OF INVESTMENT EXCHANGES AND CLEARING HOUSES

Any body corporate or unincorporated association may apply to the FSA for an order declaring it to be a recognised investment exchange or clearing house under FSAMA 2000, ss. 287(1) and 288(1). Applications are to be in such manner as may be directed but must be accompanied by copies of the applicant's rules, a copy of any guidance issued, required particulars and such other information as may reasonably be requested (ss. 287(2) and 288(2)). The required particulars are the proposed clearing arrangements to be entered into by an exchange applicant or clearing services to be provided by a clearing applicant (ss. 287(3) and 288(3)). If clearing is to be provided in respect of transactions not effected on RIEs, the criteria to be applied in determining to whom these services will be provided must be specified (s. 288(3)(b)). The FSA may also require the applicant to provide such further information as it reasonably considers necessary to determine the application (s. 289(1)).

A recognition order may be made under s. 290(1) where an application has been successful. A recognition order may be revoked, under s. 297, where either a recognised body requests or consents to it, or a body fails to satisfy the recognition requirements or any other obligation imposed under the Act. If an application is to be refused or recognition revoked, the FSA must give written notice of its intention to the body concerned (ss. 290(5) and 298(1)(a)). It must also take such other steps as it considers reasonably practicable to bring the notice to the attention of members and publish the notice in such manner as it considers appropriate (ss. 290(5) and 298(1)(b) and (c)). The notice must give reasons for the proposed decision and draw attention to the right of the body, any member of the body or any other person who is likely to be affected by the proposed order to make representations (ss. 290(5) and 298(2) and (3)). Representations must generally be made within two months of the date on which the notice is served (ss. 290(5) and 298(4)).

Instead of revoking recognition, the FSA may, under s. 296, direct the body to take specified steps (including making alterations to its rules or suspending or discontinuing such of its operations as may be specified) where it has failed, or is likely to fail, to satisfy the recognition requirements or any other obligation imposed by the FSA or under the Act (s. 296(1) and (2)). Such directions are enforceable by injunction in England and Wales or an order for specific performance in Scotland (s. 296(3)). The same notification and rights to make representations provided for in respect of refusals of applications and revocation decisions apply to the giving of directions (s. 298(1)).

An overseas investment exchange or clearing house may apply for recognition under s. 292(1). The applicant must provide an address for service in the United Kingdom. In such cases, the FSA may (but is not required to) make a recognition order under s. 292(2) where the applicant is subject in its home territory to requirements that afford investor protection equivalent to the recognition requirements and there are adequate procedures for dealing with persons who cannot complete market contracts (s. 292(3)(a) and (b)). The FSA must also consider whether the overseas applicant and the home supervisory authorities are able and willing to cooperate in the sharing of information and otherwise (s. 292(3)(c) and (d)).

The FSA is given new powers of supervision by s. 293. The FSA may issue rules requiring notice of specific events or such other information as it may reasonably require to be provided by any recognised body (s. 293(1) and (2)). Written notice must be provided where a domestic recognised body alters or revokes any of its rules or guidance or makes new rules or guidance (s. 293(5)). Changes to clearing arrangements must also be notified by such bodies (s. 293(6) and (7)). These supervision rules may be modified or disapplied in particular cases (s. 294).

An overseas investment exchange or clearing house must also, by s. 295, provide an annual report which must state whether any events have occurred which are likely to affect the continuing validity of its recognition or have any effect on competition (s. 295(1) and (2)). A copy of the report must be sent to the Treasury and the Director General of Fair Trading (s. 295(4)).

The FSA must ensure that adequate arrangements are set up for the consideration of relevant complaints against a recognised body (s. 299(1)). This, however, relates only to matters which are relevant to whether the body's recognition should be maintained (s. 299(2)). The functions of the Financial Services and Markets Tribunal may be extended by Treasury order to include review of disciplinary proceedings held by recognised investment exchanges or clearing houses either generally or one by one (s. 300(1)). Such an order may be issued where the Treasury considers it necessary to ensure that disciplinary decisions are consistent with Tribunal decisions taken under Part VIII of the Act or are in accordance with the European Human Rights Convention (s. 300(2)). In this way, recognised bodies are gradually becoming more part of the larger public functions dealt with by the Act, and less seen as separate commercial organisations.

## RECOGNITION REQUIREMENTS

Draft recognition regulations under FSAMA 2000, s. 286(1), were issued by the Treasury in February 1999. The Secretary of State is a co-signatory with the Treasury to regulations under s. 301(1), which deals with default rules (originally applied to market contracts as defined in s. 155 of the Companies Act 1989). Default rules relate to the arrangements to be taken by the investment exchange or clearing house where a person appears to be unable or is likely to be unable to complete contracts with the exchange or clearing house.

The government recognises that exchanges and clearing houses are necessarily expert in the operation of their markets and that they have strong incentives in ensuring that they function in a safe and proper manner. It was accordingly considered in the public interest to allow them a wide degree of flexibility in the determination and application of their own market rules. On recognition, such bodies are accordingly exempt from the need for authorisation under FSAMA 2000 although they are still subject to the supervision and oversight of the FSA. While they do not have to comply with the FSA's conduct of business rules, their members will if separately authorised.

The requirements set out in the recognition regulations replace the earlier provisions contained in FSA 1986, s. 39 and sch. 4. The further requirements with regard to default rules were set out in the Companies Act 1989, sch. 21.

The former general provisions with regard to financial resources, proper monitoring and the promotion and maintenance of standards are repeated. The new draft regulations, however, draw all of the relevant provisions together for the first time. They are also made more explicit in their terms, provide for more delegation of functions and allow clearing houses to be recognised on a stand-alone basis not tied to any particular investment exchange.

The proposed recognition requirements in respect of investment exchanges are set out in part I of the schedule to the draft regulations, which is reproduced in Table 20.1. The proposed requirements for recognition as a clearing house are set out in part II. These are almost identical to those proposed for applicant exchanges and correspond with the material set out in paragraphs (a), (b), (c), (d) and (e) of Table 20.1.

Special requirements are proposed in relation to exchanges or clearing houses which offer or propose to offer clearing services in respect of market contracts under s. 155(2) or (3) of the Companies Act 1989. These are set out in parts III (exchanges) and IV (clearing houses) of the schedule.

The proposed requirements are that default rules must be in place which allow for appropriate action to be taken in respect of unsettled market contracts where a member is unable to meet its obligations in respect of one or more contracts. The default rules must enable action to be taken in respect of all unsettled market contracts other than those entered into by a recognised clearing house for the purposes of or in connection with the provision of clearing services for the exchange. The effect is to ensure that all rights and liabilities between the parties to an unsettled market contract are discharged and to enable net payments to be made in all relevant cases.

**Table 20.1**    Proposed requirements for recognition of investment exchanges

---

(a)    The exchange must operate market facilities which enable persons using those facilities to enter into transactions and investments.

(b)    The exchange must be a fit and proper person and, in particular, must ensure by its constitution, rules, practices or otherwise that the systems and controls used are appropriate to the scale and nature of the exchange's business and that adequate procedures are adopted for making and amending rules and for keeping the rules under review.

(c)    The exchange must have sufficient financial resources for the proper carrying out of its regulated activities.

(d)    The exchange must be able and willing to cooperate in the sharing of information or otherwise with the FSA, any other law enforcement agency and any other person having responsibility for the supervision or regulation of any regulated activity or other financial service in the United Kingdom or overseas.

(e)    The exchange must be able and willing to promote and maintain high standards of integrity and fair dealing in the carrying on of regulated activities.

(f)    The exchange must have satisfactory arrangements for ensuring the timely discharge of the rights and liabilities of parties to transactions effected on the exchange, recording such transactions, monitoring and enforcing compliance with its rules and arrangements and investigating complaints.

(g)    Where it clears transactions other than those effected on the exchange, it must also provide satisfactory arrangements for the recording of all such transactions, monitoring and enforcing compliance and investigating complaints.

(h)    In the event of a failure of an issuer to comply with the obligation of disclosure imposed under reg. 3(1) of the Traded Securities (Disclosure) Regulations 1994 (SI 1994/188), the rules of the exchange must provide for the discontinuation of the admission of the relevant securities to trading, suspension of trading in those securities, publication of the fact that the issuer has still to comply with the obligation of disclosure and for the exchange itself to make public any information which the issuer has failed to publish.

---

## RIE AND RCH SOURCEBOOK

The FSA issued Consultation Paper 39, *RIE and RCH Sourcebook*, in January 2000. The proposed new sourcebook contains the FSA's guidance on the interpretation of the proposed recognition requirements set out by the Treasury, the new notification rules for RIEs and RCHs to replace the Financial Services (Notification by Recognised Bodies) Regulations 1995 and guidance on the approach which the FSA will take to the supervision of RIEs and RCHs.

The sourcebook incorporates the three main changes referred to in connection with the recognition regimes. A separate chapter of the sourcebook deals with assumption by the FSA of responsibility from the Treasury for the oversight of overseas investment exchanges and clearing houses.

## COMPETITION SCRUTINY

A separate competition scrutiny regime is set up for recognised bodies under Chapters II and III of Part XVIII of FSAMA 2000. This is concerned with ensuring that the rules and practices of recognised bodies do not have any significant anti-competitive effects or amount to an abuse of a dominant position. Investigations may be conducted by the Director General of Fair Trading and, following a report from the Competition Commission, directions may be given by the Treasury. The general domestic competition law is disapplied by FSAMA 2000, ss. 311 and 312.

### Practices and regulatory provisions

The competition rules generally apply to practices and regulatory provisions. Practices are those of the exchange or clearing house acting as such (s. 302(1)). Regulatory provisions include the rules, guidance or required clearing arrangements of the recognised body (s. 302(1)).

A regulatory provision or practice will be considered under s. 302(2) to have a significantly adverse effect on competition if it has, or is intended or likely to have, that effect or if its effect requires or encourages behaviour which has or is intended or likely to have that effect. Regulatory provisions or practices which require or encourage exploitation of the strength of a market position are to be assumed to have an adverse effect on competition (s. 302(3)).

### Role of the Director General of Fair Trading

FSAMA 2000, s. 303(1), requires that the FSA send to the Treasury and the Director General of Fair Trading (DGFT) a copy of any regulatory provisions with which it is provided in connection with an application for recognition as well as any information which it considers will assist him in discharging his functions in connection with an application (s. 303(2)). The DGFT must then issue a report as to whether any particular regulatory provision or combination of regulatory provisions has a significantly adverse effect on competition (s. 303(3)). Practices, accordingly, do not feature in their own right at this stage. Reasons must be given for any finding (s. 303(4)) and the report copied to the FSA, the Competition Commission and the Treasury (s. 303(5)).

### Continuing reports

The DGFT must keep under continuing review the regulatory provisions and practices of all recognised bodies (s. 304(1)). A report must be made if there is any significantly adverse effect on competition (s. 304(2)) and may be made where there is not (s. 304(3)). The same requirements as to justification and copying apply where there is an adverse effect (s. 304(4) and (5)).

## Investigations

The DGFT is given substantial powers to investigate initial or continuing competition issues (s. 305). He may by notice require any person to produce any specified or described document in the person's custody or control or provide any information at a specified time and place (s. 305(2) and (3)). If the person refuses or fails to comply, the DGFT may certify that in writing to the High Court or Court of Session in Scotland (s. 305(5) and (7)). The court may then hold the defaulter in contempt after hearing any witness or statement produced in defence (s. 305(6)). This will apply to any relevant information other than legally privileged communications and others where the defaulter has a reasonable excuse.

## Competition Commission

The Competition Commission is required to investigate any matter set out in a report issued by the DGFT which is sent to it for consideration (s. 306(1)). This may arise when the DGFT concludes that there is an adverse effect on competition, whether on an application for recognition or thereafter (s. 306(2)). The DGFT can also ask the Commission to consider one of his reports even if he finds no significant adverse effect himself (s. 306(3)). A separate report must be produced by the Commission unless no useful purpose would be served following a change in circumstances (s. 306(4)). The report must confirm whether the regulatory provisions or practices have a significant adverse effect (s. 306(6)). The provisions set out in sch. 14 concerning the role of the Commission will generally apply (s. 306(11)). Importantly, however, the test is not a pure economic test of competitive effects, since, under s. 306(7), (8) and (9), the Commission needs to consider whether the adverse effect is justified and, in this context, the conclusions should in so far as reasonably possible be consistent with the obligations imposed on the recognised body concerned under the Act. They must also be explained to facilitate understanding (s. 306(10)). Copies of the report produced must be sent to the Treasury, the FSA and the DGFT (s. 306(12)).

An application for a recognition order for an investment exchange or clearing house must be approved by the Treasury (FSAMA 2000, s. 290(2)). Under s. 307(1) and (2), unless the Treasury consider that there are exceptional circumstances, approval must be given if:

(a)   the DGFT makes a report under s. 303 but does not ask the Competition Commission to consider it under s. 306; and
(b)   the Competition Commission concludes:

(i)     that the applicant's regulatory provisions do not have a significantly adverse effect on competition; or
(ii)    that if those provisions do have that effect, the effect is justified.

On the other hand, under s. 307(3) and (4), the Treasury must refuse approval, unless they consider that there are exceptional circumstances, if the Competition Commission has concluded that the applicant's regulatory provisions have a significantly adverse effect on competition and that effect is not justified.

These provisions are intended to keep ministerial involvement in competition decision-making to the minimum.

## Treasury directions

The Treasury may issue a remedial direction to the FSA following an adverse report from the Competition Commission (s. 308(5) and (6)). If the conclusion is that the adverse effect on competition is not justified, the Treasury must give a remedial direction to the FSA (s. 308(2)) unless effective corrective action has already been taken or there are exceptional circumstances which would make it inappropriate to do so (s. 308(3)). The remedial direction may require the FSA to withdraw the body's recognition or instruct the body by a further direction to undertake such action as may be specified (s. 308(8)). The Treasury must issue (and publish) a statement explaining their action in each case (s. 309).

Any body in respect of which a request for approval by the Treasury for recognition is to be refused or other corrective action directed and any party affected must be given the opportunity to make representations before any action is taken (s. 310(2)). The representations may relate to either the DGFT's report or that of the Competition Commission, or the proposed action to be taken in response (s. 310(1)).

## MARKET INFRASTRUCTURE

In addition to clearing market counterparties, the FSA is also concerned to establish an effective supervisory and regulatory regime with regard to other service providers who support the market's infrastructure, as well as all other areas of market innovation.

Sir Howard Davies has described ATSs as including both full trading systems providing access to a range of investors with a high degree of functionality as well as looser electronic crossing networks which operate within and between groups of institutions. Their essential features are that they bring orders and sales together and provide for contract execution. The new platforms can compete with the older exchanges in terms of technological efficiency and support but even more importantly cost. There are about 12 such systems in London and a number of others across Europe (totalling around 25 at time of writing).

In light of the importance of these systems, the SEC issued a set of rules proposals on the regulation of ATSs in April 2000 following an earlier concept release in May 1997, which sought comments on the revision of the regulatory framework for organised securities markets. The April rules amendments will fundamentally expand the definition of a market under the Securities Exchange Act 1934. Where an entity is deemed an exchange, it will have to register as a national securities exchange or as an ATS to which certain additional regulatory requirements will now be applied.

In the UK, any infrastructure provider is generally required either to be recognised as an RIE or RCH or authorised to conduct a regulated activity. Recognition generally focuses on the maintenance of appropriate standards in connection with the operation of the market or clearing system. Authorisation is concerned with fitness and properness, financial resources and conduct of business compliance. An infrastructure provider will usually have the choice of either being recognised or authorised.

While this dual regime approach is continued under FSAMA 2000, the FSA is concerned that future developments, in particular, with regard to electronic trading and processing, might increase competition in the markets and lead to substantial fragmentation of formal exchanges in favour of other non-exchange based systems or OTC markets. The issues which arise with regard to such fragmentation were set out in the FSA's discussion paper on the regulation of market infrastructure in January 2000 (*The FSA's Approach to Regulation of the Market Infrastructure* (Discussion Paper D02)). The FSA is currently considering possible changes to the recognition guidance or the adoption of separate infrastructure rules for authorised firms.

This is an important issue in light of the substantial further improvements in digital communications and technological support which have become possible. It is expected that a number of further alternative trading and processing platforms will become available for various categories of securities and debt instruments. Some of the new operators in this area have already been referred to, including Jiway and UKPX, and a number of other schemes are currently being set up, or are in the course of applying for relevant recognition or authorisation. While the FSA is concerned that all of these new systems are subject to proper oversight and control, it proposes to allow the market to develop and to monitor potential areas of difficulty rather than impose overly burdensome requirements at this stage which could otherwise unnecessarily restrict growth and innovation.

# Chapter Twenty-One
# Lloyd's of London

*George Walker*

Lloyd's of London is the most famous single insurance institution in the world. Over its 300-year history, it has led the development of marine insurance internationally and more recently has been the market leader in such other areas as aviation, motor, property damage and general liability. Lloyd's has always been proud to be able to provide insurance against almost any type of event or activity.

Its long history has meant that it is unique in both its structure and operation as well as in its methods of market supervision and control. Although the Council of Lloyd's and the Lloyd's Regulatory Board, with the Lloyd's Market Board, in particular, have been able to manage the provision of insurance and underwriting facilities successfully for a long period of time, recent scandals and significant claims have called into question the ability of Lloyd's generally fully to supervise and regulate all of its members' activities. Substantial losses suffered during the late 1980s and early 1990s also raised concerns as to the ability of the institution effectively to cover all of the risk undertaken. A number of initiatives were accordingly launched to attempt to correct these potential difficulties and deficiencies. A Capital Reconstruction Renewal Plan was, in particular, announced in May 1995, which attempted to resolve outstanding litigation, close the insurance years then left open and plan for the future continuation of the market.

It was against this background that the government decided in 1997 to include Lloyd's within the new framework of market supervision and regulation which has been set up under the Financial Services and Markets Act 2000 (FSAMA 2000). This does not attempt to deal with all outstanding issues, such as corporate governance or capital provision. An external monitoring and review mechanism is, however, set up under the auspices of the FSA to ensure that Lloyd's continues to control its market in an effective manner and to provide oversight and direction as required. The core statutory provisions in this area are now in Part XIX of the Act. Many other sections of the Act will also apply to Lloyd's and its members and specific provision is to be included within the new FSA *Handbook* to deal with their activities, for example, in the Supervision Manual, Prudential Sourcebook and Conduct of Business Sourcebook.

Lloyd's will in this way be brought within the scope of general operation of the new supervisory and regulatory system, although account will be taken of the special nature of its operations and activities. Much of the success of the new framework to be established will depend upon the continued work of the Lloyd's existing board and committee structure. The Act allows them to operate in a largely autonomous manner, but now subject to external oversight and possible direction by the FSA.

## HISTORICAL ORIGIN

A coffee house set up by Edward Lloyd in Tower Street, London, was used as a meeting place for merchants and insurances. The first mention of the coffee house was in the *London Gazette* in February 1688. Merchants and shipowners would meet to discuss shipping business and agreements would be entered into to insure or underwrite particular transactions. The shipowner would pay a premium in return for which the loss of the ship or cargo would be covered by one or more underwriters. Each person providing insurance cover would write his name at the bottom or under the agreement or policy, and they were then referred to as names or underwriters from an early stage. If the risk was large, a syndicate would be formed with all of the contributing names signing under the lead underwriter.

Edward Lloyd did not provide insurance cover himself but only the premises. To develop the facilities further, he built up a network of correspondents in ports throughout Britain and elsewhere to provide information on shipping business. This information became *Lloyd's News*, which acted as a regular shipping bulletin from 1696 onwards.

After the original coffee house fell into disrepute, because of the fact that gamblers and speculators as well as legitimate underwriters took part in its business, another coffee house known as the New Lloyd's was set up in 1769 by Thomas Fielding. After a period at the Royal Exchange, Lloyd's moved into Leadenhall Street in 1928 to acquire more space and into Lime Street in 1958. The current building was opened in November 1986 at 1 Lime Street on the site of its earlier Leadenhall premises.

Lloyd's became the property of its subscribers in 1771 and the Society of Lloyd's was incorporated by s. 3 of the Lloyd's Act 1871. Further private Acts were passed in 1888, 1911, 1925 and 1951. Following the Fisher Committee investigation into whether further statutory amendment was required, the Lloyd's Act 1982 was passed. This was in turn reconsidered by the Neill Committee in 1987 in the context of the Financial Services Act 1986 to ensure, in the light of further unease about the prevailing standards at Lloyd's, that Lloyd's was able to secure protection on a basis equivalent to that called for elsewhere by that Act.

A number of further changes have since been given effect following the significant losses incurred especially between 1988 and 1992. These included the introduction of corporate capital in 1994 with members having the option of continuing to trade as individuals or with limited liability. The Members' Agents Pooling Arrangement (MAPA) was also set up, which allowed capital and names to participate in an agents' MAPA (with a consequent spread of risk) or to operate through an original or bespoke portfolio.

## STRUCTURE OF LLOYD'S

The affairs of Lloyd's are generally conducted through the Committee of Lloyd's, which consists of 16 persons elected by its members with a chairman and two deputy chairmen. Following the recommendation of the Fisher Report, a new governing council was established under the Lloyd's Act 1982 which is made up of six non-working names and three non-members of Lloyd's. The Fisher Report also recommended that the Council should have power to issue bye-laws and to suspend or exclude membership. Many of these activities are now undertaken by committees of the Council.

The regulatory work of Lloyd's is conducted through its Regulatory Division which is answerable to the Lloyd's Regulatory Board. The Division authorises entities to trade in the market, ensures that firms and individuals comply with the Lloyd's regulations through inspection visits and investigates allegations of misconduct. The Division has approximately 160 staff and is divided into a number of functional groups which include the following:

(a) *Regulatory Policy Group*. This group is responsible for the development of regulatory policy for consideration by the Lloyd's Regulatory Board. This includes undertaking specific projects or research for developing, implementing, interpreting and advising on regulatory policy in the market, including the chain of security underlying the Lloyd's policy, standards of behaviour in the market and issues affecting individual and corporate members' code of conduct. It liaises with agents and the market associations and other regulatory authorities.

(b) *Authorisations Group*. Initial registrations and approvals of any changes in relevant circumstances are dealt with through the Authorisations Group. All regulated entities and individuals are subject to registration.

(c) *Monitoring Group*. Inspections of business practices are conducted through the Monitoring Group to ensure that required standards of good management are complied with by the underwriting agents and brokers. Specific aspects of members' businesses are examined including premiums and claims control, with remedial plans being agreed in the event of any difficulties being identified. To the extent that disciplinary action may be required, this is referred to the Lloyd's Regulatory Board, which may, in turn, pass matters to the Lloyd's Investigations Committee and the Lloyd's Disciplinary Committee.

(d) *Enforcement Group*. Complaints against or concerning Lloyd's underwriters, underwriting agents or Lloyd's brokers are dealt with through the complaints department within the Enforcement Group. Investigations are conducted through the separate investigations department with disciplinary work being prepared by a regulatory proceedings team for consideration by the Council's Investigations Committee.

(e)  *Other departments.* Various other departments of Lloyd's may be involved in supervisory or regulatory activity including Market Reporting and Solvency, Market Financial Service and the International Department.

## MARKET OPERATION

The principal market participants are the names or underwriting members, the underwriting syndicates, Lloyd's brokers and underwriting agents. The names are the individuals who provide capital to cover the policies underwritten. There were up to 34,000 individual names at one point although this number has since dropped to around 6,800. Corporate members have been admitted to Lloyd's since 1994. A substantial part of Lloyd's total business is now conducted through corporate members.

Underwriting members trade through syndicates with between one or two and 3,000 members. A syndicate is distinct from a partnership in that liability is several, with each underwriting member's proportion being limited to the stated amount of any claim. There are approximately 400 underwriting syndicates and individual names may be members of one or more. Each syndicate has its own box, or table, within the Room at Lloyd's. The work of the syndicate is conducted through an active underwriter who decides which business should be covered, at what rate and subject to what conditions. Policies are said to be issued 'at' and not 'with' Lloyd's.

Business is brought to Lloyd's through Lloyd's brokers. Over 250 firms are approved by Lloyd's which allows them entry to the trading Room. Non-Lloyd's brokers have to conduct their business through a Lloyd's broker. This then becomes 'insurance arranged at Lloyd's' and not 'at Lloyd's'. The broker is obliged to provide all relevant information concerning the risk to be covered as these contracts are *uberrimae fidei*. Details are noted on a slip which is taken by the Lloyd's broker between different syndicate boxes in the Room. Depending upon the size of the coverage required, more than one box will be approached with a primary or lead underwriter 'leading' the slip by taking the first slice or line of the risk. Once the lead underwriter has determined the relevant premium and conditions of cover, this will generally be followed by all of the other underwriters who will accept a line each. Once the slip is fully subscribed, or underwritten, the transaction is closed and a policy is submitted to the Lloyd's Policy Signing Office for processing. Amendments to the cover provided are also subject to the slip procedure. Much of the risk undertaken will then not be held by the syndicate but spread, or covered, through other syndicates under a process of reinsurance.

Lloyd's brokers may also act as underwriting agents by either soliciting and managing syndicate members (a members' agency) or being responsible for the general management of one or more underwriting syndicates (a managing agency). The Lloyd's Act 1982 required that insurance brokers divest themselves of control of managing agencies to avoid any potential conflicts of interest where an underwriter may be pressurised to accept or provide more generous terms of cover.

Business may also be conducted through syndicates or separate insurance companies which comprise the London Market. These usually also operate around Lime Street. Lloyd's generally only deals in short-term risk with all syndicates being legally required to cease business and reform each year. It is accordingly not suitable for life insurance but is in competition with the larger insurance companies for all other types of business.

## THE NEW FRAMEWORK

Following the announcement that responsibility for the oversight of Lloyd's would be transferred to the FSA, a consultation paper, *The Future Regulation of Lloyd's* (Consultation Paper 16) was issued by the FSA in November 1998. This was followed by *Response Paper on Consultation Paper 16: The Future Regulation of Lloyd's* in June 1999. A separate paper, *The Lloyd's Return* (Consultation Paper 16 Lloyd's Return) was published in December 1999. A further consultation document, *Insurance Draft Interim Prudential Sourcebook* was also produced in January 2000 (Consultation Paper 41).

The primary concern of the FSA is to protect policyholders against the risk that valid claims may not be paid and members from poor-quality underwriting and inadequate monitoring and control of underwriting risks. Concentration of risk through excessive re-insurance was identified as a particular factor in the massive recent losses suffered which was compounded by a lack of transparency in relation to underwriting exposures. The FSA has, however, recognised the large amount of work undertaken within Lloyd's to identify and monitor risks and to establish appropriate regulatory requirements especially in connection with management control and financial resources. To allow this to continue, a new regulatory framework of control is to be established which will involve the FSA conducting certain supervisory functions directly, with others being discharged by Lloyd's but under the direction of the FSA.

The division of functions proposed was set out in Consultation Paper 16 (summarised in its annex C). It was intended that the FSA would generally authorise market participants, approve certain persons and acquirers of influence and monitor compliance with authorisation and approval criteria and general principles. Appropriate gateways would be established to provide for a necessary exchange of information between the FSA and Lloyd's. These would be in accordance with the rules set out in FSAMA 2000, Part XXIII. The FSA would also be directly involved with the conduct of advisory and investment-related activities including the custody and management of funds as well as the activities of former members and non-Lloyd's regulated firms which provide advice on syndicate participations.

Rules would then be issued to impose requirements on Lloyd's to discharge its regulatory powers in such areas as the prudential supervision of insurance business, management controls and managing agents and the conduct of capacity auctions.

The FSA would also review the existing Lloyd's procedures already in place. This would allow Lloyd's to continue to exercise many of its existing functions although now under the general oversight of the FSA. Having set appropriate standards, the FSA would monitor compliance and take any enforcement action as required including the withdrawal of certain functions if necessary. Day-to-day working contact would be developed between the various departments of Lloyd's and the FSA and regular meetings would be held between the chairman of the Council and other senior officials to discuss general market and policy issues.

Although half of the respondents to the November 1998 Consultation Paper would have preferred Lloyd's being brought within the full control of the FSA, it was decided that the split or dual system proposed would be adopted. Some adjustments to the specific mechanisms to be set up would, however, be made to ensure that Lloyd's activities were subject to effective supervision and control in all cases.

## THE LEGISLATION

Part XIX of FSAMA 2000 sets out the extent to which the Society of Lloyd's is subject to the general provisions of the Act and the manner in which the FSA may direct the Council of Lloyd's to exercise its rule-making powers under the Lloyd's Acts.

Section 314(1) and (2) requires the FSA to keep itself informed about the affairs of Lloyd's and its activities and to review on a continuing basis whether it should exercise its powers to issue directions under the Act. Lloyd's is accordingly not brought within the scope of full regulatory control by the FSA but allowed to continue to operate on a largely autonomous basis. This is, however, subject to the external oversight and direction of the FSA.

The Society of Lloyd's is made an authorised person by s. 315(1). Lloyd's is given permission by s. 315(2) to carry on its basic market activity (arranging deals in contracts of insurance written at Lloyd's), its secondary market activity (arranging deals in participation in syndicates) and other connected activities (s. 315(2)). FSA has its s. 45 power to vary the Society's permission on its own initiative and may exercise that power before the permission comes into force (s. 315(4)). The effect of these requirements is generally to bring the Society within the control of the FSA and to restrict its activities to traditional Lloyd's market operations.

The FSA may determine which core parts of the Act are to apply to the carrying on of an insurance market activity by Lloyd's or Lloyd's members through the issuance of an insurance market direction under s. 316(1). This may apply to the general prohibition in s. 19 or any core provision listed in s. 317(1). Insurance market activity means a regulated activity relating to contracts of insurance written at Lloyd's (s. 316(3)). Directions under s. 316 will be issued only where the interests of policyholders or potential policyholders justify doing so, there has been a failure by the Society to implement any relevant EEA provision or otherwise to ensure the effective exercise of the FSA's functions in relation to Lloyd's (s. 316(4)). Directions must be in writing (s. 316(5)) and specify each core provision, class of person and kind of activity covered (s. 316(7)).

Rather than issue an insurance market direction, the FSA may act through the Council by imposing an obligation on the Council directly or on the Society, or both, under s. 318(1). A s. 318 direction may apply to the exercise of powers generally by the body concerned or a specific power (s. 318(2)). Exercising powers through the Council does not prevent specific obligations being imposed directly on market participants. This mechanism allows the FSA a certain degree of discretion in regulating the market either through its direct or indirect involvement.

The FSA must publish a draft direction under either s. 316 or s. 318 in advance including a cost-benefit analysis and notice of entitlement to make representations unless any delay would be prejudicial to consumers (s. 319(1) and (2)). Any representations made must then be considered (s. 319(3)). An account of the representations and the FSA's response must also be published (s. 319(4)). A significant change in the final direction must be explained and justified on a cost benefit basis (s. 319(5)). These directions accordingly have something of a legislative, rather than an executive or disciplinary, character.

To deal with the issue of continuing liability following a member leaving Lloyd's, s. 320(1) provides that former underwriting members may carry out each contract they have underwritten whether they continue to be authorised or not for the purposes of the Act. The FSA may impose on a former underwriting member any requirements considered to be appropriate for the purpose of protecting policyholders against the risk of not being paid (s. 320(3)). The FSA may also make rules imposing any such requirements as it considers appropriate (s. 322(1)). Safeguards have been included in connection with the issuance and content of requirements under s. 320, including the provision of reasons and the right to make representations (s. 321(1) to (12)). The imposition of any requirement and refusal to vary or revoke it may, in particular, be referred to the Financial Services and Markets Tribunal (s. 321(11)).

The effect of these provisions is to bring the Society of Lloyd's and all relevant market participants including the former underwriting members within the general control of the FSA. Such control may be exercised through the issuance of insurance market directions which will apply specific parts of the Act to Lloyd's, or Lloyd's members, or through more specific directions addressed to the Council or Society of Lloyd's directly. This means that the regulation of the Lloyd's market and market participants should generally be consistent with the regulation of other authorised persons in the UK although the historical background and unique operation of Lloyd's will be taken fully into account. The FSA has made it clear that it will, at least, initially attempt to rely on the existing board and committee structure of Lloyd's to carry out proper market supervision and regulation on a daily basis under its general oversight. It remains to be seen how the FSA will exercise its powers over time.

## CONDUCT IN THE MARKET

While the Society of Lloyd's may issue additional rules for its members and market participants, the FSA has issued the following proposals in connection with the control of its rules. Some of the proposed rules can be made only if the relevant sections of FSAMA 2000 are applied to Lloyd's by an insurance market direction (s. 316(1) and (2) and s. 317(1)).

## Authorisation, approval of persons and grandfathering

Although the Society of Lloyd's will be automatically authorised under the Act (s. 315(1)), the structure of the Act appears to enable the FSA, where appropriate, to deprive that status of any real effect. The FSA can cancel as well as restrict or extend the necessary permission, as well as issue directions (under s. 316 or s. 318). Managing agents will be authorised by the FSA once they have demonstrated that they are fit and proper persons. Applications will be assessed on the same basis as all other financial firms. The Society may, however, still refuse admission to Lloyd's or impose additional conditions on the conduct of Lloyd's business. Members' agents and Lloyd's advisers will have to be similarly authorised.

The FSA proposes to issue separate rules under s. 59 specifying controlled functions in relation to regulated activities for which prior approval will be required. This will apply to a number of the senior management posts within the Society of Lloyd's as well as managing agents, members' agents and Lloyd's advisers.

Existing authorisations in relation to all parties will be grandfathered when the relevant provisions of FSAMA 2000 come into force subject to the FSA's right to require re-application which will be reviewed prior to the Act coming into effect. Persons performing regulated functions within authorised firms will be similarly grandfathered although Lloyd's management will have to be separately approved as they were not previously registered.

## Prudential supervision

In assuming responsibility for the supervision of Lloyd's, the FSA has stated that it has attempted to develop the highest possible standards of prudential regulatory practice having regard to the capability and resilience of its essential resources. Under the Insurance Companies Act 1982, insurance undertakings must hold adequate reserves to cover their liabilities with a solvency margin calculated by reference to premium income or claims whichever is the higher. The difficulty which arises with Lloyd's is that a large portion of the assets supporting its activities are not pooled, apart from the Central Fund which is designed only to act as a form of reserve in the event that syndicates are not able to meet their liabilities. The crisis of the late 1980s, however, demonstrated how fragile the Central Fund and market as a whole could be without effective prudential practices.

The FSA's emerging policy, therefore, in attempting to ensure that Lloyd's is subject to proper prudential supervision, is as follows:

*Solvency*   Under the Act of 1982, Lloyd's was in recent years subject to three separate solvency tests. Under the global solvency test, the members of Lloyd's collectively had to have assets sufficient to meet their liabilities plus a minimum margin of solvency calculated in accordance with specified rules with regard to the valuation of assets and liabilities. This is based on the assumption that all admissible assets are available to meet total liabilities. With the separate individual solvency test, each member had separately to confirm that they had assets available, at least, equal to their liabilities. In 1997, a third combined solvency test was introduced which required each member individually to have assets to meet liabilities plus a simplified European minimum solvency margin, with Lloyd's also being required to be able to make available centrally held resources to cover any deficit (subject to discretionary allowances for inter-syndicate re-insurance). The effect of the third test was to combine the two other tests in a way that also dealt with the problem of several liability and non-transferability of assets between members. Following consultation, it was decided only to retain the third test provided that it could be made compatible with relevant European legislation which had been implemented through the global solvency test. The FSA proposes to consider separately how the Insurance Group Directive 98/78/EC of December 1998 will be implemented. A consultation paper in this regard was subsequently issued.

*Statutory statement of business (SSOB)*   Under the FSA's proposals, Lloyd's would be required to produce an annual statutory statement of business to demonstrate how the solvency tests were met. While the FSA had initially proposed only to bring the SSOB into line with the annual returns required of insurance companies, following consultation it was also decided to develop the SSOB further to provide more relevant and detailed information. This would include technical analysis of returns at syndicate level with more general solvency, trading results and assets at the market level.

*Risk-based capital (RBC)*   In addition to the solvency test established under the Insurance Companies Act 1982, Lloyd's members have hitherto been subject to its own risk based capital requirements. These take into account, in particular, the individual syndicate exposure of each member, risk volatility and diversification within and between syndicates as well as the quality of syndicate management. Capital is then held having regard to the proportionate amount of risk placed on the Central Fund in the event of default.

The system was set up following the 1992 Walker Report on the London market excess of loss (LMX) spirals. The system imposed capacity limits on members in relation to higher-risk categories of business having regard to volatility and risk. This was then extended to apply a basic capital requirement in relation to all types of business having regard to expected loss and volatility. Historical data at Lloyd's is used to calculate business risk (including underwriting and reserving risk) and management risk. Business risk is calculated allowing for adjustments for business mix, managing agent spread and re-insurance credit as well as members' experience in underwriting the portfolio.

Loadings are then applied to this base 'RBC' number. Agents and syndicates with a low rating (one or two) are subject to a 20 per cent or 10 per cent loading or deduction, while those with three or four (the best) ratings are subject to no adjustment. The ratings are applied by the Regulatory Division. A new syndicate loading is applied to syndicates less than three years old based on certain Lloyd's projections. From 1999, a third loading of up to 15 per cent of capacity has been applied to take into account changes in market conditions having regard to different disaster scenarios. This generates a funds at Lloyd's requirement which is then adjusted to reflect the performance of a particular syndicate having regard to average performance figures. A final funds at Lloyd's figure is then determined using certain other prudential margins which are, in particular, related to capacity assumptions (see FSA Consultation Paper 16, annex D).

The FSA decided to examine the Lloyd's RBC system in further detail with a view to developing it for use as a continuing regulatory tool. While it was anticipated that the system would be retained, certain concerns had arisen with regard to its technical operation and application or implementation. The FSA was also interested in the use of aggregation analyses and more risk of ruin stress testing, which would be considered with its more general examination of the feasibility and use of the RBC system. The general objective was accordingly to allow Lloyd's to continue to develop its own system and models in cooperation with the FSA rather than have responsibility in this regard simply assumed by the FSA. Work continues and further reports are expected in this regard.

Lloyd's will be required to ensure that members continue to pay premiums into trust funds approved by the Treasury (in time the FSA) as well as existing solvency tests, valuation of assets and liability rules and audit arrangements. Lloyd's will, under FSA rules, separately be required to issue detailed provisions in relation to the solvency tests and the SSOB.

## Managing agents

The FSA will require Lloyd's to issue rules to protect the interests of policyholders including maintenance of members to support underwriting and the publication of annual accounts by syndicates. While the FSA did not originally propose to require rules to be issued to protect members as such, following consultation it decided to reconsider the agency relationship involved with a view to including appropriate provision within the *Handbook*. It proposed to consult separately on the introduction of necessary capital requirements for firms involved in regulated activities as agents. Consultation on the relevant capital requirements is to be conducted as part of the general work undertaken in relation to the Prudential Sourcebook.

## Underwriting agents

Lloyd's has already issued Core Principles for Underwriting Agents which generally reflect the FSA's principles for regulated firms, although they may require some further revision (see Table 21.1).

**Table 21.1**   Lloyd's core principles for underwriting agents

---

**1.  Integrity**   An agent should observe high standards of integrity and deal openly and fairly.

**2.  Skill, care and diligence**   An agent should act with due skill, care and diligence.

**3.  Market conduct**   An agent should observe high standards of conduct and should take all reasonable steps to avoid causing harm to the standing or reputation of Lloyd's.

**4.  Conduct towards members**   An agent should conduct the affairs of each of the members for whom it acts in a manner which does not unfairly prejudice the interests of any such member.

**5.  Information**   An agent should seek from members it advises any information about their circumstances and objectives which might reasonably be expected to be relevant in enabling it to fulfil its responsibilities to them. An agent should take all reasonable steps to give members it advises or for whom it exercises discretion, in a comprehensible and timely way, any information needed to enable them to make balanced and informed decisions. An agent should also be ready to provide members with a full and fair account of the fulfilment of its responsibilities to them.*

**6.  Conflicts of interest**   An agent should seek to avoid any conflict of interest arising, but where a conflict does arise, should make comprehensible and timely disclosure of that conflict and of the steps to be taken to ensure the fair treatment of any members affected. An agent should not unfairly put its own interest above its duty to any members for whom it acts.

**7.  Assets**   An agent should deal with assets and rights received or held on behalf of a member prudently and in accordance with the terms of any applicable trust deed or agreement with the member.

**8.  Financial resources**   An agent should maintain adequate financial resources to meet its commitments and to withstand the normal risks to which it is subject.

**9.  Internal organisation**   An agent should organise and control its internal affairs in a responsible manner, maintaining proper records and systems for the conduct of its business and the management of risk. It should have adequate arrangements to ensure that staff and others whom it employs are suitable, adequately trained and properly supervised and that it has well-defined compliance procedures.

**10.  Relations with Lloyd's**   An agent should deal with Lloyd's in an open and cooperative manner and keep Lloyd's promptly informed of anything concerning the agent which Lloyd's might reasonably expect to be disclosed to it.

*This principle does not require an agent to give the member concerned greater rights of access to documents and information than the member has under any agreement with the agent.

---

## Former members

The FSA proposed that minimum requirements, including reporting obligations, should be imposed on former members under new rules which would replicate the existing orders issued under the Insurance Companies Act 1982.

## Members' agents and Lloyd's advisers

Members' agents and Lloyd's advisers are expected to be supervised by the FSA directly. This was considered appropriate as many members' agents may become more general financial advisers and investment managers by the time that the relevant provisions of FSAMA 2000 come into force. While Lloyd's did impose its own rules, for example, in relation to the maintenance of adequate capital by members' agents and Lloyd's advisers, it would also be expected to impose additional requirements in relation to such matters as the conduct of capacity auctions. The FSA rules would deal with such matters as quality of advice and execution and compliance would be monitored by it directly. Rules would make appropriate allowance for experienced customers through the counterparty classification regime following earlier consultation on inter-professional business in October 1998. The continuing relevance of errors and omissions cover and its relationship to members' agents' capital would be reconsidered by the FSA in connection with professional indemnity insurance more generally.

## Syndicate capacity market

The FSA has accepted that Lloyd's should continue to be responsible for the running of the capacity transfer market through its Regulatory Division. The formal transfer market may in time be replaced by simple bilateral deals or acquisitions through a natural process of consolidation of the syndicates within Lloyd's. While the market would not satisfy the FSA's recognition requirements for an RIE, the conduct of the market should be subject to some continuing review and control. Following consultation, the FSA decided that it would direct Lloyd's to make appropriate rules for conduct in the market which would reflect standards imposed elsewhere especially with regard to conflicts of interest. The functioning and mechanics of the market are to be monitored over time and further action taken as appropriate.

## Custodianship and funds management

Lloyd's itself and members' funds held for underwriting purposes and members' agents were to be subject to the FSA's normal rules in connection with the holding and management of funds belonging to others following the removal of the Lloyd's-related-activities exemption in FSA 1986. This will include the premium trust funds held or managed by Lloyd's or managing agents under approved trust deeds. The trust fund regime would be continued as a parallel device to the reserves maintained by normal insurance companies. Some relaxation of the more detailed rules would be permitted to reflect the fact that the funds continued to belong to the members. The operation of these trusts would be reviewed and appropriate provisions included within the relevant sections of the new *Handbook*.

## Investigations, discipline and enforcement

It was always intended that the FSA would be able to exercise its full powers of information gathering and investigation, intervention and discipline in relation to both the Society of Lloyd's and Lloyd's participants. The exercise of these powers, however, had to take into account the fact that Lloyd's had its own internal procedures in this regard. It was accordingly accepted that delays, unnecessary duplication of effort and possible double jeopardy may arise. Effective arrangements would accordingly be set up to ensure cooperation and exchange of information and appropriate provision included within the relevant sections of the *Handbook*. With regard to the division of responsibility, including the identification of areas where the FSA would be responsible for supervising the activities of the Society itself, the FSA prepared a summary table which was set out in annex C to Consultation Paper 16 (see Table 21.2). Where both bodies may be concerned with the same issue or event, a series of guidelines would be followed to avoid any unnecessary overlap of activity and prejudice. Following consultation on the scope of the enforcement powers contained in the original Bill, the government and the FSA accepted certain adjustments which were published in the Treasury's progress report on the Bill. These changes would also be reflected in the enforcement arrangements to be set up with Lloyd's.

## Complaints

The FSA has accepted that the existing complaints arrangements should continue to be processed through Lloyd's Complaints Department. The Complaints Department will consider complaints initially which will subsequently be referred to the Financial Services Ombudsman Scheme which the Society of Lloyd's has joined. This has replaced the earlier Insurance Ombudsman Bureau. The FSA considered that the maintenance of the two-tier complaints procedures would be the most efficient and cost-effective in practice. Members would continue to be able to take complaints against other members or managing agents to the Lloyd's Complaints Department, failing which to the Lloyd's Arbitration Scheme. Complaints concerning maladministration by the Corporation of Lloyd's would still be taken to the Lloyd's Members' Ombudsman. The FSA did not intend to interfere with these established practices and arrangements.

**Table 21.2**    Investigation by the FSA and Lloyd's

1.   All Lloyd's participants should not be subject to more than one investigation or set of disciplinary proceedings for the same alleged wrongdoing unless it is appropriate for both the FSA and Lloyd's to exercise their different powers against the firm or the investigation or discipline relates to different aspects of the misconduct.

2.   Disciplinary action should not usually be taken by both bodies concurrently although there may occasionally be instances where consecutive action is appropriate (for example in relation to de-authorisation proceedings conducted by FSA following Lloyd's disciplinary proceedings).

3.   The body whose powers are most appropriate to discipline a firm for, or otherwise deal with, the apparent wrongdoing should in most cases be responsible for leading the investigation.

4.   The relative effectiveness of the FSA's or Lloyd's powers to obtain the required information and evidence should, however, be taken into account in all cases.

5.   If the FSA is investigating a concern about a Lloyd's participant it may require Lloyd's Regulatory Proceedings Department to assist by providing technical advice, information and documents or by carrying out its own enquiries and reporting its findings to the FSA.

6.   If appropriate, the FSA may formally appoint a member of Lloyd's Regulatory Proceedings Department together with a member of the FSA's staff or another competent person to investigate concerns about a Lloyd's participant.

7.   The FSA will always have power to carry out investigations itself and to take such disciplinary action as it considers appropriate.

8.   Cases of joint interest will be reviewed regularly as they develop to determine whether the lead responsibility should be transferred from Lloyd's to the FSA or vice versa.

## Compensation

Where Lloyd's members were unable to meet their liabilities to policyholders, claims could be made against the Lloyd's Central Fund. This was levied through individual member contributions of 1 per cent from 1998 for individual members and 1.5 per cent for corporate members. The Central Fund then had a value of £206 million with Lloyd's being able to make a pro rata call of £200 million from the premium trust funds without consent and further calls on consent. Lloyd's subsequently arranged with six major re-insurance groups for an additional excess cover for the Central Fund to be made available. This extended the cover up to £350 million on an annual basis and £500 million in aggregate. Compensation in relation to non-Lloyd's contracts was available through the Policyholders Protection Board and Policyholders Protection Scheme which was governed by the Policyholders Protection Acts.

In light of the security provided under the Lloyd's Central Fund arrangements, the FSA considered that Lloyd's should be exempt from the Financial Services Compensation Scheme (FSCS) which would replace, among other schemes, the Policyholders Protection Scheme. This would, however, be kept under review.

The FSA also decided, following consultation, that individual members of Lloyd's should not have access to the FSCS as they would already be covered by Lloyd's existing compensation arrangements. The FSA would, however, require Lloyd's to maintain appropriate compensation arrangements for individual members with appropriate guidance to be applied.

# Chapter Twenty-Two
# Provision of Financial Services by Members of the Professions

## Michael Blair

Part XX of the Financial Services and Markets Act 2000 (FSAMA 2000) attempts to resolve one of the long-standing structural problems confronted by the reforming process that has culminated in the Act. This problem was that presented by the 15,000 or so firms which were involved in investment business under the Financial Services Act 1986 (FSA 1986), not by virtue of authorisation by a self-regulating organisation (SRO), but because they were given a certificate, entitling them to carry on that business, by a 'recognised professional body'.

These firms, in the main, are accountancy firms and firms of solicitors. Only a few of them transact any significant amount of investment business. The others are mainly involved in their own specific professional activities, but need to have the ability to deal with aspects of investment business when they arise incidentally in the course of that professional work. A good example would be when a solicitor has recovered a substantial sum of money as damages for personal injury to a client and then wishes to be able to advise the client on how that money should be invested in the stock market or in bonds etc. in order to seek to preserve its real value and obtain a regular yield.

The device adopted in FSA 1986 to resolve this problem was threefold:

(a)  instead of authorisation by the SIB (later the FSA) an authorisation could be conferred by a certification procedure run by the firm's professional body;

(b)  the machinery of the professional body was available only if the firm in question was involved in investment business as a sideline, that is, below the proportion agreed between the SIB and the professional body (which was typically 20 per cent, though in some cases more);

(c)  any firm that went above the agreed proportion would be required to seek authorisation in the usual way, typically from an SRO.

The RPBs in recent years were those involved with accountants (four professional bodies), solicitors (three professional bodies) and actuaries (one).

With the emphasis of FSAMA 2000 shifting radically away from self-regulation, and the consequential abolition of the SROs, it was not immediately obvious how to carry forward the arrangements for professional firms. Initial policy decisions by the Treasury involved the following three elements:

(a)   any authorisation that was required would be conferred by the FSA;

(b)   the authorisation requirement would be fashioned so as to leave outside the need for authorisation those firms that merely carried on 'investment business' in an incidental way, and

(c)   although there would be no status of RPB hereafter, the FSA might wish to contract with professional bodies for the supply of monitoring services for professional firms authorised by the FSA.

Points (a) and (c) above proved relatively non-contentious, but the task of producing a workable regime to implement (b) proved surprisingly elusive. The Treasury made more than one attempt to deal with point (b), but found, in consultation with the professional bodies, that most of the formulations put forward appeared to bring into the net of regulation more firms than the broad policy intent had meant to catch. The figures, broadly, were about 15,000 firms, of which only about 2,000 were carrying on 'mainstream' investment business. The task of singling the 2,000 out from the remaining 13,000 was difficult, and, even now, the question whether Part XX achieves that aim is still unanswered. In part this is because professional firms with their reputations at stake are naturally cautious about taking any risk of committing the criminal offence of carrying on business without authorisation. Over the years 'protective authorisation' has been taken out by a large number of professional practices, and, unless the line between authorisable business and business not requiring authorisation is crystal clear, there is likely to be a continued demand for protective authorisation. Even with clarity, professional firms offering a full service to their clients are reluctant to have to inform any particular client that there is an aspect of the business of an '*homme d'affaires*' that they are unable to deliver to the client.

## THE SCHEME IN PART XX

Part XX of FSAMA 2000 deals with the general test to be applied for permitting professional firms to carry on specific regulated activities without authorisation, and also deals with the machinery put in place in order to make that test a workable one and to ensure that there is a necessary degree of consumer (or client) protection. It is convenient to take the test itself first.

## EXEMPTION: THE CONDITIONS

The central provision in Part XX is in s. 327, which specifies the conditions under which a professional firm may lawfully carry on professional activities without requiring FSA authorisation. The technical language for this is that the general prohibition in s. 19 against carrying on a regulated activity unless authorised to do so does not apply if all the conditions in s. 327 are satisfied.

The firm or person concerned must be carrying on the regulated activity in a manner which is 'incidental to the provision by him of professional services' (s. 327(4)). Further, it or he must not be remunerated by commission (any pecuniary reward or other advantage 'from a person other than his client') unless he accounts to the client for the receipt (s. 327(3)).

These are the main conditions in drawing the borderline for the professional regime. Others of significance are that the persons or firms must not carry on, or hold themselves out as carrying on, regulated activities other than those which arise out of, or are complementary to, the provision of their professional services (ss. 327(5) and s. 332(4)).

The Treasury are enabled by order to specify particular activities for which this exemption is not available, even on an incidental basis (s. 327(6)). The discussions over the placing of the borderline have singled out derivatives and pension opt-outs as possible candidates for such an order.

The general purpose, therefore, is to enable professional firms carrying on professional business to stray lawfully into the area of regulated activities without being regulated, as long as the straying is done on an incidental basis, and as long as any commission received is accounted for to the client.

The test of incidentality in s. 327(4) is enforceable in two separate ways. First, if there is a breach of s. 327, the 'general prohibition' in s. 19 does apply, and it is therefore possible for the FSA to take any of the steps normally available to it in relation to the enforcement of the perimeter set by the Act. These include prosecution under s. 401, injunctions under s. 380 and restitution under s. 382. Secondly, the test is reinforced by s. 332, which requires the professional body concerned to make rules governing the carrying on of regulated activities, which, in particular, must be designed to secure that the professional person carries on regulated activities only if they arise out of or are complementary to the provision of the professional service. Thus the Act requires that the weight of professional discipline is also available in a case of breach of this 'incidental' (or 'arising out of or complementary') requirement.

The borderline must also be visible to clients. Under s. 332(1) and (2) the FSA may make rules applying to the professional persons benefiting from the exemption in Part XX 'for the purpose of ensuring that clients are aware that such persons are not authorised persons'. And s. 333 makes it a criminal offence for members of the profession, or indeed anyone else, to describe themselves or to hold themselves out as free of the obligation to be authorised by virtue of Part XX, if that is not the case.

## THE MACHINERY TO MAKE THE EXEMPTION WORKABLE

The arrangements in Part XX start with the Treasury. Under s. 326, they may by order (made by statutory instrument) designate professional bodies for the purposes of Part XX. Any such body has to satisfy the basic condition that it has rules applicable to the carrying on by the members of profession of regulated activities which would fall within the exemption in Part XX. There is, on the face of the Act, no qualitative test about the substance, rigour and extent of those rules, but it can be expected that the Treasury will exercise their discretion in such a way as to secure that the rules are of the requisite quality. The subsequent arrangements in the hands of the FSA (see below) do involve a qualitative test.

In order to qualify for designation by the Treasury, in addition to making adequate rules, a professional body must satisfy one or more additional qualifying conditions. These are that it has statutory powers to regulate the profession, or there is a statutory provision restricting particular functions to members of the profession, or the body is recognised for other statutory purposes, or the equivalent in another EEA State of any of these.

The extension of those conditions to EEA professions seems inevitable now that 'own title' professional practice has been introduced under the Single Market arrangements. Within the UK the statutes recognising a professional body may be Scottish or Northern Irish legislation (s. 326(6)).

Once the Treasury have designated a professional body, the focus for the machinery switches to the FSA. Under s. 325, the FSA is required to keep itself informed about the way in which the designated professional bodies supervise and regulate the carrying on of the exempted activities, and the way in which the members carry on those activities. So there is a measure of oversight akin to that called for by FSA 1986 in relation to RPBs. Indeed the bodies are required to cooperate by sharing of information and in other ways in a similar way to that required under the 1986 Act.

If the FSA has concerns about a particular professional body or about a particular firm supervised and regulated by such a body, there is machinery to enable it to rectify the position. Essentially, the FSA has the power to knock out the exemption for the professional body in whole or in part (FSAMA 2000, s. 328), or to knock out a particular firm (s. 329). The test for the *general* power is that the FSA has to be satisfied that exercise of it is desirable in order to protect the interests of clients (s. 328(6)). Parliament has, in s. 328(7), directed the FSA's mind to four particular criteria that are relevant to the question of protecting the interests of clients. These are:

(a)   whether the body's arrangements are effective for securing compliance with the rules about the incidental (or 'arising out of or complementary to') border;

(b)   the effectiveness of complaints handling in relation to the exempted activities concerned;

(c)   the effectiveness of arrangements for redress to clients suffering or claiming to have suffered loss as a result of misconduct in the exempted activities area;

(d)   the body's arrangements for cooperating with the FSA.

There are separate powers about concerns over particular firms. These are contained in s. 329. The test for taking action relating to a particular firm is that the person concerned is not a fit and proper person to carry on regulated activities in accordance with s. 327. This means that it is either appropriate that the person should be subjected to full authorisation, or that the person should not be conducting regulated activities at all.

The Act sets out special machinery for both of these forms of rectifying action. The machinery for the general withdrawal or restriction of the Part XX regime (s. 330) is similar to that required by the Act in relation to the FSA's rule-making functions. The direction relating to the particular professional body has to be accompanied by a cost-benefit analysis, and must permit representations to be made. The procedure looks like a mixture between withdrawal of recognition under FSA 1986 and that available for legislative functions under FSAMA 2000. Section 330(6) also enables the consultative procedure to be set aside if the delay involved in complying with the procedure would prejudice the interests of 'consumers', who, no doubt, would largely overlap with the 'clients', as defined in s. 328(8), whose interests the FSA has to have in mind in exercising the power in the first place.

The power to knock out individual firms or persons is in s. 329. It involves assessing whether a person is 'fit and proper' to carry on regulated activities and is thus strikingly similar to the provision in s. 56 which enables the FSA to ban particular persons from the financial services industry or any part of it for not being fit and proper. The procedure for making an order under s. 329 involves delivery of a warning notice (see s. 331(1)) with the consequential rights to have the matter determined by the Financial Services and Markets Tribunal. Unlike s. 56, there appears to be no express provision for placing any resulting disqualification of a partnership, other firm or individual under Part XX on the register established under s. 347. No doubt it is envisaged that public information about persons disqualified under s. 329 will be provided for in the rules made, with the FSA's approval, by the professional body concerned under s. 332(3).

The provisions of Part XX have been welcomed by the relevant professional bodies to a greater extent than any of the previous attempts to solve the conundrum. One of the particular issues that came to the fore in the discussions after Part XX was added to the Bill for the Act related to the impact of the new structure on a firm which required FSA authorisation, because part of it was dealing with 'mainstream' regulated activities, but which also wished to continue to carry on exempted activities in the remaining parts of the firm. Broadly speaking, the firm being indivisible for this purpose, the Act does not enable the firm to be both authorised and exempted, though this conclusion arises from general principles of law and not from an express provision in the Act, of the kind made for other classes of exempted person (as to which see ss. 38(2) and 39(1)). But the extent of the regulation applied by the FSA to the part of the firm which would have been exempted had it been operating on its own need not be extensive, and, indeed, for proportionality reasons, needs to be broadly equivalent to the regime that would have been applicable had that part indeed been a separate partnership or firm.

# Chapter Twenty-Three
# Mutual Societies

## Michael Blair

Part XXI of the Financial Services and Markets Act 2000 (FSAMA 2000) deals with the dismantling of the regulatory and other public institutions concerned with the oversight of the mutual sector so far as this is required in consequence of the reforms achieved by the Act.

Most of the sections in Part XXI confer powers on the Treasury to achieve the desired results by statutory instrument. Under s. 429 of the Act all the orders envisaged by Part XXI are subject to the negative resolution procedure only.

Part XXI envisages that most of the transfers of responsibility to be made by Treasury order under it will be to the FSA. One section (s. 337) is different in that it enables complete abolition by the Treasury of the Building Societies Investor Protection Board, whose functions will be carried on hereafter by the Financial Services Compensation Scheme to be established under Part XV. Interestingly, in s. 416(3), four other bodies are abolished outright without the need for a special Treasury order of the kind required by s. 337. These are two of the other compensation schemes (Policyholders Protection Board and Deposit Protection Board) as well as the Insurance Brokers Registration Council and the Board of Banking Supervision. Not being concerned with mutual societies, it would not have been appropriate to deal with them in s. 337 and a separate section was required in Part XXVIII.

Each of the other powers enabling transfer of functions to the FSA contains power to transfer the balance of the powers to the Treasury. When the insurance functions of the Treasury were transferred to the FSA on 1 January 1999, the arrangements then made, under the Deregulation and Contracting Out Act 1994, involved a subdivision of the functions, with the principal policy staff remaining in the Treasury while the supervisory and oversight functions were transferred to the FSA. Something similar to that can be expected under the orders under Part XXI.

The institutions covered by the order making powers are as follows:

(a)   the Friendly Societies Commission (s. 334);

(b)   the Chief Registrar of Friendly Societies (s. 335) (this includes the Assistant Registrar for Scotland and the central office of the registry); and

(c)   the Building Societies Commission (s. 336).

Section 338 specifies the legislation concerning industrial and provident societies and credit unions conferring functions which are currently exercised by the Chief Registrar of Friendly Societies. The bulk of them will go to the FSA with the balance being transferred to the Treasury.

# Chapter Twenty-Four
## Auditors

*George Walker*

Auditors and accountants discharge a number of core functions in any supervisory system. The most important of these are information and data verification and confirmation of systems integrity. To the extent that a large part of the supervisory process is in practice conducted through the examination of regular prudential returns made by financial institutions, it is essential that the accuracy of the information provided can be relied on.

Every financial institution must also maintain adequate internal control systems to ensure that decisions are taken in accordance with relevant procedures and guidelines and that full and accurate records of all operations and transactions are properly collected and stored. Accountants and auditors accordingly have an essential role to play to ensure that appropriate systems and procedures have been set up and that they work effectively in practice. While the internal accountant will generally be responsible for the design and establishment of such systems, the external auditor will confirm their effective operation on an independent basis.

Actuaries have a similar role to play in assessing the liabilities of insurance companies.

## APPOINTMENT AND INFORMATION RULES

Many financial services firms are companies subject to the requirements of the Companies Act 1985 for annual accounts and reports which must be audited. FSAMA 2000, Part XXII empowers the FSA to make rules extending similar requirements to other authorised persons, such as partnerships and sole traders. The FSA may also make rules requiring authorised persons of a specified class to appoint actuaries.

### Appointment

Under FSAMA 2000, the FSA may issue rules to provide for the appointment of an auditor or actuary in cases where this has not already been required under any other enactment (s. 340(1)). The rules may specify the manner and time within which the appointment should be made, provide for notification of the appointment to the FSA and deal with remuneration and terms of office, removal and resignation (s. 340(4)). The rules may allow the FSA to make an appointment if no other appointment has been made or notified (s. 340(4)(c)). The FSA may specify in rules the qualifications and experience required of persons to be appointed as auditors or actuaries (s. 340(6) and (7)).

The FSA may make rules requiring classes of authorised persons to produce periodic financial reports which must be reported on by an auditor or actuary (s. 340(2)). The auditor or actuary may be placed under such other duties as may be required (s. 340(3)). Appointees must comply with the obligations imposed on them under the rules and will exercise such powers as may be conferred on them to discharge these functions (s. 340(5)).

### Information

Any auditor or actuary of an authorised person appointed under or as a result of FSAMA 2000 has the right of access at all times to the authorised person's books and accounts and is entitled to require any such information and explanations as are considered necessary from the authorised person's officers for the performance of his or her duties (s. 341(1)). Knowingly or recklessly giving an auditor or actuary information which is false or misleading in any material particular is an offence triable either way, with a maximum penalty on indictment of two years in prison and/or a fine (s. 346(c)). Sections 341 and 346 make provisions which are equivalent to those made for company auditors by the Companies Act 1985, s. 389A.

## DISCLOSURE BY AUDITORS TO THE FSA

### Disclosure and immunity

The problem for a regulator in relying on an auditor of a regulated person to provide information needed for regulation is that the auditor is employed by the regulated person and is thus subject to an obligation of confidentiality. FSAMA 2000 deals with this problem by exempting auditors and actuaries of authorised persons from liability for breach of duty by disclosing confidential information, in good faith, to the FSA, if the disclosure was made in the reasonable belief that it was relevant to any function of the FSA (s. 342(3)).

This exemption from liability applies to an authorised person's auditor or actuary appointed under or as a result of a statutory provision (s. 342(1) and (2)). It will therefore apply both to auditors appointed under the Companies Act 1985 and auditors and actuaries appointed under rules made by the FSA under FSAMA 2000, s. 340.

The exemption from liability applies not only to disclosure of information acquired while acting as an auditor or actuary but also to giving to the FSA the auditor's or actuary's opinion on such information (s. 342(3)(a) and (b)). It applies whether or not the FSA asked for the information or opinion (s. 342(4)) and even if the auditor's or actuary's appointment has ended (s. 342(1) and (2)).

The Treasury are empowered to make regulations prescribing when auditors and actuaries of authorised persons must communicate information and opinions to the FSA (s. 342(5)) and they are made expressly subject a duty to comply with those regulations (s. 342(6)).

Equivalent provision is made in s. 343 for disclosure of information by the present or former auditor or actuary of a person who 'has close links' with an authorised person. By s. 343(8), an entity has close links with an authorised person, A, if it is:

(a)  a parent undertaking of A;
(b)  a subsidiary undertaking of A;
(c)  a parent undertaking of a subsidiary undertaking of A; or
(d)  a subsidiary undertaking of a parent undertaking of A.

'Subsidiary undertaking' is defined by s. 343(9) to include all possible forms of subsidiary undertaking mentioned in art. 1(1) and (2) of the Seventh Company Law Directive (83/349/EEC). Although the Directive is concerned with consolidated accounts when a parent undertaking and/or one or more of its subsidiary undertakings are companies (art. 4), the definitions in art. 1 are not restricted to any particular legal form of undertaking.

**Notification on leaving office**

When an auditor or actuary of an authorised person appointed under or as a result of a statutory provision (see s. 342 above) is removed from office, resigns or is not re-appointed, he or she must notify that fact to the FSA (s. 344(1) and (2)). The FSA must also be notified of any fact or matter connected with leaving office which the auditor or actuary thinks ought to be drawn to the FSA's attention (s. 344(3)(a)). If there is no such matter or fact, the FSA must be given a notice to that effect (s. 344 (3)(b)).

**Disqualification**

If an auditor or actuary of an authorised person appointed under or as a result of a statutory provision fails to comply with a duty imposed on him or her under the Act, the FSA may disqualify him or her from acting as auditor or actuary of authorised persons generally or of a particular class of authorised persons (s. 345(1)). There is a similar power of disqualification in relation to unit trusts and OEICs (s. 249(1)) which will operate parallel to this jurisdiction.

The FSA must give the person concerned a warning notice if it is considering disqualifying him and a decision notice must be served once the decision to disqualify has been taken (s. 345(2) and (3)). The FSA may remove the disqualification if satisfied that the auditor or actuary will in future comply with the relevant obligations (s. 345(4)). This would allow the FSA to exercise or threaten to exercise its right to disqualify to ensure that all necessary information was released in particular cases. The decision to disqualify is referable to the Financial Services and Markets Tribunal by the person disqualified (s. 345(5)).

## RULES ISSUANCE

The FSA has not yet issued any rules or further guidance in relation to Part XXII. This will accordingly be considered further in subsequent editions of this *Guide*.

# Chapter Twenty-Five
# Public Record, Disclosure of Information and Cooperation

*Loretta Minghella*

Part XXIII of the Financial Services and Markets Act 2000 (FSAMA 2000) imposes three sets of obligations on the FSA in relation to its handling of information. First, it creates an obligation to create a record of certain information which must be available for public inspection. Secondly, confidential information is prohibited from disclosure except as prescribed. Thirdly, the Act places the FSA under an obligation to cooperate with other authorities in the fight against financial crime.

The information disclosure regime under the Act, which will be supplemented by regulations yet to be made, will be very important in the daily work of the FSA. There is inevitably a tension between the growing demands made on the FSA and other public bodies for increased transparency and accountability, on the one hand, and the need to respect the commercial and sometimes personal sensitivities of the information they have the powers to collect, on the other. This Part of the Act provides the FSA with a framework within which to balance these competing pressures.

It is, of course, only a small corner of the law relevant to decisions to disclose information. Such decisions will often involve consideration of other areas such as data protection, defamation, rehabilitation of offenders, common law confidentiality, public interest immunity and freedom of information laws. Previous case law on the disclosure of regulatory information has concentrated in the main on principles of statutory interpretation. It will be interesting to see in future how far arguments based on art. 8 and art. 10 of the European Convention on Human Rights begin to emerge in determining the rights and wrongs of any decision to disclose.

## THE PUBLIC RECORD TO BE MAINTAINED BY THE FSA

The FSA is required by FSAMA 2000, s. 347 to maintain a record of every person who appears to the FSA to be an authorised person, together with information about others, including authorised collective investment schemes, recognised investment exchanges and clearing houses, approved persons, and individuals prohibited from being employed in the industry.

Section 347 specifies what the record must contain and confers a duty on the FSA to include any information which it considers appropriate. The mandatory elements include information about the services which each authorised person holds himself out as able to provide, together with an address for service.

In the case of individuals in respect of whom a prohibition order has been made under s. 56 of the Act, the FSA must include at least the name of each individual and details of the effect of the order. This marks a significant departure from the scheme for publication of similar orders made under FSA 1986, s. 59. Under that Act the FSA had only limited powers to make known the names of those disqualified by it from working in the industry.

In the case of an approved person, the FSA will be obliged to publish his or her name, the name of the relevant authorised person for whom the approved person performs controlled functions and the name of any contractor through whom the functions are performed (FSAMA 2000, s. 347(2)(g)).

Entries referring to people or firms who no longer have the relevant status do not have to be deleted, but where it appears to the FSA that an entry is out of date for this reason, it must make a note on the record explaining why it takes that view (s. 347(3) and (4)).

The FSA must make the record available for inspection in legible form (s. 347(5)(a)). It must also provide certified copy entries on request, for which it may charge a fee (s. 347(5)(b)). It may go further and publish the record or any part of it (s. 347(6)(a)). The section also expressly allows the FSA to exploit the information commercially (s. 347(6)(b)).

## RESTRICTIONS ON DISCLOSURE OF CONFIDENTIAL INFORMATION

The core obligation in FSAMA 2000, s. 348, is a duty on the FSA and certain other persons not to disclose confidential information without the consent of the person who provided it and, if different, the person to whom it relates. The prohibition is lifted when disclosure is made through what are often called 'gateways'. These are statutory permissions to disclose information which depend on the purpose of disclosure and sometimes the identity of the recipient as well.

This sort of prohibition on disclosure is a common feature of the predecessor legislation and it was inevitable that some sort of confidentiality regime would be carried forward. This is because so-called 'professional secrecy' regimes are required by the Single Market Directives including the Investment Services Directive (93/22/EEC) and the Credit Institutions Directive (2000/12/EC).

The government has indicated that the new regime, including the regulations yet to be published, will be 'very similar' to those currently in place.

## What is 'confidential information'?

The words 'confidential information' are explained in s. 348(2) to (4). Confidential information must be information which relates to 'the business or other affairs of any person'. In practice, this may be difficult to distinguish from other information about a person, but it is clear from the formulation that not all information about a person is covered. In *Melton Medes Ltd* v *Securities and Investments Board* [1995] Ch 137, Lightman J made clear that similar words in FSA 1986, s. 179, required a relationship to the business and affairs of the individual or company which was not indirect or incidental.

Information is only caught by FSAMA 2000, s. 348, if it was received by the primary recipient for the purposes of, or in the discharge of, any functions of the FSA (including the FSA as Listing Authority) or of the Secretary of State under or by virtue of the Act. Information received by the FSA in other circumstances, for example, acting solely in its private capacity, or sent to it by mistake and really intended for a different authority, would not be caught. However, information received in the course of discharging statutory functions will be caught even if the information was volunteered rather than obtained in response to a requirement imposed under the Act (s. 348(3)(a)).

The Act makes plain that information received for more than one purpose is still capable of being confidential: see s. 348(3)(b), which spares argument of the kind found in relation to the Banking Act 1987 in *Bank of Credit and Commerce (International) Ltd* v *Price Waterhouse* (No. 2) [1998] Ch 84, which was overruled in some respects by the Court of Appeal in *Barings plc (in liquidation)* v *Coopers & Lybrand and others (The Independent,* 10 May 2000).

By s. 348(4)(a) information is not confidential if it has already been made available to the public without breaching s. 348. Hence information will not be confidential if it has been disclosed by the FSA in open court in the course of proceedings brought by the FSA under the Act, assuming that the relevant gateways in predecessor legislation are carried forward in the regulations to be made under s. 349. A recent decision about when information is to be regarded as 'made public' for this kind of purpose is to be found in the Court of Appeal's decision in *Barings plc (in liquidation)* v *Coopers & Lybrand and others (The Independent,* 10 May 2000).

Information will not be confidential if it is not possible to ascertain from it information relating to any particular person because it takes the form of a summary or collection of information (s. 348(4)(b)). The FSA may rely on this provision to use confidential information to compile and publish aggregated statistics about different industry sectors or products, for example.

## What is a 'primary recipient'?

The duty not to disclose confidential information applies to 'primary recipients', a term defined in s. 348(5) by reference to the official function of the recipient rather than being the first person to whom the information was passed. Primary recipients include the FSA (including in its capacity as the Listing Authority), the Secretary of State, and any of their staff. It also includes a skilled person appointed to make a report under s. 166 as well as auditors or experts instructed by the FSA or the Secretary of State. Experts include, for this purpose, investigators appointed under s. 97 by the FSA acting as Listing Authority, any person appointed by the FSA or Secretary of State to investigate under Part XI of the Act, and any person to whom monitoring responsibilities are delegated under sch. 1, para. 6.

The duty not to disclose extends from the primary recipient to any person obtaining the information directly or indirectly from a primary recipient (s. 348(1)).

## Exceptions from the prohibition from disclosure: 'gateways'

FSAMA 2000 does not prevent disclosure of confidential information for the purpose of facilitating the carrying out of a public function, where there is a 'gateway', i.e., where disclosure is permitted by Treasury regulations made under s. 349. For this purpose, 'public function' is glossed very broadly to include functions conferred by or in accordance with any provision contained in any enactment or subordinate legislation and similar functions conferred on authorities in other jurisdictions (s. 349(5)).

## Disclosure of information by the Inland Revenue

The obligations of confidence which apply to the Inland Revenue have meant that its ability to be of any assistance to the FSA in specific cases in the past has been relatively limited. FSAMA 2000, s. 350, enlarges the potential for assistance by providing that the Inland Revenue may disclose information to the FSA or the Secretary of State, despite the fact that the Finance Act 1989, s. 182, would otherwise make disclosure a criminal offence.

However, there are limits to the discretion, which mean that disclosure may only be made by or under the authority of the Commissioners of Inland Revenue (s. 350(2)) and, by s. 350(1), the disclosure must be made for the purpose of assisting an investigation (or with a view to the appointment of investigators) under s. 168. That section deals with investigations triggered by serious specific concerns rather than general investigations.

Information disclosed by the Revenue may only be used by the FSA or the Secretary of State for a narrow range of quite serious purposes beyond the investigation (or decision to investigate) itself (s. 350(4)). Those purposes include criminal proceedings brought under FSAMA 2000 or under the Criminal Justice Act 1993 (insider dealing), or to take other action under FSAMA 2000 against a person as a result of the investigation. Onward disclosure of 'Revenue information' is generally restricted to the same sort of criminal or regulatory proceedings, unless the disclosure is made by or under the authority of the Commissioners of Inland Revenue (s. 350(5)).

## Competition information

FSAMA 2000 gives the Director General of Fair Trading and the Competition Commission powers of competition scrutiny. Section 351 protects from disclosure non-public information relating to the affairs of particular individuals or bodies obtained in the course of such competition scrutiny, whether undertaken under s. 95 (scrutiny of the FSA as Listing Authority), Part X, Chapter III (scrutiny of the FSA's rules and practices) or Part XVIII, Chapter II (scrutiny of RIEs and RCHs). Such information (which is called by s. 351(5) 'competition information') may not generally be disclosed without the relevant consents for a certain period. Where it relates to the affairs of an individual, the period continues throughout the individual's lifetime (s. 351(1)(a)). If it relates to any particular business of a body, the non-disclosure period continues while that business is still being carried on (s. 351(1)(b)).

There are 'gateways' in s. 351(2) for the disclosure of competition information in a number of circumstances. These include where information is connected to the investigation or prosecution of any UK criminal offence or to help a person mentioned in the table in sch. 19 to perform a function mentioned in that table. This latter category enables 'competition information' to be disclosed, for example, to a number of other competition regulators to assist with their statutory functions.

## Consequences of breaching the prohibition

The wrongful disclosure of regulatory information in breach of the prohibition in ss. 348 and 350 will be a criminal offence, by virtue of s. 352. It may result in a prison sentence of up to two years and an unlimited fine. There is a defence if the accused can show that he did not know and had no reason to suspect that the information was confidential or that it had been disclosed by the Inland Revenue to the FSA or the Secretary of State in accordance with s. 350. It is also a defence to show that the accused has taken all reasonable precautions and exercised all due diligence to avoid committing the offence.

The disclosure of confidential information in breach of the prohibition will be unlikely in itself to give rise to civil liability: see *Melton Medes Ltd* v *Securities and Investments Board* [1995] Ch 137, in which Lightman J came to that view in relation to the similar prohibition contained in FSA 1986 s. 179.

## Removal of other restrictions on disclosure

The Treasury have the power under s. 353 to make regulations permitting disclosure for the purposes of helping particular authorities to discharge prescribed functions in the new legislative framework. There is also power to permit the disclosure of information by prescribed persons to the FSA to assist it in carrying out its functions. This will enable the confidentiality obligations to which those prescribed persons would otherwise be subject to be overridden.

## DUTY OF THE FSA TO COOPERATE WITH OTHER AUTHORITIES

The FSA is under a duty to do whatever it considers appropriate to cooperate with authorities who have similar functions, whether in the UK or overseas (s. 354(1)(a)). It is also obliged to do whatever it considers appropriate to cooperate with other authorities in the UK and overseas who have functions in relation to the prevention or detection of financial crime, whether or not they have functions similar to the FSA's (s. 354(1)(b)). Financial crime here has the same meaning as in s. 6, extending to all offences of fraud and dishonesty, market-related offences and those relating to the handling of proceeds of crime.

The duty to cooperate with other authorities does not in any way override the confidentiality obligations imposed by other sections of this Part: s. 354(2) makes clear that cooperation may include the sharing of information which the FSA is not prevented from disclosing.

The purpose of s. 354 is to roll forward the legislative support for the FSA's cooperative arrangements with other authorities, such as the Financial Fraud Information Network, for which the FSA provides a secretariat function. Legislative support was previously to be found in FSA 1986, sch. 7, para. 5, which required the FSA as 'designated agency' to 'cooperate, by the sharing of information and otherwise, with the Secretary and State and any other authority, body or person having responsibility for the supervision or regulation of investment business or other financial services'.

# Chapter Twenty-Six
## Insolvency

*Loretta Minghella*

The Financial Services and Markets Act 2000 (FSAMA 2000), Part XXIV, confers a range of powers on the FSA to deal with situations where customers are at risk because a financial services business has become insolvent. In theory, consumers often have their own rights to take action against the business in these circumstances, but may lack the knowledge or financial resources to do so.

There are, for example, provisions entitling the FSA to petition for winding up even when it is not itself a creditor, together with a right to be notified of and heard in insolvency proceedings initiated by others. The provisions of the Act in this respect are more wide-ranging than under the predecessor legislation. They operate by slight modification of the general law of insolvency, as contained in the Insolvency Act 1986, the Insolvency (Northern Ireland) Order 1989 (SI 1989/2405) and the Bankruptcy (Scotland) Act 1985.

The provisions on insolvency will assist the FSA to pursue its statutory objectives of maintaining market confidence, protecting consumers and reducing financial crime by enabling it to take action to stop firms and unauthorised persons carrying on insolvent or unlawful business. It will also help the FSA to ensure the orderly realisation and distribution of their assets.

This chapter follows the Part XXIV framework, explaining the FSA's rights and powers in relation to voluntary arrangements, administration orders, receiverships, voluntary and compulsory winding up, and bankruptcy. It also notes the Act's provisions in relation to debt avoidance, as well as supplemental provision concerning insurers.

## VOLUNTARY ARRANGEMENTS

A company in financial difficulties may seek to enter into an arrangement with its creditors for the repayment of their debts, as an alternative to going into liquidation. Where an authorised person which is a company or insolvent partnership has entered into a voluntary arrangement under Part I of the Insolvency Act 1986, s. 356 of the FSAMA 2000 gives the FSA the right to apply to the court under s. 6 of the 1986 Act. This enables the FSA to challenge the arrangement on the ground that it is in some way unfairly prejudicial or there has been some material irregularity in its establishment. The FSA may also be heard at any hearing of an application by another person under s. 6.

Similar provision is made by FSAMA 2000, s. 357, to enable the FSA to challenge a voluntary arrangement made by an authorised person who is an individual. The FSA also has a right to be heard on an application to the court by an individual who is an authorised person for an interim order imposing a moratorium pending establishment of a voluntary arrangement. At present it is not possible for a company to obtain a moratorium while seeking to establish a voluntary arrangement, except by going into administration.

Sections 356 and 357 also apply to the equivalent procedures in Northern Ireland. The position in Scotland in relation to individuals is rather different. Section 358 provides for the FSA to have rights in the alternative to an individual voluntary arrangement under Scottish law, where the debtor is an authorised person. This alternative is a voluntary trust deed whereby a person who cannot pay his debts gives his assets to a trustee, who may then arrange a settlement with creditors as an alternative to sequestration (which is the Scottish equivalent of bankruptcy). When the trustee realises that the debtor is an authorised person, he must let the FSA know by sending a copy of the trust deed together with the copy documents sent to creditors. From that point on, the FSA will have the same rights to be given notice of creditor meetings as the creditors themselves. Section 358(5) gives the FSA the right to send a representative to those meetings but does not give the representative a right to vote at them. The FSA has the same rights as creditors who were not given notice of (or who have objected to) the trust deed to petition for the sequestration of a debtor who is an authorised person (s. 358(3)).

## ADMINISTRATION ORDERS

An administration order is an order which enables a company or partnership to remain in business under the supervision of an administrator, as an alternative to winding up. FSAMA 2000, s. 359, enables the FSA to petition the court under s. 9 of the Insolvency Act 1986 (or art. 22 of the Insolvency (Northern Ireland) Order 1989) for an administration order in relation to a company or insolvent partnership which is, or has been, an authorised person or an appointed representative. The FSA may also petition for such an order in relation to a company or insolvent partnership which is or has been carrying on regulated activities without authorisation. The court may only make an administration order if it is satisfied that the entity concerned is unable to pay its debts, or is likely to become so. By virtue of FSAMA 2000, s. 359(3) and (4), the entity will be treated as unable to pay its debts if it has failed to pay any sum due under an agreement where the making or performance of the agreement is (or is part of) its regulated activity.

It is not presently possible for an insurance company to go into administration (Insolvency Act 1986, s. 8(4)(a)). However, FSAMA 2000, s. 360, enables the Treasury to make an order modifying the law in this respect.

By virtue of s. 361, any administrator of a company or insolvent partnership is under a duty to report to the FSA without delay where it appears to him that the company or partnership is or has been carrying on unauthorised regulated activity in breach of the general prohibition in s. 19.

The FSA has a range of rights under s. 362 to participate in administration proceedings as though it were a creditor. For example, s. 362(2) confers rights to be heard at a hearing at which a person other than the FSA asks the court to place in administration a person who is or was an authorised person or appointed representative or who has been carrying on regulated activities without authorisation in breach of the general prohibition. The FSA is also entitled to receive notices and documents as though it were a creditor (s. 362)(3)).

## RECEIVERSHIPS

Where a receiver has been appointed in relation to a company which is or has been an authorised person or appointed representative or which has been carrying on regulated activities in breach of the general prohibition the FSA is given by FSAMA 2000, s. 363, the same statutory rights as unsecured creditors.

The FSA may be heard at hearings for directions, at the receiver's application, about how the receiver should perform his or her functions. The FSA is entitled to apply to the court if the receiver defaults on his or her obligations to file documents, make returns and give notices and to account and make payments to the liquidator when a company goes into liquidation.

Under FSAMA 2000, s. 364, a receiver appointed in relation to a company is obliged to inform the FSA without delay if it appears to him or her that the company is or has been carrying on regulated activities without authorisation in breach of the general prohibition.

## VOLUNTARY WINDING UP

The FSA is given certain rights in relation to authorised companies which are being wound up voluntarily (FSAMA 2000, s. 365).

The rights include rights to receive notices or other documents as though the FSA were a creditor, and the right to be heard at any court hearing about the winding up. The FSA is entitled to send a representative to attend and speak at creditors' meetings. The FSA also has the right to ask the court to decide any questions arising out of the winding up or to request the court to exercise all or any of the powers which the court might exercise if it were winding up the company itself.

A liquidator in a voluntary liquidation of any company must inform the FSA if it appears that the company is, or has been, carrying on a regulated activity in contravention of the general prohibition (ss. 19 and 370).

The fact that a company is in voluntary liquidation does not prevent the FSA from petitioning to have the company wound up by the court (s. 365(6)).

By s. 366, a long-term insurer may not be wound up voluntarily without the consent of the FSA. Unless the copy of the winding-up resolution sent to the registrar of companies is accompanied by an FSA certificate of consent, the resolution has no effect.

This changes the position under predecessor legislation, whereby such winding up has not been permitted at all (Insurance Companies Act 1982, s. 55(2)), because of the potentially detrimental effect on long-term insurance policyholders. The requirement under the new Act to obtain the FSA's consent will enable the FSA to secure appropriate arrangements in respect of long-term policyholders before consent is given.

FSAMA 2000, s. 366, makes it a criminal offence for a director of such an insurer not to notify the FSA promptly on becoming aware of a notice of intention to propose a voluntary winding up. The procedure in the Companies Act 1985, s. 381A, for written resolutions of a private company cannot be used for a resolution for voluntary winding up of a long-term insurer (FSAMA 2000, s. 366(4)). This means that a general meeting must be held to approve such a resolution, which will have to be a special resolution unless the company is unable to pay its debts, and FSAMA 2000, s. 366(4), prevents the members waiving the need for 21 days' notice of a special resolution.

## WINDING UP BY THE COURT

Section 367 of FSAMA 2000 contains an important extension to the FSA's powers under FSA 1986. Under s. 72 of that Act, the FSA has been able to petition for the winding up of authorised firms and appointed representatives. Under s. 367 of the 2000 Act, the FSA may still petition for the winding up of any company or partnership which is or has been an authorised person or appointed representative. In addition, the FSA may petition for the winding up of any unauthorised company or partnership which is or has been carrying on a regulated activity in contravention of the general prohibition. The FSA's powers now also extend to Northern Ireland as well as to the rest of the United Kingdom.

The grounds on which the court may grant the petition are either that the body is unable to pay its debts (as defined) or the court is of the opinion that it is just and equitable that it should be wound up. A body is deemed unable to pay its debts if it has failed to pay a sum due under an agreement where the making or performance of that agreement is or is part of a regulated activity.

# WINDING UP PETITIONS FOR EEA AND TREATY FIRMS

Where a firm is authorised to do regulated business in the UK by virtue of an authorisation granted in another EEA State, decisions to remove its authorisation are for the home State regulator. FSAMA 2000, s. 368, therefore provides that the FSA may not present a petition to wind up such a firm except at the request of the home State regulator.

## Duties to inform the FSA in insurance cases

A person applying for the appointment of a provisional liquidator or petitioning for the winding up of an authorised person who is permitted to effect or carry out insurance contracts must serve a copy of the application or petition on the FSA (FSAMA 2000, s. 369).

## Liquidator's duty to report

A liquidator of a company must notify the FSA if it appears that the company is or has been carrying on a regulated activity in breach of the general prohibition (FSAMA 2000, ss. 19 and 370).

## The FSA's participation in a compulsory winding up

Where a person other than the FSA asks the court to wind up a firm which is or has been authorised or an appointed representative or is or has been breaching the general prohibition, the FSA is granted by FSAMA 2000, s. 371, certain rights of the kind granted in relation to other insolvency procedures. For example, the FSA has the right to be heard at the hearing of the petition and any subsequent hearing. Along with the creditors, the FSA has the right to receive information or proposals sent by the liquidator, to attend and speak at creditors' meetings and to ask the court to intervene or order a scheme to settle debts to be put to a creditors' vote.

# BANKRUPTCY

The power for the FSA to petition for the bankruptcy of an individual (in Scotland, the sequestration of his estate) is an important new power given by FSAMA 2000, s. 372, which was not available to it under FSA 1986 (or, indeed, the Banking Act 1987). The individual may be a formerly or currently authorised person, or a person who is or was carrying on business in breach of the general prohibition (s. 372(7)). The only grounds on which such a petition may be presented by the FSA are that the individual appears to be unable to pay a regulated activity debt or appears to have no reasonable prospect of being able to pay such a debt (s. 372(2)).

The first of these grounds may be established by showing that the individual has not paid a sum due under an agreement the making or performance of which was, or was part of, a regulated activity (s. 372(3) and (8)). The second may be established if the FSA has served a demand requiring the individual to produce satisfactory evidence of a reasonable prospect that he will be able to pay a relevant debt as it falls due (s. 372(4)). The FSA must show that at least three weeks have gone by without the demand being complied with or set aside in accordance with insolvency rules.

Section 373 requires an insolvency practitioner to report to the FSA evidence of unauthorised business which it appears that a bankrupt has at any time carried on. Section 374 makes provision for the FSA to participate in and receive information about bankruptcy proceedings brought by another against an individual who is or has been carrying on financial services business, as though the FSA were a creditor.

## PROVISIONS AGAINST DEBT AVOIDANCE

Under FSAMA 2000, s. 375, the FSA may apply to the court for an order where a transaction has been entered into at an undervalue, even though the FSA is not itself a victim of the transaction. The application is to be treated as made on behalf of every person who was a victim of the transaction.

Section 423 of the Insolvency Act 1986 provides that a transaction is to be treated as a transaction at an undervalue if, for example, it provides for property to be given away or sold at much less than its true value. Before interfering with such a transaction, the court must be satisfied that its purpose has been to put assets beyond the reach of creditors or otherwise to prejudice their interests.

Under FSAMA 2000, s. 375, the FSA will have to show that at the time the transaction was entered into, the debtor was carrying on a regulated activity. The FSA will also have to show that a victim of the transaction is (or was) party to an agreement with the debtor, the making or performance of which was (or was part of) a regulated activity carried on by the debtor.

Under the Insolvency Act 1986, s. 423, the court may make such order as it thinks fit to restore the position to what it would have been if the transaction had not been entered into and to protect the interests of persons who are victims of the transaction.

There are equivalent provisions in Northern Ireland, but not in Scotland.

## SUPPLEMENTAL PROVISIONS IN INSURANCE CASES

When insurance companies are in financial difficulties, special considerations arise for their regulators. Consumers do not necessarily want their money back: what they generally need is for the insurance cover to continue. The need can be particularly acute in relation to long-term insurance, where the policyholder may not now be able to arrange alternative cover. FSAMA 2000 therefore makes special provision for such companies. In particular, it provides that the liquidator must carry out any existing long-term insurance contracts with a view to a transfer of the insurer's business as a going concern, unless the court otherwise orders. This is a close parallel to provisions made for the Financial Services Compensation Scheme by ss. 216 and 217.

# Chapter Twenty-Seven
# Injunctions and Restitution

*Loretta Minghella*

The provisions of Part XXV of the Financial Services and Markets Act 2000 (FSAMA 2000) are similar to those contained in ss. 6 and 61 of the Financial Services Act 1986 (FSA 1986), pursuant to which the FSA has brought a significant number of cases for injunction and restitution since those powers were commenced in 1988. The new Act goes further in two important respects: it introduces injunction and restitution powers in relation to market abuse, and it introduces provision for the FSA to seek restitution by administrative procedure rather than through the High Court or Court of Session. The latter provision is novel for the FSA, although it was a common feature of SRO rule books.

## CONTRAVENTION OF RELEVANT REQUIREMENTS

### Definition of 'relevant requirement'

FSAMA 2000, s. 380(6), defines the concept of a relevant requirement as a requirement imposed by or under FSAMA 2000 or a requirement imposed by or under other Acts whose contravention amounts to an offence which may be prosecuted by the FSA or the Secretary of State by virtue of FSAMA 2000. Breach of a relevant requirement therefore includes a breach of an FSA principle or other rule, a breach of the provisions of s. 397 (misleading statements and practices) and a breach of the prescribed money laundering regulations or of the insider dealing provisions of the Criminal Justice Act 1993. It would also cover the classic 'perimeter' breaches: carrying on regulated activities in breach of the general prohibition, or unlawful financial promotion. (A similar result is achieved for Scotland even though the FSA and the Secretary of State do not prosecute there.)

## Injunction or interdict

Section 380 contains powers for the High Court to grant the FSA an injunction (in Scotland, an interdict by the Court of Session) where it is satisfied that there is a reasonable likelihood that any person will contravene a relevant requirement. It may also grant an injunction where it is satisfied that any person has already contravened a relevant requirement and there is a reasonable likelihood that the contravention will continue or be repeated.

Where it appears that there are steps which could be taken to remedy a contravention, the court is given powers to make an order requiring the contravener and any other person who appears to have been knowingly concerned in the contravention to take such steps as the court may direct to remedy it.

In considering what amounts to 'knowing concern' for this purpose, it is worth considering the case law on similar words in the FSA 1986. It would clearly cover a person who knew of the breach and received the unlawful proceeds of it (*Securities and Investments Board* v *Pantell SA* [1990] Ch 426). It would also cover a case where a defendant knew the facts upon which the contravention depended even if he did not realise that there was any breach (*Securities and Investments Board* v *Scandex Capital Management A/S* [1998] 1 WLR 712.

What may amount to 'remedying the contravention' is not entirely clear. Similar words in FSA 1986 were not always given a wide meaning: see, for example, *Securities and Investments Board* v *Pantell SA (No. 2)* [1993] Ch 256. Where the contravention was a misleading statement which had induced a person to enter into an investment transaction, it appears that the remedy which may be available under the 1986 Act may generally only be an order to issue a correcting statement. However, the words appear to be open to a wider meaning in the new Act since, by virtue of s. 380(5), references to remedying a contravention include references to mitigating its effect.

The other type of order which may be made under s. 380 is an order restraining someone who the court is satisfied may be a contravener, or a person knowingly concerned in a contravention, from disposing or otherwise dealing with any of his assets. Such an order would be like a freezing order (which FSA has often obtained when pursuing restitution action under ss. 6 and 61 of the 1986 Act) save that there is no requirement to show that proceedings have been commenced or are imminent.

The Secretary of State is also able to bring proceedings under FSAMA 2000, s. 380, where breach of the relevant requirement is an offence for which the Secretary of State has power to prosecute under FSAMA 2000.

## Restitution orders

The FSA or the Secretary of State may apply to the High Court (in Scotland, the Court of Session) under FSAMA 2000, s. 382, for a restitution order. This may be granted if the court is satisfied that a person has breached a relevant requirement or been knowingly concerned in the contravention and either that he has accrued profits as a result, or one or more persons have suffered loss or been otherwise adversely affected.

The court has a broad discretion as to the amount which may be awarded. This is such sum as appears to it to be just, having regard to the profits which have accrued to the wrongdoer and/or the losses or adverse effects suffered by the victims.

The FSA is bound to pay any amount received pursuant to such an order as the court may direct. The payments will be made to qualifying persons within the meaning of s. 382(8), being persons to whom the defendant's profits are attributable or those who have suffered losses or adverse effects. There is an interesting change here from the position under FSA 1986, which required such a person to have entered into a transaction with the contravener. Under the new Act, the victim's transaction may be with a third party.

FSAMA 2000, s. 382(4), gives the court power to order the defendant to supply it with accounts or other information to enable it: (a) to establish what are the relevant profits; (b) to establish what losses and adverse effects have been suffered, by whom and to what extent; and (c) to determine how any amounts are to be paid out by FSA. The court may require any such information or accounts to be verified in such manner as it may direct (s. 382(5)).

Victims of breaches of relevant requirements may have their own rights to bring proceedings (for example, rights in contract or tort) and nothing in s. 382 affects those rights (s. 382(7)). Indeed, the FSA has indicated that it is likely to regard the existence of such rights as one of the factors it takes into consideration in deciding whether it should itself seek restitution under the Act.

## MARKET ABUSE

### Injunctions

FSAMA 2000, s. 381, gives the court power to grant an injunction in market abuse cases. The power is framed in very similar terms to the power in s. 380 to grant an injunction for breach of a relevant requirement. Market abuse here has the meaning given to it in s. 118. The key difference is that the ability to apply for the injunction is reserved to the FSA rather than being shared with the Secretary of State, even though under s. 168 the Secretary of State has concurrent power to investigate apparent market abuse.

This provision of the Act caused considerable difficulty during the latter stages of the Bill. This was caused by concerns that the FSA's power to seek an injunction might be used during a takeover bid subject to the jurisdiction of the Panel on Takeovers and Mergers in a way which would undermine the Panel's ability to regulate takeovers effectively. It is now intended that these concerns be resolved by sensible working arrangements between the FSA and the Panel and close consultation in relevant cases. See further chapter 10.

## Restitution orders

The court's power in s. 383 to order restitution in cases of market abuse is very similar to its power in s. 382 to order restitution for breach of relevant requirements. As in s. 382 the ability to apply is reserved to the FSA, rather than being shared with the Secretary of State. However, there are a couple of important distinctions between restitution orders in market abuse cases and restitution orders in respect of breach of relevant requirements.

First, in market abuse restitution cases, third parties can be caught but not on the basis of 'knowing concern'. The test is different. A third party may only be the subject of a restitution order if the court is satisfied that the third party has, by act or omission, required or encouraged another person to commit what would be market abuse if the third party himself or herself had done it (s. 383(1)(b)).

Secondly, the court may not make a restitution order if it is satisfied that the defendant believed on reasonable grounds that his or her behaviour did not amount to market abuse or to requiring or encouraging market abuse as described in s. 383(1). Nor may the court make an order if is satisfied that the defendant took all reasonable precautions and exercised all due diligence to avoid behaving in a way which could give rise to such an order. There is an echo here of s. 123(2) in Part VIII.

The question what is appropriate restitution in a case of market abuse is a very complex one. FSA has indicated that it is unlikely to use this power in order to seek restitution for every market participant who happened to be active in the market at the time of the abuse (so-called 'contemporaneous traders'). Such actions *are* brought in some other jurisdictions. However, they are capable of involving a very substantial number of market participants each of whom might be alleged to be owed a very small sum, whereas the cost of the litigation may well be significant.

## RESTITUTION REQUIRED BY THE FSA

FSAMA 2000, s. 384, gives the FSA the power to order restitution on much the same basis as the court under s. 382 or s. 383 for breaches of relevant requirements and market abuse. The FSA's power is, however, more limited in scope than the court's power, in that it may only be used, so far as concerns relevant requirements, against authorised persons who have themselves breached the requirements or been knowingly concerned in the breaches of others. The power of restitution in respect of market abuse appears to be coextensive with that given to the courts.

Any money which is required to be paid is not paid via the FSA, but directly to the persons who the FSA believes are entitled to restitution.

The procedure which the FSA must use in these cases is the warning notice procedure (described more fully in chapter 28). Important features of the statutory procedure at the warning notice stage include the right to make representations and to have access to the evidence on which the FSA relies and other material which undermines its case. Where the FSA decides nevertheless to proceed, it must issue a decision notice. In contested cases, there is a right to refer the decision to the Financial Services and Markets Tribunal. Where this occurs, the decision cannot take effect, nor may it be publicised, while the matter is under review.

# Chapter Twenty-Eight
# Notices

*Loretta Minghella*

The administrative procedure to be used by the FSA in reaching key supervisory and enforcement decisions in respect of firms and individuals is prescribed in general terms largely by Part XXVI of the Financial Services and Markets Act 2000 (FSAMA 2000).

There is a simple procedure commencing with a supervisory notice for some kinds of decisions, and a more sophisticated procedure commencing with a warning notice and moving on to a decision notice and final notice for others, including disciplinary and market abuse decisions. The latter procedure involves giving access to evidence and certain rights to affected third parties (with some exceptions relating to applications to the FSA). Both procedures envisage referrals to the Financial Services and Markets Tribunal in contested cases.

The Act requires the FSA to set out the detail of its internal decision-making procedure in a statement on which it must consult and which it is obliged to follow. What would constitute the appropriate procedure was the subject of much debate, especially in the Joint Committee on Financial Services and Markets. There was much pressure during the passage of the Bill to put more detail about this in the statute than has eventually been included. However, the government did make a number of amendments in this area, particularly in relation to access to evidence.

## WARNING NOTICES

Warning notices are the first notices to be given by the FSA in the exercise of a number of its formal 'enforcement' powers. For example, the warning notice procedure applies to cases where the FSA decides to discipline authorised firms and approved persons or to impose a penalty for market abuse.

FSAMA 2000, s. 387, provides that a warning notice must state the action which the FSA intends to take and specify a reasonable period of at least 28 days within which the recipient may make representations to the FSA. The warning notice must be in writing, giving reasons for the proposed action. Where the access to evidence provisions in s. 394 apply, the notice must say so, explain what that means in terms of access to material on which the FSA has relied in making its decision, and state whether there is additional, secondary material to which the recipient must be allowed access.

Where a warning notice has been given, the FSA may extend the period specified in the notice for a response. This is likely to occur in complex cases where discussions with a view to a possible settlement are in progress. Within a reasonable time, the FSA must decide whether to go on to issue a decision notice.

## The FSA's enforcement decision-making process

FSAMA 2000, s. 396, obliges the FSA to publish a draft statement about its proposed procedures so as to enable the public to make representations about it. The FSA must have due regard to the representations made during consultation when deciding whether or not the draft statement should be amended. In publishing the settled procedure, it must state what representations were received and how it has responded to them. The FSA first consulted in 1998–9 about the components of its own procedure between warning and decision notice: *Enforcing the New Regime* (Consultation Paper 17) (1998) and *Response to Consultation Paper 17* (1999). A similar consultation procedure is intended to apply whenever the FSA seeks to amend the process: see s. 396(7).

The FSA issued its draft Enforcement Manual for consultation in August 2000: see FSA Consultation Paper 65a. This contains the draft of a detailed statement of procedure relating to warning notices. It is likely that the final statement will propose: the use of a committee including practitioners appointed by the FSA Board and separate from the staff to make disciplinary and market abuse decisions; the opportunity for recipients of warning notices to make oral and written representations to that committee; and the possibility of reaching agreement with the FSA as to the outcome, whether bilaterally or (on a one-year pilot basis) with the help of a third-party mediator.

## DECISION NOTICES

Where the FSA continues to believe that action of the kind envisaged in the warning notice is necessary, despite representations, it must proceed to issue a decision notice (FSAMA 2000, s. 387(4)). Like warning notices, decision notices must be in writing, giving reasons for the FSA's action (s. 388(1)(a) and (b)). A decision notice must state whether the access to evidence provisions in section 394 apply and if so what that means and whether any secondary material exists to which the recipient must be given access (s. 388(1)(c) and (d)). A decision notice must also give an indication of any rights to refer the decision to the Financial Services and Markets Tribunal, and the procedure for doing so (s. 388(1)(e)).

It is quite possible that a decision notice will indicate that the FSA intends to take action which is different from that stated in the warning notice which preceded it. For example, if the FSA intended to impose a penalty, it might decide, having considered representations, that the matter is less serious than it originally thought, and that a public censure would be sufficient. The Act expressly provides for the FSA to change the proposed outcome to reflect this. However, s. 388(2) precludes the FSA from proceeding directly to a decision notice under one Part of the Act where the warning notice was issued under another Part. Thus, for example, it would not be possible to issue a decision notice about a penalty for market abuse under Part VIII when the warning notice related to a proposed penalty for breach of rules applying to authorised persons and was given under Part XIV. Different procedures and different rights apply to action taken under different Parts of the Act. Section 388(2) ensures that those concerned have all the rights to which they are intended to be entitled under the Act and that the FSA cannot dilute those rights by taking the first steps in the process under a different Part.

The first or only decision notice may be given without the consent of the person to whom the warning notice was given. A recipient of a decision notice who does not agree with the action proposed in it may refer the matter to the Tribunal. If, after the issue of a decision notice, the FSA changes its mind about the action to be taken, and the recipient of the notice agrees, the FSA may issue a further decision notice stating the action the FSA now intends to take (s. 388(3) and (4)). These provisions are intended to cover cases where settlement discussions come to fruition only after the first decision notice has been issued. Even in these cases of apparent settlement, any right to refer the matter to the Tribunal is retained, thereby providing a kind of cooling-off period for the subject of the notice (s. 388(5)).

## NOTICES OF DISCONTINUANCE

Of course there will be cases where the FSA, having given a warning notice or decision notice, decides not to take the action stated. This may arise, for example, where it becomes apparent in the light of representations that the matter is much less serious than it first appeared and does not warrant disciplinary action after all. In these cases, the FSA must give a notice of discontinuance to the recipient of the original notice, identifying the proceedings which are being discontinued (s. 389). The only exception is where the decision to discontinue amounts to a decision to grant an application (e.g., for authorisation) where, of course, the person concerned will be alerted to the outcome in any event (s. 389(2)).

## FINAL NOTICES

The decision-making process may take some time, especially in complex cases. In order that the recipient of the notices is entirely clear that the matter is coming to a close, FSAMA 2000, s. 390, makes provision for the giving of final notices.

These will have to be given when the recipient of a decision notice does not refer the matter to the Tribunal. They are also required to be given when the Tribunal or Court of Appeal (or Court of Session) has made a decision following the referral of an FSA decision notice. They must be issued by the FSA when it moves to implement the Tribunal or Court decision.

Section 390 prescribes the content of the final notice, which varies according to whether it relates to a penalty, public censure, or other action. The effect of the section is to require the FSA to make plain what is now going to happen and when. For example, a final notice about a public censure must set out the terms of the statement the FSA is going to make, and give details of the manner in which, and the date on which, the statement will be published (s. 390(3)). To the extent that the notice states that the recipient must make a payment, it must require that to happen in not less than 14 days (s. 390(8)).

If a financial penalty remains unpaid after the due date, the FSA may recover it as a debt due to it, i.e., without proving the underlying facts which gave rise to the decision to impose the penalty (s. 390(9)).

Where the payment to be made is by way of restitution, and the person concerned fails to make the payment in time, the FSA may apply to the court for an injunction ordering the payment to be made (or, in Scotland, an order under the Court of Session Act 1988, s. 45) (FSAMA 2000, s. 390(10)).

## PUBLICATION

FSAMA 2000, s. 391, provides a careful balance between the competing interests relating to sensitive regulatory information about enforcement action. On the one hand, a firm or individual who is the subject of a warning notice and decision notice will generally wish to keep that matter private. On the other, the public interest in securing the transparency and accountability of the regulatory process is also significant. Generally speaking, s. 391 addresses this conflict by prohibiting the publication of proceedings until they are completed, but obliging the FSA to publish appropriate information at that point.

Section 391(1) prevents publication of warning notices and decision notices or any details about them.

Where the FSA issues a notice of discontinuance, it may publish such information as it considers appropriate about the discontinued proceedings, but it must alert the recipient of the notice to this possibility in the notice itself and obtain the recipient's consent (s. 391(2)).

When a supervisory notice takes effect (i.e., when it is no longer open to any further review under the Act), the FSA is obliged to publish such information about it as it considers appropriate (s. 391(5)). The FSA is similarly obliged to publish such information as it considers appropriate about final notices (s. 391(4)).

Two general provisions apply to any publication under s. 391. First, publication may be in any manner which the FSA considers appropriate (s. 391(7)). Secondly, the Authority is precluded from publishing information under the section if it would, in the FSA's opinion, be unfair to the person with respect to whom the action was taken or prejudicial to the interests of consumers (s. 391(6)).

## THIRD-PARTY RIGHTS

The FSA's disciplinary or supervisory action may, on occasion, be aimed at one person but may be triggered at least in part by the actions of another. For example, the FSA may take action against a firm for failing properly to supervise a particular member of staff. In these circumstances, the third party may find himself identified in an FSA notice in a way which is prejudicial to him. On ordinary public law principles, he might expect the FSA to notify him and give him an opportunity to respond: see, for example, *R* v *LAUTRO, ex parte Ross* [1993] QB 17.

Sections 393 and 394 of FSAMA 2000 give certain third parties in this position a number of rights. The rights only arise in relation to warning notices and decision notices given under the provisions of the Act listed in s. 392.

If any of the reasons in a warning notice relates to a matter which identifies a third party and the FSA believes the matter is prejudicial to him, he is entitled to be given a copy of the notice by the FSA (unless he is being given his own separate warning notice) (s. 393(1) and (2)). A similar provision applies to decision notices (s. 393(4) and (6)). Copy notices need not be given where the FSA believes this would be impracticable (s. 393(7)).

A third party who is given a copy warning notice must be given a period of at least 28 days during which he may make representations to the FSA (s. 393(3)).

Where a third party receives a copy decision notice with which he takes issue, he may refer it to the Tribunal, in so far as it is based on a reason which identifies him and is believed by the FSA to be prejudicial to him (s. 393(9)(a)). He may also refer to the Tribunal any opinion expressed by the FSA about him (s. 393(9)(b)). The copy notice must be accompanied by an indication of these rights and how to exercise them (s. 393(10)). A third party given a copy of a notice can refer it to the Tribunal only if the person who was given the original notice has a right to refer the matter to the Tribunal (s. 393(8)).

If the third party does not receive a copy decision notice but alleges that he should have done, there is provision in s. 393(11) for him to refer the alleged failure to the Tribunal but only in conjunction with an appeal against the decision or opinion contained in the notice. This right can be exercised only if the person who was given the original notice has a right to refer the matter to the Tribunal (s. 393(8)).

The access to evidence provisions in s. 394 apply to the third party receiving the copy notice as they apply to the person to whom the original notice was given but are limited to material relating to the matter which identifies the third party (s. 393(12)). The copy notice must be accompanied by a description of how section 394 applies to the third party (s. 393(13)).

There is provision in s. 393 for third parties to be kept up to date with the progress of the matter. For example, s. 393(5) provides that a third party who receives a copy warning notice is entitled to a copy of any subsequent decision notice, even if that decision notice does not relate to a matter which identifies him. Section 393(14) provides that a third party who receives a copy warning notice or decision notice must be sent a copy of any notice of discontinuance applying to the proceedings to which the earlier notice related.

## ACCESS TO FSA MATERIAL

FSAMA 2000, s. 394, makes arrangements for providing those in receipt of notices and copy notices with access to relevant material in the FSA's possession. Following amendments in the House of Lords, these provisions are broadly similar to those found in the Criminal Procedure and Investigations Act 1996, even though the procedures to which they relate are civil procedures (including restitution procedures akin to High Court claims). The provisions on access to FSA material apply to persons receiving warning notices and decision notices of the kind specified in s. 392, and those receiving copies of such notices pursuant to s. 393.

A person receiving such a notice must be given access to the material on which the FSA relied in taking the decision to give the notice. It must also give the person access to secondary material which the Authority believes might undermine that decision. Secondary material is defined in s. 394(6) as material which was not relied on but which was either considered by the FSA in reaching the decision or which was obtained by it in connection with the matter to which the notice relates.

There are a number of exceptions to the obligation to give access to material. The first relates to what is called 'excluded material': see s. 394(7). This is material which has been intercepted under warrant or which indicates that such a warrant has been issued or executed, or which is a protected item. Section 413 contains a definition of what amounts to a protected item. In broad terms, this is material covered by legal professional privilege, whether that be the FSA's privilege or another's. Where the material is withheld because it is a protected item, written notice must be given that such an item exists and is being withheld.

The second exception is where material relates to another case and was taken into account by the FSA only for comparative purposes.

The FSA is not obliged to disclose material at this stage if it believes access would not be in the public interest. Nor is it required to give access if it believes that access would not be fair, weighing in the balance the likely significance of the material to the case in question and the potential prejudice to the commercial interests of a third party if the material were to be disclosed. In these cases, the FSA must give written notice of its refusal and the reasons for it.

## FSA PROCEDURES

The FSA is obliged by FSAMA 2000, s. 395, to publish a statement about its procedures for the giving of supervisory, warning and decision notices, for which it may charge a reasonable fee. A copy must be given to the Treasury without delay. (Section 396 sets out the standard procedure for consultation on draft statements of procedure and any revision of them.)

The procedure must be designed to secure that those who decide to give notices have not been directly involved in establishing the evidence on which the decision is based. An exception is made in relation to supervisory notices in cases where the FSA considers this to be necessary to protect the interests of consumers, provided the person taking the decision is of a level of seniority laid down by the procedure.

The FSA is obliged to follow the procedure. If it fails to do so, it will not affect the validity of the notice but the failure may be taken into account by the Financial Services and Markets Tribunal in considering any matter referred to it.

## SUPERVISORY NOTICES

Part XXVI of FSAMA 2000 deals in passing with supervisory notices, and this chapter has referred to them in places as well. The term 'supervisory notice' is defined in s. 395(13). Broadly speaking supervisory notices are notices concerned with regulatory issues which may need to be referred to the Financial Services and Markets Tribunal, but where the more formal structure of warning notice and decision notice is not required. The cases concerned are:

(a)  exercise by the FSA of its own-initiative power to vary, or propose a variation of, a Part IV permission;

(b)  discontinuance or suspension (actual or proposed) of the listing of securities by the FSA as listing authority;

(c)  decisions about intervention in relation to inwardly passporting firms, though not in cases where the Directives provide for a different procedure;

(d)  decisions about intervention in relation to collective investment schemes;

(e)  decisions about former underwriting members at Lloyd's.

Of these, (a) is likely to be the one most often encountered in practice. Each of the relevant provisions sets out the procedure to be followed: see for example, s. 53.

# Chapter Twenty-Nine
# Criminal Offences and their Prosecution

## *Loretta Minghella*

The focus of the Financial Services and Markets Act 2000 (FSAMA 2000) is to establish a system of regulation applying (over and above the general law) to a restricted class of persons seeking to enjoy the special privileges of authorisation or approval. However, it also provides for a number of criminal offences of wider application. Part XXVII includes the more serious of these offences and sets out who may prosecute them (including the offence of market manipulation, described in more detail below). It provides that the FSA itself may (except in Scotland) prosecute all the offences contained in the Act. The combined position of regulator and prosecutor is rare, if not unique, amongst financial services regulators internationally.

### PROSECUTION OF OFFENCES

### What may the FSA prosecute?

FSAMA 2000, s. 401, gives the FSA power to prosecute offences contained in the Act or in subordinate legislation made under the Act. The offences created by the Act itself relate to:

(a)  carrying on or purporting to carry on a regulated activity without authorisation or exemption (s. 23);

(b)  making false claims to be authorised or exempt (s. 24);

(c)  communicating an invitation or inducement to engage in investment activity in breach of the restrictions on financial promotion (s. 25);

(d)  misleading the FSA and other contraventions in relation to the exercise of Treaty rights (sch. 4, para. 6);

(e)  performing or agreeing to perform functions in breach of a prohibition order (s. 56(4)). These are orders made by the FSA in relation to individuals appearing to it not to be fit and proper to perform functions in relation to an authorised person's regulated business;

(f)   offering new securities to the public before publishing any prospectus required by listing rules made under the Act (s. 85);

(g)   issuing an advertisement or other information specified in the listing rules, without prior approval or authorisation from the competent authority (s. 98);

(h)   giving false information to investigators appointed by the FSA or the Secretary of State and other related offences (s. 177);

(i)   failing to notify the FSA of a planned assumption of control or greater control of an authorised person, or, being a controller, failing to notify a planned reduction or surrendering of control (s. 191);

(j)   carrying on or purporting to carry on business in contravention of a consumer credit restriction or prohibition (ss. 203 and 204);

(k)   making false claims to be a person to whom the general prohibition does not apply as a result of Part XX, i.e., a member of a professional body who qualifies for the exemption outlined in s. 327 (s. 333);

(l)   providing false or misleading information to an auditor or actuary (under s. 346);

(m)   disclosing confidential information in contravention of the statutory restrictions (s. 352);

(n)   failing, as a director of an insurance company carrying on long-term insurance business, to notify the FSA of a general meeting to propose the company's voluntary winding up (s. 366);

(o)   misleading by statements and practices, contrary to s. 397;

(p)   misleading the FSA, contrary to s. 398;

(q)   refusing or failing to attend or give evidence at a Tribunal hearing or tampering with, suppressing, concealing or destroying documents which may be relevant to it (sch. 13, para. 11).

Section 402 gives the FSA power to prosecute two additional types of offence: insider dealing contrary to Part V of the Criminal Justice Act 1993, and breaches of prescribed money laundering regulations.

FSAMA 2000 does not preclude the FSA from prosecuting offences which any other private person may prosecute, such as theft and obtaining property by deception. In practice, it is not likely that the FSA will routinely prosecute such offences. However, many cases which the FSA investigates in pursuit of its statutory objectives may throw up these offences: theft often goes hand in hand with misleading statements and practices, for example. It may well be appropriate for the FSA to pursue such offences where, for example, they are incidental to offences which the Act expressly states are for the FSA to prosecute.

In all cases, the FSA power is to prosecute offences in England, Wales and Northern Ireland. In Scotland, prosecution remains the responsibility of the Lord Advocate and the procurator fiscal.

## FSA powers to prosecute: Treasury control

In exercising its power to institute proceedings for an offence, the FSA must comply with any conditions or restrictions imposed in writing by the Treasury (ss. 401(5) and 402(2)). It is not expected that the FSA will be subject to any such controls at commencement of the Act. This power might be used, for example, to require notification of an intended prosecution to the government or to require the FSA to follow the Code for Crown Prosecutors. In practice the FSA has policies and well-established working relationships with the relevant government authorities which mean that this reserve power is likely to go unused.

## Who else may prosecute?

Others are also given express statutory power to prosecute: the Secretary of State and the Director of Public Prosecutions may prosecute in England and Wales, as may the DPP for Northern Ireland in Northern Ireland (s. 401(2) and (3)). Both DPPs may give consent to any other person to prosecute; but without such consent, no private prosecution may be brought. The Director General of Fair Trading may prosecute the offence of contravening a consumer credit prohibition except in Scotland (see s. 401(4)). By virtue of s. 1 of the Criminal Justice Act 1987, the Serious Fraud Office may also prosecute any offence arising out of serious and complex fraud.

## FSA decisions to prosecute

The FSA has indicated that, although it is not a Crown prosecutor, it will follow the Code for Crown Prosecutors in deciding whether or not to prosecute. This means that decisions whether to prosecute will rest on the answer to two questions: first, is the evidence sufficient to provide a realistic prospect of conviction against the defendant on each charge, and second, having regard to all the circumstances, is criminal prosecution in the public interest?

## FSA decisions not to prosecute: cautioning policy

The FSA has also indicated that it may, in some cases, decide to issue a formal caution rather than prosecute. In these cases, it will follow the Home Office guidance on cautioning, which requires a number of conditions to be met. In particular, there must be evidence sufficient to give a realistic prospect of conviction. In addition, the offender must admit the offence, understand the significance of the caution and give his or her informed consent to its issue.

## Liaison with other prosecuting authorities

Where a case indicates possible criminality, it may be that there are a number of agencies apart from the FSA with a potential interest in the case. The FSA intends to operate under published guidelines agreed with those other agencies to ensure efficiency, effectiveness and best practice in liaison and cooperation: see Chapter 16 of FSA Consultation Paper 65a.

## SPECIFIC OFFENCES

Some of the most important offences created by FSAMA 2000 are contained in Part XXVII.

The offence in s. 397 is largely a carrying forward of s. 47 of the Financial Services Act 1986 (FSA 1986), enlarged to cover insurance contracts and the making of deposits.

The first of the two offences is created by FSAMA 2000, 397(1) and (2), which apply to a person who makes a materially false or misleading or deceptive statement, knowingly or recklessly, or who dishonestly conceals material facts. This is an offence if, in summary, the act or omission is for the purpose of inducing any other person to enter into or refrain from entering into a relevant agreement or to exercise rights conferred by such an agreement. 'Relevant agreement' is defined in s. 397(9) to mean, in effect, agreement of types to be defined in an order made by the Treasury. It is thought that the offence will be defined so as to include recklessly making a misleading statement intended to induce a person into buying a share, for example.

It is notable that this offence may be committed by any person, whether or not authorised. It is an offence commonly associated with the carrying on of unauthorised business, where that business is being carried on fraudulently. Dishonesty is not, however, an essential ingredient of the offence (except where the charge is one of concealing material facts).

Section 397(3) defines the important offence generally known as market manipulation. This makes it a criminal act to engage in any course of conduct which creates a false or misleading impression as to the market or price or value of relevant investments if that is done for the purpose of creating that impression and inducing another person to buy, sell, subscribe for or underwrite those investments or to refrain from doing so. It is also an offence if the ultimate objective is to induce a person to exercise or refrain from exercising rights conferred by those investments. 'Relevant investments' are to be defined by the Treasury (s. 397(10)).

It is suggested that, whilst it is necessary for the prosecution to show that the impression was consciously created for a particular purpose, it is not necessary to show that the person who created the impression believed that it would be false or misleading. This is borne out by s. 397(5), which makes it a defence for a defendant to prove — on the balance of probabilities — that he reasonably believed that what he did would not create a false or misleading impression. This defence would be unnecessary if the burden were on the prosecution to show that he knew that the impression created would be false or misleading.

There are some circumstances where it may be necessary or desirable to make misleading statements or create a false or misleading impression about the price, value or market in investments. For example, the FSA's rules are likely to include rules which require the proper control of information between different parts of authorised firms to make sure that inside information available in one part of the firm is not given to another part of the firm which might enable it to take inappropriate advantage of it. These rules, commonly referred to as rules on Chinese walls, are known in FSAMA 2000 as control of information rules and would be made under s. 147. The FSA's rules may also include rules expressly designed to stabilise the price of new issues of shares. These would be made under s. 144. It is a defence to a charge under s. 397(3), to prove, on the balance of probabilities, that the course of conduct was in accordance with those rules (s. 397(5)(b) and (c)). In the case of acts in conformity with price stabilisation rules, the defendant must also show that the purpose of the conduct was to stabilise the price of the investments.

### Territorial scope of offences under section 397

Section 397(6) makes express provision for the application of s. 397 to conduct outside, or having an effect outside the United Kingdom. More specifically, misleading statements may be criminal if they are made in or from the United Kingdom, even if they are made for the purpose of inducing persons located abroad. They may also be criminal if they are made in or from a place outside the United Kingdom if they are directed at inducing persons in the United Kingdom, or the agreement is, or would be, entered into here.

The offence of market manipulation is not committed unless it is committed in the United Kingdom or the false or misleading impression, whilst caused by activity outside the United Kingdom, is in fact created here.

### Sentencing

The offences in s. 397 are serious offences which are triable either way. In the magistrates' courts, a maximum sentence of six months' imprisonment may be imposed together with a fine not exceeding the statutory maximum (currently £5,000). In the Crown Court, the maximum sentence is seven years' imprisonment together with an unlimited fine.

### Misleading the FSA

FSAMA 2000, s. 398, makes it an offence knowingly or recklessly to give false or misleading information to the FSA in purported compliance with any requirement imposed by or under the Act, including requirements imposed by FSA rules.

This is an indictable but not an imprisonable offence: in the Crown Court, only a fine (albeit an unlimited one) may be imposed.

There are other offences in the Act of misleading the FSA — misleading an investigator under s. 177, for example — which carry higher sentences (in the case of s. 177, up to two years' imprisonment). Section 398 makes clear that it is a sweep-up provision: the offence which it creates applies only to behaviour which is not an offence by virtue of some other provision of the Act.

## Misleading the Director General of Fair Trading

The effect of FSAMA 2000, s. 399, is to extend the Competition Act 1998, s. 44, and make it an offence under that Act to mislead or give false information to the Director General of Fair Trading when he is exercising his functions under FSAMA 2000.

## Applications to officers of bodies corporate, members of a partnership and unincorporated associations

Where an offence is committed by a company, officers (including controllers) will also be guilty of an offence if they are shown to have consented or connived in the offence, or if it can be shown to be attributable to negligence on their part (s. 400(1) and (2)). Similar provisions extend criminal liability to partners within a partnership, and those purporting to be partners (s. 400(3) and (4)). Section 400(6) extends liability to officers and members of governing bodies of unincorporated associations. The Treasury may make an order providing for liability to extend to officers of companies and unincorporated associations formed outside the UK (s. 400(7)).

## NOTABLE DIFFERENCES FROM THE CURRENT FRAMEWORK

FSAMA 2000 contains some important extensions to the FSA's current prosecution powers. In particular, it will be able to prosecute insider dealing and the offence commonly known as market manipulation, and breach of money laundering regulations prescribed by the Treasury (ss. 401(2) and 402(1)). There will be an important cutback too, in that the FSA will not be able to prosecute a person who is permitted only to carry on certain kinds of regulated activity but who exceeds the terms of his permission (s. 20(2)(a)). (It was previously an offence to go beyond investment business to deposit taking, for example, without a separate authorisation for the purpose.) It will become more important in these circumstances to have effective tools to deal with those who do not obtain permission to do all the business they plan to do. The ability to prosecute the offence of misleading the FSA will perhaps assume a greater importance in these circumstances.

# Chapter Thirty
# Miscellaneous, Interpretation and Supplemental

*Michael Blair*

This chapter deals with Parts XXVIII, XXIX and XXX of the Financial Services and Markets Act 2000 (FSAMA 2000). Much of the material in these three final parts is technical and of no specific significance in itself, though practitioners will frequently need to consult Part XXIX at least, with its 10 sections containing definitions of different kinds. There is, however, some material of interest in Part XXVIII (miscellaneous), particularly in relation to reviews of compliance failure and in the international arena.

## REVIEWS OF COMPLIANCE FAILURES

Section 404 of FSAMA 2000 deals with schemes for reviewing past business. It came into the Bill for the Act at a relatively late stage (report stage in the House of Lords). It is designed to ensure that, if there ever were another widespread compliance failure, the regulatory system could tackle the problem, and put in place machinery to provide redress to those who had suffered from the compliance failure. The precedents to date have been, principally, the pension opt-out and transfer problems of the 1990s and, to a much lesser extent, the more recent review of possible mis-selling of free-standing additional voluntary contributions (FSAVCs). For convenience, this chapter concentrates on the pensions opt-out and transfer precedent.

In the period 1988 to 1994, there was a significant amount of 'mis-selling' in the context of the new liberalised personal pension regime introduced by the then government in the mid to late 1980s. One of these was the mis-selling of an 'opt-out'. Here, the typical case would be that of an employed person, with membership of an occupational pension scheme involving his employer's contributions as well as his own, who was encouraged to opt out of the employer's scheme and to rely, for his retirement, on a personal pension funded either from the rebate provided from government funds (linked to the State Earnings-Related Pension Scheme (SERPS)), or from his own contributions as well as the rebate. In practice, except in rare cases, it was simply not possible for those two sources of finance to make up, in terms of pension provision, for the loss of the continuing inflow of cash from the employer's contributions. It became, therefore, generally recognised that there had to be special reasons to justify advice to effect an opt-out of this kind.

A second class of 'mis-selling' was also identified over this period, which was similar but not so generally indefensible. This was the advice to transfer a lump sum from an occupational pension scheme into a personal pension. Typically, this would involve the prospective pension rights of a former employee who had not yet reached normal pension age. At that stage, between the employee leaving the company and his reaching the date when the pension came into payment, his right to a pension would be in a state of preservation (with some inflation indexation), with the trustees having made a capital provision to enable them to meet their objectives in due course. Under the reforms in the 1980s the employee became entitled to require the employer's pension fund trustees to pay out to a personal pension fund provider the 'transfer value' of his acquired but deferred rights to the occupational pension scheme. In some cases, that transfer was fully defensible as a sensible investment decision: but in many cases the personal pension, bought with the transfer value and with further contributions, could be foreseen to be too slender to support the sort of living standard that the employee might reasonably have expected on attaining normal pension age. This might have been because the transfer value was conservatively valued, or because account could not be or was not taken of discretionary benefits and improvements which the employee might in fact have obtained, even if he had no right to them. Another reason was because the amount of further contributions was not likely to be enough to fill the eventual pension needs. Finally the transfer often involved a switch from the certainty of defined benefit, in the preserved pension, to the risks of investment performance in the personal pension. For some investors, for some or all of these reasons, this was not suitable or not adequately explained.

Putting right this widespread malaise became a major priority for the regulators in the period from 1993 onward. Although the initiative was led by the SIB, using its function of oversight of the regulatory system, and the relatively restricted powers relating to that, the real compulsive force of the review was delivered by the SROs and, in particular, the Personal Investment Authority.

FSAMA 2000, s. 404 recognises that, in this respect, the old regime had the benefit that the SROs (by the membership contract) had power to do something which could not have securely been delivered under the previous legislation on its own. New machinery is therefore enabled, by a Treasury 'switch-on' order under the section requiring the affirmative approval of each House of Parliament. In that way the FSA can be authorised to establish and operate a scheme for enquiring into the specified failure, for establishing the liability of authorised persons to make redress, and for determining the amount of that redress.

The Treasury power to trigger the machinery is bounded by conditions. In particular, an order authorising the FSA to create a scheme can be made only if the FSA has reported to the Treasury about the alleged failure and asked the Treasury to make the order (s. 404(4)(a)). The FSA has to put forward details of the proposed scheme, and the Treasury have to be satisfied that the proposed scheme is 'an appropriate way of dealing with the failure' (s. 404(4)(b) and (c)).

The meat of the provision is in s. 404(6). Once the scheme has been made, then failure by an authorised person to comply with the scheme is treated as a failure to comply with rules. So all the sanctions available for breach of the FSA's rules are available to back the scheme up with the force of compulsion. Subsection (6) is, however, subject to any provision made by the scheme order concerned: so the section appears to contemplate that the Treasury may wish to pick and choose between the various remedies for failure to comply. In particular, it might be decided that the provisions of s. 150 would be disapplied in a scheme order, thus removing the possibility that a private person could bring legal proceedings against a firm for failure to comply with the scheme. The pension transfer and opt-out review was seen as an alternative, in fact if not in law, to court procedure, which might make disapplication of s. 150 a possible item in a scheme order.

## THIRD COUNTRIES: COMMUNITY MEASURES

Sections 405 to 407 of FSAMA 2000 provide the machinery to enable the United Kingdom to continue to comply with the requirements of the four leading Single Market Directives in the context of effective market access by firms in the Community into third countries.

The four Directives concerned (the Investment Services Directive (93/22/EEC), the Second Banking Coordination Directive (86/646/EEC) (since replaced by the Credit Institutions Directive (2000/12/EC)), and the twin First Life and Non-life Insurance Directives (79/267/EEC and 73/239/EEC), set up machinery enabling the Commission or the Council to take measures against countries outside the EEA if they do not allow Community financial services firms effective market access.

Most of the machinery in the relevant articles of the four Directives is of a diplomatic and political character. But, in order to give credence to the Commission or Council's negotiating position, the Directives enable the Community authorities to require the competent authorities of the member States to limit or suspend decisions about authorisation of, and about approval of controlling arrangements in relation to, bodies corporate originating in their own States. Section 405 accordingly gives the Treasury the power to direct the FSA to refuse or defer decisions on applications for Part IV permission by UK incorporated bodies. Similarly the Treasury may direct the FSA to object to proposals for acquisition of control of such bodies.

The refusal of permission and the objection to control are made automatic, without reference to the Financial Services and Markets Tribunal; and any requirement on the FSA's part to defer a decision results in a suspension of all relevant time limits (s. 407). Section 408 makes further provision, following such a Commission decision, in relation to EFTA firms which are subsidiaries of a parent governed by the law of the relevant third country: the effect is to deny the EFTA firm the passport it might otherwise have been entitled to. EFTA firm currently means a firm based in Norway, Iceland or Liechtenstein.

Interestingly, s. 405 limits the Treasury's power of direction to applications by UK companies, and to matters affecting control of UK companies. The latter seems to fit the design of the Directives, which are aimed at the third State and control of community companies passing to companies from that State. In relation to authorisation, however, the limitation to UK companies seems curious, as the Directives have no such limitation and appear to contemplate that application for authorisation by branches emanating from the third State should be refused or deferred. However, in this case, no doubt the more general power of direction in s. 410 could be used (see below).

## INTERNATIONAL OBLIGATIONS

Section 410 of FSAMA 2000 is also of some interest internationally. It contains a list of persons who may loosely be described as regulators for the purposes of the Act. These are the FSA (including its new capacity as Listing Authority), recognised investment exchanges and clearing houses (RIEs and RCHs) (though not overseas ones), persons providing settlement arrangements of the kind that can be netted in an insolvency (as to which see s. 301) and the ombudsman company (FOS) functioning under Part XVI.

If any of these bodies appears to the Treasury to be proposing to take action which would be incompatible with Community obligations or other international obligations, the Treasury can direct that the action be not taken. Equally, if positive steps are required to be taken by such a person to implement such obligations, the Treasury may require those steps to be taken. The power of the Treasury to intervene in the regulatory system established under the Act is highly restricted, but this is one of the two cases where it exists (leaving aside ss. 405 to 408), the other one being in the context of competition override.

## GAMING

Section 412 carries forward the provision, previously in FSA 1986, s. 63, which removes any threat of nullity or unenforceability as a gaming contract of any contract covered by FSAMA 2000. In the past there was some doubt as to whether, in particular, some derivatives contracts might be void or unenforceable as gaming contracts. That ancient public policy for control of antisocial bargains became inappropriate with the regulation of, in particular, investment business in 1986, though it took some litigation to establish the true width of the original 1986 provision (see *City Index Ltd* v *Leslie* [1992] 1 QB 98). Under FSAMA 2000, s. 412, any contract relating to activities to be specified by the Treasury where either or each party is acting by way of business is saved from the risk of nullity or unenforceability on the ground that it is a gaming or wagering contract.

## INTERPRETATION

Part XXIX of FSAMA 2000 deals with definitions. The bulk of these are in s. 417, which is followed by sections dealing with specific issues such as the corporation law definitions of parent, subsidiary, group and controller, etc.

## SUPPLEMENTAL PROVISIONS

Part XXX (supplemental) of FSAMA 2000 contains the closing provisions including important enabling powers for consequential amendments, transitionals and repeals. The passage of the Bill for the Act was relatively contentious, protracted and complex and the customary arrangements for transitionals and for repeals were not included in the Bill. Instead the Treasury have power, in ss. 426 and 427, to deal with all the consequential carpentry by subordinate legislation subject to the negative resolution procedure (s. 429(8)). This relegation to the secondary level of the consequential amendments and transitional arrangements means that the commencement of the legislation is likely to take a bit longer than if it had been possible to deal with the machinery for that commencement in the primary legislation.

Section 430 deals with extent, and applies the whole Act, except the provisions about open-ended investment companies, to Northern Ireland. The entire Act applies to Scotland without express mention. Financial services remains a matter within the jurisdiction of the Westminster Parliament, and is not devolved under the Scotland Act 1998 to the Scottish Parliament or Executive.

There are no provisions in sch. 20 (minor and consequential amendments) which require comment. Schedule 21, however, contains some provisions that come into force on royal assent and facilitate the further attenuation of the powers and responsibilities of the SROs while retaining them in existence until the date or principal date for commencement of the Act.

# Financial Services and Markets Act 2000

CHAPTER 8
ARRANGEMENT OF SECTIONS

PART I
THE REGULATOR

## PART IV
## PERMISSION TO CARRY ON REGULATED ACTIVITIES

### *Application for permission*

### *Permission*

### *Variation and cancellation of Part IV permission*

### *Connected persons*

### *Additional permissions*

### *Procedure*

### *References to the Tribunal*

## PART V
## PERFORMANCE OF REGULATED ACTIVITIES

### *Prohibition orders*

### *Approval*

## PART XX
## PROVISION OF FINANCIAL SERVICES BY MEMBERS
## OF THE PROFESSIONS

## PART XXI
## MUTUAL SOCIETIES

*Friendly societies*

*Building societies*

*Industrial and provident societies and credit unions*

*Supplemental*

## PART XXII
## AUDITORS AND ACTUARIES

*Appointment*

# Financial Services and Markets Act 2000

## 2000 CHAPTER 8

An Act to make provision about the regulation of financial services and markets; to provide for the transfer of certain statutory functions relating to building societies, friendly societies, industrial and provident societies and certain other mutual societies; and for connected purposes.

[14th June 2000]

BE IT ENACTED by the Queen's most Excellent Majesty, by and with the advice and consent of the Lords Spiritual and Temporal, and Commons, in this present Parliament assembled, and by the authority of the same, as follows:—

## PART I
## THE REGULATOR

### 1. The Financial Services Authority

(1) The body corporate known as the Financial Services Authority ('the Authority') is to have the functions conferred on it by or under this Act.

(2) The Authority must comply with the requirements as to its constitution set out in Schedule 1.

(3) Schedule 1 also makes provision about the status of the Authority and the exercise of certain of its functions.

*The Authority's general duties*

### 2. The Authority's general duties

(1) In discharging its general functions the Authority must, so far as is reasonably possible, act in a way—

   (a) which is compatible with the regulatory objectives; and

   (b) which the Authority considers most appropriate for the purpose of meeting those objectives.

(2) The regulatory objectives are—

   (a) market confidence;

   (b) public awareness;

   (c) the protection of consumers; and

   (d) the reduction of financial crime.

(3) In discharging its general functions the Authority must have regard to—

    (a)   the need to use its resources in the most efficient and economic way;

    (b)   the responsibilities of those who manage the affairs of authorised persons;

    (c)   the principle that a burden or restriction which is imposed on a person, or on the carrying on of an activity, should be proportionate to the benefits, considered in general terms, which are expected to result from the imposition of that burden or restriction;

    (d)   the desirability of facilitating innovation in connection with regulated activities;

    (e)   the international character of financial services and markets and the desirability of maintaining the competitive position of the United Kingdom;

    (f)   the need to minimise the adverse effects on competition that may arise from anything done in the discharge of those functions;

    (g)   the desirability of facilitating competition between those who are subject to any form of regulation by the Authority.

    (4)   The Authority's general functions are—

    (a)   its function of making rules under this Act (considered as a whole);

    (b)   its function of preparing and issuing codes under this Act (considered as a whole);

    (c)   its functions in relation to the giving of general guidance (considered as a whole); and

    (d)   its function of determining the general policy and principles by reference to which it performs particular functions.

    (5)   'General guidance' has the meaning given in section 158(5).

*The regulatory objectives*

## 3.  Market confidence

    (1)   The market confidence objective is: maintaining confidence in the financial system.

    (2)   'The financial system' means the financial system operating in the United Kingdom and includes—

    (a)   financial markets and exchanges;

    (b)   regulated activities; and

    (c)   other activities connected with financial markets and exchanges.

## 4.  Public awareness

    (1)   The public awareness objective is: promoting public understanding of the financial system.

    (2)   It includes, in particular—

    (a)   promoting awareness of the benefits and risks associated with different kinds of investment or other financial dealing; and

    (b)   the provision of appropriate information and advice.

    (3)   'The financial system' has the same meaning as in section 3.

## 5.  The protection of consumers

    (1)   The protection of consumers objective is: securing the appropriate degree of protection for consumers.

    (2)   In considering what degree of protection may be appropriate, the Authority must have regard to—

    (a)   the differing degrees of risk involved in different kinds of investment or other transaction;

    (b)   the differing degrees of experience and expertise that different consumers may have in relation to different kinds of regulated activity;

    (c)   the needs that consumers may have for advice and accurate information; and

(d)   the general principle that consumers should take responsibility for their decisions.

(3)   'Consumers' means persons—

(a)   who are consumers for the purposes of section 138; or

(b)   who, in relation to regulated activities carried on otherwise than by authorised persons, would be consumers for those purposes if the activities were carried on by authorised persons.

## 6.   The reduction of financial crime

(1)   The reduction of financial crime objective is: reducing the extent to which it is possible for a business carried on—

(a)   by a regulated person, or

(b)   in contravention of the general prohibition,

to be used for a purpose connected with financial crime.

(2)   In considering that objective the Authority must, in particular, have regard to the desirability of—

(a)   regulated persons being aware of the risk of their businesses being used in connection with the commission of financial crime;

(b)   regulated persons taking appropriate measures (in relation to their administration and employment practices, the conduct of transactions by them and otherwise) to prevent financial crime, facilitate its detection and monitor its incidence;

(c)   regulated persons devoting adequate resources to the matters mentioned in paragraph (b).

(3)   'Financial crime' includes any offence involving—

(a)   fraud or dishonesty;

(b)   misconduct in, or misuse of information relating to, a financial market; or

(c)   handling the proceeds of crime.

(4)   'Offence' includes an act or omission which would be an offence if it had taken place in the United Kingdom.

(5)   'Regulated person' means an authorised person, a recognised investment exchange or a recognised clearing house.

*Corporate governance*

## 7.   Duty of Authority to follow principles of good governance

In managing its affairs, the Authority must have regard to such generally accepted principles of good corporate governance as it is reasonable to regard as applicable to it.

*Arrangements for consulting practitioners and consumers*

## 8.   The Authority's general duty to consult

The Authority must make and maintain effective arrangements for consulting practitioners and consumers on the extent to which its general policies and practices are consistent with its general duties under section 2.

## 9.   The Practitioner Panel

(1)   Arrangements under section 8 must include the establishment and maintenance of a panel of persons (to be known as 'the Practitioner Panel') to represent the interests of practitioners.

(2)   The Authority must appoint one of the members of the Practitioner Panel to be its chairman.

(3)   The Treasury's approval is required for the appointment or dismissal of the chairman.

(4)   The Authority must have regard to any representations made to it by the Practitioner Panel.

(5)   The Authority must appoint to the Practitioner Panel such—

    (a)   individuals who are authorised persons,

    (b)   persons representing authorised persons,

    (c)   persons representing recognised investment exchanges, and

    (d)   persons representing recognised clearing houses,

as it considers appropriate.

## 10.   The Consumer Panel

(1)   Arrangements under section 8 must include the establishment and maintenance of a panel of persons (to be known as 'the Consumer Panel') to represent the interests of consumers.

(2)   The Authority must appoint one of the members of the Consumer Panel to be its chairman.

(3)   The Treasury's approval is required for the appointment or dismissal of the chairman.

(4)   The Authority must have regard to any representations made to it by the Consumer Panel.

(5)   The Authority must appoint to the Consumer Panel such consumers, or persons representing the interests of consumers, as it considers appropriate.

(6)   The Authority must secure that the membership of the Consumer Panel is such as to give a fair degree of representation to those who are using, or are or may be contemplating using, services otherwise than in connection with businesses carried on by them.

(7)   'Consumers' means persons, other than authorised persons—

    (a)   who are consumers for the purposes of section 138; or

    (b)   who, in relation to regulated activities carried on otherwise than by authorised persons, would be consumers for those purposes if the activities were carried on by authorised persons.

## 11.   Duty to consider representations by the Panels

(1)   This section applies to a representation made, in accordance with arrangements made under section 8, by the Practitioner Panel or by the Consumer Panel.

(2)   The Authority must consider the representation.

(3)   If the Authority disagrees with a view expressed, or proposal made, in the representation, it must give the Panel a statement in writing of its reasons for disagreeing.

*Reviews*

## 12.   Reviews

(1)   The Treasury may appoint an independent person to conduct a review of the economy, efficiency and effectiveness with which the Authority has used its resources in discharging its functions.

(2)   A review may be limited by the Treasury to such functions of the Authority (however described) as the Treasury may specify in appointing the person to conduct it.

(3)   A review is not to be concerned with the merits of the Authority's general policy or principles in pursuing regulatory objectives or in exercising functions under Part VI.

(4)   On completion of a review, the person conducting it must make a written report to the Treasury—

(a)   setting out the result of the review; and

(b)   making such recommendations (if any) as he considers appropriate.

(5)   A copy of the report must be—

(a)   laid before each House of Parliament; and

(b)   published in such manner as the Treasury consider appropriate.

(6)   Any expenses reasonably incurred in the conduct of a review are to be met by the Treasury out of money provided by Parliament.

(7)   'Independent' means appearing to the Treasury to be independent of the Authority.

### 13.   Right to obtain documents and information

(1)   A person conducting a review under section 12—

(a)   has a right of access at any reasonable time to all such documents as he may reasonably require for purposes of the review; and

(b)   may require any person holding or accountable for any such document to provide such information and explanation as are reasonably necessary for that purpose.

(2)   Subsection (1) applies only to documents in the custody or under the control of the Authority.

(3)   An obligation imposed on a person as a result of the exercise of powers conferred by subsection (1) is enforceable by injunction or, in Scotland, by an order for specific performance under section 45 of the Court of Session Act 1988.

*Inquiries*

### 14.   Cases in which the Treasury may arrange independent inquiries

(1)   This section applies in two cases.

(2)   The first is where it appears to the Treasury that—

(a)   events have occurred in relation to—

(i)   a collective investment scheme, or

(ii)   a person who is, or was at the time of the events, carrying on a regulated activity (whether or not as an authorised person),

which posed or could have posed a grave risk to the financial system or caused or risked causing significant damage to the interests of consumers; and

(b)   those events might not have occurred, or the risk or damage might have been reduced, but for a serious failure in—

(i)   the system established by this Act for the regulation of such schemes or of such persons and their activities; or

(ii)   the operation of that system.

(3)   The second is where it appears to the Treasury that—

(a)   events have occurred in relation to listed securities or an issuer of listed securities which caused or could have caused significant damage to holders of listed securities; and

(b)   those events might not have occurred but for a serious failure in the regulatory system established by Part VI or in its operation.

(4)   If the Treasury consider that it is in the public interest that there should be an independent inquiry into the events and the circumstances surrounding them, they may arrange for an inquiry to be held under section 15.

(5)   'Consumers' means persons—

(a)   who are consumers for the purposes of section 138; or

(b)   who, in relation to regulated activities carried on otherwise than by authorised persons, would be consumers for those purposes if the activities were carried on by authorised persons.

(6)   'The financial system' has the same meaning as in section 3.

(7)   'Listed securities' means anything which has been admitted to the official list under Part VI.

### 15.  Power to appoint person to hold an inquiry

(1)   If the Treasury decide to arrange for an inquiry to be held under this section, they may appoint such person as they consider appropriate to hold the inquiry.

(2)   The Treasury may, by a direction to the appointed person, control—

(a)   the scope of the inquiry;

(b)   the period during which the inquiry is to be held;

(c)   the conduct of the inquiry; and

(d)   the making of reports.

(3)   A direction may, in particular—

(a)   confine the inquiry to particular matters;

(b)   extend the inquiry to additional matters;

(c)   require the appointed person to discontinue the inquiry or to take only such steps as are specified in the direction;

(d)   require the appointed person to make such interim reports as are so specified.

### 16.  Powers of appointed person and procedure

(1)   The person appointed to hold an inquiry under section 15 may—

(a)   obtain such information from such persons and in such manner as he thinks fit;

(b)   make such inquiries as he thinks fit; and

(c)   determine the procedure to be followed in connection with the inquiry.

(2)   The appointed person may require any person who, in his opinion, is able to provide any information, or produce any document, which is relevant to the inquiry to provide any such information or produce any such document.

(3)   For the purposes of an inquiry, the appointed person has the same powers as the court in respect of the attendance and examination of witnesses (including the examination of witnesses abroad) and in respect of the production of documents.

(4)   'Court' means—

(a)   the High Court; or

(b)   in Scotland, the Court of Session.

### 17.  Conclusion of inquiry

(1)   On completion of an inquiry under section 15, the person holding the inquiry must make a written report to the Treasury—

(a)   setting out the result of the inquiry; and

(b)   making such recommendations (if any) as he considers appropriate.

(2)   The Treasury may publish the whole, or any part, of the report and may do so in such manner as they consider appropriate.

(3)   Subsection (4) applies if the Treasury propose to publish a report but consider that it contains material—

(a)   which relates to the affairs of a particular person whose interests would, in the opinion of the Treasury, be seriously prejudiced by publication of the material; or

(b)   the disclosure of which would be incompatible with an international obligation of the United Kingdom.

(4)   The Treasury must ensure that the material is removed before publication.

(5)   The Treasury must lay before each House of Parliament a copy of any report or part of a report published under subsection (2).

(6)   Any expenses reasonably incurred in holding an inquiry are to be met by the Treasury out of money provided by Parliament.

## 18.   Obstruction and contempt

(1)   If a person ('A')—

(a)   fails to comply with a requirement imposed on him by a person holding an inquiry under section 15, or

(b)   otherwise obstructs such an inquiry,

the person holding the inquiry may certify the matter to the High Court (or, in Scotland, the Court of Session).

(2)   The court may enquire into the matter.

(3)   If, after hearing—

(a)   any witnesses who may be produced against or on behalf of A, and

(b)   any statement made by or on behalf of A,

the court is satisfied that A would have been in contempt of court if the inquiry had been proceedings before the court, it may deal with him as if he were in contempt.

PART II
REGULATED AND PROHIBITED ACTIVITIES

*The general prohibition*

## 19.   The general prohibition

(1)   No person may carry on a regulated activity in the United Kingdom, or purport to do so, unless he is—

(a)   an authorised person; or

(b)   an exempt person.

(2)   The prohibition is referred to in this Act as the general prohibition.

*Requirement for permission*

## 20.   Authorised persons acting without permission

(1)   If an authorised person carries on a regulated activity in the United Kingdom, or purports to do so, otherwise than in accordance with permission—

(a)   given to him by the Authority under Part IV, or

(b)   resulting from any other provision of this Act,

he is to be taken to have contravened a requirement imposed on him by the Authority under this Act.

(2)   The contravention does not—

(a)   make a person guilty of an offence;

(b)   make any transaction void or unenforceable; or

(c)   (subject to subsection (3)) give rise to any right of action for breach of statutory duty.

(3)   In prescribed cases the contravention is actionable at the suit of a person who suffers loss as a result of the contravention, subject to the defences and other incidents applying to actions for breach of statutory duty.

*Financial promotion*

## 21.  Restrictions on financial promotion

(1)  A person ('A') must not, in the course of business, communicate an invitation or inducement to engage in investment activity.

(2)  But subsection (1) does not apply if—

(a)  A is an authorised person; or

(b)  the content of the communication is approved for the purposes of this section by an authorised person.

(3)  In the case of a communication originating outside the United Kingdom, subsection (1) applies only if the communication is capable of having an effect in the United Kingdom.

(4)  The Treasury may by order specify circumstances in which a person is to be regarded for the purposes of subsection (1) as—

(a)  acting in the course of business;

(b)  not acting in the course of business.

(5)  The Treasury may by order specify circumstances (which may include compliance with financial promotion rules) in which subsection (1) does not apply.

(6)  An order under subsection (5) may, in particular, provide that subsection (1) does not apply in relation to communications—

(a)  of a specified description;

(b)  originating in a specified country or territory outside the United Kingdom;

(c)  originating in a country or territory which falls within a specified description of country or territory outside the United Kingdom; or

(d)  originating outside the United Kingdom.

(7)  The Treasury may by order repeal subsection (3).

(8)  'Engaging in investment activity' means—

(a)  entering or offering to enter into an agreement the making or performance of which by either party constitutes a controlled activity; or

(b)  exercising any rights conferred by a controlled investment to acquire, dispose of, underwrite or convert a controlled investment.

(9)  An activity is a controlled activity if—

(a)  it is an activity of a specified kind or one which falls within a specified class of activity; and

(b)  it relates to an investment of a specified kind, or to one which falls within a specified class of investment.

(10)  An investment is a controlled investment if it is an investment of a specified kind or one which falls within a specified class of investment.

(11)  Schedule 2 (except paragraph 26) applies for the purposes of subsections (9) and (10) with references to section 22 being read as references to each of those subsections.

(12)  Nothing in Schedule 2, as applied by subsection (11), limits the powers conferred by subsection (9) or (10).

(13)  'Communicate' includes causing a communication to be made.

(14)  'Investment' includes any asset, right or interest.

(15)  'Specified' means specified in an order made by the Treasury.

*Regulated activities*

## 22.  The classes of activity and categories of investment

(1)  An activity is a regulated activity for the purposes of this Act if it is an activity of a specified kind which is carried on by way of business and—

(a) relates to an investment of a specified kind; or

(b) in the case of an activity of a kind which is also specified for the purposes of this paragraph, is carried on in relation to property of any kind.

(2) Schedule 2 makes provision supplementing this section.

(3) Nothing in Schedule 2 limits the powers conferred by subsection (1).

(4) 'Investment' includes any asset, right or interest.

(5) 'Specified' means specified in an order made by the Treasury.

*Offences*

## 23. Contravention of the general prohibition

(1) A person who contravenes the general prohibition is guilty of an offence and liable—

(a) on summary conviction, to imprisonment for a term not exceeding six months or a fine not exceeding the statutory maximum, or both;

(b) on conviction on indictment, to imprisonment for a term not exceeding two years or a fine, or both.

(2) In this Act 'an authorisation offence' means an offence under this section.

(3) In proceedings for an authorisation offence it is a defence for the accused to show that he took all reasonable precautions and exercised all due diligence to avoid committing the offence.

## 24. False claims to be authorised or exempt

(1) A person who is neither an authorised person nor, in relation to the regulated activity in question, an exempt person is guilty of an offence if he—

(a) describes himself (in whatever terms) as an authorised person;

(b) describes himself (in whatever terms) as an exempt person in relation to the regulated activity; or

(c) behaves, or otherwise holds himself out, in a manner which indicates (or which is reasonably likely to be understood as indicating) that he is—

(i) an authorised person; or

(ii) an exempt person in relation to the regulated activity.

(2) In proceedings for an offence under this section it is a defence for the accused to show that he took all reasonable precautions and exercised all due diligence to avoid committing the offence.

(3) A person guilty of an offence under this section is liable on summary conviction to imprisonment for a term not exceeding six months or a fine not exceeding level 5 on the standard scale, or both.

(4) But where the conduct constituting the offence involved or included the public display of any material, the maximum fine for the offence is level 5 on the standard scale multiplied by the number of days for which the display continued.

## 25. Contravention of section 21

(1) A person who contravenes section 21(1) is guilty of an offence and liable—

(a) on summary conviction, to imprisonment for a term not exceeding six months or a fine not exceeding the statutory maximum, or both;

(b) on conviction on indictment, to imprisonment for a term not exceeding two years or a fine, or both.

(2) In proceedings for an offence under this section it is a defence for the accused to show—

(a)  that he believed on reasonable grounds that the content of the communication was prepared, or approved for the purposes of section 21, by an authorised person; or

(b)  that he took all reasonable precautions and exercised all due diligence to avoid committing the offence.

*Enforceability of agreements*

## 26.  Agreements made by unauthorised persons

(1)  An agreement made by a person in the course of carrying on a regulated activity in contravention of the general prohibition is unenforceable against the other party.

(2)  The other party is entitled to recover—

(a)  any money or other property paid or transferred by him under the agreement; and

(b)  compensation for any loss sustained by him as a result of having parted with it.

(3)  'Agreement' means an agreement—

(a)  made after this section comes into force; and

(b)  the making or performance of which constitutes, or is part of, the regulated activity in question.

(4)  This section does not apply if the regulated activity is accepting deposits.

## 27.  Agreements made through unauthorised persons

(1)  An agreement made by an authorised person ('the provider')—

(a)  in the course of carrying on a regulated activity (not in contravention of the general prohibition), but

(b)  in consequence of something said or done by another person ('the third party') in the course of a regulated activity carried on by the third party in contravention of the general prohibition,

is unenforceable against the other party.

(2)  The other party is entitled to recover—

(a)  any money or other property paid or transferred by him under the agreement; and

(b)  compensation for any loss sustained by him as a result of having parted with it.

(3)  'Agreement' means an agreement—

(a)  made after this section comes into force; and

(b)  the making or performance of which constitutes, or is part of, the regulated activity in question carried on by the provider.

(4)  This section does not apply if the regulated activity is accepting deposits.

## 28.  Agreements made unenforceable by section 26 or 27

(1)  This section applies to an agreement which is unenforceable because of section 26 or 27.

(2)  The amount of compensation recoverable as a result of that section is—

(a)  the amount agreed by the parties; or

(b)  on the application of either party, the amount determined by the court.

(3)  If the court is satisfied that it is just and equitable in the circumstances of the case, it may allow—

(a)  the agreement to be enforced; or

(b)  money and property paid or transferred under the agreement to be retained.

(4)  In considering whether to allow the agreement to be enforced or (as the case may be) the money or property paid or transferred under the agreement to be retained the court must—

(a)   if the case arises as a result of section 26, have regard to the issue mentioned in subsection (5); or

(b)   if the case arises as a result of section 27, have regard to the issue mentioned in subsection (6).

(5)   The issue is whether the person carrying on the regulated activity concerned reasonably believed that he was not contravening the general prohibition by making the agreement.

(6)   The issue is whether the provider knew that the third party was (in carrying on the regulated activity) contravening the general prohibition.

(7)   If the person against whom the agreement is unenforceable—

(a)   elects not to perform the agreement, or

(b)   as a result of this section, recovers money paid or other property transferred by him under the agreement,

he must repay any money and return any other property received by him under the agreement.

(8)   If property transferred under the agreement has passed to a third party, a reference in section 26 or 27 or this section to that property is to be read as a reference to its value at the time of its transfer under the agreement.

(9)   The commission of an authorisation offence does not make the agreement concerned illegal or invalid to any greater extent than is provided by section 26 or 27.

## 29.   Accepting deposits in breach of general prohibition

(1)   This section applies to an agreement between a person ('the depositor') and another person ('the deposit-taker') made in the course of the carrying on by the deposit-taker of accepting deposits in contravention of the general prohibition.

(2)   If the depositor is not entitled under the agreement to recover without delay any money deposited by him, he may apply to the court for an order directing the deposit-taker to return the money to him.

(3)   The court need not make such an order if it is satisfied that it would not be just and equitable for the money deposited to be returned, having regard to the issue mentioned in subsection (4).

(4)   The issue is whether the deposit-taker reasonably believed that he was not contravening the general prohibition by making the agreement.

(5)   'Agreement' means an agreement—

(a)   made after this section comes into force; and

(b)   the making or performance of which constitutes, or is part of, accepting deposits.

## 30.   Enforceability of agreements resulting from unlawful communications

(1)   In this section—

'unlawful communication' means a communication in relation to which there has been a contravention of section 21(1);

'controlled agreement' means an agreement the making or performance of which by either party constitutes a controlled activity for the purposes of that section; and

'controlled investment' has the same meaning as in section 21.

(2)   If in consequence of an unlawful communication a person enters as a customer into a controlled agreement, it is unenforceable against him and he is entitled to recover—

(a)   any money or other property paid or transferred by him under the agreement; and

(b)   compensation for any loss sustained by him as a result of having parted with it.

(3)  If in consequence of an unlawful communication a person exercises any rights conferred by a controlled investment, no obligation to which he is subject as a result of exercising them is enforceable against him and he is entitled to recover—

(a)  any money or other property paid or transferred by him under the obligation; and

(b)  compensation for any loss sustained by him as a result of having parted with it.

(4)  But the court may allow—

(a)  the agreement or obligation to be enforced, or

(b)  money or property paid or transferred under the agreement or obligation to be retained,

if it is satisfied that it is just and equitable in the circumstances of the case.

(5)  In considering whether to allow the agreement or obligation to be enforced or (as the case may be) the money or property paid or transferred under the agreement to be retained the court must have regard to the issues mentioned in subsections (6) and (7).

(6)  If the applicant made the unlawful communication, the issue is whether he reasonably believed that he was not making such a communication.

(7)  If the applicant did not make the unlawful communication, the issue is whether he knew that the agreement was entered into in consequence of such a communication.

(8)  'Applicant' means the person seeking to enforce the agreement or obligation or retain the money or property paid or transferred.

(9)  Any reference to making a communication includes causing a communication to be made.

(10)  The amount of compensation recoverable as a result of subsection (2) or (3) is—

(a)  the amount agreed between the parties; or

(b)  on the application of either party, the amount determined by the court.

(11)  If a person elects not to perform an agreement or an obligation which (by virtue of subsection (2) or (3)) is unenforceable against him, he must repay any money and return any other property received by him under the agreement.

(12)  If (by virtue of subsection (2) or (3)) a person recovers money paid or property transferred by him under an agreement or obligation, he must repay any money and return any other property received by him as a result of exercising the rights in question.

(13)  If any property required to be returned under this section has passed to a third party, references to that property are to be read as references to its value at the time of its receipt by the person required to return it.

## PART III
## AUTHORISATION AND EXEMPTION

*Authorisation*

### 31.  Authorised persons

(1)  The following persons are authorised for the purposes of this Act—

(a)  a person who has a Part IV permission to carry on one or more regulated activities;

(b)  an EEA firm qualifying for authorisation under Schedule 3;

(c)  a Treaty firm qualifying for authorisation under Schedule 4;

(d)  a person who is otherwise authorised by a provision of, or made under, this Act.

(2)  In this Act 'authorised person' means a person who is authorised for the purposes of this Act.

## 32.   Partnerships and unincorporated associations

(1)   If a firm is authorised—

(a)   it is authorised to carry on the regulated activities concerned in the name of the firm; and

(b)   its authorisation is not affected by any change in its membership.

(2)   If an authorised firm is dissolved, its authorisation continues to have effect in relation to any firm which succeeds to the business of the dissolved firm.

(3)   For the purposes of this section, a firm is to be regarded as succeeding to the business of another firm only if—

(a)   the members of the resulting firm are substantially the same as those of the former firm; and

(b)   succession is to the whole or substantially the whole of the business of the former firm.

(4)   'Firm' means—

(a)   a partnership; or

(b)   an unincorporated association of persons.

(5)   'Partnership' does not include a partnership which is constituted under the law of any place outside the United Kingdom and is a body corporate.

*Ending of authorisation*

## 33.   Withdrawal of authorisation by the Authority

(1)   This section applies if—

(a)   an authorised person's Part IV permission is cancelled; and

(b)   as a result, there is no regulated activity for which he has permission.

(2)   The Authority must give a direction withdrawing that person's status as an authorised person.

## 34.   EEA firms

(1)   An EEA firm ceases to qualify for authorisation under Part II of Schedule 3 if it ceases to be an EEA firm as a result of—

(a)   having its EEA authorisation withdrawn; or

(b)   ceasing to have an EEA right in circumstances in which EEA authorisation is not required.

(2)   At the request of an EEA firm, the Authority may give a direction cancelling its authorisation under Part II of Schedule 3.

(3)   If an EEA firm has a Part IV permission, it does not cease to be an authorised person merely because it ceases to qualify for authorisation under Part II of Schedule 3.

## 35.   Treaty firms

(1)   A Treaty firm ceases to qualify for authorisation under Schedule 4 if its home State authorisation is withdrawn.

(2)   At the request of a Treaty firm, the Authority may give a direction cancelling its Schedule 4 authorisation.

(3)   If a Treaty firm has a Part IV permission, it does not cease to be an authorised person merely because it ceases to qualify for authorisation under Schedule 4.

## 36.   Persons authorised as a result of paragraph 1(1) of Schedule 5

(1)   At the request of a person authorised as a result of paragraph 1(1) of Schedule 5, the Authority may give a direction cancelling his authorisation as such a person.

(2)   If a person authorised as a result of paragraph 1(1) of Schedule 5 has a Part IV permission, he does not cease to be an authorised person merely because he ceases to be a person so authorised.

*Exercise of EEA rights by UK firms*

### 37.   Exercise of EEA rights by UK firms

Part III of Schedule 3 makes provision in relation to the exercise outside the United Kingdom of EEA rights by UK firms.

*Exemption*

### 38.   Exemption orders

(1)   The Treasury may by order ('an exemption order') provide for—

(a)   specified persons, or

(b)   persons falling within a specified class,

to be exempt from the general prohibition.

(2)   But a person cannot be an exempt person as a result of an exemption order if he has a Part IV permission.

(3)   An exemption order may provide for an exemption to have effect—

(a)   in respect of all regulated activities;

(b)   in respect of one or more specified regulated activities;

(c)   only in specified circumstances;

(d)   only in relation to specified functions;

(e)   subject to conditions.

(4)   'Specified' means specified by the exemption order.

### 39.   Exemption of appointed representatives

(1)   If a person (other than an authorised person)—

(a)   is a party to a contract with an authorised person ('his principal') which—

(i)    permits or requires him to carry on business of a prescribed description, and

(ii)   complies with such requirements as may be prescribed, and

(b)   is someone for whose activities in carrying on the whole or part of that business his principal has accepted responsibility in writing,

he is exempt from the general prohibition in relation to any regulated activity comprised in the carrying on of that business for which his principal has accepted responsibility.

(2)   A person who is exempt as a result of subsection (1) is referred to in this Act as an appointed representative.

(3)   The principal of an appointed representative is responsible, to the same extent as if he had expressly permitted it, for anything done or omitted by the representative in carrying on the business for which he has accepted responsibility.

(4)   In determining whether an authorised person has complied with a provision contained in or made under this Act, anything which a relevant person has done or omitted as respects business for which the authorised person has accepted responsibility is to be treated as having been done or omitted by the authorised person.

(5)   'Relevant person' means a person who at the material time is or was an appointed representative by virtue of being a party to a contract with the authorised person.

(6)   Nothing in subsection (4) is to cause the knowledge or intentions of an appointed representative to be attributed to his principal for the purpose of determining whether the

principal has committed an offence, unless in all the circumstances it is reasonable for them to be attributed to him.

PART IV

PERMISSION TO CARRY ON REGULATED ACTIVITIES

*Application for permission*

## 40.   Application for permission

(1)   An application for permission to carry on one or more regulated activities may be made to the Authority by—

    (a)   an individual;

    (b)   a body corporate;

    (c)   a partnership; or

    (d)   an unincorporated association.

(2)   An authorised person may not apply for permission under this section if he has a permission—

    (a)   given to him by the Authority under this Part, or

    (b)   having effect as if so given,

which is in force.

(3)   An EEA firm may not apply for permission under this section to carry on a regulated activity which it is, or would be, entitled to carry on in exercise of an EEA right, whether through a United Kingdom branch or by providing services in the United Kingdom.

(4)   A permission given by the Authority under this Part or having effect as if so given is referred to in this Act as 'a Part IV permission'.

## 41.   The threshold conditions

(1)   'The threshold conditions', in relation to a regulated activity, means the conditions set out in Schedule 6.

(2)   In giving or varying permission, or imposing or varying any requirement, under this Part the Authority must ensure that the person concerned will satisfy, and continue to satisfy, the threshold conditions in relation to all of the regulated activities for which he has or will have permission.

(3)   But the duty imposed by subsection (2) does not prevent the Authority, having due regard to that duty, from taking such steps as it considers are necessary, in relation to a particular authorised person, in order to secure its regulatory objective of the protection of consumers.

*Permission*

## 42.   Giving permission

(1)   'The applicant' means an applicant for permission under section 40.

(2)   The Authority may give permission for the applicant to carry on the regulated activity or activities to which his application relates or such of them as may be specified in the permission.

(3)   If the applicant—

    (a)   in relation to a particular regulated activity, is exempt from the general prohibition as a result of section 39(1) or an order made under section 38(1), but

    (b)   has applied for permission in relation to another regulated activity,

the application is to be treated as relating to all the regulated activities which, if permission is given, he will carry on.

(4)   If the applicant—

(a)   in relation to a particular regulated activity, is exempt from the general prohibition as a result of section 285(2) or (3), but

(b)   has applied for permission in relation to another regulated activity,

the application is to be treated as relating only to that other regulated activity.

(5)   If the applicant—

(a)   is a person to whom, in relation to a particular regulated activity, the general prohibition does not apply as a result of Part XIX, but

(b)   has applied for permission in relation to another regulated activity,

the application is to be treated as relating only to that other regulated activity.

(6)   If it gives permission, the Authority must specify the permitted regulated activity or activities, described in such manner as the Authority considers appropriate.

(7)   The Authority may—

(a)   incorporate in the description of a regulated activity such limitations (for example as to circumstances in which the activity may, or may not, be carried on) as it considers appropriate;

(b)   specify a narrower or wider description of regulated activity than that to which the application relates;

(c)   give permission for the carrying on of a regulated activity which is not included among those to which the application relates.

### 43.   Imposition of requirements

(1)   A Part IV permission may include such requirements as the Authority considers appropriate.

(2)   A requirement may, in particular, be imposed—

(a)   so as to require the person concerned to take specified action; or

(b)   so as to require him to refrain from taking specified action.

(3)   A requirement may extend to activities which are not regulated activities.

(4)   A requirement may be imposed by reference to the person's relationship with—

(a)   his group; or

(b)   other members of his group.

(5)   A requirement expires at the end of such period as the Authority may specify in the permission.

(6)   But subsection (5) does not affect the Authority's powers under section 44 or 45.

*Variation and cancellation of Part IV permission*

### 44.   Variation etc. at request of authorised person

(1)   The Authority may, on the application of an authorised person with a Part IV permission, vary the permission by—

(a)   adding a regulated activity to those for which it gives permission;

(b)   removing a regulated activity from those for which it gives permission;

(c)   varying the description of a regulated activity for which it gives permission;

(d)   cancelling a requirement imposed under section 43; or

(e)   varying such a requirement.

(2)   The Authority may, on the application of an authorised person with a Part IV permission, cancel the permission.

(3)   The Authority may refuse an application under this section if it appears to it—

(a)   that the interests of consumers, or potential consumers, would be adversely affected if the application were to be granted; and

(b)    that it is desirable in the interests of consumers, or potential consumers, for the application to be refused.

(4)    If, as a result of a variation of a Part IV permission under this section, there are no longer any regulated activities for which the authorised person concerned has permission, the Authority must, once it is satisfied that it is no longer necessary to keep the permission in force, cancel it.

(5)    The Authority's power to vary a Part IV permission under this section extends to including any provision in the permission as varied that could be included if a fresh permission were being given in response to an application under section 40.

### 45.    Variation etc. on the Authority's own initiative

(1)    The Authority may exercise its power under this section in relation to an authorised person if it appears to it that—

(a)    he is failing, or is likely to fail, to satisfy the threshold conditions;

(b)    he has failed, during a period of at least 12 months, to carry on a regulated activity for which he has a Part IV permission; or

(c)    it is desirable to exercise that power in order to protect the interests of consumers or potential consumers.

(2)    The Authority's power under this section is the power to vary a Part IV permission in any of the ways mentioned in section 44(1) or to cancel it.

(3)    If, as a result of a variation of a Part IV permission under this section, there are no longer any regulated activities for which the authorised person concerned has permission, the Authority must, once it is satisfied that it is no longer necessary to keep the permission in force, cancel it.

(4)    The Authority's power to vary a Part IV permission under this section extends to including any provision in the permission as varied that could be included if a fresh permission were being given in response to an application under section 40.

(5)    The Authority's power under this section is referred to in this Part as its own-initiative power.

### 46.    Variation of permission on acquisition of control

(1)    This section applies if it appears to the Authority that—

(a)    a person has acquired control over a UK authorised person who has a Part IV permission; but

(b)    there are no grounds for exercising its own-initiative power.

(2)    If it appears to the Authority that the likely effect of the acquisition of control on the authorised person, or on any of its activities, is uncertain the Authority may vary the authorised person's permission by—

(a)    imposing a requirement of a kind that could be imposed under section 43 on giving permission; or

(b)    varying a requirement included in the authorised person's permission under that section.

(3)    Any reference to a person having acquired control is to be read in accordance with Part XII.

### 47.    Exercise of power in support of overseas regulator

(1)    The Authority's own-initiative power may be exercised in respect of an authorised person at the request of, or for the purpose of assisting, a regulator who is—

(a)    outside the United Kingdom; and

(b)   of a prescribed kind.

(2)   Subsection (1) applies whether or not the Authority has powers which are exercisable in relation to the authorised person by virtue of any provision of Part XIII.

(3)   If a request to the Authority for the exercise of its own-initiative power has been made by a regulator who is—

(a)   outside the United Kingdom,

(b)   of a prescribed kind, and

(c)   acting in pursuance of provisions of a prescribed kind,

the Authority must, in deciding whether or not to exercise that power in response to the request, consider whether it is necessary to do so in order to comply with a Community obligation.

(4)   In deciding in any case in which the Authority does not consider that the exercise of its own-initiative power is necessary in order to comply with a Community obligation, it may take into account in particular—

(a)   whether in the country or territory of the regulator concerned, corresponding assistance would be given to a United Kingdom regulatory authority;

(b)   whether the case concerns the breach of a law, or other requirement, which has no close parallel in the United Kingdom or involves the assertion of a jurisdiction not recognised by the United Kingdom;

(c)   the seriousness of the case and its importance to persons in the United Kingdom;

(d)   whether it is otherwise appropriate in the public interest to give the assistance sought.

(5)   The Authority may decide not to exercise its own-initiative power, in response to a request, unless the regulator concerned undertakes to make such contribution towards the cost of its exercise as the Authority considers appropriate.

(6)   Subsection (5) does not apply if the Authority decides that it is necessary for it to exercise its own-initiative power in order to comply with a Community obligation.

(7)   In subsections (4) and (5) 'request' means a request of a kind mentioned in subsection (1).

## 48.   Prohibitions and restrictions

(1)   This section applies if the Authority—

(a)   on giving a person a Part IV permission, imposes an assets requirement on him; or

(b)   varies an authorised person's Part IV permission so as to alter an assets requirement imposed on him or impose such a requirement on him.

(2)   A person on whom an assets requirement is imposed is referred to in this section as 'A'.

(3)   'Assets requirement' means a requirement under section 43—

(a)   prohibiting the disposal of, or other dealing with, any of A's assets (whether in the United Kingdom or elsewhere) or restricting such disposals or dealings; or

(b)   that all or any of A's assets, or all or any assets belonging to consumers but held by A or to his order, must be transferred to and held by a trustee approved by the Authority.

(4)   If the Authority—

(a)   imposes a requirement of the kind mentioned in subsection (3)(a), and

(b)   gives notice of the requirement to any institution with whom A keeps an account,

the notice has the effects mentioned in subsection (5).

(5)   Those effects are that—

(a)   the institution does not act in breach of any contract with A if, having been instructed by A (or on his behalf) to transfer any sum or otherwise make any payment out of A's account, it refuses to do so in the reasonably held belief that complying with the instruction would be incompatible with the requirement; and

(b)   if the institution complies with such an instruction, it is liable to pay to the Authority an amount equal to the amount transferred from, or otherwise paid out of, A's account in contravention of the requirement.

(6)   If the Authority imposes a requirement of the kind mentioned in subsection (3)(b), no assets held by a person as trustee in accordance with the requirement may, while the requirement is in force, be released or dealt with except with the consent of the Authority.

(7)   If, while a requirement of the kind mentioned in subsection (3)(b) is in force, A creates a charge over any assets of his held in accordance with the requirement, the charge is (to the extent that it confers security over the assets) void against the liquidator and any of A's creditors.

(8)   Assets held by a person as trustee ('T') are to be taken to be held by T in accordance with a requirement mentioned in subsection (3)(b) only if—

(a)   A has given T written notice that those assets are to be held by T in accordance with the requirement; or

(b)   they are assets into which assets to which paragraph (a) applies have been transposed by T on the instructions of A.

(9)   A person who contravenes subsection (6) is guilty of an offence and liable on summary conviction to a fine not exceeding level 5 on the standard scale.

(10)   'Charge' includes a mortgage (or in Scotland a security over property).

(11)   Subsections (6) and (8) do not affect any equitable interest or remedy in favour of a person who is a beneficiary of a trust as a result of a requirement of the kind mentioned in subsection (3)(b).

*Connected persons*

## 49.   Persons connected with an applicant

(1)   In considering—

(a)   an application for a Part IV permission, or

(b)   whether to vary or cancel a Part IV permission,

the Authority may have regard to any person appearing to it to be, or likely to be, in a relationship with the applicant or person given permission which is relevant.

(2)   Before—

(a)   giving permission in response to an application made by a person who is connected with an EEA firm, or

(b)   cancelling or varying any permission given by the Authority to such a person,

the Authority must consult the firm's home state regulator.

(3)   A person ('A') is connected with an EEA firm if—

(a)   A is a subsidiary undertaking of the firm; or

(b)   A is a subsidiary undertaking of a parent undertaking of the firm.

*Additional permissions*

## 50.   Authority's duty to consider other permissions etc

(1)   'Additional Part IV permission' means a Part IV permission which is in force in relation to an EEA firm, a Treaty firm or a person authorised as a result of paragraph 1(1) of Schedule 5.

(2)   If the Authority is considering whether, and if so how, to exercise its own-initiative power under this Part in relation to an additional Part IV permission, it must take into account—

(a)   the home State authorisation of the authorised person concerned;

(b)   any relevant directive; and

(c)   relevant provisions of the Treaty.

*Procedure*

## 51.   Applications under this Part

(1)   An application for a Part IV permission must—

(a)   contain a statement of the regulated activity or regulated activities which the applicant proposes to carry on and for which he wishes to have permission; and

(b)   give the address of a place in the United Kingdom for service on the applicant of any notice or other document which is required or authorised to be served on him under this Act.

(2)   An application for the variation of a Part IV permission must contain a statement—

(a)   of the desired variation; and

(b)   of the regulated activity or regulated activities which the applicant proposes to carry on if his permission is varied.

(3)   Any application under this Part must—

(a)   be made in such manner as the Authority may direct; and

(b)   contain, or be accompanied by, such other information as the Authority may reasonably require.

(4)   At any time after receiving an application and before determining it, the Authority may require the applicant to provide it with such further information as it reasonably considers necessary to enable it to determine the application.

(5)   Different directions may be given, and different requirements imposed, in relation to different applications or categories of application.

(6)   The Authority may require an applicant to provide information which he is required to provide under this section in such form, or to verify it in such a way, as the Authority may direct.

## 52.   Determination of applications

(1)   An application under this Part must be determined by the Authority before the end of the period of six months beginning with the date on which it received the completed application.

(2)   The Authority may determine an incomplete application if it considers it appropriate to do so; and it must in any event determine such an application within twelve months beginning with the date on which it received the application.

(3)   The applicant may withdraw his application, by giving the Authority written notice, at any time before the Authority determines it.

(4)   If the Authority grants an application for, or for variation of, a Part IV permission, it must give the applicant written notice.

(5)   The notice must state the date from which the permission, or the variation, has effect.

(6)   If the Authority proposes—

(a)   to give a Part IV permission but to exercise its power under section 42(7)(a) or (b) or 43(1), or

(b)   to vary a Part IV permission on the application of an authorised person but to exercise its power under any of those provisions (as a result of section 44(5)),

it must give the applicant a warning notice.

(7)  If the Authority proposes to refuse an application made under this Part, it must (unless subsection (8) applies) give the applicant a warning notice.

(8)  This subsection applies if it appears to the Authority that—

(a)  the applicant is an EEA firm; and

(b)  the application is made with a view to carrying on a regulated activity in a manner in which the applicant is, or would be, entitled to carry on that activity in the exercise of an EEA right whether through a United Kingdom branch or by providing services in the United Kingdom.

(9)  If the Authority decides—

(a)  to give a Part IV permission but to exercise its power under section 42(7)(a) or (b) or 43(1),

(b)  to vary a Part IV permission on the application of an authorised person but to exercise its power under any of those provisions (as a result of section 44(5)), or

(c)  to refuse an application under this Part,

it must give the applicant a decision notice.

## 53.  Exercise of own-initiative power: procedure

(1)  This section applies to an exercise of the Authority's own-initiative power to vary an authorised person's Part IV permission.

(2)  A variation takes effect—

(a)  immediately, if the notice given under subsection (4) states that that is the case;

(b)  on such date as may be specified in the notice; or

(c)  if no date is specified in the notice, when the matter to which the notice relates is no longer open to review.

(3)  A variation may be expressed to take effect immediately (or on a specified date) only if the Authority, having regard to the ground on which it is exercising its own-initiative power, reasonably considers that it is necessary for the variation to take effect immediately (or on that date).

(4)  If the Authority proposes to vary the Part IV permission, or varies it with immediate effect, it must give the authorised person written notice.

(5)  The notice must—

(a)  give details of the variation;

(b)  state the Authority's reasons for the variation and for its determination as to when the variation takes effect;

(c)  inform the authorised person that he may make representations to the Authority within such period as may be specified in the notice (whether or not he has referred the matter to the Tribunal);

(d)  inform him of when the variation takes effect; and

(e)  inform him of his right to refer the matter to the Tribunal.

(6)  The Authority may extend the period allowed under the notice for making representations.

(7)  If, having considered any representations made by the authorised person, the Authority decides—

(a)  to vary the permission in the way proposed, or

(b)  if the permission has been varied, not to rescind the variation,

it must give him written notice.

(8)  If, having considered any representations made by the authorised person, the Authority decides—

(a) not to vary the permission in the way proposed,

(b) to vary the permission in a different way, or

(c) to rescind a variation which has effect,

it must give him written notice.

(9) A notice given under subsection (7) must inform the authorised person of his right to refer the matter to the Tribunal.

(10) A notice under subsection (8)(b) must comply with subsection (5).

(11) If a notice informs a person of his right to refer a matter to the Tribunal, it must give an indication of the procedure on such a reference.

(12) For the purposes of subsection (2)(c), whether a matter is open to review is to be determined in accordance with section 391(8).

### 54. Cancellation of Part IV permission: procedure

(1) If the Authority proposes to cancel an authorised person's Part IV permission otherwise than at his request, it must give him a warning notice.

(2) If the Authority decides to cancel an authorised person's Part IV permission otherwise than at his request, it must give him a decision notice.

*References to the Tribunal*

### 55. Right to refer matters to the Tribunal

(1) An applicant who is aggrieved by the determination of an application made under this Part may refer the matter to the Tribunal.

(2) An authorised person who is aggrieved by the exercise of the Authority's own-initiative power may refer the matter to the Tribunal.

PART V

PERFORMANCE OF REGULATED ACTIVITIES

*Prohibition orders*

### 56. Prohibition orders

(1) Subsection (2) applies if it appears to the Authority that an individual is not a fit and proper person to perform functions in relation to a regulated activity carried on by an authorised person.

(2) The Authority may make an order ('a prohibition order') prohibiting the individual from performing a specified function, any function falling within a specified description or any function.

(3) A prohibition order may relate to—

(a) a specified regulated activity, any regulated activity falling within a specified description or all regulated activities;

(b) authorised persons generally or any person within a specified class of authorised person.

(4) An individual who performs or agrees to perform a function in breach of a prohibition order is guilty of an offence and liable on summary conviction to a fine not exceeding level 5 on the standard scale.

(5) In proceedings for an offence under subsection (4) it is a defence for the accused to show that he took all reasonable precautions and exercised all due diligence to avoid committing the offence.

(6) An authorised person must take reasonable care to ensure that no function of his, in relation to the carrying on of a regulated activity, is performed by a person who is prohibited from performing that function by a prohibition order.

(7) The Authority may, on the application of the individual named in a prohibition order, vary or revoke it.

(8) This section applies to the performance of functions in relation to a regulated activity carried on by—

(a) a person who is an exempt person in relation to that activity, and

(b) a person to whom, as a result of Part XX, the general prohibition does not apply in relation to that activity,

as it applies to the performance of functions in relation to a regulated activity carried on by an authorised person.

(9) 'Specified' means specified in the prohibition order.

### 57. Prohibition orders: procedure and right to refer to Tribunal

(1) If the Authority proposes to make a prohibition order it must give the individual concerned a warning notice.

(2) The warning notice must set out the terms of the prohibition.

(3) If the Authority decides to make a prohibition order it must give the individual concerned a decision notice.

(4) The decision notice must—

(a) name the individual to whom the prohibition order applies;

(b) set out the terms of the order; and

(c) be given to the individual named in the order.

(5) A person against whom a decision to make a prohibition order is made may refer the matter to the Tribunal.

### 58. Applications relating to prohibitions: procedure and right to refer to Tribunal

(1) This section applies to an application for the variation or revocation of a prohibition order.

(2) If the Authority decides to grant the application, it must give the applicant written notice of its decision.

(3) If the Authority proposes to refuse the application, it must give the applicant a warning notice.

(4) If the Authority decides to refuse the application, it must give the applicant a decision notice.

(5) If the Authority gives the applicant a decision notice, he may refer the matter to the Tribunal.

*Approval*

### 59. Approval for particular arrangements

(1) An authorised person ('A') must take reasonable care to ensure that no person performs a controlled function under an arrangement entered into by A in relation to the carrying on by A of a regulated activity, unless the Authority approves the performance by that person of the controlled function to which the arrangement relates.

(2) An authorised person ('A') must take reasonable care to ensure that no person performs a controlled function under an arrangement entered into by a contractor of A in relation to the carrying on by A of a regulated activity, unless the Authority approves the performance by that person of the controlled function to which the arrangement relates.

(3) 'Controlled function' means a function of a description specified in rules.

(4) The Authority may specify a description of function under subsection (3) only if, in relation to the carrying on of a regulated activity by an authorised person, it is satisfied that the first, second or third condition is met.

(5)   The first condition is that the function is likely to enable the person responsible for its performance to exercise a significant influence on the conduct of the authorised person's affairs, so far as relating to the regulated activity.

(6)   The second condition is that the function will involve the person performing it in dealing with customers of the authorised person in a manner substantially connected with the carrying on of the regulated activity.

(7)   The third condition is that the function will involve the person performing it in dealing with property of customers of the authorised person in a manner substantially connected with the carrying on of the regulated activity.

(8)   Neither subsection (1) nor subsection (2) applies to an arrangement which allows a person to perform a function if the question of whether he is a fit and proper person to perform the function is reserved under any of the single market directives to an authority in a country or territory outside the United Kingdom.

(9)   In determining whether the first condition is met, the Authority may take into account the likely consequences of a failure to discharge that function properly.

(10)   'Arrangement'—

(a)   means any kind of arrangement for the performance of a function of A which is entered into by A or any contractor of his with another person; and

(b)   includes, in particular, that other person's appointment to an office, his becoming a partner or his employment (whether under a contract of service or otherwise).

(11)   'Customer', in relation to an authorised person, means a person who is using, or who is or may be contemplating using, any of the services provided by the authorised person.

## 60.  Applications for approval

(1)   An application for the Authority's approval under section 59 may be made by the authorised person concerned.

(2)   The application must—

(a)   be made in such manner as the Authority may direct; and

(b)   contain, or be accompanied by, such information as the Authority may reasonably require.

(3)   At any time after receiving the application and before determining it, the Authority may require the applicant to provide it with such further information as it reasonably considers necessary to enable it to determine the application.

(4)   The Authority may require an applicant to present information which he is required to give under this section in such form, or to verify it in such a way, as the Authority may direct.

(5)   Different directions may be given, and different requirements imposed, in relation to different applications or categories of application.

(6)   'The authorised person concerned' includes a person who has applied for permission under Part IV and will be the authorised person concerned if permission is given.

## 61.  Determination of applications

(1)   The Authority may grant an application made under section 60 only if it is satisfied that the person in respect of whom the application is made ('the candidate') is a fit and proper person to perform the function to which the application relates.

(2)   In deciding that question, the Authority may have regard (among other things) to whether the candidate, or any person who may perform a function on his behalf—

(a)   has obtained a qualification,

(b)   has undergone, or is undergoing, training, or

(c)   possesses a level of competence,

required by general rules in relation to persons performing functions of the kind to which the application relates.

(3)   The Authority must, before the end of the period of three months beginning with the date on which it receives an application made under section 60 ('the period for consideration'), determine whether—

(a)   to grant the application; or

(b)   to give a warning notice under section 62(2).

(4)   If the Authority imposes a requirement under section 60(3), the period for consideration stops running on the day on which the requirement is imposed but starts running again—

(a)   on the day on which the required information is received by the Authority; or

(b)   if the information is not provided on a single day, on the last of the days on which it is received by the Authority.

(5)   A person who makes an application under section 60 may withdraw his application by giving written notice to the Authority at any time before the Authority determines it, but only with the consent of—

(a)   the candidate; and

(b)   the person by whom the candidate is to be retained to perform the function concerned, if not the applicant.

## 62.   Applications for approval: procedure and right to refer to Tribunal

(1)   If the Authority decides to grant an application made under section 60 ('an application'), it must give written notice of its decision to each of the interested parties.

(2)   If the Authority proposes to refuse an application, it must give a warning notice to each of the interested parties.

(3)   If the Authority decides to refuse an application, it must give a decision notice to each of the interested parties.

(4)   If the Authority decides to refuse an application, each of the interested parties may refer the matter to the Tribunal.

(5)   'The interested parties', in relation to an application, are—

(a)   the applicant;

(b)   the person in respect of whom the application is made ('A'); and

(c)   the person by whom A's services are to be retained, if not the applicant.

## 63.   Withdrawal of approval

(1)   The Authority may withdraw an approval given under section 59 if it considers that the person in respect of whom it was given is not a fit and proper person to perform the function to which the approval relates.

(2)   When considering whether to withdraw its approval, the Authority may take into account any matter which it could take into account if it were considering an application made under section 60 in respect of the performance of the function to which the approval relates.

(3)   If the Authority proposes to withdraw its approval, it must give each of the interested parties a warning notice.

(4)   If the Authority decides to withdraw its approval, it must give each of the interested parties a decision notice.

(5)   If the Authority decides to withdraw its approval, each of the interested parties may refer the matter to the Tribunal.

(6)   'The interested parties', in relation to an approval, are—

(a) the person on whose application it was given ('A');

(b) the person in respect of whom it was given ('B'); and

(c) the person by whom B's services are retained, if not A.

*Conduct*

## 64. Conduct: statements and codes

(1) The Authority may issue statements of principle with respect to the conduct expected of approved persons.

(2) If the Authority issues a statement of principle under subsection (1), it must also issue a code of practice for the purpose of helping to determine whether or not a person's conduct complies with the statement of principle.

(3) A code issued under subsection (2) may specify—

(a) descriptions of conduct which, in the opinion of the Authority, comply with a statement of principle;

(b) descriptions of conduct which, in the opinion of the Authority, do not comply with a statement of principle;

(c) factors which, in the opinion of the Authority, are to be taken into account in determining whether or not a person's conduct complies with a statement of principle.

(4) The Authority may at any time alter or replace a statement or code issued under this section.

(5) If a statement or code is altered or replaced, the altered or replacement statement or code must be issued by the Authority.

(6) A statement or code issued under this section must be published by the Authority in the way appearing to the Authority to be best calculated to bring it to the attention of the public.

(7) A code published under this section and in force at the time when any particular conduct takes place may be relied on so far as it tends to establish whether or not that conduct complies with a statement of principle.

(8) Failure to comply with a statement of principle under this section does not of itself give rise to any right of action by persons affected or affect the validity of any transaction.

(9) A person is not to be taken to have failed to comply with a statement of principle if he shows that, at the time of the alleged failure, it or its associated code of practice had not been published.

(10) The Authority must, without delay, give the Treasury a copy of any statement or code which it publishes under this section.

(11) The power under this section to issue statements of principle and codes of practice—

(a) includes power to make different provision in relation to persons, cases or circumstances of different descriptions; and

(b) is to be treated for the purposes of section 2(4)(a) as part of the Authority's rule-making functions.

(12) The Authority may charge a reasonable fee for providing a person with a copy of a statement or code published under this section.

(13) 'Approved person' means a person in relation to whom the Authority has given its approval under section 59.

## 65. Statements and codes: procedure

(1) Before issuing a statement or code under section 64, the Authority must publish a draft of it in the way appearing to the Authority to be best calculated to bring it to the attention of the public.

(2)   The draft must be accompanied by —

(a)   a cost benefit analysis; and

(b)   notice that representations about the proposal may be made to the Authority within a specified time.

(3)   Before issuing the proposed statement or code, the Authority must have regard to any representations made to it in accordance with subsection (2)(b).

(4)   If the Authority issues the proposed statement or code it must publish an account, in general terms, of—

(a)   the representations made to it in accordance with subsection (2)(b); and

(b)   its response to them.

(5)   If the statement or code differs from the draft published under subsection (1) in a way which is, in the opinion of the Authority, significant—

(a)   the Authority must (in addition to complying with subsection (4)) publish details of the difference; and

(b)   those details must be accompanied by a cost benefit analysis.

(6)   Neither subsection (2)(a) nor subsection (5)(b) applies if the Authority considers—

(a)   that, making the appropriate comparison, there will be no increase in costs; or

(b)   that, making that comparison, there will be an increase in costs but the increase will be of minimal significance.

(7)   Subsections (1) to (6) do not apply if the Authority considers that the delay involved in complying with them would prejudice the interests of consumers.

(8)   A statement or code must state that it is issued under section 64.

(9)   The Authority may charge a reasonable fee for providing a copy of a draft published under subsection (1).

(10)   This section also applies to a proposal to alter or replace a statement or code.

(11)   'Cost benefit analysis' means an estimate of the costs together with an analysis of the benefits that will arise—

(a)   if the proposed statement or code is issued; or

(b)   if subsection (5)(b) applies, from the statement or code that has been issued.

(12)   'The appropriate comparison' means—

(a)   in relation to subsection (2)(a), a comparison between the overall position if the statement or code is issued and the overall position if it is not issued;

(b)   in relation to subsection (5)(b), a comparison between the overall position after the issuing of the statement or code and the overall position before it was issued.

## 66.   Disciplinary powers

(1)   The Authority may take action against a person under this section if—

(a)   it appears to the Authority that he is guilty of misconduct; and

(b)   the Authority is satisfied that it is appropriate in all the circumstances to take action against him.

(2)   A person is guilty of misconduct if, while an approved person—

(a)   he has failed to comply with a statement of principle issued under section 64; or

(b)   he has been knowingly concerned in a contravention by the relevant authorised person of a requirement imposed on that authorised person by or under this Act.

(3)   If the Authority is entitled to take action under this section against a person, it may—

(a)   impose a penalty on him of such amount as it considers appropriate; or

(b)   publish a statement of his misconduct.

(4)   The Authority may not take action under this section after the end of the period of two years beginning with the first day on which the Authority knew of the misconduct, unless proceedings in respect of it against the person concerned were begun before the end of that period.

(5)   For the purposes of subsection (4)—

(a)   the Authority is to be treated as knowing of misconduct if it has information from which the misconduct can reasonably be inferred; and

(b)   proceedings against a person in respect of misconduct are to be treated as begun when a warning notice is given to him under section 67(1).

(6)   'Approved person' has the same meaning as in section 64.

(7)   'Relevant authorised person', in relation to an approved person, means the person on whose application approval under section 59 was given.

## 67.   Disciplinary measures: procedure and right to refer to Tribunal

(1)   If the Authority proposes to take action against a person under section 66, it must give him a warning notice.

(2)   A warning notice about a proposal to impose a penalty must state the amount of the penalty.

(3)   A warning notice about a proposal to publish a statement must set out the terms of the statement.

(4)   If the Authority decides to take action against a person under section 66, it must give him a decision notice.

(5)   A decision notice about the imposition of a penalty must state the amount of the penalty.

(6)   A decision notice about the publication of a statement must set out the terms of the statement.

(7)   If the Authority decides to take action against a person under section 66, he may refer the matter to the Tribunal.

## 68.   Publication

After a statement under section 66 is published, the Authority must send a copy of it to the person concerned and to any person to whom a copy of the decision notice was given.

## 69.   Statement of policy

(1)   The Authority must prepare and issue a statement of its policy with respect to—

(a)   the imposition of penalties under section 66; and

(b)   the amount of penalties under that section.

(2)   The Authority's policy in determining what the amount of a penalty should be must include having regard to—

(a)   the seriousness of the misconduct in question in relation to the nature of the principle or requirement concerned;

(b)   the extent to which that misconduct was deliberate or reckless; and

(c)   whether the person on whom the penalty is to be imposed is an individual.

(3)   The Authority may at any time alter or replace a statement issued under this section.

(4)   If a statement issued under this section is altered or replaced, the Authority must issue the altered or replacement statement.

(5)   The Authority must, without delay, give the Treasury a copy of any statement which it publishes under this section.

(6)   A statement issued under this section must be published by the Authority in the way appearing to the Authority to be best calculated to bring it to the attention of the public.

(7)   The Authority may charge a reasonable fee for providing a person with a copy of the statement.

(8)   In exercising, or deciding whether to exercise, its power under section 66 in the case of any particular misconduct, the Authority must have regard to any statement of policy published under this section and in force at the time when the misconduct in question occurred.

## 70.   Statements of policy: procedure

(1)   Before issuing a statement under section 69, the Authority must publish a draft of the proposed statement in the way appearing to the Authority to be best calculated to bring it to the attention of the public.

(2)   The draft must be accompanied by notice that representations about the proposal may be made to the Authority within a specified time.

(3)   Before issuing the proposed statement, the Authority must have regard to any representations made to it in accordance with subsection (2).

(4)   If the Authority issues the proposed statement it must publish an account, in general terms, of—

(a)   the representations made to it in accordance with subsection (2); and

(b)   its response to them.

(5)   If the statement differs from the draft published under subsection (1) in a way which is, in the opinion of the Authority, significant, the Authority must (in addition to complying with subsection (4)) publish details of the difference.

(6)   The Authority may charge a reasonable fee for providing a person with a copy of a draft published under subsection (1).

(7)   This section also applies to a proposal to alter or replace a statement.

*Breach of statutory duty*

## 71.   Actions for damages

(1)   A contravention of section 56(6) or 59(1) or (2) is actionable at the suit of a private person who suffers loss as a result of the contravention, subject to the defences and other incidents applying to actions for breach of statutory duty.

(2)   In prescribed cases, a contravention of that kind which would be actionable at the suit of a private person is actionable at the suit of a person who is not a private person, subject to the defences and other incidents applying to actions for breach of statutory duty.

(3)   'Private person' has such meaning as may be prescribed.

## PART VI
## OFFICIAL LISTING

*The competent authority*

## 72.   The competent authority

(1)   On the coming into force of this section, the functions conferred on the competent authority by this Part are to be exercised by the Authority.

(2)   Schedule 7 modifies this Act in its application to the Authority when it acts as the competent authority.

(3)   But provision is made by Schedule 8 allowing some or all of those functions to be transferred by the Treasury so as to be exercisable by another person.

### 73. General duty of the competent authority

(1) In discharging its general functions the competent authority must have regard to—

(a)   the need to use its resources in the most efficient and economic way;

(b)   the principle that a burden or restriction which is imposed on a person should be proportionate to the benefits, considered in general terms, which are expected to arise from the imposition of that burden or restriction;

(c)   the desirability of facilitating innovation in respect of listed securities;

(d)   the international character of capital markets and the desirability of maintaining the competitive position of the United Kingdom;

(e)   the need to minimise the adverse effects on competition of anything done in the discharge of those functions;

(f)   the desirability of facilitating competition in relation to listed securities.

(2)   The competent authority's general functions are—

(a)   its function of making rules under this Part (considered as a whole);

(b)   its functions in relation to the giving of general guidance in relation to this Part (considered as a whole);

(c)   its function of determining the general policy and principles by reference to which it performs particular functions under this Part.

*The official list*

### 74. The official list

(1)   The competent authority must maintain the official list.

(2)   The competent authority may admit to the official list such securities and other things as it considers appropriate.

(3)   But—

(a)   nothing may be admitted to the official list except in accordance with this Part; and

(b)   the Treasury may by order provide that anything which falls within a description or category specified in the order may not be admitted to the official list.

(4)   The competent authority may make rules ('listing rules') for the purposes of this Part.

(5)   In the following provisions of this Part—

'security' means anything which has been, or may be, admitted to the official list; and

'listing' means being included in the official list in accordance with this Part.

*Listing*

### 75. Applications for listing

(1)   Admission to the official list may be granted only on an application made to the competent authority in such manner as may be required by listing rules.

(2)   No application for listing may be entertained by the competent authority unless it is made by, or with the consent of, the issuer of the securities concerned.

(3)   No application for listing may be entertained by the competent authority in respect of securities which are to be issued by a body of a prescribed kind.

(4)   The competent authority may not grant an application for listing unless it is satisfied that—

(a)   the requirements of listing rules (so far as they apply to the application), and

(b)   any other requirements imposed by the authority in relation to the application, are complied with.

(5)   An application for listing may be refused if, for a reason relating to the issuer, the competent authority considers that granting it would be detrimental to the interests of investors.

(6)   An application for listing securities which are already officially listed in another EEA State may be refused if the issuer has failed to comply with any obligations to which he is subject as a result of that listing.

## 76.   Decision on application

(1)   The competent authority must notify the applicant of its decision on an application for listing—

(a)   before the end of the period of six months beginning with the date on which the application is received; or

(b)   if within that period the authority has required the applicant to provide further information in connection with the application, before the end of the period of six months beginning with the date on which that information is provided.

(2)   If the competent authority fails to comply with subsection (1), it is to be taken to have decided to refuse the application.

(3)   If the competent authority decides to grant an application for listing, it must give the applicant written notice.

(4)   If the competent authority proposes to refuse an application for listing, it must give the applicant a warning notice.

(5)   If the competent authority decides to refuse an application for listing, it must give the applicant a decision notice.

(6)   If the competent authority decides to refuse an application for listing, the applicant may refer the matter to the Tribunal.

(7)   If securities are admitted to the official list, their admission may not be called in question on the ground that any requirement or condition for their admission has not been complied with.

## 77.   Discontinuance and suspension of listing

(1)   The competent authority may, in accordance with listing rules, discontinue the listing of any securities if satisfied that there are special circumstances which preclude normal regular dealings in them.

(2)   The competent authority may, in accordance with listing rules, suspend the listing of any securities.

(3)   If securities are suspended under subsection (2) they are to be treated, for the purposes of sections 96 and 99, as still being listed.

(4)   This section applies to securities whenever they were admitted to the official list.

(5)   If the competent authority discontinues or suspends the listing of any securities, the issuer may refer the matter to the Tribunal.

## 78.   Discontinuance or suspension: procedure

(1)   A discontinuance or suspension takes effect—

(a)   immediately, if the notice under subsection (2) states that that is the case;

(b)   in any other case, on such date as may be specified in that notice.

(2)   If the competent authority—

(a)   proposes to discontinue or suspend the listing of securities, or

(b)   discontinues or suspends the listing of securities with immediate effect,

it must give the issuer of the securities written notice.

(3)   The notice must—

(a)   give details of the discontinuance or suspension;

(b)   state the competent authority's reasons for the discontinuance or suspension and for choosing the date on which it took effect or takes effect;

(c)   inform the issuer of the securities that he may make representations to the competent authority within such period as may be specified in the notice (whether or not he has referred the matter to the Tribunal);

(d)   inform him of the date on which the discontinuance or suspension took effect or will take effect; and

(e)   inform him of his right to refer the matter to the Tribunal.

(4)   The competent authority may extend the period within which representations may be made to it.

(5)   If, having considered any representations made by the issuer of the securities, the competent authority decides—

(a)   to discontinue or suspend the listing of the securities, or

(b)   if the discontinuance or suspension has taken effect, not to cancel it,

the competent authority must give the issuer of the securities written notice.

(6)   A notice given under subsection (5) must inform the issuer of the securities of his right to refer the matter to the Tribunal.

(7)   If a notice informs a person of his right to refer a matter to the Tribunal, it must give an indication of the procedure on such a reference.

(8)   If the competent authority decides—

(a)   not to discontinue or suspend the listing of the securities, or

(b)   if the discontinuance or suspension has taken effect, to cancel it,

the competent authority must give the issuer of the securities written notice.

(9)   The effect of cancelling a discontinuance is that the securities concerned are to be readmitted, without more, to the official list.

(10)   If the competent authority has suspended the listing of securities and proposes to refuse an application by the issuer of the securities for the cancellation of the suspension, it must give him a warning notice.

(11)   The competent authority must, having considered any representations made in response to the warning notice—

(a)   if it decides to refuse the application, give the issuer of the securities a decision notice;

(b)   if it grants the application, give him written notice of its decision.

(12)   If the competent authority decides to refuse an application for the cancellation of the suspension of listed securities, the applicant may refer the matter to the Tribunal.

(13)   'Discontinuance' means a discontinuance of listing under section 77(1).

(14)   'Suspension' means a suspension of listing under section 77(2).

*Listing particulars*

## 79.   Listing particulars and other documents

(1)   Listing rules may provide that securities (other than new securities) of a kind specified in the rules may not be admitted to the official list unless—

(a)   listing particulars have been submitted to, and approved by, the competent authority and published; or

(b)   in such cases as may be specified by listing rules, such document (other than listing particulars or a prospectus of a kind required by listing rules) as may be so specified has been published.

(2) 'Listing particulars' means a document in such form and containing such information as may be specified in listing rules.

(3) For the purposes of this Part, the persons responsible for listing particulars are to be determined in accordance with regulations made by the Treasury.

(4) Nothing in this section affects the competent authority's general power to make listing rules.

## 80. General duty of disclosure in listing particulars

(1) Listing particulars submitted to the competent authority under section 79 must contain all such information as investors and their professional advisers would reasonably require, and reasonably expect to find there, for the purpose of making an informed assessment of—

(a)  the assets and liabilities, financial position, profits and losses, and prospects of the issuer of the securities; and

(b)  the rights attaching to the securities.

(2) That information is required in addition to any information required by—

(a)  listing rules, or

(b)  the competent authority,

as a condition of the admission of the securities to the official list.

(3) Subsection (1) applies only to information—

(a)  within the knowledge of any person responsible for the listing particulars; or

(b)  which it would be reasonable for him to obtain by making enquiries.

(4) In determining what information subsection (1) requires to be included in listing particulars, regard must be had (in particular) to—

(a)  the nature of the securities and their issuer;

(b)  the nature of the persons likely to consider acquiring them;

(c)  the fact that certain matters may reasonably be expected to be within the knowledge of professional advisers of a kind which persons likely to acquire the securities may reasonably be expected to consult; and

(d)  any information available to investors or their professional advisers as a result of requirements imposed on the issuer of the securities by a recognised investment exchange, by listing rules or by or under any other enactment.

## 81. Supplementary listing particulars

(1) If at any time after the preparation of listing particulars which have been submitted to the competent authority under section 79 and before the commencement of dealings in the securities concerned following their admission to the official list—

(a)  there is a significant change affecting any matter contained in those particulars the inclusion of which was required by—

(i)   section 80,

(ii)  listing rules, or

(iii) the competent authority, or

(b)  a significant new matter arises, the inclusion of information in respect of which would have been so required if it had arisen when the particulars were prepared,

the issuer must, in accordance with listing rules, submit supplementary listing particulars of the change or new matter to the competent authority, for its approval and, if they are approved, publish them.

(2) 'Significant' means significant for the purpose of making an informed assessment of the kind mentioned in section 80(1).

(3)   If the issuer of the securities is not aware of the change or new matter in question, he is not under a duty to comply with subsection (1) unless he is notified of the change or new matter by a person responsible for the listing particulars.

(4)   But it is the duty of any person responsible for those particulars who is aware of such a change or new matter to give notice of it to the issuer.

(5)   Subsection (1) applies also as respects matters contained in any supplementary listing particulars previously published under this section in respect of the securities in question.

## 82.   Exemptions from disclosure

(1)   The competent authority may authorise the omission from listing particulars of any information, the inclusion of which would otherwise be required by section 80 or 81, on the ground—

(a)   that its disclosure would be contrary to the public interest;

(b)   that its disclosure would be seriously detrimental to the issuer; or

(c)   in the case of securities of a kind specified in listing rules, that its disclosure is unnecessary for persons of the kind who may be expected normally to buy or deal in securities of that kind.

(2)   But—

(a)   no authority may be granted under subsection (1)(b) in respect of essential information; and

(b)   no authority granted under subsection (1)(b) extends to any such information.

(3)   The Secretary of State or the Treasury may issue a certificate to the effect that the disclosure of any information (including information that would otherwise have to be included in listing particulars for which they are themselves responsible) would be contrary to the public interest.

(4)   The competent authority is entitled to act on any such certificate in exercising its powers under subsection (1)(a).

(5)   This section does not affect any powers of the competent authority under listing rules made as a result of section 101(2).

(6)   'Essential information' means information which a person considering acquiring securities of the kind in question would be likely to need in order not to be misled about any facts which it is essential for him to know in order to make an informed assessment.

(7)   'Listing particulars' includes supplementary listing particulars.

## 83.   Registration of listing particulars

(1)   On or before the date on which listing particulars are published as required by listing rules, a copy of the particulars must be delivered for registration to the registrar of companies.

(2)   A statement that a copy has been delivered to the registrar must be included in the listing particulars when they are published.

(3)   If there has been a failure to comply with subsection (1) in relation to listing particulars which have been published—

(a)   the issuer of the securities in question, and

(b)   any person who is a party to the publication and aware of the failure,

is guilty of an offence.

(4)   A person guilty of an offence under subsection (3) is liable—

(a)   on summary conviction, to a fine not exceeding the statutory maximum;

(b)   on conviction on indictment, to a fine.

(5)   'Listing particulars' includes supplementary listing particulars.

(6)   'The registrar of companies' means—

(a)   if the securities are, or are to be, issued by a company incorporated in Great Britain whose registered office is in England and Wales, the registrar of companies in England and Wales;

(b)   if the securities are, or are to be, issued by a company incorporated in Great Britain whose registered office is in Scotland, the registrar of companies in Scotland;

(c)   if the securities are, or are to be, issued by a company incorporated in Northern Ireland, the registrar of companies for Northern Ireland; and

(d)   in any other case, any of those registrars.

*Prospectuses*

## 84.   Prospectuses

(1)   Listing rules must provide that no new securities for which an application for listing has been made may be admitted to the official list unless a prospectus has been submitted to, and approved by, the competent authority and published.

(2)   'New securities' means securities which are to be offered to the public in the United Kingdom for the first time before admission to the official list.

(3)   'Prospectus' means a prospectus in such form and containing such information as may be specified in listing rules.

(4)   Nothing in this section affects the competent authority's general power to make listing rules.

## 85.   Publication of prospectus

(1)   If listing rules made under section 84 require a prospectus to be published before particular new securities are admitted to the official list, it is unlawful for any of those securities to be offered to the public in the United Kingdom before the required prospectus is published.

(2)   A person who contravenes subsection (1) is guilty of an offence and liable—

(a)   on summary conviction, to imprisonment for a term not exceeding three months or a fine not exceeding level 5 on the standard scale;

(b)   on conviction on indictment, to imprisonment for a term not exceeding two years or a fine, or both.

(3)   A person is not to be regarded as contravening subsection (1) merely because a prospectus does not fully comply with the requirements of listing rules as to its form or content.

(4)   But subsection (3) does not affect the question whether any person is liable to pay compensation under section 90.

(5)   Any contravention of subsection (1) is actionable, at the suit of a person who suffers loss as a result of the contravention, subject to the defences and other incidents applying to actions for breach of statutory duty.

## 86.   Application of this Part to prospectuses

(1)   The provisions of this Part apply in relation to a prospectus required by listing rules as they apply in relation to listing particulars.

(2)   In this Part—

(a)   any reference to listing particulars is to be read as including a reference to a prospectus; and

(b)   any reference to supplementary listing particulars is to be read as including a reference to a supplementary prospectus.

## 87. Approval of prospectus where no application for listing

(1)   Listing rules may provide for a prospectus to be submitted to and approved by the competent authority if—

    (a)   securities are to be offered to the public in the United Kingdom for the first time;

    (b)   no application for listing of the securities has been made under this Part; and

    (c)   the prospectus is submitted by, or with the consent of, the issuer of the securities.

(2)   'Non-listing prospectus' means a prospectus submitted to the competent authority as a result of any listing rules made under subsection (1).

(3)   Listing rules made under subsection (1) may make provision—

    (a)   as to the information to be contained in, and the form of, a non-listing prospectus; and

    (b)   as to the timing and manner of publication of a non-listing prospectus.

(4)   The power conferred by subsection (3)(b) is subject to such provision made by or under any other enactment as the Treasury may by order specify.

(5)   Schedule 9 modifies provisions of this Part as they apply in relation to non-listing prospectuses.

*Sponsors*

## 88. Sponsors

(1)   Listing rules may require a person to make arrangements with a sponsor for the performance by the sponsor of such services in relation to him as may be specified in the rules.

(2)   'Sponsor' means a person approved by the competent authority for the purposes of the rules.

(3)   Listing rules made by virtue of subsection (1) may—

    (a)   provide for the competent authority to maintain a list of sponsors;

    (b)   specify services which must be performed by a sponsor;

    (c)   impose requirements on a sponsor in relation to the provision of services or specified services;

    (d)   specify the circumstances in which a person is qualified for being approved as a sponsor.

(4)   If the competent authority proposes—

    (a)   to refuse a person's application for approval as a sponsor, or

    (b)   to cancel a person's approval as a sponsor,

it must give him a warning notice.

(5)   If, after considering any representations made in response to the warning notice, the competent authority decides—

    (a)   to grant the application for approval, or

    (b)   not to cancel the approval,

it must give the person concerned, and any person to whom a copy of the warning notice was given, written notice of its decision.

(6)   If, after considering any representations made in response to the warning notice, the competent authority decides—

    (a)   to refuse to grant the application for approval, or

    (b)   to cancel the approval,

it must give the person concerned a decision notice.

(7)   A person to whom a decision notice is given under this section may refer the matter to the Tribunal.

**89. Public censure of sponsor**

(1)  Listing rules may make provision for the competent authority, if it considers that a sponsor has contravened a requirement imposed on him by rules made as a result of section 88(3)(c), to publish a statement to that effect.

(2)  If the competent authority proposes to publish a statement it must give the sponsor a warning notice setting out the terms of the proposed statement.

(3)  If, after considering any representations made in response to the warning notice, the competent authority decides to make the proposed statement, it must give the sponsor a decision notice setting out the terms of the statement.

(4)  A sponsor to whom a decision notice is given under this section may refer the matter to the Tribunal.

*Compensation*

**90. Compensation for false or misleading particulars**

(1)  Any person responsible for listing particulars is liable to pay compensation to a person who has—

(a)  acquired securities to which the particulars apply; and

(b)  suffered loss in respect of them as a result of—

(i)  any untrue or misleading statement in the particulars; or

(ii)  the omission from the particulars of any matter required to be included by section 80 or 81.

(2)  Subsection (1) is subject to exemptions provided by Schedule 10.

(3)  If listing particulars are required to include information about the absence of a particular matter, the omission from the particulars of that information is to be treated as a statement in the listing particulars that there is no such matter.

(4)  Any person who fails to comply with section 81 is liable to pay compensation to any person who has—

(a)  acquired securities of the kind in question; and

(b)  suffered loss in respect of them as a result of the failure.

(5)  Subsection (4) is subject to exemptions provided by Schedule 10.

(6)  This section does not affect any liability which may be incurred apart from this section.

(7)  References in this section to the acquisition by a person of securities include references to his contracting to acquire them or any interest in them.

(8)  No person shall, by reason of being a promoter of a company or otherwise, incur any liability for failing to disclose information which he would not be required to disclose in listing particulars in respect of a company's securities—

(a)  if he were responsible for those particulars; or

(b)  if he is responsible for them, which he is entitled to omit by virtue of section 82.

(9)  The reference in subsection (8) to a person incurring liability includes a reference to any other person being entitled as against that person to be granted any civil remedy or to rescind or repudiate an agreement.

(10)  'Listing particulars', in subsection (1) and Schedule 10, includes supplementary listing particulars.

*Penalties*

**91. Penalties for breach of listing rules**

(1)  If the competent authority considers that—

    (a)   an issuer of listed securities, or

    (b)   an applicant for listing,

has contravened any provision of listing rules, it may impose on him a penalty of such amount as it considers appropriate.

   (2)   If, in such a case, the competent authority considers that a person who was at the material time a director of the issuer or applicant was knowingly concerned in the contravention, it may impose on him a penalty of such amount as it considers appropriate.

   (3)   If the competent authority is entitled to impose a penalty on a person under this section in respect of a particular matter it may, instead of imposing a penalty on him in respect of that matter, publish a statement censuring him.

   (4)   Nothing in this section prevents the competent authority from taking any other steps which it has power to take under this Part.

   (5)   A penalty under this section is payable to the competent authority.

   (6)   The competent authority may not take action against a person under this section after the end of the period of two years beginning with the first day on which it knew of the contravention unless proceedings against that person, in respect of the contravention, were begun before the end of that period.

   (7)   For the purposes of subsection (6)—

    (a)   the competent authority is to be treated as knowing of a contravention if it has information from which the contravention can reasonably be inferred; and

    (b)   proceedings against a person in respect of a contravention are to be treated as begun when a warning notice is given to him under section 92.

## 92.  Procedure

   (1)   If the competent authority proposes to take action against a person under section 91, it must give him a warning notice.

   (2)   A warning notice about a proposal to impose a penalty must state the amount of the proposed penalty.

   (3)   A warning notice about a proposal to publish a statement must set out the terms of the proposed statement.

   (4)   If the competent authority decides to take action against a person under section 91, it must give him a decision notice.

   (5)   A decision notice about the imposition of a penalty must state the amount of the penalty.

   (6)   A decision notice about the publication of a statement must set out the terms of the statement.

   (7)   If the competent authority decides to take action against a person under section 91, he may refer the matter to the Tribunal.

## 93.  Statement of policy

   (1)   The competent authority must prepare and issue a statement ('its policy statement') of its policy with respect to—

    (a)   the imposition of penalties under section 91; and

    (b)   the amount of penalties under that section.

   (2)   The competent authority's policy in determining what the amount of a penalty should be must include having regard to—

    (a)   the seriousness of the contravention in question in relation to the nature of the requirement contravened;

    (b)   the extent to which that contravention was deliberate or reckless; and

(c)   whether the person on whom the penalty is to be imposed is an individual.

(3)   The competent authority may at any time alter or replace its policy statement.

(4)   If its policy statement is altered or replaced, the competent authority must issue the altered or replacement statement.

(5)   In exercising, or deciding whether to exercise, its power under section 91 in the case of any particular contravention, the competent authority must have regard to any policy statement published under this section and in force at the time when the contravention in question occurred.

(6)   The competent authority must publish a statement issued under this section in the way appearing to the competent authority to be best calculated to bring it to the attention of the public.

(7)   The competent authority may charge a reasonable fee for providing a person with a copy of the statement.

(8)   The competent authority must, without delay, give the Treasury a copy of any policy statement which it publishes under this section.

### 94.  Statements of policy: procedure

(1)   Before issuing a statement under section 93, the competent authority must publish a draft of the proposed statement in the way appearing to the competent authority to be best calculated to bring it to the attention of the public.

(2)   The draft must be accompanied by notice that representations about the proposal may be made to the competent authority within a specified time.

(3)   Before issuing the proposed statement, the competent authority must have regard to any representations made to it in accordance with subsection (2).

(4)   If the competent authority issues the proposed statement it must publish an account, in general terms, of—

(a)   the representations made to it in accordance with subsection (2); and

(b)   its response to them.

(5)   If the statement differs from the draft published under subsection (1) in a way which is, in the opinion of the competent authority, significant, the competent authority must (in addition to complying with subsection (4)) publish details of the difference.

(6)   The competent authority may charge a reasonable fee for providing a person with a copy of a draft published under subsection (1).

(7)   This section also applies to a proposal to alter or replace a statement.

*Competition*

### 95.  Competition scrutiny

(1)   The Treasury may by order provide for—

(a)   regulating provisions, and

(b)   the practices of the competent authority in exercising its functions under this Part ('practices'),

to be kept under review.

(2)   Provision made as a result of subsection (1) must require the person responsible for keeping regulating provisions and practices under review to consider—

(a)   whether any regulating provision or practice has a significantly adverse effect on competition; or

(b)   whether two or more regulating provisions or practices taken together have, or a particular combination of regulating provisions and practices has, such an effect.

(3)   An order under this section may include provision corresponding to that made by any provision of Chapter III of Part X.

(4)   Subsection (3) is not to be read as in any way restricting the power conferred by subsection (1).

(5)   Subsections (6) to (8) apply for the purposes of provision made by or under this section.

(6)   Regulating provisions or practices have a significantly adverse effect on competition if—

(a)   they have, or are intended or likely to have, that effect; or

(b)   the effect that they have, or are intended or likely to have, is to require or encourage behaviour which has, or is intended or likely to have, a significantly adverse effect on competition.

(7)   If regulating provisions or practices have, or are intended or likely to have, the effect of requiring or encouraging exploitation of the strength of a market position they are to be taken to have, or be intended or be likely to have, an adverse effect on competition.

(8)   In determining whether any of the regulating provisions or practices have, or are intended or likely to have, a particular effect, it may be assumed that the persons to whom the provisions concerned are addressed will act in accordance with them.

(9)   'Regulating provisions' means—

(a)   listing rules,

(b)   general guidance given by the competent authority in connection with its functions under this Part.

*Miscellaneous*

## 96.   Obligations of issuers of listed securities

(1)   Listing rules may—

(a)   specify requirements to be complied with by issuers of listed securities; and

(b)   make provision with respect to the action that may be taken by the competent authority in the event of non-compliance.

(2)   If the rules require an issuer to publish information, they may include provision authorising the competent authority to publish it in the event of his failure to do so.

(3)   This section applies whenever the listed securities were admitted to the official list.

## 97.   Appointment by competent authority of persons to carry out investigations

(1)   Subsection (2) applies if it appears to the competent authority that there are circumstances suggesting that—

(a)   there may have been a breach of listing rules;

(b)   a person who was at the material time a director of an issuer of listed securities has been knowingly concerned in a breach of listing rules by that issuer;

(c)   a person who was at the material time a director of a person applying for the admission of securities to the official list has been knowingly concerned in a breach of listing rules by that applicant;

(d)   there may have been a contravention of section 83, 85 or 98.

(2)   The competent authority may appoint one or more competent persons to conduct an investigation on its behalf.

(3)   Part XI applies to an investigation under subsection (2) as if—

(a)   the investigator were appointed under section 167(1);

(b)   references to the investigating authority in relation to him were to the competent authority;

(c)   references to the offences mentioned in section 168 were to those mentioned in subsection (1)(d);

(d)   references to an authorised person were references to the person under investigation.

## 98.   Advertisements etc in connection with listing applications

(1)   If listing particulars are, or are to be, published in connection with an application for listing, no advertisement or other information of a kind specified by listing rules may be issued in the United Kingdom unless the contents of the advertisement or other information have been submitted to the competent authority and that authority has—

(a)   approved those contents; or

(b)   authorised the issue of the advertisement or information without such approval.

(2)   A person who contravenes subsection (1) is guilty of an offence and liable—

(a)   on summary conviction, to a fine not exceeding the statutory maximum;

(b)   on conviction on indictment, to imprisonment for a term not exceeding two years or a fine, or both.

(3)   A person who issues an advertisement or other information to the order of another person is not guilty of an offence under subsection (2) if he shows that he believed on reasonable grounds that the advertisement or information had been approved, or its issue authorised, by the competent authority.

(4)   If information has been approved, or its issue has been authorised, under this section, neither the person issuing it nor any person responsible for, or for any part of, the listing particulars incurs any civil liability by reason of any statement in or omission from the information if that information and the listing particulars, taken together, would not be likely to mislead persons of the kind likely to consider acquiring the securities in question.

(5)   The reference in subsection (4) to a person incurring civil liability includes a reference to any other person being entitled as against that person to be granted any civil remedy or to rescind or repudiate an agreement.

## 99.   Fees

(1)   Listing rules may require the payment of fees to the competent authority in respect of—

(a)   applications for listing;

(b)   the continued inclusion of securities in the official list;

(c)   applications under section 88 for approval as a sponsor; and

(d)   continued inclusion of sponsors in the list of sponsors.

(2)   In exercising its powers under subsection (1), the competent authority may set such fees as it considers will (taking account of the income it expects as the competent authority) enable it—

(a)   to meet expenses incurred in carrying out its functions under this Part or for any incidental purpose;

(b)   to maintain adequate reserves; and

(c)   in the case of the Authority, to repay the principal of, and pay any interest on, any money which it has borrowed and which has been used for the purpose of meeting expenses incurred in relation to—

(i)   its assumption of functions from the London Stock Exchange Limited in relation to the official list; and

    (ii)   its assumption of functions under this Part.

(3)   In fixing the amount of any fee which is to be payable to the competent authority, no account is to be taken of any sums which it receives, or expects to receive, by way of penalties imposed by it under this Part.

(4)   Subsection (2)(c) applies whether expenses were incurred before or after the coming into force of this Part.

(5)   Any fee which is owed to the competent authority under any provision made by or under this Part may be recovered as a debt due to it.

## 100.  Penalties

(1)   In determining its policy with respect to the amount of penalties to be imposed by it under this Part, the competent authority must take no account of the expenses which it incurs, or expects to incur, in discharging its functions under this Part.

(2)   The competent authority must prepare and operate a scheme for ensuring that the amounts paid to it by way of penalties imposed under this Part are applied for the benefit of issuers of securities admitted to the official list.

(3)   The scheme may, in particular, make different provision with respect to different classes of issuer.

(4)   Up to date details of the scheme must be set out in a document ('the scheme details').

(5)   The scheme details must be published by the competent authority in the way appearing to it to be best calculated to bring them to the attention of the public.

(6)   Before making the scheme, the competent authority must publish a draft of the proposed scheme in the way appearing to it to be best calculated to bring it to the attention of the public.

(7)   The draft must be accompanied by notice that representations about the proposals may be made to the competent authority within a specified time.

(8)   Before making the scheme, the competent authority must have regard to any representations made to it under subsection (7).

(9)   If the competent authority makes the proposed scheme, it must publish an account, in general terms, of—

    (a)   the representations made to it in accordance with subsection (7); and

    (b)   its response to them.

(10)   If the scheme differs from the draft published under subsection (6) in a way which is, in the opinion of the competent authority, significant the competent authority must (in addition to complying with subsection (9)) publish details of the difference.

(11)   The competent authority must, without delay, give the Treasury a copy of any scheme details published by it.

(12)   The competent authority may charge a reasonable fee for providing a person with a copy of—

    (a)   a draft published under subsection (6);

    (b)   scheme details.

(13)   Subsections (6) to (10) and (12) apply also to a proposal to alter or replace the scheme.

## 101.  Listing rules: general provisions

(1)   Listing rules may make different provision for different cases.

(2)   Listing rules may authorise the competent authority to dispense with or modify the application of the rules in particular cases and by reference to any circumstances.

(3)    Listing rules must be made by an instrument in writing.

(4)    Immediately after an instrument containing listing rules is made, it must be printed and made available to the public with or without payment.

(5)    A person is not to be taken to have contravened any listing rule if he shows that at the time of the alleged contravention the instrument containing the rule had not been made available as required by subsection (4).

(6)    The production of a printed copy of an instrument purporting to be made by the competent authority on which is endorsed a certificate signed by an officer of the authority authorised by it for that purpose and stating—

(a)    that the instrument was made by the authority,

(b)    that the copy is a true copy of the instrument, and

(c)    that on a specified date the instrument was made available to the public as required by subsection (4),

is evidence (or in Scotland sufficient evidence) of the facts stated in the certificate.

(7)    A certificate purporting to be signed as mentioned in subsection (6) is to be treated as having been properly signed unless the contrary is shown.

(8)    A person who wishes in any legal proceedings to rely on a rule-making instrument may require the Authority to endorse a copy of the instrument with a certificate of the kind mentioned in subsection (6).

## 102.    Exemption from liability in damages

(1)    Neither the competent authority nor any person who is, or is acting as, a member, officer or member of staff of the competent authority is to be liable in damages for anything done or omitted in the discharge, or purported discharge, of the authority's functions.

(2)    Subsection (1) does not apply—

(a)    if the act or omission is shown to have been in bad faith; or

(b)    so as to prevent an award of damages made in respect of an act or omission on the ground that the act or omission was unlawful as a result of section 6(1) of the Human Rights Act 1998.

## 103.    Interpretation of this Part

(1)    In this Part—

'application' means an application made under section 75;

'issuer', in relation to anything which is or may be admitted to the official list, has such meaning as may be prescribed by the Treasury;

'listing' has the meaning given in section 74(5);

'listing particulars' has the meaning given in section 79(2);

'listing rules' has the meaning given in section 74(4);

'new securities' has the meaning given in section 84(2);

'the official list' means the list maintained as the official list by the Authority immediately before the coming into force of section 74, as that list has effect for the time being;

'security' (except in section 74(2)) has the meaning given in section 74(5).

(2)    In relation to any function conferred on the competent authority by this Part, any reference in this Part to the competent authority is to be read as a reference to the person by whom that function is for the time being exercisable.

(3)    If, as a result of an order under Schedule 8, different functions conferred on the competent authority by this Part are exercisable by different persons, the powers conferred by section 91 are exercisable by such person as may be determined in accordance with the provisions of the order.

(4)   For the purposes of this Part, a person offers securities if, and only if, as principal—

(a)   he makes an offer which, if accepted, would give rise to a contract for their issue or sale by him or by another person with whom he has made arrangements for their issue or sale; or

(b)   he invites a person to make such an offer.

(5)   'Offer' and 'offeror' are to be read accordingly.

(6)   For the purposes of this Part, the question whether a person offers securities to the public in the United Kingdom is to be determined in accordance with Schedule 11.

(7)   For the purposes of subsection (4) 'sale' includes any disposal for valuable consideration.

## PART VII
## CONTROL OF BUSINESS TRANSFERS

### 104.   Control of business transfers

No insurance business transfer scheme or banking business transfer scheme is to have effect unless an order has been made in relation to it under section 111(1).

### 105.   Insurance business transfer schemes

(1)   A scheme is an insurance business transfer scheme if it—

(a)   satisfies one of the conditions set out in subsection (2);

(b)   results in the business transferred being carried on from an establishment of the transferee in an EEA State; and

(c)   is not an excluded scheme.

(2)   The conditions are that—

(a)   the whole or part of the business carried on in one or more member States by a UK authorised person who has permission to effect or carry out contracts of insurance ('the authorised person concerned') is to be transferred to another body ('the transferee');

(b)   the whole or part of the business, so far as it consists of reinsurance, carried on in the United Kingdom through an establishment there by an EEA firm qualifying for authorisation under Schedule 3 which has permission to effect or carry out contracts of insurance ('the authorised person concerned') is to be transferred to another body ('the transferee');

(c)   the whole or part of the business carried on in the United Kingdom by an authorised person who is neither a UK authorised person nor an EEA firm but who has permission to effect or carry out contracts of insurance ('the authorised person concerned') is to be transferred to another body ('the transferee').

(3)   A scheme is an excluded scheme for the purposes of this section if it falls within any of the following cases:

### CASE 1

Where the authorised person concerned is a friendly society.

### CASE 2

Where—

(a)   the authorised person concerned is a UK authorised person;

(b)   the business to be transferred under the scheme is business which consists of the effecting or carrying out of contracts of reinsurance in one or more EEA States other than the United Kingdom; and (c)　the scheme has been approved by a court in an EEA State other than the United Kingdom or by the host state regulator.

## CASE 3

Where—

(a)　the authorised person concerned is a UK authorised person;

(b)　the business to be transferred under the scheme is carried on in one or more countries or territories (none of which is an EEA State) and does not include policies of insurance (other than reinsurance) against risks arising in an EEA State; and

(c)　the scheme has been approved by a court in a country or territory other than an EEA State or by the authority responsible for the supervision of that business in a country or territory in which it is carried on.

## CASE 4

Where the business to be transferred under the scheme is the whole of the business of the authorised person concerned and—

(a)　consists solely of the effecting or carrying out of contracts of reinsurance, or

(b)　all the policyholders are controllers of the firm or of firms within the same group as the firm which is the transferee,

and, in either case, all of the policyholders who will be affected by the transfer have consented to it.

(4)　The parties to a scheme which falls within Case 2, 3 or 4 may apply to the court for an order sanctioning the scheme as if it were an insurance business transfer scheme.

(5)　Subsection (6) applies if the scheme involves a compromise or arrangement falling within section 427A of the Companies Act 1985 (or Article 420A of the Companies (Northern Ireland) Order 1986).

(6)　Sections 425 to 427 of that Act (or Articles 418 to 420 of that Order) have effect as modified by section 427A of that Act (or Article 420A of that Order) in relation to that compromise or arrangement.

(7)　But subsection (6) does not affect the operation of this Part in relation to the scheme.

(8)　'UK authorised person' means a body which is an authorised person and which—

(a)　is incorporated in the United Kingdom; or

(b)　is an unincorporated association formed under the law of any part of the United Kingdom.

(9)　'Establishment' means, in relation to a person, his head office or a branch of his.

## 106.　Banking business transfer schemes

(1)　A scheme is a banking business transfer scheme if it—

(a)　satisfies one of the conditions set out in subsection (2);

(b)　is one under which the whole or part of the business to be transferred includes the accepting of deposits; and

(c)　is not an excluded scheme.

(2)　The conditions are that—

(a)　the whole or part of the business carried on by a UK authorised person who has permission to accept deposits ('the authorised person concerned') is to be transferred to another body ('the transferee');

(b)　the whole or part of the business carried on in the United Kingdom by an authorised person who is not a UK authorised person but who has permission to accept deposits ('the authorised person concerned') is to be transferred to another body which will carry it on in the United Kingdom ('the transferee').

(3)  A scheme is an excluded scheme for the purposes of this section if—

(a)  the authorised person concerned is a building society or a credit union; or

(b)  the scheme is a compromise or arrangement to which section 427A(1) of the Companies Act 1985 or Article 420A of the Companies (Northern Ireland) Order 1986 (mergers and divisions of public companies) applies.

(4)  For the purposes of subsection (2)(a) it is immaterial whether or not the business to be transferred is carried on in the United Kingdom.

(5)  'UK authorised person' has the same meaning as in section 105.

(6)  'Building society' has the meaning given in the Building Societies Act 1986.

(7)  'Credit union' means a credit union within the meaning of—

(a)  the Credit Unions Act 1979;

(b)  the Credit Unions (Northern Ireland) Order 1985.

### 107.  Application for order sanctioning transfer scheme

(1)  An application may be made to the court for an order sanctioning an insurance business transfer scheme or a banking business transfer scheme.

(2)  An application may be made by—

(a)  the authorised person concerned;

(b)  the transferee; or

(c)   both.

(3)  The application must be made—

(a)  if the authorised person concerned and the transferee are registered or have their head offices in the same jurisdiction, to the court in that jurisdiction;

(b)  if the authorised person concerned and the transferee are registered or have their head offices in different jurisdictions, to the court in either jurisdiction;

(c)  if the transferee is not registered in the United Kingdom and does not have his head office there, to the court which has jurisdiction in relation to the authorised person concerned.

(4)  'Court' means—

(a)  the High Court; or

(b)  in Scotland, the Court of Session.

### 108.  Requirements on applicants

(1)  The Treasury may by regulations impose requirements on applicants under section 107.

(2)  The court may not determine an application under that section if the applicant has failed to comply with a prescribed requirement.

(3)  The regulations may, in particular, include provision—

(a)  as to the persons to whom, and periods within which, notice of an application must be given;

(b)  enabling the court to waive a requirement of the regulations in prescribed circumstances.

### 109.  Scheme reports

(1)  An application under section 107 in respect of an insurance business transfer scheme must be accompanied by a report on the terms of the scheme ('a scheme report').

(2)  A scheme report may be made only by a person—

(a)   appearing to the Authority to have the skills necessary to enable him to make a proper report; and

(b)   nominated or approved for the purpose by the Authority.

(3)   A scheme report must be made in a form approved by the Authority.

## 110.   Right to participate in proceedings

On an application under section 107, the following are also entitled to be heard—

(a)   the Authority, and

(b)   any person (including an employee of the authorised person concerned or of the transferee) who alleges that he would be adversely affected by the carrying out of the scheme.

## 111.   Sanction of the court for business transfer schemes

(1)   This section sets out the conditions which must be satisfied before the court may make an order under this section sanctioning an insurance business transfer scheme or a banking business transfer scheme.

(2)   The court must be satisfied that—

(a)   the appropriate certificates have been obtained (as to which see Parts I and II of Schedule 12);

(b)   the transferee has the authorisation required (if any) to enable the business, or part, which is to be transferred to be carried on in the place to which it is to be transferred (or will have it before the scheme takes effect).

(3)   The court must consider that, in all the circumstances of the case, it is appropriate to sanction the scheme.

## 112.   Effect of order sanctioning business transfer scheme

(1)   If the court makes an order under section 111(1), it may by that or any subsequent order make such provision (if any) as it thinks fit—

(a)   for the transfer to the transferee of the whole or any part of the undertaking concerned and of any property or liabilities of the authorised person concerned;

(b)   for the allotment or appropriation by the transferee of any shares, debentures, policies or other similar interests in the transferee which under the scheme are to be allotted or appropriated to or for any other person;

(c)   for the continuation by (or against) the transferee of any pending legal proceedings by (or against) the authorised person concerned;

(d)   with respect to such incidental, consequential and supplementary matters as are, in its opinion, necessary to secure that the scheme is fully and effectively carried out.

(2)   An order under subsection (1)(a) may—

(a)   transfer property or liabilities whether or not the authorised person concerned otherwise has the capacity to effect the transfer in question;

(b)   make provision in relation to property which was held by the authorised person concerned as trustee;

(c)   make provision as to future or contingent rights or liabilities of the authorised person concerned, including provision as to the construction of instruments (including wills) under which such rights or liabilities may arise;

(d)   make provision as to the consequences of the transfer in relation to any retirement benefits scheme (within the meaning of section 611 of the Income and Corporation Taxes Act 1988) operated by or on behalf of the authorised person concerned.

(3)   If an order under subsection (1) makes provision for the transfer of property or liabilities—

(a)  the property is transferred to and vests in, and

(b)  the liabilities are transferred to and become liabilities of,

the transferee as a result of the order.

(4)  But if any property or liability included in the order is governed by the law of any country or territory outside the United Kingdom, the order may require the authorised person concerned, if the transferee so requires, to take all necessary steps for securing that the transfer to the transferee of the property or liability is fully effective under the law of that country or territory.

(5)  Property transferred as the result of an order under subsection (1) may, if the court so directs, vest in the transferee free from any charge which is (as a result of the scheme) to cease to have effect.

(6)  An order under subsection (1) which makes provision for the transfer of property is to be treated as an instrument of transfer for the purposes of the provisions mentioned in subsection (7) and any other enactment requiring the delivery of an instrument of transfer for the registration of property.

(7)  The provisions are—

(a)  section 183(1) of the Companies Act 1985;

(b)  Article 193(1) and (2) of the Companies (Northern Ireland) Order 1986.

(8)  If the court makes an order under section 111(1) in relation to an insurance business transfer scheme, it may by that or any subsequent order make such provision (if any) as it thinks fit—

(a)  for dealing with the interests of any person who, within such time and in such manner as the court may direct, objects to the scheme;

(b)  for the dissolution, without winding up, of the authorised person concerned;

(c)  for the reduction, on such terms and subject to such conditions (if any) as it thinks fit, of the benefits payable under—

(i)  any description of policy, or

(ii)  policies generally,

entered into by the authorised person concerned and transferred as a result of the scheme.

(9)  If, in the case of an insurance business transfer scheme, the authorised person concerned is not an EEA firm, it is immaterial for the purposes of subsection (1)(a), (c) or (d) or subsection (2), (3) or (4) that the law applicable to any of the contracts of insurance included in the transfer is the law of an EEA State other than the United Kingdom.

(10)  The transferee must, if an insurance or banking business transfer scheme is sanctioned by the court, deposit two office copies of the order made under subsection (1) with the Authority within 10 days of the making of the order.

(11)  But the Authority may extend that period.

(12)  'Property' includes property, rights and powers of any description.

(13)  'Liabilities' includes duties.

(14)  'Shares' and 'debentures' have the same meaning as in—

(a)  the Companies Act 1985; or

(b)  in Northern Ireland, the Companies (Northern Ireland) Order 1986.

(15)  'Charge' includes a mortgage (or, in Scotland, a security over property).

## 113. Appointment of actuary in relation to reduction of benefits

(1)  This section applies if an order has been made under section 111(1).

(2)  The court making the order may, on the application of the Authority, appoint an independent actuary—

(a)   to investigate the business transferred under the scheme; and

(b)   to report to the Authority on any reduction in the benefits payable under policies entered into by the authorised person concerned that, in the opinion of the actuary, ought to be made.

## 114.   Rights of certain policyholders

(1)   This section applies in relation to an insurance business transfer scheme if—

(a)   the authorised person concerned is an authorised person other than an EEA firm qualifying for authorisation under Schedule 3;

(b)   the court has made an order under section 111 in relation to the scheme; and

(c)   an EEA State other than the United Kingdom is, as regards any policy included in the transfer which evidences a contract of insurance, the State of the commitment or the EEA State in which the risk is situated ('the EEA State concerned').

(2)   The court must direct that notice of the making of the order, or the execution of any instrument, giving effect to the transfer must be published by the transferee in the EEA State concerned.

(3)   A notice under subsection (2) must specify such period as the court may direct as the period during which the policyholder may exercise any right which he has to cancel the policy.

(4)   The order or instrument mentioned in subsection (2) does not bind the policyholder if—

(a)   the notice required under that subsection is not published; or

(b)   the policyholder cancels the policy during the period specified in the notice given under that subsection.

(5)   The law of the EEA State concerned governs—

(a)   whether the policyholder has a right to cancel the policy; and

(b)   the conditions, if any, subject to which any such right may be exercised.

(6)   Paragraph 6 of Schedule 12 applies for the purposes of this section as it applies for the purposes of that Schedule.

### Business transfers outside the United Kingdom

## 115.   Certificates for purposes of insurance business transfers overseas

Part III of Schedule 12 makes provision about certificates which the Authority may issue in relation to insurance business transfers taking place outside the United Kingdom.

## 116.   Effect of insurance business transfers authorised in other EEA States

(1)   This section applies if, as a result of an authorised transfer, an EEA firm falling within paragraph 5(d) of Schedule 3 transfers to another body all its rights and obligations under any UK policies.

(2)   This section also applies if, as a result of an authorised transfer, a company authorised in an EEA State other than the United Kingdom under Article 27 of the first life insurance directive, or Article 23 of the first non-life insurance directive, transfers to another body all its rights and obligations under any UK policies.

(3)   If appropriate notice of the execution of an instrument giving effect to the transfer is published, the instrument has the effect in law—

(a)   of transferring to the transferee all the transferor's rights and obligations under the UK policies to which the instrument applies, and

(b)   if the instrument so provides, of securing the continuation by or against the transferee of any legal proceedings by or against the transferor which relate to those rights and obligations.

(4)   No agreement or consent is required before subsection (3) has the effects mentioned.

(5)   'Authorised transfer' means—

(a)   in subsection (1), a transfer authorised in the home State of the EEA firm in accordance with—

(i)    Article 11 of the third life directive; or

(ii)   Article 12 of the third non-life directive; and

(b)   in subsection (2), a transfer authorised in an EEA State other than the United Kingdom in accordance with—

(i)    Article 31a of the first life directive; or

(ii)   Article 28a of the first non-life directive.

(6)   'UK policy' means a policy evidencing a contract of insurance (other than a contract of reinsurance) to which the applicable law is the law of any part of the United Kingdom.

(7)   'Appropriate notice' means—

(a)   if the UK policy evidences a contract of insurance in relation to which an EEA State other than the United Kingdom is the State of the commitment, notice given in accordance with the law of that State;

(b)   if the UK policy evidences a contract of insurance where the risk is situated in an EEA State other than the United Kingdom, notice given in accordance with the law of that EEA State;

(c)   in any other case, notice given in accordance with the applicable law.

(8)   Paragraph 6 of Schedule 12 applies for the purposes of this section as it applies for the purposes of that Schedule.

### Modifications

### 117.   Power to modify this Part

The Treasury may by regulations—

(a)   provide for prescribed provisions of this Part to have effect in relation to prescribed cases with such modifications as may be prescribed;

(b)   make such amendments to any provision of this Part as they consider appropriate for the more effective operation of that or any other provision of this Part.

### PART VIII
### PENALTIES FOR MARKET ABUSE

### Market abuse

### 118.   Market abuse

(1)   For the purposes of this Act, market abuse is behaviour (whether by one person alone or by two or more persons jointly or in concert)—

(a)   which occurs in relation to qualifying investments traded on a market to which this section applies;

(b)   which satisfies any one or more of the conditions set out in subsection (2); and

(c)   which is likely to be regarded by a regular user of that market who is aware of the behaviour as a failure on the part of the person or persons concerned to observe the standard of behaviour reasonably expected of a person in his or their position in relation to the market.

(2)   The conditions are that—

(a)   the behaviour is based on information which is not generally available to those using the market but which, if available to a regular user of the market, would or would be likely to be regarded by him as relevant when deciding the terms on which transactions in investments of the kind in question should be effected;

(b)   the behaviour is likely to give a regular user of the market a false or misleading impression as to the supply of, or demand for, or as to the price or value of, investments of the kind in question;

(c)   a regular user of the market would, or would be likely to, regard the behaviour as behaviour which would, or would be likely to, distort the market in investments of the kind in question.

(3)   The Treasury may by order prescribe (whether by name or by description)—

(a)   the markets to which this section applies; and

(b)   the investments which are qualifying investments in relation to those markets.

(4)   The order may prescribe different investments or descriptions of investment in relation to different markets or descriptions of market.

(5)   Behaviour is to be disregarded for the purposes of subsection (1) unless it occurs—

(a)   in the United Kingdom; or

(b)   in relation to qualifying investments traded on a market to which this section applies which is situated in the United Kingdom or which is accessible electronically in the United Kingdom.

(6)   For the purposes of this section, the behaviour which is to be regarded as occurring in relation to qualifying investments includes behaviour which—

(a)   occurs in relation to anything which is the subject matter, or whose price or value is expressed by reference to the price or value, of those qualifying investments; or

(b)   occurs in relation to investments (whether qualifying or not) whose subject matter is those qualifying investments.

(7)   Information which can be obtained by research or analysis conducted by, or on behalf of, users of a market is to be regarded for the purposes of this section as being generally available to them.

(8)   Behaviour does not amount to market abuse if it conforms with a rule which includes a provision to the effect that behaviour conforming with the rule does not amount to market abuse.

(9)   Any reference in this Act to a person engaged in market abuse is a reference to a person engaged in market abuse whether alone or with one or more other persons.

(10)   In this section—

'behaviour' includes action or inaction;

'investment' is to be read with section 22 and Schedule 2;

'regular user', in relation to a particular market, means a reasonable person who regularly deals on that market in investments of the kind in question.

*The code*

## 119.   The code

(1)   The Authority must prepare and issue a code containing such provisions as the Authority considers will give appropriate guidance to those determining whether or not behaviour amounts to market abuse.

(2)   The code may among other things specify—

(a)   descriptions of behaviour that, in the opinion of the Authority, amount to market abuse;

(b)   descriptions of behaviour that, in the opinion of the Authority, do not amount to market abuse;

(c)   factors that, in the opinion of the Authority, are to be taken into account in determining whether or not behaviour amounts to market abuse.

(3)  The code may make different provision in relation to persons, cases or circumstances of different descriptions.

(4)  The Authority may at any time alter or replace the code.

(5)  If the code is altered or replaced, the altered or replacement code must be issued by the Authority.

(6)  A code issued under this section must be published by the Authority in the way appearing to the Authority to be best calculated to bring it to the attention of the public.

(7)  The Authority must, without delay, give the Treasury a copy of any code published under this section.

(8)  The Authority may charge a reasonable fee for providing a person with a copy of the code.

**120.  Provisions included in the Authority's code by reference to the City Code**

(1)  The Authority may include in a code issued by it under section 119 ('the Authority's code') provision to the effect that in its opinion behaviour conforming with the City Code—

(a)  does not amount to market abuse;

(b)  does not amount to market abuse in specified circumstances; or

(c)  does not amount to market abuse if engaged in by a specified description of person.

(2)  But the Treasury's approval is required before any such provision may be included in the Authority's code.

(3)  If the Authority's code includes provision of a kind authorised by subsection (1), the Authority must keep itself informed of the way in which the Panel on Takeovers and Mergers interprets and administers the relevant provisions of the City Code.

(4)  'City Code' means the City Code on Takeovers and Mergers issued by the Panel as it has effect at the time when the behaviour occurs.

(5)  'Specified' means specified in the Authority's code.

**121.  Codes: procedure**

(1)  Before issuing a code under section 119, the Authority must publish a draft of the proposed code in the way appearing to the Authority to be best calculated to bring it to the attention of the public.

(2)  The draft must be accompanied by—

(a)  a cost benefit analysis; and

(b)  notice that representations about the proposal may be made to the Authority within a specified time.

(3)  Before issuing the proposed code, the Authority must have regard to any representations made to it in accordance with subsection (2)(b).

(4)  If the Authority issues the proposed code it must publish an account, in general terms, of—

(a)  the representations made to it in accordance with subsection (2)(b); and

(b)  its response to them.

(5)  If the code differs from the draft published under subsection (1) in a way which is, in the opinion of the Authority, significant—

(a)  the Authority must (in addition to complying with subsection (4)) publish details of the difference; and

(b)  those details must be accompanied by a cost benefit analysis.

(6)  Subsections (1) to (5) do not apply if the Authority considers that there is an urgent need to publish the code.

(7)  Neither subsection (2)(a) nor subsection (5)(b) applies if the Authority considers—

(a)   that, making the appropriate comparison, there will be no increase in costs; or

(b)   that, making that comparison, there will be an increase in costs but the increase will be of minimal significance.

(8)   The Authority may charge a reasonable fee for providing a person with a copy of a draft published under subsection (1).

(9)   This section also applies to a proposal to alter or replace a code.

(10)   'Cost benefit analysis' means an estimate of the costs together with an analysis of the benefits that will arise—

(a)   if the proposed code is issued; or

(b)   if subsection (5)(b) applies, from the code that has been issued.

(11)   'The appropriate comparison' means—

(a)   in relation to subsection (2)(a), a comparison between the overall position if the code is issued and the overall position if it is not issued;

(b)   in relation to subsection (5)(b), a comparison between the overall position after the issuing of the code and the overall position before it was issued.

### 122.   Effect of the code

(1)   If a person behaves in a way which is described (in the code in force under section 119 at the time of the behaviour) as behaviour that, in the Authority's opinion, does not amount to market abuse that behaviour of his is to be taken, for the purposes of this Act, as not amounting to market abuse.

(2)   Otherwise, the code in force under section 119 at the time when particular behaviour occurs may be relied on so far as it indicates whether or not that behaviour should be taken to amount to market abuse.

*Power to impose penalties*

### 123.   Power to impose penalties in cases of market abuse

(1)   If the Authority is satisfied that a person ('A')—

(a)   is or has engaged in market abuse, or

(b)   by taking or refraining from taking any action has required or encouraged another person or persons to engage in behaviour which, if engaged in by A, would amount to market abuse,

it may impose on him a penalty of such amount as it considers appropriate.

(2)   But the Authority may not impose a penalty on a person if, having considered any representations made to it in response to a warning notice, there are reasonable grounds for it to be satisfied that—

(a)   he believed, on reasonable grounds, that his behaviour did not fall within paragraph (a) or (b) of subsection (1), or

(b)   he took all reasonable precautions and exercised all due diligence to avoid behaving in a way which fell within paragraph (a) or (b) of that subsection.

(3)   If the Authority is entitled to impose a penalty on a person under this section it may, instead of imposing a penalty on him, publish a statement to the effect that he has engaged in market abuse.

*Statement of policy*

### 124.   Statement of policy

(1)   The Authority must prepare and issue a statement of its policy with respect to—

(a)   the imposition of penalties under section 123; and

(b)    the amount of penalties under that section.

(2)    The Authority's policy in determining what the amount of a penalty should be must include having regard to—

(a)    whether the behaviour in respect of which the penalty is to be imposed had an adverse effect on the market in question and, if it did, how serious that effect was;

(b)    the extent to which that behaviour was deliberate or reckless; and

(c)    whether the person on whom the penalty is to be imposed is an individual.

(3)    A statement issued under this section must include an indication of the circumstances in which the Authority is to be expected to regard a person as—

(a)    having a reasonable belief that his behaviour did not amount to market abuse; or

(b)    having taken reasonable precautions and exercised due diligence to avoid engaging in market abuse.

(4)    The Authority may at any time alter or replace a statement issued under this section.

(5)    If a statement issued under this section is altered or replaced, the Authority must issue the altered or replacement statement.

(6)    In exercising, or deciding whether to exercise, its power under section 123 in the case of any particular behaviour, the Authority must have regard to any statement published under this section and in force at the time when the behaviour concerned occurred.

(7)    A statement issued under this section must be published by the Authority in the way appearing to the Authority to be best calculated to bring it to the attention of the public.

(8)    The Authority may charge a reasonable fee for providing a person with a copy of a statement published under this section.

(9)    The Authority must, without delay, give the Treasury a copy of any statement which it publishes under this section.

## 125.    Statement of policy: procedure

(1)    Before issuing a statement of policy under section 124, the Authority must publish a draft of the proposed statement in the way appearing to the Authority to be best calculated to bring it to the attention of the public.

(2)    The draft must be accompanied by notice that representations about the proposal may be made to the Authority within a specified time.

(3)    Before issuing the proposed statement, the Authority must have regard to any representations made to it in accordance with subsection (2).

(4)    If the Authority issues the proposed statement it must publish an account, in general terms, of—

(a)    the representations made to it in accordance with subsection (2); and

(b)    its response to them.

(5)    If the statement differs from the draft published under subsection (1) in a way which is, in the opinion of the Authority, significant, the Authority must (in addition to complying with subsection (4)) publish details of the difference.

(6)    The Authority may charge a reasonable fee for providing a person with a copy of a draft published under subsection (1).

(7)    This section also applies to a proposal to alter or replace a statement.

*Procedure*

## 126.    Warning notices

(1)    If the Authority proposes to take action against a person under section 123, it must give him a warning notice.

(2)   A warning notice about a proposal to impose a penalty must state the amount of the proposed penalty.

(3)   A warning notice about a proposal to publish a statement must set out the terms of the proposed statement.

### 127.   Decision notices and right to refer to Tribunal

(1)   If the Authority decides to take action against a person under section 123, it must give him a decision notice.

(2)   A decision notice about the imposition of a penalty must state the amount of the penalty.

(3)   A decision notice about the publication of a statement must set out the terms of the statement.

(4)   If the Authority decides to take action against a person under section 123, that person may refer the matter to the Tribunal.

*Miscellaneous*

### 128.   Suspension of investigations

(1)   If the Authority considers it desirable or expedient because of the exercise or possible exercise of a power relating to market abuse, it may direct a recognised investment exchange or recognised clearing house—

(a)   to terminate, suspend or limit the scope of any inquiry which the exchange or clearing house is conducting under its rules; or

(b)   not to conduct an inquiry which the exchange or clearing house proposes to conduct under its rules.

(2)   A direction under this section—

(a)   must be given to the exchange or clearing house concerned by notice in writing; and

(b)   is enforceable, on the application of the Authority, by injunction or, in Scotland, by an order under section 45 of the Court of Session Act 1988.

(3)   The Authority's powers relating to market abuse are its powers—

(a)   to impose penalties under section 123; or

(b)   to appoint a person to conduct an investigation under section 168 in a case falling within subsection (2)(d) of that section.

### 129.   Power of court to impose penalty in cases of market abuse

(1)   The Authority may on an application to the court under section 381 or 383 request the court to consider whether the circumstances are such that a penalty should be imposed on the person to whom the application relates.

(2)   The court may, if it considers it appropriate, make an order requiring the person concerned to pay to the Authority a penalty of such amount as it considers appropriate.

### 130.   Guidance

(1)   The Treasury may from time to time issue written guidance for the purpose of helping relevant authorities to determine the action to be taken in cases where behaviour occurs which is behaviour—

(a)   with respect to which the power in section 123 appears to be exercisable; and

(b)   which appears to involve the commission of an offence under section 397 of this Act or Part V of the Criminal Justice Act 1993 (insider dealing).

(2)   The Treasury must obtain the consent of the Attorney General and the Secretary of State before issuing any guidance under this section.

(3)   In this section 'relevant authorities'—

(a)   in relation to England and Wales, means the Secretary of State, the Authority, the Director of the Serious Fraud Office and the Director of Public Prosecutions;

(b)   in relation to Northern Ireland, means the Secretary of State, the Authority, the Director of the Serious Fraud Office and the Director of Public Prosecutions for Northern Ireland.

(4)   Subsections (1) to (3) do not apply to Scotland.

(5)   In relation to Scotland, the Lord Advocate may from time to time, after consultation with the Treasury, issue written guidance for the purpose of helping the Authority to determine the action to be taken in cases where behaviour mentioned in subsection (1) occurs.

### 131.   Effect on transactions

The imposition of a penalty under this Part does not make any transaction void or unenforceable.

PART IX
## HEARINGS AND APPEALS

### 132.   The Financial Services and Markets Tribunal

(1)   For the purposes of this Act, there is to be a tribunal known as the Financial Services and Markets Tribunal (but referred to in this Act as 'the Tribunal').

(2)   The Tribunal is to have the functions conferred on it by or under this Act.

(3)   The Lord Chancellor may by rules make such provision as appears to him to be necessary or expedient in respect of the conduct of proceedings before the Tribunal.

(4)   Schedule 13 is to have effect as respects the Tribunal and its proceedings (but does not limit the Lord Chancellor's powers under this section).

### 133.   Proceedings: general provision

(1)   A reference to the Tribunal under this Act must be made before the end of—

(a)   the period of 28 days beginning with the date on which the decision notice or supervisory notice in question is given; or

(b)   such other period as may be specified in rules made under section 132.

(2)   Subject to rules made under section 132, the Tribunal may allow a reference to be made after the end of that period.

(3)   On a reference the Tribunal may consider any evidence relating to the subject-matter of the reference, whether or not it was available to the Authority at the material time.

(4)   On a reference the Tribunal must determine what (if any) is the appropriate action for the Authority to take in relation to the matter referred to it.

(5)   On determining a reference, the Tribunal must remit the matter to the Authority with such directions (if any) as the Tribunal considers appropriate for giving effect to its determination.

(6)   In determining a reference made as a result of a decision notice, the Tribunal may not direct the Authority to take action which the Authority would not, as a result of section 388(2), have had power to take when giving the decision notice.

(7)   In determining a reference made as a result of a supervisory notice, the Tribunal may not direct the Authority to take action which would have otherwise required the giving of a decision notice.

(8)   The Tribunal may, on determining a reference, make recommendations as to the Authority's regulating provisions or its procedures.

(9) The Authority must not take the action specified in a decision notice—

(a) during the period within which the matter to which the decision notice relates may be referred to the Tribunal; and

(b) if the matter is so referred, until the reference, and any appeal against the Tribunal's determination, has been finally disposed of.

(10) The Authority must act in accordance with the determination of, and any direction given by, the Tribunal.

(11) An order of the Tribunal may be enforced—

(a) as if it were an order of a county court; or

(b) in Scotland, as if it were an order of the Court of Session.

(12) 'Supervisory notice' has the same meaning as in section 395.

*Legal assistance before the Tribunal*

### 134. Legal assistance scheme

(1) The Lord Chancellor may by regulations establish a scheme governing the provision of legal assistance in connection with proceedings before the Tribunal.

(2) If the Lord Chancellor establishes a scheme under subsection (1), it must provide that a person is eligible for assistance only if—

(a) he falls within subsection (3); and

(b) he fulfils such other criteria (if any) as may be prescribed as a result of section 135(1)(d).

(3) A person falls within this subsection if he is an individual who has referred a matter to the Tribunal under section 127(4).

(4) In this Part of this Act 'the legal assistance scheme' means any scheme in force under subsection (1).

### 135. Provisions of the legal assistance scheme

(1) The legal assistance scheme may, in particular, make provision as to—

(a) the kinds of legal assistance that may be provided;

(b) the persons by whom legal assistance may be provided;

(c) the manner in which applications for legal assistance are to be made;

(d) the criteria on which eligibility for legal assistance is to be determined;

(e) the persons or bodies by whom applications are to be determined;

(f) appeals against refusals of applications;

(g) the revocation or variation of decisions;

(h) its administration and the enforcement of its provisions.

(2) Legal assistance under the legal assistance scheme may be provided subject to conditions or restrictions, including conditions as to the making of contributions by the person to whom it is provided.

### 136. Funding of the legal assistance scheme

(1) The Authority must pay to the Lord Chancellor such sums at such times as he may, from time to time, determine in respect of the anticipated or actual cost of legal assistance provided in connection with proceedings before the Tribunal under the legal assistance scheme.

(2) In order to enable it to pay any sum which it is obliged to pay under subsection (1), the Authority must make rules requiring the payment to it by authorised persons or any class of authorised person of specified amounts or amounts calculated in a specified way.

(3) Sums received by the Lord Chancellor under subsection (1) must be paid into the Consolidated Fund.

(4)   The Lord Chancellor must, out of money provided by Parliament fund the cost of legal assistance provided in connection with proceedings before the Tribunal under the legal assistance scheme.

(5)   Subsection (6) applies if, as respects a period determined by the Lord Chancellor, the amount paid to him under subsection (1) as respects that period exceeds the amount he has expended in that period under subsection (4).

(6)   The Lord Chancellor must—

(a)   repay, out of money provided by Parliament, the excess to the Authority; or

(b)   take the excess into account on the next occasion on which he makes a determination under subsection (1).

(7)   The Authority must make provision for any sum repaid to it under subsection (6)(a)—

(a)   to be distributed among—

(i)   the authorised persons on whom a levy was imposed in the period in question as a result of rules made under subsection (2); or

(ii)   such of those persons as it may determine;

(b)   to be applied in order to reduce any amounts which those persons, or such of them as it may determine, are or will be liable to pay to the Authority, whether under rules made under subsection (2) or otherwise; or

(c)   to be partly so distributed and partly so applied.

(8)   If the Authority considers that it is not practicable to deal with any part of a sum repaid to it under subsection (6)(a) in accordance with provision made by it as a result of subsection (7), it may, with the consent the Lord Chancellor, apply or dispose of that part of that sum in such manner as it considers appropriate.

(9)   'Specified' means specified in the rules.

*Appeals*

### 137.   Appeal on a point of law

(1)   A party to a reference to the Tribunal may with permission appeal—

(a)   to the Court of Appeal, or

(b)   in Scotland, to the Court of Session,

on a point of law arising from a decision of the Tribunal disposing of the reference.

(2)   'Permission' means permission given by the Tribunal or by the Court of Appeal or (in Scotland) the Court of Session.

(3)   If, on an appeal under subsection (1), the court considers that the decision of the Tribunal was wrong in law, it may—

(a)   remit the matter to the Tribunal for rehearing and determination by it; or

(b)   itself make a determination.

(4)   An appeal may not be brought from a decision of the Court of Appeal under subsection (3) except with the leave of—

(a)   the Court of Appeal; or

(b)   the House of Lords.

(5)   An appeal lies, with the leave of the Court of Session or the House of Lords, from any decision of the Court of Session under this section, and such leave may be given on such terms as to costs, expenses or otherwise as the Court of Session or the House of Lords may determine.

(6)   Rules made under section 132 may make provision for regulating or prescribing any matters incidental to or consequential on an appeal under this section.

PART X
RULES AND GUIDANCE

CHAPTER I
RULE-MAKING POWERS

**138.  General rule-making power**

(1)  The Authority may make such rules applying to authorised persons—

(a)  with respect to the carrying on by them of regulated activities, or

(b)  with respect to the carrying on by them of activities which are not regulated activities,

as appear to it to be necessary or expedient for the purpose of protecting the interests of consumers.

(2)  Rules made under this section are referred to in this Act as the Authority's general rules.

(3)  The Authority's power to make general rules is not limited by any other power which it has to make regulating provisions.

(4)  The Authority's general rules may make provision applying to authorised persons even though there is no relationship between the authorised persons to whom the rules will apply and the persons whose interests will be protected by the rules.

(5)  General rules may contain requirements which take into account, in the case of an authorised person who is a member of a group, any activity of another member of the group.

(6)  General rules may not—

(a)  make provision prohibiting an EEA firm from carrying on, or holding itself out as carrying on, any activity which it has permission conferred by Part II of Schedule 3 to carry on in the United Kingdom;

(b)  make provision, as respects an EEA firm, about any matter responsibility for which is, under any of the single market directives, reserved to the firm's home state regulator.

(7)  'Consumers' means persons—

(a)  who use, have used, or are or may be contemplating using, any of the services provided by—

(i)  authorised persons in carrying on regulated activities; or

(ii)  persons acting as appointed representatives;

(b)  who have rights or interests which are derived from, or are otherwise attributable to, the use of any such services by other persons; or

(c)  who have rights or interests which may be adversely affected by the use of any such services by persons acting on their behalf or in a fiduciary capacity in relation to them.

(8)  If an authorised person is carrying on a regulated activity in his capacity as a trustee, the persons who are, have been or may be beneficiaries of the trust are to be treated as persons who use, have used or are or may be contemplating using services provided by the authorised person in his carrying on of that activity.

(9)  For the purposes of subsection (7) a person who deals with an authorised person in the course of the authorised person's carrying on of a regulated activity is to be treated as using services provided by the authorised person in carrying on those activities.

**139.  Miscellaneous ancillary matters**

(1)  Rules relating to the handling of money held by an authorised person in specified circumstances ('clients' money') may—

(a)  make provision which results in that clients' money being held on trust in accordance with the rules;

(b)   treat two or more accounts as a single account for specified purposes (which may include the distribution of money held in the accounts);

(c)   authorise the retention by the authorised person of interest accruing on the clients' money; and

(d)   make provision as to the distribution of such interest which is not to be retained by him.

(2)   An institution with which an account is kept in pursuance of rules relating to the handling of clients' money does not incur any liability as constructive trustee if money is wrongfully paid from the account, unless the institution permits the payment—

(a)   with knowledge that it is wrongful; or

(b)   having deliberately failed to make enquiries in circumstances in which a reasonable and honest person would have done so.

(3)   In the application of subsection (1) to Scotland, the reference to money being held on trust is to be read as a reference to its being held as agent for the person who is entitled to call for it to be paid over to him or to be paid on his direction or to have it otherwise credited to him.

(4)   Rules may—

(a)   confer rights on persons to rescind agreements with, or withdraw offers to, authorised persons within a specified period; and

(b)   make provision, in respect of authorised persons and persons exercising those rights, for the restitution of property and the making or recovery of payments where those rights are exercised.

(5)   'Rules' means general rules.

(6)   'Specified' means specified in the rules.

## 140.   Restriction on managers of authorised unit trust schemes

(1)   The Authority may make rules prohibiting an authorised person who has permission to act as the manager of an authorised unit trust scheme from carrying on a specified activity.

(2)   Such rules may specify an activity which is not a regulated activity.

## 141.   Insurance business rules

(1)   The Authority may make rules prohibiting an authorised person who has permission to effect or carry out contracts of insurance from carrying on a specified activity.

(2)   Such rules may specify an activity which is not a regulated activity.

(3)   The Authority may make rules in relation to contracts entered into by an authorised person in the course of carrying on business which consists of the effecting or carrying out of contracts of long-term insurance.

(4)   Such rules may, in particular—

(a)   restrict the descriptions of property or indices of the value of property by reference to which the benefits under such contracts may be determined;

(b)   make provision, in the interests of the protection of policyholders, for the substitution of one description of property, or index of value, by reference to which the benefits under a contract are to be determined for another such description of property or index.

(5)   Rules made under this section are referred to in this Act as insurance business rules.

## 142.   Insurance business: regulations supplementing Authority's rules

(1)   The Treasury may make regulations for the purpose of preventing a person who is not an authorised person but who—

(a)   is a parent undertaking of an authorised person who has permission to effect or carry out contracts of insurance, and

(b)   falls within a prescribed class,

from doing anything to lessen the effectiveness of asset identification rules.

(2)   'Asset identification rules' means rules made by the Authority which require an authorised person who has permission to effect or carry out contracts of insurance to identify assets which belong to him and which are maintained in respect of a particular aspect of his business.

(3)   The regulations may, in particular, include provision—

(a)   prohibiting the payment of dividends;

(b)   prohibiting the creation of charges;

(c)   making charges created in contravention of the regulations void.

(4)   The Treasury may by regulations provide that, in prescribed circumstances, charges created in contravention of asset identification rules are void.

(5)   A person who contravenes regulations under subsection (1) is guilty of an offence and liable on summary conviction to a fine not exceeding level 5 on the standard scale.

(6)   'Charges' includes mortgages (or in Scotland securities over property).

## 143.   Endorsement of codes etc

(1)   The Authority may make rules ('endorsing rules')—

(a)   endorsing the City Code on Takeovers and Mergers issued by the Panel on Takeovers and Mergers;

(b)   endorsing the Rules Governing Substantial Acquisitions of Shares issued by the Panel.

(2)   Endorsement may be—

(a)   as respects all authorised persons; or

(b)   only as respects a specified kind of authorised person.

(3)   At any time when endorsing rules are in force, and if asked to do so by the Panel, the Authority may exercise its powers under Part IV or section 66 as if failure to comply with an endorsed provision was a ground entitling the Authority to exercise those powers.

(4)   At any time when endorsing rules are in force and if asked to do so by the Panel, the Authority may exercise its powers under Part XIII, XIV or XXV as if the endorsed provisions were rules applying to the persons in respect of whom they are endorsed.

(5)   For the purposes of subsections (3) and (4), a failure to comply with a requirement imposed, or ruling given, under an endorsed provision is to be treated as a failure to comply with the endorsed provision under which that requirement was imposed or ruling was given.

(6)   If endorsed provisions are altered, subsections (3) and (4) apply to them as altered, but only if before the alteration the Authority has notified the Panel (and has not withdrawn its notification) that it is satisfied with the Panel's consultation procedures.

(7)   'Consultation procedures' means procedures designed to provide an opportunity for persons likely to be affected by alterations to those provisions to make representations about proposed alterations to any of those provisions.

(8)   Subsections (1), (2)(d), (4), (5), (6)(a) and (12) of section 155 apply (with the necessary modifications) to a proposal to give notification of the kind mentioned in subsection (6) as they apply to a proposal to make endorsing rules.

(9)   This section applies in relation to particular provisions of the code or rules mentioned in subsection (1) as it applies to the code or the rules.

*Specific rules*

**144.  Price stabilising rules**

(1)   The Authority may make rules ('price stabilising rules') as to—

(a)   the circumstances and manner in which,

(b)   the conditions subject to which, and

(c)   the time when or the period during which,

action may be taken for the purpose of stabilising the price of investments of specified kinds.

(2)   Price stabilising rules—

(a)   are to be made so as to apply only to authorised persons;

(b)   may make different provision in relation to different kinds of investment.

(3)   The Authority may make rules which, for the purposes of section 397(5)(b), treat a person who acts or engages in conduct—

(a)   for the purpose of stabilising the price of investments, and

(b)   in conformity with such provisions corresponding to price stabilising rules and made by a body or authority outside the United Kingdom as may be specified in the rules under this subsection,

as acting, or engaging in that conduct, for that purpose and in conformity with price stabilising rules.

(4)   The Treasury may by order impose limitations on the power to make rules under this section.

(5)   Such an order may, in particular—

(a)   specify the kinds of investment in relation to which price stabilising rules may make provision;

(b)   specify the kinds of investment in relation to which rules made under subsection (3) may make provision;

(c)   provide for price stabilising rules to make provision for action to be taken for the purpose of stabilising the price of investments only in such circumstances as the order may specify;

(d)   provide for price stabilising rules to make provision for action to be taken for that purpose only at such times or during such periods as the order may specify.

(6)   If provisions specified in rules made under subsection (3) are altered, the rules continue to apply to those provisions as altered, but only if before the alteration the Authority has notified the body or authority concerned (and has not withdrawn its notification) that it is satisfied with its consultation procedures.

(7)   'Consultation procedures' has the same meaning as in section 143.

**145.  Financial promotion rules**

(1)   The Authority may make rules applying to authorised persons about the communication by them, or their approval of the communication by others, of invitations or inducements—

(a)   to engage in investment activity; or

(b)   to participate in a collective investment scheme.

(2)   Rules under this section may, in particular, make provision about the form and content of communications.

(3)   Subsection (1) applies only to communications which—

(a)   if made by a person other than an authorised person, without the approval of an authorised person, would contravene section 21(1);

(b)   may be made by an authorised person without contravening section 238(1).

(4) 'Engage in investment activity' has the same meaning as in section 21.

(5) The Treasury may by order impose limitations on the power to make rules under this section.

## 146. Money laundering rules

The Authority may make rules in relation to the prevention and detection of money laundering in connection with the carrying on of regulated activities by authorised persons.

## 147. Control of information rules

(1) The Authority may make rules ('control of information rules') about the disclosure and use of information held by an authorised person ('A').

(2) Control of information rules may—

(a) require the withholding of information which A would otherwise have to disclose to a person ('B') for or with whom A does business in the course of carrying on any regulated or other activity;

(b) specify circumstances in which A may withhold information which he would otherwise have to disclose to B;

(c) require A not to use for the benefit of B information A holds which A would otherwise have to use in that way;

(d) specify circumstances in which A may decide not to use for the benefit of B information A holds which A would otherwise have to use in that way.

*Modification or waiver*

## 148. Modification or waiver of rules

(1) This section applies in relation to the following—

(a) auditors and actuaries rules;

(b) control of information rules;

(c) financial promotion rules;

(d) general rules;

(e) insurance business rules;

(f) money laundering rules; and

(g) price stabilising rules.

(2) The Authority may, on the application or with the consent of an authorised person, direct that all or any of the rules to which this section applies—

(a) are not to apply to the authorised person; or

(b) are to apply to him with such modifications as may be specified in the direction.

(3) An application must be made in such manner as the Authority may direct.

(4) The Authority may not give a direction unless it is satisfied that—

(a) compliance by the authorised person with the rules, or with the rules as unmodified, would be unduly burdensome or would not achieve the purpose for which the rules were made; and

(b) the direction would not result in undue risk to persons whose interests the rules are intended to protect.

(5) A direction may be given subject to conditions.

(6) Unless it is satisfied that it is inappropriate or unnecessary to do so, a direction must be published by the Authority in such a way as it thinks most suitable for bringing the direction to the attention of—

(a) those likely to be affected by it; and

(b)　others who may be likely to make an application for a similar direction.

(7)　In deciding whether it is satisfied as mentioned in subsection (6), the Authority must—

(a)　take into account whether the direction relates to a rule contravention of which is actionable in accordance with section 150;

(b)　consider whether its publication would prejudice, to an unreasonable degree, the commercial interests of the authorised person concerned or any other member of his immediate group; and

(c)　consider whether its publication would be contrary to an international obligation of the United Kingdom.

(8)　For the purposes of paragraphs (b) and (c) of subsection (7), the Authority must consider whether it would be possible to publish the direction without either of the consequences mentioned in those paragraphs by publishing it without disclosing the identity of the authorised person concerned.

(9)　The Authority may—

(a)　revoke a direction; or

(b)　vary it on the application, or with the consent, of the authorised person to whom it relates.

(10)　'Direction' means a direction under subsection (2).

(11)　'Immediate group', in relation to an authorised person ('A'), means—

(a)　A;

(b)　a parent undertaking of A;

(c)　a subsidiary undertaking of A;

(d)　a subsidiary undertaking of a parent undertaking of A;

(e)　a parent undertaking of a subsidiary undertaking of A.

*Contravention of rules*

## 149.　Evidential provisions

(1)　If a particular rule so provides, contravention of the rule does not give rise to any of the consequences provided for by other provisions of this Act.

(2)　A rule which so provides must also provide—

(a)　that contravention may be relied on as tending to establish contravention of such other rule as may be specified; or

(b)　that compliance may be relied on as tending to establish compliance with such other rule as may be specified.

(3)　A rule may include the provision mentioned in subsection (1) only if the Authority considers that it is appropriate for it also to include the provision required by subsection (2).

## 150.　Actions for damages

(1)　A contravention by an authorised person of a rule is actionable at the suit of a private person who suffers loss as a result of the contravention, subject to the defences and other incidents applying to actions for breach of statutory duty.

(2)　If rules so provide, subsection (1) does not apply to contravention of a specified provision of those rules.

(3)　In prescribed cases, a contravention of a rule which would be actionable at the suit of a private person is actionable at the suit of a person who is not a private person, subject to the defences and other incidents applying to actions for breach of statutory duty.

(4)   In subsections (1) and (3) 'rule' does not include—
(a)   listing rules; or
(b)   a rule requiring an authorised person to have or maintain financial resources.
(5)   'Private person' has such meaning as may be prescribed.

### 151.   Limits on effect of contravening rules

(1)   A person is not guilty of an offence by reason of a contravention of a rule made by the Authority.
(2)   No such contravention makes any transaction void or unenforceable.

*Procedural provisions*

### 152.   Notification of rules to the Treasury

(1)   If the Authority makes any rules, it must give a copy to the Treasury without delay.
(2)   If the Authority alters or revokes any rules, it must give written notice to the Treasury without delay.
(3)   Notice of an alteration must include details of the alteration.

### 153.   Rule-making instruments

(1)   Any power conferred on the Authority to make rules is exercisable in writing.
(2)   An instrument by which rules are made by the Authority ('a rule-making instrument') must specify the provision under which the rules are made.
(3)   To the extent to which a rule-making instrument does not comply with subsection (2), it is void.
(4)   A rule-making instrument must be published by the Authority in the way appearing to the Authority to be best calculated to bring it to the attention of the public.
(5)   The Authority may charge a reasonable fee for providing a person with a copy of a rule-making instrument.
(6)   A person is not to be taken to have contravened any rule made by the Authority if he shows that at the time of the alleged contravention the rule-making instrument concerned had not been made available in accordance with this section.

### 154.   Verification of rules

(1)   The production of a printed copy of a rule-making instrument purporting to be made by the Authority—
(a)   on which is endorsed a certificate signed by a member of the Authority's staff authorised by it for that purpose, and
(b)   which contains the required statements,
is evidence (or in Scotland sufficient evidence) of the facts stated in the certificate.
(2)   The required statements are—
(a)   that the instrument was made by the Authority;
(b)   that the copy is a true copy of the instrument; and
(c)   that on a specified date the instrument was made available to the public in accordance with section 153(4).
(3)   A certificate purporting to be signed as mentioned in subsection (1) is to be taken to have been properly signed unless the contrary is shown.
(4)   A person who wishes in any legal proceedings to rely on a rule-making instrument may require the Authority to endorse a copy of the instrument with a certificate of the kind mentioned in subsection (1).

**155.  Consultation**

(1)  If the Authority proposes to make any rules, it must publish a draft of the proposed rules in the way appearing to it to be best calculated to bring them to the attention of the public.

(2)  The draft must be accompanied by—

(a)  a cost benefit analysis;

(b)  an explanation of the purpose of the proposed rules;

(c)  an explanation of the Authority's reasons for believing that making the proposed rules is compatible with its general duties under section 2; and

(d)  notice that representations about the proposals may be made to the Authority within a specified time.

(3)  In the case of a proposal to make rules under a provision mentioned in subsection (9), the draft must also be accompanied by details of the expected expenditure by reference to which the proposal is made.

(4)  Before making the proposed rules, the Authority must have regard to any representations made to it in accordance with subsection (2)(d).

(5)  If the Authority makes the proposed rules, it must publish an account, in general terms, of—

(a)  the representations made to it in accordance with subsection (2)(d); and

(b)  its response to them.

(6)  If the rules differ from the draft published under subsection (1) in a way which is, in the opinion of the Authority, significant—

(a)  the Authority must (in addition to complying with subsection (5)) publish details of the difference; and

(b)  those details must be accompanied by a cost benefit analysis.

(7)  Subsections (1) to (6) do not apply if the Authority considers that the delay involved in complying with them would be prejudicial to the interests of consumers.

(8)  Neither subsection (2)(a) nor subsection (6)(b) applies if the Authority considers—

(a)  that, making the appropriate comparison, there will be no increase in costs; or

(b)  that, making that comparison, there will be an increase in costs but the increase will be of minimal significance.

(9)  Neither subsection (2)(a) nor subsection (6)(b) requires a cost benefit analysis to be carried out in relation to rules made under—

(a)  section 136(2);

(b)  subsection (1) of section 213 as a result of subsection (4) of that section;

(c)  section 234;

(d)  paragraph 17 of Schedule 1.

(10)  'Cost benefit analysis' means an estimate of the costs together with an analysis of the benefits that will arise—

(a)  if the proposed rules are made; or

(b)  if subsection (6) applies, from the rules that have been made.

(11)  'The appropriate comparison' means—

(a)  in relation to subsection (2)(a), a comparison between the overall position if the rules are made and the overall position if they are not made;

(b)  in relation to subsection (6)(b), a comparison between the overall position after the making of the rules and the overall position before they were made.

(12)  The Authority may charge a reasonable fee for providing a person with a copy of a draft published under subsection (1).

**156.  General supplementary powers**

(1)  Rules made by the Authority may make different provision for different cases and may, in particular, make different provision in respect of different descriptions of authorised person, activity or investment.

(2)  Rules made by the Authority may contain such incidental, supplemental, consequential and transitional provision as the Authority considers appropriate.

## CHAPTER II
## GUIDANCE

**157.  Guidance**

(1)  The Authority may give guidance consisting of such information and advice as it considers appropriate—

  (a)  with respect to the operation of this Act and of any rules made under it;

  (b)  with respect to any matters relating to functions of the Authority;

  (c)  for the purpose of meeting the regulatory objectives;

  (d)  with respect to any other matters about which it appears to the Authority to be desirable to give information or advice.

(2)  The Authority may give financial or other assistance to persons giving information or advice of a kind which the Authority could give under this section.

(3)  If the Authority proposes to give guidance to regulated persons generally, or to a class of regulated person, in relation to rules to which those persons are subject, subsections (1), (2) and (4) to (10) of section 155 apply to the proposed guidance as they apply to proposed rules.

(4)  The Authority may—

  (a)  publish its guidance;

  (b)  offer copies of its published guidance for sale at a reasonable price; and

  (c)  if it gives guidance in response to a request made by any person, make a reasonable charge for that guidance.

(5)  In this Chapter, references to guidance given by the Authority include references to any recommendation made by the Authority to persons generally, to regulated persons generally or to any class of regulated person.

(6)  'Regulated person' means any—

  (a)  authorised person;

  (b)  person who is otherwise subject to rules made by the Authority.

**158.  Notification of guidance to the Treasury**

(1)  On giving any general guidance, the Authority must give the Treasury a copy of the guidance without delay.

(2)  If the Authority alters any of its general guidance, it must give written notice to the Treasury without delay.

(3)  The notice must include details of the alteration.

(4)  If the Authority revokes any of its general guidance, it must give written notice to the Treasury without delay.

(5)  'General guidance' means guidance given by the Authority under section 157 which is—

  (a)  given to persons generally, to regulated persons generally or to a class of regulated person;

   (b)   intended to have continuing effect; and

   (c)   given in writing or other legible form.

  (6)   'Regulated person' has the same meaning as in section 157.

## CHAPTER III
## COMPETITION SCRUTINY

### 159.  Interpretation

  (1)   In this Chapter—

'Director' means the Director General of Fair Trading;

'practices', in relation to the Authority, means practices adopted by the Authority in the exercise of functions under this Act;

'regulating provisions' means any—

     (a)   rules;

     (b)   general guidance (as defined by section 158(5));

     (c)   statement issued by the Authority under section 64;

     (d)   code issued by the Authority under section 64 or 119.

  (2)   For the purposes of this Chapter, regulating provisions or practices have a significantly adverse effect on competition if—

    (a)   they have, or are intended or likely to have, that effect; or

    (b)   the effect that they have, or are intended or likely to have, is to require or encourage behaviour which has, or is intended or likely to have, a significantly adverse effect on competition.

  (3)   If regulating provisions or practices have, or are intended or likely to have, the effect of requiring or encouraging exploitation of the strength of a market position they are to be taken, for the purposes of this Chapter, to have an adverse effect on competition.

  (4)   In determining under this Chapter whether any of the regulating provisions have, or are likely to have, a particular effect, it may be assumed that the persons to whom the provisions concerned are addressed will act in accordance with them.

### 160.  Reports by Director General of Fair Trading

  (1)   The Director must keep the regulating provisions and the Authority's practices under review.

  (2)   If at any time the Director considers that—

    (a)   a regulating provision or practice has a significantly adverse effect on competition, or

    (b)   two or more regulating provisions or practices taken together, or a particular combination of regulating provisions and practices, have such an effect,

he must make a report to that effect.

  (3)   If at any time the Director considers that—

    (a)   a regulating provision or practice does not have a significantly adverse effect on competition, or

    (b)   two or more regulating provisions or practices taken together, or a particular combination of regulating provisions and practices, do not have any such effect,

he may make a report to that effect.

  (4)   A report under subsection (2) must include details of the adverse effect on competition.

  (5)   If the Director makes a report under subsection (2) he must—

(a)    send a copy of it to the Treasury, the Competition Commission and the Authority; and

(b)    publish it in the way appearing to him to be best calculated to bring it to the attention of the public.

(6)    If the Director makes a report under subsection (3)—

(a)    he must send a copy of it to the Treasury, the Competition Commission and the Authority; and

(b)    he may publish it.

(7)    Before publishing a report under this section the Director must, so far as practicable, exclude any matter which relates to the private affairs of a particular individual the publication of which, in the opinion of the Director, would or might seriously and prejudicially affect his interests.

(8)    Before publishing such a report the Director must, so far as practicable, exclude any matter which relates to the affairs of a particular body the publication of which, in the opinion of the Director, would or might seriously and prejudicially affect its interests.

(9)    Subsections (7) and (8) do not apply in relation to copies of a report which the Director is required to send under subsection (5)(a) or (6)(a).

(10)    For the purposes of the law of defamation, absolute privilege attaches to any report of the Director under this section.

## 161.    Power of Director to request information

(1)    For the purpose of investigating any matter with a view to its consideration under section 160, the Director may exercise the powers conferred on him by this section.

(2)    The Director may by notice in writing require any person to produce to him or to a person appointed by him for the purpose, at a time and place specified in the notice, any document which—

(a)    is specified or described in the notice; and

(b)    is a document in that person's custody or under his control.

(3)    The Director may by notice in writing—

(a)    require any person carrying on any business to provide him with such information as may be specified or described in the notice; and

(b)    specify the time within which, and the manner and form in which, any such information is to be provided.

(4)    A requirement may be imposed under subsection (2) or (3)(a) only in respect of documents or information which relate to any matter relevant to the investigation.

(5)    If a person ('the defaulter') refuses, or otherwise fails, to comply with a notice under this section, the Director may certify that fact in writing to the court and the court may enquire into the case.

(6)    If, after hearing any witness who may be produced against or on behalf of the defaulter and any statement which may be offered in defence, the court is satisfied that the defaulter did not have a reasonable excuse for refusing or otherwise failing to comply with the notice, the court may deal with the defaulter as if he were in contempt.

(7)    'Court' means—

(a)    the High Court; or

(b)    in relation to Scotland, the Court of Session.

## 162.    Consideration by Competition Commission

(1)    If the Director—

    (a)   makes a report under section 160(2), or

    (b)   asks the Commission to consider a report that he has made under section 160(3), the Commission must investigate the matter.

    (2)   The Commission must then make its own report on the matter unless it considers that, as a result of a change of circumstances, no useful purpose would be served by a report.

    (3)   If the Commission decides in accordance with subsection (2) not to make a report, it must make a statement setting out the change of circumstances which resulted in that decision.

    (4)   A report made under this section must state the Commission's conclusion as to whether—

    (a)   the regulating provision or practice which is the subject of the report has a significantly adverse effect on competition; or

    (b)   the regulating provisions or practices, or combination of regulating provisions and practices, which are the subject of the report have such an effect.

    (5)   A report under this section stating the Commission's conclusion that there is a significantly adverse effect on competition must also—

    (a)   state whether the Commission considers that that effect is justified; and

    (b)   if it states that the Commission considers that it is not justified, state its conclusion as to what action, if any, ought to be taken by the Authority.

    (6)   Subsection (7) applies whenever the Commission is considering, for the purposes of this section, whether a particular adverse effect on competition is justified.

    (7)   The Commission must ensure, so far as that is reasonably possible, that the conclusion it reaches is compatible with the functions conferred, and obligations imposed, on the Authority by or under this Act.

    (8)   A report under this section must contain such an account of the Commission's reasons for its conclusions as is expedient, in the opinion of the Commission, for facilitating proper understanding of them.

    (9)   Schedule 14 supplements this section.

    (10)   If the Commission makes a report under this section it must send a copy to the Treasury, the Authority and the Director.

## 163.  Role of the Treasury

    (1)   This section applies if the Competition Commission makes a report under section 162(2) which states its conclusion that there is a significantly adverse effect on competition.

    (2)   If the Commission's conclusion, as stated in the report, is that the adverse effect on competition is not justified, the Treasury must give a direction to the Authority requiring it to take such action as may be specified in the direction.

    (3)   But subsection (2) does not apply if the Treasury consider—

    (a)   that, as a result of action taken by the Authority in response to the Commission's report, it is unnecessary for them to give a direction; or

    (b)   that the exceptional circumstances of the case make it inappropriate or unnecessary for them to do so.

    (4)   In considering the action to be specified in a direction under subsection (2), the Treasury must have regard to any conclusion of the Commission included in the report because of section 162(5)(b).

    (5)   Subsection (6) applies if—

    (a)   the Commission's conclusion, as stated in its report, is that the adverse effect on competition is justified; but

(b)   the Treasury consider that the exceptional circumstances of the case require them to act.

(6)   The Treasury may give a direction to the Authority requiring it to take such action—

(a)   as they consider to be necessary in the light of the exceptional circumstances of the case; and

(b)   as may be specified in the direction.

(7)   The Authority may not be required as a result of this section to take any action—

(a)   that it would not have power to take in the absence of a direction under this section; or

(b)   that would otherwise be incompatible with any of the functions conferred, or obligations imposed, on it by or under this Act.

(8)   Subsection (9) applies if the Treasury are considering—

(a)   whether subsection (2) applies and, if so, what action is to be specified in a direction under that subsection; or

(b)   whether to give a direction under subsection (6).

(9)   The Treasury must—

(a)   do what they consider appropriate to allow the Authority, and any other person appearing to the Treasury to be affected, an opportunity to make representations; and

(b)   have regard to any such representations.

(10)   If, in reliance on subsection (3)(a) or (b), the Treasury decline to act under subsection (2), they must make a statement to that effect, giving their reasons.

(11)   If the Treasury give a direction under this section they must make a statement giving—

(a)   details of the direction; and

(b)   if the direction is given under subsection (6), their reasons for giving it.

(12)   The Treasury must—

(a)   publish any statement made under this section in the way appearing to them best calculated to bring it to the attention of the public; and

(b)   lay a copy of it before Parliament.

## 164.   The Competition Act 1998

(1)   The Chapter I prohibition does not apply to an agreement the parties to which consist of or include—

(a)   an authorised person, or

(b)   a person who is otherwise subject to the Authority's regulating provisions,

to the extent to which the agreement consists of provisions the inclusion of which in the agreement is encouraged by any of the Authority's regulating provisions.

(2)   The Chapter I prohibition does not apply to the practices of an authorised person or a person who is otherwise subject to the regulating provisions to the extent to which the practices are encouraged by any of the Authority's regulating provisions.

(3)   The Chapter II prohibition does not apply to conduct of—

(a)   an authorised person, or

(b)   a person who is otherwise subject to the Authority's regulating provisions,

to the extent to which the conduct is encouraged by any of the Authority's regulating provisions.

(4)   'The Chapter I prohibition' means the prohibition imposed by section 2(1) of the Competition Act 1998.

(5)   'The Chapter II prohibition' means the prohibition imposed by section 18(1) of that Act.

## PART XI
## INFORMATION GATHERING AND INVESTIGATIONS

*Powers to gather information*

**165. Authority's power to require information**

(1) The Authority may, by notice in writing given to an authorised person, require him—

(a) to provide specified information or information of a specified description; or

(b) to produce specified documents or documents of a specified description.

(2) The information or documents must be provided or produced—

(a) before the end of such reasonable period as may be specified; and

(b) at such place as may be specified.

(3) An officer who has written authorisation from the Authority to do so may require an authorised person without delay—

(a) to provide the officer with specified information or information of a specified description; or

(b) to produce to him specified documents or documents of a specified description.

(4) This section applies only to information and documents reasonably required in connection with the exercise by the Authority of functions conferred on it by or under this Act.

(5) The Authority may require any information provided under this section to be provided in such form as it may reasonably require.

(6) The Authority may require—

(a) any information provided, whether in a document or otherwise, to be verified in such manner, or

(b) any document produced to be authenticated in such manner,

as it may reasonably require.

(7) The powers conferred by subsections (1) and (3) may also be exercised to impose requirements on—

(a) a person who is connected with an authorised person;

(b) an operator, trustee or depositary of a scheme recognised under section 270 or 272 who is not an authorised person;

(c) a recognised investment exchange or recognised clearing house.

(8) 'Authorised person' includes a person who was at any time an authorised person but who has ceased to be an authorised person.

(9) 'Officer' means an officer of the Authority and includes a member of the Authority's staff or an agent of the Authority.

(10) 'Specified' means—

(a) in subsections (1) and (2), specified in the notice; and

(b) in subsection (3), specified in the authorisation.

(11) For the purposes of this section, a person is connected with an authorised person ('A') if he is or has at any relevant time been—

(a) a member of A's group;

(b) a controller of A;

(c) any other member of a partnership of which A is a member; or

(d) in relation to A, a person mentioned in Part I of Schedule 15.

**166. Reports by skilled persons**

(1) The Authority may, by notice in writing given to a person to whom subsection (2) applies, require him to provide the Authority with a report on any matter about which the

Authority has required or could require the provision of information or production of documents under section 165.

(2) This subsection applies to—

   (a) an authorised person ('A'),

   (b) any other member of A's group,

   (c) a partnership of which A is a member, or

   (d) a person who has at any relevant time been a person falling within paragraph (a), (b) or (c),

who is, or was at the relevant time, carrying on a business.

(3) The Authority may require the report to be in such form as may be specified in the notice.

(4) The person appointed to make a report required by subsection (1) must be a person—

   (a) nominated or approved by the Authority; and

   (b) appearing to the Authority to have the skills necessary to make a report on the matter concerned.

(5) It is the duty of any person who is providing (or who at any time has provided) services to a person to whom subsection (2) applies in relation to a matter on which a report is required under subsection (1) to give a person appointed to provide such a report all such assistance as the appointed person may reasonably require.

(6) The obligation imposed by subsection (5) is enforceable, on the application of the Authority, by an injunction or, in Scotland, by an order for specific performance under section 45 of the Court of Session Act 1988.

*Appointment of investigators*

**167. Appointment of persons to carry out general investigations**

(1) If it appears to the Authority or the Secretary of State ('the investigating authority') that there is good reason for doing so, the investigating authority may appoint one or more competent persons to conduct an investigation on its behalf into—

   (a) the nature, conduct or state of the business of an authorised person or of an appointed representative;

   (b) a particular aspect of that business; or

   (c) the ownership or control of an authorised person.

(2) If a person appointed under subsection (1) thinks it necessary for the purposes of his investigation, he may also investigate the business of a person who is or has at any relevant time been—

   (a) a member of the group of which the person under investigation ('A') is part; or

   (b) a partnership of which A is a member.

(3) If a person appointed under subsection (1) decides to investigate the business of any person under subsection (2) he must give that person written notice of his decision.

(4) The power conferred by this section may be exercised in relation to a former authorised person (or appointed representative) but only in relation to—

   (a) business carried on at any time when he was an authorised person (or appointed representative); or

   (b) the ownership or control of a former authorised person at any time when he was an authorised person.

(5) 'Business' includes any part of a business even if it does not consist of carrying on regulated activities.

## 168.  Appointment of persons to carry out investigations in particular cases

(1)  Subsection (3) applies if it appears to an investigating authority that there are circumstances suggesting that—

(a)  a person may have contravened any regulation made under section 142; or

(b)  a person may be guilty of an offence under section 177, 191, 346 or 398(1) or under Schedule 4.

(2)  Subsection (3) also applies if it appears to an investigating authority that there are circumstances suggesting that—

(a)  an offence under section 24(1) or 397 or under Part V of the Criminal Justice Act 1993 may have been committed;

(b)  there may have been a breach of the general prohibition;

(c)  there may have been a contravention of section 21 or 238; or

(d)  market abuse may have taken place.

(3)  The investigating authority may appoint one or more competent persons to conduct an investigation on its behalf.

(4)  Subsection (5) applies if it appears to the Authority that there are circumstances suggesting that—

(a)  a person may have contravened section 20;

(b)  a person may be guilty of an offence under prescribed regulations relating to money laundering;

(c)  an authorised person may have contravened a rule made by the Authority;

(d)  an individual may not be a fit and proper person to perform functions in relation to a regulated activity carried on by an authorised or exempt person;

(e)  an individual may have performed or agreed to perform a function in breach of a prohibition order;

(f)  an authorised or exempt person may have failed to comply with section 56(6);

(g)  an authorised person may have failed to comply with section 59(1) or (2);

(h)  a person in relation to whom the Authority has given its approval under section 59 may not be a fit and proper person to perform the function to which that approval relates; or

(i)  a person may be guilty of misconduct for the purposes of section 66.

(5)  The Authority may appoint one or more competent persons to conduct an investigation on its behalf.

(6)  'Investigating authority' means the Authority or the Secretary of State.

*Assistance to overseas regulators*

## 169.  Investigations etc in support of overseas regulator

(1)  At the request of an overseas regulator, the Authority may—

(a)  exercise the power conferred by section 165; or

(b)  appoint one or more competent persons to investigate any matter.

(2)  An investigator has the same powers as an investigator appointed under section 168(3) (as a result of subsection (1) of that section).

(3)  If the request has been made by a competent authority in pursuance of any Community obligation the Authority must, in deciding whether or not to exercise its investigative power, consider whether its exercise is necessary to comply with any such obligation.

(4)  In deciding whether or not to exercise its investigative power, the Authority may take into account in particular—

(a)   whether in the country or territory of the overseas regulator concerned, corresponding assistance would be given to a United Kingdom regulatory authority;

(b)   whether the case concerns the breach of a law, or other requirement, which has no close parallel in the United Kingdom or involves the assertion of a jurisdiction not recognised by the United Kingdom;

(c)   the seriousness of the case and its importance to persons in the United Kingdom;

(d)   whether it is otherwise appropriate in the public interest to give the assistance sought.

(5)   The Authority may decide that it will not exercise its investigative power unless the overseas regulator undertakes to make such contribution towards the cost of its exercise as the Authority considers appropriate.

(6)   Subsections (4) and (5) do not apply if the Authority considers that the exercise of its investigative power is necessary to comply with a Community obligation.

(7)   If the Authority has appointed an investigator in response to a request from an overseas regulator, it may direct the investigator to permit a representative of that regulator to attend, and take part in, any interview conducted for the purposes of the investigation.

(8)   A direction under subsection (7) is not to be given unless the Authority is satisfied that any information obtained by an overseas regulator as a result of the interview will be subject to safeguards equivalent to those contained in Part XXIII.

(9)   The Authority must prepare a statement of its policy with respect to the conduct of interviews in relation to which a direction under subsection (7) has been given.

(10)   The statement requires the approval of the Treasury.

(11)   If the Treasury approve the statement, the Authority must publish it.

(12)   No direction may be given under subsection (7) before the statement has been published.

(13)   'Overseas regulator' has the same meaning as in section 195.

(14)   'Investigative power' means one of the powers mentioned in subsection (1).

(15)   'Investigator' means a person appointed under subsection (1)(b).

*Conduct of investigations*

**170.   Investigations: general**

(1)   This section applies if an investigating authority appoints one or more competent persons ('investigators') under section 167 or 168(3) or (5) to conduct an investigation on its behalf.

(2)   The investigating authority must give written notice of the appointment of an investigator to the person who is the subject of the investigation ('the person under investigation').

(3)   Subsections (2) and (9) do not apply if —

(a)   the investigator is appointed as a result of section 168(1) or (4) and the investigating authority believes that the notice required by subsection (2) or (9) would be likely to result in the investigation being frustrated; or

(b)   the investigator is appointed as a result of subsection (2) of section 168.

(4)   A notice under subsection (2) must—

(a)   specify the provisions under which, and as a result of which, the investigator was appointed; and

(b)   state the reason for his appointment.

(5)   Nothing prevents the investigating authority from appointing a person who is a member of its staff as an investigator.

(6)   An investigator must make a report of his investigation to the investigating authority.

(7)   The investigating authority may, by a direction to an investigator, control—

(a)   the scope of the investigation;

(b)   the period during which the investigation is to be conducted;

(c)   the conduct of the investigation; and

(d)   the reporting of the investigation.

(8)   A direction may, in particular—

(a)   confine the investigation to particular matters;

(b)   extend the investigation to additional matters;

(c)   require the investigator to discontinue the investigation or to take only such steps as are specified in the direction;

(d)   require the investigator to make such interim reports as are so specified.

(9)   If there is a change in the scope or conduct of the investigation and, in the opinion of the investigating authority, the person subject to investigation is likely to be significantly prejudiced by not being made aware of it, that person must be given written notice of the change.

(10)   'Investigating authority', in relation to an investigator, means—

(a)   the Authority, if the Authority appointed him;

(b)   the Secretary of State, if the Secretary of State appointed him.

## 171.   Powers of persons appointed under section 167

(1)   An investigator may require the person who is the subject of the investigation ('the person under investigation') or any person connected with the person under investigation—

(a)   to attend before the investigator at a specified time and place and answer questions; or

(b)   otherwise to provide such information as the investigator may require.

(2)   An investigator may also require any person to produce at a specified time and place any specified documents or documents of a specified description.

(3)   A requirement under subsection (1) or (2) may be imposed only so far as the investigator concerned reasonably considers the question, provision of information or production of the document to be relevant to the purposes of the investigation.

(4)   For the purposes of this section and section 172, a person is connected with the person under investigation ('A') if he is or has at any relevant time been—

(a)   a member of A's group;

(b)   a controller of A;

(c)   a partnership of which A is a member; or

(d)   in relation to A, a person mentioned in Part I or II of Schedule 15.

(5)   'Investigator' means a person conducting an investigation under section 167.

(6)   'Specified' means specified in a notice in writing.

## 172.   Additional power of persons appointed as a result of section 168(1) or (4)

(1)   An investigator has the powers conferred by section 171.

(2)   An investigator may also require a person who is neither the subject of the investigation ('the person under investigation') nor a person connected with the person under investigation—

(a)   to attend before the investigator at a specified time and place and answer questions; or

(b)   otherwise to provide such information as the investigator may require for the purposes of the investigation.

(3)   A requirement may only be imposed under subsection (2) if the investigator is satisfied that the requirement is necessary or expedient for the purposes of the investigation.

(4)   'Investigator' means a person appointed as a result of subsection (1) or (4) of section 168.

(5)   'Specified' means specified in a notice in writing.

## 173.   Powers of persons appointed as a result of section 168(2)

(1)   Subsections (2) to (4) apply if an investigator considers that any person ('A') is or may be able to give information which is or may be relevant to the investigation.

(2)   The investigator may require A—

(a)   to attend before him at a specified time and place and answer questions; or

(b)   otherwise to provide such information as he may require for the purposes of the investigation.

(3)   The investigator may also require A to produce at a specified time and place any specified documents or documents of a specified description which appear to the investigator to relate to any matter relevant to the investigation.

(4)   The investigator may also otherwise require A to give him all assistance in connection with the investigation which A is reasonably able to give.

(5)   'Investigator' means a person appointed under subsection (3) of section 168 (as a result of subsection (2) of that section).

## 174.   Admissibility of statements made to investigators

(1)   A statement made to an investigator by a person in compliance with an information requirement is admissible in evidence in any proceedings, so long as it also complies with any requirements governing the admissibility of evidence in the circumstances in question.

(2)   But in criminal proceedings in which that person is charged with an offence to which this subsection applies or in proceedings in relation to action to be taken against that person under section 123—

(a)   no evidence relating to the statement may be adduced, and

(b)   no question relating to it may be asked,

by or on behalf of the prosecution or (as the case may be) the Authority, unless evidence relating to it is adduced, or a question relating to it is asked, in the proceedings by or on behalf of that person.

(3)   Subsection (2) applies to any offence other than one—

(a)   under section 177(4) or 398;

(b)   under section 5 of the Perjury Act 1911 (false statements made otherwise than on oath);

(c)   under section 44(2) of the Criminal Law (Consolidation)(Scotland) Act 1995 (false statements made otherwise than on oath); or

(d)   under Article 10 of the Perjury (Northern Ireland) Order 1979.

(4)   'Investigator' means a person appointed under section 167 or 168(3) or (5).

(5)   'Information requirement' means a requirement imposed by an investigator under section 171, 172, 173 or 175.

## 175.   Information and documents: supplemental provisions

(1)   If the Authority or an investigator has power under this Part to require a person to produce a document but it appears that the document is in the possession of a third person, that power may be exercised in relation to the third person.

(2)   If a document is produced in response to a requirement imposed under this Part, the person to whom it is produced may—

(a)   take copies or extracts from the document; or

(b)   require the person producing the document, or any relevant person, to provide an explanation of the document.

(3)   If a person who is required under this Part to produce a document fails to do so, the Authority or an investigator may require him to state, to the best of his knowledge and belief, where the document is.

(4)   A lawyer may be required under this Part to furnish the name and address of his client.

(5)   No person may be required under this Part to disclose information or produce a document in respect of which he owes an obligation of confidence by virtue of carrying on the business of banking unless—

(a)   he is the person under investigation or a member of that person's group;

(b)   the person to whom the obligation of confidence is owed is the person under investigation or a member of that person's group;

(c)   the person to whom the obligation of confidence is owed consents to the disclosure or production; or

(d)   the imposing on him of a requirement with respect to such information or document has been specifically authorised by the investigating authority.

(6)   If a person claims a lien on a document, its production under this Part does not affect the lien.

(7)   'Relevant person', in relation to a person who is required to produce a document, means a person who—

(a)   has been or is or is proposed to be a director or controller of that person;

(b)   has been or is an auditor of that person;

(c)   has been or is an actuary, accountant or lawyer appointed or instructed by that person; or

(d)   has been or is an employee of that person.

(8)   'Investigator' means a person appointed under section 167 or 168(3) or (5).

## 176.   Entry of premises under warrant

(1)   A justice of the peace may issue a warrant under this section if satisfied on information on oath given by or on behalf of the Secretary of State, the Authority or an investigator that there are reasonable grounds for believing that the first, second or third set of conditions is satisfied.

(2)   The first set of conditions is—

(a)   that a person on whom an information requirement has been imposed has failed (wholly or in part) to comply with it; and

(b)   that on the premises specified in the warrant—

(i)   there are documents which have been required; or

(ii)   there is information which has been required.

(3)   The second set of conditions is—

(a)   that the premises specified in the warrant are premises of an authorised person or an appointed representative;

(b)   that there are on the premises documents or information in relation to which an information requirement could be imposed; and

(c)   that if such a requirement were to be imposed—

(i)   it would not be complied with; or

(ii)   the documents or information to which it related would be removed, tampered with or destroyed.

(4)   The third set of conditions is—

(a)   that an offence mentioned in section 168 for which the maximum sentence on conviction on indictment is two years or more has been (or is being) committed by any person;

(b)   that there are on the premises specified in the warrant documents or information relevant to whether that offence has been (or is being) committed;

(c)   that an information requirement could be imposed in relation to those documents or information; and

(d)   that if such a requirement were to be imposed—

(i)   it would not be complied with; or

(ii)   the documents or information to which it related would be removed, tampered with or destroyed.

(5)   A warrant under this section shall authorise a constable—

(a)   to enter the premises specified in the warrant;

(b)   to search the premises and take possession of any documents or information appearing to be documents or information of a kind in respect of which a warrant under this section was issued ('the relevant kind') or to take, in relation to any such documents or information, any other steps which may appear to be necessary for preserving them or preventing interference with them;

(c)   to take copies of, or extracts from, any documents or information appearing to be of the relevant kind;

(d)   to require any person on the premises to provide an explanation of any document or information appearing to be of the relevant kind or to state where it may be found; and

(e)   to use such force as may be reasonably necessary.

(6)   In England and Wales, sections 15(5) to (8) and section 16 of the Police and Criminal Evidence Act 1984 (execution of search warrants and safeguards) apply to warrants issued under this section.

(7)   In Northern Ireland, Articles 17(5) to (8) and 18 of the Police and Criminal Evidence (Northern Ireland) Order 1989 apply to warrants issued under this section.

(8)   Any document of which possession is taken under this section may be retained—

(a)   for a period of three months; or

(b)   if within that period proceedings to which the document is relevant are commenced against any person for any criminal offence, until the conclusion of those proceedings.

(9)   In the application of this section to Scotland—

(a)   for the references to a justice of the peace substitute references to a justice of the peace or a sheriff; and

(b)   for the references to information on oath substitute references to evidence on oath.

(10)   'Investigator' means a person appointed under section 167 or 168(3) or (5).

(11)   'Information requirement' means a requirement imposed—

(a)   by the Authority under section 165 or 175; or

(b)   by an investigator under section 171, 172, 173 or 175.

*Offences*

**177.   Offences**

(1)   If a person other than the investigator ('the defaulter') fails to comply with a requirement imposed on him under this Part the person imposing the requirement may certify that fact in writing to the court.

(2)  If the court is satisfied that the defaulter failed without reasonable excuse to comply with the requirement, it may deal with the defaulter (and in the case of a body corporate, any director or officer) as if he were in contempt.

(3)  A person who knows or suspects that an investigation is being or is likely to be conducted under this Part is guilty of an offence if—

(a)  he falsifies, conceals, destroys or otherwise disposes of a document which he knows or suspects is or would be relevant to such an investigation, or

(b)  he causes or permits the falsification, concealment, destruction or disposal of such a document,

unless he shows that he had no intention of concealing facts disclosed by the documents from the investigator.

(4)  A person who, in purported compliance with a requirement imposed on him under this Part—

(a)  provides information which he knows to be false or misleading in a material particular, or

(b)  recklessly provides information which is false or misleading in a material particular,

is guilty of an offence.

(5)  A person guilty of an offence under subsection (3) or (4) is liable—

(a)  on summary conviction, to imprisonment for a term not exceeding six months or a fine not exceeding the statutory maximum, or both;

(b)  on conviction on indictment, to imprisonment for a term not exceeding two years or a fine, or both.

(6)  Any person who intentionally obstructs the exercise of any rights conferred by a warrant under section 176 is guilty of an offence and liable on summary conviction to imprisonment for a term not exceeding three months or a fine not exceeding level 5 on the standard scale, or both.

(7)  'Court' means—

(a)  the High Court;

(b)  in Scotland, the Court of Session.

## PART XII
## CONTROL OVER AUTHORISED PERSONS

### *Notice of control*

### 178.  Obligation to notify the Authority

(1)  If a step which a person proposes to take would result in his acquiring—

(a)  control over a UK authorised person,

(b)  an additional kind of control over a UK authorised person, or

(c)  an increase in a relevant kind of control which he already has over a UK authorised person,

he must notify the Authority of his proposal.

(2)  A person who, without himself taking any such step, acquires any such control or additional or increased control must notify the Authority before the end of the period of 14 days beginning with the day on which he first becomes aware that he has acquired it.

(3)  A person who is under the duty to notify the Authority imposed by subsection (1) must also give notice to the Authority on acquiring, or increasing, the control in question.

(4)  In this Part 'UK authorised person' means an authorised person who—

(a)   is a body incorporated in, or an unincorporated association formed under the law of, any part of the United Kingdom; and

(b)   is not a person authorised as a result of paragraph 1 of Schedule 5.

(5)   A notice under subsection (1) or (2) is referred to in this Part as 'a notice of control'.

*Acquiring, increasing and reducing control*

### 179.  Acquiring control

(1)   For the purposes of this Part, a person ('the acquirer') acquires control over a UK authorised person ('A') on first falling within any of the cases in subsection (2).

(2)   The cases are where the acquirer—

(a)   holds 10% or more of the shares in A;

(b)   is able to exercise significant influence over the management of A by virtue of his shareholding in A;

(c)   holds 10% or more of the shares in a parent undertaking ('P') of A;

(d)   is able to exercise significant influence over the management of P by virtue of his shareholding in P;

(e)   is entitled to exercise, or control the exercise of, 10% or more of the voting power in A;

(f)   is able to exercise significant influence over the management of A by virtue of his voting power in A;

(g)   is entitled to exercise, or control the exercise of, 10% or more of the voting power in P; or

(h)   is able to exercise significant influence over the management of P by virtue of his voting power in P.

(3)   In subsection (2) 'the acquirer' means—

(a)   the acquirer;

(b)   any of the acquirer's associates; or

(c)   the acquirer and any of his associates.

(4)   For the purposes of this Part, each of the following is to be regarded as a kind of control—

(a)   control arising as a result of the holding of shares in A;

(b)   control arising as a result of the holding of shares in P;

(c)   control arising as a result of the entitlement to exercise, or control the exercise of, voting power in A;

(d)   control arising as a result of the entitlement to exercise, or control the exercise of, voting power in P.

(5)   For the purposes of this section and sections 180 and 181, 'associate', 'shares' and 'voting power' have the same meaning as in section 422.

### 180.  Increasing control

(1)   For the purposes of this Part, a controller of a person ('A') who is a UK authorised person increases his control over A if—

(a)   the percentage of shares held by the controller in A increases by any of the steps mentioned in subsection (2);

(b)   the percentage of shares held by the controller in a parent undertaking ('P') of A increases by any of the steps mentioned in subsection (2);

(c)   the percentage of voting power which the controller is entitled to exercise, or control the exercise of, in A increases by any of the steps mentioned in subsection (2);

(d)   the percentage of voting power which the controller is entitled to exercise, or control the exercise of, in P increases by any of the steps mentioned in subsection (2); or

(e)   the controller becomes a parent undertaking of A.

(2)   The steps are—

(a)   from below 10% to 10% or more but less than 20%;

(b)   from below 20% to 20% or more but less than 33%;

(c)   from below 33% to 33% or more but less than 50%;

(d)   from below 50% to 50% or more.

(3)   In paragraphs (a) to (d) of subsection (1) 'the controller' means—

(a)   the controller;

(b)   any of the controller's associates; or

(c)   the controller and any of his associates.

(4)   In the rest of this Part 'acquiring control' or 'having control' includes—

(a)   acquiring or having an additional kind of control; or

(b)   acquiring an increase in a relevant kind of control, or having increased control of a relevant kind.

### 181.   Reducing control

(1)   For the purposes of this Part, a controller of a person ('A') who is a UK authorised person reduces his control over A if—

(a)   the percentage of shares held by the controller in A decreases by any of the steps mentioned in subsection (2),

(b)   the percentage of shares held by the controller in a parent undertaking ('P') of A decreases by any of the steps mentioned in subsection (2),

(c)   the percentage of voting power which the controller is entitled to exercise, or control the exercise of, in A decreases by any of the steps mentioned in subsection (2),

(d)   the percentage of voting power which the controller is entitled to exercise, or control the exercise of, in P decreases by any of the steps mentioned in subsection (2), or

(e)   the controller ceases to be a parent undertaking of A,

unless the controller ceases to have the kind of control concerned over A as a result.

(2)   The steps are—

(a)   from 50% or more to 33% or more but less than 50%;

(b)   from 33% or more to 20% or more but less than 33%;

(c)   from 20% or more to 10% or more but less than 20%;

(d)   from 10% or more to less than 10%.

(3)   In paragraphs (a) to (d) of subsection (1) 'the controller' means—

(a)   the controller;

(b)   any of the controller's associates; or

(c)   the controller and any of his associates.

*Acquiring or increasing control: procedure*

### 182.   Notification

(1)   A notice of control must—

(a)   be given to the Authority in writing; and

(b)   include such information and be accompanied by such documents as the Authority may reasonably require.

(2)   The Authority may require the person giving a notice of control to provide such additional information or documents as it reasonably considers necessary in order to enable it to determine what action it is to take in response to the notice.

(3)    Different requirements may be imposed in different circumstances.

## 183.   Duty of Authority in relation to notice of control

(1)    The Authority must, before the end of the period of three months beginning with the date on which it receives a notice of control ('the period for consideration'), determine whether—

   (a)   to approve of the person concerned having the control to which the notice relates; or

   (b)   to serve a warning notice under subsection (3) or section 185(3).

(2)    Before doing so, the Authority must comply with such requirements as to consultation with competent authorities outside the United Kingdom as may be prescribed.

(3)    If the Authority proposes to give the person concerned a notice of objection under section 186(1), it must give him a warning notice.

## 184.   Approval of acquisition of control

(1)    If the Authority decides to approve of the person concerned having the control to which the notice relates it must notify that person of its approval in writing without delay.

(2)    If the Authority fails to comply with subsection (1) of section 183 it is to be treated as having given its approval and notified the person concerned at the end of the period fixed by that subsection.

(3)    The Authority's approval remains effective only if the person to whom it relates acquires the control in question—

   (a)   before the end of such period as may be specified in the notice; or

   (b)   if no period is specified, before the end of the period of one year beginning with the date—

      (i)    of the notice of approval;

      (ii)   on which the Authority is treated as having given approval under subsection (2); or

      (iii)  of a decision on a reference to the Tribunal which results in the person concerned receiving approval.

## 185.   Conditions attached to approval

(1)    The Authority's approval under section 184 may be given unconditionally or subject to such conditions as the Authority considers appropriate.

(2)    In imposing any conditions, the Authority must have regard to its duty under section 41.

(3)    If the Authority proposes to impose conditions on a person it must give him a warning notice.

(4)    If the Authority decides to impose conditions on a person it must give him a decision notice.

(5)    A person who is subject to a condition imposed under this section may apply to the Authority—

   (a)   for the condition to be varied; or

   (b)   for the condition to be cancelled.

(6)    The Authority may, on its own initiative, cancel a condition imposed under this section.

(7)    If the Authority has given its approval to a person subject to a condition, he may refer to the Tribunal—

   (a)   the imposition of the condition; or

(b)   the Authority's decision to refuse an application made by him under subsection (5).

## 186.   Objection to acquisition of control

(1)   On considering a notice of control, the Authority may give a decision notice under this section to the person acquiring control ('the acquirer') unless it is satisfied that the approval requirements are met.

(2)   The approval requirements are that—

(a)   the acquirer is a fit and proper person to have the control over the authorised person that he has or would have if he acquired the control in question; and

(b)   the interests of consumers would not be threatened by the acquirer's control or by his acquiring that control.

(3)   In deciding whether the approval requirements are met, the Authority must have regard, in relation to the control that the acquirer—

(a)   has over the authorised person concerned ('A'), or

(b)   will have over A if the proposal to which the notice of control relates is carried into effect,

to its duty under section 41 in relation to each regulated activity carried on by A.

(4)   If the Authority gives a notice under this section but considers that the approval requirements would be met if the person to whom a notice is given were to take, or refrain from taking, a particular step, the notice must identify that step.

(5)   A person to whom a notice under this section is given may refer the matter to the Tribunal.

(6)   'Consumers' means persons who are consumers for the purposes of section 138.

## 187.   Objection to existing control

(1)   If the Authority is not satisfied that the approval requirements are met, it may give a decision notice under this section to a person if he has failed to comply with a duty to notify imposed by section 178.

(2)   If the failure relates to subsection (1) or (2) of that section, the Authority may (instead of giving a notice under subsection (1)) approve the acquisition of the control in question by the person concerned as if he had given it a notice of control.

(3)   The Authority may also give a decision notice under this section to a person who is a controller of a UK authorised person if the Authority becomes aware of matters as a result of which it is satisfied that—

(a)   the approval requirements are not met with respect to the controller; or

(b)   a condition imposed under section 185 required that person to do (or refrain from doing) a particular thing and the condition has been breached as a result of his failing to do (or doing) that thing.

(4)   A person to whom a notice under this section is given may refer the matter to the Tribunal.

(5)   'Approval requirements' has the same meaning as in section 186.

## 188.   Notices of objection under section 187: procedure

(1)   If the Authority proposes to give a notice of objection to a person under section 187, it must give him a warning notice.

(2)   Before doing so, the Authority must comply with such requirements as to consultation with competent authorities outside the United Kingdom as may be prescribed.

(3)   If the Authority decides to give a warning notice under this section, it must do so before the end of the period of three months beginning—

(a)   in the case of a notice to be given under section 187(1), with the date on which it became aware of the failure to comply with the duty in question;

(b)   in the case of a notice to be given under section 187(3), with the date on which it became aware of the matters in question.

(4)   The Authority may require the person concerned to provide such additional information or documents as it considers reasonable.

(5)   Different requirements may be imposed in different circumstances.

(6)   In this Part 'notice of objection' means a notice under section 186 or 187.

*Improperly acquired shares*

## 189.   Improperly acquired shares

(1)   The powers conferred by this section are exercisable if a person has acquired, or has continued to hold, any shares in contravention of—

(a)   a notice of objection; or

(b)   a condition imposed on the Authority's approval.

(2)   The Authority may by notice in writing served on the person concerned ('a restriction notice') direct that any such shares which are specified in the notice are, until further notice, subject to one or more of the following restrictions—

(a)   a transfer of (or agreement to transfer) those shares, or in the case of unissued shares any transfer of (or agreement to transfer) the right to be issued with them, is void;

(b)   no voting rights are to be exercisable in respect of the shares;

(c)   no further shares are to be issued in right of them or in pursuance of any offer made to their holder;

(d)   except in a liquidation, no payment is to be made of any sums due from the body corporate on the shares, whether in respect of capital or otherwise.

(3)   The court may, on the application of the Authority, order the sale of any shares to which this section applies and, if they are for the time being subject to any restriction under subsection (2), that they are to cease to be subject to that restriction.

(4)   No order may be made under subsection (3)—

(a)   until the end of the period within which a reference may be made to the Tribunal in respect of the notice of objection; and

(b)   if a reference is made, until the matter has been determined or the reference withdrawn.

(5)   If an order has been made under subsection (3), the court may, on the application of the Authority, make such further order relating to the sale or transfer of the shares as it thinks fit.

(6)   If shares are sold in pursuance of an order under this section, the proceeds of sale, less the costs of the sale, must be paid into court for the benefit of the persons beneficially interested in them; and any such person may apply to the court for the whole or part of the proceeds to be paid to him.

(7)   This section applies—

(a)   in the case of an acquirer falling within section 178(1), to all the shares—

(i)   in the authorised person which the acquirer has acquired;

(ii)   which are held by him or an associate of his; and

(iii)   which were not so held immediately before he became a person with control over the authorised person;

(b)   in the case of an acquirer falling within section 178(2), to all the shares held by him or an associate of his at the time when he first became aware that he had acquired control over the authorised person; and

(c) to all the shares in an undertaking ('C')—

    (i) which are held by the acquirer or an associate of his, and

    (ii) which were not so held before he became a person with control in relation to the authorised person,

where C is the undertaking in which shares were acquired by the acquirer (or an associate of his) and, as a result, he became a person with control in relation to that authorised person.

(8) A copy of the restriction notice must be served on—

    (a) the authorised person to whose shares it relates; and

    (b) if it relates to shares held by an associate of that authorised person, on that associate.

(9) The jurisdiction conferred by this section may be exercised by the High Court and the Court of Session.

*Reducing control: procedure*

### 190. Notification

(1) If a step which a controller of a UK authorised person proposes to take would result in his—

    (a) ceasing to have control of a relevant kind over the authorised person, or

    (b) reducing a relevant kind of control over that person,

he must notify the Authority of his proposal.

(2) A controller of a UK authorised person who, without himself taking any such step, ceases to have that control or reduces that control must notify the Authority before the end of the period of 14 days beginning with the day on which he first becomes aware that—

    (a) he has ceased to have the control in question; or

    (b) he has reduced that control.

(3) A person who is under the duty to notify the Authority imposed by subsection (1) must also give a notice to the Authority—

    (a) on ceasing to have the control in question; or

    (b) on reducing that control.

(4) A notice under this section must—

    (a) be given to the Authority in writing; and

    (b) include details of the extent of the control (if any) which the person concerned will retain (or still retains) over the authorised person concerned.

*Offences*

### 191. Offences under this Part

(1) A person who fails to comply with the duty to notify the Authority imposed on him by section 178(1) or 190(1) is guilty of an offence.

(2) A person who fails to comply with the duty to notify the Authority imposed on him by section 178(2) or 190(2) is guilty of an offence.

(3) If a person who has given a notice of control to the Authority carries out the proposal to which the notice relates, he is guilty of an offence if—

    (a) the period of three months beginning with the date on which the Authority received the notice is still running; and

    (b) the Authority has not responded to the notice by either giving its approval or giving him a warning notice under section 183(3) or 185(3).

(4) A person to whom the Authority has given a warning notice under section 183(3) is guilty of an offence if he carries out the proposal to which the notice relates before the Authority has decided whether to give him a notice of objection.

(5)   A person to whom a notice of objection has been given is guilty of an offence if he acquires the control to which the notice applies at a time when the notice is still in force.

(6)   A person guilty of an offence under subsection (1), (2), (3) or (4) is liable on summary conviction to a fine not exceeding level 5 on the standard scale.

(7)   A person guilty of an offence under subsection (5) is liable—

(a)   on summary conviction, to a fine not exceeding the statutory maximum; and

(b)   on conviction on indictment, to imprisonment for a term not exceeding two years or a fine, or both.

(8)   A person guilty of an offence under subsection (5) is also liable on summary conviction to a fine not exceeding one tenth of the statutory maximum for each day on which the offence has continued.

(9)   It is a defence for a person charged with an offence under subsection (1) to show that he had, at the time of the alleged offence, no knowledge of the act or circumstances by virtue of which the duty to notify the Authority arose.

(10)   If a person—

(a)   was under the duty to notify the Authority imposed by section 178(1) or 190(1) but had no knowledge of the act or circumstances by virtue of which that duty arose, but

(b)   subsequently becomes aware of that act or those circumstances,

he must notify the Authority before the end of the period of 14 days beginning with the day on which he first became so aware.

(11)   A person who fails to comply with the duty to notify the Authority imposed by subsection (10) is guilty of an offence and liable, on summary conviction, to a fine not exceeding level 5 on the standard scale.

*Miscellaneous*

**192.   Power to change definitions of control etc**

The Treasury may by order—

(a)   provide for exemptions from the obligations to notify imposed by sections 178 and 190;

(b)   amend section 179 by varying, or removing, any of the cases in which a person is treated as having control over a UK authorised person or by adding a case;

(c)   amend section 180 by varying, or removing, any of the cases in which a person is treated as increasing control over a UK authorised person or by adding a case;

(d)   amend section 181 by varying, or removing, any of the cases in which a person is treated as reducing his control over a UK authorised person or by adding a case;

(e)   amend section 422 by varying, or removing, any of the cases in which a person is treated as being a controller of a person or by adding a case.

PART XIII

INCOMING FIRMS: INTERVENTION BY AUTHORITY

*Interpretation*

**193.   Interpretation of this Part**

(1)   In this Part—

'additional procedure' means the procedure described in section 199;

'incoming firm' means—

(a)   an EEA firm which is exercising, or has exercised, its right to carry on a regulated activity in the United Kingdom in accordance with Schedule 3; or

(b)   a Treaty firm which is exercising, or has exercised, its right to carry on a regulated activity in the United Kingdom in accordance with Schedule 4; and

'power of intervention' means the power conferred on the Authority by section 196.

(2)   In relation to an incoming firm which is an EEA firm, expressions used in this Part and in Schedule 3 have the same meaning in this Part as they have in that Schedule.

### 194.   General grounds on which power of intervention is exercisable

(1)   The Authority may exercise its power of intervention in respect of an incoming firm if it appears to it that—

(a)   the firm has contravened, or is likely to contravene, a requirement which is imposed on it by or under this Act (in a case where the Authority is responsible for enforcing compliance in the United Kingdom);

(b)   the firm has, in purported compliance with any requirement imposed by or under this Act, knowingly or recklessly given the Authority information which is false or misleading in a material particular; or

(c)   it is desirable to exercise the power in order to protect the interests of actual or potential customers.

(2)   Subsection (3) applies to an incoming EEA firm falling within sub-paragraph (a) or (b) of paragraph 5 of Schedule 3 which is exercising an EEA right to carry on any Consumer Credit Act business in the United Kingdom.

(3)   The Authority may exercise its power of intervention in respect of the firm if the Director General of Fair Trading has informed the Authority that—

(a)   the firm,

(b)   any of the firm's employees, agents or associates (whether past or present), or

(c)   if the firm is a body corporate, a controller of the firm or an associate of such a controller,

has done any of the things specified in paragraphs (a) to (d) of section 25(2) of the Consumer Credit Act 1974.

(4)   'Associate', 'Consumer Credit Act business' and 'controller' have the same meaning as in section 203.

### 195.   Exercise of power in support of overseas regulator

(1)   The Authority may exercise its power of intervention in respect of an incoming firm at the request of, or for the purpose of assisting, an overseas regulator.

(2)   Subsection (1) applies whether or not the Authority's power of intervention is also exercisable as a result of section 194.

(3)   'An overseas regulator' means an authority in a country or territory outside the United Kingdom—

(a)   which is a home state regulator; or

(b)   which exercises any function of a kind mentioned in subsection (4).

(4)   The functions are—

(a)   a function corresponding to any function of the Authority under this Act;

(b)   a function corresponding to any function exercised by the competent authority under Part VI in relation to the listing of shares;

(c)   a function corresponding to any function exercised by the Secretary of State under the Companies Act 1985;

(d)   a function in connection with—

(i)   the investigation of conduct of the kind prohibited by Part V of the Criminal Justice Act 1993 (insider dealing); or

(ii)    the enforcement of rules (whether or not having the force of law) relating to such conduct;

(e)    a function prescribed by regulations made for the purposes of this subsection which, in the opinion of the Treasury, relates to companies or financial services.

(5)    If—

(a)    a request to the Authority for the exercise of its power of intervention has been made by a home state regulator in pursuance of a Community obligation, or

(b)    a home state regulator has notified the Authority that an EEA firm's EEA authorisation has been withdrawn,

the Authority must, in deciding whether or not to exercise its power of intervention, consider whether exercising it is necessary in order to comply with a Community obligation.

(6)    In deciding in any case in which the Authority does not consider that the exercise of its power of intervention is necessary in order to comply with a Community obligation, it may take into account in particular—

(a)    whether in the country or territory of the overseas regulator concerned, corresponding assistance would be given to a United Kingdom regulatory authority;

(b)    whether the case concerns the breach of a law, or other requirement, which has no close parallel in the United Kingdom or involves the assertion of a jurisdiction not recognised by the United Kingdom;

(c)    the seriousness of the case and its importance to persons in the United Kingdom;

(d)    whether it is otherwise appropriate in the public interest to give the assistance sought.

(7)    The Authority may decide not to exercise its power of intervention, in response to a request, unless the regulator concerned undertakes to make such contribution to the cost of its exercise as the Authority considers appropriate.

(8)    Subsection (7) does not apply if the Authority decides that it is necessary for it to exercise its power of intervention in order to comply with a Community obligation.

## 196.    The power of intervention

If the Authority is entitled to exercise its power of intervention in respect of an incoming firm under this Part, it may impose any requirement in relation to the firm which it could impose if—

(a)    the firm's permission was a Part IV permission; and

(b)    the Authority was entitled to exercise its power under that Part to vary that permission.

*Exercise of power of intervention*

## 197.    Procedure on exercise of power of intervention

(1)    A requirement takes effect—

(a)    immediately, if the notice given under subsection (3) states that that is the case;

(b)    on such date as may be specified in the notice; or

(c)    if no date is specified in the notice, when the matter to which it relates is no longer open to review.

(2)    A requirement may be expressed to take effect immediately (or on a specified date) only if the Authority, having regard to the ground on which it is exercising its power of intervention, considers that it is necessary for the requirement to take effect immediately (or on that date).

(3)   If the Authority proposes to impose a requirement under section 196 on an incoming firm, or imposes such a requirement with immediate effect, it must give the firm written notice.

(4)   The notice must—

    (a)   give details of the requirement;

    (b)   inform the firm of when the requirement takes effect;

    (c)   state the Authority's reasons for imposing the requirement and for its determination as to when the requirement takes effect;

    (d)   inform the firm that it may make representations to the Authority within such period as may be specified in the notice (whether or not it has referred the matter to the Tribunal); and

    (e)   inform it of its right to refer the matter to the Tribunal.

(5)   The Authority may extend the period allowed under the notice for making representations.

(6)   If, having considered any representations made by the firm, the Authority decides—

    (a)   to impose the requirement proposed, or

    (b)   if it has been imposed, not to rescind the requirement,

it must give it written notice.

(7)   If, having considered any representations made by the firm, the Authority decides—

    (a)   not to impose the requirement proposed,

    (b)   to impose a different requirement from that proposed, or

    (c)   to rescind a requirement which has effect,

it must give it written notice.

(8)   A notice given under subsection (6) must inform the firm of its right to refer the matter to the Tribunal.

(9)   A notice under subsection (7)(b) must comply with subsection (4).

(10)   If a notice informs a person of his right to refer a matter to the Tribunal, it must give an indication of the procedure on such a reference.

## 198.   Power to apply to court for injunction in respect of certain overseas insurance companies

(1)   This section applies if the Authority has received a request made in respect of an incoming EEA firm in accordance with—

    (a)   Article 20.5 of the first non-life insurance directive; or

    (b)   Article 24.5 of the first life insurance directive.

(2)   The court may, on an application made to it by the Authority with respect to the firm, grant an injunction restraining (or in Scotland an interdict prohibiting) the firm disposing of or otherwise dealing with any of its assets.

(3)   If the court grants an injunction, it may by subsequent orders make provision for such incidental, consequential and supplementary matters as it considers necessary to enable the Authority to perform any of its functions under this Act.

(4)   'The court' means—

    (a)   the High Court; or

    (b)   in Scotland, the Court of Session.

## 199.   Additional procedure for EEA firms in certain cases

(1)   This section applies if it appears to the Authority that its power of intervention is exercisable in relation to an EEA firm exercising EEA rights in the United Kingdom ('an incoming EEA firm') in respect of the contravention of a relevant requirement.

(2)   A requirement is relevant if—

(a)   it is imposed by the Authority under this Act; and

(b)   as respects its contravention, any of the single market directives provides that a procedure of the kind set out in the following provisions of this section is to apply.

(3)   The Authority must, in writing, require the firm to remedy the situation.

(4)   If the firm fails to comply with the requirement under subsection (3) within a reasonable time, the Authority must give a notice to that effect to the firm's home state regulator requesting it—

(a)   to take all appropriate measures for the purpose of ensuring that the firm remedies the situation which has given rise to the notice; and

(b)   to inform the Authority of the measures it proposes to take or has taken or the reasons for not taking such measures.

(5)   Except as mentioned in subsection (6), the Authority may not exercise its power of intervention unless satisfied—

(a)   that the firm's home state regulator has failed or refused to take measures for the purpose mentioned in subsection (4)(a); or

(b)   that the measures taken by the home state regulator have proved inadequate for that purpose.

(6)   If the Authority decides that it should exercise its power of intervention in respect of the incoming EEA firm as a matter of urgency in order to protect the interests of consumers, it may exercise that power—

(a)   before complying with subsections (3) and (4); or

(b)   where it has complied with those subsections, before it is satisfied as mentioned in subsection (5).

(7)   In such a case the Authority must at the earliest opportunity inform the firm's home state regulator and the Commission.

(8)   If—

(a)   the Authority has (by virtue of subsection (6)) exercised its power of intervention before complying with subsections (3) and (4) or before it is satisfied as mentioned in subsection (5), and

(b)   the Commission decides under any of the single market directives that the Authority must rescind or vary any requirement imposed in the exercise of its power of intervention,

the Authority must in accordance with the decision rescind or vary the requirement.

*Supplemental*

## 200.   Rescission and variation of requirements

(1)   The Authority may rescind or vary a requirement imposed in exercise of its power of intervention on its own initiative or on the application of the person subject to the requirement.

(2)   The power of the Authority on its own initiative to rescind a requirement is exercisable by written notice given by the Authority to the person concerned, which takes effect on the date specified in the notice.

(3)   Section 197 applies to the exercise of the power of the Authority on its own initiative to vary a requirement as it applies to the imposition of a requirement.

(4)   If the Authority proposes to refuse an application for the variation or rescission of a requirement, it must give the applicant a warning notice.

(5)   If the Authority decides to refuse an application for the variation or rescission of a requirement—

(a)   the Authority must give the applicant a decision notice; and

(b)   that person may refer the matter to the Tribunal.

### 201.   Effect of certain requirements on other persons

If the Authority, in exercising its power of intervention, imposes on an incoming firm a requirement of a kind mentioned in subsection (3) of section 48, the requirement has the same effect in relation to the firm as it would have in relation to an authorised person if it had been imposed on the authorised person by the Authority acting under section 45.

### 202.   Contravention of requirement imposed under this Part

(1)   Contravention of a requirement imposed by the Authority under this Part does not—

(a)   make a person guilty of an offence;

(b)   make any transaction void or unenforceable; or

(c)   (subject to subsection (2)) give rise to any right of action for breach of statutory duty.

(2)   In prescribed cases the contravention is actionable at the suit of a person who suffers loss as a result of the contravention, subject to the defences and other incidents applying to actions for breach of statutory duty.

*Powers of Director General of Fair Trading*

### 203.   Power to prohibit the carrying on of Consumer Credit Act business

(1)   If it appears to the Director General of Fair Trading ('the Director') that subsection (4) has been, or is likely to be, contravened as respects a consumer credit EEA firm, he may by written notice given to the firm impose on the firm a consumer credit prohibition.

(2)   If it appears to the Director that a restriction imposed under section 204 on an EEA consumer credit firm has not been complied with, he may by written notice given to the firm impose a consumer credit prohibition.

(3)   'Consumer credit prohibition' means a prohibition on carrying on, or purporting to carry on, in the United Kingdom any Consumer Credit Act business which consists of or includes carrying on one or more listed activities.

(4)   This subsection is contravened as respects a firm if—

(a)   the firm or any of its employees, agents or associates (whether past or present), or

(b)   if the firm is a body corporate, any controller of the firm or an associate of any such controller,

does any of the things specified in paragraphs (a) to (d) of section 25(2) of the Consumer Credit Act 1974.

(5)   A consumer credit prohibition may be absolute or may be imposed—

(a)   for such period,

(b)   until the occurrence of such event, or

(c)   until such conditions are complied with,

as may be specified in the notice given under subsection (1) or (2).

(6)   Any period, event or condition so specified may be varied by the Director on the application of the firm concerned.

(7)   A consumer credit prohibition may be withdrawn by written notice served by the Director on the firm concerned, and any such notice takes effect on such date as is specified in the notice.

(8)   Schedule 16 has effect as respects consumer credit prohibitions and restrictions under section 204.

(9)   A firm contravening a prohibition under this section is guilty of an offence and liable—

(a)   on summary conviction, to a fine not exceeding the statutory maximum;

(b)   on conviction on indictment, to a fine.

(10)   In this section and section 204—

'a consumer credit EEA firm' means an EEA firm falling within any of paragraphs (a) to (c) of paragraph 5 of Schedule 3 whose EEA authorisation covers any Consumer Credit Act business;

'Consumer Credit Act business' means consumer credit business, consumer hire business or ancillary credit business;

'consumer credit business', 'consumer hire business' and 'ancillary credit business' have the same meaning as in the Consumer Credit Act 1974;

'listed activity' means an activity listed in the Annex to the second banking co-ordination directive or the Annex to the investment services directive;

'associate' has the same meaning as in section 25(2) of the Consumer Credit Act 1974;

'controller' has the meaning given by section 189(1) of that Act.

## 204.   Power to restrict the carrying on of Consumer Credit Act business

(1)   In this section 'restriction' means a direction that a consumer credit EEA firm may not carry on in the United Kingdom, otherwise than in accordance with such condition or conditions as may be specified in the direction, any Consumer Credit Act business which—

(a)   consists of or includes carrying on any listed activity; and

(b)   is specified in the direction.

(2)   If it appears to the Director that the situation as respects a consumer credit EEA firm is such that the powers conferred by section 203(1) are exercisable, the Director may, instead of imposing a prohibition, impose such restriction as appears to him desirable.

(3)   A restriction—

(a)   may be withdrawn, or

(b)   may be varied with the agreement of the firm concerned,

by written notice served by the Director on the firm, and any such notice takes effect on such date as is specified in the notice.

(4)   A firm contravening a restriction is guilty of an offence and liable—

(a)   on summary conviction, to a fine not exceeding the statutory maximum;

(b)   on conviction on indictment, to a fine.

## PART XIV
## DISCIPLINARY MEASURES

## 205.   Public censure

If the Authority considers that an authorised person has contravened a requirement imposed on him by or under this Act, the Authority may publish a statement to that effect.

## 206.   Financial penalties

(1)   If the Authority considers that an authorised person has contravened a requirement imposed on him by or under this Act, it may impose on him a penalty, in respect of the contravention, of such amount as it considers appropriate.

(2)   The Authority may not in respect of any contravention both require a person to pay a penalty under this section and withdraw his authorisation under section 33.

(3)   A penalty under this section is payable to the Authority.

## 207.   Proposal to take disciplinary measures

(1)   If the Authority proposes—

    (a)   to publish a statement in respect of an authorised person (under section 205), or

    (b)   to impose a penalty on an authorised person (under section 206),

it must give the authorised person a warning notice.

    (2)   A warning notice about a proposal to publish a statement must set out the terms of the statement.

    (3)   A warning notice about a proposal to impose a penalty, must state the amount of the penalty.

### 208.  Decision notice

    (1)   If the Authority decides—

    (a)   to publish a statement under section 205 (whether or not in the terms proposed), or

    (b)   to impose a penalty under section 206 (whether or not of the amount proposed),

it must without delay give the authorised person concerned a decision notice.

    (2)   In the case of a statement, the decision notice must set out the terms of the statement.

    (3)   In the case of a penalty, the decision notice must state the amount of the penalty.

    (4)   If the Authority decides to—

    (a)   publish a statement in respect of an authorised person under section 205, or

    (b)   impose a penalty on an authorised person under section 206,

the authorised person may refer the matter to the Tribunal.

### 209.  Publication

After a statement under section 205 is published, the Authority must send a copy of it to the authorised person and to any person on whom a copy of the decision notice was given under section 393(4).

### 210.  Statements of policy

    (1)   The Authority must prepare and issue a statement of its policy with respect to—

    (a)   the imposition of penalties under this Part; and

    (b)   the amount of penalties under this Part.

    (2)   The Authority's policy in determining what the amount of a penalty should be must include having regard to—

    (a)   the seriousness of the contravention in question in relation to the nature of the requirement contravened;

    (b)   the extent to which that contravention was deliberate or reckless; and

    (c)   whether the person on whom the penalty is to be imposed is an individual.

    (3)   The Authority may at any time alter or replace a statement issued under this section.

    (4)   If a statement issued under this section is altered or replaced, the Authority must issue the altered or replacement statement.

    (5)   The Authority must, without delay, give the Treasury a copy of any statement which it publishes under this section.

    (6)   A statement issued under this section must be published by the Authority in the way appearing to the Authority to be best calculated to bring it to the attention of the public.

    (7)   In exercising, or deciding whether to exercise, its power under section 206 in the case of any particular contravention, the Authority must have regard to any statement published under this section and in force at the time when the contravention in question occurred.

    (8)   The Authority may charge a reasonable fee for providing a person with a copy of the statement.

### 211.   Statements of policy: procedure

(1)   Before issuing a statement under section 210, the Authority must publish a draft of the proposed statement in the way appearing to the Authority to be best calculated to bring it to the attention of the public.

(2)   The draft must be accompanied by notice that representations about the proposal may be made to the Authority within a specified time.

(3)   Before issuing the proposed statement, the Authority must have regard to any representations made to it in accordance with subsection (2).

(4)   If the Authority issues the proposed statement it must publish an account, in general terms, of—

    (a)   the representations made to it in accordance with subsection (2); and

    (b)   its response to them.

(5)   If the statement differs from the draft published under subsection (1) in a way which is, in the opinion of the Authority, significant, the Authority must (in addition to complying with subsection (4)) publish details of the difference.

(6)   The Authority may charge a reasonable fee for providing a person with a copy of a draft published under subsection (1).

(7)   This section also applies to a proposal to alter or replace a statement.

## PART XV
## THE FINANCIAL SERVICES COMPENSATION SCHEME

*The scheme manager*

### 212.   The scheme manager

(1)   The Authority must establish a body corporate ('the scheme manager') to exercise the functions conferred on the scheme manager by or under this Part.

(2)   The Authority must take such steps as are necessary to ensure that the scheme manager is, at all times, capable of exercising those functions.

(3)   The constitution of the scheme manager must provide for it to have—

    (a)   a chairman; and

    (b)   a board (which must include the chairman) whose members are the scheme manager's directors.

(4)   The chairman and other members of the board must be persons appointed, and liable to removal from office, by the Authority (acting, in the case of the chairman, with the approval of the Treasury).

(5)   But the terms of their appointment (and in particular those governing removal from office) must be such as to secure their independence from the Authority in the operation of the compensation scheme.

(6)   The scheme manager is not to be regarded as exercising functions on behalf of the Crown.

(7)   The scheme manager's board members, officers and staff are not to be regarded as Crown servants.

*The scheme*

### 213.   The compensation scheme

(1)   The Authority must by rules establish a scheme for compensating persons in cases where relevant persons are unable, or are likely to be unable, to satisfy claims against them.

(2)   The rules are to be known as the Financial Services Compensation Scheme (but are referred to in this Act as 'the compensation scheme').

(3)   The compensation scheme must, in particular, provide for the scheme manager—

(a)   to assess and pay compensation, in accordance with the scheme, to claimants in respect of claims made in connection with regulated activities carried on (whether or not with permission) by relevant persons; and

(b)   to have power to impose levies on authorised persons, or any class of authorised person, for the purpose of meeting its expenses (including in particular expenses incurred, or expected to be incurred, in paying compensation, borrowing or insuring risks).

(4)   The compensation scheme may provide for the scheme manager to have power to impose levies on authorised persons, or any class of authorised person, for the purpose of recovering the cost (whenever incurred) of establishing the scheme.

(5)   In making any provision of the scheme by virtue of subsection (3)(b), the Authority must take account of the desirability of ensuring that the amount of the levies imposed on a particular class of authorised person reflects, so far as practicable, the amount of the claims made, or likely to be made, in respect of that class of person.

(6)   An amount payable to the scheme manager as a result of any provision of the scheme made by virtue of subsection (3)(b) or (4) may be recovered as a debt due to the scheme manager.

(7)   Sections 214 to 217 make further provision about the scheme but are not to be taken as limiting the power conferred on the Authority by subsection (1).

(8)   In those sections 'specified' means specified in the scheme.

(9)   In this Part (except in sections 219, 220 or 224) 'relevant person' means a person who was—

(a)   an authorised person at the time the act or omission giving rise to the claim against him took place; or

(b)   an appointed representative at that time.

(10)   But a person who, at that time—

(a)   qualified for authorisation under Schedule 3, and

(b)   fell within a prescribed category,

is not to be regarded as a relevant person in relation to any activities for which he had permission as a result of any provision of, or made under, that Schedule unless he had elected to participate in the scheme in relation to those activities at that time.

*Provisions of the scheme*

## 214.   General

(1)   The compensation scheme may, in particular, make provision—

(a)   as to the circumstances in which a relevant person is to be taken (for the purposes of the scheme) to be unable, or likely to be unable, to satisfy claims made against him;

(b)   for the establishment of different funds for meeting different kinds of claim;

(c)   for the imposition of different levies in different cases;

(d)   limiting the levy payable by a person in respect of a specified period;

(e)   for repayment of the whole or part of a levy in specified circumstances;

(f)   for a claim to be entertained only if it is made by a specified kind of claimant;

(g)   for a claim to be entertained only if it falls within a specified kind of claim;

(h)   as to the procedure to be followed in making a claim;

(i)   for the making of interim payments before a claim is finally determined;

(j)   limiting the amount payable on a claim to a specified maximum amount or a maximum amount calculated in a specified manner;

(k) for payment to be made, in specified circumstances, to a person other than the claimant.

(2) Different provision may be made with respect to different kinds of claim.

(3) The scheme may provide for the determination and regulation of matters relating to the scheme by the scheme manager.

(4) The scheme, or particular provisions of the scheme, may be made so as to apply only in relation to—

(a) activities carried on,

(b) claimants,

(c) matters arising, or

(d) events occurring,

in specified territories, areas or localities.

(5) The scheme may provide for a person who—

(a) qualifies for authorisation under Schedule 3, and

(b) falls within a prescribed category,

to elect to participate in the scheme in relation to some or all of the activities for which he has permission as a result of any provision of, or made under, that Schedule.

(6) The scheme may provide for the scheme manager to have power—

(a) in specified circumstances,

(b) but only if the scheme manager is satisfied that the claimant is entitled to receive a payment in respect of his claim—

(i) under a scheme which is comparable to the compensation scheme, or

(ii) as the result of a guarantee given by a government or other authority,

to make a full payment of compensation to the claimant and recover the whole or part of the amount of that payment from the other scheme or under that guarantee.

## 215. Rights of the scheme in relevant person's insolvency

(1) The compensation scheme may, in particular, make provision—

(a) as to the effect of a payment of compensation under the scheme in relation to rights or obligations arising out of the claim against a relevant person in respect of which the payment was made;

(b) for conferring on the scheme manager a right of recovery against that person.

(2) Such a right of recovery conferred by the scheme does not, in the event of the relevant person's insolvency, exceed such right (if any) as the claimant would have had in that event.

(3) If a person other than the scheme manager presents a petition under section 9 of the 1986 Act or Article 22 of the 1989 Order in relation to a company or partnership which is a relevant person, the scheme manager has the same rights as are conferred on the Authority by section 362.

(4) If a person other than the scheme manager presents a petition for the winding up of a body which is a relevant person, the scheme manager has the same rights as are conferred on the Authority by section 371.

(5) If a person other than the scheme manager presents a bankruptcy petition to the court in relation to an individual who, or an entity which, is a relevant person, the scheme manager has the same rights as are conferred on the Authority by section 374.

(6) Insolvency rules may be made for the purpose of integrating any procedure for which provision is made as a result of subsection (1) into the general procedure on the administration of a company or partnership or on a winding-up, bankruptcy or sequestration.

(7) 'Bankruptcy petition' means a petition to the court—

(a)   under section 264 of the 1986 Act or Article 238 of the 1989 Order for a bankruptcy order to be made against an individual;

(b)   under section 5 of the 1985 Act for the sequestration of the estate of an individual; or

(c)   under section 6 of the 1985 Act for the sequestration of the estate belonging to or held for or jointly by the members of an entity mentioned in subsection (1) of that section.

(8)   'Insolvency rules' are—

(a)   for England and Wales, rules made under sections 411 and 412 of the 1986 Act;

(b)   for Scotland, rules made by order by the Treasury, after consultation with the Scottish Ministers, for the purposes of this section; and

(c)   for Northern Ireland, rules made under Article 359 of the 1989 Order and section 55 of the Judicature (Northern Ireland) Act 1978.

(9)   'The 1985 Act', 'the 1986 Act', 'the 1989 Order' and 'court' have the same meaning as in Part XXIV.

## 216.   Continuity of long-term insurance policies

(1)   The compensation scheme may, in particular, include provision requiring the scheme manager to make arrangements for securing continuity of insurance for policyholders, or policyholders of a specified class, of relevant long-term insurers.

(2)   'Relevant long-term insurers' means relevant persons who—

(a)   have permission to effect or carry out contracts of long-term insurance; and

(b)   are unable, or likely to be unable, to satisfy claims made against them.

(3)   The scheme may provide for the scheme manager to take such measures as appear to him to be appropriate—

(a)   for securing or facilitating the transfer of a relevant long-term insurer's business so far as it consists of the carrying out of contracts of long-term insurance, or of any part of that business, to another authorised person;

(b)   for securing the issue by another authorised person to the policyholders concerned of policies in substitution for their existing policies.

(4)   The scheme may also provide for the scheme manager to make payments to the policyholders concerned—

(a)   during any period while he is seeking to make arrangements mentioned in subsection (1);

(b)   if it appears to him that it is not reasonably practicable to make such arrangements.

(5)   A provision of the scheme made by virtue of section 213(3)(b) may include power to impose levies for the purpose of meeting expenses of the scheme manager incurred in—

(a)   taking measures as a result of any provision of the scheme made by virtue of subsection (3);

(b)   making payments as a result of any such provision made by virtue of subsection (4).

## 217.   Insurers in financial difficulties

(1)   The compensation scheme may, in particular, include provision for the scheme manager to have power to take measures for safeguarding policyholders, or policyholders of a specified class, of relevant insurers.

(2)   'Relevant insurers' means relevant persons who—

(a)   have permission to effect or carry out contracts of insurance; and

(b)   are in financial difficulties.

(3)   The measures may include such measures as the scheme manager considers appropriate for—

(a)   securing or facilitating the transfer of a relevant insurer's business so far as it consists of the carrying out of contracts of insurance, or of any part of that business, to another authorised person;

(b)   giving assistance to the relevant insurer to enable it to continue to effect or carry out contracts of insurance.

(4)   The scheme may provide—

(a)   that if measures of a kind mentioned in subsection (3)(a) are to be taken, they should be on terms appearing to the scheme manager to be appropriate, including terms reducing, or deferring payment of, any of the things to which any of those who are eligible policyholders in relation to the relevant insurer are entitled in their capacity as such;

(b)   that if measures of a kind mentioned in subsection (3)(b) are to be taken, they should be conditional on the reduction of, or the deferment of the payment of, the things to which any of those who are eligible policyholders in relation to the relevant insurer are entitled in their capacity as such;

(c)   for ensuring that measures of a kind mentioned in subsection (3)(b) do not benefit to any material extent persons who were members of a relevant insurer when it began to be in financial difficulties or who had any responsibility for, or who may have profited from, the circumstances giving rise to its financial difficulties, except in specified circumstances;

(d)   for requiring the scheme manager to be satisfied that any measures he proposes to take are likely to cost less than it would cost to pay compensation under the scheme if the relevant insurer became unable, or likely to be unable, to satisfy claims made against him.

(5)   The scheme may provide for the Authority to have power—

(a)   to give such assistance to the scheme manager as it considers appropriate for assisting the scheme manager to determine what measures are practicable or desirable in the case of a particular relevant insurer;

(b)   to impose constraints on the taking of measures by the scheme manager in the case of a particular relevant insurer;

(c)   to require the scheme manager to provide it with information about any particular measures which the scheme manager is proposing to take.

(6)   The scheme may include provision for the scheme manager to have power—

(a)   to make interim payments in respect of eligible policyholders of a relevant insurer;

(b)   to indemnify any person making payments to eligible policyholders of a relevant insurer.

(7)   A provision of the scheme made by virtue of section 213(3)(b) may include power to impose levies for the purpose of meeting expenses of the scheme manager incurred in—

(a)   taking measures as a result of any provision of the scheme made by virtue of subsection (1);

(b)   making payments or giving indemnities as a result of any such provision made by virtue of subsection (6).

(8)   'Financial difficulties' and 'eligible policyholders' have such meanings as may be specified.

*Annual report*

## 218.   Annual report

(1)   At least once a year, the scheme manager must make a report to the Authority on the discharge of its functions.

(2)  The report must—

(a)  include a statement setting out the value of each of the funds established by the compensation scheme; and

(b)  comply with any requirements specified in rules made by the Authority.

(3)  The scheme manager must publish each report in the way it considers appropriate.

*Information and documents*

**219.  Scheme manager's power to require information**

(1)  The scheme manager may, by notice in writing given to the relevant person in respect of whom a claim is made under the scheme or to a person otherwise involved, require that person—

(a)  to provide specified information or information of a specified description; or

(b)  to produce specified documents or documents of a specified description.

(2)  The information or documents must be provided or produced—

(a)  before the end of such reasonable period as may be specified; and

(b)  in the case of information, in such manner or form as may be specified.

(3)  This section applies only to information and documents the provision or production of which the scheme manager considers—

(a)  to be necessary for the fair determination of the claim; or

(b)  to be necessary (or likely to be necessary) for the fair determination of other claims made (or which it expects may be made) in respect of the relevant person concerned.

(4)  If a document is produced in response to a requirement imposed under this section, the scheme manager may—

(a)  take copies or extracts from the document; or

(b)  require the person producing the document to provide an explanation of the document.

(5)  If a person who is required under this section to produce a document fails to do so, the scheme manager may require the person to state, to the best of his knowledge and belief, where the document is.

(6)  If the relevant person is insolvent, no requirement may be imposed under this section on a person to whom section 220 or 224 applies.

(7)  If a person claims a lien on a document, its production under this Part does not affect the lien.

(8)  'Relevant person' has the same meaning as in section 224.

(9)  'Specified' means specified in the notice given under subsection (1).

(10)  A person is involved in a claim made under the scheme if he was knowingly involved in the act or omission giving rise to the claim.

**220.  Scheme manager's power to inspect information held by liquidator etc**

(1)  For the purpose of assisting the scheme manager to discharge its functions in relation to a claim made in respect of an insolvent relevant person, a person to whom this section applies must permit a person authorised by the scheme manager to inspect relevant documents.

(2)  A person inspecting a document under this section may take copies of, or extracts from, the document.

(3)  This section applies to—

(a)  the administrative receiver, administrator, liquidator or trustee in bankruptcy of an insolvent relevant person;

(b)   the permanent trustee, within the meaning of the Bankruptcy (Scotland) Act 1985, on the estate of an insolvent relevant person.

(4)   This section does not apply to a liquidator, administrator or trustee in bankruptcy who is—

(a)   the Official Receiver;

(b)   the Official Receiver for Northern Ireland; or

(c)   the Accountant in Bankruptcy.

(5)   'Relevant person' has the same meaning as in section 224.

### 221.   Powers of court where information required

(1)   If a person ('the defaulter')—

(a)   fails to comply with a requirement imposed under section 219, or

(b)   fails to permit documents to be inspected under section 220,

the scheme manager may certify that fact in writing to the court and the court may enquire into the case.

(2)   If the court is satisfied that the defaulter failed without reasonable excuse to comply with the requirement (or to permit the documents to be inspected), it may deal with the defaulter (and, in the case of a body corporate, any director or officer) as if he were in contempt.

(3)   'Court' means—

(a)   the High Court;

(b)   in Scotland, the Court of Session.

*Miscellaneous*

### 222.   Statutory immunity

(1)   Neither the scheme manager nor any person who is, or is acting as, its board member, officer or member of staff is to be liable in damages for anything done or omitted in the discharge, or purported discharge, of the scheme manager's functions.

(2)   Subsection (1) does not apply—

(a)   if the act or omission is shown to have been in bad faith; or

(b)   so as to prevent an award of damages made in respect of an act or omission on the ground that the act or omission was unlawful as a result of section 6(1) of the Human Rights Act 1998.

### 223.   Management expenses

(1)   The amount which the scheme manager may recover, from the sums levied under the scheme, as management expenses attributable to a particular period may not exceed such amount as may be fixed by the scheme as the limit applicable to that period.

(2)   In calculating the amount of any levy to be imposed by the scheme manager, no amount may be included to reflect management expenses unless the limit mentioned in subsection (1) has been fixed by the scheme.

(3)   'Management expenses' means expenses incurred, or expected to be incurred, by the scheme manager in connection with its functions under this Act other than those incurred—

(a)   in paying compensation;

(b)   as a result of any provision of the scheme made by virtue of section 216(3) or (4) or 217(1) or (6).

### 224.   Scheme manager's power to inspect documents held by Official Receiver etc

(1)   If, as a result of the insolvency or bankruptcy of a relevant person, any documents have come into the possession of a person to whom this section applies, he must permit any

person authorised by the scheme manager to inspect the documents for the purpose of establishing—

    (a)   the identity of persons to whom the scheme manager may be liable to make a payment in accordance with the compensation scheme; or

    (b)   the amount of any payment which the scheme manager may be liable to make.

    (2)   A person inspecting a document under this section may take copies or extracts from the document.

    (3)   In this section 'relevant person' means a person who was—

    (a)   an authorised person at the time the act or omission which may give rise to the liability mentioned in subsection (1)(a) took place; or

    (b)   an appointed representative at that time.

    (4)   But a person who, at that time—

    (a)   qualified for authorisation under Schedule 3, and

    (b)   fell within a prescribed category,

is not to be regarded as a relevant person for the purposes of this section in relation to any activities for which he had permission as a result of any provision of, or made under, that Schedule unless he had elected to participate in the scheme in relation to those activities at that time.

    (5)   This section applies to—

    (a)   the Official Receiver;

    (b)   the Official Receiver for Northern Ireland; and

    (c)   the Accountant in Bankruptcy.

## PART XVI
## THE OMBUDSMAN SCHEME

### *The scheme*

### 225.  The scheme and the scheme operator

    (1)   This Part provides for a scheme under which certain disputes may be resolved quickly and with minimum formality by an independent person.

    (2)   The scheme is to be administered by a body corporate ('the scheme operator').

    (3)   The scheme is to be operated under a name chosen by the scheme operator but is referred to in this Act as 'the ombudsman scheme'.

    (4)   Schedule 17 makes provision in connection with the ombudsman scheme and the scheme operator.

### 226.  Compulsory jurisdiction

    (1)   A complaint which relates to an act or omission of a person ('the respondent') in carrying on an activity to which compulsory jurisdiction rules apply is to be dealt with under the ombudsman scheme if the conditions mentioned in subsection (2) are satisfied.

    (2)   The conditions are that—

    (a)   the complainant is eligible and wishes to have the complaint dealt with under the scheme;

    (b)   the respondent was an authorised person at the time of the act or omission to which the complaint relates; and

    (c)   the act or omission to which the complaint relates occurred at a time when compulsory jurisdiction rules were in force in relation to the activity in question.

    (3)   'Compulsory jurisdiction rules' means rules—

(a)   made by the Authority for the purposes of this section; and

(b)   specifying the activities to which they apply.

(4)   Only activities which are regulated activities, or which could be made regulated activities by an order under section 22, may be specified.

(5)   Activities may be specified by reference to specified categories (however described).

(6)   A complainant is eligible, in relation to the compulsory jurisdiction of the ombudsman scheme, if he falls within a class of person specified in the rules as eligible.

(7)   The rules—

(a)   may include provision for persons other than individuals to be eligible; but

(b)   may not provide for authorised persons to be eligible except in specified circumstances or in relation to complaints of a specified kind.

(8)   The jurisdiction of the scheme which results from this section is referred to in this Act as the 'compulsory jurisdiction'.

## 227.  Voluntary jurisdiction

(1)   A complaint which relates to an act or omission of a person ('the respondent') in carrying on an activity to which voluntary jurisdiction rules apply is to be dealt with under the ombudsman scheme if the conditions mentioned in subsection (2) are satisfied.

(2)   The conditions are that—

(a)   the complainant is eligible and wishes to have the complaint dealt with under the scheme;

(b)   at the time of the act or omission to which the complaint relates, the respondent was participating in the scheme;

(c)   at the time when the complaint is referred under the scheme, the respondent has not withdrawn from the scheme in accordance with its provisions;

(d)   the act or omission to which the complaint relates occurred at a time when voluntary jurisdiction rules were in force in relation to the activity in question; and

(e)   the complaint cannot be dealt with under the compulsory jurisdiction.

(3)   'Voluntary jurisdiction rules' means rules—

(a)   made by the scheme operator for the purposes of this section; and

(b)   specifying the activities to which they apply.

(4)   The only activities which may be specified in the rules are activities which are, or could be, specified in compulsory jurisdiction rules.

(5)   Activities may be specified by reference to specified categories (however described).

(6)   The rules require the Authority's approval.

(7)   A complainant is eligible, in relation to the voluntary jurisdiction of the ombudsman scheme, if he falls within a class of person specified in the rules as eligible.

(8)   The rules may include provision for persons other than individuals to be eligible.

(9)   A person qualifies for participation in the ombudsman scheme if he falls within a class of person specified in the rules in relation to the activity in question.

(10)   Provision may be made in the rules for persons other than authorised persons to participate in the ombudsman scheme.

(11)   The rules may make different provision in relation to complaints arising from different activities.

(12)   The jurisdiction of the scheme which results from this section is referred to in this Act as the 'voluntary jurisdiction'.

(13)   In such circumstances as may be specified in voluntary jurisdiction rules, a complaint—

(a)   which relates to an act or omission occurring at a time before the rules came into force, and

(b)   which could have been dealt with under a scheme which has to any extent been replaced by the voluntary jurisdiction,

is to be dealt with under the ombudsman scheme even though paragraph (b) or (d) of subsection (2) would otherwise prevent that.

(14)   In such circumstances as may be specified in voluntary jurisdiction rules, a complaint is to be dealt with under the ombudsman scheme even though—

(a)   paragraph (b) or (d) of subsection (2) would otherwise prevent that, and

(b)   the complaint is not brought within the scheme as a result of subsection (13),

but only if the respondent has agreed that complaints of that kind were to be dealt with under the scheme.

*Determination of complaints*

### 228.   Determination under the compulsory jurisdiction

(1)   This section applies only in relation to the compulsory jurisdiction.

(2)   A complaint is to be determined by reference to what is, in the opinion of the ombudsman, fair and reasonable in all the circumstances of the case.

(3)   When the ombudsman has determined a complaint he must give a written statement of his determination to the respondent and to the complainant.

(4)   The statement must—

(a)   give the ombudsman's reasons for his determination;

(b)   be signed by him; and

(c)   require the complainant to notify him in writing, before a date specified in the statement, whether he accepts or rejects the determination.

(5)   If the complainant notifies the ombudsman that he accepts the determination, it is binding on the respondent and the complainant and final.

(6)   If, by the specified date, the complainant has not notified the ombudsman of his acceptance or rejection of the determination he is to be treated as having rejected it.

(7)   The ombudsman must notify the respondent of the outcome.

(8)   A copy of the determination on which appears a certificate signed by an ombudsman is evidence (or in Scotland sufficient evidence) that the determination was made under the scheme.

(9)   Such a certificate purporting to be signed by an ombudsman is to be taken to have been duly signed unless the contrary is shown.

### 229.   Awards

(1)   This section applies only in relation to the compulsory jurisdiction.

(2)   If a complaint which has been dealt with under the scheme is determined in favour of the complainant, the determination may include—

(a)   an award against the respondent of such amount as the ombudsman considers fair compensation for loss or damage (of a kind falling within subsection (3)) suffered by the complainant ('a money award');

(b)   a direction that the respondent take such steps in relation to the complainant as the ombudsman considers just and appropriate (whether or not a court could order those steps to be taken).

(3)   A money award may compensate for—

(a)   financial loss; or

(b)   any other loss, or any damage, of a specified kind.

(4)   The Authority may specify the maximum amount which may be regarded as fair compensation for a particular kind of loss or damage specified under subsection (3)(b).

(5)   A money award may not exceed the monetary limit; but the ombudsman may, if he considers that fair compensation requires payment of a larger amount, recommend that the respondent pay the complainant the balance.

(6)   The monetary limit is such amount as may be specified.

(7)   Different amounts may be specified in relation to different kinds of complaint.

(8)   A money award—

(a)   may provide for the amount payable under the award to bear interest at a rate and as from a date specified in the award; and

(b)   is enforceable by the complainant in accordance with Part III of Schedule 17.

(9)   Compliance with a direction under subsection (2)(b)—

(a)   is enforceable by an injunction; or

(b)   in Scotland, is enforceable by an order under section 45 of the Court of Session Act 1988.

(10)   Only the complainant may bring proceedings for an injunction or proceedings for an order.

(11)   'Specified' means specified in compulsory jurisdiction rules.

## 230.   Costs

(1)   The scheme operator may by rules ('costs rules') provide for an ombudsman to have power, on determining a complaint under the compulsory jurisdiction, to award costs in accordance with the provisions of the rules.

(2)   Costs rules require the approval of the Authority.

(3)   Costs rules may not provide for the making of an award against the complainant in respect of the respondent's costs.

(4)   But they may provide for the making of an award against the complainant in favour of the scheme operator, for the purpose of providing a contribution to resources deployed in dealing with the complaint, if in the opinion of the ombudsman—

(a)   the complainant's conduct was improper or unreasonable; or

(b)   the complainant was responsible for an unreasonable delay.

(5)   Costs rules may authorise an ombudsman making an award in accordance with the rules to order that the amount payable under the award bears interest at a rate and as from a date specified in the order.

(6)   An amount due under an award made in favour of the scheme operator is recoverable as a debt due to the scheme operator.

(7)   Any other award made against the respondent is to be treated as a money award for the purposes of paragraph 16 of Schedule 17.

*Information*

## 231.   Ombudsman's power to require information

(1)   An ombudsman may, by notice in writing given to a party to a complaint, require that party—

(a)   to provide specified information or information of a specified description; or

(b)   to produce specified documents or documents of a specified description.

(2)  The information or documents must be provided or produced—

(a)  before the end of such reasonable period as may be specified; and

(b)  in the case of information, in such manner or form as may be specified.

(3)  This section applies only to information and documents the production of which the ombudsman considers necessary for the determination of the complaint.

(4)  If a document is produced in response to a requirement imposed under this section, the ombudsman may—

(a)  take copies or extracts from the document; or

(b)  require the person producing the document to provide an explanation of the document.

(5)  If a person who is required under this section to produce a document fails to do so, the ombudsman may require him to state, to the best of his knowledge and belief, where the document is.

(6)  If a person claims a lien on a document, its production under this Part does not affect the lien.

(7)  'Specified' means specified in the notice given under subsection (1).

## 232.  Powers of court where information required

(1)  If a person ('the defaulter') fails to comply with a requirement imposed under section 231, the ombudsman may certify that fact in writing to the court and the court may enquire into the case.

(2)  If the court is satisfied that the defaulter failed without reasonable excuse to comply with the requirement, it may deal with the defaulter (and, in the case of a body corporate, any director or officer) as if he were in contempt.

(3)  'Court' means—

(a)  the High Court;

(b)  in Scotland, the Court of Session.

## 233.  Data protection

In section 31 of the Data Protection Act 1998 (regulatory activity), after subsection (4), insert—

'(4A)  Personal data processed for the purpose of discharging any function which is conferred by or under Part XVI of the Financial Services and Markets Act 2000 on the body established by the Financial Services Authority for the purposes of that Part are exempt from the subject information provisions in any case to the extent to which the application of those provisions to the data would be likely to prejudice the proper discharge of the function.'

*Funding*

## 234.  Industry funding

(1)  For the purpose of funding—

(a)  the establishment of the ombudsman scheme (whenever any relevant expense is incurred), and

(b)  its operation in relation to the compulsory jurisdiction,

the Authority may make rules requiring the payment to it or to the scheme operator, by authorised persons or any class of authorised person of specified amounts (or amounts calculated in a specified way).

(2)  'Specified' means specified in the rules.

## PART XVII
## COLLECTIVE INVESTMENT SCHEMES

### CHAPTER I
### INTERPRETATION

### 235.  Collective investment schemes

(1)   In this Part 'collective investment scheme' means any arrangements with respect to property of any description, including money, the purpose or effect of which is to enable persons taking part in the arrangements (whether by becoming owners of the property or any part of it or otherwise) to participate in or receive profits or income arising from the acquisition, holding, management or disposal of the property or sums paid out of such profits or income.

(2)   The arrangements must be such that the persons who are to participate ('participants') do not have day-to-day control over the management of the property, whether or not they have the right to be consulted or to give directions.

(3)   The arrangements must also have either or both of the following characteristics—

(a)   the contributions of the participants and the profits or income out of which payments are to be made to them are pooled;

(b)   the property is managed as a whole by or on behalf of the operator of the scheme.

(4)   If arrangements provide for such pooling as is mentioned in subsection (3)(a) in relation to separate parts of the property, the arrangements are not to be regarded as constituting a single collective investment scheme unless the participants are entitled to exchange rights in one part for rights in another.

(5)   The Treasury may by order provide that arrangements do not amount to a collective investment scheme—

(a)   in specified circumstances; or

(b)   if the arrangements fall within a specified category of arrangement.

### 236.  Open-ended investment companies

(1)   In this Part 'an open-ended investment company' means a collective investment scheme which satisfies both the property condition and the investment condition.

(2)   The property condition is that the property belongs beneficially to, and is managed by or on behalf of, a body corporate ('BC') having as its purpose the investment of its funds with the aim of—

(a)   spreading investment risk; and

(b)   giving its members the benefit of the results of the management of those funds by or on behalf of that body.

(3)   The investment condition is that, in relation to BC, a reasonable investor would, if he were to participate in the scheme—

(a)   expect that he would be able to realize, within a period appearing to him to be reasonable, his investment in the scheme (represented, at any given time, by the value of shares in, or securities of, BC held by him as a participant in the scheme); and

(b)   be satisfied that his investment would be realized on a basis calculated wholly or mainly by reference to the value of property in respect of which the scheme makes arrangements.

(4)   In determining whether the investment condition is satisfied, no account is to be taken of any actual or potential redemption or repurchase of shares or securities under—

(a)   Chapter VII of Part V of the Companies Act 1985;

(b)   Chapter VII of Part VI of the Companies (Northern Ireland) Order 1986;

(c)   corresponding provisions in force in another EEA State; or

(d)   provisions in force in a country or territory other than an EEA state which the Treasury have, by order, designated as corresponding provisions.

(5)   The Treasury may by order amend the definition of 'an open-ended investment company' for the purposes of this Part.

### 237.   Other definitions

(1)   In this Part 'unit trust scheme' means a collective investment scheme under which the property is held on trust for the participants.

(2)   In this Part—

'trustee', in relation to a unit trust scheme, means the person holding the property in question on trust for the participants;

'depositary', in relation to—

(a)   a collective investment scheme which is constituted by a body incorporated by virtue of regulations under section 262, or

(b)   any other collective investment scheme which is not a unit trust scheme,

means any person to whom the property subject to the scheme is entrusted for safekeeping;

'the operator', in relation to a unit trust scheme with a separate trustee, means the manager and in relation to an open-ended investment company, means that company;

'units' means the rights or interests (however described) of the participants in a collective investment scheme.

(3)   In this Part—

'an authorised unit trust scheme' means a unit trust scheme which is authorised for the purposes of this Act by an authorisation order in force under section 243;

'an authorised open-ended investment company' means a body incorporated by virtue of regulations under section 262 in respect of which an authorisation order is in force under any provision made in such regulations by virtue of subsection (2)(l) of that section;

'a recognised scheme' means a scheme recognised under section 264, 270 or 272.

## CHAPTER II
## RESTRICTIONS ON PROMOTION

### 238.   Restrictions on promotion

(1)   An authorised person must not communicate an invitation or inducement to participate in a collective investment scheme.

(2)   But that is subject to the following provisions of this section and to section 239.

(3)   Subsection (1) applies in the case of a communication originating outside the United Kingdom only if the communication is capable of having an effect in the United Kingdom.

(4)   Subsection (1) does not apply in relation to—

(a)   an authorised unit trust scheme;

(b)   a scheme constituted by an authorised open-ended investment company; or

(c)   a recognised scheme.

(5)   Subsection (1) does not apply to anything done in accordance with rules made by the Authority for the purpose of exempting from that subsection the promotion otherwise than to the general public of schemes of specified descriptions.

(6)    The Treasury may by order specify circumstances in which subsection (1) does not apply.

(7)    An order under subsection (6) may, in particular, provide that subsection (1) does not apply in relation to communications—

(a)    of a specified description;

(b)    originating in a specified country or territory outside the United Kingdom;

(c)    originating in a country or territory which falls within a specified description of country or territory outside the United Kingdom; or

(d)    originating outside the United Kingdom.

(8)    The Treasury may by order repeal subsection (3).

(9)    'Communicate' includes causing a communication to be made.

(10)    'Promotion otherwise than to the general public' includes promotion in a way designed to reduce, so far as possible, the risk of participation by persons for whom participation would be unsuitable.

(11)    'Participate', in relation to a collective investment scheme, means become a participant (within the meaning given by section 235(2)) in the scheme.

### 239.    Single property schemes

(1)    The Treasury may by regulations make provision for exempting single property schemes from section 238(1).

(2)    For the purposes of subsection (1) a single property scheme is a scheme which has the characteristics mentioned in subsection (3) and satisfies such other requirements as are prescribed by the regulations conferring the exemption.

(3)    The characteristics are—

(a)    that the property subject to the scheme (apart from cash or other assets held for management purposes) consists of—

(i)    a single building (or a single building with ancillary buildings) managed by or on behalf of the operator of the scheme, or

(ii)    a group of adjacent or contiguous buildings managed by him or on his behalf as a single enterprise,

with or without ancillary land and with or without furniture, fittings or other contents of the building or buildings in question; and

(b)    that the units of the participants in the scheme are either dealt in on a recognised investment exchange or offered on terms such that any agreement for their acquisition is conditional on their admission to dealings on such an exchange.

(4)    If regulations are made under subsection (1), the Authority may make rules imposing duties or liabilities on the operator and (if any) the trustee or depositary of a scheme exempted by the regulations.

(5)    The rules may include, to such extent as the Authority thinks appropriate, provision for purposes corresponding to those for which provision can be made under section 248 in relation to authorised unit trust schemes.

### 240.    Restriction on approval of promotion

(1)    An authorised person may not approve for the purposes of section 21 the content of a communication relating to a collective investment scheme if he would be prohibited by section 238(1) from effecting the communication himself or from causing it to be communicated.

(2)    For the purposes of determining in any case whether there has been a contravention of section 21(1), an approval given in contravention of subsection (1) is to be regarded as not having been given.

### 241.  Actions for damages
If an authorised person contravenes a requirement imposed on him by section 238 or 240, section 150 applies to the contravention as it applies to a contravention mentioned in that section.

## CHAPTER III
## AUTHORISED UNIT TRUST SCHEMES

*Applications for authorisation*

### 242.  Applications for authorisation of unit trust schemes
(1)  Any application for an order declaring a unit trust scheme to be an authorised unit trust scheme must be made to the Authority by the manager and trustee, or proposed manager and trustee, of the scheme.

(2)  The manager and trustee (or proposed manager and trustee) must be different persons.

(3)  The application—
(a)  must be made in such manner as the Authority may direct; and
(b)  must contain or be accompanied by such information as the Authority may reasonably require for the purpose of determining the application.

(4)  At any time after receiving an application and before determining it, the Authority may require the applicants to provide it with such further information as it reasonably considers necessary to enable it to determine the application.

(5)  Different directions may be given, and different requirements imposed, in relation to different applications.

(6)  The Authority may require applicants to present information which they are required to give under this section in such form, or to verify it in such a way, as the Authority may direct.

### 243.  Authorisation orders
(1)  If, on an application under section 242 in respect of a unit trust scheme, the Authority—
(a)  is satisfied that the scheme complies with the requirements set out in this section,
(b)  is satisfied that the scheme complies with the requirements of the trust scheme rules, and
(c)  has been provided with a copy of the trust deed and a certificate signed by a solicitor to the effect that it complies with such of the requirements of this section or those rules as relate to its contents,
the Authority may make an order declaring the scheme to be an authorised unit trust scheme.

(2)  If the Authority makes an order under subsection (1), it must give written notice of the order to the applicant.

(3)  In this Chapter 'authorisation order' means an order under subsection (1).

(4)  The manager and the trustee must be persons who are independent of each other.

(5)  The manager and the trustee must each—
(a)  be a body corporate incorporated in the United Kingdom or another EEA State, and
(b)  have a place of business in the United Kingdom,
and the affairs of each must be administered in the country in which it is incorporated.

(6)  If the manager is incorporated in another EEA State, the scheme must not be one which satisfies the requirements prescribed for the purposes of section 264.

(7)   The manager and the trustee must each be an authorised person and the manager must have permission to act as manager and the trustee must have permission to act as trustee.

(8)   The name of the scheme must not be undesirable or misleading.

(9)   The purposes of the scheme must be reasonably capable of being successfully carried into effect.

(10)   The participants must be entitled to have their units redeemed in accordance with the scheme at a price—

(a)   related to the net value of the property to which the units relate; and

(b)   determined in accordance with the scheme.

(11)   But a scheme is to be treated as complying with subsection (10) if it requires the manager to ensure that a participant is able to sell his units on an investment exchange at a price not significantly different from that mentioned in that subsection.

## 244.   Determination of applications

(1)   An application under section 242 must be determined by the Authority before the end of the period of six months beginning with the date on which it receives the completed application.

(2)   The Authority may determine an incomplete application if it considers it appropriate to do so; and it must in any event determine such an application within twelve months beginning with the date on which it first receives the application.

(3)   The applicant may withdraw his application, by giving the Authority written notice, at any time before the Authority determines it.

*Applications refused*

## 245.   Procedure when refusing an application

(1)   If the Authority proposes to refuse an application made under section 242 it must give each of the applicants a warning notice.

(2)   If the Authority decides to refuse the application—

(a)   it must give each of the applicants a decision notice; and

(b)   either applicant may refer the matter to the Tribunal.

*Certificates*

## 246.   Certificates

(1)   If the manager or trustee of a unit trust scheme which complies with the conditions necessary for it to enjoy the rights conferred by any relevant Community instrument so requests, the Authority may issue a certificate to the effect that the scheme complies with those conditions.

(2)   Such a certificate may be issued on the making of an authorisation order in respect of the scheme or at any subsequent time.

*Rules*

## 247.   Trust scheme rules

(1)   The Authority may make rules ('trust scheme rules') as to—

(a)   the constitution, management and operation of authorised unit trust schemes;

(b)   the powers, duties, rights and liabilities of the manager and trustee of any such scheme;

(c)   the rights and duties of the participants in any such scheme; and

  (d)   the winding up of any such scheme.
  (2)   Trust scheme rules may, in particular, make provision—
    (a)   as to the issue and redemption of the units under the scheme;
    (b)   as to the expenses of the scheme and the means of meeting them;
    (c)   for the appointment, removal, powers and duties of an auditor for the scheme;
    (d)   for restricting or regulating the investment and borrowing powers exercisable in relation to the scheme;
    (e)   requiring the keeping of records with respect to the transactions and financial position of the scheme and for the inspection of those records;
    (f)   requiring the preparation of periodical reports with respect to the scheme and the provision of those reports to the participants and to the Authority; and
    (g)   with respect to the amendment of the scheme.
  (3)   Trust scheme rules may make provision as to the contents of the trust deed, including provision requiring any of the matters mentioned in subsection (2) to be dealt with in the deed.
  (4)   But trust scheme rules are binding on the manager, trustee and participants independently of the contents of the trust deed and, in the case of the participants, have effect as if contained in it.
  (5)   If—
    (a)   a modification is made of the statutory provisions in force in Great Britain or Northern Ireland relating to companies,
    (b)   the modification relates to the rights and duties of persons who hold the beneficial title to any shares in a company without also holding the legal title, and
    (c)   it appears to the Treasury that, for the purpose of assimilating the law relating to authorised unit trust schemes to the law relating to companies as so modified, it is expedient to modify the rule-making powers conferred on the Authority by this section,
the Treasury may by order make such modifications of those powers as they consider appropriate.

## 248.  Scheme particulars rules

  (1)   The Authority may make rules ('scheme particulars rules') requiring the manager of an authorised unit trust scheme—
    (a)   to submit scheme particulars to the Authority; and
    (b)   to publish scheme particulars or make them available to the public on request.
  (2)   'Scheme particulars' means particulars in such form, containing such information about the scheme and complying with such requirements, as are specified in scheme particulars rules.
  (3)   Scheme particulars rules may require the manager of an authorised unit trust scheme to submit, and to publish or make available, revised or further scheme particulars if there is a significant change affecting any matter—
    (a)   which is contained in scheme particulars previously published or made available; and
    (b)   whose inclusion in those particulars was required by the rules.
  (4)   Scheme particulars rules may require the manager of an authorised unit trust scheme to submit, and to publish or make available, revised or further scheme particulars if—
    (a)   a significant new matter arises; and
    (b)   the inclusion of information in respect of that matter would have been required in previous particulars if it had arisen when those particulars were prepared.

(5) Scheme particulars rules may provide for the payment, by the person or persons who in accordance with the rules are treated as responsible for any scheme particulars, of compensation to any qualifying person who has suffered loss as a result of—

(a) any untrue or misleading statement in the particulars; or

(b) the omission from them of any matter required by the rules to be included.

(6) 'Qualifying person' means a person who—

(a) has become or agreed to become a participant in the scheme; or

(b) although not being a participant, has a beneficial interest in units in the scheme.

(7) Scheme particulars rules do not affect any liability which any person may incur apart from the rules.

## 249. Disqualification of auditor for breach of trust scheme rules

(1) If it appears to the Authority that an auditor has failed to comply with a duty imposed on him by trust scheme rules, it may disqualify him from being the auditor for any authorised unit trust scheme or authorised open—ended investment company.

(2) Subsections (2) to (5) of section 345 have effect in relation to disqualification under subsection (1) as they have effect in relation to disqualification under subsection (1) of that section.

## 250. Modification or waiver of rules

(1) In this section 'rules' means—

(a) trust scheme rules; or

(b) scheme particulars rules.

(2) The Authority may, on the application or with the consent of any person to whom any rules apply, direct that all or any of the rules—

(a) are not to apply to him as respects a particular scheme; or

(b) are to apply to him, as respects a particular scheme, with such modifications as may be specified in the direction.

(3) The Authority may, on the application or with the consent of the manager and trustee of a particular scheme acting jointly, direct that all or any of the rules—

(a) are not to apply to the scheme; or

(b) are to apply to the scheme with such modifications as may be specified in the direction.

(4) Subsections (3) to (9) and (11) of section 148 have effect in relation to a direction under subsection (2) as they have effect in relation to a direction under section 148(2) but with the following modifications—

(a) subsection (4)(a) is to be read as if the words 'by the authorised person' were omitted;

(b) any reference to the authorised person (except in subsection (4)(a)) is to be read as a reference to the person mentioned in subsection (2); and

(c) subsection (7)(b) is to be read, in relation to a participant of the scheme, as if the word 'commercial' were omitted.

(5) Subsections (3) to (9) and (11) of section 148 have effect in relation to a direction under subsection (3) as they have effect in relation to a direction under section 148(2) but with the following modifications—

(a) subsection (4)(a) is to be read as if the words 'by the authorised person' were omitted;

(b) subsections (7)(b) and (11) are to be read as if references to the authorised person were references to each of the manager and the trustee of the scheme;

(c) subsection (7)(b) is to be read, in relation to a participant of the scheme, as if the word 'commercial' were omitted;

(d)   subsection (8) is to be read as if the reference to the authorised person concerned were a reference to the scheme concerned and to its manager and trustee; and

(e)   subsection (9) is to be read as if the reference to the authorised person were a reference to the manager and trustee of the scheme acting jointly.

*Alterations*

### 251.   Alteration of schemes and changes of manager or trustee

(1)   The manager of an authorised unit trust scheme must give written notice to the Authority of any proposal to alter the scheme or to replace its trustee.

(2)   Any notice given in respect of a proposal to alter the scheme involving a change in the trust deed must be accompanied by a certificate signed by a solicitor to the effect that the change will not affect the compliance of the deed with the trust scheme rules.

(3)   The trustee of an authorised unit trust scheme must give written notice to the Authority of any proposal to replace the manager of the scheme.

(4)   Effect is not to be given to any proposal of which notice has been given under subsection (1) or (3) unless—

(a)   the Authority, by written notice, has given its approval to the proposal; or

(b)   one month, beginning with the date on which the notice was given, has expired without the manager or trustee having received from the Authority a warning notice under section 252 in respect of the proposal.

(5)   The Authority must not approve a proposal to replace the manager or the trustee of an authorised unit trust scheme unless it is satisfied that, if the proposed replacement is made, the scheme will continue to comply with the requirements of section 243(4) to (7).

### 252.   Procedure when refusing approval of change of manager or trustee

(1)   If the Authority proposes to refuse approval of a proposal to replace the trustee or manager of an authorised unit trust scheme, it must give a warning notice to the person by whom notice of the proposal was given under section 251(1) or (3).

(2)   If the Authority proposes to refuse approval of a proposal to alter an authorised unit trust scheme it must give separate warning notices to the manager and the trustee of the scheme.

(3)   To be valid the warning notice must be received by that person before the end of one month beginning with the date on which notice of the proposal was given.

(4)   If, having given a warning notice to a person, the Authority decides to refuse approval—

(a)   it must give him a decision notice; and

(b)   he may refer the matter to the Tribunal.

*Exclusion clauses*

### 253.   Avoidance of exclusion clauses

Any provision of the trust deed of an authorised unit trust scheme is void in so far as it would have the effect of exempting the manager or trustee from liability for any failure to exercise due care and diligence in the discharge of his functions in respect of the scheme.

*Ending of authorisation*

### 254.   Revocation of authorisation order otherwise than by consent

(1)   An authorisation order may be revoked by an order made by the Authority if it appears to the Authority that—

(a)   one or more of the requirements for the making of the order are no longer satisfied;

(b)   the manager or trustee of the scheme concerned has contravened a requirement imposed on him by or under this Act;

(c)   the manager or trustee of the scheme has, in purported compliance with any such requirement, knowingly or recklessly given the Authority information which is false or misleading in a material particular;

(d)   no regulated activity is being carried on in relation to the scheme and the period of that inactivity began at least twelve months earlier; or

(e)   none of paragraphs (a) to (d) applies, but it is desirable to revoke the authorisation order in order to protect the interests of participants or potential participants in the scheme.

(2)   For the purposes of subsection (1)(e), the Authority may take into account any matter relating to—

(a)   the scheme;

(b)   the manager or trustee;

(c)   any person employed by or associated with the manager or trustee in connection with the scheme;

(d)   any director of the manager or trustee;

(e)   any person exercising influence over the manager or trustee;

(f)   any body corporate in the same group as the manager or trustee;

(g)   any director of any such body corporate;

(h)   any person exercising influence over any such body corporate.

### 255.  Procedure

(1)   If the Authority proposes to make an order under section 254 revoking an authorisation order ('a revoking order'), it must give separate warning notices to the manager and the trustee of the scheme.

(2)   If the Authority decides to make a revoking order, it must without delay give each of them a decision notice and either of them may refer the matter to the Tribunal.

### 256.  Requests for revocation of authorisation order

(1)   An authorisation order may be revoked by an order made by the Authority at the request of the manager or trustee of the scheme concerned.

(2)   If the Authority makes an order under subsection (1), it must give written notice of the order to the manager and trustee of the scheme concerned.

(3)   The Authority may refuse a request to make an order under this section if it considers that—

(a)   the public interest requires that any matter concerning the scheme should be investigated before a decision is taken as to whether the authorisation order should be revoked; or

(b)   revocation would not be in the interests of the participants or would be incompatible with a Community obligation.

(4)   If the Authority proposes to refuse a request under this section, it must give separate warning notices to the manager and the trustee of the scheme.

(5)   If the Authority decides to refuse the request, it must without delay give each of them a decision notice and either of them may refer the matter to the Tribunal.

*Powers of intervention*

### 257.  Directions

(1)   The Authority may give a direction under this section if it appears to the Authority that—

(a)   one or more of the requirements for the making of an authorisation order are no longer satisfied;

(b)   the manager or trustee of an authorised unit trust scheme has contravened, or is likely to contravene, a requirement imposed on him by or under this Act;

(c)   the manager or trustee of such a scheme has, in purported compliance with any such requirement, knowingly or recklessly given the Authority information which is false or misleading in a material particular; or

(d)   none of paragraphs (a) to (c) applies, but it is desirable to give a direction in order to protect the interests of participants or potential participants in such a scheme.

(2)   A direction under this section may—

(a)   require the manager of the scheme to cease the issue or redemption, or both the issue and redemption, of units under the scheme;

(b)   require the manager and trustee of the scheme to wind it up.

(3)   If the authorisation order is revoked, the revocation does not affect any direction under this section which is then in force.

(4)   A direction may be given under this section in relation to a scheme in the case of which the authorisation order has been revoked if a direction under this section was already in force at the time of revocation.

(5)   If a person contravenes a direction under this section, section 150 applies to the contravention as it applies to a contravention mentioned in that section.

(6)   The Authority may, either on its own initiative or on the application of the manager or trustee of the scheme concerned, revoke or vary a direction given under this section if it appears to the Authority—

(a)   in the case of revocation, that it is no longer necessary for the direction to take effect or continue in force;

(b)   in the case of variation, that the direction should take effect or continue in force in a different form.

## 258.   Applications to the court

(1)   If the Authority could give a direction under section 257, it may also apply to the court for an order—

(a)   removing the manager or the trustee, or both the manager and the trustee, of the scheme; and

(b)   replacing the person or persons removed with a suitable person or persons nominated by the Authority.

(2)   The Authority may nominate a person for the purposes of subsection (1)(b) only if it is satisfied that, if the order was made, the requirements of section 243(4) to (7) would be complied with.

(3)   If it appears to the Authority that there is no person it can nominate for the purposes of subsection (1)(b), it may apply to the court for an order—

(a)   removing the manager or the trustee, or both the manager and the trustee, of the scheme; and

(b)   appointing an authorised person to wind up the scheme.

(4)   On an application under this section the court may make such order as it thinks fit.

(5)   The court may, on the application of the Authority, rescind any such order as is mentioned in subsection (3) and substitute such an order as is mentioned in subsection (1).

(6)   The Authority must give written notice of the making of an application under this section to the manager and trustee of the scheme concerned.

(7) The jurisdiction conferred by this section may be exercised by—

(a) the High Court;

(b) in Scotland, the Court of Session.

### 259. Procedure on giving directions under section 257 and varying them on Authority's own initiative

(1) A direction takes effect—

(a) immediately, if the notice given under subsection (3) states that that is the case;

(b) on such date as may be specified in the notice; or

(c) if no date is specified in the notice, when the matter to which it relates is no longer open to review.

(2) A direction may be expressed to take effect immediately (or on a specified date) only if the Authority, having regard to the ground on which it is exercising its power under section 257, considers that it is necessary for the direction to take effect immediately (or on that date).

(3) If the Authority proposes to give a direction under section 257, or gives such a direction with immediate effect, it must give separate written notice to the manager and the trustee of the scheme concerned.

(4) The notice must—

(a) give details of the direction;

(b) inform the person to whom it is given of when the direction takes effect;

(c) state the Authority's reasons for giving the direction and for its determination as to when the direction takes effect;

(d) inform the person to whom it is given that he may make representations to the Authority within such period as may be specified in it (whether or not he has referred the matter to the Tribunal); and

(e) inform him of his right to refer the matter to the Tribunal.

(5) If the direction imposes a requirement under section 257(2)(a), the notice must state that the requirement has effect until—

(a) a specified date; or

(b) a further direction.

(6) If the direction imposes a requirement under section 257(2)(b), the scheme must be wound up—

(a) by a date specified in the notice; or

(b) if no date is specified, as soon as practicable.

(7) The Authority may extend the period allowed under the notice for making representations.

(8) If, having considered any representations made by a person to whom the notice was given, the Authority decides—

(a) to give the direction in the way proposed, or

(b) if it has been given, not to revoke the direction,

it must give separate written notice to the manager and the trustee of the scheme concerned.

(9) If, having considered any representations made by a person to whom the notice was given, the Authority decides—

(a) not to give the direction in the way proposed,

(b) to give the direction in a way other than that proposed, or

(c) to revoke a direction which has effect,

it must give separate written notice to the manager and the trustee of the scheme concerned.

(10) A notice given under subsection (8) must inform the person to whom it is given of his right to refer the matter to the Tribunal.

(11) A notice under subsection (9)(b) must comply with subsection (4).

(12) If a notice informs a person of his right to refer a matter to the Tribunal, it must give an indication of the procedure on such a reference.

(13) This section applies to the variation of a direction on the Authority's own initiative as it applies to the giving of a direction.

(14) For the purposes of subsection (1)(c), whether a matter is open to review is to be determined in accordance with section 391(8).

**260. Procedure: refusal to revoke or vary direction**

(1) If on an application under section 257(6) for a direction to be revoked or varied the Authority proposes—

(a) to vary the direction otherwise than in accordance with the application, or

(b) to refuse to revoke or vary the direction,

it must give the applicant a warning notice.

(2) If the Authority decides to refuse to revoke or vary the direction—

(a) it must give the applicant a decision notice; and

(b) the applicant may refer the matter to the Tribunal.

**261. Procedure: revocation of direction and grant of request for variation**

(1) If the Authority decides on its own initiative to revoke a direction under section 257 it must give separate written notices of its decision to the manager and trustee of the scheme.

(2) If on an application under section 257(6) for a direction to be revoked or varied the Authority decides to revoke the direction or vary it in accordance with the application, it must give the applicant written notice of its decision.

(3) A notice under this section must specify the date on which the decision takes effect.

(4) The Authority may publish such information about the revocation or variation, in such way, as it considers appropriate.

CHAPTER IV
OPEN-ENDED INVESTMENT COMPANIES

**262. Open-ended investment companies**

(1) The Treasury may by regulations make provision for—

(a) facilitating the carrying on of collective investment by means of open—ended investment companies;

(b) regulating such companies.

(2) The regulations may, in particular, make provision—

(a) for the incorporation and registration in Great Britain of bodies corporate;

(b) for a body incorporated by virtue of the regulations to take such form as may be determined in accordance with the regulations;

(c) as to the purposes for which such a body may exist, the investments which it may issue and otherwise as to its constitution;

(d) as to the management and operation of such a body and the management of its property;

(e) as to the powers, duties, rights and liabilities of such a body and of other persons, including—

(i) the directors or sole director of such a body;

(ii) its depositary (if any);

(iii)   its shareholders, and persons who hold the beneficial title to shares in it without holding the legal title;

(iv)   its auditor; and

(v)   any persons who act or purport to act on its behalf;

(f)   as to the merger of one or more such bodies and the division of such a body;

(g)   for the appointment and removal of an auditor for such a body;

(h)   as to the winding up and dissolution of such a body;

(i)   for such a body, or any director or depositary of such a body, to be required to comply with directions given by the Authority;

(j)   enabling the Authority to apply to a court for an order removing and replacing any director or depositary of such a body;

(k)   for the carrying out of investigations by persons appointed by the Authority or the Secretary of State;

(l)   corresponding to any provision made in relation to unit trust schemes by Chapter III of this Part.

(3)   Regulations under this section may—

(a)   impose criminal liability;

(b)   confer functions on the Authority;

(c)   in the case of provision made by virtue of subsection (2)(l), authorise the making of rules by the Authority;

(d)   confer jurisdiction on any court or on the Tribunal;

(e)   provide for fees to be charged by the Authority in connection with the carrying out of any of its functions under the regulations (including fees payable on a periodical basis);

(f)   modify, exclude or apply (with or without modifications) any primary or subordinate legislation (including any provision of, or made under, this Act);

(g)   make consequential amendments, repeals and revocations of any such legislation;

(h)   modify or exclude any rule of law.

(4)   The provision that may be made by virtue of subsection (3)(f) includes provision extending or adapting any power to make subordinate legislation.

(5)   Regulations under this section may, in particular—

(a)   revoke the Open-Ended Investment Companies (Investment Companies with Variable Capital) Regulations 1996; and

(b)   provide for things done under or in accordance with those regulations to be treated as if they had been done under or in accordance with regulations under this section.

### 263.   Amendment of section 716 Companies Act 1985

In section 716(1) of the Companies Act 1985 (prohibition on formation of companies with more than 20 members unless registered under the Act etc.), after 'this Act,' insert 'is incorporated by virtue of regulations made under section 262 of the Financial Services and Markets Act 2000'.

CHAPTER V

RECOGNISED OVERSEAS SCHEMES

*Schemes constituted in other EEA States*

### 264.   Schemes constituted in other EEA States

(1)   A collective investment scheme constituted in another EEA State is a recognised scheme if—

(a)   it satisfies such requirements as are prescribed for the purposes of this section; and

(b)   not less than two months before inviting persons in the United Kingdom to become participants in the scheme, the operator of the scheme gives notice to the Authority of his intention to do so, specifying the way in which the invitation is to be made.

(2)   But this section does not make the scheme a recognised scheme if within two months of receiving the notice under subsection (1) the Authority notifies—

(a)   the operator of the scheme, and

(b)   the authorities of the State in question who are responsible for the authorisation of collective investment schemes,

that the way in which the invitation is to be made does not comply with the law in force in the United Kingdom.

(3)   The notice to be given to the Authority under subsection (1)—

(a)   must be accompanied by a certificate from the authorities mentioned in subsection (2)(b) to the effect that the scheme complies with the conditions necessary for it to enjoy the rights conferred by any relevant Community instrument;

(b)   must contain the address of a place in the United Kingdom for the service on the operator of notices or other documents required or authorised to be served on him under this Act; and

(c)   must contain or be accompanied by such other information and documents as may be prescribed.

(4)   A notice given by the Authority under subsection (2) must—

(a)   give the reasons for which the Authority considers that the law in force in the United Kingdom will not be complied with; and

(b)   specify a reasonable period (which may not be less than 28 days) within which any person to whom it is given may make representations to the Authority.

(5)   For the purposes of this section a collective investment scheme is constituted in another EEA State if—

(a)   it is constituted under the law of that State by a contract or under a trust and is managed by a body corporate incorporated under that law; or

(b)   it takes the form of an open-ended investment company incorporated under that law.

(6)   The operator of a recognised scheme may give written notice to the Authority that he desires the scheme to be no longer recognised by virtue of this section.

(7)   On the giving of notice under subsection (6), the scheme ceases to be a recognised scheme.

### 265.   Representations and references to the Tribunal

(1)   This section applies if any representations are made to the Authority, before the period for making representations has ended, by a person to whom a notice was given by the Authority under section 264(2).

(2)   The Authority must, within a reasonable period, decide in the light of those representations whether or not to withdraw its notice.

(3)   If the Authority withdraws its notice the scheme is a recognised scheme from the date on which the notice is withdrawn.

(4)   If the Authority decides not to withdraw its notice, it must give a decision notice to each person to whom the notice under section 264(2) was given.

(5)   The operator of the scheme to whom the decision notice is given may refer the matter to the Tribunal.

**266.  Disapplication of rules**

(1)   Apart from—

(a)   financial promotion rules, and

(b)   rules under section 283(1),

rules made by the Authority under this Act do not apply to the operator, trustee or depositary of a scheme in relation to the carrying on by him of regulated activities for which he has permission in that capacity.

(2)   'Scheme' means a scheme which is a recognised scheme by virtue of section 264.

**267.  Power of Authority to suspend promotion of scheme**

(1)   Subsection (2) applies if it appears to the Authority that the operator of a scheme has communicated an invitation or inducement in relation to the scheme in a manner contrary to financial promotion rules.

(2)   The Authority may direct that—

(a)   the exemption from subsection (1) of section 238 provided by subsection (4)(c) of that section is not to apply in relation to the scheme; and

(b)   subsection (5) of that section does not apply with respect to things done in relation to the scheme.

(3)   A direction under subsection (2) has effect—

(a)   for a specified period;

(b)   until the occurrence of a specified event; or

(c)   until specified conditions are complied with.

(4)   The Authority may, either on its own initiative or on the application of the operator of the scheme concerned, vary a direction given under subsection (2) if it appears to the Authority that the direction should take effect or continue in force in a different form.

(5)   The Authority may, either on its own initiative or on the application of the operator of the recognised scheme concerned, revoke a direction given under subsection (2) if it appears to the Authority—

(a)   that the conditions specified in the direction have been complied with; or

(b)   that it is no longer necessary for the direction to take effect or continue in force.

(6)   If an event is specified, the direction ceases to have effect (unless revoked earlier) on the occurrence of that event.

(7)   For the purposes of this section and sections 268 and 269—

(a)   the scheme's home State is the EEA State in which the scheme is constituted (within the meaning given by section 264);

(b)   the competent authorities in the scheme's home State are the authorities in that State who are responsible for the authorisation of collective investment schemes.

(8)   'Scheme' means a scheme which is a recognised scheme by virtue of section 264.

(9)   'Specified', in relation to a direction, means specified in it.

**268.  Procedure on giving directions under section 267 and varying them on Authority's own initiative**

(1)   A direction under section 267 takes effect—

(a)   immediately, if the notice given under subsection (3)(a) states that that is the case;

(b)   on such date as may be specified in the notice; or

(c)   if no date is specified in the notice, when the matter to which it relates is no longer open to review.

(2)   A direction may be expressed to take effect immediately (or on a specified date) only if the Authority, having regard to its reasons for exercising its power under section

267, considers that it is necessary for the direction to take effect immediately (or on that date).

(3)   If the Authority proposes to give a direction under section 267, or gives such a direction with immediate effect, it must—

(a)   give the operator of the scheme concerned written notice; and

(b)   inform the competent authorities in the scheme's home State of its proposal or (as the case may be) of the direction.

(4)   The notice must—

(a)   give details of the direction;

(b)   inform the operator of when the direction takes effect;

(c)   state the Authority's reasons for giving the direction and for its determination as to when the direction takes effect;

(d)   inform the operator that he may make representations to the Authority within such period as may be specified in it (whether or not he has referred the matter to the Tribunal); and

(e)   inform him of his right to refer the matter to the Tribunal.

(5)   The Authority may extend the period allowed under the notice for making representations.

(6)   Subsection (7) applies if, having considered any representations made by the operator, the Authority decides—

(a)   to give the direction in the way proposed, or

(b)   if it has been given, not to revoke the direction.

(7)   The Authority must—

(a)   give the operator of the scheme concerned written notice; and

(b)   inform the competent authorities in the scheme's home State of the direction.

(8)   Subsection (9) applies if, having considered any representations made by a person to whom the notice was given, the Authority decides—

(a)   not to give the direction in the way proposed,

(b)   to give the direction in a way other than that proposed, or

(c)   to revoke a direction which has effect.

(9)   The Authority must—

(a)   give the operator of the scheme concerned written notice; and

(b)   inform the competent authorities in the scheme's home State of its decision.

(10)   A notice given under subsection (7)(a) must inform the operator of his right to refer the matter to the Tribunal.

(11)   A notice under subsection (9)(a) given as a result of subsection (8)(b) must comply with subsection (4).

(12)   If a notice informs a person of his right to refer a matter to the Tribunal, it must give an indication of the procedure on such a reference.

(13)   This section applies to the variation of a direction on the Authority's own initiative as it applies to the giving of a direction.

(14)   For the purposes of subsection (1)(c), whether a matter is open to review is to be determined in accordance with section 391(8).

### 269.   Procedure on application for variation or revocation of direction

(1)   If, on an application under subsection (4) or (5) of section 267, the Authority proposes—

(a)   to vary a direction otherwise than in accordance with the application, or

(b)   to refuse the application,

it must give the operator of the scheme concerned a warning notice.

(2)   If, on such an application, the Authority decides—

(a)   to vary a direction otherwise than in accordance with the application, or

(b)   to refuse the application,

it must give the operator of the scheme concerned a decision notice.

(3)   If the application is refused, the operator of the scheme may refer the matter to the Tribunal.

(4)   If, on such an application, the Authority decides to grant the application it must give the operator of the scheme concerned written notice.

(5)   If the Authority decides on its own initiative to revoke a direction given under section 267 it must give the operator of the scheme concerned written notice.

(6)   The Authority must inform the competent authorities in the scheme's home State of any notice given under this section.

*Schemes authorised in designated countries or territories*

**270.   Schemes authorised in designated countries or territories**

(1)   A collective investment scheme which is not a recognised scheme by virtue of section 264 but is managed in, and authorised under the law of, a country or territory outside the United Kingdom is a recognised scheme if—

(a)   that country or territory is designated for the purposes of this section by an order made by the Treasury;

(b)   the scheme is of a class specified by the order;

(c)   the operator of the scheme has given written notice to the Authority that he wishes it to be recognised; and

(d)   either—

(i)   the Authority, by written notice, has given its approval to the scheme's being recognised; or

(ii)   two months, beginning with the date on which notice was given under paragraph (c), have expired without the operator receiving a warning notice from the Authority under section 271.

(2)   The Treasury may not make an order designating any country or territory for the purposes of this section unless satisfied—

(a)   that the law and practice under which relevant collective investment schemes are authorised and supervised in that country or territory affords to investors in the United Kingdom protection at least equivalent to that provided for them by or under this Part in the case of comparable authorised schemes; and

(b)   that adequate arrangements exist, or will exist, for co-operation between the authorities of the country or territory responsible for the authorisation and supervision of relevant collective investment schemes and the Authority.

(3)   'Relevant collective investment schemes' means collective investment schemes of the class or classes to be specified by the order.

(4)   'Comparable authorised schemes' means whichever of the following the Treasury consider to be the most appropriate, having regard to the class or classes of scheme to be specified by the order—

(a)   authorised unit trust schemes;

(b)   authorised open-ended investment companies;

(c)   both such unit trust schemes and such companies.

(5)   If the Treasury are considering whether to make an order designating a country or territory for the purposes of this section—

(a)   the Treasury must ask the Authority for a report—

(i)   on the law and practice of that country or territory in relation to the authorisation and supervision of relevant collective investment schemes,

(ii)   on any existing or proposed arrangements for co-operation between it and the authorities responsible in that country or territory for the authorisation and supervision of relevant collective investment schemes,

having regard to the Treasury's need to be satisfied as mentioned in subsection (2);

(b)   the Authority must provide the Treasury with such a report; and

(c)   the Treasury must have regard to it in deciding whether to make the order.

(6)   The notice to be given by the operator under subsection (1)(c)—

(a)   must contain the address of a place in the United Kingdom for the service on the operator of notices or other documents required or authorised to be served on him under this Act; and

(b)   must contain or be accompanied by such information and documents as may be specified by the Authority.

## 271.   Procedure

(1)   If the Authority proposes to refuse approval of a scheme's being a recognised scheme by virtue of section 270, it must give the operator of the scheme a warning notice.

(2)   To be valid the warning notice must be received by the operator before the end of two months beginning with the date on which notice was given under section 270(1)(c).

(3)   If, having given a warning notice, the Authority decides to refuse approval—

(a)   it must give the operator of the scheme a decision notice; and

(b)   the operator may refer the matter to the Tribunal.

*Individually recognised overseas schemes*

## 272.   Individually recognised overseas schemes

(1)   The Authority may, on the application of the operator of a collective investment scheme which—

(a)   is managed in a country or territory outside the United Kingdom,

(b)   does not satisfy the requirements prescribed for the purposes of section 264,

(c)   is not managed in a country or territory designated for the purposes of section 270 or, if it is so managed, is of a class not specified by the designation order, and

(d)   appears to the Authority to satisfy the requirements set out in the following provisions of this section,

make an order declaring the scheme to be a recognised scheme.

(2)   Adequate protection must be afforded to participants in the scheme.

(3)   The arrangements for the scheme's constitution and management must be adequate.

(4)   The powers and duties of the operator and, if the scheme has a trustee or depositary, of the trustee or depositary must be adequate.

(5)   In deciding whether the matters mentioned in subsection (3) or (4) are adequate, the Authority must have regard to—

(a)   any rule of law, and

(b)   any matters which are, or could be, the subject of rules,

applicable in relation to comparable authorised schemes.

(6) 'Comparable authorised schemes' means whichever of the following the Authority considers the most appropriate, having regard to the nature of scheme in respect of which the application is made—

  (a)   authorised unit trust schemes;

  (b)   authorised open-ended investment companies;

  (c)   both such unit trust schemes and such companies.

(7)   The scheme must take the form of an open—ended investment company or (if it does not take that form) the operator must be a body corporate.

(8)   The operator of the scheme must—

  (a)   if an authorised person, have permission to act as operator;

  (b)   if not an authorised person, be a fit and proper person to act as operator.

(9)   The trustee or depositary (if any) of the scheme must—

  (a)   if an authorised person, have permission to act as trustee or depositary;

  (b)   if not an authorised person, be a fit and proper person to act as trustee or depositary.

(10)   The operator and the trustee or depositary (if any) of the scheme must be able and willing to co-operate with the Authority by the sharing of information and in other ways.

(11)   The name of the scheme must not be undesirable or misleading.

(12)   The purposes of the scheme must be reasonably capable of being successfully carried into effect.

(13)   The participants must be entitled to have their units redeemed in accordance with the scheme at a price related to the net value of the property to which the units relate and determined in accordance with the scheme.

(14)   But a scheme is to be treated as complying with subsection (13) if it requires the operator to ensure that a participant is able to sell his units on an investment exchange at a price not significantly different from that mentioned in that subsection.

(15)   Subsection (13) is not to be read as imposing a requirement that the participants must be entitled to have their units redeemed (or sold as mentioned in subsection (14)) immediately following a demand to that effect.

### 273.   Matters that may be taken into account

For the purposes of subsections (8)(b) and (9)(b) of section 272, the Authority may take into account any matter relating to—

  (a)   any person who is or will be employed by or associated with the operator, trustee or depositary in connection with the scheme;

  (b)   any director of the operator, trustee or depositary;

  (c)   any person exercising influence over the operator, trustee or depositary;

  (d)   any body corporate in the same group as the operator, trustee or depositary;

  (e)   any director of any such body corporate;

  (f)   any person exercising influence over any such body corporate.

### 274.   Applications for recognition of individual schemes

(1)   An application under section 272 for an order declaring a scheme to be a recognised scheme must be made to the Authority by the operator of the scheme.

(2)   The application—

  (a)   must be made in such manner as the Authority may direct;

  (b)   must contain the address of a place in the United Kingdom for the service on the operator of notices or other documents required or authorised to be served on him under this Act;

(c) must contain or be accompanied by such information as the Authority may reasonably require for the purpose of determining the application.

(3) At any time after receiving an application and before determining it, the Authority may require the applicant to provide it with such further information as it reasonably considers necessary to enable it to determine the application.

(4) Different directions may be given, and different requirements imposed, in relation to different applications.

(5) The Authority may require an applicant to present information which he is required to give under this section in such form, or to verify it in such a way, as the Authority may direct.

### 275. Determination of applications

(1) An application under section 272 must be determined by the Authority before the end of the period of six months beginning with the date on which it receives the completed application.

(2) The Authority may determine an incomplete application if it considers it appropriate to do so; and it must in any event determine such an application within twelve months beginning with the date on which it first receives the application.

(3) If the Authority makes an order under section 272(1), it must give written notice of the order to the applicant.

### 276. Procedure when refusing an application

(1) If the Authority proposes to refuse an application made under section 272 it must give the applicant a warning notice.

(2) If the Authority decides to refuse the application—

(a) it must give the applicant a decision notice; and

(b) the applicant may refer the matter to the Tribunal.

### 277. Alteration of schemes and changes of operator, trustee or depositary

(1) The operator of a scheme recognised by virtue of section 272 must give written notice to the Authority of any proposed alteration to the scheme.

(2) Effect is not to be given to any such proposal unless—

(a) the Authority, by written notice, has given its approval to the proposal; or

(b) one month, beginning with the date on which notice was given under subsection (1), has expired without the Authority having given written notice to the operator that it has decided to refuse approval.

(3) At least one month before any replacement of the operator, trustee or depositary of such a scheme, notice of the proposed replacement must be given to the Authority—

(a) by the operator, trustee or depositary (as the case may be); or

(b) by the person who is to replace him.

*Schemes recognised under sections 270 and 272*

### 278. Rules as to scheme particulars

The Authority may make rules imposing duties or liabilities on the operator of a scheme recognised under section 270 or 272 for purposes corresponding to those for which rules may be made under section 248 in relation to authorised unit trust schemes.

### 279. Revocation of recognition

The Authority may direct that a scheme is to cease to be recognised by virtue of section 270 or revoke an order under section 272 if it appears to the Authority—

(a)   that the operator, trustee or depositary of the scheme has contravened a requirement imposed on him by or under this Act;

(b)   that the operator, trustee or depositary of the scheme has, in purported compliance with any such requirement, knowingly or recklessly given the Authority information which is false or misleading in a material particular;

(c)   in the case of an order under section 272, that one or more of the requirements for the making of the order are no longer satisfied; or

(d)   that none of paragraphs (a) to (c) applies, but it is undesirable in the interests of the participants or potential participants that the scheme should continue to be recognised.

### 280.  Procedure

(1)   If the Authority proposes to give a direction under section 279 or to make an order under that section revoking a recognition order, it must give a warning notice to the operator and (if any) the trustee or depositary of the scheme.

(2)   If the Authority decides to give a direction or make an order under that section—

(a)   it must without delay give a decision notice to the operator and (if any) the trustee or depositary of the scheme; and

(b)   the operator or the trustee or depositary may refer the matter to the Tribunal.

### 281.  Directions

(1)   In this section a 'relevant recognised scheme' means a scheme recognised under section 270 or 272.

(2)   If it appears to the Authority that—

(a)   the operator, trustee or depositary of a relevant recognised scheme has contravened, or is likely to contravene, a requirement imposed on him by or under this Act,

(b)   the operator, trustee or depositary of such a scheme has, in purported compliance with any such requirement, knowingly or recklessly given the Authority information which is false or misleading in a material particular,

(c)   one or more of the requirements for the recognition of a scheme under section 272 are no longer satisfied, or

(d)   none of paragraphs (a) to (c) applies, but the exercise of the power conferred by this section is desirable in order to protect the interests of participants or potential participants in a relevant recognised scheme who are in the United Kingdom,

it may direct that the scheme is not to be a recognised scheme for a specified period or until the occurrence of a specified event or until specified conditions are complied with.

### 282.  Procedure on giving directions under section 281 and varying them otherwise than as requested

(1)   A direction takes effect—

(a)   immediately, if the notice given under subsection (3) states that that is the case;

(b)   on such date as may be specified in the notice; or

(c)   if no date is specified in the notice, when the matter to which it relates is no longer open to review.

(2)   A direction may be expressed to take effect immediately (or on a specified date) only if the Authority, having regard to the ground on which it is exercising its power under section 281, considers that it is necessary for the direction to take effect immediately (or on that date).

(3)   If the Authority proposes to give a direction under section 281, or gives such a direction with immediate effect, it must give separate written notice to the operator and (if any) the trustee or depositary of the scheme concerned.

(4)　The notice must—

(a)　give details of the direction;

(b)　inform the person to whom it is given of when the direction takes effect;

(c)　state the Authority's reasons for giving the direction and for its determination as to when the direction takes effect;

(d)　inform the person to whom it is given that he may make representations to the Authority within such period as may be specified in it (whether or not he has referred the matter to the Tribunal); and

(e)　inform him of his right to refer the matter to the Tribunal.

(5)　The Authority may extend the period allowed under the notice for making representations.

(6)　If, having considered any representations made by a person to whom the notice was given, the Authority decides—

(a)　to give the direction in the way proposed, or

(b)　if it has been given, not to revoke the direction,

it must give separate written notice to the operator and (if any) the trustee or depositary of the scheme concerned.

(7)　If, having considered any representations made by a person to whom the notice was given, the Authority decides—

(a)　not to give the direction in the way proposed,

(b)　to give the direction in a way other than that proposed, or

(c)　to revoke a direction which has effect,

it must give separate written notice to the operator and (if any) the trustee or depositary of the scheme concerned.

(8)　A notice given under subsection (6) must inform the person to whom it is given of his right to refer the matter to the Tribunal.

(9)　A notice under subsection (7)(b) must comply with subsection (4).

(10)　If a notice informs a person of his right to refer a matter to the Tribunal, it must give an indication of the procedure on such a reference.

(11)　This section applies to the variation of a direction on the Authority's own initiative as it applies to the giving of a direction.

(12)　For the purposes of subsection (1)(c), whether a matter is open to review is to be determined in accordance with section 391(8).

*Facilities and information in UK*

**283.　Facilities and information in UK**

(1)　The Authority may make rules requiring operators of recognised schemes to maintain in the United Kingdom, or in such part or parts of it as may be specified, such facilities as the Authority thinks desirable in the interests of participants and as are specified in rules.

(2)　The Authority may by notice in writing require the operator of any recognised scheme to include such explanatory information as is specified in the notice in any communication of his which—

(a)　is a communication of an invitation or inducement of a kind mentioned in section 21(1); and

(b)　names the scheme.

(3)　In the case of a communication originating outside the United Kingdom, subsection (2) only applies if the communication is capable of having an effect in the United Kingdom.

CHAPTER VI
INVESTIGATIONS

**284.  Power to investigate**

(1)   An investigating authority may appoint one or more competent persons to investigate on its behalf—

(a)   the affairs of, or of the manager or trustee of, any authorised unit trust scheme,

(b)   the affairs of, or of the operator, trustee or depositary of, any recognised scheme so far as relating to activities carried on in the United Kingdom, or

(c)   the affairs of, or of the operator, trustee or depositary of, any other collective investment scheme except a body incorporated by virtue of regulations under section 262, if it appears to the investigating authority that it is in the interests of the participants or potential participants to do so or that the matter is of public concern.

(2)   A person appointed under subsection (1) to investigate the affairs of, or of the manager, trustee, operator or depositary of, any scheme (scheme 'A'), may also, if he thinks it necessary for the purposes of that investigation, investigate—

(a)   the affairs of, or of the manager, trustee, operator or depositary of, any other such scheme as is mentioned in subsection (1) whose manager, trustee, operator or depositary is the same person as the manager, trustee, operator or depositary of scheme A;

(b)   the affairs of such other schemes and persons (including bodies incorporated by virtue of regulations under section 262 and the directors and depositaries of such bodies) as may be prescribed.

(3)   If the person appointed to conduct an investigation under this section ('B') considers that a person ('C') is or may be able to give information which is relevant to the investigation, B may require C—

(a)   to produce to B any documents in C's possession or under his control which appear to B to be relevant to the investigation,

(b)   to attend before B, and

(c)   otherwise to give B all assistance in connection with the investigation which C is reasonably able to give,

and it is C's duty to comply with that requirement.

(4)   Subsections (5) to (9) of section 170 apply if an investigating authority appoints a person under this section to conduct an investigation on its behalf as they apply in the case mentioned in subsection (1) of that section.

(5)   Section 174 applies to a statement made by a person in compliance with a requirement imposed under this section as it applies to a statement mentioned in that section.

(6)   Subsections (2) to (4) and (6) of section 175 and section 177 have effect as if this section were contained in Part XI.

(7)   Subsections (1) to (9) of section 176 apply in relation to a person appointed under subsection (1) as if—

(a)   references to an investigator were references to a person so appointed;

(b)   references to an information requirement were references to a requirement imposed under section 175 or under subsection (3) by a person so appointed;

(c)   the premises mentioned in subsection (3)(a) were the premises of a person whose affairs are the subject of an investigation under this section or of an appointed representative of such a person.

(8)   No person may be required under this section to disclose information or produce a document in respect of which he owes an obligation of confidence by virtue of carrying on the business of banking unless subsection (9) or (10) applies.

(9)   This subsection applies if—

(a)   the person to whom the obligation of confidence is owed consents to the disclosure or production; or

(b)   the imposing on the person concerned of a requirement with respect to information or a document of a kind mentioned in subsection (8) has been specifically authorised by the investigating authority.

(10)   This subsection applies if the person owing the obligation of confidence or the person to whom it is owed is—

(a)   the manager, trustee, operator or depositary of any collective investment scheme which is under investigation;

(b)   the director of a body incorporated by virtue of regulations under section 262 which is under investigation;

(c)   any other person whose own affairs are under investigation.

(11)   'Investigating authority' means the Authority or the Secretary of State.

## PART XVIII
## RECOGNISED INVESTMENT EXCHANGES AND CLEARING HOUSES

### CHAPTER I
### EXEMPTION

*General*

### 285.   Exemption for recognised investment exchanges and clearing houses

(1)   In this Act—

(a)   'recognised investment exchange' means an investment exchange in relation to which a recognition order is in force; and

(b)   'recognised clearing house' means a clearing house in relation to which a recognition order is in force.

(2)   A recognised investment exchange is exempt from the general prohibition as respects any regulated activity—

(a)   which is carried on as a part of the exchange's business as an investment exchange; or

(b)   which is carried on for the purposes of, or in connection with, the provision of clearing services by the exchange.

(3)   A recognised clearing house is exempt from the general prohibition as respects any regulated activity which is carried on for the purposes of, or in connection with, the provision of clearing services by the clearing house.

### 286.   Qualification for recognition

(1)   The Treasury may make regulations setting out the requirements—

(a)   which must be satisfied by an investment exchange or clearing house if it is to qualify as a body in respect of which the Authority may make a recognition order under this Part; and

(b)   which, if a recognition order is made, it must continue to satisfy if it is to remain a recognised body.

(2) But if regulations contain provision as to the default rules of an investment exchange or clearing house, or as to proceedings taken under such rules by such a body, they require the approval of the Secretary of State.

(3) 'Default rules' means rules of an investment exchange or clearing house which provide for the taking of action in the event of a person's appearing to be unable, or likely to become unable, to meet his obligations in respect of one or more market contracts connected with the exchange or clearing house.

(4) 'Market contract' means—

(a) a contract to which Part VII of the Companies Act 1989 applies as a result of section 155 of that Act or a contract to which Part V of the Companies (No. 2) (Northern Ireland) Order 1990 applies as a result of Article 80 of that Order; and

(b) such other kind of contract as may be prescribed.

(5) Requirements resulting from this section are referred to in this Part as 'recognition requirements'.

*Applications for recognition*

### 287. Application by an investment exchange

(1) Any body corporate or unincorporated association may apply to the Authority for an order declaring it to be a recognised investment exchange for the purposes of this Act.

(2) The application must be made in such manner as the Authority may direct and must be accompanied by—

(a) a copy of the applicant's rules;

(b) a copy of any guidance issued by the applicant;

(c) the required particulars; and

(d) such other information as the Authority may reasonably require for the purpose of determining the application.

(3) The required particulars are—

(a) particulars of any arrangements which the applicant has made, or proposes to make, for the provision of clearing services in respect of transactions effected on the exchange;

(b) if the applicant proposes to provide clearing services in respect of transactions other than those effected on the exchange, particulars of the criteria which the applicant will apply when determining to whom it will provide those services.

### 288. Application by a clearing house

(1) Any body corporate or unincorporated association may apply to the Authority for an order declaring it to be a recognised clearing house for the purposes of this Act.

(2) The application must be made in such manner as the Authority may direct and must be accompanied by—

(a) a copy of the applicant's rules;

(b) a copy of any guidance issued by the applicant;

(c) the required particulars; and

(d) such other information as the Authority may reasonably require for the purpose of determining the application.

(3) The required particulars are—

(a) if the applicant makes, or proposes to make, clearing arrangements with a recognised investment exchange, particulars of those arrangements;

(b)   if the applicant proposes to provide clearing services for persons other than recognised investment exchanges, particulars of the criteria which it will apply when determining to whom it will provide those services.

## 289.   Applications: supplementary.

(1)   At any time after receiving an application and before determining it, the Authority may require the applicant to provide such further information as it reasonably considers necessary to enable it to determine the application.

(2)   Information which the Authority requires in connection with an application must be provided in such form, or verified in such manner, as the Authority may direct.

(3)   Different directions may be given, or requirements imposed, by the Authority with respect to different applications.

## 290.   Recognition orders.

(1)   If it appears to the Authority that the applicant satisfies the recognition requirements applicable in its case, the Authority may make a recognition order declaring the applicant to be—

(a)   a recognised investment exchange, if the application is made under section 287;

(b)   a recognised clearing house, if it is made under section 288.

(2)   The Treasury's approval of the making of a recognition order is required under section 307.

(3)   In considering an application, the Authority may have regard to any information which it considers is relevant to the application.

(4)   A recognition order must specify a date on which it is to take effect.

(5)   Section 298 has effect in relation to a decision to refuse to make a recognition order—

(a)   as it has effect in relation to a decision to revoke such an order; and

(b)   as if references to a recognised body were references to the applicant.

(6)   Subsection (5) does not apply in a case in which the Treasury have failed to give their approval under section 307.

## 291.   Liability in relation to recognised body's regulatory functions

(1)   A recognised body and its officers and staff are not to be liable in damages for anything done or omitted in the discharge of the recognised body's regulatory functions unless it is shown that the act or omission was in bad faith.

(2)   But subsection (1) does not prevent an award of damages made in respect of an act or omission on the ground that the act or omission was unlawful as a result of section 6(1) of the Human Rights Act 1998.

(3)   'Regulatory functions' means the functions of the recognised body so far as relating to, or to matters arising out of, the obligations to which the body is subject under or by virtue of this Act.

## 292.   Overseas investment exchanges and overseas clearing houses

(1)   An application under section 287 or 288 by an overseas applicant must contain the address of a place in the United Kingdom for the service on the applicant of notices or other documents required or authorised to be served on it under this Act.

(2)   If it appears to the Authority that an overseas applicant satisfies the requirements of subsection (3) it may make a recognition order declaring the applicant to be—

(a)   a recognised investment exchange;

(b)   a recognised clearing house.

(3)   The requirements are that—

(a)   investors are afforded protection equivalent to that which they would be afforded if the body concerned were required to comply with recognition requirements;

(b)   there are adequate procedures for dealing with a person who is unable, or likely to become unable, to meet his obligations in respect of one or more market contracts connected with the investment exchange or clearing house;

(c)   the applicant is able and willing to co-operate with the Authority by the sharing of information and in other ways;

(d)   adequate arrangements exist for co-operation between the Authority and those responsible for the supervision of the applicant in the country or territory in which the applicant's head office is situated.

(4)   In considering whether it is satisfied as to the requirements mentioned in subsection (3)(a) and (b), the Authority is to have regard to—

(a)   the relevant law and practice of the country or territory in which the applicant's head office is situated;

(b)   the rules and practices of the applicant.

(5)   In relation to an overseas applicant and a body or association declared to be a recognised investment exchange or recognised clearing house by a recognition order made by virtue of subsection (2)—

(a)   the reference in section 313(2) to recognition requirements is to be read as a reference to matters corresponding to the matters in respect of which provision is made in the recognition requirements;

(b)   sections 296(1) and 297(2) have effect as if the requirements mentioned in section 296(1)(a) and section 297(2)(a) were those of subsection (3)(a), (b), and (c) of this section;

(c)   section 297(2) has effect as if the grounds on which a recognition order may be revoked under that provision included the ground that in the opinion of the Authority arrangements of the kind mentioned in subsection (3)(d) no longer exist.

*Supervision*

### 293.  Notification requirements

(1)   The Authority may make rules requiring a recognised body to give it—

(a)   notice of such events relating to the body as may be specified; and

(b)   such information in respect of those events as may be specified.

(2)   The rules may also require a recognised body to give the Authority, at such times or in respect of such periods as may be specified, such information relating to the body as may be specified.

(3)   An obligation imposed by the rules extends only to a notice or information which the Authority may reasonably require for the exercise of its functions under this Act.

(4)   The rules may require information to be given in a specified form and to be verified in a specified manner.

(5)   If a recognised body—

(a)   alters or revokes any of its rules or guidance, or

(b)   makes new rules or issues new guidance,

it must give written notice to the Authority without delay.

(6)   If a recognised investment exchange makes a change—

(a)   in the arrangements it makes for the provision of clearing services in respect of transactions effected on the exchange, or

(b)   in the criteria which it applies when determining to whom it will provide clearing services,
it must give written notice to the Authority without delay.

(7)   If a recognised clearing house makes a change—

(a)   in the recognised investment exchanges for whom it provides clearing services, or

(b)   in the criteria which it applies when determining to whom (other than recognised investment exchanges) it will provide clearing services,
it must give written notice to the Authority without delay.

(8)   Subsections (5) to (7) do not apply to an overseas investment exchange or an overseas clearing house.

(9)   'Specified' means specified in the Authority's rules.

## 294.   Modification or waiver of rules

(1)   The Authority may, on the application or with the consent of a recognised body, direct that rules made under section 293 or 295—

(a)   are not to apply to the body; or

(b)   are to apply to the body with such modifications as may be specified in the direction.

(2)   An application must be made in such manner as the Authority may direct.

(3)   Subsections (4) to (6) apply to a direction given under subsection (1).

(4)   The Authority may not give a direction unless it is satisfied that—

(a)   compliance by the recognised body with the rules, or with the rules as unmodified, would be unduly burdensome or would not achieve the purpose for which the rules were made; and

(b)   the direction would not result in undue risk to persons whose interests the rules are intended to protect.

(5)   A direction may be given subject to conditions.

(6)   The Authority may—

(a)   revoke a direction; or

(b)   vary it on the application, or with the consent, of the recognised body to which it relates.

## 295.   Notification: overseas investment exchanges and overseas clearing houses

(1)   At least once a year, every overseas investment exchange and overseas clearing house must provide the Authority with a report.

(2)   The report must contain a statement as to whether any events have occurred which are likely—

(a)   to affect the Authority's assessment of whether it is satisfied as to the requirements set out in section 292(3); or

(b)   to have any effect on competition.

(3)   The report must also contain such information as may be specified in rules made by the Authority.

(4)   The investment exchange or clearing house must provide the Treasury and the Director with a copy of the report.

## 296.   Authority's power to give directions

(1)   This section applies if it appears to the Authority that a recognised body—

(a)   has failed, or is likely to fail, to satisfy the recognition requirements; or

(b)   has failed to comply with any other obligation imposed on it by or under this Act.

(2)   The Authority may direct the body to take specified steps for the purpose of securing the body's compliance with—

(a)   the recognition requirements; or

(b)   any obligation of the kind in question.

(3)   A direction under this section is enforceable, on the application of the Authority, by an injunction or, in Scotland, by an order for specific performance under section 45 of the Court of Session Act 1988.

(4)   The fact that a rule made by a recognised body has been altered in response to a direction given by the Authority does not prevent it from being subsequently altered or revoked by the recognised body.

## 297.   Revoking recognition

(1)   A recognition order may be revoked by an order made by the Authority at the request, or with the consent, of the recognised body concerned.

(2)   If it appears to the Authority that a recognised body—

(a)   is failing, or has failed, to satisfy the recognition requirements, or

(b)   is failing, or has failed, to comply with any other obligation imposed on it by or under this Act,

it may make an order revoking the recognition order for that body even though the body does not wish the order to be made.

(3)   An order under this section ('a revocation order') must specify the date on which it is to take effect.

(4)   In the case of a revocation order made under subsection (2), the specified date must not be earlier than the end of the period of three months beginning with the day on which the order is made.

(5)   A revocation order may contain such transitional provisions as the Authority thinks necessary or expedient.

## 298.   Directions and revocation: procedure

(1)   Before giving a direction under section 296, or making a revocation order under section 297(2), the Authority must—

(a)   give written notice of its intention to do so to the recognised body concerned;

(b)   take such steps as it considers reasonably practicable to bring the notice to the attention of members (if any) of that body; and

(c)   publish the notice in such manner as it thinks appropriate for bringing it to the attention of other persons who are, in its opinion, likely to be affected.

(2)   A notice under subsection (1) must—

(a)   state why the Authority intends to give the direction or make the order; and

(b)   draw attention to the right to make representations conferred by subsection (3).

(3)   Before the end of the period for making representations—

(a)   the recognised body,

(b)   any member of that body, and

(c)   any other person who is likely to be affected by the proposed direction or revocation order,

may make representations to the Authority.

(4)   The period for making representations is—

(a)   two months beginning—

(i)   with the date on which the notice is served on the recognised body; or

(ii)   if later, with the date on which the notice is published; or

(b)  such longer period as the Authority may allow in the particular case.

(5)  In deciding whether to—

(a)  give a direction, or

(b)  make a revocation order,

the Authority must have regard to any representations made in accordance with subsection (3).

(6)  When the Authority has decided whether to give a direction under section 296 or to make the proposed revocation order, it must—

(a)  give the recognised body written notice of its decision; and

(b)  if it has decided to give a direction or make an order, take such steps as it considers reasonably practicable for bringing its decision to the attention of members of the body or of other persons who are, in the Authority's opinion, likely to be affected.

(7)  If the Authority considers it essential to do so, it may give a direction under section 296—

(a)  without following the procedure set out in this section; or

(b)  if the Authority has begun to follow that procedure, regardless of whether the period for making representations has expired.

(8)  If the Authority has, in relation to a particular matter, followed the procedure set out in subsections (1) to (5), it need not follow it again if, in relation to that matter, it decides to take action other than that specified in its notice under subsection (1).

## 299.  Complaints about recognised bodies

(1)  The Authority must make arrangements for the investigation of any relevant complaint about a recognised body.

(2)  'Relevant complaint' means a complaint which the Authority considers is relevant to the question of whether the body concerned should remain a recognised body.

## 300.  Extension of functions of Tribunal

(1)  If the Treasury are satisfied that the condition mentioned in subsection (2) is satisfied, they may by order confer functions on the Tribunal with respect to disciplinary proceedings—

(a)  of one or more investment exchanges in relation to which a recognition order under section 290 is in force or of such investment exchanges generally, or

(b)  of one or more clearing houses in relation to which a recognition order under that section is in force or of such clearing houses generally.

(2)  The condition is that it is desirable to exercise the power conferred under subsection (1) with a view to ensuring that—

(a)  decisions taken in disciplinary proceedings with respect to which functions are to be conferred on the Tribunal are consistent with—

(i)  decisions of the Tribunal in cases arising under Part VIII; and

(ii)  decisions taken in other disciplinary proceedings with respect to which the Tribunal has functions as a result of an order under this section; or

(b)  the disciplinary proceedings are in accordance with the Convention rights.

(3)  An order under this section may modify or exclude any provision made by or under this Act with respect to proceedings before the Tribunal.

(4)  'Disciplinary proceedings' means proceedings under the rules of an investment exchange or clearing house in relation to market abuse by persons subject to the rules.

(5)  'The Convention rights' has the meaning given in section 1 of the Human Rights Act 1998.

*Other matters*

### 301.  Supervision of certain contracts

(1)   The Secretary of State and the Treasury, acting jointly, may by regulations provide for—

(a)   Part VII of the Companies Act 1989 (financial markets and insolvency), and

(b)   Part V of the Companies (No. 2) (Northern Ireland) Order 1990,

to apply to relevant contracts as it applies to contracts connected with a recognised body.

(2)   'Relevant contracts' means contracts of a prescribed description in relation to which settlement arrangements are provided by a person for the time being included in a list ('the list') maintained by the Authority for the purposes of this section.

(3)   Regulations may be made under this section only if the Secretary of State and the Treasury are satisfied, having regard to the extent to which the relevant contracts concerned are contracts of a kind dealt in by persons supervised by the Authority, that it is appropriate for the arrangements mentioned in subsection (2) to be supervised by the Authority.

(4)   The approval of the Treasury is required for—

(a)   the conditions set by the Authority for admission to the list; and

(b)   the arrangements for admission to, and removal from, the list.

(5)   If the Treasury withdraw an approval given by them under subsection (4), all regulations made under this section and then in force are to be treated as suspended.

(6)   But if—

(a)   the Authority changes the conditions or arrangements (or both), and

(b)   the Treasury give a fresh approval under subsection (4),

the suspension of the regulations ends on such date as the Treasury may, in giving the fresh approval, specify.

(7)   The Authority must—

(a)   publish the list as for the time being in force; and

(b)   provide a certified copy of it to any person who wishes to refer to it in legal proceedings.

(8)   A certified copy of the list is evidence (or in Scotland sufficient evidence) of the contents of the list.

(9)   A copy of the list which purports to be certified by or on behalf of the Authority is to be taken to have been duly certified unless the contrary is shown.

(10)   Regulations under this section may, in relation to a person included in the list—

(a)   apply (with such exceptions, additions and modifications as appear to the Secretary of State and the Treasury to be necessary or expedient) such provisions of, or made under, this Act as they consider appropriate;

(b)   provide for the provisions of Part VII of the Companies Act 1989 and Part V of the Companies (No. 2) (Northern Ireland) Order 1990 to apply (with such exceptions, additions or modifications as appear to the Secretary of State and the Treasury to be necessary or expedient).

## CHAPTER II
## COMPETITION SCRUTINY

### 302.  Interpretation

(1)   In this Chapter and Chapter III—

'practices' means—

(a)   in relation to a recognised investment exchange, the practices of the exchange in its capacity as such; and

(b)   in relation to a recognised clearing house, the practices of the clearing house in respect of its clearing arrangements;

'regulatory provisions' means—

(a)   the rules of an investment exchange or a clearing house;

(b)   any guidance issued by an investment exchange or clearing house;

(c)   in the case of an investment exchange, the arrangements and criteria mentioned in section 287(3);

(d)   in the case of a clearing house, the arrangements and criteria mentioned in section 288(3).,

(2)   For the purposes of this Chapter, regulatory provisions or practices have a significantly adverse effect on competition if—

(a)   they have, or are intended or likely to have, that effect; or

(b)   the effect that they have, or are intended or likely to have, is to require or encourage behaviour which has, or is intended or likely to have, a significantly adverse effect on competition.

(3)   If regulatory provisions or practices have, or are intended or likely to have, the effect of requiring or encouraging exploitation of the strength of a market position they are to be taken, for the purposes of this Chapter, to have an adverse effect on competition.

(4)   In determining under this Chapter whether any regulatory provisions have, or are intended or likely to have, a particular effect, it may be assumed that persons to whom the provisions concerned are addressed will act in accordance with them.

*Role of Director General of Fair Trading*

### 303.   Initial report by Director

(1)   The Authority must send to the Treasury and to the Director a copy of any regulatory provisions with which it is provided on an application for recognition under section 287 or 288.

(2)   The Authority must send to the Director such information in its possession as a result of the application for recognition as it considers will assist him in discharging his functions in connection with the application.

(3)   The Director must issue a report as to whether—

(a)   a regulatory provision of which a copy has been sent to him under subsection (1) has a significantly adverse effect on competition; or

(b)   a combination of regulatory provisions so copied to him have such an effect.

(4)   If the Director's conclusion is that one or more provisions have a significantly adverse effect on competition, he must state his reasons for that conclusion.

(5)   When the Director issues a report under subsection (3), he must send a copy of it to the Authority, the Competition Commission and the Treasury.

### 304.   Further reports by Director

(1)   The Director must keep under review the regulatory provisions and practices of recognised bodies.

(2)   If at any time the Director considers that—

(a)   a regulatory provision or practice has a significantly adverse effect on competition, or

(b)   regulatory provisions or practices, or a combination of regulating provisions and practices have such an effect,

he must make a report.

(3)　If at any time the Director considers that—

(a)　a regulatory provision or practice does not have a significantly adverse effect on competition, or

(b)　regulatory provisions or practices, or a combination of regulatory provisions and practices do not have any such effect,

he may make a report to that effect.

(4)　A report under subsection (2) must contain details of the adverse effect on competition.

(5)　If the Director makes a report under subsection (2), he must—

(a)　send a copy of it to the Treasury, to the Competition Commission and to the Authority; and

(b)　publish it in the way appearing to him to be best calculated to bring it to the attention of the public.

(6)　If the Director makes a report under subsection (3)—

(a)　he must send a copy of it to the Treasury, to the Competition Commission and to the Authority; and

(b)　he may publish it.

(7)　Before publishing a report under this section, the Director must, so far as practicable, exclude any matter which relates to the private affairs of a particular individual the publication of which, in the opinion of the Director, would or might seriously and prejudicially affect his interests.

(8)　Before publishing such a report, the Director must exclude any matter which relates to the affairs of a particular body the publication of which, in the opinion of the Director, would or might seriously and prejudicially affect its interests.

(9)　Subsections (7) and (8) do not apply to the copy of a report which the Director is required to send to the Treasury, the Competition Commission and the Authority under subsection (5)(a) or (6)(a).

(10)　For the purposes of the law of defamation, absolute privilege attaches to any report of the Director under this section.

### 305.　Investigations by Director

(1)　For the purpose of investigating any matter with a view to its consideration under section 303 or 304, the Director may exercise the powers conferred on him by this section.

(2)　The Director may by notice in writing require any person to produce to him or to a person appointed by him for the purpose, at a time and place specified in the notice, any document which—

(a)　is specified or described in the notice; and

(b)　is a document in that person's custody or under his control.

(3)　The Director may by notice in writing—

(a)　require any person carrying on any business to provide him with such information as may be specified or described in the notice; and

(b)　specify the time within which, and the manner and form in which, any such information is to be provided.

(4)　A requirement may be imposed under subsection (2) or (3)(a) only in respect of documents or information which relate to any matter relevant to the investigation.

(5)　If a person ('the defaulter') refuses, or otherwise fails, to comply with a notice under this section, the Director may certify that fact in writing to the court and the court may enquire into the case.

(6) If, after hearing any witness who may be produced against or on behalf of the defaulter and any statement which may be offered in defence, the court is satisfied that the defaulter did not have a reasonable excuse for refusing or otherwise failing to comply with the notice, the court may deal with the defaulter as if he were in contempt.

(7) In this section, 'the court' means—

(a) the High Court; or

(b) in Scotland, the Court of Session.

*Role of Competition Commission*

### 306. Consideration by Competition Commission

(1) If subsection (2) or (3) applies, the Commission must investigate the matter which is the subject of the Director's report.

(2) This subsection applies if the Director sends to the Competition Commission a report—

(a) issued by him under section 303(3) which concludes that one or more regulatory provisions have a significantly adverse effect on competition, or

(b) made by him under section 304(2).

(3) This subsection applies if the Director asks the Commission to consider a report—

(a) issued by him under section 303(3) which concludes that one or more regulatory provisions do not have a significantly adverse effect on competition, or

(b) made by him under section 304(3).

(4) The Commission must then make its own report on the matter unless it considers that, as a result of a change of circumstances, no useful purpose would be served by a report.

(5) If the Commission decides in accordance with subsection (4) not to make a report, it must make a statement setting out the change of circumstances which resulted in that decision.

(6) A report made under this section must state the Commission's conclusion as to whether—

(a) the regulatory provision or practice which is the subject of the report has a significantly adverse effect on competition, or

(b) the regulatory provisions or practices or combination of regulatory provisions and practices which are the subject of the report have such an effect.

(7) A report under this section stating the Commission's conclusion that there is a significantly adverse effect on competition must also—

(a) state whether the Commission considers that that effect is justified; and

(b) if it states that the Commission considers that it is not justified, state its conclusion as to what action, if any, the Treasury ought to direct the Authority to take.

(8) Subsection (9) applies whenever the Commission is considering, for the purposes of this section, whether a particular adverse effect on competition is justified.

(9) The Commission must ensure, so far as that is reasonably possible, that the conclusion it reaches is compatible with the obligations imposed on the recognised body concerned by or under this Act.

(10) A report under this section must contain such an account of the Commission's reasons for its conclusions as is expedient, in the opinion of the Commission, for facilitating proper understanding of them.

(11) The provisions of Schedule 14 (except paragraph 2(b)) apply for the purposes of this section as they apply for the purposes of section 162.

(12) If the Commission makes a report under this section it must send a copy to the Treasury, the Authority and the Director.

*Role of the Treasury*

### 307.    Recognition orders: role of the Treasury

(1)    Subsection (2) applies if, on an application for a recognition order—

(a)    the Director makes a report under section 303 but does not ask the Competition Commission to consider it under section 306;

(b)    the Competition Commission concludes—

(i)    that the applicant's regulatory provisions do not have a significantly adverse effect on competition; or

(ii)    that if those provisions do have that effect, the effect is justified.

(2)    The Treasury may refuse to approve the making of the recognition order only if they consider that the exceptional circumstances of the case make it inappropriate for them to give their approval.

(3)    Subsection (4) applies if, on an application for a recognition order, the Competition Commission concludes—

(a)    that the applicant's regulatory provisions have a significantly adverse effect on competition; and

(b)    that that effect is not justified.

(4)    The Treasury must refuse to approve the making of the recognition order unless they consider that the exceptional circumstances of the case make it inappropriate for them to refuse their approval.

### 308.    Directions by the Treasury

(1)    This section applies if the Competition Commission makes a report under section 306(4) (other than a report on an application for a recognition order) which states the Commission's conclusion that there is a significantly adverse effect on competition.

(2)    If the Commission's conclusion, as stated in the report, is that the adverse effect on competition is not justified, the Treasury must give a remedial direction to the Authority.

(3)    But subsection (2) does not apply if the Treasury consider—

(a)    that, as a result of action taken by the Authority or the recognised body concerned in response to the Commission's report, it is unnecessary for them to give a direction; or

(b)    that the exceptional circumstances of the case make it inappropriate or unnecessary for them to do so.

(4)    In considering the action to be specified in a remedial direction, the Treasury must have regard to any conclusion of the Commission included in the report because of section 306(7)(b).

(5)    Subsection (6) applies if—

(a)    the Commission's conclusion, as stated in its report, is that the adverse effect on competition is justified; but

(b)    the Treasury consider that the exceptional circumstances of the case require them to act.

(6)    The Treasury may give a direction to the Authority requiring it to take such action—

(a)    as they consider to be necessary in the light of the exceptional circumstances of the case; and

(b)    as may be specified in the direction.

(7)    If the action specified in a remedial direction is the giving by the Authority of a direction—

(a)    the direction to be given must be compatible with the recognition requirements applicable to the recognised body in relation to which it is given; and

(b)   subsections (3) and (4) of section 296 apply to it as if it were a direction given under that section.

(8)   'Remedial direction' means a direction requiring the Authority—

(a)   to revoke the recognition order for the body concerned; or

(b)   to give such directions to the body concerned as may be specified in it.

### 309.   Statements by the Treasury

(1)   If, in reliance on subsection (3)(a) or (b) of section 308, the Treasury decline to act under subsection (2) of that section, they must make a statement to that effect, giving their reasons.

(2)   If the Treasury give a direction under section 308 they must make a statement giving—

(a)   details of the direction; and

(b)   f the direction is given under subsection (6) of that section, their reasons for giving it.

(3)   The Treasury must—

(a)   publish any statement made under this section in the way appearing to them best calculated to bring it to the attention of the public; and

(b)   lay a copy of it before Parliament.

### 310.   Procedure on exercise of certain powers by the Treasury

(1)   Subsection (2) applies if the Treasury are considering—

(a)   whether to refuse their approval under section 307;

(b)   whether section 308(2) applies; or

(c)   whether to give a direction under section 308(6).

(2)   The Treasury must—

(a)   take such steps as they consider appropriate to allow the exchange or clearing house concerned, and any other person appearing to the Treasury to be affected, an opportunity to make representations—

(i)   about any report made by the Director under section 303 or 304 or by the Competition Commission under section 306;

(ii)   as to whether, and if so how, the Treasury should exercise their powers under section 307 or 308; and

(b)   have regard to any such representations.

### CHAPTER III
### EXCLUSION FROM THE COMPETITION ACT 1998

### 311.   The Chapter I prohibition

(1)   The Chapter I prohibition does not apply to an agreement for the constitution of a recognised body to the extent to which the agreement relates to the regulatory provisions of that body.

(2)   If the conditions set out in subsection (3) are satisfied, the Chapter I prohibition does not apply to an agreement for the constitution of—

(a)   an investment exchange which is not a recognised investment exchange, or

(b)   a clearing house which is not a recognised clearing house,

to the extent to which the agreement relates to the regulatory provisions of that body.

(3)   The conditions are that—

(a)   the body has applied for a recognition order in accordance with the provisions of this Act; and

(b)  the application has not been determined.

(4)  The Chapter I prohibition does not apply to a recognised body's regulatory provisions.

(5)  The Chapter I prohibition does not apply to a decision made by a recognised body to the extent to which the decision relates to any of that body's regulatory provisions or practices.

(6)  The Chapter I prohibition does not apply to practices of a recognised body.

(7)  The Chapter I prohibition does not apply to an agreement the parties to which consist of or include—

(a)  a recognised body, or

(b)  a person who is subject to the rules of a recognised body,

to the extent to which the agreement consists of provisions the inclusion of which is required or encouraged by any of the body's regulatory provisions or practices.

(8)  If a recognised body's recognition order is revoked, this section is to have effect as if that body had continued to be recognised until the end of the period of six months beginning with the day on which the revocation took effect.

(9)  'The Chapter I prohibition' means the prohibition imposed by section 2(1) of the Competition Act 1998.

(10)  Expressions used in this section which are also used in Part I of the Competition Act 1998 are to be interpreted in the same way as for the purposes of that Part of that Act.

## 312.  The Chapter II prohibition

(1)  The Chapter II prohibition does not apply to—

(a)  practices of a recognised body;

(b)  the adoption or enforcement of such a body's regulatory provisions;

(c)  any conduct which is engaged in by such a body or by a person who is subject to the rules of such a body to the extent to which it is encouraged or required by the regulatory provisions of the body.

(2)  The Chapter II prohibition means the prohibition imposed by section 18(1) of the Competition Act 1998.

### CHAPTER IV

*Interpretation*

## 313.  Interpretation of Part XVIII

(1)  In this Part—

'application' means an application for a recognition order made under section 287 or 288;

'applicant' means a body corporate or unincorporated association which has applied for a recognition order;

'Director' means the Director General of Fair Trading;

'overseas applicant' means a body corporate or association which has neither its head office nor its registered office in the United Kingdom and which has applied for a recognition order;

'overseas investment exchange' means a body corporate or association which has neither its head office nor its registered office in the United Kingdom and in relation to which a recognition order is in force;

'overseas clearing house' means a body corporate or association which has neither its head office nor its registered office in the United Kingdom and in relation to which a recognition order is in force;

'recognised body' means a recognised investment exchange or a recognised clearing house;

'recognised clearing house' has the meaning given in section 285;

'recognised investment exchange' has the meaning given in section 285;

'recognition order' means an order made under section 290 or 292;

'recognition requirements' has the meaning given by section 286;

'remedial direction' has the meaning given in section 308(8);

'revocation order' has the meaning given in section 297.

(2)   References in this Part to rules of an investment exchange (or a clearing house) are to rules made, or conditions imposed, by the investment exchange (or the clearing house) with respect to—

(a)   recognition requirements;

(b)   admission of persons to, or their exclusion from the use of, its facilities; or

(c)   matters relating to its constitution.

(3)   References in this Part to guidance issued by an investment exchange are references to guidance issued, or any recommendation made, in writing or other legible form and intended to have continuing effect, by the investment exchange to—

(a)   all or any class of its members or users, or

(b)   persons seeking to become members of the investment exchange or to use its facilities,

with respect to any of the matters mentioned in subsection (2)(a) to (c).

(4)   References in this Part to guidance issued by a clearing house are to guidance issued, or any recommendation made, in writing or other legible form and intended to have continuing effect, by the clearing house to—

(a)   all or any class of its members, or

(b)   persons using or seeking to use its services,

with respect to the provision by it or its members of clearing services.

PART XIX

LLOYD'S

*General*

**314.   Authority's general duty**

(1)   The Authority must keep itself informed about—

(a)   the way in which the Council supervises and regulates the market at Lloyd's; and

(b)   the way in which regulated activities are being carried on in that market.

(2)   The Authority must keep under review the desirability of exercising—

(a)   any of its powers under this Part;

(b)   any powers which it has in relation to the Society as a result of section 315.

*The Society*

**315.   The Society: authorisation and permission**

(1)   The Society is an authorised person.

(2)   The Society has permission to carry on a regulated activity of any of the following kinds—

(a)   arranging deals in contracts of insurance written at Lloyd's ('the basic market activity');

(b)   arranging deals in participation in Lloyd's syndicates ('the secondary market activity'); and

(c)   an activity carried on in connection with, or for the purposes of, the basic or secondary market activity.

(3)   For the purposes of Part IV, the Society's permission is to be treated as if it had been given on an application for permission under that Part.

(4)   The power conferred on the Authority by section 45 may be exercised in anticipation of the coming into force of the Society's permission (or at any other time).

(5)   The Society is not subject to any requirement of this Act concerning the registered office of a body corporate.

*Power to apply Act to Lloyd's underwriting*

### 316.   Direction by Authority

(1)   The general prohibition or (if the general prohibition is not applied under this section) a core provision applies to the carrying on of an insurance market activity by—

(a)   a member of the Society, or

(b)   the members of the Society taken together,

only if the Authority so directs.

(2)   A direction given under subsection (1) which applies a core provision is referred to in this Part as 'an insurance market direction'.

(3)   In subsection (1)—

'core provision' means a provision of this Act mentioned in section 317; and

'insurance market activity' means a regulated activity relating to contracts of insurance written at Lloyd's.

(4)   In deciding whether to give a direction under subsection (1), the Authority must have particular regard to—

(a)   the interests of policyholders and potential policyholders;

(b)   any failure by the Society to satisfy an obligation to which it is subject as a result of a provision of the law of another EEA State which—

(i)   gives effect to any of the insurance directives; and

(ii)   is applicable to an activity carried on in that State by a person to whom this section applies;

(c)   the need to ensure the effective exercise of the functions which the Authority has in relation to the Society as a result of section 315.

(5)   A direction under subsection (1) must be in writing.

(6)   A direction under subsection (1) applying the general prohibition may apply it in relation to different classes of person.

(7)   An insurance market direction—

(a)   must specify each core provision, class of person and kind of activity to which it applies;

(b)   may apply different provisions in relation to different classes of person and different kinds of activity.

(8)   A direction under subsection (1) has effect from the date specified in it, which may not be earlier than the date on which it is made.

(9)   A direction under subsection (1) must be published in the way appearing to the Authority to be best calculated to bring it to the attention of the public.

(10)   The Authority may charge a reasonable fee for providing a person with a copy of the direction.

(11)   The Authority must, without delay, give the Treasury a copy of any direction which it gives under this section.

**317. The core provisions**

(1) The core provisions are Parts V, X, XI, XII, XIV, XV, XVI, XXII and XXIV, sections 384 to 386 and Part XXVI.

(2) References in an applied core provision to an authorised person are (where necessary) to be read as references to a person in the class to which the insurance market direction applies.

(3) An insurance market direction may provide that a core provision is to have effect, in relation to persons to whom the provision is applied by the direction, with modifications.

**318. Exercise of powers through Council**

(1) The Authority may give a direction under this subsection to the Council or to the Society (acting through the Council) or to both.

(2) A direction under subsection (1) is one given to the body concerned—

(a) in relation to the exercise of its powers generally with a view to achieving, or in support of, a specified objective; or

(b) in relation to the exercise of a specified power which it has, whether in a specified manner or with a view to achieving, or in support of, a specified objective.

(3) 'Specified' means specified in the direction.

(4) A direction under subsection (1) may be given—

(a) instead of giving a direction under section 316(1); or

(b) if the Authority considers it necessary or expedient to do so, at the same time as, or following, the giving of such a direction.

(5) A direction may also be given under subsection (1) in respect of underwriting agents as if they were among the persons mentioned in section 316(1).

(6) A direction under this section—

(a) does not, at any time, prevent the exercise by the Authority of any of its powers;

(b) must be in writing.

(7) A direction under subsection (1) must be published in the way appearing to the Authority to be best calculated to bring it to the attention of the public.

(8) The Authority may charge a reasonable fee for providing a person with a copy of the direction.

(9) The Authority must, without delay, give the Treasury a copy of any direction which it gives under this section.

**319. Consultation**

(1) Before giving a direction under section 316 or 318, the Authority must publish a draft of the proposed direction.

(2) The draft must be accompanied by—

(a) a cost benefit analysis; and

(b) notice that representations about the proposed direction may be made to the Authority within a specified time.

(3) Before giving the proposed direction, the Authority must have regard to any representations made to it in accordance with subsection (2)(b).

(4) If the Authority gives the proposed direction it must publish an account, in general terms, of—

(a) the representations made to it in accordance with subsection (2)(b); and

(b) its response to them.

(5) If the direction differs from the draft published under subsection (1) in a way which is, in the opinion of the Authority, significant—

(a)   the Authority must (in addition to complying with subsection (4)) publish details of the difference; and

(b)   those details must be accompanied by a cost benefit analysis.

(6)   Subsections (1) to (5) do not apply if the Authority considers that the delay involved in complying with them would be prejudicial to the interests of consumers.

(7)   Neither subsection (2)(a) nor subsection (5)(b) applies if the Authority considers—

(a)   that, making the appropriate comparison, there will be no increase in costs; or

(b)   that, making that comparison, there will be an increase in costs but the increase will be of minimal significance.

(8)   The Authority may charge a reasonable fee for providing a person with a copy of a draft published under subsection (1).

(9)   When the Authority is required to publish a document under this section it must do so in the way appearing to it to be best calculated to bring it to the attention of the public.

(10)   'Cost benefit analysis' means an estimate of the costs together with an analysis of the benefits that will arise—

(a)   if the proposed direction is given; or

(b)   if subsection (5)(b) applies, from the direction that has been given.

(11)   'The appropriate comparison' means—

(a)   in relation to subsection (2)(a), a comparison between the overall position if the direction is given and the overall position if it is not given;

(b)   in relation to subsection (5)(b), a comparison between the overall position after the giving of the direction and the overall position before it was given.

*Former underwriting members*

### 320.   Former underwriting members

(1)   A former underwriting member may carry out each contract of insurance that he has underwritten at Lloyd's whether or not he is an authorised person.

(2)   If he is an authorised person, any Part IV permission that he has does not extend to his activities in carrying out any of those contracts.

(3)   The Authority may impose on a former underwriting member such requirements as appear to it to be appropriate for the purpose of protecting policyholders against the risk that he may not be able to meet his liabilities.

(4)   A person on whom a requirement is imposed may refer the matter to the Tribunal.

### 321.   Requirements imposed under section 320

(1)   A requirement imposed under section 320 takes effect—

(a)   immediately, if the notice given under subsection (2) states that that is the case;

(b)   in any other case, on such date as may be specified in that notice.

(2)   If the Authority proposes to impose a requirement on a former underwriting member ('A') under section 320, or imposes such a requirement on him which takes effect immediately, it must give him written notice.

(3)   The notice must—

(a)   give details of the requirement;

(b)   state the Authority's reasons for imposing it;

(c)   inform A that he may make representations to the Authority within such period as may be specified in the notice (whether or not he has referred the matter to the Tribunal);

(d)   inform him of the date on which the requirement took effect or will take effect; and

(e)   inform him of his right to refer the matter to the Tribunal.

(4)   The Authority may extend the period allowed under the notice for making representations.

(5)   If, having considered any representations made by A, the Authority decides—

(a)   to impose the proposed requirement, or

(b)   if it has been imposed, not to revoke it,

it must give him written notice.

(6)   If the Authority decides—

(a)   not to impose a proposed requirement, or

(b)   to revoke a requirement that has been imposed,

it must give A written notice.

(7)   If the Authority decides to grant an application by A for the variation or revocation of a requirement, it must give him written notice of its decision.

(8)   If the Authority proposes to refuse an application by A for the variation or revocation of a requirement it must give him a warning notice.

(9)   If the Authority, having considered any representations made in response to the warning notice, decides to refuse the application, it must give A a decision notice.

(10)   A notice given under—

(a)   subsection (5), or

(b)   subsection (9) in the case of a decision to refuse the application,

must inform A of his right to refer the matter to the Tribunal.

(11)   If the Authority decides to refuse an application for a variation or revocation of the requirement, the applicant may refer the matter to the Tribunal.

(12)   If a notice informs a person of his right to refer a matter to the Tribunal, it must give an indication of the procedure on such a reference.

### 322.   Rules applicable to former underwriting members

(1)   The Authority may make rules imposing such requirements on persons to whom the rules apply as appear to it to be appropriate for protecting policyholders against the risk that those persons may not be able to meet their liabilities.

(2)   The rules may apply to—

(a)   former underwriting members generally; or

(b)   to a class of former underwriting member specified in them.

(3)   Section 319 applies to the making of proposed rules under this section as it applies to the giving of a proposed direction under section 316.

(4)   Part X (except sections 152 to 154) does not apply to rules made under this section.

*Transfers of business done at Lloyd's*

### 323.   Transfer schemes

The Treasury may by order provide for the application of any provision of Part VII (with or without modification) in relation to schemes for the transfer of the whole or any part of the business carried on by one or more members of the Society or former underwriting members.

*Supplemental*

### 324.   Interpretation of this Part

(1)   In this Part—

'arranging deals', in relation to the investments to which this Part applies, has the same meaning as in paragraph 3 of Schedule 2;

'former underwriting member' means a person ceasing to be an underwriting member of the Society on, or at any time after, 24 December 1996; and

'participation in Lloyd's syndicates', in relation to the secondary market activity, means the investment described in sub-paragraph (1) of paragraph 21 of Schedule 2.

(2)    A term used in this Part which is defined in Lloyd's Act 1982 has the same meaning as in that Act.

## PART XX
## PROVISION OF FINANCIAL SERVICES BY MEMBERS OF THE PROFESSIONS

### 325.    Authority's general duty

(1)    The Authority must keep itself informed about—

(a)    the way in which designated professional bodies supervise and regulate the carrying on of exempt regulated activities by members of the professions in relation to which they are established;

(b)    the way in which such members are carrying on exempt regulated activities.

(2)    In this Part—

'exempt regulated activities' means regulated activities which may, as a result of this Part, be carried on by members of a profession which is supervised and regulated by a designated professional body without breaching the general prohibition; and

'members', in relation to a profession, means persons who are entitled to practise the profession in question and, in practising it, are subject to the rules of the body designated in relation to that profession, whether or not they are members of that body.

(3)    The Authority must keep under review the desirability of exercising any of its powers under this Part.

(4)    Each designated professional body must co—operate with the Authority, by the sharing of information and in other ways, in order to enable the Authority to perform its functions under this Part.

### 326.    Designation of professional bodies

(1)    The Treasury may by order designate bodies for the purposes of this Part.

(2)    A body designated under subsection (1) is referred to in this Part as a designated professional body.

(3)    The Treasury may designate a body under subsection (1) only if they are satisfied that—

(a)    the basic condition, and

(b)    one or more of the additional conditions,

are met in relation to it.

(4)    The basic condition is that the body has rules applicable to the carrying on by members of the profession in relation to which it is established of regulated activities which, if the body were to be designated, would be exempt regulated activities.

(5)    The additional conditions are that—

(a)    the body has power under any enactment to regulate the practice of the profession;

(b)    being a member of the profession is a requirement under any enactment for the exercise of particular functions or the holding of a particular office;

(c)    the body has been recognised for the purpose of any enactment other than this Act and the recognition has not been withdrawn;

(d)    the body is established in an EEA State other than the United Kingdom and in that State—

(i)    the body has power corresponding to that mentioned in paragraph (a);

(ii)    there is a requirement in relation to the body corresponding to that mentioned in paragraph (b); or

(iii)    the body is recognised in a manner corresponding to that mentioned in paragraph (c).

(6)    'Enactment' includes an Act of the Scottish Parliament, Northern Ireland legislation and subordinate legislation (whether made under an Act, an Act of the Scottish Parliament or Northern Ireland legislation).

(7)    'Recognised' means recognised by—

(a)    a Minister of the Crown;

(b)    the Scottish Ministers;

(c)    a Northern Ireland Minister;

(d)    a Northern Ireland department or its head.

### 327.  Exemption from the general prohibition

(1)    The general prohibition does not apply to the carrying on of a regulated activity by a person ('P') if—

(a)    the conditions set out in subsections (2) to (7) are satisfied; and

(b)    there is not in force—

(i)    a direction under section 328, or

(ii)    an order under section 329,

which prevents this subsection from applying to the carrying on of that activity by him.

(2)    P must be—

(a)    a member of a profession; or

(b)    controlled or managed by one or more such members.

(3)    P must not receive from a person other than his client any pecuniary reward or other advantage, for which he does not account to his client, arising out of his carrying on of any of the activities.

(4)    The manner of the provision by P of any service in the course of carrying on the activities must be incidental to the provision by him of professional services.

(5)    P must not carry on, or hold himself out as carrying on, a regulated activity other than—

(a)    one which rules made as a result of section 332(3) allow him to carry on; or

(b)    one in relation to which he is an exempt person.

(6)    The activities must not be of a description, or relate to an investment of a description, specified in an order made by the Treasury for the purposes of this subsection.

(7)    The activities must be the only regulated activities carried on by P (other than regulated activities in relation to which he is an exempt person).

(8)    'Professional services' means services—

(a)    which do not constitute carrying on a regulated activity, and

(b)    the provision of which is supervised and regulated by a designated professional body.

### 328.  Directions in relation to the general prohibition

(1)    The Authority may direct that section 327(1) is not to apply to the extent specified in the direction.

(2)    A direction under subsection (1)—

(a)    must be in writing;

(b)    may be given in relation to different classes of person or different descriptions of regulated activity.

(3)	A direction under subsection (1) must be published in the way appearing to the Authority to be best calculated to bring it to the attention of the public.

(4)	The Authority may charge a reasonable fee for providing a person with a copy of the direction.

(5)	The Authority must, without delay, give the Treasury a copy of any direction which it gives under this section.

(6)	The Authority may exercise the power conferred by subsection (1) only if it is satisfied that it is desirable in order to protect the interests of clients.

(7)	In considering whether it is so satisfied, the Authority must have regard amongst other things to the effectiveness of any arrangements made by any designated professional body—

(a)	for securing compliance with rules made under section 332(1);

(b)	for dealing with complaints against its members in relation to the carrying on by them of exempt regulated activities;

(c)	in order to offer redress to clients who suffer, or claim to have suffered, loss as a result of misconduct by its members in their carrying on of exempt regulated activities;

(d)	for co-operating with the Authority under section 325(4).

(8)	In this Part 'clients' means—

(a)	persons who use, have used or are or may be contemplating using, any of the services provided by a member of a profession in the course of carrying on exempt regulated activities;

(b)	persons who have rights or interests which are derived from, or otherwise attributable to, the use of any such services by other persons; or

(c)	persons who have rights or interests which may be adversely affected by the use of any such services by persons acting on their behalf or in a fiduciary capacity in relation to them.

(9)	If a member of a profession is carrying on an exempt regulated activity in his capacity as a trustee, the persons who are, have been or may be beneficiaries of the trust are to be treated as persons who use, have used or are or may be contemplating using services provided by that person in his carrying on of that activity.

## 329.	Orders in relation to the general prohibition

(1)	Subsection (2) applies if it appears to the Authority that a person to whom, as a result of section 327(1), the general prohibition does not apply is not a fit and proper person to carry on regulated activities in accordance with that section.

(2)	The Authority may make an order disapplying section 327(1) in relation to that person to the extent specified in the order.

(3)	The Authority may, on the application of the person named in an order under subsection (1), vary or revoke it.

(4)	'Specified' means specified in the order.

(5)	If a partnership is named in an order under this section, the order is not affected by any change in its membership.

(6)	If a partnership named in an order under this section is dissolved, the order continues to have effect in relation to any partnership which succeeds to the business of the dissolved partnership.

(7)	For the purposes of subsection (6), a partnership is to be regarded as succeeding to the business of another partnership only if—

(a)	the members of the resulting partnership are substantially the same as those of the former partnership; and

(b)	succession is to the whole or substantially the whole of the business of the former partnership.

**330.   Consultation**

(1)   Before giving a direction under section 328(1), the Authority must publish a draft of the proposed direction.

(2)   The draft must be accompanied by—

(a)   a cost benefit analysis; and

(b)   notice that representations about the proposed direction may be made to the Authority within a specified time.

(3)   Before giving the proposed direction, the Authority must have regard to any representations made to it in accordance with subsection (2)(b).

(4)   If the Authority gives the proposed direction it must publish an account, in general terms, of—

(a)   the representations made to it in accordance with subsection (2)(b); and

(b)   its response to them.

(5)   If the direction differs from the draft published under subsection (1) in a way which is, in the opinion of the Authority, significant—

(a)   the Authority must (in addition to complying with subsection (4)) publish details of the difference; and

(b)   those details must be accompanied by a cost benefit analysis.

(6)   Subsections (1) to (5) do not apply if the Authority considers that the delay involved in complying with them would prejudice the interests of consumers.

(7)   Neither subsection (2)(a) nor subsection (5)(b) applies if the Authority considers—

(a)   that, making the appropriate comparison, there will be no increase in costs; or

(b)   that, making that comparison, there will be an increase in costs but the increase will be of minimal significance.

(8)   The Authority may charge a reasonable fee for providing a person with a copy of a draft published under subsection (1).

(9)   When the Authority is required to publish a document under this section it must do so in the way appearing to it to be best calculated to bring it to the attention of the public.

(10)   'Cost benefit analysis' means an estimate of the costs together with an analysis of the benefits that will arise—

(a)   if the proposed direction is given; or

(b)   if subsection (5)(b) applies, from the direction that has been given.

(11)   'The appropriate comparison' means—

(a)   in relation to subsection (2)(a), a comparison between the overall position if the direction is given and the overall position if it is not given;

(b)   in relation to subsection (5)(b), a comparison between the overall position after the giving of the direction and the overall position before it was given.

**331.   Procedure on making or varying orders under section 329**

(1)   If the Authority proposes to make an order under section 329, it must give the person concerned a warning notice.

(2)   The warning notice must set out the terms of the proposed order.

(3)   If the Authority decides to make an order under section 329, it must give the person concerned a decision notice.

(4)   The decision notice must—

(a)   name the person to whom the order applies;

(b)   set out the terms of the order; and

(c)   be given to the person named in the order.

(5)   Subsections (6) to (8) apply to an application for the variation or revocation of an order under section 329.

(6)   If the Authority decides to grant the application, it must give the applicant written notice of its decision.

(7)   If the Authority proposes to refuse the application, it must give the applicant a warning notice.

(8)   If the Authority decides to refuse the application, it must give the applicant a decision notice.

(9)   A person—

(a)   against whom the Authority have decided to make an order under section 329, or

(b)   whose application for the variation or revocation of such an order the Authority had decided to refuse,

may refer the matter to the Tribunal.

(10)   The Authority may not make an order under section 329 unless—

(a)   the period within which the decision to make to the order may be referred to the Tribunal has expired and no such reference has been made; or

(b)   if such a reference has been made, the reference has been determined.

### 332.   Rules in relation to persons to whom the general prohibition does not apply

(1)   The Authority may make rules applicable to persons to whom, as a result of section 327(1), the general prohibition does not apply.

(2)   The power conferred by subsection (1) is to be exercised for the purpose of ensuring that clients are aware that such persons are not authorised persons.

(3)   A designated professional body must make rules—

(a)   applicable to members of the profession in relation to which it is established who are not authorised persons; and

(b)   governing the carrying on by those members of regulated activities (other than regulated activities in relation to which they are exempt persons).

(4)   Rules made in compliance with subsection (3) must be designed to secure that, in providing a particular professional service to a particular client, the member carries on only regulated activities which arise out of, or are complementary to, the provision by him of that service to that client.

(5)   Rules made by a designated professional body under subsection (3) require the approval of the Authority.

### 333.   False claims to be a person to whom the general prohibition does not apply

(1)   A person who—

(a)   describes himself (in whatever terms) as a person to whom the general prohibition does not apply, in relation to a particular regulated activity, as a result of this Part, or

(b)   behaves, or otherwise holds himself out, in a manner which indicates (or which is reasonably likely to be understood as indicating) that he is such a person,

is guilty of an offence if he is not such a person.

(2)   In proceedings for an offence under this section it is a defence for the accused to show that he took all reasonable precautions and exercised all due diligence to avoid committing the offence.

(3)   A person guilty of an offence under this section is liable on summary conviction to imprisonment for a term not exceeding six months or a fine not exceeding level 5 on the standard scale, or both.

(4)   But where the conduct constituting the offence involved or included the public display of any material, the maximum fine for the offence is level 5 on the standard scale multiplied by the number of days for which the display continued.

## PART XXI
## MUTUAL SOCIETIES

*Friendly societies*

### 334.   The Friendly Societies Commission

(1)   The Treasury may by order provide—

(a)   for any functions of the Friendly Societies Commission to be transferred to the Authority;

(b)   for any functions of the Friendly Societies Commission which have not been, or are not being, transferred to the Authority to be transferred to the Treasury.

(2)   If the Treasury consider it appropriate to do so, they may by order provide for the Friendly Societies Commission to cease to exist on a day specified in or determined in accordance with the order.

(3)   The enactments relating to friendly societies which are mentioned in Part I of Schedule 18 are amended as set out in that Part.

(4)   Part II of Schedule 18—

(a)   removes certain restrictions on the ability of incorporated friendly societies to form subsidiaries and control corporate bodies; and

(b)   makes connected amendments.

### 335.   The Registry of Friendly Societies

(1)   The Treasury may by order provide—

(a)   for any functions of the Chief Registrar of Friendly Societies, or of an assistant registrar of friendly societies for the central registration area, to be transferred to the Authority;

(b)   for any of their functions which have not been, or are not being, transferred to the Authority to be transferred to the Treasury.

(2)   The Treasury may by order provide—

(a)   for any functions of the central office of the registry of friendly societies to be transferred to the Authority;

(b)   for any functions of that office which have not been, or are not being, transferred to the Authority to be transferred to the Treasury.

(3)   The Treasury may by order provide—

(a)   for any functions of the assistant registrar of friendly societies for Scotland to be transferred to the Authority;

(b)   for any functions of the assistant registrar which have not been, or are not being, transferred to the Authority to be transferred to the Treasury.

(4)   If the Treasury consider it appropriate to do so, they may by order provide for—

(a)   the office of Chief Registrar of Friendly Societies,

(b)   the office of assistant registrar of friendly societies for the central registration area,

(c)   the central office, or

(d)   the office of assistant registrar of friendly societies for Scotland,

to cease to exist on a day specified in or determined in accordance with the order.

*Building societies*

**336. The Building Societies Commission**

(1) The Treasury may by order provide—

(a) for any functions of the Building Societies Commission to be transferred to the Authority;

(b) for any functions of the Building Societies Commission which have not been, or are not being, transferred to the Authority to be transferred to the Treasury.

(2) If the Treasury consider it appropriate to do so, they may by order provide for the Building Societies Commission to cease to exist on a day specified in or determined in accordance with the order.

(3) The enactments relating to building societies which are mentioned in Part III of Schedule 18 are amended as set out in that Part.

**337. The Building Societies Investor Protection Board**

The Treasury may by order provide for the Building Societies Investor Protection Board to cease to exist on a day specified in or determined in accordance with the order.

*Industrial and provident societies and credit unions*

**338. Industrial and provident societies and credit unions**

(1) The Treasury may by order provide for the transfer to the Authority of any functions conferred by—

(a) the Industrial and Provident Societies Act 1965;

(b) the Industrial and Provident Societies Act 1967;

(c) the Friendly and Industrial and Provident Societies Act 1968;

(d) the Industrial and Provident Societies Act 1975;

(e) the Industrial and Provident Societies Act 1978;

(f) the Credit Unions Act 1979.

(2) The Treasury may by order provide for the transfer to the Treasury of any functions under those enactments which have not been, or are not being, transferred to the Authority.

(3) The enactments relating to industrial and provident societies which are mentioned in Part IV of Schedule 18 are amended as set out in that Part.

(4) The enactments relating to credit unions which are mentioned in Part V of Schedule 18 are amended as set out in that Part.

*Supplemental*

**339. Supplemental provisions**

(1) The additional powers conferred by section 428 on a person making an order under this Act include power for the Treasury, when making an order under section 334, 335, 336 or 338 which transfers functions, to include provision—

(a) for the transfer of any functions of a member of the body, or servant or agent of the body or person, whose functions are transferred by the order;

(b) for the transfer of any property, rights or liabilities held, enjoyed or incurred by any person in connection with transferred functions;

(c) for the carrying on and completion by or under the authority of the person to whom functions are transferred of any proceedings, investigations or other matters commenced, before the order takes effect, by or under the authority of the person from whom the functions are transferred;

(d)    amending any enactment relating to transferred functions in connection with their exercise by, or under the authority of, the person to whom they are transferred;

(e)    for the substitution of the person to whom functions are transferred for the person from whom they are transferred, in any instrument, contract or legal proceedings made or begun before the order takes effect.

(2)    The additional powers conferred by section 428 on a person making an order under this Act include power for the Treasury, when making an order under section 334(2), 335(4), 336(2) or 337, to include provision—

(a)    for the transfer of any property, rights or liabilities held, enjoyed or incurred by any person in connection with the office or body which ceases to have effect as a result of the order;

(b)    for the carrying on and completion by or under the authority of such person as may be specified in the order of any proceedings, investigations or other matters commenced, before the order takes effect, by or under the authority of the person whose office, or the body which, ceases to exist as a result of the order;

(c)    amending any enactment which makes provision with respect to that office or body;

(d)    for the substitution of the Authority, the Treasury or such other body as may be specified in the order in any instrument, contract or legal proceedings made or begun before the order takes effect.

(3)    On or after the making of an order under any of sections 334 to 338 ('the original order'), the Treasury may by order make any incidental, supplemental, consequential or transitional provision which they had power to include in the original order.

(4)    A certificate issued by the Treasury that property vested in a person immediately before an order under this Part takes effect has been transferred as a result of the order is conclusive evidence of the transfer.

(5)    Subsections (1) and (2) are not to be read as affecting in any way the powers conferred by section 428.

## PART XXII
## AUDITORS AND ACTUARIES

*Appointment*

**340.    Appointment**

(1)    Rules may require an authorised person, or an authorised person falling within a specified class—

(a)    to appoint an auditor, or

(b)    to appoint an actuary,

if he is not already under an obligation to do so imposed by another enactment.

(2)    Rules may require an authorised person, or an authorised person falling within a specified class—

(a)    to produce periodic financial reports; and

(b)    to have them reported on by an auditor or an actuary.

(3)    Rules may impose such other duties on auditors of, or actuaries acting for, authorised persons as may be specified.

(4)    Rules under subsection (1) may make provision—

(a)    specifying the manner in which and time within which an auditor or actuary is to be appointed;

(b)  requiring the Authority to be notified of an appointment;

(c)  enabling the Authority to make an appointment if no appointment has been made or notified;

(d)  as to remuneration;

(e)  as to the term of office, removal and resignation of an auditor or actuary.

(5)  An auditor or actuary appointed as a result of rules under subsection (1), or on whom duties are imposed by rules under subsection (3)—

(a)  must act in accordance with such provision as may be made by rules; and

(b)  is to have such powers in connection with the discharge of his functions as may be provided by rules.

(6)  In subsections (1) to (3) 'auditor' or 'actuary' means an auditor, or actuary, who satisfies such requirements as to qualifications, experience and other matters (if any) as may be specified.

(7)  'Specified' means specified in rules.

*Information*

**341.  Access to books etc**

(1)  An appointed auditor of, or an appointed actuary acting for, an authorised person—

(a)  has a right of access at all times to the authorised person's books, accounts and vouchers; and

(b)  is entitled to require from the authorised person's officers such information and explanations as he reasonably considers necessary for the performance of his duties as auditor or actuary.

(2)  'Appointed' means appointed under or as a result of this Act.

**342.  Information given by auditor or actuary to the Authority**

(1)  This section applies to a person who is, or has been, an auditor of an authorised person appointed under or as a result of a statutory provision.

(2)  This section also applies to a person who is, or has been, an actuary acting for an authorised person and appointed under or as a result of a statutory provision.

(3)  An auditor or actuary does not contravene any duty to which he is subject merely because he gives to the Authority—

(a)  information on a matter of which he has, or had, become aware in his capacity as auditor of, or actuary acting for, the authorised person, or

(b)  his opinion on such a matter,

if he is acting in good faith and he reasonably believes that the information or opinion is relevant to any functions of the Authority.

(4)  Subsection (3) applies whether or not the auditor or actuary is responding to a request from the Authority.

(5)  The Treasury may make regulations prescribing circumstances in which an auditor or actuary must communicate matters to the Authority as mentioned in subsection (3).

(6)  It is the duty of an auditor or actuary to whom any such regulations apply to communicate a matter to the Authority in the circumstances prescribed by the regulations.

(7)  The matters to be communicated to the Authority in accordance with the regulations may include matters relating to persons other than the authorised person concerned.

**343.  Information given by auditor or actuary to the Authority: persons with close links**

(1)  This section applies to a person who—

(a)   is, or has been, an auditor of an authorised person appointed under or as a result of a statutory provision; and

(b)   is, or has been, an auditor of a person ('CL') who has close links with the authorised person.

(2)   This section also applies to a person who—

(a)   is, or has been, an actuary acting for an authorised person and appointed under or as a result of a statutory provision; and

(b)   is, or has been, an actuary acting for a person ('CL') who has close links with the authorised person.

(3)   An auditor or actuary does not contravene any duty to which he is subject merely because he gives to the Authority—

(a)   information on a matter concerning the authorised person of which he has, or had, become aware in his capacity as auditor of, or actuary acting for, CL, or

(b)   his opinion on such a matter,

if he is acting in good faith and he reasonably believes that the information or opinion is relevant to any functions of the Authority.

(4)   Subsection (3) applies whether or not the auditor or actuary is responding to a request from the Authority.

(5)   The Treasury may make regulations prescribing circumstances in which an auditor or actuary must communicate matters to the Authority as mentioned in subsection (3).

(6)   It is the duty of an auditor or actuary to whom any such regulations apply to communicate a matter to the Authority in the circumstances prescribed by the regulations.

(7)   The matters to be communicated to the Authority in accordance with the regulations may include matters relating to persons other than the authorised person concerned.

(8)   CL has close links with the authorised person concerned ('A') if CL is—

(a)   a parent undertaking of A;

(b)   a subsidiary undertaking of A;

(c)   a parent undertaking of a subsidiary undertaking of A; or

(d)   a subsidiary undertaking of a parent undertaking of A.

(9)   'Subsidiary undertaking' includes all the instances mentioned in Article 1(1) and (2) of the Seventh Company Law Directive in which an entity may be a subsidiary of an undertaking.

### 344.   Duty of auditor or actuary resigning etc to give notice

(1)   This section applies to an auditor or actuary to whom section 342 applies.

(2)   He must without delay notify the Authority if he—

(a)   is removed from office by an authorised person;

(b)   resigns before the expiry of his term of office with such a person; or

(c)   is not re-appointed by such a person.

(3)   If he ceases to be an auditor of, or actuary acting for, such a person, he must without delay notify the Authority—

(a)   of any matter connected with his so ceasing which he thinks ought to be drawn to the Authority's attention; or

(b)   that there is no such matter.

*Disqualification*

### 345.   Disqualification

(1)   If it appears to the Authority that an auditor or actuary to whom section 342 applies has failed to comply with a duty imposed on him under this Act, it may disqualify him from

being the auditor of, or (as the case may be) from acting as an actuary for, any authorised person or any particular class of authorised person.

(2)   If the Authority proposes to disqualify a person under this section it must give him a warning notice.

(3)   If it decides to disqualify him it must give him a decision notice.

(4)   The Authority may remove any disqualification imposed under this section if satisfied that the disqualified person will in future comply with the duty in question.

(5)   A person who has been disqualified under this section may refer the matter to the Tribunal.

*Offence*

### 346.   Provision of false or misleading information to auditor or actuary

(1)   An authorised person who knowingly or recklessly gives an appointed auditor or actuary information which is false or misleading in a material particular is guilty of an offence and liable—

(a)   on summary conviction, to imprisonment for a term not exceeding six months or a fine not exceeding the statutory maximum, or both;

(b)   on conviction on indictment, to imprisonment for a term not exceeding two years or a fine, or both.

(2)   Subsection (1) applies equally to an officer, controller or manager of an authorised person.

(3)   'Appointed' means appointed under or as a result of this Act.

PART XXIII
PUBLIC RECORD, DISCLOSURE OF INFORMATION AND CO-OPERATION

*The public record*

### 347.   The record of authorised persons etc

(1)   The Authority must maintain a record of every—

(a)   person who appears to the Authority to be an authorised person;

(b)   authorised unit trust scheme;

(c)   authorised open-ended investment company;

(d)   recognised scheme;

(e)   recognised investment exchange;

(f)   recognised clearing house;

(g)   individual to whom a prohibition order relates;

(h)   approved person; and

(i)   person falling within such other class (if any) as the Authority may determine.

(2)   The record must include such information as the Authority considers appropriate and at least the following information—

(a)   in the case of a person appearing to the Authority to be an authorised person—

(i)   information as to the services which he holds himself out as able to provide; and

(ii)   any address of which the Authority is aware at which a notice or other document may be served on him;

(b)   in the case of an authorised unit trust scheme, the name and address of the manager and trustee of the scheme;

(c)   in the case of an authorised open-ended investment company, the name and address of—

    (i)    the company;

    (ii)   if it has only one director, the director; and

    (iii)  its depositary (if any);

  (d)   in the case of a recognised scheme, the name and address of—

    (i)    the operator of the scheme; and

    (ii)   any representative of the operator in the United Kingdom;

  (e)   in the case of a recognised investment exchange or recognised clearing house, the name and address of the exchange or clearing house;

  (f)   in the case of an individual to whom a prohibition order relates—

    (i)    his name; and

    (ii)   details of the effect of the order;

  (g)   in the case of a person who is an approved person—

    (i)    his name;

    (ii)   the name of the relevant authorised person;

    (iii)  if the approved person is performing a controlled function under an arrangement with a contractor of the relevant authorised person, the name of the contractor.

(3)   If it appears to the Authority that a person in respect of whom there is an entry in the record as a result of one of the paragraphs of subsection (1) has ceased to be a person to whom that paragraph applies, the Authority may remove the entry from the record.

(4)   But if the Authority decides not to remove the entry, it must—

  (a)   make a note to that effect in the record; and

  (b)   state why it considers that the person has ceased to be a person to whom that paragraph applies.

(5)   The Authority must—

  (a)   make the record available for inspection by members of the public in a legible form at such times and in such place or places as the Authority may determine; and

  (b)   provide a certified copy of the record, or any part of it, to any person who asks for it—

    (i)    on payment of the fee (if any) fixed by the Authority; and

    (ii)   in a form (either written or electronic) in which it is legible to the person asking for it.

(6)   The Authority may—

  (a)   publish the record, or any part of it;

  (b)   exploit commercially the information contained in the record, or any part of that information.

(7)   'Authorised unit trust scheme', 'authorised open-ended investment company' and 'recognised scheme' have the same meaning as in Part XVII, and associated expressions are to be read accordingly.

(8)   'Approved person' means a person in relation to whom the Authority has given its approval under section 59 and 'controlled function' and 'arrangement' have the same meaning as in that section.

(9)   'Relevant authorised person' has the meaning given in section 66.

*Disclosure of information*

## 348. Restrictions on disclosure of confidential information by Authority etc

(1)   Confidential information must not be disclosed by a primary recipient, or by any person obtaining the information directly or indirectly from a primary recipient, without the consent of—

(a) the person from whom the primary recipient obtained the information; and

(b) if different, the person to whom it relates.

(2) In this Part 'confidential information' means information which—

(a) relates to the business or other affairs of any person;

(b) was received by the primary recipient for the purposes of, or in the discharge of, any functions of the Authority, the competent authority for the purposes of Part VI or the Secretary of State under any provision made by or under this Act; and

(c) is not prevented from being confidential information by subsection (4).

(3) It is immaterial for the purposes of subsection (2) whether or not the information was received—

(a) by virtue of a requirement to provide it imposed by or under this Act;

(b) for other purposes as well as purposes mentioned in that subsection.

(4) Information is not confidential information if—

(a) it has been made available to the public by virtue of being disclosed in any circumstances in which, or for any purposes for which, disclosure is not precluded by this section; or

(b) it is in the form of a summary or collection of information so framed that it is not possible to ascertain from it information relating to any particular person.

(5) Each of the following is a primary recipient for the purposes of this Part—

(a) the Authority;

(b) any person exercising functions conferred by Part VI on the competent authority;

(c) the Secretary of State;

(d) a person appointed to make a report under section 166;

(e) any person who is or has been employed by a person mentioned in paragraphs (a) to (c);

(f) any auditor or expert instructed by a person mentioned in those paragraphs.

(6) In subsection (5)(f) 'expert' includes—

(a) a competent person appointed by the competent authority under section 97;

(b) a competent person appointed by the Authority or the Secretary of State to conduct an investigation under Part XI;

(c) any body or person appointed under paragraph 6 of Schedule 1 to perform a function on behalf of the Authority.

### 349. Exceptions from section 348

(1) Section 348 does not prevent a disclosure of confidential information which is—

(a) made for the purpose of facilitating the carrying out of a public function; and

(b) permitted by regulations made by the Treasury under this section.

(2) The regulations may, in particular, make provision permitting the disclosure of confidential information or of confidential information of a prescribed kind—

(a) by prescribed recipients, or recipients of a prescribed description, to any person for the purpose of enabling or assisting the recipient to discharge prescribed public functions;

(b) by prescribed recipients, or recipients of a prescribed description, to prescribed persons, or persons of prescribed descriptions, for the purpose of enabling or assisting those persons to discharge prescribed public functions;

(c) by the Authority to the Treasury or the Secretary of State for any purpose;

(d) by any recipient if the disclosure is with a view to or in connection with prescribed proceedings.

(3) The regulations may also include provision—

(a)  making any permission to disclose confidential information subject to conditions (which may relate to the obtaining of consents or any other matter);

(b)  restricting the uses to which confidential information disclosed under the regulations may be put.

(4)  In relation to confidential information, each of the following is a 'recipient'—

(a)  a primary recipient;

(b)  a person obtaining the information directly or indirectly from a primary recipient.

(5)  'Public functions' includes—

(a)  functions conferred by or in accordance with any provision contained in any enactment or subordinate legislation;

(b)  functions conferred by or in accordance with any provision contained in the Community Treaties or any Community instrument;

(c)  similar functions conferred on persons by or under provisions having effect as part of the law of a country or territory outside the United Kingdom;

(d)  functions exercisable in relation to prescribed disciplinary proceedings.

(6)  'Enactment' includes—

(a)  an Act of the Scottish Parliament;

(b)  Northern Ireland legislation.

(7)  'Subordinate legislation' has the meaning given in the Interpretation Act 1978 and also includes an instrument made under an Act of the Scottish Parliament or under Northern Ireland legislation.

## 350.  Disclosure of information by the Inland Revenue

(1)  No obligation as to secrecy imposed by statute or otherwise prevents the disclosure of Revenue information to—

(a)  the Authority, or

(b)  the Secretary of State,

if the disclosure is made for the purpose of assisting in the investigation of a matter under section 168 or with a view to the appointment of an investigator under that section.

(2)  A disclosure may only be made under subsection (1) by or under the authority of the Commissioners of Inland Revenue.

(3)  Section 348 does not apply to Revenue information.

(4)  Information obtained as a result of subsection (1) may not be used except—

(a)  for the purpose of deciding whether to appoint an investigator under section 168;

(b)  in the conduct of an investigation under section 168;

(c)  in criminal proceedings brought against a person under this Act or the Criminal Justice Act 1993 as a result of an investigation under section 168;

(d)  for the purpose of taking action under this Act against a person as a result of an investigation under section 168;

(e)  in proceedings before the Tribunal as a result of action taken as mentioned in paragraph (d).

(5)  Information obtained as a result of subsection (1) may not be disclosed except—

(a)  by or under the authority of the Commissioners of Inland Revenue;

(b)  in proceedings mentioned in subsection (4)(c) or (e) or with a view to their institution.

(6)  Subsection (5) does not prevent the disclosure of information obtained as a result of subsection (1) to a person to whom it could have been disclosed under subsection (1).

(7)  'Revenue information' means information held by a person which it would be an offence under section 182 of the Finance Act 1989 for him to disclose.

### 351.  Competition information

(1)   A person is guilty of an offence if he has competition information (whether or not it was obtained by him) and improperly discloses it—

    (a)   if it relates to the affairs of an individual, during that individual's lifetime;

    (b)   if it relates to any particular business of a body, while that business continues to be carried on.

(2)   For the purposes of subsection (1) a disclosure is improper unless it is made—

    (a)   with the consent of the person from whom it was obtained and, if different—

        (i)     the individual to whose affairs the information relates, or

        (ii)    the person for the time being carrying on the business to which the information relates;

    (b)   to facilitate the performance by a person mentioned in the first column of the table set out in Part I of Schedule 19 of a function mentioned in the second column of that table;

    (c)   in pursuance of a Community obligation;

    (d)   for the purpose of criminal proceedings in any part of the United Kingdom;

    (e)   in connection with the investigation of any criminal offence triable in the United Kingdom or any part of the United Kingdom;

    (f)   with a view to the institution of, or otherwise for the purposes of, civil proceedings brought under or in connection with—

        (i)     a competition provision; or

        (ii)    a specified enactment.

(3)   A person guilty of an offence under this section is liable—

    (a)   on summary conviction, to a fine not exceeding the statutory maximum;

    (b)   on conviction on indictment, to imprisonment for a term not exceeding two years or to a fine or to both.

(4)   Section 348 does not apply to competition information.

(5)   'Competition information' means information which—

    (a)   relates to the affairs of a particular individual or body;

    (b)   is not otherwise in the public domain; and

    (c)   was obtained under or by virtue of a competition provision.

(6)   'Competition provision' means any provision of—

    (a)   an order made under section 95;

    (b)   Chapter III of Part X; or

    (c)   Chapter II of Part XVIII.

(7)   'Specified enactment' means an enactment specified in Part II of Schedule 19.

### 352.  Offences

(1)   A person who discloses information in contravention of section 348 or 350(5) is guilty of an offence.

(2)   A person guilty of an offence under subsection (1) is liable—

    (a)   on summary conviction, to imprisonment for a term not exceeding three months or a fine not exceeding the statutory maximum, or both;

    (b)   on conviction on indictment, to imprisonment for a term not exceeding two years or a fine, or both.

(3)   A person is guilty of an offence if, in contravention of any provision of regulations made under section 349, he uses information which has been disclosed to him in accordance with the regulations.

(4)  A person is guilty of an offence if, in contravention of subsection (4) of section 350, he uses information which has been disclosed to him in accordance with that section.

(5)  A person guilty of an offence under subsection (3) or (4) is liable on summary conviction to imprisonment for a term not exceeding three months or a fine not exceeding level 5 on the standard scale, or both.

(6)  In proceedings for an offence under this section it is a defence for the accused to prove—

(a)  that he did not know and had no reason to suspect that the information was confidential information or that it had been disclosed in accordance with section 350;

(b)  that he took all reasonable precautions and exercised all due diligence to avoid committing the offence.

### 353.  Removal of other restrictions on disclosure

(1)  The Treasury may make regulations permitting the disclosure of any information, or of information of a prescribed kind—

(a)  by prescribed persons for the purpose of assisting or enabling them to discharge prescribed functions under this Act or any rules or regulations made under it;

(b)  by prescribed persons, or persons of a prescribed description, to the Authority for the purpose of assisting or enabling the Authority to discharge prescribed functions.

(2)  Regulations under this section may not make any provision in relation to the disclosure of confidential information by primary recipients or by any person obtaining confidential information directly or indirectly from a primary recipient.

(3)  If a person discloses any information as permitted by regulations under this section the disclosure is not to be taken as a contravention of any duty to which he is subject.

*Co-operation*

### 354.  Authority's duty to co-operate with others

(1)  The Authority must take such steps as it considers appropriate to co-operate with other persons (whether in the United Kingdom or elsewhere) who have functions—

(a)  similar to those of the Authority; or

(b)  in relation to the prevention or detection of financial crime.

(2)  Co-operation may include the sharing of information which the Authority is not prevented from disclosing.

(3)  'Financial crime' has the same meaning as in section 6.

PART XXIV
INSOLVENCY

*Interpretation*

### 355.  Interpretation of this Part

(1)  In this Part—

'the 1985 Act' means the Bankruptcy (Scotland) Act 1985;

'the 1986 Act' means the Insolvency Act 1986;

'the 1989 Order' means the Insolvency (Northern Ireland) Order 1989;

'body' means a body of persons—

(a)  over which the court has jurisdiction under any provision of, or made under, the 1986 Act (or the 1989 Order); but

(b)  which is not a building society, a friendly society or an industrial and provident society; and 'court' means—

(a)   the court having jurisdiction for the purposes of the 1985 Act or the 1986 Act; or

(b)   in Northern Ireland, the High Court.

(2)   In this Part 'insurer' has such meaning as may be specified in an order made by the Treasury.

*Voluntary arrangements*

### 356.   Authority's powers to participate in proceedings: company voluntary arrangements

(1)   This section applies if a voluntary arrangement has been approved under Part I of the 1986 Act (or Part II of the 1989 Order) in respect of a company or insolvent partnership which is an authorised person.

(2)   The Authority may make an application to the court in relation to the company or insolvent partnership under section 6 of the 1986 Act (or Article 19 of the 1989 Order).

(3)   If a person other than the Authority makes an application to the court in relation to the company or insolvent partnership under either of those provisions, the Authority is entitled to be heard at any hearing relating to the application.

### 357.   Authority's powers to participate in proceedings: individual voluntary arrangements

(1)   The Authority is entitled to be heard on an application by an individual who is an authorised person under section 253 of the 1986 Act (or Article 227 of the 1989 Order).

(2)   Subsections (3) to (6) apply if such an order is made on the application of such a person.

(3)   A person appointed for the purpose by the Authority is entitled to attend any meeting of creditors of the debtor summoned under section 257 of the 1986 Act (or Article 231 of the 1989 Order).

(4)   Notice of the result of a meeting so summoned is to be given to the Authority by the chairman of the meeting.

(5)   The Authority may apply to the court—

(a)   under section 262 of the 1986 Act (or Article 236 of the 1989 Order); or

(b)   under section 263 of the 1986 Act (or Article 237 of the 1989 Order).

(6)   If a person other than the Authority makes an application to the court under any provision mentioned in subsection (5), the Authority is entitled to be heard at any hearing relating to the application.

### 358.   Authority's powers to participate in proceedings: trust deeds for creditors in Scotland

(1)   This section applies where a trust deed has been granted by or on behalf of a debtor who is an authorised person.

(2)   The trustee must, as soon as practicable after he becomes aware that the debtor is an authorised person, send to the Authority—

(a)   in every case, a copy of the trust deed;

(b)   where any other document or information is sent to every creditor known to the trustee in pursuance of paragraph 5(1)(c) of Schedule 5 to the 1985 Act, a copy of such document or information.

(3)   Paragraph 7 of that Schedule applies to the Authority as if it were a qualified creditor who has not been sent a copy of the notice as mentioned in paragraph 5(1)(c) of the Schedule.

(4)   The Authority must be given the same notice as the creditors of any meeting of creditors held in relation to the trust deed.

(5)   A person appointed for the purpose by the Authority is entitled to attend and participate in (but not to vote at) any such meeting of creditors as if the Authority were a creditor under the deed.

(6)   This section does not affect any right the Authority has as a creditor of a debtor who is an authorised person.

(7)   Expressions used in this section and in the 1985 Act have the same meaning in this section as in that Act.

*Administration orders*

### 359.   Petitions

(1)   The Authority may present a petition to the court under section 9 of the 1986 Act (or Article 22 of the 1989 Order) in relation to a company or insolvent partnership which—

(a)   is, or has been, an authorised person;

(b)   is, or has been, an appointed representative; or

(c)   is carrying on, or has carried on, a regulated activity in contravention of the general prohibition.

(2)   Subsection (3) applies in relation to a petition presented by the Authority by virtue of this section.

(3)   If the company or partnership is in default on an obligation to pay a sum due and payable under an agreement, it is to be treated for the purpose of section 8(1)(a) of the 1986 Act (or Article 21(1)(a) of the 1989 Order) as unable to pay its debts.

(4)   'Agreement' means an agreement the making or performance of which constitutes or is part of a regulated activity carried on by the company or partnership.

(5)   'Company' means—

(a)   a company to which section 8 of the 1986 Act applies; or

(b)   in relation to Northern Ireland, a company to which Article 21 of the 1989 Order applies.

### 360.   Insurers

(1)   The Treasury may by order provide that such provisions of Part II of the 1986 Act (or Part III of the 1989 Order) as may be specified are to apply in relation to insurers with such modifications as may be specified.

(2)   An order under this section—

(a)   may provide that such provisions of this Part as may be specified are to apply in relation to the administration of insurers in accordance with the order with such modifications as may be specified; and

(b)   requires the consent of the Secretary of State.

(3)   'Specified' means specified in the order.

### 361.   Administrator's duty to report to Authority

(1)   If—

(a)   an administration order is in force in relation to a company or partnership by virtue of a petition presented by a person other than the Authority, and

(b)   it appears to the administrator that the company or partnership is carrying on, or has carried on, a regulated activity in contravention of the general prohibition,

the administrator must report the matter to the Authority without delay.

(2) 'An administration order' means an administration order under Part II of the 1986 Act (or Part III of the 1989 Order).

**362. Authority's powers to participate in proceedings**

(1) This section applies if a person other than the Authority presents a petition to the court under section 9 of the 1986 Act (or Article 22 of the 1989 Order) in relation to a company or partnership which—

(a) is, or has been, an authorised person;

(b) is, or has been, an appointed representative; or

(c) is carrying on, or has carried on, a regulated activity in contravention of the general prohibition.

(2) The Authority is entitled to be heard—

(a) at the hearing of the petition; and

(b) at any other hearing of the court in relation to the company or partnership under Part II of the 1986 Act (or Part III of the 1989 Order).

(3) Any notice or other document required to be sent to a creditor of the company or partnership must also be sent to the Authority.

(4) The Authority may apply to the court under section 27 of the 1986 Act (or Article 39 of the 1989 Order); and on such an application, section 27(1)(a) (or Article 39(1)(a)) has effect with the omission of the words '(including at least himself)'.

(5) A person appointed for the purpose by the Authority is entitled—

(a) to attend any meeting of creditors of the company or partnership summoned under any enactment;

(b) to attend any meeting of a committee established under section 26 of the 1986 Act (or Article 38 of the 1989 Order); and

(c) to make representations as to any matter for decision at such a meeting.

(6) If, during the course of the administration of a company, a compromise or arrangement is proposed between the company and its creditors, or any class of them, the Authority may apply to the court under section 425 of the Companies Act 1985 (or Article 418 of the Companies (Northern Ireland) Order 1986).

*Receivership*

**363. Authority's powers to participate in proceedings**

(1) This section applies if a receiver has been appointed in relation to a company which—

(a) is, or has been, an authorised person;

(b) is, or has been, an appointed representative; or

(c) is carrying on, or has carried on, a regulated activity in contravention of the general prohibition.

(2) The Authority is entitled to be heard on an application made under section 35 or 63 of the 1986 Act (or Article 45 of the 1989 Order).

(3) The Authority is entitled to make an application under section 41(1)(a) or 69(1)(a) of the 1986 Act (or Article 51(1)(a) of the 1989 Order).

(4) A report under section 48(1) or 67(1) of the 1986 Act (or Article 58(1) of the 1989 Order) must be sent by the person making it to the Authority.

(5) A person appointed for the purpose by the Authority is entitled—

(a) to attend any meeting of creditors of the company summoned under any enactment;

(b) to attend any meeting of a committee established under section 49 or 68 of the 1986 Act (or Article 59 of the 1989 Order); and

(c)  to make representations as to any matter for decision at such a meeting.

## 364.  Receiver's duty to report to Authority

If—

(a)  a receiver has been appointed in relation to a company, and

(b)  it appears to the receiver that the company is carrying on, or has carried on, a regulated activity in contravention of the general prohibition,

the receiver must report the matter to the Authority without delay.

*Voluntary winding up*

## 365.  Authority's powers to participate in proceedings

(1)  This section applies in relation to a company which—

(a)  is being wound up voluntarily;

(b)  is an authorised person; and

(c)  is not an insurer effecting or carrying out contracts of long-term insurance.

(2)  The Authority may apply to the court under section 112 of the 1986 Act (or Article 98 of the 1989 Order) in respect of the company.

(3)  The Authority is entitled to be heard at any hearing of the court in relation to the voluntary winding up of the company.

(4)  Any notice or other document required to be sent to a creditor of the company must also be sent to the Authority.

(5)  A person appointed for the purpose by the Authority is entitled—

(a)  to attend any meeting of creditors of the company summoned under any enactment;

(b)  to attend any meeting of a committee established under section 101 of the 1986 Act (or Article 87 of the 1989 Order); and

(c)  to make representations as to any matter for decision at such a meeting.

(6)  The voluntary winding up of the company does not bar the right of the Authority to have it wound up by the court.

(7)  If, during the course of the winding up of the company, a compromise or arrangement is proposed between the company and its creditors, or any class of them, the Authority may apply to the court under section 425 of the Companies Act 1985 (or Article 418 of the Companies (Northern Ireland) Order 1986).

## 366.  Insurers effecting or carrying out long-term contracts of insurance

(1)  An insurer effecting or carrying out contracts of long-term insurance may not be wound up voluntarily without the consent of the Authority.

(2)  If notice of a general meeting of such an insurer is given, specifying the intention to propose a resolution for voluntary winding up of the insurer, a director of the insurer must notify the Authority as soon as practicable after he becomes aware of it.

(3)  A person who fails to comply with subsection (2) is guilty of an offence and liable on summary conviction to a fine not exceeding level 5 on the standard scale.

(4)  The following provisions do not apply in relation to a winding-up resolution—

(a)  sections 378(3) and 381A of the Companies Act 1985 ('the 1985 Act'); and

(b)  Articles 386(3) and 389A of the Companies (Northern Ireland) Order 1986 ('the 1986 Order').

(5)  A copy of a winding-up resolution forwarded to the registrar of companies in accordance with section 380 of the 1985 Act (or Article 388 of the 1986 Order) must be accompanied by a certificate issued by the Authority stating that it consents to the voluntary winding up of the insurer.

(6)   If subsection (5) is complied with, the voluntary winding up is to be treated as having commenced at the time the resolution was passed.

(7)   If subsection (5) is not complied with, the resolution has no effect.

(8)   'Winding-up resolution' means a resolution for voluntary winding up of an insurer effecting or carrying out contracts of long-term insurance.

*Winding up by the court*

### 367.   Winding-up petitions

(1)   The Authority may present a petition to the court for the winding up of a body which—

(a)   is, or has been, an authorised person;

(b)   is, or has been, an appointed representative; or

(c)   is carrying on, or has carried on, a regulated activity in contravention of the general prohibition.

(2)   In subsection (1) 'body' includes any partnership.

(3)   On such a petition, the court may wind up the body if—

(a)   the body is unable to pay its debts within the meaning of section 123 or 221 of the 1986 Act (or Article 103 or 185 of the 1989 Order); or

(b)   the court is of the opinion that it is just and equitable that it should be wound up.

(4)   If a body is in default on an obligation to pay a sum due and payable under an agreement, it is to be treated for the purpose of subsection (3)(a) as unable to pay its debts.

(5)   'Agreement' means an agreement the making or performance of which constitutes or is part of a regulated activity carried on by the body concerned.

(6)   Subsection (7) applies if a petition is presented under subsection (1) for the winding up of a partnership—

(a)   on the ground mentioned in subsection (3)(b); or

(b)   in Scotland, on a ground mentioned in subsection (3)(a) or (b).

(7)   The court has jurisdiction, and the 1986 Act (or the 1989 Order) has effect, as if the partnership were an unregistered company as defined by section 220 of that Act (or Article 184 of that Order).

### 368.   Winding-up petitions: EEA and Treaty firms

The Authority may not present a petition to the court under section 367 for the winding up of—

(a)   an EEA firm which qualifies for authorisation under Schedule 3, or

(b)   a Treaty firm which qualifies for authorisation under Schedule 4,

unless it has been asked to do so by the home state regulator of the firm concerned.

### 369.   Insurers: service of petition etc on Authority

(1)   If a person other than the Authority presents a petition for the winding up of an authorised person with permission to effect or carry out contracts of insurance, the petitioner must serve a copy of the petition on the Authority.

(2)   If a person other than the Authority applies to have a provisional liquidator appointed under section 135 of the 1986 Act (or Article 115 of the 1989 Order) in respect of an authorised person with permission to effect or carry out contracts of insurance, the applicant must serve a copy of the application on the Authority.

### 370.   Liquidator's duty to report to Authority

If—

(a)   a company is being wound up voluntarily or a body is being wound up on a petition presented by a person other than the Authority, and

(b)   it appears to the liquidator that the company or body is carrying on, or has carried on, a regulated activity in contravention of the general prohibition,

the liquidator must report the matter to the Authority without delay.

### 371.   Authority's powers to participate in proceedings

(1)   This section applies if a person other than the Authority presents a petition for the winding up of a body which—

(a)   is, or has been, an authorised person;

(b)   is, or has been, an appointed representative; or

(c)   is carrying on, or has carried on, a regulated activity in contravention of the general prohibition.

(2)   The Authority is entitled to be heard—

(a)   at the hearing of the petition; and

(b)   at any other hearing of the court in relation to the body under or by virtue of Part IV or V of the 1986 Act (or Part V or VI of the 1989 Order).

(3)   Any notice or other document required to be sent to a creditor of the body must also be sent to the Authority.

(4)   A person appointed for the purpose by the Authority is entitled—

(a)   to attend any meeting of creditors of the body;

(b)   to attend any meeting of a committee established for the purposes of Part IV or V of the 1986 Act under section 101 of that Act or under section 141 or 142 of that Act;

(c)   to attend any meeting of a committee established for the purposes of Part V or VI of the 1989 Order under Article 87 of that Order or under Article 120 of that Order; and

(d)   to make representations as to any matter for decision at such a meeting.

(5)   If, during the course of the winding up of a company, a compromise or arrangement is proposed between the company and its creditors, or any class of them, the Authority may apply to the court under section 425 of the Companies Act 1985 (or Article 418 of the Companies (Northern Ireland) Order 1986).

*Bankruptcy*

### 372.   Petitions

(1)   The Authority may present a petition to the court—

(a)   under section 264 of the 1986 Act (or Article 238 of the 1989 Order) for a bankruptcy order to be made against an individual; or

(b)   under section 5 of the 1985 Act for the sequestration of the estate of an individual.

(2)   But such a petition may be presented only on the ground that—

(a)   the individual appears to be unable to pay a regulated activity debt; or

(b)   the individual appears to have no reasonable prospect of being able to pay a regulated activity debt.

(3)   An individual appears to be unable to pay a regulated activity debt if he is in default on an obligation to pay a sum due and payable under an agreement.

(4)   An individual appears to have no reasonable prospect of being able to pay a regulated activity debt if—

(a)   the Authority has served on him a demand requiring him to establish to the satisfaction of the Authority that there is a reasonable prospect that he will be able to pay a sum payable under an agreement when it falls due;

(b)   at least three weeks have elapsed since the demand was served; and

(c)   the demand has been neither complied with nor set aside in accordance with rules.

(5)    A demand made under subsection (4)(a) is to be treated for the purposes of the 1986 Act (or the 1989 Order) as if it were a statutory demand under section 268 of that Act (or Article 242 of that Order).

(6)    For the purposes of a petition presented in accordance with subsection (1)(b)—

    (a)   the Authority is to be treated as a qualified creditor; and

    (b)   a ground mentioned in subsection (2) constitutes apparent insolvency.

(7)    'Individual' means an individual—

    (a)   who is, or has been, an authorised person; or

    (b)   who is carrying on, or has carried on, a regulated activity in contravention of the general prohibition.

(8)    'Agreement' means an agreement the making or performance of which constitutes or is part of a regulated activity carried on by the individual concerned.

(9)    'Rules' means—

    (a)   in England and Wales, rules made under section 412 of the 1986 Act;

    (b)   in Scotland, rules made by order by the Treasury, after consultation with the Scottish Ministers, for the purposes of this section; and

    (c)   in Northern Ireland, rules made under Article 359 of the 1989 Order.

### 373.  Insolvency practitioner's duty to report to Authority

(1)    If—

    (a)   a bankruptcy order or sequestration award is in force in relation to an individual by virtue of a petition presented by a person other than the Authority, and

    (b)   it appears to the insolvency practitioner that the individual is carrying on, or has carried on, a regulated activity in contravention of the general prohibition,

the insolvency practitioner must report the matter to the Authority without delay.

(2)    'Bankruptcy order' means a bankruptcy order under Part IX of the 1986 Act (or Part IX of the 1989 Order).

(3)    'Sequestration award' means an award of sequestration under section 12 of the 1985 Act.

(4)    'Individual' includes an entity mentioned in section 374(1)(c).

### 374.  Authority's powers to participate in proceedings

(1)    This section applies if a person other than the Authority presents a petition to the court—

    (a)   under section 264 of the 1986 Act (or Article 238 of the 1989 Order) for a bankruptcy order to be made against an individual;

    (b)   under section 5 of the 1985 Act for the sequestration of the estate of an individual; or

    (c)   under section 6 of the 1985 Act for the sequestration of the estate belonging to or held for or jointly by the members of an entity mentioned in subsection (1) of that section.

(2)    The Authority is entitled to be heard—

    (a)   at the hearing of the petition; and

    (b)   at any other hearing in relation to the individual or entity under—

       (i)   Part IX of the 1986 Act;

       (ii)   Part IX of the 1989 Order; or

       (iii)   the 1985 Act.

(3)    A copy of the report prepared under section 274 of the 1986 Act (or Article 248 of the 1989 Order) must also be sent to the Authority.

(4)    A person appointed for the purpose by the Authority is entitled—

(a)   to attend any meeting of creditors of the individual or entity;

(b)   to attend any meeting of a committee established under section 301 of the 1986 Act (or Article 274 of the 1989 Order);

(c)   to attend any meeting of commissioners held under paragraph 17 or 18 of Schedule 6 to the 1985 Act; and

(d)   to make representations as to any matter for decision at such a meeting.

(5)   'Individual' means an individual who—

(a)   is, or has been, an authorised person; or

(b)   is carrying on, or has carried on, a regulated activity in contravention of the general prohibition.

(6)   'Entity' means an entity which—

(a)   is, or has been, an authorised person; or

(b)   is carrying on, or has carried on, a regulated activity in contravention of the general prohibition.

*Provisions against debt avoidance*

### 375.   Authority's right to apply for an order

(1)   The Authority may apply for an order under section 423 of the 1986 Act (or Article 367 of the 1989 Order) in relation to a debtor if—

(a)   at the time the transaction at an undervalue was entered into, the debtor was carrying on a regulated activity (whether or not in contravention of the general prohibition); and

(b)   a victim of the transaction is or was party to an agreement entered into with the debtor, the making or performance of which constituted or was part of a regulated activity carried on by the debtor.

(2)   An application made under this section is to be treated as made on behalf of every victim of the transaction to whom subsection (1)(b) applies.

(3)   Expressions which are given a meaning in Part XVI of the 1986 Act (or Article 367, 368 or 369 of the 1989 Order) have the same meaning when used in this section.

*Supplemental provisions concerning insurers*

### 376.   Continuation of contracts of long-term insurance where insurer in liquidation

(1)   This section applies in relation to the winding up of an insurer which effects or carries out contracts of long-term insurance.

(2)   Unless the court otherwise orders, the liquidator must carry on the insurer's business so far as it consists of carrying out the insurer's contracts of long-term insurance with a view to its being transferred as a going concern to a person who may lawfully carry out those contracts.

(3)   In carrying on the business, the liquidator—

(a)   may agree to the variation of any contracts of insurance in existence when the winding up order is made; but

(b)   must not effect any new contracts of insurance.

(4)   If the liquidator is satisfied that the interests of the creditors in respect of liabilities of the insurer attributable to contracts of long-term insurance effected by it require the appointment of a special manager, he may apply to the court.

(5)   On such an application, the court may appoint a special manager to act during such time as the court may direct.

(6)   The special manager is to have such powers, including any of the powers of a receiver or manager, as the court may direct.

(7)   Section 177(5) of the 1986 Act (or Article 151(5) of the 1989 Order) applies to a special manager appointed under subsection (5) as it applies to a special manager appointed under section 177 of the 1986 Act (or Article 151 of the 1989 Order).

(8)   If the court thinks fit, it may reduce the value of one or more of the contracts of long-term insurance effected by the insurer.

(9)   Any reduction is to be on such terms and subject to such conditions (if any) as the court thinks fit.

(10)   The court may, on the application of an official, appoint an independent actuary to investigate the insurer's business so far as it consists of carrying out its contracts of long-term insurance and to report to the official—

(a)   on the desirability or otherwise of that part of the insurer's business being continued; and

(b)   on any reduction in the contracts of long-term insurance effected by the insurer that may be necessary for successful continuation of that part of the insurer's business.

(11)   'Official' means—

(a)   the liquidator;

(b)   a special manager appointed under subsection (5); or

(c)   the Authority.

(12)   The liquidator may make an application in the name of the insurer and on its behalf under Part VII without obtaining the permission that would otherwise be required by section 167 of, and Schedule 4 to, the 1986 Act (or Article 142 of, and Schedule 2 to, the 1989 Order).

## 377.   Reducing the value of contracts instead of winding up

(1)   This section applies in relation to an insurer which has been proved to be unable to pay its debts.

(2)   If the court thinks fit, it may reduce the value of one or more of the insurer's contracts instead of making a winding up order.

(3)   Any reduction is to be on such terms and subject to such conditions (if any) as the court thinks fit.

## 378.   Treatment of assets on winding up

(1)   The Treasury may by regulations provide for the treatment of the assets of an insurer on its winding up.

(2)   The regulations may, in particular, provide for—

(a)   assets representing a particular part of the insurer's business to be available only for meeting liabilities attributable to that part of the insurer's business;

(b)   separate general meetings of the creditors to be held in respect of liabilities attributable to a particular part of the insurer's business.

## 379.   Winding-up rules

(1)   Winding-up rules may include provision—

(a)   for determining the amount of the liabilities of an insurer to policyholders of any class or description for the purpose of proof in a winding up; and

(b)   generally for carrying into effect the provisions of this Part with respect to the winding up of insurers.

(2)   Winding-up rules may, in particular, make provision for all or any of the following matters—

(a)   the identification of assets and liabilities;

(b)   the apportionment, between assets of different classes or descriptions, of—

      (i)    the costs, charges and expenses of the winding up; and

      (ii)   any debts of the insurer of a specified class or description;

   (c)   the determination of the amount of liabilities of a specified description;

   (d)   the application of assets for meeting liabilities of a specified description;

   (e)   the application of assets representing any excess of a specified description.

(3)   'Specified' means specified in winding-up rules.

(4)   'Winding-up rules' means rules made under section 411 of the 1986 Act (or Article 359 of the 1989 Order).

(5)   Nothing in this section affects the power to make winding—up rules under the 1986 Act or the 1989 Order.

## PART XXV
## INJUNCTIONS AND RESTITUTION

*Injunctions*

### 380.  Injunctions

(1)   If, on the application of the Authority or the Secretary of State, the court is satisfied—

   (a)   that there is a reasonable likelihood that any person will contravene a relevant requirement, or

   (b)   that any person has contravened a relevant requirement and that there is a reasonable likelihood that the contravention will continue or be repeated,

the court may make an order restraining (or in Scotland an interdict prohibiting) the contravention.

(2)   If on the application of the Authority or the Secretary of State the court is satisfied—

   (a)   that any person has contravened a relevant requirement, and

   (b)   that there are steps which could be taken for remedying the contravention,

the court may make an order requiring that person, and any other person who appears to have been knowingly concerned in the contravention, to take such steps as the court may direct to remedy it.

(3)   If, on the application of the Authority or the Secretary of State, the court is satisfied that any person may have—

   (a)   contravened a relevant requirement, or

   (b)   been knowingly concerned in the contravention of such a requirement,

it may make an order restraining (or in Scotland an interdict prohibiting) him from disposing of, or otherwise dealing with, any assets of his which it is satisfied he is reasonably likely to dispose of or otherwise deal with.

(4)   The jurisdiction conferred by this section is exercisable by the High Court and the Court of Session.

(5)   In subsection (2), references to remedying a contravention include references to mitigating its effect.

(6)   'Relevant requirement'—

   (a)   in relation to an application by the Authority, means a requirement—

      (i)    which is imposed by or under this Act; or

      (ii)   which is imposed by or under any other Act and whose contravention constitutes an offence which the Authority has power to prosecute under this Act;

   (b)   in relation to an application by the Secretary of State, means a requirement which is imposed by or under this Act and whose contravention constitutes an offence which the Secretary of State has power to prosecute under this Act.

(7)   In the application of subsection (6) to Scotland—

(a)   in paragraph (a)(ii) for 'which the Authority has power to prosecute under this Act' substitute 'mentioned in paragraph (a) or (b) of section 402(1)'; and

(b)   in paragraph (b) omit 'which the Secretary of State has power to prosecute under this Act'.

### 381.   Injunctions in cases of market abuse

(1)   If, on the application of the Authority, the court is satisfied—

(a)   that there is a reasonable likelihood that any person will engage in market abuse, or

(b)   that any person is or has engaged in market abuse and that there is a reasonable likelihood that the market abuse will continue or be repeated,

the court may make an order restraining (or in Scotland an interdict prohibiting) the market abuse.

(2)   If on the application of the Authority the court is satisfied—

(a)   that any person is or has engaged in market abuse, and

(b)   that there are steps which could be taken for remedying the market abuse,

the court may make an order requiring him to take such steps as the court may direct to remedy it.

(3)   Subsection (4) applies if, on the application of the Authority, the court is satisfied that any person—

(a)   may be engaged in market abuse; or

(b)   may have been engaged in market abuse.

(4)   The court make an order restraining (or in Scotland an interdict prohibiting) the person concerned from disposing of, or otherwise dealing with, any assets of his which it is satisfied that he is reasonably likely to dispose of, or otherwise deal with.

(5)   The jurisdiction conferred by this section is exercisable by the High Court and the Court of Session.

(6)   In subsection (2), references to remedying any market abuse include references to mitigating its effect.

*Restitution orders*

### 382.   Restitution orders

(1)   The court may, on the application of the Authority or the Secretary of State, make an order under subsection (2) if it is satisfied that a person has contravened a relevant requirement, or been knowingly concerned in the contravention of such a requirement, and—

(a)   that profits have accrued to him as a result of the contravention; or

(b)   that one or more persons have suffered loss or been otherwise adversely affected as a result of the contravention.

(2)   The court may order the person concerned to pay to the Authority such sum as appears to the court to be just having regard—

(a)   in a case within paragraph (a) of subsection (1), to the profits appearing to the court to have accrued;

(b)   in a case within paragraph (b) of that subsection, to the extent of the loss or other adverse effect;

(c)   in a case within both of those paragraphs, to the profits appearing to the court to have accrued and to the extent of the loss or other adverse effect.

(3)   Any amount paid to the Authority in pursuance of an order under subsection (2) must be paid by it to such qualifying person or distributed by it among such qualifying persons as the court may direct.

(4)   On an application under subsection (1) the court may require the person concerned to supply it with such accounts or other information as it may require for any one or more of the following purposes—

(a)   establishing whether any and, if so, what profits have accrued to him as mentioned in paragraph (a) of that subsection;

(b)   establishing whether any person or persons have suffered any loss or adverse effect as mentioned in paragraph (b) of that subsection and, if so, the extent of that loss or adverse effect; and

(c)   determining how any amounts are to be paid or distributed under subsection (3).

(5)   The court may require any accounts or other information supplied under subsection (4) to be verified in such manner as it may direct.

(6)   The jurisdiction conferred by this section is exercisable by the High Court and the Court of Session.

(7)   Nothing in this section affects the right of any person other than the Authority or the Secretary of State to bring proceedings in respect of the matters to which this section applies.

(8)   'Qualifying person' means a person appearing to the court to be someone—

(a)   to whom the profits mentioned in subsection (1)(a) are attributable; or

(b)   who has suffered the loss or adverse effect mentioned in subsection (1)(b).

(9)   'Relevant requirement'—

(a)   in relation to an application by the Authority, means a requirement—

(i)   which is imposed by or under this Act; or

(ii)   which is imposed by or under any other Act and whose contravention constitutes an offence which the Authority has power to prosecute under this Act;

(b)   in relation to an application by the Secretary of State, means a requirement which is imposed by or under this Act and whose contravention constitutes an offence which the Secretary of State has power to prosecute under this Act.

(10)   In the application of subsection (9) to Scotland—

(a)   in paragraph (a)(ii) for 'which the Authority has power to prosecute under this Act' substitute 'mentioned in paragraph (a) or (b) of section 402(1)'; and

(b)   in paragraph (b) omit 'which the Secretary of State has power to prosecute under this Act'.

### 383.   Restitution orders in cases of market abuse

(1)   The court may, on the application of the Authority, make an order under subsection (4) if it is satisfied that a person ('the person concerned')—

(a)   has engaged in market abuse, or

(b)   by taking or refraining from taking any action has required or encouraged another person or persons to engage in behaviour which, if engaged in by the person concerned, would amount to market abuse,

and the condition mentioned in subsection (2) is fulfilled.

(2)   The condition is—

(a)   that profits have accrued to the person concerned as a result; or

(b)   that one or more persons have suffered loss or been otherwise adversely affected as a result.

(3)   But the court may not make an order under subsection (4) if it is satisfied that—

(a)   the person concerned believed, on reasonable grounds, that his behaviour did not fall within paragraph (a) or (b) of subsection (1); or

(b)   he took all reasonable precautions and exercised all due diligence to avoid behaving in a way which fell within paragraph (a) or (b) of subsection (1).

(4)   The court may order the person concerned to pay to the Authority such sum as appears to the court to be just having regard—

(a)   in a case within paragraph (a) of subsection (2), to the profits appearing to the court to have accrued;

(b)   in a case within paragraph (b) of that subsection, to the extent of the loss or other adverse effect;

(c)   in a case within both of those paragraphs, to the profits appearing to the court to have accrued and to the extent of the loss or other adverse effect.

(5)   Any amount paid to the Authority in pursuance of an order under subsection (4) must be paid by it to such qualifying person or distributed by it among such qualifying persons as the court may direct.

(6)   On an application under subsection (1) the court may require the person concerned to supply it with such accounts or other information as it may require for any one or more of the following purposes—

(a)   establishing whether any and, if so, what profits have accrued to him as mentioned in subsection (2)(a);

(b)   establishing whether any person or persons have suffered any loss or adverse effect as mentioned in subsection (2)(b) and, if so, the extent of that loss or adverse effect; and

(c)   determining how any amounts are to be paid or distributed under subsection (5).

(7)   The court may require any accounts or other information supplied under subsection (6) to be verified in such manner as it may direct.

(8)   The jurisdiction conferred by this section is exercisable by the High Court and the Court of Session.

(9)   Nothing in this section affects the right of any person other than the Authority to bring proceedings in respect of the matters to which this section applies.

(10)   'Qualifying person' means a person appearing to the court to be someone—

(a)   to whom the profits mentioned in paragraph (a) of subsection (2) are attributable; or

(b)   who has suffered the loss or adverse effect mentioned in paragraph (b) of that subsection.

*Restitution required by Authority*

### 384.   Power of Authority to require restitution

(1)   The Authority may exercise the power in subsection (5) if it is satisfied that an authorised person ('the person concerned') has contravened a relevant requirement, or been knowingly concerned in the contravention of such a requirement, and—

(a)   that profits have accrued to him as a result of the contravention; or

(b)   that one or more persons have suffered loss or been otherwise adversely affected as a result of the contravention.

(2)   The Authority may exercise the power in subsection (5) if it is satisfied that a person ('the person concerned')—

(a)   has engaged in market abuse, or

(b)   by taking or refraining from taking any action has required or encouraged another person or persons to engage in behaviour which, if engaged in by the person concerned, would amount to market abuse,

and the condition mentioned in subsection (3) is fulfilled,

(3)   The condition is—

(a)   that profits have accrued to the person concerned as a result of the market abuse; or

(b)   that one or more persons have suffered loss or been otherwise adversely affected as a result of the market abuse.

(4)   But the Authority may not exercise that power as a result of subsection (2) if, having considered any representations made to it in response to a warning notice, there are reasonable grounds for it to be satisfied that—

(a)   the person concerned believed, on reasonable grounds, that his behaviour did not fall within paragraph (a) or (b) of that subsection; or

(b)   he took all reasonable precautions and exercised all due diligence to avoid behaving in a way which fell within paragraph (a) or (b) of that subsection.

(5)   The power referred to in subsections (1) and (2) is a power to require the person concerned, in accordance with such arrangements as the Authority considers appropriate, to pay to the appropriate person or distribute among the appropriate persons such amount as appears to the Authority to be just having regard—

(a)   in a case within paragraph (a) of subsection (1) or (3), to the profits appearing to the Authority to have accrued;

(b)   in a case within paragraph (b) of subsection (1) or (3), to the extent of the loss or other adverse effect;

(c)   in a case within paragraphs (a) and (b) of subsection (1) or (3), to the profits appearing to the Authority to have accrued and to the extent of the loss or other adverse effect.

(6)   'Appropriate person' means a person appearing to the Authority to be someone—

(a)   to whom the profits mentioned in paragraph (a) of subsection (1) or (3) are attributable; or

(b)   who has suffered the loss or adverse effect mentioned in paragraph (b) of subsection (1) or (3).

(7)   'Relevant requirement' means—

(a)   a requirement imposed by or under this Act; and

(b)   a requirement which is imposed by or under any other Act and whose contravention constitutes an offence in relation to which this Act confers power to prosecute on the Authority.

(8)   In the application of subsection (7) to Scotland, in paragraph (b) for 'in relation to which this Act confers power to prosecute on the Authority' substitute 'mentioned in paragraph (a) or (b) of section 402(1)'.

### 385.   Warning notices

(1)   If the Authority proposes to exercise the power under section 384(5) in relation to a person, it must give him a warning notice.

(2)   A warning notice under this section must specify the amount which the Authority proposes to require the person concerned to pay or distribute as mentioned in section 384(5).

### 386.   Decision notices

(1)   If the Authority decides to exercise the power under section 384(5), it must give a decision notice to the person in relation to whom the power is exercised.

(2)   The decision notice must—

(a)   state the amount that he is to pay or distribute as mentioned in section 384(5);

(b)   identify the person or persons to whom that amount is to be paid or among whom that amount is to be distributed; and

(c)   state the arrangements in accordance with which the payment or distribution is to be made.

(3)   If the Authority decides to exercise the power under section 384(5), the person in relation to whom it is exercised may refer the matter to the Tribunal.

## PART XXVI
## NOTICES

*Warning notices*

**387.**—(1)   A warning notice must—

(a)   state the action which the Authority proposes to take;

(b)   be in writing;

(c)   give reasons for the proposed action;

(d)   state whether section 394 applies; and

(e)   if that section applies, describe its effect and state whether any secondary material exists to which the person concerned must be allowed access under it.

(2)   The warning notice must specify a reasonable period (which may not be less than 28 days) within which the person to whom it is given may make representations to the Authority.

(3)   The Authority may extend the period specified in the notice.

(4)   The Authority must then decide, within a reasonable period, whether to give the person concerned a decision notice.

*Decision notices*

**388.**—(1)   A decision notice must—

(a)   be in writing;

(b)   give the Authority's reasons for the decision to take the action to which the notice relates;

(c)   state whether section 394 applies;

(d)   if that section applies, describe its effect and state whether any secondary material exists to which the person concerned must be allowed access under it; and

(e)   give an indication of—

(i)   any right to have the matter referred to the Tribunal which is given by this Act; and

(ii)   the procedure on such a reference.

(2)   If the decision notice was preceded by a warning notice, the action to which the decision notice relates must be action under the same Part as the action proposed in the warning notice.

(3)   The Authority may, before it takes the action to which a decision notice ('the original notice') relates, give the person concerned a further decision notice which relates to different action in respect of the same matter.

(4)   The Authority may give a further decision notice as a result of subsection (3) only if the person to whom the original notice was given consents.

(5)   If the person to whom a decision notice is given under subsection (3) had the right to refer the matter to which the original decision notice related to the Tribunal, he has that right as respects the decision notice under subsection (3).

*Conclusion of proceedings*

### 389.   Notices of discontinuance

(1)   If the Authority decides not to take—

(a)   the action proposed in a warning notice, or

(b)   the action to which a decision notice relates,

it must give a notice of discontinuance to the person to whom the warning notice or decision notice was given.

(2)   But subsection (1) does not apply if the discontinuance of the proceedings concerned results in the granting of an application made by the person to whom the warning or decision notice was given.

(3)   A notice of discontinuance must identify the proceedings which are being discontinued.

### 390.   Final notices

(1)   If the Authority has given a person a decision notice and the matter was not referred to the Tribunal within the period mentioned in section 133(1), the Authority must, on taking the action to which the decision notice relates, give the person concerned and any person to whom the decision notice was copied a final notice.

(2)   If the Authority has given a person a decision notice and the matter was referred to the Tribunal, the Authority must, on taking action in accordance with any directions given by—

(a)   the Tribunal, or

(b)   the court under section 137,

give that person and any person to whom the decision notice was copied a final notice.

(3)   A final notice about a statement must—

(a)   set out the terms of the statement;

(b)   give details of the manner in which, and the date on which, the statement will be published.

(4)   A final notice about an order must—

(a)   set out the terms of the order;

(b)   state the date from which the order has effect.

(5)   A final notice about a penalty must—

(a)   state the amount of the penalty;

(b)   state the manner in which, and the period within which, the penalty is to be paid;

(c)   give details of the way in which the penalty will be recovered if it is not paid by the date stated in the notice.

(6)   A final notice about a requirement to make a payment or distribution in accordance with section 384(5) must state—

(a)   the persons to whom,

(b)   the manner in which, and

(c)   the period within which,

it must be made.

(7)   In any other case, the final notice must—

(a)  give details of the action being taken;

(b)  state the date on which the action is to be taken.

(8)  The period stated under subsection (5)(b) or (6)(c) may not be less than 14 days beginning with the date on which the final notice is given.

(9)  If all or any of the amount of a penalty payable under a final notice is outstanding at the end of the period stated under subsection (5)(b), the Authority may recover the outstanding amount as a debt due to it.

(10)  If all or any of a required payment or distribution has not been made at the end of a period stated in a final notice under subsection (6)(c), the obligation to make the payment is enforceable, on the application of the Authority, by injunction or, in Scotland, by an order under section 45 of the Court of Session Act 1988.

*Publication*

**391.  Publication**

(1)  Neither the Authority nor a person to whom a warning notice or decision notice is given or copied may publish the notice or any details concerning it.

(2)  A notice of discontinuance must state that, if the person to whom the notice is given consents, the Authority may publish such information as it considers appropriate about the matter to which the discontinued proceedings related.

(3)  A copy of a notice of discontinuance must be accompanied by a statement that, if the person to whom the notice is copied consents, the Authority may publish such information as it considers appropriate about the matter to which the discontinued proceedings related, so far as relevant to that person.

(4)  The Authority must publish such information about the matter to which a final notice relates as it considers appropriate.

(5)  When a supervisory notice takes effect, the Authority must publish such information about the matter to which the notice relates as it considers appropriate.

(6)  But the Authority may not publish information under this section if publication of it would, in its opinion, be unfair to the person with respect to whom the action was taken or prejudicial to the interests of consumers.

(7)  Information is to be published under this section in such manner as the Authority considers appropriate.

(8)  For the purposes of determining when a supervisory notice takes effect, a matter to which the notice relates is open to review if—

(a)  the period during which any person may refer the matter to the Tribunal is still running;

(b)  the matter has been referred to the Tribunal but has not been dealt with;

(c)  the matter has been referred to the Tribunal and dealt with but the period during which an appeal may be brought against the Tribunal's decision is still running; or

(d)  such an appeal has been brought but has not been determined.

(9)  'Notice of discontinuance' means a notice given under section 389.

(10)  'Supervisory notice' has the same meaning as in section 395.

(11)  'Consumers' means persons who are consumers for the purposes of section 138.

*Third party rights and access to evidence*

**392.  Application of sections 393 and 394**

Sections 393 and 394 apply to—

(a)   a warning notice given in accordance with section 54(1), 57(1), 63(3), 67(1), 88(4)(b), 89(2), 92(1), 126(1), 207(1), 255(1), 280(1), 331(1), 345(2) (whether as a result of subsection (1) of that section or section 249(1)) or 385(1);

(b)   a decision notice given in accordance with section 54(2), 57(3), 63(4), 67(4), 88(6)(b), 89(3), 92(4), 127(1), 208(1), 255(2), 280(2), 331(3), 345(3) (whether as a result of subsection (1) of that section or section 249(1)) or 386(1).

### 393.   Third party rights

(1)   If any of the reasons contained in a warning notice to which this section applies relates to a matter which—

(a)   identifies a person ('the third party') other than the person to whom the notice is given, and

(b)   in the opinion of the Authority, is prejudicial to the third party,

a copy of the notice must be given to the third party.

(2)   Subsection (1) does not require a copy to be given to the third party if the Authority—

(a)   has given him a separate warning notice in relation to the same matter; or

(b)   gives him such a notice at the same time as it gives the warning notice which identifies him.

(3)   The notice copied to a third party under subsection (1) must specify a reasonable period (which may not be less than 28 days) within which he may make representations to the Authority.

(4)   If any of the reasons contained in a decision notice to which this section applies relates to a matter which—

(a)   identifies a person ('the third party') other than the person to whom the decision notice is given, and

(b)   in the opinion of the Authority, is prejudicial to the third party,

a copy of the notice must be given to the third party.

(5)   If the decision notice was preceded by a warning notice, a copy of the decision notice must (unless it has been given under subsection (4)) be given to each person to whom the warning notice was copied.

(6)   Subsection (4) does not require a copy to be given to the third party if the Authority—

(a)   has given him a separate decision notice in relation to the same matter; or

(b)   gives him such a notice at the same time as it gives the decision notice which identifies him.

(7)   Neither subsection (1) nor subsection (4) requires a copy of a notice to be given to a third party if the Authority considers it impracticable to do so.

(8)   Subsections (9) to (11) apply if the person to whom a decision notice is given has a right to refer the matter to the Tribunal.

(9)   A person to whom a copy of the notice is given under this section may refer to the Tribunal—

(a)   the decision in question, so far as it is based on a reason of the kind mentioned in subsection (4); or

(b)   any opinion expressed by the Authority in relation to him.

(10)   The copy must be accompanied by an indication of the third party's right to make a reference under subsection (9) and of the procedure on such a reference.

(11)   A person who alleges that a copy of the notice should have been given to him, but was not, may refer to the Tribunal the alleged failure and—

(a) the decision in question, so far as it is based on a reason of the kind mentioned in subsection (4); or

(b) any opinion expressed by the Authority in relation to him.

(12) Section 394 applies to a third party as it applies to the person to whom the notice to which this section applies was given, in so far as the material which the Authority must disclose under that section relates to the matter which identifies the third party.

(13) A copy of a notice given to a third party under this section must be accompanied by a description of the effect of section 394 as it applies to him.

(14) Any person to whom a warning notice or decision notice was copied under this section must be given a copy of a notice of discontinuance applicable to the proceedings to which the warning notice or decision notice related.

## 394. Access to Authority material

(1) If the Authority gives a person ('A') a notice to which this section applies, it must—

(a) allow him access to the material on which it relied in taking the decision which gave rise to the obligation to give the notice;

(b) allow him access to any secondary material which, in the opinion of the Authority, might undermine that decision.

(2) But the Authority does not have to allow A access to material under subsection (1) if the material is excluded material or it—

(a) relates to a case involving a person other than A; and

(b) was taken into account by the Authority in A's case only for purposes of comparison with other cases.

(3) The Authority may refuse A access to particular material which it would otherwise have to allow him access to if, in its opinion, allowing him access to the material—

(a) would not be in the public interest; or

(b) would not be fair, having regard to—

(i) the likely significance of the material to A in relation to the matter in respect of which he has been given a notice to which this section applies; and

(ii) the potential prejudice to the commercial interests of a person other than A which would be caused by the material's disclosure.

(4) If the Authority does not allow A access to material because it is excluded material consisting of a protected item, it must give A written notice of—

(a) the existence of the protected item; and

(b) the Authority's decision not to allow him access to it.

(5) If the Authority refuses under subsection (3) to allow A access to material, it must give him written notice of—

(a) the refusal; and

(b) the reasons for it.

(6) 'Secondary material' means material, other than material falling within paragraph (a) of subsection (1) which—

(a) was considered by the Authority in reaching the decision mentioned in that paragraph; or

(b) was obtained by the Authority in connection with the matter to which the notice to which this section applies relates but which was not considered by it in reaching that decision.

(7) 'Excluded material' means material which—

(a) has been intercepted in obedience to a warrant issued under any enactment relating to the interception of communications;

(b)   indicates that such a warrant has been issued or that material has been intercepted in obedience to such a warrant; or

(c)   is a protected item (as defined in section 413).

*The Authority's procedures*

### 395.   The Authority's procedures

(1)   The Authority must determine the procedure that it proposes to follow in relation to the giving of—

(a)   supervisory notices; and

(b)   warning notices and decision notices.

(2)   That procedure must be designed to secure, among other things, that the decision which gives rise to the obligation to give any such notice is taken by a person not directly involved in establishing the evidence on which that decision is based.

(3)   But the procedure may permit a decision which gives rise to an obligation to give a supervisory notice to be taken by a person other than a person mentioned in subsection (2) if—

(a)   the Authority considers that, in the particular case, it is necessary in order to protect the interests of consumers; and

(b)   the person taking the decision is of a level of seniority laid down by the procedure.

(4)   A level of seniority laid down by the procedure for the purposes of subsection (3)(b) must be appropriate to the importance of the decision.

(5)   The Authority must issue a statement of the procedure.

(6)   The statement must be published in the way appearing to the Authority to be best calculated to bring it to the attention of the public.

(7)   The Authority may charge a reasonable fee for providing a person with a copy of the statement.

(8)   The Authority must, without delay, give the Treasury a copy of any statement which it issues under this section.

(9)   When giving a supervisory notice, or a warning notice or decision notice, the Authority must follow its stated procedure.

(10)   If the Authority changes the procedure in a material way, it must publish a revised statement.

(11)   The Authority's failure in a particular case to follow its procedure as set out in the latest published statement does not affect the validity of a notice given in that case.

(12)   But subsection (11) does not prevent the Tribunal from taking into account any such failure in considering a matter referred to it.

(13)   'Supervisory notice' means a notice given in accordance with section—

(a)   53(4), (7) or (8)(b);

(b)   78(2) or (5);

(c)   197(3), (6) or (7)(b);

(d)   259(3), (8) or (9)(b);

(e)   268(3), (7)(a) or (9)(a) (as a result of subsection (8)(b));

(f)   282(3), (6) or (7)(b);

(g)   321(2) or (5).

### 396.   Statements under section 395: consultation

(1)   Before issuing a statement of procedure under section 395, the Authority must publish a draft of the proposed statement in the way appearing to the Authority to be best calculated to bring it to the attention of the public.

(2)   The draft must be accompanied by notice that representations about the proposal may be made to the Authority within a specified time.

(3)   Before issuing the proposed statement of procedure, the Authority must have regard to any representations made to it in accordance with subsection (2).

(4)   If the Authority issues the proposed statement of procedure it must publish an account, in general terms, of—

(a)   the representations made to it in accordance with subsection (2); and

(b)   its response to them.

(5)   If the statement of procedure differs from the draft published under subsection (1) in a way which is, in the opinion of the Authority, significant, the Authority must (in addition to complying with subsection (4)) publish details of the difference.

(6)   The Authority may charge a reasonable fee for providing a person with a copy of a draft published under subsection (1).

(7)   This section also applies to a proposal to revise a statement of policy.

PART XXVII
OFFENCES

*Miscellaneous offences*

### 397.  Misleading statements and practices

(1)   This subsection applies to a person who—

(a)   makes a statement, promise or forecast which he knows to be misleading, false or deceptive in a material particular;

(b)   dishonestly conceals any material facts whether in connection with a statement, promise or forecast made by him or otherwise; or

(c)   recklessly makes (dishonestly or otherwise) a statement, promise or forecast which is misleading, false or deceptive in a material particular.

(2)   A person to whom subsection (1) applies is guilty of an offence if he makes the statement, promise or forecast or conceals the facts for the purpose of inducing, or is reckless as to whether it may induce, another person (whether or not the person to whom the statement, promise or forecast is made)—

(a)   to enter or offer to enter into, or to refrain from entering or offering to enter into, a relevant agreement; or

(b)   to exercise, or refrain from exercising, any rights conferred by a relevant investment.

(3)   Any person who does any act or engages in any course of conduct which creates a false or misleading impression as to the market in or the price or value of any relevant investments is guilty of an offence if he does so for the purpose of creating that impression and of thereby inducing another person to acquire, dispose of, subscribe for or underwrite those investments or to refrain from doing so or to exercise, or refrain from exercising, any rights conferred by those investments.

(4)   In proceedings for an offence under subsection (2) brought against a person to whom subsection (1) applies as a result of paragraph (a) of that subsection, it is a defence for him to show that the statement, promise or forecast was made in conformity with price stabilising rules or control of information rules.

(5)   In proceedings brought against any person for an offence under subsection (3) it is a defence for him to show—

(a)   that he reasonably believed that his act or conduct would not create an impression that was false or misleading as to the matters mentioned in that subsection;

(b)   that he acted or engaged in the conduct—

   (i)   for the purpose of stabilising the price of investments; and

   (ii)   in conformity with price stabilising rules; or

(c)   that he acted or engaged in the conduct in conformity with control of information rules.

(6)   Subsections (1) and (2) do not apply unless—

(a)   the statement, promise or forecast is made in or from, or the facts are concealed in or from, the United Kingdom or arrangements are made in or from the United Kingdom for the statement, promise or forecast to be made or the facts to be concealed;

(b)   the person on whom the inducement is intended to or may have effect is in the United Kingdom; or

(c)   the agreement is or would be entered into or the rights are or would be exercised in the United Kingdom.

(7)   Subsection (3) does not apply unless—

   (a)   the act is done, or the course of conduct is engaged in, in the United Kingdom; or

(b)   the false or misleading impression is created there.

(8)   A person guilty of an offence under this section is liable—

(a)   on summary conviction, to imprisonment for a term not exceeding six months or a fine not exceeding the statutory maximum, or both;

(b)   on conviction on indictment, to imprisonment for a term not exceeding seven years or a fine, or both.

(9)   'Relevant agreement' means an agreement—

(a)   the entering into or performance of which by either party constitutes an activity of a specified kind or one which falls within a specified class of activity; and

(b)   which relates to a relevant investment.

(10)   'Relevant investment' means an investment of a specified kind or one which falls within a prescribed class of investment.

(11)   Schedule 2 (except paragraphs 25 and 26) applies for the purposes of subsections (9) and (10) with references to section 22 being read as references to each of those subsections.

(12)   Nothing in Schedule 2, as applied by subsection (11), limits the power conferred by subsection (9) or (10).

(13)   'Investment' includes any asset, right or interest.

(14)   'Specified' means specified in an order made by the Treasury.

## 398.   Misleading the Authority: residual cases

(1)   A person who, in purported compliance with any requirement imposed by or under this Act, knowingly or recklessly gives the Authority information which is false or misleading in a material particular is guilty of an offence.

(2)   Subsection (1) applies only to a requirement in relation to which no other provision of this Act creates an offence in connection with the giving of information.

(3)   A person guilty of an offence under this section is liable—

(a)   on summary conviction, to a fine not exceeding the statutory maximum;

(b)   on conviction on indictment, to a fine.

## 399.   Misleading the Director General of Fair Trading

Section 44 of the Competition Act 1998 (offences connected with the provision of false or misleading information) applies in relation to any function of the Director General of Fair Trading under this Act as if it were a function under Part I of that Act.

*Bodies corporate and partnerships*

**400.   Offences by bodies corporate etc**

(1)   If an offence under this Act committed by a body corporate is shown—

(a)   to have been committed with the consent or connivance of an officer, or

(b)   to be attributable to any neglect on his part,

the officer as well as the body corporate is guilty of the offence and liable to be proceeded against and punished accordingly.

(2)   If the affairs of a body corporate are managed by its members, subsection (1) applies in relation to the acts and defaults of a member in connection with his functions of management as if he were a director of the body.

(3)   If an offence under this Act committed by a partnership is shown—

(a)   to have been committed with the consent or connivance of a partner, or

(b)   to be attributable to any neglect on his part,

the partner as well as the partnership is guilty of the offence and liable to be proceeded against and punished accordingly.

(4)   In subsection (3) 'partner' includes a person purporting to act as a partner.

(5)   'Officer', in relation to a body corporate, means—

(a)   a director, member of the committee of management, chief executive, manager, secretary or other similar officer of the body, or a person purporting to act in any such capacity; and

(b)   an individual who is a controller of the body.

(6)   If an offence under this Act committed by an unincorporated association (other than a partnership) is shown—

(a)   to have been committed with the consent or connivance of an officer of the association or a member of its governing body, or

(b)   to be attributable to any neglect on the part of such an officer or member,

that officer or member as well as the association is guilty of the offence and liable to be proceeded against and punished accordingly.

(7)   Regulations may provide for the application of any provision of this section, with such modifications as the Treasury consider appropriate, to a body corporate or unincorporated association formed or recognised under the law of a territory outside the United Kingdom.

*Institution of proceedings*

**401.   Proceedings for offences**

(1)   In this section 'offence' means an offence under this Act or subordinate legislation made under this Act.

(2)   Proceedings for an offence may be instituted in England and Wales only—

(a)   by the Authority or the Secretary of State; or

(b)   by or with the consent of the Director of Public Prosecutions.

(3)   Proceedings for an offence may be instituted in Northern Ireland only—

(a)   by the Authority or the Secretary of State; or

(b)   by or with the consent of the Director of Public Prosecutions for Northern Ireland.

(4)   Except in Scotland, proceedings for an offence under section 203 may also be instituted by the Director General of Fair Trading.

(5)   In exercising its power to institute proceedings for an offence, the Authority must comply with any conditions or restrictions imposed in writing by the Treasury.

(6)   Conditions or restrictions may be imposed under subsection (5) in relation to—

(a)   proceedings generally; or

(b)   such proceedings, or categories of proceedings, as the Treasury may direct.

## 402.   Power of the Authority to institute proceedings for certain other offences

(1)   Except in Scotland, the Authority may institute proceedings for an offence under—

(a)   Part V of the Criminal Justice Act 1993 (insider dealing); or

(b)   prescribed regulations relating to money laundering.

(2)   In exercising its power to institute proceedings for any such offence, the Authority must comply with any conditions or restrictions imposed in writing by the Treasury.

(3)   Conditions or restrictions may be imposed under subsection (2) in relation to—

(a)   proceedings generally; or

(b)   such proceedings, or categories of proceedings, as the Treasury may direct.

## 403.   Jurisdiction and procedure in respect of offences

(1)   A fine imposed on an unincorporated association on its conviction of an offence is to be paid out of the funds of the association.

(2)   Proceedings for an offence alleged to have been committed by an unincorporated association must be brought in the name of the association (and not in that of any of its members).

(3)   Rules of court relating to the service of documents are to have effect as if the association were a body corporate.

(4)   In proceedings for an offence brought against an unincorporated association—

(a)   section 33 of the Criminal Justice Act 1925 and Schedule 3 to the Magistrates' Courts Act 1980 (procedure) apply as they do in relation to a body corporate;

(b)   section 70 of the Criminal Procedure (Scotland) Act 1995 (procedure) applies as if the association were a body corporate;

(c)   section 18 of the Criminal Justice (Northern Ireland) Act 1945 and Schedule 4 to the Magistrates' Courts (Northern Ireland) Order 1981 (procedure) apply as they do in relation to a body corporate.

(5)   Summary proceedings for an offence may be taken—

(a)   against a body corporate or unincorporated association at any place at which it has a place of business;

(b)   against an individual at any place where he is for the time being.

(6)   Subsection (5) does not affect any jurisdiction exercisable apart from this section.

(7)   'Offence' means an offence under this Act.

### PART XXVIII
### MISCELLANEOUS

*Schemes for reviewing past business*

## 404.   Schemes for reviewing past business

(1)   Subsection (2) applies if the Treasury are satisfied that there is evidence suggesting—

(a)   that there has been a widespread or regular failure on the part of authorised persons to comply with rules relating to a particular kind of activity; and

(b)   that, as a result, private persons have suffered (or will suffer) loss in respect of which authorised persons are (or will be) liable to make payments ('compensation payments').

(2)   The Treasury may by order ('a scheme order') authorise the Authority to establish and operate a scheme for—

(a)   determining the nature and extent of the failure;

(b)   establishing the liability of authorised persons to make compensation payments; and

(c)   determining the amounts payable by way of compensation payments.

(3)   An authorised scheme must be made so as to comply with specified requirements.

(4)   A scheme order may be made only if—

(a)   the Authority has given the Treasury a report about the alleged failure and asked them to make a scheme order;

(b)   the report contains details of the scheme which the Authority propose to make; and

(c)   the Treasury are satisfied that the proposed scheme is an appropriate way of dealing with the failure.

(5)   A scheme order may provide for specified provisions of or made under this Act to apply in relation to any provision of, or determination made under, the resulting authorised scheme subject to such modifications (if any) as may be specified.

(6)   For the purposes of this Act, failure on the part of an authorised person to comply with any provision of an authorised scheme is to be treated (subject to any provision made by the scheme order concerned) as a failure on his part to comply with rules.

(7)   The Treasury may prescribe circumstances in which loss suffered by a person ('A') acting in a fiduciary or other prescribed capacity is to be treated, for the purposes of an authorised scheme, as suffered by a private person in relation to whom A was acting in that capacity.

(8)   This section applies whenever the failure in question occurred.

(9)   'Authorised scheme' means a scheme authorised by a scheme order.

(10)   'Private person' has such meaning as may be prescribed.

(11)   'Specified' means specified in a scheme order.

*Third countries*

## 405.   Directions

(1)   For the purpose of implementing a third country decision, the Treasury may direct the Authority to—

(a)   refuse an application for permission under Part IV made by a body incorporated in, or formed under the law of, any part of the United Kingdom;

(b)   defer its decision on such an application either indefinitely or for such period as may be specified in the direction;

(c)   give a notice of objection to a person who has served a notice of control to the effect that he proposes to acquire a 50% stake in a UK authorised person; or

(d)   give a notice of objection to a person who has acquired a 50% stake in a UK authorised person without having served the required notice of control.

(2)   A direction may also be given in relation to—

(a)   any person falling within a class specified in the direction;

(b)   future applications, notices of control or acquisitions.

(3)   The Treasury may revoke a direction at any time.

(4)   But revocation does not affect anything done in accordance with the direction before it was revoked.

(5)   'Third country decision' means a decision of the Council or the Commission under—

(a)   Article 7(5) of the investment services directive;

(b)   Article 9(4) of the second banking co-ordination directive;

    (c)   Article 29b(4) of the first non-life insurance directive; or

    (d)   Article 32b(4) of the first life insurance directive.

### 406.  Interpretation of section 405

(1)   For the purposes of section 405, a person ('the acquirer') acquires a 50% stake in a UK authorised person ('A') on first falling within any of the cases set out in subsection (2).

(2)   The cases are where the acquirer—

    (a)   holds 50% or more of the shares in A;

    (b)   holds 50% or more of the shares in a parent undertaking ('P') of A;

    (c)   is entitled to exercise, or control the exercise of, 50% or more of the voting power in A; or

    (d)   is entitled to exercise, or control the exercise of, 50% or more of the voting power in P.

(3)   In subsection (2) 'the acquirer' means—

    (a)   the acquirer;

    (b)   any of the acquirer's associates; or

    (c)   the acquirer and any of his associates.

(4)   'Associate', 'shares' and 'voting power' have the same meaning as in section 422.

### 407.  Consequences of a direction under section 405

(1)   If the Authority refuses an application for permission as a result of a direction under section 405(1)(a)—

    (a)   subsections (7) to (9) of section 52 do not apply in relation to the refusal; but

    (b)   the Authority must notify the applicant of the refusal and the reasons for it.

(2)   If the Authority defers its decision on an application for permission as a result of a direction under section 405(1)(b)—

    (a)   the time limit for determining the application mentioned in section 52(1) or (2) stops running on the day of the deferral and starts running again (if at all) on the day the period specified in the direction (if any) ends or the day the direction is revoked; and

    (b)   the Authority must notify the applicant of the deferral and the reasons for it.

(3)   If the Authority gives a notice of objection to a person as a result of a direction under section 405(1)(c) or (d)—

    (a)   sections 189 and 191 have effect as if the notice was a notice of objection within the meaning of Part XII; and

    (b)   the Authority must state in the notice the reasons for it.

### 408.  EFTA firms

(1)   If a third country decision has been taken, the Treasury may make a determination in relation to an EFTA firm which is a subsidiary undertaking of a parent undertaking which is governed by the law of the country to which the decision relates.

(2)   'Determination' means a determination that the firm concerned does not qualify for authorisation under Schedule 3 even if it satisfies the conditions in paragraph 13 or 14 of that Schedule.

(3)   A determination may also be made in relation to any firm falling within a class specified in the determination.

(4)   The Treasury may withdraw a determination at any time.

(5)   But withdrawal does not affect anything done in accordance with the determination before it was withdrawn.

(6)   If the Treasury make a determination in respect of a particular firm, or withdraw such a determination, they must give written notice to that firm.

(7) The Treasury must publish notice of any determination (or the withdrawal of any determination)—

(a) in such a way as they think most suitable for bringing the determination (or withdrawal) to the attention of those likely to be affected by it; and

(b) on, or as soon as practicable after, the date of the determination (or withdrawal).

(8) 'EFTA firm' means a firm, institution or undertaking which—

(a) is an EEA firm as a result of paragraph 5(a), (b) or (d) of Schedule 3; and

(b) is incorporated in, or formed under the law of, an EEA State which is not a member State.

(9) 'Third country decision' has the same meaning as in section 405.

### 409. Gibraltar

(1) The Treasury may by order—

(a) modify Schedule 3 so as to provide for Gibraltar firms of a specified description to qualify for authorisation under that Schedule in specified circumstances;

(b) modify Schedule 3 so as to make provision in relation to the exercise by UK firms of rights under the law of Gibraltar which correspond to EEA rights;

(c) modify Schedule 4 so as to provide for Gibraltar firms of a specified description to qualify for authorisation under that Schedule in specified circumstances;

(d) modify section 264 so as to make provision in relation to collective investment schemes constituted under the law of Gibraltar;

(e) provide for the Authority to be able to give notice under section 264(2) on grounds relating to the law of Gibraltar;

(f) provide for this Act to apply to a Gibraltar recognised scheme as if the scheme were a scheme recognised under section 264.

(2) The fact that a firm may qualify for authorisation under Schedule 3 as a result of an order under subsection (1) does not prevent it from applying for a Part IV permission.

(3) 'Gibraltar firm' means a firm which has its head office in Gibraltar or is otherwise connected with Gibraltar.

(4) 'Gibraltar recognised scheme' means a collective investment scheme—

(a) constituted in an EEA State other than the United Kingdom, and

(b) recognised in Gibraltar under provisions which appear to the Treasury to give effect to the provisions of a relevant Community instrument.

(5) 'Specified' means specified in the order.

(6) 'UK firm' and 'EEA right' have the same meaning as in Schedule 3.

*International obligations*

### 410. International obligations

(1) If it appears to the Treasury that any action proposed to be taken by a relevant person would be incompatible with Community obligations or any other international obligations of the United Kingdom, they may direct that person not to take that action.

(2) If it appears to the Treasury that any action which a relevant person has power to take is required for the purpose of implementing any such obligations, they may direct that person to take that action.

(3) A direction under this section—

(a) may include such supplemental or incidental requirements as the Treasury consider necessary or expedient; and

(b)    is enforceable, on an application made by the Treasury, by injunction or, in Scotland, by an order for specific performance under section 45 of the Court of Session Act 1988.

(4)    'Relevant person' means—

(a)    the Authority;

(b)    any person exercising functions conferred by Part VI on the competent authority;

(c)    any recognised investment exchange (other than one which is an overseas investment exchange);

(d)    any recognised clearing house (other than one which is an overseas clearing house);

(e)    a person included in the list maintained under section 301; or

(f)    the scheme operator of the ombudsman scheme.

*Tax treatment of levies and repayments*

### 411.    Tax treatment of levies and repayments

(1)    In the Income and Corporation Taxes Act 1988 ('the 1988 Act'), in section 76 (expenses of management: insurance companies), for subsections (7) and (7A) substitute—

'(7)    For the purposes of this section any sums paid by a company by way of a levy shall be treated as part of its expenses of management.

(7A)    'Levy' means—

(a)    a payment required under rules made under section 136(2) of the Financial Services and Markets Act 2000 ('the Act of 2000');

(b)    a levy imposed under the Financial Services Compensation Scheme;

(c)    a payment required under rules made under section 234 of the Act of 2000;

(d)    a payment required in accordance with the standard terms fixed under paragraph 18 of Schedule 17 to the Act of 2000.'

(2)    After section 76 of the 1988 Act insert—

### '76A.    Levies and repayments under the Financial Services and Markets Act 2000

(1)    In computing the amount of the profits to be charged under Case I of Schedule D arising from a trade carried on by an authorised person (other than an investment company)—

(a)    to the extent that it would not be deductible apart from this section, any sum expended by the authorised person in paying a levy may be deducted as an allowable expense;

(b)    any payment which is made to the authorised person as a result of a repayment provision is to be treated as a trading receipt.

(2)    "Levy" has the meaning given in section 76(7A).

(3)    "Repayment provision" means any provision made by virtue of—

(a)    section 136(7) of the Financial Services and Markets Act 2000 ("the Act of 2000");

(b)    section 214(1)(e) of the Act of 2000.

(4)    "Authorised person" has the same meaning as in the Act of 2000.

### 76B.    Levies and repayments under the Financial Services and Markets Act 2000: investment companies

(1)    For the purposes of section 75 any sums paid by an investment company—

(a)    by way of a levy, or

(b)   as a result of an award of costs under costs rules,

shall be treated as part of its expenses of management.

(2)   If a payment is made to an investment company as a result of a repayment provision, the company shall be charged to tax under Case VI of Schedule D on the amount of that payment.

(3)   ''Levy'' has the meaning given in section 76(7A).

(4)   ''Costs rules'' means—

(a)   rules made under section 230 of the Financial Services and Markets Act 2000;

(b)   provision relating to costs contained in the standard terms fixed under paragraph 18 of Schedule 17 to that Act.

(5)   ''Repayment provision'' has the meaning given in section 76A(3).'

*Gaming contracts*

**412.   Gaming contracts**

(1)   No contract to which this section applies is void or unenforceable because of—

(a)   section 18 of the Gaming Act 1845, section 1 of the Gaming Act 1892 or Article 170 of the Betting, Gaming, Lotteries and Amusements (Northern Ireland) Order 1985; or

(b)   any rule of the law of Scotland under which a contract by way of gaming or wagering is not legally enforceable.

(2)   This section applies to a contract if—

(a)   it is entered into by either or each party by way of business;

(b)   the entering into or performance of it by either party constitutes an activity of a specified kind or one which falls within a specified class of activity; and

(c)   it relates to an investment of a specified kind or one which falls within a specified class of investment.

(3)   Part II of Schedule 2 applies for the purposes of subsection (2)(c), with the references to section 22 being read as references to that subsection.

(4)   Nothing in Part II of Schedule 2, as applied by subsection (3), limits the power conferred by subsection (2)(c).

(5)   'Investment' includes any asset, right or interest.

(6)   'Specified' means specified in an order made by the Treasury.

*Limitation on powers to require documents*

**413.   Protected items**

(1)   A person may not be required under this Act to produce, disclose or permit the inspection of protected items.

(2)   'Protected items' means—

(a)   communications between a professional legal adviser and his client or any person representing his client which fall within subsection (3);

(b)   communications between a professional legal adviser, his client or any person representing his client and any other person which fall within subsection (3) (as a result of paragraph (b) of that subsection);

(c)   items which—

(i)   are enclosed with, or referred to in, such communications;

(ii)   fall within subsection (3); and

(iii)   are in the possession of a person entitled to possession of them.

(3)   A communication or item falls within this subsection if it is made—

    (a)   in connection with the giving of legal advice to the client; or

    (b)   in connection with, or in contemplation of, legal proceedings and for the purposes of those proceedings.

(4)   A communication or item is not a protected item if it is held with the intention of furthering a criminal purpose.

*Service of notices*

## 414.  Service of notices

(1)   The Treasury may by regulations make provision with respect to the procedure to be followed, or rules to be applied, when a provision of or made under this Act requires a notice, direction or document of any kind to be given or authorises the imposition of a requirement.

(2)   The regulations may, in particular, make provision—

    (a)   as to the manner in which a document must be given;

    (b)   as to the address to which a document must be sent;

    (c)   requiring, or allowing, a document to be sent electronically;

    (d)   for treating a document as having been given, or as having been received, on a date or at a time determined in accordance with the regulations;

    (e)   as to what must, or may, be done if the person to whom a document is required to be given is not an individual;

    (f)   as to what must, or may, be done if the intended recipient of a document is outside the United Kingdom.

(3)   Subsection (1) applies however the obligation to give a document is expressed (and so, in particular, includes a provision which requires a document to be served or sent).

(4)   Section 7 of the Interpretation Act 1978 (service of notice by post) has effect in relation to provisions made by or under this Act subject to any provision made by regulations under this section.

*Jurisdiction*

## 415.  Jurisdiction in civil proceedings

(1)   Proceedings arising out of any act or omission (or proposed act or omission) of—

    (a)   the Authority,

    (b)   the competent authority for the purposes of Part VI,

    (c)   the scheme manager, or

    (d)   the scheme operator,

in the discharge or purported discharge of any of its functions under this Act may be brought before the High Court or the Court of Session.

(2)   The jurisdiction conferred by subsection (1) is in addition to any other jurisdiction exercisable by those courts.

*Removal of certain unnecessary provisions*

## 416.  Provisions relating to industrial assurance and certain other enactments

(1)   The following enactments are to cease to have effect—

    (a)   the Industrial Assurance Act 1923;

    (b)   the Industrial Assurance and Friendly Societies Act 1948;

    (c)   the Insurance Brokers (Registration) Act 1977.

(2)   The Industrial Assurance (Northern Ireland) Order 1979 is revoked.

(3)   The following bodies are to cease to exist—

(a)   the Insurance Brokers Registration Council;

(b)   the Policyholders Protection Board;

(c)   the Deposit Protection Board;

(d)   the Board of Banking Supervision.

(4)   If the Treasury consider that, as a consequence of any provision of this section, it is appropriate to do so, they may by order make any provision of a kind that they could make under this Act (and in particular any provision of a kind mentioned in section 339) with respect to anything done by or under any provision of Part XXI.

(5)   Subsection (4) is not to be read as affecting in any way any other power conferred on the Treasury by this Act.

## PART XXIX
## INTERPRETATION

### 417.   Definitions

(1)   In this Act—

'appointed representative' has the meaning given in section 39(2);

'auditors and actuaries rules' means rules made under section 340;

'authorisation offence' has the meaning given in section 23(2);

'authorised open-ended investment company' has the meaning given in section 237(3);

'authorised person' has the meaning given in section 31(2);

'the Authority' means the Financial Services Authority;

'body corporate' includes a body corporate constituted under the law of a country or territory outside the United Kingdom;

'chief executive'—

(a)   in relation to a body corporate whose principal place of business is within the United Kingdom, means an employee of that body who, alone or jointly with one or more others, is responsible under the immediate authority of the directors, for the conduct of the whole of the business of that body; and

(b)   in relation to a body corporate whose principal place of business is outside the United Kingdom, means the person who, alone or jointly with one or more others, is responsible for the conduct of its business within the United Kingdom;

'collective investment scheme' has the meaning given in section 235;

'the Commission' means the European Commission (except in provisions relating to the Competition Commission);

'the compensation scheme' has the meaning given in section 213(2);

'control of information rules' has the meaning given in section 147(1);

'director', in relation to a body corporate, includes—

(a)   a person occupying in relation to it the position of a director (by whatever name called); and

(b)   a person in accordance with whose directions or instructions (not being advice given in a professional capacity) the directors of that body are accustomed to act;

'documents' includes information recorded in any form and, in relation to information recorded otherwise than in legible form, references to its production include references to producing a copy of the information in legible form;

'exempt person', in relation to a regulated activity, means a person who is exempt from the general prohibition in relation to that activity as a result of an exemption order made under section 38(1) or as a result of section 39(1) or 285(2) or (3);

'financial promotion rules' means rules made under section 145;

'friendly society' means an incorporated or registered friendly society;

'general prohibition' has the meaning given in section 19(2);

'general rules' has the meaning given in section 138(2);

'incorporated friendly society' means a society incorporated under the Friendly Societies Act 1992;

'industrial and provident society' means a society registered or deemed to be registered under the Industrial and Provident Societies Act 1965 or the Industrial and Provident Societies Act (Northern Ireland) 1969;

'market abuse' has the meaning given in section 118;

'Minister of the Crown' has the same meaning as in the Ministers of the Crown Act 1975;

'money laundering rules' means rules made under section 146;

'notice of control' has the meaning given in section 178(5);

'the ombudsman scheme' has the meaning given in section 225(3);

'open-ended investment company' has the meaning given in section 236;

'Part IV permission' has the meaning given in section 40(4);

'partnership' includes a partnership constituted under the law of a country or territory outside the United Kingdom;

'prescribed' (where not otherwise defined) means prescribed in regulations made by the Treasury;

'price stabilising rules' means rules made under section 144;

'private company' has the meaning given in section 1(3) of the Companies Act 1985 or in Article 12(3) of the Companies (Northern Ireland) Order 1986;

'prohibition order' has the meaning given in section 56(2);

'recognised clearing house' and 'recognised investment exchange' have the meaning given in section 285;

'registered friendly society' means a society which is—

    (a)   a friendly society within the meaning of section 7(1)(a) of the Friendly Societies Act 1974; and

    (b)   registered within the meaning of that Act;

'regulated activity' has the meaning given in section 22;

'regulating provisions' has the meaning given in section 159(1);

'regulatory objectives' means the objectives mentioned in section 2;

'regulatory provisions' has the meaning given in section 302;

'rule' means a rule made by the Authority under this Act;

'rule-making instrument' has the meaning given in section 153;

'the scheme manager' has the meaning given in section 212(1);

'the scheme operator' has the meaning given in section 225(2);

'scheme particulars rules' has the meaning given in section 248(1);

'Seventh Company Law Directive' means the European Council Seventh Company Law Directive of 13 June 1983 on consolidated accounts (No. 83/349/EEC);

'threshold conditions', in relation to a regulated activity, has the meaning given in section 41;

'the Treaty' means the treaty establishing the European Community;

'trust scheme rules' has the meaning given in section 247(1);

'UK authorised person' has the meaning given in section 178(4); and

'unit trust scheme' has the meaning given in section 237.

(2)   In the application of this Act to Scotland, references to a matter being actionable at the suit of a person are to be read as references to the matter being actionable at the instance of that person.

(3)   For the purposes of any provision of this Act authorising or requiring a person to do anything within a specified number of days no account is to be taken of any day which is a public holiday in any part of the United Kingdom.

**418.   Carrying on regulated activities in the United Kingdom**

(1)   In the four cases described in this section, a person who—

(a)   is carrying on a regulated activity, but

(b)   would not otherwise be regarded as carrying it on in the United Kingdom,

is, for the purposes of this Act, to be regarded as carrying it on in the United Kingdom.

(2)   The first case is where—

(a)   his registered office (or if he does not have a registered office his head office) is in the United Kingdom;

(b)   he is entitled to exercise rights under a single market directive as a UK firm; and

(c)   he is carrying on in another EEA State a regulated activity to which that directive applies.

(3)   The second case is where—

(a)   his registered office (or if he does not have a registered office his head office) is in the United Kingdom;

(b)   he is the manager of a scheme which is entitled to enjoy the rights conferred by an instrument which is a relevant Community instrument for the purposes of section 264; and

(c)   persons in another EEA State are invited to become participants in the scheme.

(4)   The third case is where—

(a)   his registered office (or if he does not have a registered office his head office) is in the United Kingdom;

(b)   the day-to-day management of the carrying on of the regulated activity is the responsibility of—

(i)   his registered office (or head office); or

(ii)   another establishment maintained by him in the United Kingdom.

(5)   The fourth case is where—

(a)   his head office is not in the United Kingdom; but

(b)   the activity is carried on from an establishment maintained by him in the United Kingdom.

(6)   For the purposes of subsections (2) to (5) it is irrelevant where the person with whom the activity is carried on is situated.

**419.   Carrying on regulated activities by way of business**

(1)   The Treasury may by order make provision—

(a)   as to the circumstances in which a person who would otherwise not be regarded as carrying on a regulated activity by way of business is to be regarded as doing so;

(b)   as to the circumstances in which a person who would otherwise be regarded as carrying on a regulated activity by way of business is to be regarded as not doing so.

(2)   An order under subsection (1) may be made so as to apply—

(a)   generally in relation to all regulated activities;

(b)   in relation to a specified category of regulated activity; or

(c)   in relation to a particular regulated activity.

(3) An order under subsection (1) may be made so as to apply—

(a) for the purposes of all provisions;

(b) for a specified group of provisions; or

(c) for a specified provision.

(4) 'Provision' means a provision of, or made under, this Act.

(5) Nothing in this section is to be read as affecting the provisions of section 428(3).

### 420. Parent and subsidiary undertaking

(1) In this Act, except in relation to an incorporated friendly society, 'parent undertaking' and 'subsidiary undertaking' have the same meaning as in Part VII of the Companies Act 1985 (or Part VIII of the Companies (Northern Ireland) Order 1986).

(2) But—

(a) 'parent undertaking' also includes an individual who would be a parent undertaking for the purposes of those provisions if he were taken to be an undertaking (and 'subsidiary undertaking' is to be read accordingly);

(b) 'subsidiary undertaking' also includes, in relation to a body incorporated in or formed under the law of an EEA State other than the United Kingdom, an undertaking which is a subsidiary undertaking within the meaning of any rule of law in force in that State for purposes connected with implementation of the Seventh Company Law Directive (and 'parent undertaking' is to be read accordingly).

(3) In this Act 'subsidiary undertaking', in relation to an incorporated friendly society, means a body corporate of which the society has control within the meaning of section 13(9)(a) or (aa) of the Friendly Societies Act 1992 (and 'parent undertaking' is to be read accordingly).

### 421. Group

(1) In this Act 'group', in relation to a person ('A'), means A and any person who is—

(a) a parent undertaking of A;

(b) a subsidiary undertaking of A;

(c) a subsidiary undertaking of a parent undertaking of A;

(d) a parent undertaking of a subsidiary undertaking of A;

(e) an undertaking in which A or an undertaking mentioned in paragraph (a), (b), (c) or (d) has a participating interest;

(f) if A or an undertaking mentioned in paragraph (a) or (d) is a building society, an associated undertaking of the society; or

(g) if A or an undertaking mentioned in paragraph (a) or (d) is an incorporated friendly society, a body corporate of which the society has joint control (within the meaning of section 13(9)(c) or (cc) of the Friendly Societies Act 1992).

(2) 'Participating interest' has the same meaning as in Part VII of the Companies Act 1985 or Part VIII of the Companies (Northern Ireland) Order 1986; but also includes an interest held by an individual which would be a participating interest for the purposes of those provisions if he were taken to be an undertaking.

(3) 'Associated undertaking' has the meaning given in section 119(1) of the Building Societies Act 1986.

### 422. Controller

(1) In this Act 'controller', in relation to an undertaking ('A'), means a person who falls within any of the cases in subsection (2).

(2) The cases are where the person—

   (a)   holds 10% or more of the shares in A;

   (b)   is able to exercise significant influence over the management of A by virtue of his shareholding in A;

   (c)   holds 10% or more of the shares in a parent undertaking ('P') of A;

   (d)   is able to exercise significant influence over the management of P by virtue of his shareholding in P;

   (e)   is entitled to exercise, or control the exercise of, 10% or more of the voting power in A;

   (f)   is able to exercise significant influence over the management of A by virtue of his voting power in A;

   (g)   is entitled to exercise, or control the exercise of, 10% or more of the voting power in P; or

   (h)   is able to exercise significant influence over the management of P by virtue of his voting power in P.

   (3)   In subsection (2) 'the person' means—

   (a)   the person;

   (b)   any of the person's associates; or

   (c)   the person and any of his associates.

   (4)   'Associate', in relation to a person ('H') holding shares in an undertaking ('C') or entitled to exercise or control the exercise of voting power in relation to another undertaking ('D'), means—

   (a)   the spouse of H;

   (b)   a child or stepchild of H (if under 18);

   (c)   the trustee of any settlement under which H has a life interest in possession (or in Scotland a life interest);

   (d)   an undertaking of which H is a director;

   (e)   a person who is an employee or partner of H;

   (f)   if H is an undertaking—

      (i)   a director of H;

      (ii)   a subsidiary undertaking of H;

      (iii)   a director or employee of such a subsidiary undertaking; and

   (g)   if H has with any other person an agreement or arrangement with respect to the acquisition, holding or disposal of shares or other interests in C or D or under which they undertake to act together in exercising their voting power in relation to C or D, that other person.

   (5)   'Settlement', in subsection (4)(c), includes any disposition or arrangement under which property is held on trust (or subject to a comparable obligation).

   (6)   'Shares'—

   (a)   in relation to an undertaking with a share capital, means allotted shares;

   (b)   in relation to an undertaking with capital but no share capital, means rights to share in the capital of the undertaking;

   (c)   in relation to an undertaking without capital, means interests—

      (i)   conferring any right to share in the profits, or liability to contribute to the losses, of the undertaking; or

      (ii)   giving rise to an obligation to contribute to the debts or expenses of the undertaking in the event of a winding up.

   (7)   'Voting power', in relation to an undertaking which does not have general meetings at which matters are decided by the exercise of voting rights, means the right under the

constitution of the undertaking to direct the overall policy of the undertaking or alter the terms of its constitution.

### 423. Manager

(1)   In this Act, except in relation to a unit trust scheme or a registered friendly society, 'manager' means an employee who—

(a)   under the immediate authority of his employer is responsible, either alone or jointly with one or more other persons, for the conduct of his employer's business; or

(b)   under the immediate authority of his employer or of a person who is a manager by virtue of paragraph (a) exercises managerial functions or is responsible for maintaining accounts or other records of his employer.

(2)   If the employer is not an individual, references in subsection (1) to the authority of the employer are references to the authority—

(a)   in the case of a body corporate, of the directors;

(b)   in the case of a partnership, of the partners; and

(c)   in the case of an unincorporated association, of its officers or the members of its governing body.

(3)   'Manager', in relation to a body corporate, means a person (other than an employee of the body) who is appointed by the body to manage any part of its business and includes an employee of the body corporate (other than the chief executive) who, under the immediate authority of a director or chief executive of the body corporate, exercises managerial functions or is responsible for maintaining accounts or other records of the body corporate.

### 424. Insurance

(1)   In this Act, references to—

(a)   contracts of insurance,

(b)   reinsurance,

(c)   contracts of long-term insurance,

(d)   contracts of general insurance,

are to be read with section 22 and Schedule 2.

(2)   In this Act 'policy' and 'policyholder', in relation to a contract of insurance, have such meaning as the Treasury may by order specify.

(3)   The law applicable to a contract of insurance, the effecting of which constitutes the carrying on of a regulated activity, is to be determined, if it is of a prescribed description, in accordance with regulations made by the Treasury.

### 425. Expressions relating to authorisation elsewhere in the single market

(1)   In this Act—

(a)   'EEA authorisation', 'EEA firm', 'EEA right', 'EEA State', 'first life insurance directive', 'first non-life insurance directive', 'insurance directives', 'investment services directive', 'single market directives' and 'second banking co-ordination directive' have the meaning given in Schedule 3; and

(b)   'home state regulator', in relation to an EEA firm, has the meaning given in Schedule 3.

(2)   In this Act—

(a)   'home state authorisation' has the meaning given in Schedule 4;

(b)   'Treaty firm' has the meaning given in Schedule 4; and

(c)   'home state regulator', in relation to a Treaty firm, has the meaning given in Schedule 4.

## PART XXX
## SUPPLEMENTAL

**426.  Consequential and supplementary provision**

(1)   A Minister of the Crown may by order make such incidental, consequential, transitional or supplemental provision as he considers necessary or expedient for the general purposes, or any particular purpose, of this Act or in consequence of any provision made by or under this Act or for giving full effect to this Act or any such provision.

(2)   An order under subsection (1) may, in particular, make provision—

(a)   for enabling any person by whom any powers will become exercisable, on a date set by or under this Act, by virtue of any provision made by or under this Act to take before that date any steps which are necessary as a preliminary to the exercise of those powers;

(b)   for applying (with or without modifications) or amending, repealing or revoking any provision of or made under an Act passed before this Act or in the same Session;

(c)   dissolving any body corporate established by any Act passed, or instrument made, before the passing of this Act;

(d)   for making savings, or additional savings, from the effect of any repeal or revocation made by or under this Act.

(3)   Amendments made under this section are additional, and without prejudice, to those made by or under any other provision of this Act.

(4)   No other provision of this Act restricts the powers conferred by this section.

**427.  Transitional provisions**

(1)   Subsections (2) and (3) apply to an order under section 426 which makes transitional provisions or savings.

(2)   The order may, in particular—

(a)   if it makes provision about the authorisation and permission of persons who before commencement were entitled to carry on any activities, also include provision for such persons not to be treated as having any authorisation or permission (whether on an application to the Authority or otherwise);

(b)   make provision enabling the Authority to require persons of such descriptions as it may direct to re-apply for permissions having effect by virtue of the order;

(c)   make provision for the continuation as rules of such provisions (including primary and subordinate legislation) as may be designated in accordance with the order by the Authority, including provision for the modification by the Authority of provisions designated;

(d)   make provision about the effect of requirements imposed, liabilities incurred and any other things done before commencement, including provision for and about investigations, penalties and the taking or continuing of any other action in respect of contraventions;

(e)   make provision for the continuation of disciplinary and other proceedings begun before commencement, including provision about the decisions available to bodies before which such proceedings take place and the effect of their decisions;

(f)   make provision as regards the Authority's obligation to maintain a record under section 347 as respects persons in relation to whom provision is made by the order.

(3)   The order may—

(a)   confer functions on the Treasury, the Secretary of State, the Authority, the scheme manager, the scheme operator, members of the panel established under paragraph 4 of Schedule 17, the Competition Commission or the Director General of Fair Trading;

(b)   confer jurisdiction on the Tribunal;

(c)   provide for fees to be charged in connection with the carrying out of functions conferred under the order;

(d)   modify, exclude or apply (with or without modifications) any primary or subordinate legislation (including any provision of, or made under, this Act).

(4)   In subsection (2) 'commencement' means the commencement of such provisions of this Act as may be specified by the order.

### 428.   Regulations and orders

(1)   Any power to make an order which is conferred on a Minister of the Crown by this Act and any power to make regulations which is conferred by this Act is exercisable by statutory instrument.

(2)   The Lord Chancellor's power to make rules under section 132 is exercisable by statutory instrument.

(3)   Any statutory instrument made under this Act may—

(a)   contain such incidental, supplemental, consequential and transitional provision as the person making it considers appropriate; and

(b)   make different provision for different cases.

### 429.   Parliamentary control of statutory instruments

(1)   No order is to be made under—

(a)   section 144(4), 192(b) or (e), 236(5), 404 or 419, or

(b)   paragraph 1 of Schedule 8,

unless a draft of the order has been laid before Parliament and approved by a resolution of each House.

(2)   No regulations are to be made under section 262 unless a draft of the regulations has been laid before Parliament and approved by a resolution of each House.

(3)   An order to which, if it is made, subsection (4) or (5) will apply is not to be made unless a draft of the order has been laid before Parliament and approved by a resolution of each House.

(4)   This subsection applies to an order under section 21 if—

(a)   it is the first order to be made, or to contain provisions made, under section 21(4);

(b)   it varies an order made under section 21(4) so as to make section 21(1) apply in circumstances in which it did not previously apply;

(c)   it is the first order to be made, or to contain provision made, under section 21(5);

(d)   it varies a previous order made under section 21(5) so as to make section 21(1) apply in circumstances in which it did not, as a result of that previous order, apply;

(e)   it is the first order to be made, or to contain provisions made, under section 21(9) or (10);

(f)   it adds one or more activities to those that are controlled activities for the purposes of section 21; or

(g)   it adds one or more investments to those which are controlled investments for the purposes of section 21.

(5)   This subsection applies to an order under section 38 if—

(a)   it is the first order to be made, or to contain provisions made, under that section; or

(b)   it contains provisions restricting or removing an exemption provided by an earlier order made under that section.

(6)   An order containing a provision to which, if the order is made, subsection (7) will apply is not to be made unless a draft of the order has been laid before Parliament and approved by a resolution of each House.

(7) This subsection applies to a provision contained in an order if—

(a) it is the first to be made in the exercise of the power conferred by subsection (1) of section 326 or it removes a body from those for the time being designated under that subsection; or

(b) it is the first to be made in the exercise of the power conferred by subsection (6) of section 327 or it adds a description of regulated activity or investment to those for the time being specified for the purposes of that subsection.

(8) Any other statutory instrument made under this Act, apart from one made under section 431(2) or to which paragraph 26 of Schedule 2 applies, shall be subject to annulment in pursuance of a resolution of either House of Parliament.

## 430. Extent

(1) This Act, except Chapter IV of Part XVII, extends to Northern Ireland.

(2) Except where Her Majesty by Order in Council provides otherwise, the extent of any amendment or repeal made by or under this Act is the same as the extent of the provision amended or repealed.

(3) Her Majesty may by Order in Council provide for any provision of or made under this Act relating to a matter which is the subject of other legislation which extends to any of the Channel Islands or the Isle of Man to extend there with such modifications (if any) as may be specified in the Order.

## 431. Commencement

(1) The following provisions come into force on the passing of this Act—

(a) this section;

(b) sections 428, 430 and 433;

(c) paragraphs 1 and 2 of Schedule 21.

(2) The other provisions of this Act come into force on such day as the Treasury may by order appoint; and different days may be appointed for different purposes.

## 432. Minor and consequential amendments, transitional provisions and repeals

(1) Schedule 20 makes minor and consequential amendments.

(2) Schedule 21 makes transitional provisions.

(3) The enactments set out in Schedule 22 are repealed.

## 433. Short title

This Act may be cited as the Financial Services and Markets Act 2000.

SCHEDULES

**Section 1**                    SCHEDULE 1
THE FINANCIAL SERVICES AUTHORITY

PART I
GENERAL

*Interpretation*

1.—(1) In this Schedule—

'the 1985 Act' means the Companies Act 1985;

'non-executive committee' means the committee maintained under paragraph 3;

'functions', in relation to the Authority, means functions conferred on the Authority by or under any provision of this Act.

(2)  For the purposes of this Schedule, the following are the Authority's legislative functions—

  (a)  making rules;

  (b)  issuing codes under section 64 or 119;

  (c)  issuing statements under section 64, 69, 124 or 210;

  (d)  giving directions under section 316, 318 or 328;

  (e)  issuing general guidance (as defined by section 158(5)).

### Constitution

2.—(1)  The constitution of the Authority must continue to provide for the Authority to have—

  (a)  a chairman; and

  (b)  a governing body.

  (2)  The governing body must include the chairman.

  (3)  The chairman and other members of the governing body must be appointed, and be liable to removal from office, by the Treasury.

  (4)  The validity of any act of the Authority is not affected—

  (a)  by a vacancy in the office of chairman; or

  (b)  by a defect in the appointment of a person as a member of the governing body or as chairman.

### Non-executive members of the governing body

3.—(1)  The Authority must secure—

  (a)  that the majority of the members of its governing body are non-executive members; and

  (b)  that a committee of its governing body, consisting solely of the non-executive members, is set up and maintained for the purposes of discharging the functions conferred on the committee by this Schedule.

  (2)  The members of the non-executive committee are to be appointed by the Authority.

  (3)  The non-executive committee is to have a chairman appointed by the Treasury from among its members.

### Functions of the non-executive committee

4.—(1)  In this paragraph 'the committee' means the non-executive committee.

  (2)  The non-executive functions are functions of the Authority but must be discharged by the committee.

  (3)  The non-executive functions are—

  (a)  keeping under review the question whether the Authority is, in discharging its functions in accordance with decisions of its governing body, using its resources in the most efficient and economic way;

  (b)  keeping under review the question whether the Authority's internal financial controls secure the proper conduct of its financial affairs; and

  (c)  determining the remuneration of—

    (i)  the chairman of the Authority's governing body; and

    (ii)  the executive members of that body.

  (4)  The function mentioned in sub-paragraph (3)(b) and those mentioned in sub-paragraph (3)(c) may be discharged on behalf of the committee by a sub-committee.

  (5)  Any sub-committee of the committee—

    (a)    must have as its chairman the chairman of the committee; but

    (b)    may include persons other than members of the committee.

(6)    The committee must prepare a report on the discharge of its functions for inclusion in the Authority's annual report to the Treasury under paragraph 10.

(7)    The committee's report must relate to the same period as that covered by the Authority's report.

*Arrangements for discharging functions*

5.—(1)    The Authority may make arrangements for any of its functions to be discharged by a committee, sub-committee, officer or member of staff of the Authority.

(2)    But in exercising its legislative functions, the Authority must act through its governing body.

(3)    Sub-paragraph (1) does not apply to the non-executive functions.

*Monitoring and enforcement*

6.—(1)    The Authority must maintain arrangements designed to enable it to determine whether persons on whom requirements are imposed by or under this Act are complying with them.

(2)    Those arrangements may provide for functions to be performed on behalf of the Authority by any body or person who, in its opinion, is competent to perform them.

(3)    The Authority must also maintain arrangements for enforcing the provisions of, or made under, this Act.

(4)    Sub-paragraph (2) does not affect the Authority's duty under sub-paragraph (1).

*Arrangements for the investigation of complaints*

7.—(1)    The Authority must—

    (a)    make arrangements ('the complaints scheme') for the investigation of complaints arising in connection with the exercise of, or failure to exercise, any of its functions (other than its legislative functions); and

    (b)    appoint an independent person ('the investigator') to be responsible for the conduct of investigations in accordance with the complaints scheme.

(2)    The complaints scheme must be designed so that, as far as reasonably practicable, complaints are investigated quickly.

(3)    The Treasury's approval is required for the appointment or dismissal of the investigator.

(4)    The terms and conditions on which the investigator is appointed must be such as, in the opinion of the Authority, are reasonably designed to secure—

    (a)    that he will be free at all times to act independently of the Authority; and

    (b)    that complaints will be investigated under the complaints scheme without favouring the Authority.

(5)    Before making the complaints scheme, the Authority must publish a draft of the proposed scheme in the way appearing to the Authority best calculated to bring it to the attention of the public.

(6)    The draft must be accompanied by notice that representations about it may be made to the Authority within a specified time.

(7)    Before making the proposed complaints scheme, the Authority must have regard to any representations made to it in accordance with sub-paragraph (6).

(8)   If the Authority makes the proposed complaints scheme, it must publish an account, in general terms, of—

(a)   the representations made to it in accordance with sub-paragraph (6); and

(b)   its response to them.

(9)   If the complaints scheme differs from the draft published under sub-paragraph (5) in a way which is, in the opinion of the Authority, significant the Authority must (in addition to complying with sub-paragraph (8)) publish details of the difference.

(10)   The Authority must publish up-to-date details of the complaints scheme including, in particular, details of—

(a)   the provision made under paragraph 8(5); and

(b)   the powers which the investigator has to investigate a complaint.

(11)   Those details must be published in the way appearing to the Authority to be best calculated to bring them to the attention of the public.

(12)   The Authority must, without delay, give the Treasury a copy of any details published by it under this paragraph.

(13)   The Authority may charge a reasonable fee for providing a person with a copy of—

(a)   a draft published under sub-paragraph (5);

(b)   details published under sub-paragraph (10).

(14)   Sub-paragraphs (5) to (9) and (13)(a) also apply to a proposal to alter or replace the complaints scheme.

### Investigation of complaints

8.—(1)   The Authority is not obliged to investigate a complaint in accordance with the complaints scheme which it reasonably considers would be more appropriately dealt with in another way (for example by referring the matter to the Tribunal or by the institution of other legal proceedings).

(2)   The complaints scheme must provide—

(a)   for reference to the investigator of any complaint which the Authority is investigating; and

(b)   for him—

(i)   to have the means to conduct a full investigation of the complaint;

(ii)   to report on the result of his investigation to the Authority and the complainant; and

(iii)   to be able to publish his report (or any part of it) if he considers that it (or the part) ought to be brought to the attention of the public.

(3)   If the Authority has decided not to investigate a complaint, it must notify the investigator.

(4)   If the investigator considers that a complaint of which he has been notified under sub-paragraph (3) ought to be investigated, he may proceed as if the complaint had been referred to him under the complaints scheme.

(5)   The complaints scheme must confer on the investigator the power to recommend, if he thinks it appropriate, that the Authority—

(a)   makes a compensatory payment to the complainant,

(b)   remedies the matter complained of,

or takes both of those steps.

(6)   The complaints scheme must require the Authority, in a case where the investigator—

(a)   has reported that a complaint is well-founded, or

(b)   has criticised the Authority in his report,

to inform the investigator and the complainant of the steps which it proposes to take in response to the report.

(7)   The investigator may require the Authority to publish the whole or a specified part of the response.

(8)   The investigator may appoint a person to conduct the investigation on his behalf but subject to his direction.

(9)   Neither an officer nor an employee of the Authority may be appointed under sub-paragraph (8).

(10)   Sub-paragraph (2) is not to be taken as preventing the Authority from making arrangements for the initial investigation of a complaint to be conducted by the Authority.

### Records

9.   The Authority must maintain satisfactory arrangements for—
   (a)   recording decisions made in the exercise of its functions; and
   (b)   the safe-keeping of those records which it considers ought to be preserved.

### Annual report

10.—(1)   At least once a year the Authority must make a report to the Treasury on—
   (a)   the discharge of its functions;
   (b)   the extent to which, in its opinion, the regulatory objectives have been met;
   (c)   its consideration of the matters mentioned in section 2(3); and
   (d)   such other matters as the Treasury may from time to time direct.

(2)   The report must be accompanied by—
   (a)   the report prepared by the non-executive committee under paragraph 4(6); and
   (b)   such other reports or information, prepared by such persons, as the Treasury may from time to time direct.

(3)   The Treasury must lay before Parliament a copy of each report received by them under this paragraph.

(4)   The Treasury may—
   (a)   require the Authority to comply with any provisions of the 1985 Act about accounts and their audit which would not otherwise apply to it; or
   (b)   direct that any such provision of that Act is to apply to the Authority with such modifications as are specified in the direction.

(5)   Compliance with any requirement imposed under sub-paragraph (4)(a) or (b) is enforceable by injunction or, in Scotland, an order under section 45(b) of the Court of Session Act 1988.

(6)   Proceedings under sub-paragraph (5) may be brought only by the Treasury.

### Annual public meeting

11.—(1)   Not later than three months after making a report under paragraph 10, the Authority must hold a public meeting ('the annual meeting') for the purposes of enabling that report to be considered.

(2)   The Authority must organise the annual meeting so as to allow—
   (a)   a general discussion of the contents of the report which is being considered; and
   (b)   a reasonable opportunity for those attending the meeting to put questions to the Authority about the way in which it discharged, or failed to discharge, its functions during the period to which the report relates.

(3)   But otherwise the annual meeting is to be organised and conducted in such a way as the Authority considers appropriate.

(4)   The Authority must give reasonable notice of its annual meeting.

(5)   That notice must—

    (a)   give details of the time and place at which the meeting is to be held;

    (b)   set out the proposed agenda for the meeting;

    (c)   indicate the proposed duration of the meeting;

    (d)   give details of the Authority's arrangements for enabling persons to attend; and

    (e)   be published by the Authority in the way appearing to it to be most suitable for bringing the notice to the attention of the public.

(6)   If the Authority proposes to alter any of the arrangements which have been included in the notice given under sub-paragraph (4) it must—

    (a)   give reasonable notice of the alteration; and

    (b)   publish that notice in the way appearing to the Authority to be best calculated to bring it to the attention of the public.

*Report of annual meeting*

12.   Not later than one month after its annual meeting, the Authority must publish a report of the proceedings of the meeting.

PART II
STATUS

13.   In relation to any of its functions—

    (a)   the Authority is not to be regarded as acting on behalf of the Crown; and

    (b)   its members, officers and staff are not to be regarded as Crown servants.

*Exemption from requirement of 'limited' in Authority's name*

14.   The Authority is to continue to be exempt from the requirements of the 1985 Act relating to the use of 'limited' as part of its name.

15.   If the Secretary of State is satisfied that any action taken by the Authority makes it inappropriate for the exemption given by paragraph 14 to continue he may, after consulting the Treasury, give a direction removing it.

PART III
PENALTIES AND FEES

*Penalties*

16.—(1)   In determining its policy with respect to the amounts of penalties to be imposed by it under this Act, the Authority must take no account of the expenses which it incurs, or expects to incur, in discharging its functions.

(2)   The Authority must prepare and operate a scheme for ensuring that the amounts paid to the Authority by way of penalties imposed under this Act are applied for the benefit of authorised persons.

(3)   The scheme may, in particular, make different provision with respect to different classes of authorised person.

(4)   Up to date details of the scheme must be set out in a document ('the scheme details').

(5)   The scheme details must be published by the Authority in the way appearing to it to be best calculated to bring them to the attention of the public.

(6)   Before making the scheme, the Authority must publish a draft of the proposed scheme in the way appearing to the Authority to be best calculated to bring it to the attention of the public.

(7)   The draft must be accompanied by notice that representations about the proposals may be made to the Authority within a specified time.

(8)   Before making the scheme, the Authority must have regard to any representations made to it in accordance with sub-paragraph (7).

(9)   If the Authority makes the proposed scheme, it must publish an account, in general terms, of—

(a)   the representations made to it in accordance with sub-paragraph (7); and

(b)   its response to them.

(10)   If the scheme differs from the draft published under sub-paragraph (6) in a way which is, in the opinion of the Authority, significant the Authority must (in addition to complying with sub-paragraph (9)) publish details of the difference.

(11)   The Authority must, without delay, give the Treasury a copy of any scheme details published by it.

(12)   The Authority may charge a reasonable fee for providing a person with a copy of—

(a)   a draft published under sub-paragraph (6);

(b)   scheme details.

(13)   Sub-paragraphs (6) to (10) and (12)(a) also apply to a proposal to alter or replace the complaints scheme.

*Fees*

17.—(1)   The Authority may make rules providing for the payment to it of such fees, in connection with the discharge of any of its functions under or as a result of this Act, as it considers will (taking account of its expected income from fees and charges provided for by any other provision of this Act) enable it—

(a)   to meet expenses incurred in carrying out its functions or for any incidental purpose;

(b)   to repay the principal of, and pay any interest on, any money which it has borrowed and which has been used for the purpose of meeting expenses incurred in relation to its assumption of functions under this Act or the Bank of England Act 1998; and

(c)   to maintain adequate reserves.

(2)   In fixing the amount of any fee which is to be payable to the Authority, no account is to be taken of any sums which the Authority receives, or expects to receive, by way of penalties imposed by it under this Act.

(3)   Sub-paragraph (1)(b) applies whether expenses were incurred before or after the coming into force of this Act or the Bank of England Act 1998.

(4)   Any fee which is owed to the Authority under any provision made by or under this Act may be recovered as a debt due to the Authority.

*Services for which fees may not be charged*

18.   The power conferred by paragraph 17 may not be used to require—

(a)   a fee to be paid in respect of the discharge of any of the Authority's functions under paragraphs 13, 14, 19 or 20 of Schedule 3; or

(b)   a fee to be paid by any person whose application for approval under section 59 has been granted.

PART IV
MISCELLANEOUS

*Exemption from liability in damages*

19.—(1)  Neither the Authority nor any person who is, or is acting as, a member, officer or member of staff of the Authority is to be liable in damages for anything done or omitted in the discharge, or purported discharge, of the Authority's functions.

(2)  Neither the investigator appointed under paragraph 7 nor a person appointed to conduct an investigation on his behalf under paragraph 8(8) is to be liable in damages for anything done or omitted in the discharge, or purported discharge, of his functions in relation to the investigation of a complaint.

(3)  Neither sub-paragraph (1) nor sub-paragraph (2) applies—

(a)  if the act or omission is shown to have been in bad faith; or

(b)  so as to prevent an award of damages made in respect of an act or omission on the ground that the act or omission was unlawful as a result of section 6(1) of the Human Rights Act 1998.

*Disqualification for membership of House of Commons*

20.  In Part III of Schedule 1 to the House of Commons Disqualification Act 1975 (disqualifying offices), insert at the appropriate place—
'Member of the governing body of the Financial Services Authority'.

*Disqualification for membership of Northern Ireland Assembly*

21.  In Part III of Schedule 1 to the Northern Ireland Assembly Disqualification Act 1975 (disqualifying offices), insert at the appropriate place—
'Member of the governing body of the Financial Services Authority'.

**Section 22(2)**                    SCHEDULE 2
REGULATED ACTIVITIES

PART I
REGULATED ACTIVITIES

*General*

1.  The matters with respect to which provision may be made under section 22(1) in respect of activities include, in particular, those described in general terms in this Part of this Schedule.

*Dealing in investments*

2.—(1)  Buying, selling, subscribing for or underwriting investments or offering or agreeing to do so, either as a principal or as an agent.

(2)  In the case of an investment which is a contract of insurance, that includes carrying out the contract.

*Arranging deals in investments*

3.  Making, or offering or agreeing to make—

(a)  arrangements with a view to another person buying, selling, subscribing for or underwriting a particular investment;

(b)  arrangements with a view to a person who participates in the arrangements buying, selling, subscribing for or underwriting investments.

*Deposit taking*

4.   Accepting deposits.

*Safekeeping and administration of assets*

5.—(1)   Safeguarding and administering assets belonging to another which consist of or include investments or offering or agreeing to do so.

(2)   Arranging for the safeguarding and administration of assets belonging to another, or offering or agreeing to do so.

*Managing investments*

6.   Managing, or offering or agreeing to manage, assets belonging to another person where—

(a)   the assets consist of or include investments; or

(b)   the arrangements for their management are such that the assets may consist of or include investments at the discretion of the person managing or offering or agreeing to manage them.

*Investment advice*

7.   Giving or offering or agreeing to give advice to persons on—

(a)   buying, selling, subscribing for or underwriting an investment; or

(b)   exercising any right conferred by an investment to acquire, dispose of, underwrite or convert an investment.

*Establishing collective investment schemes*

8.   Establishing, operating or winding up a collective investment scheme, including acting as—

(a)   trustee of a unit trust scheme;

(b)   depositary of a collective investment scheme other than a unit trust scheme; or

(c)   sole director of a body incorporated by virtue of regulations under section 262.

*Using computer-based systems for giving investment instructions*

9.—(1)   Sending on behalf of another person instructions relating to an investment by means of a computer-based system which enables investments to be transferred without a written instrument.

(2)   Offering or agreeing to send such instructions by such means on behalf of another person.

(3)   Causing such instructions to be sent by such means on behalf of another person.

(4)   Offering or agreeing to cause such instructions to be sent by such means on behalf of another person.

## PART II
## INVESTMENTS

*General*

10.   The matters with respect to which provision may be made under section 22(1) in respect of investments include, in particular, those described in general terms in this Part of this Schedule.

*Securities*

11.—(1)  Shares or stock in the share capital of a company.

(2)  'Company' includes—

(a)  any body corporate (wherever incorporated), and

(b)  any unincorporated body constituted under the law of a country or territory outside the United Kingdom,

other than an open-ended investment company.

*Instruments creating or acknowledging indebtedness*

12.  Any of the following—

(a)  debentures;

(b)  debenture stock;

(c)  loan stock;

(d)  bonds;

(e)  certificates of deposit;

(f)  any other instruments creating or acknowledging a present or future indebtedness.

*Government and public securities*

13.—(1)  Loan stock, bonds and other instruments—

(a)  creating or acknowledging indebtedness; and

(b)  issued by or on behalf of a government, local authority or public authority.

(2)  'Government, local authority or public authority' means—

(a)  the government of the United Kingdom, of Northern Ireland, or of any country or territory outside the United Kingdom;

(b)  a local authority in the United Kingdom or elsewhere;

(c)  any international organisation the members of which include the United Kingdom or another member State.

*Instruments giving entitlement to investments*

14.—(1)  Warrants or other instruments entitling the holder to subscribe for any investment.

(2)  It is immaterial whether the investment is in existence or identifiable.

*Certificates representing securities*

15.  Certificates or other instruments which confer contractual or property rights—

(a)  in respect of any investment held by someone other than the person on whom the rights are conferred by the certificate or other instrument; and

(b)  the transfer of which may be effected without requiring the consent of that person.

*Units in collective investment schemes*

16.—(1)  Shares in or securities of an open-ended investment company.

(2)  Any right to participate in a collective investment scheme.

*Options*

17.  Options to acquire or dispose of property.

*Futures*

18.  Rights under a contract for the sale of a commodity or property of any other description under which delivery is to be made at a future date.

*Contracts for differences*

19.   Rights under—
    (a)   a contract for differences; or
    (b)   any other contract the purpose or pretended purpose of which is to secure a profit or avoid a loss by reference to fluctuations in—
        (i)   the value or price of property of any description; or
        (ii)   an index or other factor designated for that purpose in the contract.

*Contracts of insurance*

20.   Rights under a contract of insurance, including rights under contracts falling within head C of Schedule 2 to the Friendly Societies Act 1992.

*Participation in Lloyd's syndicates*

21.—(1)   The underwriting capacity of a Lloyd's syndicate.
    (2)   A person's membership (or prospective membership) of a Lloyd's syndicate.

*Deposits*

22.   Rights under any contract under which a sum of money (whether or not denominated in a currency) is paid on terms under which it will be repaid, with or without interest or a premium, and either on demand or at a time or in circumstances agreed by or on behalf of the person making the payment and the person receiving it.

*Loans secured on land*

23.—(1)   Rights under any contract under which—
    (a)   one person provides another with credit; and
    (b)   the obligation of the borrower to repay is secured on land.
    (2)   'Credit' includes any cash loan or other financial accommodation.
    (3)   'Cash' includes money in any form.

*Rights in investments*

24.   Any right or interest in anything which is an investment as a result of any other provision made under section 22(1).

## PART III
## SUPPLEMENTAL PROVISIONS

*The order-making power*

25.—(1)   An order under section 22(1) may—
    (a)   provide for exemptions;
    (b)   confer powers on the Treasury or the Authority;
    (c)   authorise the making of regulations or other instruments by the Treasury for purposes of, or connected with, any relevant provision;
    (d)   authorise the making of rules or other instruments by the Authority for purposes of, or connected with, any relevant provision;
    (e)   make provision in respect of any information or document which, in the opinion of the Treasury or the Authority, is relevant for purposes of, or connected with, any relevant provision;
    (f)   make such consequential, transitional or supplemental provision as the Treasury consider appropriate for purposes of, or connected with, any relevant provision.

(2)   Provision made as a result of sub-paragraph (1)(f) may amend any primary or subordinate legislation, including any provision of, or made under, this Act.

(3)   'Relevant provision' means any provision—

    (a)   of section 22 or this Schedule; or

    (b)   made under that section or this Schedule.

*Parliamentary control*

26.—(1)   This paragraph applies to the first order made under section 22(1).

(2)   This paragraph also applies to any subsequent order made under section 22(1) which contains a statement by the Treasury that, in their opinion, the effect (or one of the effects) of the proposed order would be that an activity which is not a regulated activity would become a regulated activity.

(3)   An order to which this paragraph applies—

    (a)   must be laid before Parliament after being made; and

    (b)   ceases to have effect at the end of the relevant period unless before the end of that period the order is approved by a resolution of each House of Parliament (but without that affecting anything done under the order or the power to make a new order).

(4)   'Relevant period' means a period of twenty-eight days beginning with the day on which the order is made.

(5)   In calculating the relevant period no account is to be taken of any time during which Parliament is dissolved or prorogued or during which both Houses are adjourned for more than four days.

*Interpretation*

27.—(1)   In this Schedule—

    'buying' includes acquiring for valuable consideration;

    'offering' includes inviting to treat;

    'property' includes currency of the United Kingdom or any other country or territory; and

    'selling' includes disposing for valuable consideration.

(2)   In sub-paragraph (1) 'disposing' includes—

    (a)   in the case of an investment consisting of rights under a contract—

        (i)   surrendering, assigning or converting those rights; or

        (ii)   assuming the corresponding liabilities under the contract;

    (b)   in the case of an investment consisting of rights under other arrangements, assuming the corresponding liabilities under the contract or arrangements;

    (c)   in the case of any other investment, issuing or creating the investment or granting the rights or interests of which it consists.

(3)   In this Schedule references to an instrument include references to any record (whether or not in the form of a document).

**Section 31(1)(b) and 37**          SCHEDULE 3
EEA PASSPORT RIGHTS

PART I
DEFINED TERMS

*The single market directives*

1.   'The single market directives' means—

(a)   the first banking co-ordination directive;
(b)   the second banking co-ordination directive;
(c)   the insurance directives; and
(d)   the investment services directive.

### The banking co-ordination directives

2.—(1)   'The first banking co-ordination directive' means the Council Directive of 12 December 1977 on the co-ordination of laws, regulations and administrative provisions relating to the taking up and pursuit of the business of credit institutions (No. 77/780/EEC).

(2)   'The second banking co-ordination directive' means the Council Directive of 15 December 1989 on the co-ordination of laws, etc, relating to the taking up and pursuit of the business of credit institutions and amending Directive 77/780/EEC (No. 89/646/EEC).

### The insurance directives

3.—(1)   'The insurance directives' means the first, second and third non-life insurance directives and the first, second and third life insurance directives.

(2)   'First non-life insurance directive' means the Council Directive of 24 July 1973 on the co-ordination of laws, regulations and administrative provisions relating to the taking up and pursuit of the business of direct insurance other than life assurance (No. 73/239/EEC).

(3)   'Second non-life insurance directive' means the Council Directive of 22 June 1988 on the co-ordination of laws, etc, and laying down provisions to facilitate the effective exercise of freedom to provide services and amending Directive 73/239/EEC (No. 88/357/EEC).

(4)   'Third non-life insurance directive' means the Council Directive of 18 June 1992 on the co-ordination of laws, etc, and amending Directives 73/239/EEC and 88/357/EEC (No. 92/49/EEC).

(5)   'First life insurance directive' means the Council Directive of 5 March 1979 on the co-ordination of laws, regulations and administrative provisions relating to the taking up and pursuit of the business of direct life assurance (No. 79/267/EEC).

(6)   'Second life insurance directive' means the Council Directive of 8 November 1990 on the co-ordination of laws, etc, and laying down provisions to facilitate the effective exercise of freedom to provide services and amending Directive 79/267/EEC (No. 90/619/EEC).

(7)   'Third life insurance directive' means the Council Directive of 10 November 1992 on the co-ordination of laws, etc, and amending Directives 79/267/EEC and 90/619/EEC (No. 92/96/EEC).

### The investment services directive

4.   'The investment services directive' means the Council Directive of 10 May 1993 on investment services in the securities field (No. 93/22/EEC).

### EEA firm

5.   'EEA firm' means any of the following if it does not have its head office in the United Kingdom—

(a)   an investment firm (as defined in Article 1.2 of the investment services directive) which is authorised (within the meaning of Article 3) by its home state regulator;

(b)   a credit institution (as defined in Article 1 of the first banking co-ordination directive) which is authorised (within the meaning of Article 1) by its home state regulator;

(c)   a financial institution (as defined in Article 1 of the second banking co-ordination directive) which is a subsidiary of the kind mentioned in Article 18.2 and which fulfils the conditions in Article 18; or

(d)   an undertaking pursuing the activity of direct insurance (within the meaning of Article 1 of the first life insurance directive or of the first non-life insurance directive) which has received authorisation under Article 6 from its home state regulator.

### EEA authorisation

6.   'EEA authorisation' means authorisation granted to an EEA firm by its home state regulator for the purpose of the relevant single market directive.

### EEA right

7.   'EEA right' means the entitlement of a person to establish a branch, or provide services, in an EEA State other than that in which he has his head office—

(a)   in accordance with the Treaty as applied in the EEA; and

(b)   subject to the conditions of the relevant single market directive.

### EEA State

8.   'EEA State' means a State which is a contracting party to the agreement on the European Economic Area signed at Oporto on 2 May 1992 as it has effect for the time being.

### Home state regulator

9.   'Home state regulator' means the competent authority (within the meaning of the relevant single market directive) of an EEA State (other than the United Kingdom) in relation to the EEA firm concerned.

### UK firm

10.   'UK firm' means a person whose head office is in the UK and who has an EEA right to carry on activity in an EEA State other than the United Kingdom.

### Host state regulator

11.   'Host state regulator' means the competent authority (within the meaning of the relevant single market directive) of an EEA State (other than the United Kingdom) in relation to a UK firm's exercise of EEA rights there.

## PART II
## EXERCISE OF PASSPORT RIGHTS BY EEA FIRMS

### Firms qualifying for authorisation

12.—(1)   Once an EEA firm which is seeking to establish a branch in the United Kingdom in exercise of an EEA right satisfies the establishment conditions, it qualifies for authorisation.

(2)   Once an EEA firm which is seeking to provide services in the United Kingdom in exercise of an EEA right satisfies the service conditions, it qualifies for authorisation.

### Establishment

13.—(1)   The establishment conditions are that—

(a)   the Authority has received notice ('a consent notice') from the firm's home state regulator that it has given the firm consent to establish a branch in the United Kingdom;

(b)   the consent notice—

    (i)    is given in accordance with the relevant single market directive;

    (ii)   identifies the activities to which consent relates; and

    (iii)  includes such other information as may be prescribed; and

    (c)   the firm has been informed of the applicable provisions or two months have elapsed beginning with the date when the Authority received the consent notice.

(2)   If the Authority has received a consent notice, it must—

    (a)   prepare for the firm's supervision;

    (b)   notify the firm of the applicable provisions (if any); and

    (c)   if the firm falls within paragraph 5(d), notify its home state regulator of the applicable provisions (if any).

(3)   A notice under sub-paragraph (2)(b) or (c) must be given before the end of the period of two months beginning with the day on which the Authority received the consent notice.

(4)   For the purposes of this paragraph—

    'applicable provisions' means the host state rules with which the firm is required to comply when carrying on a permitted activity through a branch in the United Kingdom;

    'host state rules' means rules—

        (a)   made in accordance with the relevant single market directive; and

        (b)   which are the responsibility of the United Kingdom (both as to implementation and as to supervision of compliance) in accordance with that directive; and

    'permitted activity' means an activity identified in the consent notice.

*Services*

14.—(1)   The service conditions are that—

    (a)   the firm has given its home state regulator notice of its intention to provide services in the United Kingdom ('a notice of intention');

    (b)   if the firm falls within paragraph 5(a) or (d), the Authority has received notice ('a regulator's notice') from the firm's home state regulator containing such information as may be prescribed; and

    (c)   if the firm falls within paragraph 5(d), its home state regulator has informed it that the regulator's notice has been sent to the Authority.

(2)   If the Authority has received a regulator's notice or, where none is required by sub-paragraph (1), has been informed of the firm's intention to provide services in the United Kingdom, it must—

    (a)   prepare for the firm's supervision; and

    (b)   notify the firm of the applicable provisions (if any).

(3)   A notice under sub-paragraph (2)(b) must be given before the end of the period of two months beginning on the day on which the Authority received the regulator's notice, or was informed of the firm's intention.

(4)   For the purposes of this paragraph—

    'applicable provisions' means the host state rules with which the firm is required to comply when carrying on a permitted activity by providing services in the United Kingdom;

    'host state rules' means rules—

        (a)   made in accordance with the relevant single market directive; and

        (b)   which are the responsibility of the United Kingdom (both as to implementation and as to supervision of compliance) in accordance with that directive; and

    'permitted activity' means an activity identified in—

        (a)   the regulator's notice; or

        (b)   where none is required by sub-paragraph (1), the notice of intention.

*Grant of permission*

15.—(1)   On qualifying for authorisation as a result of paragraph 12, a firm has, in respect of each permitted activity which is a regulated activity, permission to carry it on through its United Kingdom branch (if it satisfies the establishment conditions) or by providing services in the United Kingdom (if it satisfies the service conditions).

(2)   The permission is to be treated as being on terms equivalent to those appearing from the consent notice, regulator's notice or notice of intention.

(3)   Sections 21, 39(1) and 147(1) of the Consumer Credit Act 1974 (business requiring a licence under that Act) do not apply in relation to the carrying on of a permitted activity which is Consumer Credit Act business by a firm which qualifies for authorisation as a result of paragraph 12, unless the Director General of Fair Trading has exercised the power conferred on him by section 203 in relation to the firm.

(4)   'Consumer Credit Act business' has the same meaning as in section 203.

*Effect of carrying on regulated activity when not qualified for authorisation*

16.—(1)   This paragraph applies to an EEA firm which is not qualified for authorisation under paragraph 12.

(2)   Section 26 does not apply to an agreement entered into by the firm.

(3)   Section 27 does not apply to an agreement in relation to which the firm is a third party for the purposes of that section.

(4)   Section 29 does not apply to an agreement in relation to which the firm is the deposit-taker.

*Continuing regulation of EEA firms*

17.   Regulations may—

(a)   modify any provision of this Act which is an applicable provision (within the meaning of paragraph 13 or 14) in its application to an EEA firm qualifying for authorisation;

(b)   make provision as to any change (or proposed change) of a prescribed kind relating to an EEA firm or to an activity that it carries on in the United Kingdom and as to the procedure to be followed in relation to such cases;

(c)   provide that the Authority may treat an EEA firm's notification that it is to cease to carry on regulated activity in the United Kingdom as a request for cancellation of its qualification for authorisation under this Schedule.

*Giving up right to authorisation*

18.   Regulations may provide that in prescribed circumstances an EEA firm falling within paragraph 5(c) may, on following the prescribed procedure—

(a)   have its qualification for authorisation under this Schedule cancelled; and

(b)   seek to become an authorised person by applying for a Part IV permission.

## PART III
## EXERCISE OF PASSPORT RIGHTS BY UK FIRMS

*Establishment*

19.—(1)   A UK firm may not exercise an EEA right to establish a branch unless three conditions are satisfied.

(2)   The first is that the firm has given the Authority, in the specified way, notice of its intention to establish a branch ('a notice of intention') which—

(a)   identifies the activities which it seeks to carry on through the branch; and

(b)   includes such other information as may be specified.

(3)   The activities identified in a notice of intention may include activities which are not regulated activities.

(4)   The second is that the Authority has given notice in specified terms ('a consent notice') to the host state regulator.

(5)   The third is that—

(a)   the host state regulator has notified the firm (or, where the EEA right in question derives from any of the insurance directives, the Authority) of the applicable provisions; or

(b)   two months have elapsed beginning with the date on which the Authority gave the consent notice.

(6)   If the firm's EEA right derives from the investment services directive or the second banking coordination directive and the first condition is satisfied, the Authority must give a consent notice to the host state regulator unless it has reason to doubt the adequacy of the firm's resources or its administrative structure.

(7)   If the firm's EEA right derives from any of the insurance directives and the first condition is satisfied, the Authority must give a consent notice unless it has reason—

(a)   to doubt the adequacy of the firm's resources or its administrative structure, or

(b)   to question the reputation, qualifications or experience of the directors or managers of the firm or the person proposed as the branch's authorised agent for the purposes of those directives,

in relation to the business to be conducted through the proposed branch.

(8)   If the Authority proposes to refuse to give a consent notice it must give the firm concerned a warning notice.

(9)   If the firm's EEA right derives from any of the insurance directives and the host state regulator has notified it of the applicable provisions, the Authority must inform the firm of those provisions.

(10)   Rules may specify the procedure to be followed by the Authority in exercising its functions under this paragraph.

(11)   If the Authority gives a consent notice it must give written notice that it has done so to the firm concerned.

(12)   If the Authority decides to refuse to give a consent notice—

(a)   it must, within three months beginning with the date when it received the notice of intention, give the person who gave that notice a decision notice to that effect; and

(b)   that person may refer the matter to the Tribunal.

(13)   In this paragraph, 'applicable provisions' means the host state rules with which the firm will be required to comply when conducting business through the proposed branch in the EEA State concerned.

(14)   In sub-paragraph (13), 'host state rules' means rules—

(a)   made in accordance with the relevant single market directive; and

(b)   which are the responsibility of the EEA State concerned (both as to implementation and as to supervision of compliance) in accordance with that directive.

(15)   'Specified' means specified in rules.

*Services*

20.—(1)   A UK firm may not exercise an EEA right to provide services unless the firm has given the Authority, in the specified way, notice of its intention to provide services ('a notice of intention') which—

(a)    identifies the activities which it seeks to carry out by way of provision of services; and

(b)    includes such other information as may be specified.

(2)    The activities identified in a notice of intention may include activities which are not regulated activities.

(3)    If the firm's EEA right derives from the investment services directive or a banking co-ordination directive, the Authority must, within one month of receiving a notice of intention, send a copy of it to the host state regulator.

(4)    When the Authority sends the copy under sub-paragraph (3), it must give written notice to the firm concerned.

(5)    If the firm concerned's EEA right derives from the investment services directive, it must not provide the services to which its notice of intention relates until it has received written notice from the Authority under sub-paragraph (4).

(6)    'Specified' means specified in rules.

### Offence relating to exercise of passport rights

21.—(1)    If a UK firm which is not an authorised person contravenes the prohibition imposed by—

(a)    sub-paragraph (1) of paragraph 19, or

(b)    sub-paragraph (1) or (5) of paragraph 20,

it is guilty of an offence.

(2)    A firm guilty of an offence under sub-paragraph (1) is liable—

(a)    on summary conviction, to a fine not exceeding the statutory maximum; or

(b)    on conviction on indictment, to a fine.

(3)    In proceedings for an offence under sub-paragraph (1), it is a defence for the firm to show that it took all reasonable precautions and exercised all due diligence to avoid committing the offence.

### Continuing regulation of UK firms

22.—(1)    Regulations may make such provision as the Treasury consider appropriate in relation to a UK firm's exercise of EEA rights, and may in particular provide for the application (with or without modification) of any provision of, or made under, this Act in relation to an activity of a UK firm.

(2)    Regulations may—

(a)    make provision as to any change (or proposed change) of a prescribed kind relating to a UK firm or to an activity that it carries on and as to the procedure to be followed in relation to such cases;

(b)    make provision with respect to the consequences of the firm's failure to comply with a provision of the regulations.

(3)    Where a provision of the kind mentioned in sub-paragraph (2) requires the Authority's consent to a change (or proposed change)—

(a)    consent may be refused only on prescribed grounds; and

(b)    if the Authority decides to refuse consent, the firm concerned may refer the matter to the Tribunal.

23.—(1)    Sub-paragraph (2) applies if a UK firm—

(a)    has a Part IV permission; and

(b)    is exercising an EEA right to carry on any Consumer Credit Act business in an EEA State other than the United Kingdom.

(2) The Authority may exercise its power under section 45 in respect of the firm if the Director of Fair Trading has informed the Authority that—

(a) the firm,

(b) any of the firm's employees, agents or associates (whether past or present), or

(c) if the firm is a body corporate, a controller of the firm or an associate of such a controller,

has done any of the things specified in paragraphs (a) to (d) of section 25(2) of the Consumer Credit Act 1974.

(3) 'Associate', 'Consumer Credit Act business' and 'controller' have the same meaning as in section 203.

24.—(1) Sub-paragraph (2) applies if a UK firm—

(a) is not required to have a Part IV permission in relation to the business which it is carrying on; and

(b) is exercising the right conferred by Article 18.2 of the second banking co-ordination directive to carry on that business in an EEA State other than the United Kingdom.

(2) If requested to do so by the host state regulator in the EEA State in which the UK firm's business is being carried on, the Authority may impose any requirement in relation to the firm which it could impose if—

(a) the firm had a Part IV permission in relation to the business which it is carrying on; and

(b) the Authority was entitled to exercise its power under that Part to vary that permission.

**Section 31(1)(c)**        SCHEDULE 4
                           TREATY RIGHTS

*Definitions*

1. In this Schedule—

'consumers' means persons who are consumers for the purposes of section 138;

'Treaty firm' means a person—

(a) whose head office is situated in an EEA State (its 'home state') other than the United Kingdom; and

(b) which is recognised under the law of that State as its national; and

'home state regulator', in relation to a Treaty firm, means the competent authority of the firm's home state for the purpose of its home state authorisation (as to which see paragraph 3(1)(a)).

*Firms qualifying for authorisation*

2. Once a Treaty firm which is seeking to carry on a regulated activity satisfies the conditions set out in paragraph 3(1), it qualifies for authorisation.

*Exercise of Treaty rights*

3.—(1) The conditions are that—

(a) the firm has received authorisation ('home state authorisation') under the law of its home state to carry on the regulated activity in question ('the permitted activity');

(b) the relevant provisions of the law of the firm's home state—

(i) afford equivalent protection; or

(ii)   satisfy the conditions laid down by a Community instrument for the co-ordination or approximation of laws, regulations or administrative provisions of member States relating to the carrying on of that activity; and

(c)   the firm has no EEA right to carry on that activity in the manner in which it is seeking to carry it on.

(2)   A firm is not to be regarded as having home state authorisation unless its home state regulator has so informed the Authority in writing.

(3)   Provisions afford equivalent protection if, in relation to the firm's carrying on of the permitted activity, they afford consumers protection which is at least equivalent to that afforded by or under this Act in relation to that activity.

(4)   A certificate issued by the Treasury that the provisions of the law of a particular EEA State afford equivalent protection in relation to the activities specified in the certificate is conclusive evidence of that fact.

### Permission

4.—(1)   On qualifying for authorisation under this Schedule, a Treaty firm has permission to carry on each permitted activity through its United Kingdom branch or by providing services in the United Kingdom.

(2)   The permission is to be treated as being on terms equivalent to those to which the firm's home state authorisation is subject.

(3)   If, on qualifying for authorisation under this Schedule, a firm has a Part IV permission which includes permission to carry on a permitted activity, the Authority must give a direction cancelling the permission so far as it relates to that activity.

(4)   The Authority need not give a direction under sub-paragraph (3) if it considers that there are good reasons for not doing so.

### Notice to Authority

5.—(1)   Sub-paragraph (2) applies to a Treaty firm which—

(a)   qualifies for authorisation under this Schedule, but

(b)   is not carrying on in the United Kingdom the regulated activity, or any of the regulated activities, which it has permission to carry on there.

(2)   At least seven days before it begins to carry on such a regulated activity, the firm must give the Authority written notice of its intention to do so.

(3)   If a Treaty firm to which sub-paragraph (2) applies has given notice under that sub-paragraph, it need not give such a notice if it again becomes a firm to which that sub-paragraph applies.

(4)   Subsections (1), (3) and (6) of section 51 apply to a notice under sub-paragraph (2) as they apply to an application for a Part IV permission.

### Offences

6.—(1)   A person who contravenes paragraph 5(2) is guilty of an offence.

(2)   In proceedings against a person for an offence under sub-paragraph (1) it is a defence for him to show that he took all reasonable precautions and exercised all due diligence to avoid committing the offence.

(3)   A person is guilty of an offence if in, or in connection with, a notice given by him under paragraph 5(2) he—

(a)   provides information which he knows to be false or misleading in a material particular; or

(b) recklessly provides information which is false or misleading in a material particular.

(4) A person guilty of an offence under this paragraph is liable—

(a) on summary conviction, to a fine not exceeding the statutory maximum;

(b) on conviction on indictment, to a fine.

**Section 36**                    SCHEDULE 5
PERSONS CONCERNED IN COLLECTIVE INVESTMENT SCHEMES

*Authorisation*

1.—(1) A person who for the time being is an operator, trustee or depositary of a recognised collective investment scheme is an authorised person.

(2) 'Recognised' means recognised by virtue of section 264.

(3) An authorised open-ended investment company is an authorised person.

*Permission*

2.—(1) A person authorised as a result of paragraph 1(1) has permission to carry on, so far as it is a regulated activity—

(a) any activity, appropriate to the capacity in which he acts in relation to the scheme, of the kind described in paragraph 8 of Schedule 2;

(b) any activity in connection with, or for the purposes of, the scheme.

(2) A person authorised as a result of paragraph 1(3) has permission to carry on, so far as it is a regulated activity—

(a) the operation of the scheme;

(b) any activity in connection with, or for the purposes of, the operation of the scheme.

**Section 41**                    SCHEDULE 6
THRESHOLD CONDITIONS

PART I
PART IV PERMISSION

*Legal status*

1.—(1) If the regulated activity concerned is the effecting or carrying out of contracts of insurance the authorised person must be a body corporate, a registered friendly society or a member of Lloyd's.

(2) If the person concerned appears to the Authority to be seeking to carry on, or to be carrying on, a regulated activity constituting accepting deposits, it must be—

(a) a body corporate; or

(b) a partnership.

*Location of offices*

2.—(1) If the person concerned is a body corporate constituted under the law of any part of the United Kingdom—

(a) its head office, and

(b) if it has a registered office, that office,

must be in the United Kingdom.

(2) If the person concerned has its head office in the United Kingdom but is not a body corporate, it must carry on business in the United Kingdom.

*Close links*

3.—(1)  If the person concerned ('A') has close links with another person ('CL') the Authority must be satisfied—

(a)  that those links are not likely to prevent the Authority's effective supervision of A; and

(b)  if it appears to the Authority that CL is subject to the laws, regulations or administrative provisions of a territory which is not an EEA State ('the foreign provisions'), that neither the foreign provisions, nor any deficiency in their enforcement, would prevent the Authority's effective supervision of A.

(2)  A has close links with CL if—

(a)  CL is a parent undertaking of A;

(b)  CL is a subsidiary undertaking of A;

(c)  CL is a parent undertaking of a subsidiary undertaking of A;

(d)  CL is a subsidiary undertaking of a parent undertaking of A;

(e)  CL owns or controls 20% or more of the voting rights or capital of A; or

(f)  A owns or controls 20% or more of the voting rights or capital of CL.

(3)  'Subsidiary undertaking' includes all the instances mentioned in Article 1(1) and (2) of the Seventh Company Law Directive in which an entity may be a subsidiary of an undertaking.

*Adequate resources*

4.—(1)  The resources of the person concerned must, in the opinion of the Authority, be adequate in relation to the regulated activities that he seeks to carry on, or carries on.

(2)  In reaching that opinion, the Authority may—

(a)  take into account the person's membership of a group and any effect which that membership may have; and

(b)  have regard to—

(i)  the provision he makes and, if he is a member of a group, which other members of the group make in respect of liabilities (including contingent and future liabilities); and

(ii)  the means by which he manages and, if he is a member of a group, which other members of the group manage the incidence of risk in connection with his business.

*Suitability*

5.  The person concerned must satisfy the Authority that he is a fit and proper person having regard to all the circumstances, including—

(a)  his connection with any person;

(b)  the nature of any regulated activity that he carries on or seeks to carry on; and

(c)  the need to ensure that his affairs are conducted soundly and prudently.

## PART II
## AUTHORISATION

*Authorisation under Schedule 3*

6.  In relation to an EEA firm qualifying for authorisation under Schedule 3, the conditions set out in paragraphs 1 and 3 to 5 apply, so far as relevant, to—

(a)  an application for permission under Part IV;

(b)  exercise of the Authority's own-initiative power under section 45 in relation to a Part IV permission.

*Authorisation under Schedule 4*

7.   In relation to a person who qualifies for authorisation under Schedule 4, the conditions set out in paragraphs 1 and 3 to 5 apply, so far as relevant, to—

(a)   an application for an additional permission;

(b)   the exercise of the Authority's own-initiative power under section 45 in relation to additional permission.

## PART III
## ADDITIONAL CONDITIONS

8.—(1)   If this paragraph applies to the person concerned, he must, for the purposes of such provisions of this Act as may be specified, satisfy specified additional conditions.

(2)   This paragraph applies to a person who—

(a)   has his head office outside the EEA; and

(b)   appears to the Authority to be seeking to carry on a regulated activity relating to insurance business.

(3)   'Specified' means specified in, or in accordance with, an order made by the Treasury.

9.   The Treasury may by order—

(a)   vary or remove any of the conditions set out in Parts I and II;

(b)   add to those conditions.

**Section 72(2)**            SCHEDULE 7
THE AUTHORITY AS COMPETENT AUTHORITY FOR PART VI

*General*

1.   This Act applies in relation to the Authority when it is exercising functions under Part VI as the competent authority subject to the following modifications.

*The Authority's general functions*

2.   In section 2—

(a)   subsection (4)(a) does not apply to listing rules;

(b)   subsection (4)(c) does not apply to general guidance given in relation to Part VI; and

(c)   subsection (4)(d) does not apply to functions under Part VI.

*Duty to consult*

3.   Section 8 does not apply.

*Rules*

4.—(1)   Sections 149, 153, 154 and 156 do not apply.

(2)   Section 155 has effect as if—

(a)   the reference in subsection (2)(c) to the general duties of the Authority under section 2 were a reference to its duty under section 73; and

(b)   section 99 were included in the provisions referred to in subsection (9).

*Statements of policy*

5.—(1)   Paragraph 5 of Schedule 1 has effect as if the requirement to act through the Authority's governing body applied also to the exercise of its functions of publishing statements under section 93.

(2)   Paragraph 1 of Schedule 1 has effect as if section 93 were included in the provisions referred to in sub-paragraph (2)(d).

*Penalties*

6.   Paragraph 16 of Schedule 1 does not apply in relation to penalties under Part VI (for which separate provision is made by section 100).

*Fees*

7.   Paragraph 17 of Schedule 1 does not apply in relation to fees payable under Part VI (for which separate provision is made by section 99).

*Exemption from liability in damages*

8.   Schedule 1 has effect as if—
   (a)   sub-paragraph (1) of paragraph 19 were omitted (similar provision being made in relation to the competent authority by section 102); and
   (b)   for the words from the beginning to '(a)' in sub-paragraph (3) of that paragraph, there were substituted 'Sub-paragraph (2) does not apply'.

**Section 72(3)** | SCHEDULE 8
TRANSFER OF FUNCTIONS UNDER PART VI

*The power to transfer*

1.—(1)   The Treasury may by order provide for any function conferred on the competent authority which is exercisable for the time being by a particular person to be transferred so as to be exercisable by another person.
   (2)   An order may be made under this paragraph only if—
   (a)   the person from whom the relevant functions are to be transferred has agreed in writing that the order should be made;
   (b)   the Treasury are satisfied that the manner in which, or efficiency with which, the functions are discharged would be significantly improved if they were transferred to the transferee; or
   (c)   the Treasury are satisfied that it is otherwise in the public interest that the order should be made.

*Supplemental*

2.—(1)   An order under this Schedule does not affect anything previously done by any person ('the previous authority') in the exercise of functions which are transferred by the order to another person ('the new authority').
   (2)   Such an order may, in particular, include provision—
   (a)   modifying or excluding any provision of Part VI, IX or XXVI in its application to any such functions;
   (b)   for reviews similar to that made, in relation to the Authority, by section 12;
   (c)   imposing on the new authority requirements similar to those imposed, in relation to the Authority, by sections 152, 155 and 354;
   (d)   as to the giving of guidance by the new authority;
   (e)   for the delegation by the new authority of the exercise of functions under Part VI and as to the consequences of delegation;

(f)   for the transfer of any property, rights or liabilities relating to any such functions from the previous authority to the new authority;

(g)   for the carrying on and completion by the new authority of anything in the process of being done by the previous authority when the order takes effect;

(h)   for the substitution of the new authority for the previous authority in any instrument, contract or legal proceedings;

(i)   for the transfer of persons employed by the previous authority to the new authority and as to the terms on which they are to transfer;

(j)   making such amendments to any primary or subordinate legislation (including any provision of, or made under, this Act) as the Treasury consider appropriate in consequence of the transfer of functions effected by the order.

(3)   Nothing in this paragraph is to be taken as restricting the powers conferred by section 428.

3.   If the Treasury have made an order under paragraph 1 ('the transfer order') they may, by a separate order made under this paragraph, make any provision of a kind that could have been included in the transfer order.

**Section 87(5)**                SCHEDULE 9
                      NON-LISTING PROSPECTUSES

*General application of Part VI*

1.   The provisions of Part VI apply in relation to a non-listing prospectus as they apply in relation to listing particulars but with the modifications made by this Schedule.

*References to listing particulars*

2.—(1)   Any reference to listing particulars is to be read as a reference to a prospectus.

(2)   Any reference to supplementary listing particulars is to be read as a reference to a supplementary prospectus.

*General duty of disclosure*

3.—(1)   In section 80(1), for 'section 79' substitute 'section 87'.

(2)   In section 80(2), omit 'as a condition of the admission of the securities to the official list'.

*Supplementary prospectuses*

4.   In section 81(1), for 'section 79 and before the commencement of dealings in the securities concerned following their admission to the official list' substitute 'section 87 and before the end of the period during which the offer to which the prospectus relates remains open'.

*Exemption from liability for compensation*

5.—(1)   In paragraphs 1(3) and 2(3) of Schedule 10, for paragraph (d) substitute—

'(d)   the securities were acquired after such a lapse of time that he ought in the circumstances to be reasonably excused and, if the securities are dealt in on an approved exchange, he continued in that belief until after the commencement of dealings in the securities on that exchange.'

(2)   After paragraph 8 of that Schedule, insert—

*'Meaning of "approved exchange"*

9.   "Approved exchange" has such meaning as may be prescribed.'

*Advertisements*

6.   In section 98(1), for 'If listing particulars are, or are to be, published in connection with an application for listing,' substitute 'If a prospectus is, or is to be, published in connection with an application for approval, then, until the end of the period during which the offer to which the prospectus relates remains open,'.

*Fees*

7.   Listing rules made under section 99 may require the payment of fees to the competent authority in respect of a prospectus submitted for approval under section 87.

**Section 90(2) and (5)**            SCHEDULE 10
                                    COMPENSATION: EXEMPTIONS

*Statements believed to be true*

1.—(1)   In this paragraph 'statement' means—

(a)   any untrue or misleading statement in listing particulars; or

(b)   the omission from listing particulars of any matter required to be included by section 80 or 81.

(2)   A person does not incur any liability under section 90(1) for loss caused by a statement if he satisfies the court that, at the time when the listing particulars were submitted to the competent authority, he reasonably believed (having made such enquiries, if any, as were reasonable) that—

(a)   the statement was true and not misleading, or

(b)   the matter whose omission caused the loss was properly omitted,

and that one or more of the conditions set out in sub-paragraph (3) are satisfied.

(3)   The conditions are that—

(a)   he continued in his belief until the time when the securities in question were acquired;

(b)   they were acquired before it was reasonably practicable to bring a correction to the attention of persons likely to acquire them;

(c)   before the securities were acquired, he had taken all such steps as it was reasonable for him to have taken to secure that a correction was brought to the attention of those persons;

(d)   he continued in his belief until after the commencement of dealings in the securities following their admission to the official list and they were acquired after such a lapse of time that he ought in the circumstances to be reasonably excused.

*Statements by experts*

2.—(1)   In this paragraph 'statement' means a statement included in listing particulars which—

(a)   purports to be made by, or on the authority of, another person as an expert; and

(b)   is stated to be included in the listing particulars with that other person's consent.

(2)   A person does not incur any liability under section 90(1) for loss in respect of any securities caused by a statement if he satisfies the court that, at the time when the listing particulars were submitted to the competent authority, he reasonably believed that the other person—

(a)   was competent to make or authorise the statement, and

(b)   had consented to its inclusion in the form and context in which it was included,

and that one or more of the conditions set out in sub-paragraph (3) are satisfied.

(3)   The conditions are that—

(a)   he continued in his belief until the time when the securities were acquired;

(b)   they were acquired before it was reasonably practicable to bring the fact that the expert was not competent, or had not consented, to the attention of persons likely to acquire the securities in question;

(c)   before the securities were acquired he had taken all such steps as it was reasonable for him to have taken to secure that that fact was brought to the attention of those persons;

(d)   he continued in his belief until after the commencement of dealings in the securities following their admission to the official list and they were acquired after such a lapse of time that he ought in the circumstances to be reasonably excused.

### Corrections of statements

3.—(1)   In this paragraph 'statement' has the same meaning as in paragraph 1.

(2)   A person does not incur liability under section 90(1) for loss caused by a statement if he satisfies the court—

(a)   that before the securities in question were acquired, a correction had been published in a manner calculated to bring it to the attention of persons likely to acquire the securities; or

(b)   that he took all such steps as it was reasonable for him to take to secure such publication and reasonably believed that it had taken place before the securities were acquired.

(3)   Nothing in this paragraph is to be taken as affecting paragraph 1.

### Corrections of statements by experts

4.—(1)   In this paragraph 'statement' has the same meaning as in paragraph 2.

(2)   A person does not incur liability under section 90(1) for loss caused by a statement if he satisfies the court—

(a)   that before the securities in question were acquired, the fact that the expert was not competent or had not consented had been published in a manner calculated to bring it to the attention of persons likely to acquire the securities; or

(b)   that he took all such steps as it was reasonable for him to take to secure such publication and reasonably believed that it had taken place before the securities were acquired.

(3)   Nothing in this paragraph is to be taken as affecting paragraph 2.

### Official statements

5.   A person does not incur any liability under section 90(1) for loss resulting from—

(a)   a statement made by an official person which is included in the listing particulars, or

(b)   a statement contained in a public official document which is included in the listing particulars,

if he satisfies the court that the statement is accurately and fairly reproduced.

### False or misleading information known about

6.   A person does not incur any liability under section 90(1) or (4) if he satisfies the court that the person suffering the loss acquired the securities in question with knowledge—

(a)   that the statement was false or misleading,

(b)   of the omitted matter, or

(c)  of the change or new matter,

as the case may be.

*Belief that supplementary listing particulars not called for*

7.  A person does not incur any liability under section 90(4) if he satisfies the court that he reasonably believed that the change or new matter in question was not such as to call for supplementary listing particulars.

*Meaning of 'expert'*

8.  'Expert' includes any engineer, valuer, accountant or other person whose profession, qualifications or experience give authority to a statement made by him.

**Section 103(6)**                          SCHEDULE 11
                                    OFFERS OF SECURITIES

*The general rule*

1.—(1)  A person offers securities to the public in the United Kingdom if—

(a)  to the extent that the offer is made to persons in the United Kingdom, it is made to the public; and

(b)  the offer is not an exempt offer.

(2)  For this purpose, an offer which is made to any section of the public, whether selected—

(a)  as members or debenture holders of a body corporate,

(b)  as clients of the person making the offer, or

(c)  in any other manner,

is to be regarded as made to the public.

*Exempt offers*

2.—(1)  For the purposes of this Schedule, an offer of securities is an 'exempt offer' if, to the extent that the offer is made to persons in the United Kingdom—

(a)  the condition specified in any of paragraphs 3 to 24 is satisfied in relation to the offer; or

(b)  the condition specified in one relevant paragraph is satisfied in relation to part, but not the whole, of the offer and, in relation to each other part of the offer, the condition specified in a different relevant paragraph is satisfied.

(2)  The relevant paragraphs are 3 to 8, 12 to 18 and 21.

*Offers for business purposes*

3.  The securities are offered to persons—

(a)  whose ordinary activities involve them in acquiring, holding, managing or disposing of investments (as principal or agent) for the purposes of their businesses, or

(b)  who it is reasonable to expect will acquire, hold, manage or dispose of investments (as principal or agent) for the purposes of their businesses,

or are otherwise offered to persons in the context of their trades, professions or occupations.

*Offers to limited numbers*

4.—(1)  The securities are offered to no more than fifty persons.

(2)  In determining whether this condition is satisfied, the offer is to be taken together with any other offer of the same securities which was—

(a)    made by the same person;

(b)    open at any time within the period of 12 months ending with the date on which the offer is first made; and

(c)    not an offer to the public in the United Kingdom by virtue of this condition being satisfied.

(3)   For the purposes of this paragraph—

(a)    the making of an offer of securities to trustees or members of a partnership in their capacity as such, or

(b)    the making of such an offer to any other two or more persons jointly,

is to be treated as the making of an offer to a single person.

### *Clubs and associations*

5.    The securities are offered to the members of a club or association (whether or not incorporated) and the members can reasonably be regarded as having a common interest with each other and with the club or association in the affairs of the club or association and in what is to be done with the proceeds of the offer.

### *Restricted circles*

6.—(1)   The securities are offered to a restricted circle of persons whom the offeror reasonably believes to be sufficiently knowledgeable to understand the risks involved in accepting the offer.

(2)   In determining whether a person is sufficiently knowledgeable to understand the risks involved in accepting an offer of securities, any information supplied by the person making the offer is to be disregarded, apart from information about—

(a)    the issuer of the securities; or

(b)    if the securities confer the right to acquire other securities, the issuer of those other securities.

### *Underwriting agreements*

7.    The securities are offered in connection with a genuine invitation to enter into an underwriting agreement with respect to them.

### *Offers to public authorities*

8.—(1)   The securities are offered to a public authority.

(2)   'Public authority' means—

(a)    the government of the United Kingdom;

(b)    the government of any country or territory outside the United Kingdom;

(c)    a local authority in the United Kingdom or elsewhere;

(d)    any international organisation the members of which include the United Kingdom or another EEA State; and

(e)    such other bodies, if any, as may be specified.

### *Maximum consideration*

9.—(1)   The total consideration payable for the securities cannot exceed 40,000 euros (or an equivalent amount).

(2)   In determining whether this condition is satisfied, the offer is to be taken together with any other offer of the same securities which was—

(a)   made by the same person;

(b)   open at any time within the period of 12 months ending with the date on which the offer is first made; and

(c)   not an offer to the public in the United Kingdom by virtue of this condition being satisfied.

(3)   An amount (in relation to an amount denominated in euros) is an 'equivalent amount' if it is an amount of equal value, calculated at the latest practicable date before (but in any event not more than 3 days before) the date on which the offer is first made, denominated wholly or partly in another currency or unit of account.

### Minimum consideration

10.—(1)   The minimum consideration which may be paid by any person for securities acquired by him pursuant to the offer is at least 40,000 euros (or an equivalent amount).

(2)   Paragraph 9(3) also applies for the purposes of this paragraph.

### Securities denominated in euros

11.—(1)   The securities are denominated in amounts of at least 40,000 euros (or an equivalent amount).

(2)   Paragraph 9(3) also applies for the purposes of this paragraph.

### Takeovers

12.—(1)   The securities are offered in connection with a takeover offer.

(2)   'Takeover offer' means—

(a)   an offer to acquire shares in a body incorporated in the United Kingdom which is a takeover offer within the meaning of the takeover provisions (or would be such an offer if those provisions applied in relation to any body corporate);

(b)   an offer to acquire all or substantially all of the shares, or of the shares of a particular class, in a body incorporated outside the United Kingdom; or

(c)   an offer made to all the holders of shares, or of shares of a particular class, in a body corporate to acquire a specified proportion of those shares.

(3)   'The takeover provisions' means—

(a)   Part XIIIA of the Companies Act 1985; or

(b)   in relation to Northern Ireland, Part XIVA of the Companies (Northern Ireland) Order 1986.

(4)   For the purposes of sub-paragraph (2)(b), any shares which the offeror or any associate of his holds or has contracted to acquire are to be disregarded.

(5)   For the purposes of sub-paragraph (2)(c), the following are not to be regarded as holders of the shares in question—

(a)   the offeror;

(b)   any associate of the offeror; and

(c)   any person whose shares the offeror or any associate of the offeror has contracted to acquire.

(6)   'Associate' has the same meaning as in—

(a)   section 430E of the Companies Act 1985; or

(b)   in relation to Northern Ireland, Article 423E of the Companies (Northern Ireland) Order 1986.

*Mergers*

13. The securities are offered in connection with a merger (within the meaning of Council Directive No. 78/855/EEC).

*Free shares*

14.—(1) The securities are shares and are offered free of charge to any or all of the holders of shares in the issuer.

(2) 'Holders of shares' means the persons who at the close of business on a date—

(a) specified in the offer, and

(b) falling within the period of 60 days ending with the date on which the offer is first made,

were holders of such shares.

*Exchange of shares*

15. The securities—

(a) are shares, or investments of a specified kind relating to shares, in a body corporate, and

(b) are offered in exchange for shares in the same body corporate,

and the offer cannot result in any increase in the issued share capital of the body corporate.

*Qualifying persons*

16.—(1) The securities are issued by a body corporate and are offered—

(a) by the issuer, by a body corporate connected with the issuer or by a relevant trustee;

(b) only to qualifying persons; and

(c) on terms that a contract to acquire any such securities may be entered into only by the qualifying person to whom they were offered or, if the terms of the offer so permit, any qualifying person.

(2) A person is a 'qualifying person', in relation to an issuer, if he is a genuine employee or former employee of the issuer or of another body corporate in the same group or the wife, husband, widow, widower or child or stepchild under the age of eighteen of such an employee or former employee.

(3) In relation to an issuer of securities, 'connected with' has such meaning as may be prescribed.

(4) 'Group' and 'relevant trustee' have such meaning as may be prescribed.

*Convertible securities*

17.—(1) The securities result from the conversion of convertible securities and listing particulars (or a prospectus) relating to the convertible securities were (or was) published in the United Kingdom under or by virtue of Part VI or such other provisions applying in the United Kingdom as may be specified.

(2) 'Convertible securities' means securities of a specified kind which can be converted into, or exchanged for, or which confer rights to acquire, other securities.

(3) 'Conversion' means conversion into or exchange for, or the exercise of rights conferred by the securities to acquire, other securities.

*Charities*

18. The securities are issued by—

   (a)  a charity within the meaning of—
      (i)   section 96(1) of the Charities Act 1993, or
      (ii)   section 35 of the Charities Act (Northern Ireland) 1964,
   (b)  a recognised body within the meaning of section 1(7) of the Law Reform (Miscellaneous Provisions) (Scotland) Act 1990,
   (c)  a housing association within the meaning of—
      (i)   section 5(1) of the Housing Act 1985,
      (ii)   section 1 of the Housing Associations Act 1985, or
      (iii)   Article 3 of the Housing (Northern Ireland) Order 1992,
   (d)  an industrial or provident society registered in accordance with—
      (i)   section 1(2)(b) of the Industrial and Provident Societies Act 1965, or
      (ii)   section 1(2)(b) of the Industrial and Provident Societies Act 1969, or
   (e)  a non-profit making association or body, recognised by the country or territory in which it is established, with objectives similar to those of a body falling within any of paragraphs (a) to (c),
and the proceeds of the offer will be used for the purposes of the issuer's objectives.

### Building societies etc.

19.   The securities offered are shares which are issued by, or ownership of which entitles the holder to membership of or to obtain the benefit of services provided by—
   (a)  a building society incorporated under the law of, or of any part of, the United Kingdom;
   (b)  any body incorporated under the law of, or of any part of, the United Kingdom relating to industrial and provident societies or credit unions; or
   (c)  a body of a similar nature established in another EEA State.

### Euro-securities

20.—(1)   The securities offered are Euro-securities and no advertisement relating to the offer is issued in the United Kingdom, or is caused to be so issued—
   (a)  by the issuer of the Euro-securities;
   (b)  by any credit institution or other financial institution through which the Euro-securities may be acquired pursuant to the offer; or
   (c)  by any body corporate which is a member of the same group as the issuer or any of those institutions.
   (2)  But sub-paragraph (1) does not apply to an advertisement of a prescribed kind.
   (3)  'Euro-securities' means investments which—
   (a)  are to be underwritten and distributed by a syndicate at least two of the members of which have their registered offices in different countries or territories;
   (b)  are to be offered on a significant scale in one or more countries or territories, other than the country or territory in which the issuer has its registered office; and
   (c)  may be acquired pursuant to the offer only through a credit institution or other financial institution.
   (4)  'Credit institution' means a credit institution as defined in Article 1 of Council Directive No 77/780/EEC.
   (5)  'Financial institution' means a financial institution as defined in Article 1 of Council Directive No 89/646/EEC.
   (6)  'Underwritten' means underwritten by whatever means, including by acquisition or subscription, with a view to resale.

*Same class securities*

21.   The securities are of the same class, and were issued at the same time, as securities in respect of which a prospectus has been published under or by virtue of—

  (a)   Part VI;
  (b)   Part III of the Companies Act 1985; or
  (c)   such other provisions applying in the United Kingdom as may be specified.

*Short date securities*

22.   The securities are investments of a specified kind with a maturity of less than one year from their date of issue.

*Government and public securities*

23.—(1)   The securities are investments of a specified kind creating or acknowledging indebtedness issued by or on behalf of a public authority.

  (2)   'Public authority' means—

  (a)   the government of the United Kingdom;
  (b)   the government of any country or territory outside the United Kingdom;
  (c)   a local authority in the United Kingdom or elsewhere;
  (d)   any international organisation the members of which include the United Kingdom or another EEA State; and
  (e)   such other bodies, if any, as may be specified.

*Non-transferable securities*

24.   The securities are not transferable.

*General definitions*

25.   For the purposes of this Schedule—

  'shares' has such meaning as may be specified; and
  'specified' means specified in an order made by the Treasury.

**Sections 111(2) and 115**          SCHEDULE 12
TRANSFER SCHEMES: CERTIFICATES

PART I
INSURANCE BUSINESS TRANSFER SCHEMES

1.—(1)   For the purposes of section 111(2) the appropriate certificates, in relation to an insurance business transfer scheme, are—

  (a)   a certificate under paragraph 2;
  (b)   if sub-paragraph (2) applies, a certificate under paragraph 3;
  (c)   if sub-paragraph (3) applies, a certificate under paragraph 4;
  (d)   if sub-paragraph (4) applies, a certificate under paragraph 5.

  (2)   This sub-paragraph applies if—

  (a)   the authorised person concerned is a UK authorised person which has received authorisation under Article 6 of the first life insurance directive or of the first non-life insurance directive from the Authority; and

  (b)   the establishment from which the business is to be transferred under the proposed insurance business transfer scheme is in an EEA State other than the United Kingdom.

  (3)   This sub-paragraph applies if—

(a)   the authorised person concerned has received authorisation under Article 6 of the first life insurance directive from the Authority;

(b)   the proposed transfer relates to business which consists of the effecting or carrying out of contracts of long-term insurance; and

(c)   as regards any policy which is included in the proposed transfer and which evidences a contract of insurance (other than reinsurance), an EEA State other than the United Kingdom is the State of the commitment.

(4)   This sub-paragraph applies if—

(a)   the authorised person concerned has received authorisation under Article 6 of the first non-life insurance directive from the Authority;

(b)   the business to which the proposed insurance business transfer scheme relates is business which consists of the effecting or carrying out of contracts of general insurance; and

(c)   as regards any policy which is included in the proposed transfer and which evidences a contract of insurance (other than reinsurance), the risk is situated in an EEA State other than the United Kingdom.

*Certificates as to margin of solvency*

2.—(1)   A certificate under this paragraph is to be given—

(a)   by the relevant authority; or

(b)   in a case in which there is no relevant authority, by the Authority.

(2)   A certificate given under sub-paragraph (1)(a) is one certifying that, taking the proposed transfer into account—

(a)   the transferee possesses, or will possess before the scheme takes effect, the necessary margin of solvency; or

(b)   there is no necessary margin of solvency applicable to the transferee.

(3)   A certificate under sub-paragraph (1)(b) is one certifying that the Authority has received from the authority which it considers to be the authority responsible for supervising persons who effect or carry out contracts of insurance in the place to which the business is to be transferred that, taking the proposed transfer into account—

(a)   the transferee possesses or will possess before the scheme takes effect the margin of solvency required under the law applicable in that place; or

(b)   there is no such margin of solvency applicable to the transferee.

(4)   'Necessary margin of solvency' means the margin of solvency required in relation to the transferee, taking the proposed transfer into account, under the law which it is the responsibility of the relevant authority to apply.

(5)   'Margin of solvency' means the excess of the value of the assets of the transferee over the amount of its liabilities.

(6)   'Relevant authority' means—

(a)   if the transferee is an EEA firm falling within paragraph 5(d) of Schedule 3, its home state regulator;

(b)   if the transferee is a Swiss general insurer, the authority responsible in Switzerland for supervising persons who effect or carry out contracts of insurance;

(c)   if the transferee is an authorised person not falling within paragraph (a) or (b), the Authority.

(7)   In sub-paragraph (6), any reference to a transferee of a particular description includes a reference to a transferee who will be of that description if the proposed scheme takes effect.

(8) 'Swiss general insurer' means a body—

    (a) whose head office is in Switzerland;

    (b) which has permission to carry on regulated activities consisting of the effecting and carrying out of contracts of general insurance; and

    (c) whose permission is not restricted to the effecting or carrying out of contracts of reinsurance.

### Certificates as to consent

3. A certificate under this paragraph is one given by the Authority and certifying that the host State regulator has been notified of the proposed scheme and that—

    (a) that regulator has responded to the notification; or

    (b) that it has not responded but the period of three months beginning with the notification has elapsed.

### Certificates as to long-term business

4. A certificate under this paragraph is one given by the Authority and certifying that the authority responsible for supervising persons who effect or carry out contracts of insurance in the State of the commitment has been notified of the proposed scheme and that—

    (a) that authority has consented to the proposed scheme; or

    (b) the period of three months beginning with the notification has elapsed and that authority has not refused its consent.

### Certificates as to general business

5. A certificate under this paragraph is one given by the Authority and certifying that the authority responsible for supervising persons who effect or carry out contracts of insurance in the EEA State in which the risk is situated has been notified of the proposed scheme and that—

    (a) that authority has consented to the proposed scheme; or

    (b) the period of three months beginning with the notification has elapsed and that authority has not refused its consent.

### Interpretation of Part I

6.—(1) 'State of the commitment', in relation to a commitment entered into at any date, means—

    (a) if the policyholder is an individual, the State in which he had his habitual residence at that date;

    (b) if the policyholder is not an individual, the State in which the establishment of the policyholder to which the commitment relates was situated at that date.

(2) 'Commitment' means a commitment represented by contracts of insurance of a prescribed class.

(3) References to the EEA State in which a risk is situated are—

    (a) if the insurance relates to a building or to a building and its contents (so far as the contents are covered by the same policy), to the EEA State in which the building is situated;

    (b) if the insurance relates to a vehicle of any type, to the EEA State of registration;

    (c) in the case of policies of a duration of four months or less covering travel or holiday risks (whatever the class concerned), to the EEA State in which the policyholder took out the policy;

(d)   in a case not covered by paragraphs (a) to (c)—

(i)   if the policyholder is an individual, to the EEA State in which he has his habitual residence at the date when the contract is entered into; and

(ii)   otherwise, to the EEA State in which the establishment of the policyholder to which the policy relates is situated at that date.

## PART II
### BANKING BUSINESS TRANSFER SCHEMES

7.—(1)   For the purposes of section 111(2) the appropriate certificates, in relation to a banking business transfer scheme, are—

(a)   a certificate under paragraph 8; and

(b)   if sub-paragraph (2) applies, a certificate under paragraph 9.

(2)   This sub-paragraph applies if the authorised person concerned or the transferee is an EEA firm falling within paragraph 5(b) of Schedule 3.

*Certificates as to financial resources*

8.—(1)   A certificate under this paragraph is one given by the relevant authority and certifying that, taking the proposed transfer into account, the transferee possesses, or will possess before the scheme takes effect, adequate financial resources.

(2)   'Relevant authority' means—

(a)   if the transferee is a person with a Part IV permission or with permission under Schedule 4, the Authority;

(b)   if the transferee is an EEA firm falling within paragraph 5(b) of Schedule 3, its home state regulator;

(c)   if the transferee does not fall within paragraph (a) or (b), the authority responsible for the supervision of the transferee's business in the place in which the transferee has its head office.

(3)   In sub-paragraph (2), any reference to a transferee of a particular description of person includes a reference to a transferee who will be of that description if the proposed banking business transfer scheme takes effect.

*Certificates as to consent of home state regulator*

9.   A certificate under this paragraph is one given by the Authority and certifying that the home State regulator of the authorised person concerned or of the transferee has been notified of the proposed scheme and that—

(a)   the home State regulator has responded to the notification; or

(b)   the period of three months beginning with the notification has elapsed.

## PART III
### INSURANCE BUSINESS TRANSFERS EFFECTED OUTSIDE THE UNITED KINGDOM

10.—(1)   This paragraph applies to a proposal to execute under provisions corresponding to Part VII in a country or territory other than the United Kingdom an instrument transferring all the rights and obligations of the transferor under general or long-term insurance policies, or under such descriptions of such policies as may be specified in the instrument, to the transferee if any of the conditions in sub-paragraphs (2), (3) or (4) is met in relation to it.

(2)   The transferor is an EEA firm falling within paragraph 5(d) of Schedule 3 and the transferee is an authorised person whose margin of solvency is supervised by the Authority.

(3)    The transferor is a company authorised in an EEA State other than the United Kingdom under Article 27 of the first life insurance directive, or Article 23 of the first non-life insurance directive and the transferee is a UK authorised person which has received authorisation under Article 6 of either of those directives.

(4)    The transferor is a Swiss general insurer and the transferee is a UK authorised person which has received authorisation under Article 6 of the first life insurance directive or the first non-life insurance directive.

(5)    In relation to a proposed transfer to which this paragraph applies, the Authority may, if it is satisfied that the transferee possesses the necessary margin of solvency, issue a certificate to that effect.

(6)    'Necessary margin of solvency' means the margin of solvency which the transferee, taking the proposed transfer into account, is required by the Authority to maintain.

(7)    'Swiss general insurer' has the same meaning as in paragraph 2.

(8)    'General policy' means a policy evidencing a contract which, if it had been effected by the transferee, would have constituted the carrying on of a regulated activity consisting of the effecting of contracts of general insurance.

(9)    'Long-term policy' means a policy evidencing a contract which, if it had been effected by the transferee, would have constituted the carrying on of a regulated activity consisting of the effecting of contracts of long-term insurance.

**Section 132(4)**                    SCHEDULE 13
                    THE FINANCIAL SERVICES AND MARKETS TRIBUNAL

PART I
GENERAL

*Interpretation*

1.    In this Schedule—
         'panel of chairmen' means the panel established under paragraph 3(1);
         'lay panel' means the panel established under paragraph 3(4);
         'rules' means rules made by the Lord Chancellor under section 132.

PART II
THE TRIBUNAL

*President*

2.—(1)    The Lord Chancellor must appoint one of the members of the panel of chairmen to preside over the discharge of the Tribunal's functions.

(2)    The member so appointed is to be known as the President of the Financial Services and Markets Tribunal (but is referred to in this Act as 'the President').

(3)    The Lord Chancellor may appoint one of the members of the panel of chairmen to be Deputy President.

(4)    The Deputy President is to have such functions in relation to the Tribunal as the President may assign to him.

(5)    The Lord Chancellor may not appoint a person to be the President or Deputy President unless that person—

     (a)    has a ten year general qualification within the meaning of section 71 of the Courts and Legal Services Act 1990;

     (b)    is an advocate or solicitor in Scotland of at least ten years' standing; or

(c)  is—

   (i)   a member of the Bar of Northern Ireland of at least ten years' standing; or

   (ii)   a solicitor of the Supreme Court of Northern Ireland of at least ten years' standing.

(6)  If the President (or Deputy President) ceases to be a member of the panel of chairmen, he also ceases to be the President (or Deputy President).

(7)  The functions of the President may, if he is absent or is otherwise unable to act, be discharged—

   (a)   by the Deputy President; or

   (b)   if there is no Deputy President or he too is absent or otherwise unable to act, by a person appointed for that purpose from the panel of chairmen by the Lord Chancellor.

### Panels

3.—(1)  The Lord Chancellor must appoint a panel of persons for the purposes of serving as chairmen of the Tribunal.

(2)  A person is qualified for membership of the panel of chairmen if—

   (a)   he has a seven year general qualification within the meaning of section 71 of the Courts and Legal Services Act 1990;

   (b)   he is an advocate or solicitor in Scotland of at least seven years' standing; or

   (c)   he is—

      (i)   a member of the Bar of Northern Ireland of at least seven years' standing; or

      (ii)   a solicitor of the Supreme Court of Northern Ireland of at least seven years' standing.

(3)  The panel of chairmen must include at least one member who is a person of the kind mentioned in sub-paragraph (2)(b).

(4)  The Lord Chancellor must also appoint a panel of persons who appear to him to be qualified by experience or otherwise to deal with matters of the kind that may be referred to the Tribunal.

### Terms of office etc

4.—(1)  Subject to the provisions of this Schedule, each member of the panel of chairmen and the lay panel is to hold and vacate office in accordance with the terms of his appointment.

(2)  The Lord Chancellor may remove a member of either panel (including the President) on the ground of incapacity or misbehaviour.

(3)  A member of either panel—

   (a)   may at any time resign office by notice in writing to the Lord Chancellor;

   (b)   is eligible for re-appointment if he ceases to hold office.

### Remuneration and expenses

5.  The Lord Chancellor may pay to any person, in respect of his service—

   (a)   as a member of the Tribunal (including service as the President or Deputy President), or

   (b)   as a person appointed under paragraph 7(4),

such remuneration and allowances as he may determine.

### Staff

6.—(1)  The Lord Chancellor may appoint such staff for the Tribunal as he may determine.

(2)  The remuneration of the Tribunal's staff is to be defrayed by the Lord Chancellor.

(3) Such expenses of the Tribunal as the Lord Chancellor may determine are to be defrayed by the Lord Chancellor.

## PART III
## CONSTITUTION OF TRIBUNAL

7.—(1) On a reference to the Tribunal, the persons to act as members of the Tribunal for the purposes of the reference are to be selected from the panel of chairmen or the lay panel in accordance with arrangements made by the President for the purposes of this paragraph ('the standing arrangements').

(2) The standing arrangements must provide for at least one member to be selected from the panel of chairmen.

(3) If while a reference is being dealt with, a person serving as member of the Tribunal in respect of the reference becomes unable to act, the reference may be dealt with by—

(a) the other members selected in respect of that reference; or

(b) if it is being dealt with by a single member, such other member of the panel of chairmen as may be selected in accordance with the standing arrangements for the purposes of the reference.

(4) If it appears to the Tribunal that a matter before it involves a question of fact of special difficulty, it may appoint one or more experts to provide assistance.

## PART IV
## TRIBUNAL PROCEDURE

8. For the purpose of dealing with references, or any matter preliminary or incidental to a reference, the Tribunal must sit at such times and in such place or places as the Lord Chancellor may direct.

9. Rules made by the Lord Chancellor under section 132 may, in particular, include provision—

(a) as to the manner in which references are to be instituted;

(b) for the holding of hearings in private in such circumstances as may be specified in the rules;

(c) as to the persons who may appear on behalf of the parties;

(d) for a member of the panel of chairmen to hear and determine interlocutory matters arising on a reference;

(e) for the suspension of decisions of the Authority which have taken effect;

(f) as to the withdrawal of references;

(g) as to the registration, publication and proof of decisions and orders.

### Practice directions

10. The President of the Tribunal may give directions as to the practice and procedure to be followed by the Tribunal in relation to references to it.

### Evidence

11.—(1) The Tribunal may by summons require any person to attend, at such time and place as is specified in the summons, to give evidence or to produce any document in his custody or under his control which the Tribunal considers it necessary to examine.

(2) The Tribunal may—

(a)   take evidence on oath and for that purpose administer oaths; or

(b)   instead of administering an oath, require the person examined to make and subscribe a declaration of the truth of the matters in respect of which he is examined.

(3)   A person who without reasonable excuse—

(a)   refuses or fails—

(i)    to attend following the issue of a summons by the Tribunal, or

(ii)   to give evidence, or

(b)   alters, suppresses, conceals or destroys, or refuses to produce a document which he may be required to produce for the purposes of proceedings before the Tribunal, is guilty of an offence.

(4)   A person guilty of an offence under sub-paragraph (3)(a) is liable on summary conviction to a fine not exceeding the statutory maximum.

(5)   A person guilty of an offence under sub-paragraph (3)(b) is liable—

(a)   on summary conviction, to a fine not exceeding the statutory maximum;

(b)   on conviction on indictment, to imprisonment for a term not exceeding two years or a fine or both.

### Decisions of Tribunal

12.—(1)   A decision of the Tribunal may be taken by a majority.

(2)   The decision must—

(a)   state whether it was unanimous or taken by a majority;

(b)   be recorded in a document which—

(i)    contains a statement of the reasons for the decision; and

(ii)   is signed and dated by the member of the panel of chairmen dealing with the reference.

(3)   The Tribunal must—

(a)   inform each party of its decision; and

(b)   as soon as reasonably practicable, send to each party and, if different, to any authorised person concerned, a copy of the document mentioned in sub-paragraph (2).

(4)   The Tribunal must send the Treasury a copy of its decision.

### Costs

13.—(1)   If the Tribunal considers that a party to any proceedings on a reference has acted vexatiously, frivolously or unreasonably it may order that party to pay to another party to the proceedings the whole or part of the costs or expenses incurred by the other party in connection with the proceedings.

(2)   If, in any proceedings on a reference, the Tribunal considers that a decision of the Authority which is the subject of the reference was unreasonable it may order the Authority to pay to another party to the proceedings the whole or part of the costs or expenses incurred by the other party in connection with the proceedings.

**Section 162**                    SCHEDULE 14
ROLE OF THE COMPETITION COMMISSION

### Provision of information by Treasury

1.—(1)   The Treasury's powers under this paragraph are to be exercised only for the purpose of assisting the Commission in carrying out an investigation under section 162.

(2)   The Treasury may give to the Commission—

(a)   any information in their possession which relates to matters falling within the scope of the investigation; and

(b)   other assistance in relation to any such matters.

(3)   In carrying out an investigation under section 162, the Commission must have regard to any information given to it under this paragraph.

### Consideration of matters arising on a report

2.   In considering any matter arising from a report made by the Director under section 160, the Commission must have regard to—

(a)   any representations made to it in connection with the matter by any person appearing to the Commission to have a substantial interest in the matter; and

(b)   any cost benefit analysis prepared by the Authority (at any time) in connection with the regulatory provision or practice, or any of the regulatory provisions or practices, which are the subject of the report.

### Applied provisions

3.—(1)   The provisions mentioned in sub-paragraph (2) are to apply in relation to the functions of the Commission under section 162 as they apply in relation to the functions of the Commission in relation to a reference to the Commission under the Fair Trading Act 1973.

(2)   The provisions are—

(a)   section 82(2), (3) and (4) of the Fair Trading Act 1973 (general provisions about reports);

(b)   section 85 of that Act (attendance of witnesses and production of documents);

(c)   section 93B of that Act (false or misleading information);

(d)   section 24 of the Competition Act 1980 (modifications of provisions about the performance of the Commission's functions);

(d)   Part II of Schedule 7 to the Competition Act 1998 (performance by the Commission of its general functions).

(3)   But the reference in paragraph 15(7)(b) in Schedule 7 to the 1998 Act to section 75(5) of that Act is to be read as a reference to the power of the Commission to decide not to make a report in accordance with section 162(2).

### Publication of reports

4.—(1)   If the Commission makes a report under section 162, it must publish it in such a way as appears to it to be best calculated to bring it to the attention of the public.

(2)   Before publishing the report the Commission must, so far as practicable, exclude any matter which relates to the private affairs of a particular individual the publication of which, in the opinion of the Commission, would or might seriously and prejudicially affect his interests.

(3)   Before publishing the report the Commission must, so far as practicable, also exclude any matter which relates to the affairs of a particular body the publication of which, in the opinion of the Commission, would or might seriously and prejudicially affect its interests.

(4)   Sub-paragraphs (2) and (3) do not apply in relation to copies of a report which the Commission is required to send under section 162(10).

**Sections 165(11) and 171(4)**          SCHEDULE 15
INFORMATION AND INVESTIGATIONS: CONNECTED PERSONS

PART I
RULES FOR SPECIFIC BODIES

*Corporate bodies*

1.   If the authorised person ('BC') is a body corporate, a person who is or has been—
   (a)   an officer or manager of BC or of a parent undertaking of BC;
   (b)   an employee of BC;
   (c)   an agent of BC or of a parent undertaking of BC.

*Partnerships*

2.   If the authorised person ('PP') is a partnership, a person who is or has been a member, manager, employee or agent of PP.

*Unincorporated associations*

3.   If the authorised person ('UA') is an unincorporated association of persons which is neither a partnership nor an unincorporated friendly society, a person who is or has been an officer, manager, employee or agent of UA.

*Friendly societies*

4.—(1)   If the authorised person ('FS') is a friendly society, a person who is or has been an officer, manager or employee of FS.

   (2)   In relation to FS, 'officer' and 'manager' have the same meaning as in section 119(1) of the Friendly Societies Act 1992.

*Building societies*

5.—(1)   If the authorised person ('BS') is a building society, a person who is or has been an officer or employee of BS.

   (2)   In relation to BS, 'officer' has the same meaning as it has in section 119(1) of the Building Societies Act 1986.

*Individuals*

6.   If the authorised person ('IP') is an individual, a person who is or has been an employee or agent of IP.

*Application to sections 171 and 172*

7.   For the purposes of sections 171 and 172, if the person under investigation is not an authorised person the references in this Part of this Schedule to an authorised person are to be taken to be references to the person under investigation.

PART II
ADDITIONAL RULES

8.   A person who is, or at the relevant time was, the partner, manager, employee, agent, appointed representative, banker, auditor, actuary or solicitor of—
   (a)   the person under investigation ('A');
   (b)   a parent undertaking of A;

(c)   a subsidiary undertaking of A;

(d)   a subsidiary undertaking of a parent undertaking of A; or

(e)   a parent undertaking of a subsidiary undertaking of A.

**Section 203(8)**             SCHEDULE 16

## PROHIBITIONS AND RESTRICTIONS IMPOSED BY DIRECTOR GENERAL OF FAIR TRADING

*Preliminary*

1.   In this Schedule—

'appeal period' has the same meaning as in the Consumer Credit Act 1974;

'prohibition' means a consumer credit prohibition under section 203;

'restriction' means a restriction under section 204.

*Notice of prohibition or restriction*

2.—(1)   This paragraph applies if the Director proposes, in relation to a firm—

(a)   to impose a prohibition;

(b)   to impose a restriction; or

(c)   to vary a restriction otherwise than with the agreement of the firm.

(2)   The Director must by notice—

(a)   inform the firm of his proposal, stating his reasons; and

(b)   invite the firm to submit representations in accordance with paragraph 4.

(3)   If he imposes the prohibition or restriction or varies the restriction, the Director may give directions authorising the firm to carry into effect agreements made before the coming into force of the prohibition, restriction or variation.

(4)   A prohibition, restriction or variation is not to come into force before the end of the appeal period.

(5)   If the Director imposes a prohibition or restriction or varies a restriction, he must serve a copy of the prohibition, restriction or variation—

(a)   on the Authority; and

(b)   on the firm's home state regulator.

*Application to revoke prohibition or restriction*

3.—(1)   This paragraph applies if the Director proposes to refuse an application made by a firm for the revocation of a prohibition or restriction.

(2)   The Director must by notice—

(a)   inform the firm of the proposed refusal, stating his reasons; and

(b)   invite the firm to submit representations in accordance with paragraph 4.

*Representations to Director*

4.—(1)   If this paragraph applies to an invitation to submit representations, the Director must invite the firm, within 21 days after the notice containing the invitation is given to it or such longer period as he may allow—

(a)   to submit its representations in writing to him; and

(b)   to give notice to him, if the firm thinks fit, that it wishes to make representations orally.

(2)   If notice is given under sub-paragraph (1)(b), the Director must arrange for the oral representations to be heard.

(3)   The Director must give the firm notice of his determination.

### Appeals

5.   Section 41 of the Consumer Credit Act 1974 (appeals to the Secretary of State) has effect as if—
  (a)   the following determinations were mentioned in column 1 of the table set out at the end of that section—
    (i)    imposition of a prohibition or restriction or the variation of a restriction; and
    (ii)   refusal of an application for the revocation of a prohibition or restriction; and
  (b)   the firm concerned were mentioned in column 2 of that table in relation to those determinations.

**Section 225(4)**  
SCHEDULE 17<br>THE OMBUDSMAN SCHEME

PART I<br>GENERAL

Interpretation

1.   In this Schedule—
  'ombudsman' means a person who is a member of the panel; and
  'the panel' means the panel established under paragraph 4.

PART II<br>THE SCHEME OPERATOR

Establishment by the Authority

2.—(1)   The Authority must establish a body corporate to exercise the functions conferred on the scheme operator by or under this Act.
  (2)   The Authority must take such steps as are necessary to ensure that the scheme operator is, at all times, capable of exercising those functions.

Constitution

3.—(1)   The constitution of the scheme operator must provide for it to have—
  (a)   a chairman; and
  (b)   a board (which must include the chairman) whose members are the scheme operator's directors.
  (2)   The chairman and other members of the board must be persons appointed, and liable to removal from office, by the Authority (acting, in the case of the chairman, with the approval of the Treasury).
  (3)   But the terms of their appointment (and in particular those governing removal from office) must be such as to secure their independence from the Authority in the operation of the scheme.
  (4)   The function of making voluntary jurisdiction rules under section 227 and the functions conferred by paragraphs 4, 5, 7, 9 or 14 may be exercised only by the board.
  (5)   The validity of any act of the scheme operator is unaffected by—
  (a)   a vacancy in the office of chairman; or
  (b)   a defect in the appointment of a person as chairman or as a member of the board.

*The panel of ombudsmen*

4.—(1)   The scheme operator must appoint and maintain a panel of persons, appearing to it to have appropriate qualifications and experience, to act as ombudsmen for the purposes of the scheme.

(2)   A person's appointment to the panel is to be on such terms (including terms as to the duration and termination of his appointment and as to remuneration) as the scheme operator considers—

(a)   consistent with the independence of the person appointed; and

(b)   otherwise appropriate.

*The Chief Ombudsman*

5.—(1)   The scheme operator must appoint one member of the panel to act as Chief Ombudsman.

(2)   The Chief Ombudsman is to be appointed on such terms (including terms as to the duration and termination of his appointment) as the scheme operator considers appropriate.

*Status*

6.—(1)   The scheme operator is not to be regarded as exercising functions on behalf of the Crown.

(2)   The scheme operator's board members, officers and staff are not to be regarded as Crown servants.

(3)   Appointment as Chief Ombudsman or to the panel or as a deputy ombudsman does not confer the status of Crown servant.

*Annual reports*

7.—(1)   At least once a year—

(a)   the scheme operator must make a report to the Authority on the discharge of its functions; and

(b)   the Chief Ombudsman must make a report to the Authority on the discharge of his functions.

(2)   Each report must distinguish between functions in relation to the scheme's compulsory jurisdiction and functions in relation to its voluntary jurisdiction.

(3)   Each report must also comply with any requirements specified in rules made by the Authority.

(4)   The scheme operator must publish each report in the way it considers appropriate.

*Guidance*

8.   The scheme operator may publish guidance consisting of such information and advice as it considers appropriate and may charge for it or distribute it free of charge.

*Budget*

9.—(1)   The scheme operator must, before the start of each of its financial years, adopt an annual budget which has been approved by the Authority.

(2)   The scheme operator may, with the approval of the Authority, vary the budget for a financial year at any time after its adoption.

(3)   The annual budget must include an indication of—

(a)   the distribution of resources deployed in the operation of the scheme, and

(b)   the amounts of income of the scheme operator arising or expected to arise from the operation of the scheme,
distinguishing between the scheme's compulsory and voluntary jurisdiction.

### *Exemption from liability in damages*

10.—(1)   No person is to be liable in damages for anything done or omitted in the discharge, or purported discharge, of any functions under this Act in relation to the compulsory jurisdiction.££   (2)   Sub-paragraph (1) does not apply—

(a)   if the act or omission is shown to have been in bad faith; or

(b)   so as to prevent an award of damages made in respect of an act or omission on the ground that the act or omission was unlawful as a result of section 6(1) of the Human Rights Act 1998.

### *Privilege*

11.   For the purposes of the law relating to defamation, proceedings in relation to a complaint which is subject to the compulsory jurisdiction are to be treated as if they were proceedings before a court.

## PART III
## THE COMPULSORY JURISDICTION

### *Introduction*

12.   This Part of this Schedule applies only in relation to the compulsory jurisdiction.

### *Authority's procedural rules*

13.—(1)   The Authority must make rules providing that a complaint is not to be entertained unless the complainant has referred it under the ombudsman scheme before the applicable time limit (determined in accordance with the rules) has expired.

(2)   The rules may provide that an ombudsman may extend that time limit in specified circumstances.

(3)   The Authority may make rules providing that a complaint is not to be entertained (except in specified circumstances) if the complainant has not previously communicated its substance to the respondent and given him a reasonable opportunity to deal with it.

(4)   The Authority may make rules requiring an authorised person who may become subject to the compulsory jurisdiction as a respondent to establish such procedures as the Authority considers appropriate for the resolution of complaints which—

(a)   may be referred to the scheme; and

(b)   arise out of activity to which the Authority's powers under Part X do not apply.

### *The scheme operator's rules*

14.—(1)   The scheme operator must make rules, to be known as 'scheme rules', which are to set out the procedure for reference of complaints and for their investigation, consideration and determination by an ombudsman.

(2)   Scheme rules may, among other things—

(a)   specify matters which are to be taken into account in determining whether an act or omission was fair and reasonable;

(b)   provide that a complaint may, in specified circumstances, be dismissed without consideration of its merits;

(c)   provide for the reference of a complaint, in specified circumstances and with the consent of the complainant, to another body with a view to its being determined by that body instead of by an ombudsman;

(d)   make provision as to the evidence which may be required or admitted, the extent to which it should be oral or written and the consequences of a person's failure to produce any information or document which he has been required (under section 231 or otherwise) to produce;

(e)   allow an ombudsman to fix time limits for any aspect of the proceedings and to extend a time limit;

(f)   provide for certain things in relation to the reference, investigation or consideration (but not determination) of a complaint to be done by a member of the scheme operator's staff instead of by an ombudsman;

(g)   make different provision in relation to different kinds of complaint.

(3)   The circumstances specified under sub-paragraph (2)(b) may include the following—

(a)   the ombudsman considers the complaint frivolous or vexatious;

(b)   legal proceedings have been brought concerning the subject-matter of the complaint and the ombudsman considers that the complaint is best dealt with in those proceedings; or

(c)   the ombudsman is satisfied that there are other compelling reasons why it is inappropriate for the complaint to be dealt with under the ombudsman scheme.

(4)   If the scheme operator proposes to make any scheme rules it must publish a draft of the proposed rules in the way appearing to it to be best calculated to bring them to the attention of persons appearing to it to be likely to be affected.

(5)   The draft must be accompanied by a statement that representations about the proposals may be made to the scheme operator within a time specified in the statement.

(6).  Before making the proposed scheme rules, the scheme operator must have regard to any representations made to it under sub-paragraph (5).

(7)   The consent of the Authority is required before any scheme rules may be made.

*Fees*

15.—(1)   Scheme rules may require a respondent to pay to the scheme operator such fees as may be specified in the rules.

(2)   The rules may, among other things—

(a)   provide for the scheme operator to reduce or waive a fee in a particular case;

(b)   set different fees for different stages of the proceedings on a complaint;

(c)   provide for fees to be refunded in specified circumstances;

(d)   make different provision for different kinds of complaint.

*Enforcement of money awards*

16.   A money award, including interest, which has been registered in accordance with scheme rules may—

(a)   if a county court so orders in England and Wales, be recovered by execution issued from the county court (or otherwise) as if it were payable under an order of that court;

(b)   be enforced in Northern Ireland as a money judgment under the Judgments Enforcement (Northern Ireland) Order 1981;

(c)   be enforced in Scotland by the sheriff, as if it were a judgment or order of the sheriff and whether or not the sheriff could himself have granted such judgment or order.

## PART IV
## THE VOLUNTARY JURISDICTION

### *Introduction*

17.  This Part of this Schedule applies only in relation to the voluntary jurisdiction.

### *Terms of reference to the scheme*

18.—(1)  Complaints are to be dealt with and determined under the voluntary jurisdiction on standard terms fixed by the scheme operator with the approval of the Authority.

(2)  Different standard terms may be fixed with respect to different matters or in relation to different cases.

(3)  The standard terms may, in particular—

(a)  require the making of payments to the scheme operator by participants in the scheme of such amounts, and at such times, as may be determined by the scheme operator;

(b)  make provision as to the award of costs on the determination of a complaint.

(4)  The scheme operator may not vary any of the standard terms or add or remove terms without the approval of the Authority.

(5)  The standard terms may include provision to the effect that (unless acting in bad faith) none of the following is to be liable in damages for anything done or omitted in the discharge or purported discharge of functions in connection with the voluntary jurisdiction—

(a)  the scheme operator;

(b)  any member of its governing body;

(c)  any member of its staff;

(d)  any person acting as an ombudsman for the purposes of the scheme.

### *Delegation by and to other schemes*

19.—(1)  The scheme operator may make arrangements with a relevant body—

(a)  for the exercise by that body of any part of the voluntary jurisdiction of the ombudsman scheme on behalf of the scheme; or

(b)  for the exercise by the scheme of any function of that body as if it were part of the voluntary jurisdiction of the scheme.

(2)  A 'relevant body' is one which the scheme operator is satisfied—

(a)  is responsible for the operation of a broadly comparable scheme (whether or not established by statute) for the resolution of disputes; and

(b)  in the case of arrangements under sub-paragraph (1)(a), will exercise the jurisdiction in question in a way compatible with the requirements imposed by or under this Act in relation to complaints of the kind concerned.

(3)  Such arrangements require the approval of the Authority.

### *Voluntary jurisdiction rules: procedure*

20.—(1)  If the scheme operator makes voluntary jurisdiction rules, it must give a copy to the Authority without delay.

(2)  If the scheme operator revokes any such rules, it must give written notice to the Authority without delay.

(3)  The power to make voluntary jurisdiction rules is exercisable in writing.

(4)  Immediately after making voluntary jurisdiction rules, the scheme operator must arrange for them to be printed and made available to the public.

(5)   The scheme operator may charge a reasonable fee for providing a person with a copy of any voluntary jurisdiction rules.

### Verification of the rules

21.—(1)   The production of a printed copy of voluntary jurisdiction rules purporting to be made by the scheme operator—

(a)   on which is endorsed a certificate signed by a member of the scheme operator's staff authorised by the scheme operator for that purpose, and

(b)   which contains the required statements,

is evidence (or in Scotland sufficient evidence) of the facts stated in the certificate.

(2)   The required statements are—

(a)   that the rules were made by the scheme operator;

(b)   that the copy is a true copy of the rules; and

(c)   that on a specified date the rules were made available to the public in accordance with paragraph 20(4).

(3)   A certificate purporting to be signed as mentioned in sub-paragraph (1) is to be taken to have been duly signed unless the contrary is shown.

### Consultation

22.—(1)   If the scheme operator proposes to make voluntary jurisdiction rules, it must publish a draft of the proposed rules in the way appearing to it to be best calculated to bring them to the attention of the public.

(2)   The draft must be accompanied by—

(a)   an explanation of the proposed rules; and

(b)   a statement that representations about the proposals may be made to the scheme operator within a specified time.

(3)   Before making any voluntary jurisdiction rules, the scheme operator must have regard to any representations made to it in accordance with sub-paragraph (2)(b).

(4)   If voluntary jurisdiction rules made by the scheme operator differ from the draft published under sub-paragraph (1) in a way which the scheme operator considers significant, the scheme operator must publish a statement of the difference.

**Section 334, 336 and 338**             SCHEDULE 18
                                          MUTUALS

PART I
FRIENDLY SOCIETIES

### The Friendly Societies Act 1974 (c. 46)

1.   Omit sections 4 (provision for separate registration areas) and 10 (societies registered in one registration area carrying on business in another).

2.   In section 7 (societies which may be registered), in subsection (2)(b), for 'in the central registration area or in Scotland' substitute 'in the United Kingdom, the Channel Islands or the Isle of Man'.

3.   In section 11 (additional registration requirements for societies with branches), omit 'and where any such society has branches in more than one registration area, section 10 above shall apply to that society'.

4.  In section 99(4) (punishment of fraud etc and recovery of property misapplied), omit 'in the central registration area'.

### The Friendly Societies Act 1992 (c. 40)

5.  Omit sections 31 to 36A (authorisation of friendly societies business).

6.  In section 37 (restrictions on combinations of business), omit subsections (1), (1A) and (7A) to (9).

7.  Omit sections 38 to 43 (restrictions on business of certain authorised societies).

8.  Omit sections 44 to 50 (regulation of friendly societies business).

### PART II
### FRIENDLY SOCIETIES: SUBSIDIARIES AND CONTROLLED BODIES

#### Interpretation

9.  In this Part of this Schedule—
'the 1992 Act' means the Friendly Societies Act 1992; and
'section 13' means section 13 of that Act.

#### Qualifying bodies

10.—(1)  Subsections (2) to (5) of section 13 (incorporated friendly societies allowed to form or acquire control or joint control only of qualifying bodies) cease to have effect.
(2)  As a result, omit—
(a)  subsections (8) and (11) of that section, and
(b)  Schedule 7 to the 1992 Act (activities which may be carried on by a subsidiary of, or body jointly controlled by, an incorporated friendly society).

#### Bodies controlled by societies

11.  In section 13(9) (defined terms), after paragraph (a) insert—
'(aa)  an incorporated friendly society also has control of a body corporate if the body corporate is itself a body controlled in one of the ways mentioned in paragraph (a)(i), (ii) or (iii) by a body corporate of which the society has control;'.

#### Joint control by societies

12.  In section 13(9), after paragraph (c) insert—
'(cc)  an incorporated friendly society also has joint control of a body corporate if—
(i)  a subsidiary of the society has joint control of the body corporate in a way mentioned in paragraph (c)(i), (ii) or (iii);
(ii)  a body corporate of which the society has joint control has joint control of the body corporate in such a way; or
(iii)  the body corporate is controlled in a way mentioned in paragraph (a)(i), (ii) or (iii) by a body corporate of which the society has joint control;'.

#### Acquisition of joint control

13.  In section 13(9), in the words following paragraph (d), after 'paragraph (c)' insert 'or (cc)'.

*Amendment of Schedule 8 to the 1992 Act*

14.—(1)   Schedule 8 to the 1992 Act (provisions supplementing section 13) is amended as follows.

(2)   Omit paragraph 3(2).

(3)   After paragraph 3 insert—

'3A.—(1)   A body is to be treated for the purposes of section 13(9) as having the right to appoint to a directorship if—

(a)   a person's appointment to the directorship follows necessarily from his appointment as an officer of that body; or

(b)   the directorship is held by the body itself.

(2)   A body ('B') and some other person ('P') together are to be treated, for the purposes of section 13(9), as having the right to appoint to a directorship if—

(a)   P is a body corporate which has directors and a person's appointment to the directorship follows necessarily from his appointment both as an officer of B and a director of P;

(b)   P is a body corporate which does not have directors and a person's appointment to the directorship follows necessarily from his appointment both as an officer of B and as a member of P's managing body; or

(c)   the directorship is held jointly by B and P.

(3)   For the purposes of section 13(9), a right to appoint (or remove) which is exercisable only with the consent or agreement of another person must be left out of account unless no other person has a right to appoint (or remove) in relation to that directorship.

(4)   Nothing in this paragraph is to be read as restricting the effect of section 13(9).'

(4)   In paragraph 9 (exercise of certain rights under instruction by, or in the interests of, incorporated friendly society) insert at the end 'or in the interests of any body over which the society has joint control'.

*Consequential amendments*

15.—(1)   Section 52 of the 1992 Act is amended as follows.

(2)   In subsection (2), omit paragraph (d).

(3)   In subsection (3), for '(4) below' substitute '(2)'.

(4)   For subsection (4) substitute—

'(4)   A court may not make an order under subsection (5) unless it is satisfied that one or more of the conditions mentioned in subsection (2) are satisfied.'

(5)   In subsection (5), omit the words from 'or, where' to the end.

*References in other enactments*

16.   References in any provision of, or made under, any enactment to subsidiaries of, or bodies jointly controlled by, an incorporated friendly society are to be read as including references to bodies which are such subsidiaries or bodies as a result of any provision of this Part of this Schedule.

## PART III
## BUILDING SOCIETIES

*The Building Societies Act 1986 (c. 53)*

17.   Omit section 9 (initial authorisation to raise funds and borrow money).

18.   Omit Schedule 3 (supplementary provisions about authorisation).

## PART IV
## INDUSTRIAL AND PROVIDENT SOCIETIES

*The Industrial and Provident Societies Act 1965 (c.12)*

19. Omit section 8 (provision for separate registration areas for Scotland and for England, Wales and the Channel Islands).

20. Omit section 70 (scale of fees to be paid in respect of transactions and inspection of documents).

## PART V
## CREDIT UNIONS

*The Credit Unions Act 1979 (c. 34)*

21. In section 6 (minimum and maximum number of members), omit subsections (2) to (6).

22. In section 11 (loans), omit subsections (2) and (6).

23. Omit sections 11B (loans approved by credit unions), 11C (grant of certificates of approval) and 11D (withdrawal of certificates of approval).

24. In section 12, omit subsections (4) and (5).

25. In section 14, omit subsections (2), (3), (5) and (6).

26. In section 28 (offences), omit subsection (2).'

**Section 351**　　　　　　　　　SCHEDULE 19
COMPETITION INFORMATION

## PART I
## PERSONS AND FUNCTIONS FOR THE PURPOSES OF SECTION 351

1. The Table set out after this paragraph has effect for the purposes of section 351(3)(b).

TABLE

| *Person* | *Function* |
|---|---|
| 1. The Commission. | Any function of the Commission under Community law relating to competition. |
| 2. The Comptroller and Auditor General. | Any function of his. |
| 3. A Minister of the Crown. | Any function of his under a specified enactment. |
| 4. Director General of Telecommunications. | Any function of his under a specified enactment. |
| 5. Director General of Gas Supply. | Any function of his under a specified enactment. |
| 6. The Director General of Gas for Northern Ireland. | Any function of his under a specified enactment. |
| 7. The Director General of Electricity Supply. | Any function of his under a specified enactment. |

| Person | Function |
|---|---|
| 8. The Director General of Electricity Supply for Northern Ireland. | Any function of his under a specified enactment. |
| 9. The Director General of Water Services. | Any function of his under a specified enactment. |
| 10. The Civil Aviation Authority. | Any function of that authority under a specified enactment. |
| 11. The Rail Regulator. | Any function of his under a specified enactment. |
| 12. The Director General of Fair Trading. | Any function of his under a specified enactment. |
| 13. The Competition Commission. | Any function of the Competition Commission under a specified enactment. |
| 14. The Authority. | Any function of the Authority under a specified enactment. |
| 15. A person of a description specified in an order made by the Treasury. | Any function of his which is specified in the order. |

## PART II
## THE ENACTMENTS

1. The Fair Trading Act 1973
2. The Consumer Credit Act 1974
3. The Estate Agents Act 1979
4. The Competition Act 1980
5. The Telecommunications Act 1984
6. The Airports Act 1986
7. The Gas Act 1986
8. The Control of Misleading Advertisements Regulations 1988
9. The Electricity Act 1989
10. The Broadcasting Act 1990
11. The Water Industry Act 1991
12. The Electricity (Northern Ireland) Order 1992
13. The Railways Act 1993
14. Part IV of the Airports (Northern Ireland) Order 1994
15. The Gas (Northern Ireland) Order 1996
16. The EC Competition (Articles 88 and 89) Enforcement Regulations 1996
17. The Unfair Terms in Consumer Contracts Regulations 1999
18. This Act.
19. An enactment specified for the purposes of this paragraph in an order made by the Treasury.

**Section 432(1)**                    SCHEDULE 20
                         MINOR AND CONSEQUENTIAL AMENDMENTS

*The House of Commons Disqualification Act 1975 (c. 24)*

1. In Part III of Schedule 1 to the House of Commons Disqualification Act 1975 (disqualifying offices)—

(a)  omit—
  'Any member of the Financial Services Tribunal in receipt of remuneration'; and
(b)  at the appropriate place, insert—
  'Any member, in receipt of remuneration, of a panel of persons who may be selected
  to act as members of the Financial Services and Markets Tribunal'.

### *The Northern Ireland Assembly Disqualification Act 1975 (c. 25)*

2.  In Part III of Schedule 1 to the Northern Ireland Assembly Disqualification Act 1975
(disqualifying offices)—
  (a)  omit—
    'Any member of the Financial Services Tribunal in receipt of remuneration'; and
  (b)  at the appropriate place, insert—
    'Any member, in receipt of remuneration, of a panel of persons who may be selected
    to act as members of the Financial Services and Markets Tribunal'.

### *The Civil Jurisdiction and Judgments Act 1982 (c. 27)*

3.  In paragraph 10 of Schedule 5 to the Civil Jurisdiction and Judgments Act 1982
(proceedings excluded from the operation of Schedule 4 to that Act), for 'section 188 of the
Financial Services Act 1986' substitute 'section 415 of the Financial Services and Markets
Act 2000'.

### *The Income and Corporation Taxes Act 1988 (c. 1)*

4.—(1)  The Income and Corporation Taxes Act 1988 is amended as follows.
  (2)  In section 76 (expenses of management: insurance companies), in subsection (8),
omit the definitions of—
    'the 1986 Act';
    authorised person';
    investment business';
    investor';
    investor protection scheme';
    prescribed'; and
    recognised self-regulating organisation'.
  (3)  In section 468 (authorised unit trusts), in subsections (6) and (8), for '78 of the
Financial Services Act 1986' substitute '243 of the Financial Services and Markets Act 2000'.
  (4)  In section 469(7) (other unit trust schemes), for 'Financial Services Act 1986'
substitute 'Financial Services and Markets Act 2000'.
  (5)  In section 728 (information in relation to transfers of securities), in subsection (7)(a),
for 'Financial Services Act 1986' substitute 'Financial Services and Markets Act 2000'.
  (6)  In section 841(3) (power to apply certain provisions of the Tax Acts to recognised
investment exchange), for 'Financial Services Act 1986' substitute 'Financial Services and
Markets Act 2000'.

### *The Finance Act 1991 (c. 31)*

5.—(1)  The Finance Act 1991 is amended as follows.
  (2)  In section 47 (investor protection schemes), omit subsections (1), (2) and (4).
  (3)  In section 116 (investment exchanges and clearing houses: stamp duty), in subsection (4)(b), for 'Financial Services Act 1986' substitute 'Financial Services and Markets Act
2000'.

*The Tribunals and Inquiries Act 1992 (c. 53)*

6.—(1)   The Tribunals and Inquiries Act 1992 is amended as follows.

(2)   In Schedule 1 (tribunals under supervision of the Council on Tribunals), for the entry relating to financial services and paragraph 18, substitute—

'Financial services and        18.   The Financial Services and
markets                                 Markets Tribunal.'

*The Judicial Pensions and Retirement Act 1993 (c. 8)*

7.—(1)   The Judicial Pensions and Retirement Act 1993 is amended as follows.

(2)   In Schedule 1 (offices which may be qualifying offices), in Part II, after the entry relating to the President or chairman of the Transport Tribunal insert—
President or Deputy President of the Financial Services and Markets Tribunal'

(3)   In Schedule 5 (relevant offices in relation to retirement provisions)—

(a)   omit the entry—
Member of the Financial Services Tribunal appointed by the Lord Chancellor'; and

(b)   at the end insert—
Member of the Financial Services and Markets Tribunal'.

**Section 432(2)**                    SCHEDULE 21
                    TRANSITIONAL PROVISIONS AND SAVINGS

*Self-regulating organisations*

1.—(1)   No new application under section 9 of the 1986 Act (application for recognition) may be entertained.

(2)   No outstanding application made under that section before the passing of this Act may continue to be entertained.

(3)   After the date which is the designated date for a recognised self-regulating organisation—

(a)   the recognition order for that organisation may not be revoked under section 11 of the 1986 Act (revocation of recognition);

(b)   no application may be made to the court under section 12 of the 1986 Act (compliance orders) with respect to that organisation.

(4)   The powers conferred by section 13 of the 1986 Act (alteration of rules for protection of investors) may not be exercised.

(5)   'Designated date' means such date as the Treasury may by order designate.

(6)   Sub-paragraph (3) does not apply to a recognised self-regulating organisation in respect of which a notice of intention to revoke its recognition order was given under section 11(3) of the 1986 Act before the passing of this Act if that notice has not been withdrawn.

(7)   Expenditure incurred by the Authority in connection with the winding up of any body which was, immediately before the passing of this Act, a recognised self-regulating organisation is to be treated as having been incurred in connection with the discharge by the Authority of functions under this Act.

(8)   'Recognised self-regulating organisation' means an organisation which, immediately before the passing of this Act, was such an organisation for the purposes of the 1986 Act.

(9)   'The 1986 Act' means the Financial Services Act 1986.

*Self-regulating organisations for friendly societies*

2.—(1)   No new application under paragraph 2 of Schedule 11 to the 1986 Act (application for recognition) may be entertained.

(2)  No outstanding application made under that paragraph before the passing of this Act may continue to be entertained.

(3)  After the date which is the designated date for a recognised self-regulating organisation for friendly societies—

(a)  the recognition order for that organisation may not be revoked under paragraph 5 of Schedule 11 to the 1986 Act (revocation of recognition);

(b)  no application may be made to the court under paragraph 6 of that Schedule (compliance orders) with respect to that organisation.

(4)  'Designated date' means such date as the Treasury may by order designate.

(5)  Sub-paragraph (3) does not apply to a recognised self-regulating organisation for friendly societies in respect of which a notice of intention to revoke its recognition order was given under section 11(3) of the 1986 Act (as applied by paragraph 5(2) of that Schedule) before the passing of this Act if that notice has not been withdrawn.

(6)  Expenditure incurred by the Authority in connection with the winding up of any body which was, immediately before the passing of this Act, a recognised self-regulating organisation for friendly societies is to be treated as having been incurred in connection with the discharge by the Authority of functions under this Act.

(7)  'Recognised self-regulating organisation for friendly societies' means an organisation which, immediately before the passing of this Act, was such an organisation for the purposes of the 1986 Act.

(8)  'The 1986 Act' means the Financial Services Act 1986.

**Section 432(5)** SCHEDULE 22
REPEALS

| Chapter | Short title | Extent of repeal |
|---|---|---|
| 1923 c. 8. | The Industrial Assurance Act 1923. | The whole Act. |
| 1948 c. 39. | The Industrial Assurance and Friendly Societies Act 1948. | The whole Act. |
| 1965 c. 12. | The Industrial and Provident Societies Act 1965. | Section 8. Section 70. |
| 1974 c. 46. | The Friendly Societies Act 1974. | Section 4. Section 10. In section 11, from 'and where' to 'that society'. In section 99(4), 'in the central registration area'. |
| 1975 c. 24. | The House of Commons Disqualification Act 1975. | In Schedule 1, in Part III, 'Any member of the Financial Services Tribunal in receipt of remuneration'. |
| 1975 c. 25. | The Northern Ireland Assembly Disqualification Act 1975. | In Schedule 1, in Part III, 'Any member of the Financial Services Tribunal in receipt of remuneration'. |

| Chapter | Short title | Extent of repeal |
|---|---|---|
| 1977 c. 46. | The Insurance Brokers (Registration) Act 1977. | The whole Act. |
| 1979 c. 34. | The Credit Unions Act 1979. | Section 6(2) to (6).<br>Section 11(2) and (6).<br>Sections 11B, 11C and 11D.<br>Section 12(4) and (5).<br>In section 14, subsections (2), (3), (5) and (6).<br>Section 28(2). |
| 1986 c. 53. | The Building Societies Act 1986. | Section 9.<br>Schedule 3. |
| 1988 c. 1. | The Income and Corporation Taxes Act 1988. | In section 76, in subsection (8), the definitions of 'the 1986 Act', 'authorised person', 'investment business', 'investor', 'investor protection scheme', 'prescribed' and 'recognised self-regulating organisation'. |
| 1991 c. 31. | The Finance Act 1991. | In section 47, subsections (1), (2) and (4). |
| 1992 c. 40. | The Friendly Societies Act 1992. | In section 13, subsections (2) to (5), (8) and (11).<br>Sections 31 to 36.<br>In section 37, subsections (1), (1A) and (7A) to (9).<br>Sections 38 to 50.<br>In section 52, subsection (2)(d) and, in subsection (5), the words from 'or where' to the end.<br>Schedule 7.<br>In Schedule 8, paragraph 3(2). |
| 1993 c. 8. | The Judicial Pensions and Retirement Act 1993. | In Schedule 5, 'Member of the Financial Services Tribunal appointed by the Lord Chancellor'. |

# Index

Index